HERIOT–WATT UNIVERSITY

An Illustrated History

HERIOT–WATT UNIVERSITY

An Illustrated History

Patrick N. O'Farrell

PEARSON
Education

Published by Pearson Education Limited

Pearson Education Limited
Edinburgh Gate
Harlow
Essex CM20 2JE

and Associated Companies throughout the world.

First published 2004
© Heriot-Watt University

ISBN 0 273 69605 X

Designed by Michelle Cannatella
Typeset in 10.5/14.5 pt Garamond by Fakenham Photosetting Ltd
Printed in the UK by The Bath Press, CPI Group, Bath, UK

British Library Cataloguing-in-Publication Data
A CIP catalogue record for this book is available from the British Library.

Contents

Prologue

An announcement appeared in *The Scotsman* on 13 October 1821 advertising places at a new educational foundation, the Edinburgh School of Arts.

SCHOOL OF ARTS

FOR THE

BETTER EDUCATION OF THE MECHANICS OF EDINBURGH

The Directors hereby give notice, that this institution will be opened on Tuesday 16 October, when a lecture on Chemistry will be delivered by Dr. Fyfe at half past eight o' clock in the evening, in the Freemasons' Hall, Niddry Street.

Tickets are now ready for delivery at the Shop of Mr. Bryson, No. 8, South Bridge; and it is requested that those who mean to enter as students will do so without delay. No-one can be admitted who has not entered his name at Mr. Bryson's.

The Catalogue of the Library is now printed, and may be had at Mr. Bryson's.

The inaugural meeting of the school on 16 October 1821 was held in the old St Cecilia's concert hall in Niddry Street, in the heart of Edinburgh's Old Town. Having been acquired by the Freemasons in 1803, the orchestra space was converted into a rostrum with room for apparatus and with surrounding seats in concentric circles. Presided over by Lord Provost Arbuthnot, some 272 students, together with invited friends, the directors, subscribers and several 'most distinguished individuals' packed the hall so that by 'half past eight the room was completely filled, and some hundreds went away who could not procure admission'[1]. The objects of the institution were explained by Leonard Horner, the secretary and founder, in a 'short but luminous address' in which he cited the examples of great Scottish inventors and indulged the hope that 'other Watts, and other Rennies, will arise within the walls of the School of Arts'[2]. Thereafter, the first lecture on chemistry was delivered to the assembled throng by Dr Andrew Fyfe, son of a distinguished Edinburgh professor who was to be for many years a leading light in the school as a teacher, director and secretary, eventually becoming himself a professor at Aberdeen. *The Scotsman*, a Whig newspaper, endorsed the endeavour:

> Its tendency is in every point of view beneficial. Such an institution . . . brings down philosophy from the airy regions of speculation to guide the hand of industry in active life. Scientific principles and practical skill have hitherto been too much strangers. . . . Let an individual who falls in with a young man of an inquisitive and ingenious disposition, but in poor circumstances, give him a ticket to attend the School of Arts.[3]

Within a month of the launch of the school, no less than 452 students were enrolled at a fee of 15 shillings per annum and no further tickets were issued due to the pressure on accommodation.[4] Horner described its initial success as 'beyond my most sanguine expectations' and Lord Henry Cockburn declared, 'Horner's School of Arts has been opened gloriously. He is a most useful citizen, and it is of great importance to have such a person here, not of the law.'[5]

The packed audience at St Cecilia's Hall on that autumn evening in 1821 would not have realised the significance of the meeting. For that night was the birth of the mechanics' institute movement that would spread worldwide. The curriculum and form of governance in Edinburgh would influence numerous individual institutes from Britain to Australia; and the Edinburgh School of Arts would evolve into a university with an international reputation in research and teaching, reaching out to over 15,000 students in 140 countries across the world.

Notes

[1] *The Scotsman*, 20 October 1821.

[2] HWUA, SA 1/1/1, *Annual Report of the Directors*, 1821–22, p. 15v.

[3] *The Scotsman*, 20 October 1821.

[4] HWUA, SA 1/1/1, 1821–22, *op. cit.*, pp. 15–16.

[5] Lyell, K. (1890) *A Memoir of Leonard Horner, London*, Vol. 1, p. 196.

Preface

Nennius, the ninth-century compiler of annals, innocently and disarmingly began one of his works with the words, 'I made a heap of everything I could find.' In this book I have tried to avoid the order of the heap by selecting what I perceive to be the important events, personalities, changes and trends in the long history of an institution. It is no more than the first word on the subject; it makes no claim to be the last. In an attempt to alleviate tedium, the generic fate of institutional histories (where dullness is seen as the sine qua non of serious academic scholarship), I have tried to relieve the monotonous march of history by emphasising the personal idiosyncrasies and philosophies of the key players on the stage. Some, one could argue, richly deserve the obscurity to which history, perhaps mercifully, has consigned them. There is always the possibility, however, of discovering some mute inglorious Milton. As these pages will show, Heriot-Watt had many outstanding scholars on the staff and produced a number of brilliant students who distinguished themselves in the arts and sciences, politics, engineering, administration and in many other areas. Just as obituaries find it difficult to speak anything but good of the dead, books of this sort struggle in vain to avoid piety. Heriot-Watt has been a place to work and play, and spend long hours in earnest tutorial and corridor talk as well as on frivolous pursuits, to make friends, and for some to find their life partners.

The history of institutions is frequently conceived in organic terms, modelled as a human or as an organism of one sort or another, with the inevitable vocabulary of seeds, saplings, growth and longevity. Although metaphors such as these may occasionally illuminate, they are more likely to blur our reasoning. This book tells the history of Heriot-Watt in an utterly unreconstructed manner. It follows, for the most part, the chronology of events and it makes much of significant changes and influential personalities. The book is also idiosyncratic. I enjoyed writing it but there may be those who think I should have left it unwritten. Not only was I dealing with other things while researching it but, more importantly, I am not a historian and as successively dean of a faculty and assistant principal from 1992 to 2002, I was an actor in the drama which is told. As a result, this is not the definitive history of the university, and like all histories, it is not an impartial and objective account, although I strived to be as fair as possible. It is a biography of an institution written by one who was closely involved and remains deeply attached.

Many friends and colleagues helped me in a multitude of ways and I ask them to accept my thanks. Here I have space only to mention by name some of those who gave me particularly valued assistance. One of the distinguishing marks of Heriot-Watt is that it has a fine and extensive archive, established by Dr Norman Reid, who was committed to ensuring that the university's most important contemporary records would be preserved for future historians. Under the highly professional and enlightened direction of Ann Jones since 1995, this archive has been my major working territory and I have had the good fortune to be able to rely on a deeply committed team – Ann Jones, Pamela McIntyre, Margaret-Ann Stewart, Brian Kelvin, Angela Edgar and Helen Taylor – all of whom lent stalwart support throughout. Ann Jones and Pamela McIntyre supplied great professional expertise, working assiduously to track down obscure sources, suggesting promising lines of investigation, correcting my numerous errors, and conducting oral interviews. Without their energy, knowledge and enthusiasm this book could not have been written. Angela Edgar located an excellent collection of illustrative images from the archive and other sources. Within the archive's sources, the papers and tape recordings of the late Alex Anderson, former librarian, have been especially valuable. In addition, members of all departments of Heriot-Watt, too many to list individually, have given advice and help in providing information about research strengths and departmental histories. Maureen McMillan was especially helpful in responding to queries about the Riccarton estate. I also owe a debt of gratitude to the Carnegie Trust for awarding me a research grant, and to Principal Archer, who invited me to write the book.

Many friends, to whom I am indebted, have read parts or all of the text. Their suggestions were invariably helpful even if I did not respond to all of them, so the text remains my responsibility. My special gratitude for their comments on sections of the book goes to Professor Brian Gowenlock, Ms Ann Jones, Professor Robin Knops, Professor Sir Alistair MacFarlane, Mr Richard McGookin, Dr Greg Michaelson, Dr Norman Reid, and Mr Charles Ritchie. One friend who is not a Heriot-Watt alumnus but a professional historian, Professor Alex Tyrrell of La Trobe University, Melbourne, has been particularly helpful in suggesting numerous invaluable references, while steering me gently away from pitfalls.

Editors and designers of Pearson Education have contributed significantly, with the supportiveness and attention to detail for which they are renowned, to improve my text and produce a book which gives pleasure as well as food for thought.

I am deeply grateful to Jane Seber and Diann MacDonald, whose continued good humour enabled them to survive the typing of a lengthy manuscript made no easier by my particular Irish variety of illegibility. Diann MacDonald has been my conscientious, indefatigable aide in preparing the manuscript for publication.

Finally, I should like to thank my wife, Susan, for her patience during the five-year period of composition. This book is dedicated to her and my three daughters.

Patrick N. O'Farrell
May 2004

About the Author

Born in Ireland, Professor Patrick N. O'Farrell completed both an undergraduate degree in Natural Sciences and a doctorate at Trinity College, Dublin. He worked at Queen's University Belfast, the University of Ulster and Cardiff University before moving to Heriot-Watt University in 1986, where he was Dean of the Faculty of Economics and Social Studies and Assistant Principal.

Professor O'Farrell has published ten books and monographs and over 100 research papers in refereed journals. The major themes of his research include: transport economics, regional economic development, foreign direct investment, industrial closures, entrepreneurship, research methodology, and inter-regional and international comparisons of the competitiveness of small manufacturing firms and business service companies.

Married with three grown-up daughters, Professor O'Farrell is currently Pro-Vice-Chancellor of Swansea University.

Chapter One

The Edinburgh School of Arts and the Mechanics' Institute Movement

Education is not the filling of
a pail, but the lighting of a fire.
W. B. Yeats

The North Bridge connecting the Old and New Town, Edinburgh. J. D. Swarbreck, October 1837

An Enlightened City? Edinburgh in the Early Nineteenth Century

The establishment of the world's first mechanics' institute in Edinburgh, an elegant city dominated by education, finance and the law, begs the question as to why Edinburgh should have pioneered this form of adult education for the working class and not one of the great new centres of English industry such as Birmingham, Manchester or Leeds. What kind of a city was Edinburgh at this time? Were other educational opportunities available for working-class people in Edinburgh in the early nineteenth century? What was the nature of the philosophical and intellectual air that the founders were breathing that inspired the foundation of the School of Arts? What factors stimulated the establishment of other mechanics' institutes? What ideological perspectives informed the governance and curriculum of the institutes? What social, behavioural and moral benefits did the middle-class philanthropist founders expect the working-class students to derive from the limited educational programmes on offer? How did the working-class movement respond to this educational initiative and its underlying social control agenda? How did the Edinburgh School of Arts influence the wider mechanics' institute movement? These issues will be addressed in this chapter as a background to the development of Leonard Horner's plans for the Edinburgh School of Arts in Chapter 2.

The long Napoleonic wars, during which the Scots had fought alongside the English and learned to hate their old allies, the French, had only recently ended, thereby drawing these two parts of Britain together.[1] Although the condition of many buildings in the Old Town was not good – the collapse of a tenement in 1751 led to a survey and the demolition of a considerable number[2] – the late eighteenth century witnessed its crowning glory. It was an area vibrant with the hidden pulse of history – where ladies were borne in gilded sedan chairs, where among its bookshops and taverns wandered men whose books were read and acclaimed at home and abroad: Adam Smith, David Hume, Robert Adam, Adam Ferguson, Walter Scott and James Hutton. This had been the stage trodden by Mary Queen of Scots and John Knox; while Robert Burns, James Boswell and Dr Johnson also explored its wynds and visited its hostelries. Although stripped of its parliament, in cultural matters Edinburgh in the early nineteenth century still functioned as the focus of a vast empire of science. Edinburgh University graduates emigrated to staff the medical and technical services of the British Empire and, as we shall see, founded the University of London and several English mechanics' institutes.[3]

Edinburgh Castle and the Nor Loch. By Alexander Nasmyth, National Gallery of Scotland

In 1755 the population of the capital, the largest town in Scotland, was 57,000. From then the expansion of the city – until arrested by the economic crisis of 1825 – was even more conspicuous than that of Glasgow: the population grew from 90,768 in 1801 to 191,221 by 1851. Drainage of the Nor' Loch (later to become Princes Street Gardens), which constrained expansion of the Old Town to the north, began in 1759 and the North Bridge across it, with additional balusters to prevent pedestrians being blown off, was completed in 1772. This facilitated the northward march of the city. The noblemen, lawyers and wealthy citizens had occupied the middle floors of the Old Town's tenements while the poor lived in squalid conditions in the cellars and attics.[4] From the 1780s the aristocracy, together with the leaders of the professions and business – by means of an exceptional feat of planning – had created the New Town, a physical symbol of Edinburgh's leading role in the Enlightenment. The 'tide of gentility' rolled northward and westward from the Old Town, while the professional classes also moved out of the crowded tenements to mansions in the New Town, north of Princes Street, to be followed by the merchants. This fundamental redistribution of population in the city intensified the spatial segregation of social classes during the nineteenth century. By 1830 the New Town had 5,000 houses and 40,000 people, approaching one-quarter of the population of Edinburgh. The New Town was an essentially professional rather than aristocratic society, retaining the bourgeois emphasis on family training and religious observance, professional standards of responsibility and the enjoyment of a sober intellectual culture.[5] Social recognition still followed distinction in the law, church and medicine. The development of the southern suburbs as a genteel residential area did not proceed apace until the 1870s.

There were now two Edinburghs, not one; social unity, an attractive feature of old Edinburgh, had disappeared. The living conditions in the Old Town, already bad in 1821 when the School of Arts was founded, degenerated further to become a major concentration of misery and vice exacerbated by uprooted people, victims of poor harvests and the economic depression of 1824–25.[6] The area available for housing was restricted; further encroachment was made by construction of railways which reached Waverley Station in 1846 and breweries at the Holyrood end of Canongate.[7] The Cowgate, which had once been the fashionable street, fell into decay. The tall crow-stepped houses vacated by the middle classes – typically flats of five or six rooms – were repeatedly subdivided and cheaply partitioned into single-room units for the working class. The average size of a one-roomed house in Edinburgh in 1861 was approximately 14 feet by 11.5 feet, but this did not prevent the householders taking in lodgers.[8] By the 1820s there were some 50,000 people occupying the tenements of the Old Town.[9] The congestion and overcrowding were intensified by an increasing population of semi-skilled and unskilled workers, many of them migrants from the Highlands, and Irish immigrants (navvies digging the Union Canal and later the railways). By 1851, when there were 12,514 Irish-born people living in Edinburgh (there were only 8,443 English),[10] some 29 per cent of the population aged from 16 to 60 in the Old Town, but only 2 per cent in the New Town, had been born in Ireland.[11] Population densities continued to increase so that by 1865 there were 646 people to the acre in the Tron district of the high street[12] (equivalent today to a quarter of a million people living on the university's Riccarton campus), 'an area which had been allowed to decay into a festering slum'. The reality of these slums was described in graphic terms by Dr Alexander Miller, a gynaecologist in Edinburgh, in response to an official investigation of sanitary conditions of the labouring classes in 1842:

> The dwellings of the poor are generally very filthy ... always ill ventilated. ... Many of them, besides, are damp and partly underground. ... A few of the lowest have a bedstead, but by far the larger portion have none; these make up a kind of bed on the floor with straw, on which a whole family are huddled together, some naked and others in the same clothes they had worn during the day.[13]

The squalid overcrowded wynds of Edinburgh's Old Town were a major health hazard for their inhabitants

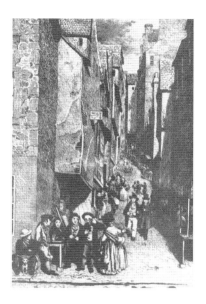

The North Bridge connecting the Old and New Town, Edinburgh. J. D. Swarbreck, October 1837. Photograph: Douglas McBride

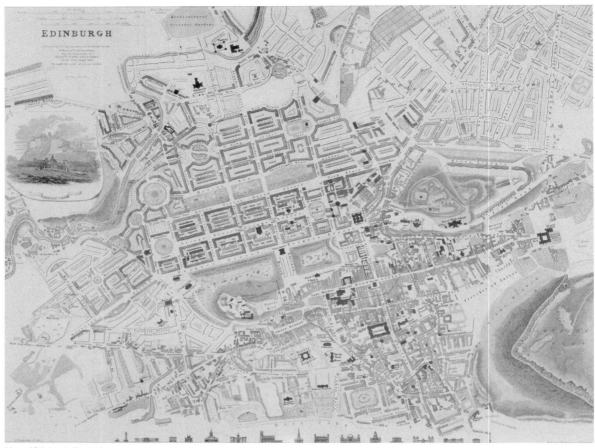

EDINBURGH

Map of Edinburgh illustrating the contrast between the Old Town and the New Town, 1834. Photograph: Douglas McBride

It was the congested and squalid tenement dwellings, the open drains and the utter destitution exposed by probings of social investigators that aroused critical comment from observers such as Dickens and Engels. Engels observed:

> It is evident that in the dwellings of the poor of Edinburgh a want of cleanliness reigns. ... [O]n the bedposts chickens roost at night, dogs and horses share the dwellings with human beings, and the natural consequence is a shocking stench with filth and swarms of vermin.[14]

With no public services or sanitation, an absence of piped water, and sewage thrown from windows of tenements into the streets and wynds, disease was rife. This was another aspect of enlightened Edinburgh, a city of stark contrasts: New Town and Old Town, elegance and degradation, humanity and cruelty. This dichotomy was symbolised in the career of Deacon Brodie, a respectable citizen and member of the town council, who was also by night an intrepid burglar; and who provided the inspiration for R. L. Stevenson's Jekyll and Hyde story.

Charles Dickens, after a visit to poor inhabitants of the Old Town in 1858, commented, '[I] saw more poverty and sickness than I had ever saw before.'[15] Hence, during the period 1821 to 1837, when the Edinburgh School of Arts was located in Niddry Street, the area from where it drew many of its students was among the worst in Europe for drunkenness, vagrancy, hunger and malnutrition. Life for many in Edinburgh during the first half of the nineteenth century was competitive, brutal and short; mere survival was a major preoccupation in the damp closes and stinking wynds of tenements. Whisky cost 10d a bottle, tea 8s a pound, and 10s a week was a good wage for those fortunate enough to find work.[16]

The need for action to turn the tide against advancing squalor was underlined in November 1863 by the collapse of a tenement in the high street, killing 35 people. In a report of 1865 by Dr Littlejohn, the first medical officer of health, he made a series of sensible recommendations, including the knocking down of many filthy houses, the regular inspection of cow byres in the city, weekly lifting of manure, compulsory introduction of water closets, and limits on the numbers in each flat.[17] Eventually measures of sanitary reform around 1866, including the laying of sewers, began to change conditions in the Old Town. Improvements also occurred as successive waves of urbanisation created extensive new working-class industrial districts, and population densities in the Old Town were reduced by slum clearance and spontaneous movement.

It is also important to analyse the employment structure of Edinburgh in the early nineteenth century in order to understand the occupational background of people enrolling for courses at the new mechanics' institute. During the first stage of the Industrial Revolution in Scotland, from the foundation of the first cotton mill in Rothesay in 1778 until around 1830 when the iron industry developed, cotton became the country's major industry. Edinburgh was largely unaffected since the mills were concentrated predominantly in the Clyde Valley, especially Lanarkshire. The second phase of the Industrial Revolution in Scotland – when the metal industries became dominant – commenced in the 1830s and extended to about 1880. Production concentrated in the Old Monkland area so that Edinburgh again was relatively uninvolved.

The economic base of Edinburgh during the formative years of the School of Arts was strikingly different from that of Glasgow. The capital in 1831 had more middle-class occupations than did Glasgow[18] – there were opportunities for professional people in the banks, courts and insurance firms – while its working classes revealed a markedly craft bias.[19] The census of 1851 confirms the existence of a conspicuous proportion of craft workers in the city: masons (1,873), cabinet makers (1,310), carpenters (1,776), printers (1,578), painters and glaziers (1,262), bakers (1,198) and blacksmiths (1,473) had a long tradition for excellence behind them. Since there was almost no textile industry, most women were employed in domestic service – 16,601 at the 1851 census – reflecting the size of the middle-class market. The city was a hive of small workshops producing goods demanded by the local 'luxury' market such as leather, glass, brass, jewellery, rubber, as well as quality clothing, boot and shoemakers. The major cluster of publishing houses – Edinburgh rivalled London as a centre of printing and publishing – stimulated a supply of papermakers, printing and papermaking machine shops. The city was also the leading Scottish centre in brewing, while its position as Scotland's financial capital was confirmed by the growth of its insurance and investment companies, and the presence of the head offices of the major Scottish banks. The status of Edinburgh was further enhanced as the leading ecclesiastical, legal and educational centre of Scotland. It was the small shopkeeper, the clerk and self-employed craftsman who comprised the local petty bourgeoisie and beneath them existed a reserve of semi-skilled and general labour. The division between the skilled and unskilled worker in the nineteenth century was institutional, forming a deep schism through the working class.[20] Hence the industrial working class in nineteenth-century Edinburgh was characterised by considerable occupational diversity, with a relatively high proportion of skilled labour in many local industries.

Educational Provision: Schools

Scotland has always remained devoted to the concept of education: the first education act in European history was passed in Scotland in 1496. In January 1561 John Knox placed before a convention of nobility and lairds a draft of a national programme for spiritual reform. The Book of Discipline was not a philosophical document, but the strict and visionary social theology behind it is apparent in every clause.[21] Knox sought to create God's earthly commonwealth in the Kingdom of Scotland. Through its courts the Church would enforce the moral standards of the godly commonwealth, but mere punishment would not be enough: as all men and women were born wicked, the Church would have to take preventive measures by providing a virtuous education for children.[22] The whole system of discipline, therefore, was to be supplemented by a national scheme for education. To this end 'we judge it necessary that every several church have a schoolmaster appointed'.[23] For the poor, if necessary, the education may be given free. This was a breathtaking vision – that education would be offered to every Scottish child – and, although never fully realised, Smout considered that by 1780 the Lowland Scot could boast with some justice of having a more extensive and liberal educational system than any in Europe.[24]

In some parishes in the Lowlands tax-supported schools were set up; but where population increased or the parish was extensive, other schools had to be provided, either by charity or by private enterprise, to supplement the national system and maintain even the semblance of provision for all.[25] In the large towns, however, the system of parish schools was not successful and when the population increased in the nineteenth century there were large numbers of uneducated children; while in the Highlands there was a heavy reliance on the haphazard application of charity.[26] Universal education and literacy came to Scotland only in the late nineteenth century.

Private provision grew in the cities so that by 1831 private schools, in which the Church had no say, were three times as numerous as parochial schools.[27] At elementary level, a wide mix of provision emerged, including parish schools of the traditional kind, Church of Scotland schools, Catholic schools and schools run by subscription or as private ventures. There were about 500,000 children of school age (between 5 and 13) in Scotland by 1837; of these, 18 per cent (90,000) escaped education and attended no school at all, and of the remainder about half attended schools with no inspection.[28] In the early 1830s a report on the Canongate parish, within the local catchment of the Edinburgh School of Arts, estimated that in a population of over 10,000, only half of the children of school age attended any kind of school.[29] The parish school was an equalising agency in so far as it was a common school designed for the education of the children of all classes, although it was neither compulsory nor free.[30]

The Scots had developed a perspective towards mass education 'significantly different from the untrusting and hostile attitude still dominant among the rulers of England'.[31] So, despite its defects, the Scottish parochial system was vastly superior to the charity schools of England.[32] When the ability to write a signature was first measured, after the civil registration of marriages was introduced in 1855, Scotland had a literacy rate of 89 per cent for men and 77 per cent for women, compared with 70 per cent and 59 per cent for England and Wales in the same year.[33] Even in Scotland, however, there was no belief in democratic equality of opportunity in education; it was never intended that formal education for the masses should go far beyond the three Rs.[34] Even where children came to school, especially in urban areas, few could remain in education after the age of 11. It was the demand for child labour in industry that was inimical to school attendance and, despite the Factory Acts, the extent of such employment grew rapidly in the mid nineteenth century in Scotland.[35] This economic pressure on the mass of the population led to an inegalitarian system by putting advanced education beyond their reach.

The parochial schools could not cope with the demand for elementary education in urban areas. The Church of Scotland, under the influence of Thomas Chalmers, supplemented the parochial schools with Church 'sessional' and 'General Assembly' schools in the towns, partly assisted by public finance after 1834 when the government began to give grants to schools in Scotland. There were eight active sessional schools in Edinburgh by 1840, run by educational societies or supported by endowments, which provided education for some 4,000 children drawn from the poorer classes.[36] The system did allow most working men to acquire some basic skills and a small number of boys (never girls) to proceed to more advanced study. It was for the individual to demonstrate his worthiness to succeed through sacrifice and hard work, and this fitted in with the Calvinistic ideal which had always emphasised qualities of character and the moral virtue of the struggle with poverty.[37]

Throughout the later eighteenth century and the first four decades of the nineteenth century, the Church of Scotland was riven with dispute which saw the emergence of two distinct groupings, Moderate and Evangelical. In the first third of the nineteenth century it was the Evangelicals who established a majority and began to set the dominant tone in Scottish spiritual life. The issue of patronage – the conflict regarding who was to have the primary say in the appointment of a minister, the congregation (the Evangelical view) or the patrons (usually the landlords) – was a particular source of contention which reached crisis point in the General Assembly of 1843, leading to the 'Disruption', when Thomas Chalmers led two-fifths of the ministers out of the Church of Scotland to set up the Free Church.[38] The new body commenced at once to build its own churches and schools, often in places where a parochial school already existed. Thus, in some districts there was overlapping, whereas in others there remained a deficiency in school places.[39] Scottish elementary education therefore became fragmented – there were now several educational bodies including the old Kirk, the new Kirk, United Presbyterians, the Roman Catholic Church and Episcopalians – and stimulated, although little beyond the bare rudiments were taught. The situation was a mess, with only a small minority attending the parochial schools of the Church of Scotland. In any given community many overlapping small-scale institutions competed where one of a larger size would have sufficed.[40] One striking feature of the Scottish school-level education in the nineteenth century was its academic bias. An emphasis on verbalism was inevitable in a system which owed so much of its inspiration to the Platonism of sixteenth-century divines: in the schools, the classics, especially Latin, ruled.[41] Verbalism also led to an overvaluing of the examinable and a heavy emphasis on teaching towards certificates. Games and hobbies played a much smaller role in the life of the school than in England. Except in the large towns, there were few secondary schools in Scotland before the

Education Act (Scotland) of 1872; the work of its lower forms was done by the so-called elementary school, that of its higher forms by the universities. For the urban working class, the school system prior to 1872 offered scant opportunity for social mobility, since the elementary schools which had multiplied during the earlier part of the century rarely matched the parish school model, and since scholarships to secondary schools hardly existed.[42]

Educational Provision: Universities

The three pre-Reformation universities of St Andrews (1411), Glasgow (1451) and King's College, Aberdeen (1495) were ecclesiastical foundations, whereas the University of Edinburgh was established by the initiative of the town council in 1582.[43] From an early date, access to university in Scotland was easier than in almost any other country: in the mid nineteenth century the ratio of university students to the population was six times that of England, where entry was restricted to Anglicans.[44] The 'lad of pairts' whose parents made major sacrifices to give him a chance and who trudged miles daily to attend school or university in the hope of becoming a lawyer, doctor or colonial governor is more than a mythical source of local pride. Unlike Oxford and Cambridge, Scottish universities offered an instruction that was inexpensive. There was no entrance exam; students came directly from parish schools to university. The parish schoolmasters taught Latin, mathematics and perhaps Greek, and the universities articulated with these schools by admitting boys at 14 or 15 (or even younger) and junior classes were provided at the start of the university course.[45] Scottish universities, therefore, were in some measure doing the work of secondary schools. The student body was relatively diverse, and the universities were not characterised by the kind of social barriers that made Oxford and Cambridge places of privilege. The distinctiveness of the Scottish university experience was deemed worthy of comment by English visitors. The Victorian essayist Walter Bagehot observed that 'the teaching of Scotland seems to have been designed to teach man to write essays and articles [whereas] . . . the compact, exclusive learning of England is inferior in this respect to the general diversified, omnipotent information of the North'.[46]

Professors at Scottish universities were usually paid a small fixed salary, but the bulk of their income came from fees paid directly by students, and so they competed for class enrolments. Dr Thomas Charles Hope, for example, earned about £2,000 per academic session.[47] Lord Cockburn revealed Hope's popularity in a letter in 1826:

> Dr Thomas Charles Hope, lectures to ladies on Chemistry. He receives 300 of them by a back window, . . . each of them brings a beau, and the ladies declare that there never was anything so delightful as these chemical flirtations. The Doctor is in absolute ecstasy with his audience of veils and feathers . . . the only thing that inwardly corrodes him, is that in an evil moment, . . . he published that he was to give the fees to found a chemical prize, and that he can't now retract, though the fees amount to about £700. . . . Horrible – I wish some of his experiments would blow him up. Each female student would get a bit of him.[48]

His private chemistry classes for wealthy women were being held in Edinburgh at exactly the same time as Dr Andrew Fyfe was lecturing in the same subject to a class of artisans at the Edinburgh School of Arts, for which he received approximately £32 per annum. This created a culture in which professors had a direct interest in asserting a monopoly of instruction in their subject. Professors, fearing for their fees, frustrated any plans for expansion, or the institution of new chairs. Consequently, whereas Scottish universities flourished in the eighteenth century, by the middle of the nineteenth century their reputation had declined due to a strong conservatism and reluctance by the professoriate to expand as a consequence of payment by results.[49]

The university curriculum during the first two years of study was at a comparatively elementary level.[50] Classics provided a common groundwork on which the arts curriculum constructed a philosophically centred education. There were six traditional subjects: Latin, Greek, mathematics, logic, moral philosophy and natural philosophy (i.e. physics). A distinctive feature of the Scottish educational tradition, as in France and Germany, was the emphasis on the key discipline of moral philosophy, combining what would now be classified as philosophy, politics, economics, psychology and sociology. Scottish universities were thus highly differentiated from the Oxbridge model: the Scottish 'professorial' system challenged the Oxbridge 'tutorial' one; nineteenth-century Scottish university students were drawn from a much wider social spectrum than the small elite educated at Oxbridge; and after a struggle, women were admitted much earlier, in 1892. The effort to get to university and the poverty endured once there prompted Lyon Playfair, a Liberal Scottish University MP, to comment, 'The English universities . . . teach men how to spend £1,000 a year with dignity and intelligence while the Scottish universities teach them how to make £1,000 a year with dignity and intelligence.'[51] No subject was studied in depth, prompting Dr Johnson to observe that in Scotland every man had a mouthful of learning but no man had a bellyful.[52] In general, lectures were not supplemented by tutorials, and many students (except at Aberdeen), although undertaking sufficient studies to gain them a degree, did not care to go through the expensive ritual of actually receiving it.[53] Scottish and English universities were at one, however, in seeing their principal mission as teaching; it was only in the 1850s that there began to emerge the German idea of a university which combined teaching and research.

Steam Intellect in Edinburgh

Edinburgh's middle classes expressed their interests through a multiplicity of religious, philanthropic and educational activities. There were societies for the control of begging, the provision of relief, the distribution of bibles and tracts; and there was an organised concern for savings banks, church extension and temperance. Increasingly during the 1820s, a more secular enthusiasm sought expression in classes on political economy and general enlightenment associated with cheap literature and phrenology. The 'steam intellect' movement – provision of educational opportunities for the working class – is most commonly represented by mechanics' institutes, such as the Edinburgh School of Arts. The phenomenon, however, also embraced a vast complex of institutions and associations, including mutual improvement societies – important forms of working-class self-help – that existed side by side with public lectures, adult libraries and lecture societies. Hence the facilities for acquiring some scientific knowledge were far from negligible. The development of steam intellect in Britain was voluntary, haphazard and incidental. It is clear that mechanics' institutes were forced to compete with other, often antagonistic, purveyors of steam intellect. The culture of steam intellect provided a forum – between work and formal education – for the upward mobility of workers into the lower middle class.[54] Natural sciences lay at the heart of the steam intellect movement. The steam engine sat on the lecturer's table, as did the geological hammer, the butterfly net, the phrenological bust and the globe. For many working men the steam intellect movement provided some opportunity for entry into a new field, as well as repeated association with members of the bourgeoisie.

It is useful, therefore, to set the establishment of the Edinburgh School of Arts in the context of other steam intellect associations in the locality. Edinburgh, like

Princess Street with the commencement of the building of the Royal Institution, 1825. By Alexander Nasmyth, National Gallery of Scotland

London, created its own science on a very significant scale. Edinburgh's intellectual life was dominated by lawyers, teachers and medical men so that the city, its university and the cultural activists were profoundly cosmopolitan at heart. A plethora of scientific, medical and technical organisations catered for local men of science, including the prestigious Royal Society of Edinburgh, the iconoclastic Phrenological Society, the utilitarian Scottish Society of Arts and the Edinburgh School of Arts, while the *Edinburgh Review* evaluated science from a Whig perspective. There was also a pioneering initiative directed towards the social and educational needs of the working class. In 1816, at the height of the economic crisis following the Napoleonic Wars, Robert Owen articulated an early version of socialism by announcing a practical plan for the establishment of cooperative communities to remedy unemployment. Abram Combe (brother of George, the phrenologist) visited New Lanark in 1820 and had met Owen. Abram, a tanner whose works adjoined the family's brewery, was quickly converted to Owen's theories.[55] In 1821, the year the Edinburgh School of Arts was founded, Abram started a 'Practical Society' to carry out Owen's socialist principles, launching a New-Lanark-style school in Edinburgh for some 130 children and involving 500 to 600 families, opening a cooperative society and holding evening instruction, enlivened by dancing and social meetings.[56] This was the socialist alternative to the School of Arts – controlled by middle-class Whigs – but as so often happened, funds were lacking, the initial enthusiasm waned, and members drifted away.[57]

A decade after Leonard Horner and Edinburgh Whigs established the School of Arts for the scientific instruction of artisans, the Edinburgh Association for Procuring Instruction in Useful and Entertaining Science was set up in 1832. This society, called the Edinburgh Philosophical Association (EPA) from 1835, was founded by the petit bourgeoisie – the 'respectable' upwardly mobile clerks and small shopkeepers.[58] The origin of the EPA may be traced back to George Combe's popular lectures on phrenology which he began offering to Edinburgh in 1825 for audiences of over 100.[59] Unlike the School of Arts, the Philosophical Association was controlled by those social groups which the organisation was designed to instruct: its management was in the hands of its members who claimed to be 'respectable tradesmen' and generally above the class who work for day wages.[60] Not surprisingly, a somewhat patronising attitude was expressed towards the Edinburgh School of Arts:

> Edinburgh's 'mechanics' having been provided for by Horner's School of Arts were now joined in Science by our 'shopkeepers and clerks' who naturally insisted on a separate and more elevated institution.[61]

The lectures were cheap: courses of 25 lectures in geology were available from 7s 6d, chemistry for 10s 6d, phrenology and physiology for 10s 6d, or the lot for £1. The early range of subjects was soon supplemented by botany, education, natural philosophy, astronomy, zoology, natural history, and non-scientific subjects such as oratory, constitutional history, drama, and vocal harmony.[62] The association was very successful and within a year of its foundation its lectures were reaching several thousand of Edinburgh's mercantile classes.

In 1836 Combe set up the Society for Aiding the General Diffusion of Science. Combe approached Leonard Horner and was rebuffed, Horner mistakenly assuming that he was being asked to become a director of the Philosophical Association and not of the new Society for Diffusion.[63] Horner objected to the governance of the EPA with its management vested in the persons to be instructed. The Society for the General Diffusion of Science was an innovative idea; yet within months of its birth, the enterprise failed because of the hostile reaction of the EPA, concerned about the social control over scientific culture.[64] The existence of the EPA explicitly catering for the scientific appetite of the lower middle classes was clearly a major reason why the School of Arts recruited a predominantly artisan clientele for much longer than comparable English mechanics' institutes.

Another element in the supply of steam intellect in Edinburgh was educational publications aimed at the working class. The brothers William and Robert Chambers – Robert was a subscriber to the School of Arts from 1837 – built up a successful publishing business in Edinburgh in the 1820s. From 1832 to 1836, *Chambers' Historical Newspaper* appeared monthly (sold at three halfpence) to comment on the news from a Whig and often unorthodox perspective. Their most important publication, however, was *Chambers' Edinburgh Journal*, a regular magazine for the reading public among the working and lower middle classes. First published in February 1832, its intention was announced in an opening address as providing the labouring classes with instruction and worthwhile entertainment, but avoiding politics.[65] An active supporter of the Whig cause during the struggle for the Reform Bill, William Chambers was content to have working-class readers accept wholesome advice. 'Taking advantage of the growing taste for cheap literature, let me lead it, if possible, in a proper direction,' was his aim.[66] *Chambers' Edinburgh Journal* became an instant success, selling 50,000 in the first few days: by 1845 circulation approached 90,000.[67] But despite the aim to appeal to the working class, it appears that the readership lay chiefly among artisans and the lower middle class, especially small shopkeepers. There was no certainty, therefore, that steam intellect initiatives actually reached the working classes.

The Scottish Enlightenment and Utilitarianism

Leonard Horner, Lord Brougham and other Scots pioneers of the mechanics' institute movement were children of the Scottish Enlightenment. Horner was influenced by his brother, Francis, and through his reading of political economy he became a disciple of the utilitarian school of thought. What gave Scottish intellectual life its particular vigour was an interest in contemporary changes, which extended over the widest field of social activity and learning, and was inspired by the conviction (which Bacon had first promulgated) that the advancement of knowledge depends on its application, that learning must be put to social use. There was a belief by Enlightenment educationists that education can change man's nature; that man was a rational being and therefore capable of advancing to perfection.[68] The roots of these ideas drew directly on a psychological

The overcrowded slums of 'Auld Reekie' viewed from Edinburgh Castle in the early nineteenth century. Drawn by J. Ewbank, engraved by W. H. Lizars

theory which, though stemming directly from materialist philosophy, also owed much to developments in anatomy and medicine; that advanced by David Hartley in his *Observations of Man* (1748), the scientific treatise on psychology.[69] Associationism provided a rational, materialist theory of human learning, one which led logically to the conclusion that man's mind is formed by his circumstances; that is, by education conceived in its broadest sense. Hartley argued that ideas – developing on the foundation of physiological processes in the brain – inevitably became 'associated' together in a certain order in the mind. From this it followed that, by organising a person's experiences according to a definitive pattern, it was possible to exercise a formative influence on mental development.[70] The central position of education in the political doctrine of utilitarianism is based on Hartley's theory of the association of ideas. According to Hartley's associationist theory, the developed mind was the result of successive sense impressions which built up a pattern (or sequence) of associated ideas determining the individual's thoughts and feelings: 'All simple ideas are copies of impressions; . . . all complex ideas are only simple ideas united by the principle of association.'[71]

For James Mill, a Scotsman educated at Edinburgh University, 'his fundamental doctrine was the formation of all human character by circumstances, through the universal principle of association, and the consequent unlimited possibility of improving the moral and intellectual condition of mankind by education'.[72] James Mill came to London in 1802 to earn a living as a journalist and formed a friendship with Jeremy Bentham that was to act as a nucleus of the Radical Movement. Mill outlined the Radical theory of education in an article in the *Encyclopaedia Britannica* in 1818, 'the first attempt', as Cavanagh put it, 'at a completely scientific treatment of education'.[73] As an associationist, he clearly believed in the power of education (conceived in its widest sense) to lift the mass of the people to a high intellectual level. He saw education not so much as a panacea for the downtrodden but as a lever to raise them to any height.[74] In theory then, all are capable of improvement; all should have the benefit of enlightenment which will conduce to happiness – the end and aim of education. Education, if properly directed, could therefore determine the thoughts and so the character of men. Mill envisaged educational change as part of an essential aspect of a wider social transformation. It was the guiding aim of the utilitarians to transform what was a closed society controlled by hereditary landlords in their own interests into a free society directed by the middle class, those most qualified to govern in the interests of all.[75]

Mill, a Radical, wrote a series of articles in which he argued that the 'liberal' Whig party (then in opposition) was no less determined to maintain aristocratic rule than the Tories. He supported the concept of universal suffrage as a means of uniting the mass of the people behind the middle class for the destruction of aristocratic oligarchy; and with it, he advocated the idea of universal education. Mill envisaged an enlightened democracy under the political and economic leadership of the middle class who he believed would exercise their power in the interests of all. Profoundly convinced of the power of reason, he was certain that it was only necessary to place the facts of political economy before the working classes for them to understand that their interests lay in giving their support to the industrial capitalist, the institution of property and the middle class generally.[76] Radicalism was the political expression of the enlightened middle class. The Whig attitude to popular education differed slightly from that of the Radicals. Whig spokesmen, although prepared to work for a measure of educational advance, saw it as a means of habituating the people to the existing social order and the dominance of the landed aristocracy rather than, in the case of the Radicals, consolidating support for the middle class.

Mill envisaged educational change as part of an essential aspect of wider social transformation.[77] Education was an essential accompaniment of an enlarged franchise. There was a contradiction, however, at the heart of utilitarian educational philosophy that became clear when Mill posed and answered the question, What is the sort of education required for the different classes of society?[78] Mill denies that the human race should be divided into two classes, but acquiesces in existing class relations and proposes to perpetuate them.[79] A higher degree of education is reserved for those who are not obliged to labour since they live on the labour of others. In spite of glowing phrases about universal enlightenment, Mill envisaged a system restricted on class lines, thereby revealing the contradiction at the heart of the utilitarian theory of education. This was the philosophy underpinning the actions of Horner and the middle-class Whigs of Edinburgh in their venture to provide scientific education for the artisans of the city.

An Experiment in Education: The Anderson Institution

There is evidence that Glasgow was the city where tuition in natural philosophy, admitting mechanics and artisans as students, was pioneered in the late eighteenth century. Dr Thomas Garnett was the first professor of natural philosophy in the Anderson Institution (founded in 1796 and later called the Glasgow Royal Technical College, now Strathclyde University). Garnett delivered popular evening courses in natural philosophy and chemistry, and was succeeded in 1799 by Dr George Birkbeck (1760–1841), a Quaker from Settle and a graduate in medicine from Edinburgh University.[80] But Birkbeck's first lecture course for working tradesmen, 'upon the mechanical properties of solid and fluid bodies', was given gratuitously in the autumn of 1800.[81] These were not the first classes to admit skilled artisans, as Birkbeck later claimed, for John Anderson (1726–1796) and others had delivered classes earlier. However, in 1800 at Anderson's Institution in Glasgow, George Birkbeck gave the first course designed specifically and exclusively for working tradesmen, and he gave it free.[82] Only this first course was free of charge; nominal fees were introduced for subsequent courses.[83] Kelly has emphasised, however, that Birkbeck, who founded the London Mechanics' Institute in 1823, which became Birkbeck College in 1907, pioneered a free mechanics *class*; the idea of an *institution* was still in the future.[84] The seed sown in Glasgow was later to bear institutional fruit in Edinburgh, although the middle-class directors of the Edinburgh School of Arts never provided tuition gratis for the artisans.

Anderson, born in Dumbartonshire and educated at Glasgow University, was appointed to the chair of oriental languages at the university, a subject for which he had no particular competence but was merely a stepping-stone to the more congenial post of professor of natural philosophy, which he held from 1757 until his death in 1796.[85] Anderson, known to the students as Jolly Jack Phosphorus, delivered a course in experimental philosophy which was open not only to students of the university but also to non-matriculated members of the general public who could attend *anti-toga* (without a gown) on Tuesdays and Thursdays.[86] These classes, held in the evenings, were attended by up to 200 people a year, including craftsmen from differing trades, to whom he gave free tickets.[87] After a lifetime spent in quarrelling with his academic colleagues at Glasgow University, Anderson died in 1796 bequeathing almost his entire fortune for the establishment of a rival institution, the Anderson Institution.

When Anderson began lecturing on experimental philosophy in 1757 he was able to draw on the equipment, new experimental methods and ideas of Robert Dick, professor of natural philosophy at Glasgow between 1751 and 1757.[88] Also, in Glasgow University itself, numerous lectures had been open to the public from early in the eighteenth century: both William Cullen and Joseph Black (who first introduced the concept of latent heat) – lecturers in chemistry from 1746 and 1756, respectively – encouraged attendance at their classes by manufacturing workers.[89] It is clear that in chemistry, natural philosophy and political economy the staff of Glasgow were heavily involved with manufacturing industry and the populace of the city before the arrival of John Anderson. His role was more catalytic than pioneering, by carrying on the struggle to provide suitable education for the industrial working classes.

The Origin and Early Evolution of Mechanics' Institutes

The foundation in 1821 of the Edinburgh School of Arts represented the start of Leonard Horner's efforts for working-class education, and was the original source of the movement which, during the next few years, was to spread rapidly throughout Britain and abroad. It is important to view the establishment of the Edinburgh School of Arts in the context of the wider debate informing the development of adult education during the first half of the nineteenth century, and to outline the contrasting philosophies of the principal advocates of mechanics' institutes which were to influence heavily the nature of the educational curriculum.

The origin of mechanics' institutes[90] has been the subject of many confused and contradictory statements. The movement was like most important historical processes, the outcome of a complex set of factors operating to produce similar results in a variety of locations.[91] Thomas Kelly, the biographer of George Birkbeck, discussed the origin of mechanics' institutes with reference to four major contributory factors.[92] First, the pace of technological change in industry meant an increased need for workers to acquire some rudimentary scientific knowledge. Second, since the early eighteenth century there had been a growing popular interest in science. A third factor was the general movement for the provision of popular education, and a fourth was the working-class struggle for political and economic reform. From the perspective of Kelly's first factor, the development of mechanics' institutes was a response to the increasing complexity of industrial processes as a consequence of the Industrial Revolution. The economic appeal of the early institutes, however, including, as we shall see, the Edinburgh School of Arts, was not, as is often supposed, due to the increasing division of labour in factories. At the foundation of the Edinburgh School of Arts in 1821, the factory system had made limited impact outside the Lancashire cotton areas; the typical workman was a craftsman working on his own or in a small enterprise. It was in a watch and clockmaker's, not a factory, that Leonard Horner outlined to Robert Bryson his ideas for educating the Edinburgh mechanics.

The second influential factor, the growth of interest in science, had expressed itself in the rapid spread of popular scientific lecturing from the early eighteenth century attended largely by middle-class audiences. Science had a broad meaning in the early nineteenth century, defined as a body of knowledge – an intellectual style – and a mode of communication. Some of the science lecturing was organised by universities; Glasgow, for example, provided in the statutes of 1727 that 'any person, not a student as said is, may attend the lessons of Experimental Philosophy without a gown',[93] and so the enthusiasm for some scientific knowledge spread to skilled craftsmen. This was accompanied by calls for the modernisation of the school curriculum; in 1796 Adam Smith, arguing for the advantages a nation would derive from extending popular education, proclaimed the value of geometry and mechanics in primary education.[94] The *Edinburgh Review* lent the cause of mechanics' institutes much support by means of regular articles and declared that 'the sacred thirst for science is become epidemic, and we look forward to the day when the laws of matter and of mind shall be known to all men'.[95] And Southey rhymed:

> That needful knowledge in this age of light,
> Should not, by birth, be every Briton's right?[96]

However, educational advances are related to changes in social structure, even if they do not necessarily cause them, and a determination to preserve the existing order involves opposition to such advances. Even in the early nineteenth century there were some who fought bitterly against any educational provision for the working class as being detrimental to the interests of society. The Anglican Bishop of London in 1803 affirmed that 'men of considerable ability say that it is safest both for the Government and the religion of the country to let the lower classes remain in that state of ignorance in which nature has originally placed them'.[97] Mr Davies Giddy's speech in a Commons debate in 1807 also characterises this perspective:

> Giving education to the labouring classes of the poor ... would be prejudicial to their morals and happiness; it would teach them to despise their lot in life instead of making them good servants in agriculture and other laborious employments. Instead of teaching them subordination it would render them fractious and refractory.[98]

These tensions will be explored later when it will be shown that some groups were implacably opposed to the existence of mechanics' institutes.

Although it gradually came to be accepted that society should provide for the broader educational needs of the working classes (and progress came earlier in Scotland than in England), the class factor influenced the *nature* of provision since one key aspect of science in the nineteenth century was its low status. Classical education became a sign of social privilege, and science was identified with 'useful knowledge', a popular term in the 1820s, to be studied as a vocational subject rather than as part of a liberal education. This low status of science subjects released them from the objections levelled against other forms of education for the working classes, that they would raise the labourer above his station.[99]

Third, as Kelly suggested, the rise of mechanics' institutes may also be regarded as forming part of a more general movement for popular education. The idea that education should be an obligation owed by society to its citizens only gained acceptance in Britain around 1800. In the early nineteenth century there were reports of grown men returning to school seeking the education they had missed when younger; in winter it was common for farm labourers in Aberdeenshire to 'tak a raith at the coontin'.[100] The movement to develop adult education in the early nineteenth century was assisted by the endeavours of two main groups of philanthropic patrons with humanitarian and religious motives:[101] evangelical churchmen – William Wilberforce, Zachary Macaulay and others – and Quakers, notably William Allen. Few periods of British history have been so passionately committed to reform as the early decades of the nineteenth century and the educational work of these groups took place alongside other philanthropic and humanitarian endeavours. Britons campaigned zealously to abolish slavery, for trade unionism, parliamentary reform, temperance and factory reform. Adopting a different perspective was the Whig–Radical group – Jeremy Bentham, James Mill, and in parliament Joseph Hume, Henry Brougham and others – which was inspired predominantly by the ideal of social justice.

Finally, the urge to create mechanics' institutes must be considered in relation to the wider movement for political and economic improvement of workers, initiated not by the paternalistic middle class but by the workers themselves. The major focus in the early nineteenth century was the agitation for the reform of Parliament. Adult education, in the political sense, formed an important part of the programme. The mechanics' institutes should be viewed as part of the general pattern of working-class aspirations. Many of those who joined them were active also in other phases of the working-class movement, and were looking to the institutes to help, an expectation that was largely unfulfilled.[102]

Credit for the first full-scale proposals for mechanics' institutes is generally ascribed to Thomas Dick, a Secession Church schoolmaster from the small Perthshire weaving town of Methven who in a letter to the *Monthly Magazine* in 1814 indulged the hope that 'the period is fast approaching when the ignorance and superstition of former ages shall be dispelled and the gates of the temple of science thrown open to all'.[103] He outlined a scheme 'for the establishment of literary and philosophical societies, among the middling and lower ranks of the community ... for the purpose of diffusing information, as well as making improvements and discoveries in art and science'.[104]

The inauguration of the first ever mechanics' institute in Edinburgh on 16 October 1821 stimulated other similar educational initiatives. Some time before July 1823 a school of arts was also established by one Samuel Brown in Haddington, the precursor of which had been a system of 'itinerating libraries' with books, chiefly of a religious character, circulating between a score of centres in East Lothian. Samuel Smiles, later the author of *Self Help*, was a lecturer there when he was a young man. Meanwhile, in Glasgow, friction arose between Anderson's institution and its mechanics class. The mechanics wished to have their own management and they seceded and formed an independent school of arts, the Glasgow Mechanics' Institution, on 5 November 1823.[105] Hence, by the end of

1823, five mechanics' institutes were in existence in Scotland, at Edinburgh, Glasgow, Greenock, Haddington and Kilmarnock, together with one in London. From the three major original centres in Edinburgh, Glasgow and London, the institutes sponsored by local dissenters, radicals of various hues, especially Whigs, and reform-minded civil leaders, spread rapidly throughout Britain. The year 1824 witnessed new institutes in Scotland, at Aberdeen, Hawick and Dundee, one in Wales and nine in England.[106] The vintage year was 1825, when around 70 new institutes were founded, doubtless as a result of the favourable economic climate of the period, and they were concentrated mainly in London, Scotland and the industrial counties of northern England.[107] The work of Birkbeck was also known abroad, and for Americans, who always felt comfortable in the assurances of an Old World precedent, it partly inspired the founding of the New York Mechanic and Scientific Institution as early as 1822 and the Franklin Institute in Philadelphia in 1824.[108]

Dangerous Knowledge? Radicals and Reaction

The educational thinking of radical movements in the early nineteenth century inherited a detailed philosophy and a framework elaborated by French radical philosophers of the eighteenth century.[109] Henry Brougham, a Whig who was inspired not so much by religion as by utilitarianism and a Benthamite ideal of social justice, was a moving spirit in the foundation of the *Edinburgh Review* in 1802, together with Francis, later Lord Jeffrey, and Leonard Horner's brother, the political economist Francis, later to become a crusading MP against the slave trade.[110] The *Edinburgh Review* became the most influential journal in the United Kingdom, publishing regular supportive articles on mechanics' institutes. Brougham became the acknowledged champion of public education in the early nineteenth century.[111] From his efforts arose the principles that govern modern policy towards education: state capital grants to establish new schools, government inspection of schools, and attempts by the state to ensure an adequate supply of schoolteachers.[112] Brougham set himself up as a type of clearing house of advice for institutions all over the country.[113] His greatest service, however, was the publication, in 1825, of his pamphlet *Practical Observations upon the Education of the People, Addressed to the Working Classes and their Employers,* dedicated to Birkbeck,[114] in which he outlined a general plan for establishing and managing mechanics' institutes throughout Great Britain. Brougham argued in the face of those who saw the education of working men as a danger, that a greater threat to good public order was ignorance. Working men, if given the opportunity to advance their education, would be 'the effectual friends of improvement in all our institutions. The possession of knowledge ... gives them a direct *interest* in the peace and good order of the community, and renders them solicitous to avoid whatever may disturb it.'[115]

Brougham explicitly assumed that workers had the time and money to devote to self-education, whereas a high proportion of the population in the 1820s were too ground down by poverty and too exhausted by protracted labour to do other than eke out a short life in ignorance. Yet Brougham argued that 'no such scheme can ... spread over the country ... unless its support is derived from those who are chiefly to reap the benefits'.[116] Furthermore, Brougham suggested that to be successful, mechanics' institutes should be both self-supporting and self-managing, suggesting that the mechanics 'should have the principal share in the management',[117] and that 'the people themselves must be the great agents in accomplishing the works of their own instruction'.[118] Majority worker representation on the board of directors, as urged by Brougham, did not necessarily mean 'workers control'. Brougham was also the founding spirit and chairman of the Society for the Diffusion of Useful Knowledge (SDUK),

Henry Brougham, 1st Baron Brougham and Vaux. By James Stewart, Scottish National Portrait Gallery

established in 1826, and many of its 46-member committee, which included Leonard Horner, had links with the utilitarian school of philosophy; the other common element of the committee was a belief in Whig politics.[119] The diffusion of knowledge was seen as a great panacea by both Radical and Whig. The main aim of the Radicals in supporting the SDUK was to propagate the doctrine of the unity of interest of employer and employee, the latter having the duty to follow where the former led. It was not that SDUK *could* not disseminate knowledge among the people; it was that they *would* not.[120] No work on political economy was ever circulated. The middle classes were condescending and condemnatory when they had no intention of being so. They tried to impose their standards and ideology, especially political economy, on people whose needs were different.

It was no surprise that Brougham's ideas and proposals attracted critical reaction from Tories, most notably from the anonymous 'Country Gentleman' who, in 1826, argued that 'it was just as ridiculous to try and elevate the beasts of the field as to teach tailors and cobblers the beautiful system of geometry'.[121] The outcome of the work of Brougham's institutes, Country Gentleman claimed, would be precisely the social upheaval which Brougham and his colleagues said they were attempting to avert. Our ancestors, Country Gentleman asserted, 'wisely confined the superior sort of education to birth and wealth ... and given a stable social order, there is no justification for altering the distribution of knowledge in society, and every reason for keeping it as it is'.[122] The *St James's Chronicle* echoed this opinion, writing of mechanics' institutes: 'A scheme more completely adapted for the destruction of this Empire could not have been invented by the author of evil himself.'[123]

An earlier expression of hostility to this form of adult education occurred in *Blackwood's Edinburgh Magazine* in a review of Brougham's *Practical Observations* in May 1825. This journal, which was rejuvenated by the Tories in response to the founding of the *Scotsman* as a liberal weekly, having described Lord Brougham as 'without question the most fanatical and outrageous party-man in the three Kingdoms',[124] reminded its readers that 'whenever the lower orders of any great state have obtained a smattering of knowledge, they have generally used it to produce national ruin'.[125] Men like Brougham 'should be scrupulously prevented from interfering in any shape with the "education of the people", the opinions and schemes of these persons are things *to be judged of by the educated* and not to be *taught to the uneducated*'.[126] The whole mechanics' institute movement was

calculated to take the working classes from the guidance of their superiors ... to make these mechanics the corrupters and petty demagogues of the working orders generally; to dissolve the bonds between the poor and the rich, create insubordination, and ferment those animosities which unfortunately prevail so much already between servants and masters; to injure industry, good workmanship and morals.[127]

Brougham, Horner, the Whigs and the *Edinburgh Review*, however, sought to *prevent* insubordination and the dissolution of such bonds by leading and directing the new forces, lest they build up of their own accord to the tempest.[128] Although there is a note of conviction in Brougham's writings which commands respect, a measure of the opposition shown towards mechanics' institutes was due to the personal antagonism he aroused; exception was taken to the 'spirit of faction and violence' which was said to be 'mingled with all his projects'.[129] There was biting satire in the advertisement of his functions at the University of London: 'Mr. Henry Brougham will inculcate the principles of subordination, respect for superiors, admiration of virtue, and the regulation of temper, and give lectures upon the cultivation of silk in cold climates.'[130]

The Brougham pamphlet, despite bitter opposition from some quarters, was a major catalyst in the subsequent establishment of mechanics' institutes. Glasgow differed from Edinburgh in adopting Brougham's ideas of democratic management in the hands of the mechanics, although later it was compelled to rely on the support of the wealthy.[131] The diffusion of new institutes was related to the progress of the Industrial Revolution, to the urbanisation of the population consequent on that revolution, and in particular to the need for skilled workers. The origins of the mechanics' institutes varied according to local circumstances and personalities but, in general, the lead was taken by the middle classes. The manufacturers, merchants, bankers and petit bourgeoisie were not slow to realise that it was in their interest, as well as of the workers themselves, that their employees should be better educated. The local aristocracy frequently gave the movement their approval, but they did not take the initiative.[132]

The Development of Mechanics' Institutes: Alternative Ideological Perspectives

lthough the mechanics' institutes performed important economic functions in an industrialising society by providing scientific education for artisans, the founding of the institutes, like much of British educational policy in the early nineteenth century, was also partly informed by an interest in social control. Middle-class social reform effort was motivated less by humanitarianism than by the threat that an increasingly articulate and organised working class posed to ordered society. This is not to deny that the reformers were interested in improving the education of artisans and mechanics'; they were, but only if it did not unleash forces which might threaten everything held dear by respectable middle-class society.

Middle-class patronage in the early years of most mechanics' institutes was the norm, not only to provide the necessary finance and to guide the working men in the art of committee work, but also to exercise social control. Like most philanthropic efforts of this kind, there lay behind the pious rhetoric and noble sentiments well-defined ideological objectives. During the early nineteenth century there were two contrasting ideological positions underpinning the movements for adult education in general and for mechanics' institutes in particular. The first of these perspectives was that of the natural theologians who combined advocacy of adult education with adherence to evangelical Christianity, reconciling science and religion in the belief that scientific study revealed God's purposes in nature. This ideology was articulated by three individuals, George Miller of Dunbar, Samuel Brown of Haddington and Thomas Dick of Methven, two of whom, Miller and Dick, wrote books on natural theology.[133] The salient feature associated with these writers was a blending of Enlightenment scientific interests with evangelical Christianity combined with a desire to see the 'sentiments of the lower classes' acquire their 'proper tone'.[134] Education as an antidote to crime was a central feature of the debate, but rescuing the poor for religion and the maintenance of the existing social structure were key facets of the agenda.

The alternative ideology informing the mechanics' institute movement, 'value-free science', although a secular one, in no way reflected anti-religious sentiments; it stressed man's ingenuity in applying the laws of nature rather than God's ingenuity reflected through the laws of nature.[135] The rhetoric associated with the secular science of the mechanics' institutes set before the working class the vision of a future central to which is the belief that there is an internal logic underlying the inevitable advance of science, technology and capitalist-inspired economic growth. The physical sciences taught at the mechanics' institutes were associated, at the level of rhetoric, with the notion of technological progress, whereas for a natural theologian such as Dick, science was seen primarily as the embodiment of God's design, rather than the man-made world of machinery and industrial processes:

> One subordinate use of the knowledge derived from this science [natural philosophy] is to enable us to construct all those mechanical engines which facilitate human labour. . . . A still nobler and higher use to which philosophy is subservient, is to demonstrate the wisdom and intelligence of the Great First Cause of all things.[136]

Dick disapproved of the secular 'value-free' approach which characterised the larger institutes and of the highly restricted curriculum of chemistry, mechanics and mathematics, and sought to broaden the subject range to include the fundamental principles of religion.[137]

Despite the differences between value-free science and the natural theologians, their many similarities must not be underrated, especially the shared belief in social control. Both groups attributed little educational value to imaginative literature, being deemed unfit for the minds of the working class; and both accepted the notion of a social class hierarchy, that the middle and upper classes were endowed with a superior sort of knowledge, while conversely the knowledge of the lower orders was in important ways defective. As Shapin and Barnes have suggested, a number of polar opposites were used to contrast the top and bottom of the social hierarchy: the thinking of the working classes was regarded as 'superficial' rather than 'profound'; based on sense data rather than abstract organising principles; it was 'fragmented', failing to perceive the connections between phenomena which gave the upper classes an integrated overall understanding of issues; and it did not take proper account of the consequences of actions.[138] These views on the mentality of the lower orders influenced proposals for curricula in the mechanics' institutes. Hence natural theology and value-free science represented differences of emphasis within a more general educational crusade against traditional working-class culture.

From the beginning, however, powerful interests worked against the success of the institutes, as originally conceived. While some Tories displayed a similar spirit of enlightenment, the old guard of the Tory party viewed the institutes with suspicion as potential nests of revolution and political dissent, and were antipathetic on the grounds that this might disturb the foundations of a rigidly structured society.[139] Attempts to extend scientific education to adult workers provoked less hostility from Scottish Tories since the parochial schools system was widely accepted and it was less exceptional for the poor to be literate.[140] Similarly, Church of England and Roman Catholic clergy, with one or two exceptions, were suspicious of encouraging large working-class gatherings, no matter how laudable their purpose, and were antagonised by the practice of eschewing religious instruction. Despite Brougham's protestations that a thinking workman could be a devout workman, the portion of the Church of England which had earlier opposed even the teaching of reading and writing to poor children continued to believe otherwise.[141] Conversely, Nonconformist ministers, especially Unitarians with their rationalist ideals, were keen advocates.[142] The opposition of the Church of England may have been due in part to the activity of dissenters in that 'some of Mr. Brougham's leading co-operators are Unitarians, and consequently members of a sect hostile to the Established Church'.[143]

The Curriculum of Mechanics' Institutes

The curriculum introduced initially by most mechanics' institutes was predominantly scientific; 'pure' rather than 'applied'; factual rather than theoretical or speculative; and simplified in presentation. There is little evidence, even of an anecdotal nature, as to the pedagogical methods used in the various institutes, although the lectorial style was almost universal.[144] Brougham was a strong advocate of the lecture as the basic teaching mode. He argued that 'much may thus be taught, even without any other instruction; but, combined with reading, and subservient to it, the effects of public lectures are great indeed'.[145] This view did not go unchallenged. *Edinburgh Blackwood's Magazine* declared that lectures were 'almost wholly useless for teaching working men, for the first time, the arts and sciences'.[146] The Edinburgh School of Arts, where the emphasis was placed on a restricted scientific curriculum and on forming habits of self-discipline and obedience which industry demanded of its labouring classes, was widely cited as the purest example of the original ideas. It was generally assumed that the children of the working classes would themselves become manual workers and that they should receive an education appropriate to their station in life.[147]

Natural theologians inclined towards astronomy, physiology and phrenology since these subjects yielded examples of God's design in nature. The science of the institutes was not, however, solely informed by the natural theological perspective; after all, chemistry, natural philosophy and mathematics were initially the core of the curriculum in Edinburgh and many other institutes, reflecting local institutional politics (see later). The emphasis on a restricted menu of certain sciences was justified by their value neutrality and objectivity, free of disturbing political implications. Conversely, the mechanics' institutes were reluctant to consider social and political issues. 'Religion and politic', wrote Holyoake, were 'the terrors of Mechanics' Institutions.'[148] Consequently, the exclusion of theological subjects from the curriculum resulted in the study of science developing without any direct connection with religious teaching, and concern was expressed by clerical writers that this would lead to scepticism with regard to the existence and providence of God.[149] Brougham, however, responded that 'the more widely science diffused the better will the Author of all things be known'.[150]

The issue of including political economy on the institutes' curricula divided the natural theologians from the radical Whigs. Part of the corpus of knowledge pursued by the literati of the Enlightenment in Scotland was concerned with a dynamic analysis of history, economics, politics and society; indeed, the subject of political economy was developed in Scotland and the lineage from Adam Smith to Dugald Stewart and writers such as Jeffrey and Francis Horner, who introduced it to the wider public, was clear and uninterrupted. The natural theologians were suspicious of subjects such as political economy, whereas Henry Brougham, who produced *Political Philosophy* in 1840, stressed its importance in promoting social harmony in times of economic crisis:

> I can hardly imagine . . . a greater service being rendered to the men than expounding to them the true principles of mutual relations of population and wages. . . . The peace of the country, and the stability of the government, could not more effectively be secured than by the universal diffusion of this kind of knowledge.[151]

Ironically, the lecturers in political economy were perceived frequently by their Scottish audience not as disinterested scholars but as 'employers' spokesmen sheltering behind a facade of religious, scientific and philanthropic notions'.[152]

Religious, political and political economy literature was almost universally banned from the institutes' libraries, and few (not including Edinburgh) made available fiction or newspapers, seen as a fatuous distraction from the serious business of learning.[153] This was supported by *Edinburgh Blackwood's Magazine*, which asserted that 'the mass of mechanics are grossly ignorant . . . every one knows that a profusion of most pernicious publications would incessantly court their attention'.[154] Controversial topics in politics or religion were studiously avoided;[155] the educational ethos would have met with the unreserved approval of Thomas Gradgrind. The founders of these institutes succumbed to the common fallacy, not unknown even today, that men who worked with machinery would be interested in science rather than politics, economics, literature or travel, anything that afforded relaxation from the heavy burden of their daily toil. Such a narrow curriculum led to a falling off in attendance at many institutes and drove many workers to return to the conviviality of the public house.

In designing the scientific curricula for the artisans, those features of knowledge which facilitated speculative thinking or which exposed its theoretical assumptions and hence weakened its credibility, were usually avoided.[156] The Reverend Thomas Chalmers, the Evangelical leader, political conservative and later professor of moral philosophy at St Andrews, argued by analogy with missionary work that it had been found more expedient to 'let down English knowledge and philosophy to the capacity and station of the Hindoos' than to attempt to 'raise the Hindoos to the level of English knowledge and philosophy'.[157] Even Brougham suggested that, in teaching the 'multitude' geometry,

> it is not necessary to go through the whole steps of that beautiful system by which … truths are connected with the few simple definitions and axioms: enough will be accomplished, if they are made to perceive the nature of geometrical investigation, and learn the leading properties of a figure.[158]

An organ of the Church of Scotland approved of the Edinburgh School of Arts curriculum and teaching, but was critical of workers spending their time

> in puzzling [their] brains in algebra … or in wandering in the thorny path of metaphysics, or in the ill-macadamized roads of even physics themselves, where the lecturers … stand waving their rods over kittle curves and conic sections, and statements of the differential calculus, rather than in showing by experiment how things really are in nature.[159]

Science for the artisan concentrated on facts and laws, not theoretically informed or subject to revision, in stark contrast to the metaphysical science of the Scottish academic tradition.[160]

The Link between Curriculum, Behaviour and Morals

The benefits to be expected from mechanics' institutes went far beyond enhancing scientific knowledge. A knowledge of science, Brougham insisted, 'would make him [the mechanic] better and a happier, as well as a wiser man, if he soared a little into those regions of purer science where happily neither doubt can cloud, nor passion ruffle our serene path'.[161] As has been shown, the natural theologians and supporters of value-free science shared a set of assumptions about how the lower-class mind functioned and were confident that there was something especially effective about scientific education in achieving social control of the working class by transforming their values, behaviour and morals to make them more docile, less troublesome and better disciplined.[162] If the Industrial Revolution was to be successful, there had to be fundamental changes in attitudes to work by the working classes. The older, flexible attitudes had to be supplanted by a sterner ethic emphasising the virtues of punctuality, discipline and sobriety, and the mechanics' institutes were seen as the vehicle through which to inculcate such values. The behaviour, manners and morals of the lower classes were, for Dick, an affront to Christian decency and he reasoned that scientific education, with its demands for systematic thought and discipline, afforded a means for effecting their reformation.[163] Mechanics' institutes would require the artisans to exercise self-discipline and exhibit a formality of conduct not usually associated with alternative places of assembly, such as the public house. Thus, for too many sponsors of adult education, such as Dick, intellectual development, moral reform and progress in civility were inextricably interwoven: knowledge, morals and manners were to be altered by the same educational process.[164] In short, mechanics' institutes, through the means of a scientific education, would fill the workmen's spare time with 'occupations calculated to make him feel contented with his lot'[165] and dissuade the working man from drunkenness, debauchery, promiscuity and the adoption of objectionable political notions.

Family life would also be transformed. Speakers at mechanics' institutes made frequent reference to artisans who would henceforth be peacefully occupied in the 'bosom of their families',[166] the 'intelligent father' crowned with a 'sacred halo', teaching natural philosophy to 'listening innocence and virtue'.[167] Domestic harmony was assured as the mechanic returned home 'to a cheerful wife, a clean house, and a smiling offspring',[168] although it is difficult to imagine the mechanic actually seeing much of his offspring given that he would have been attending courses at the School of Arts several nights each week and not returning home until 10.30 P.M.

The Philanthropists and Social Class Division

Contemporary accounts emphasised the 'benevolent' and 'philanthropic' motives of individuals: Hudson, the early historian of adult education writing in 1851, was confident that he was living in 'an age of philanthropy and good will to all men. The middle classes vie with the rich in providing the great and good work of education'.[169] J. V. Smith, however, has questioned the extent to which individuals were imbued with a glow of disinterested philanthropy.[170] Those who were most prominent in establishing mechanics' institutes had a sectional interest in trying to ensure they would encourage a positive attitude of the artisans towards capital. There is anecdotal evidence that this aim was successfully achieved. Members of mechanics' institutes were said to be rarely involved in 'trades' unions, and to dissociate themselves from rash policies and crude ideas', and few were 'seen in the arena of political strife'.[171] Similarly, when the societal function of social mobility through education was declared, it was always within a limited context, one reflecting the social imagery of the period. Watt, Franklin, Rennie, Ferguson and Stephenson were repeatedly mentioned as representatives of the social ultimate, but never Anderson, Bentham, Brougham or Birkbeck, even though these latter four were all concerned with the formation of working-class education.[172] Hence the vision of social mobility offered to the working-class artisans was a very narrow one. Engels 'had often heard working men, whose fustian jackets scarcely held together, speak upon geological, astronomical, and other subjects'[173] with great knowledge. Only the exceptional man, however, could expect to rise out of the class into which he had been born.

For natural theologians, such as Thomas Dick, the principle of subordination of ranks was divinely ordained:

> On the divinity of rank . . . is founded a great proportion of those moral laws which God hath promulgated . . . for regulating the inclinations and conduct of mankind.[174]

There was a concern 'not to abolish the distinction between rich and poor or to shatter the traditionalist theory of orders, ranks and degrees, but rather to justify both by introducing a new leaven of righteousness'.[175] Indeed the 'higher elevation' of the 'superior classes' depended on the improvement of 'the common people', who 'are the ground on which . . . the palaces and pyramids of society are raised'.[176]

Hence among the more important social connotations were a social structure in which those who performed good works were sharply differentiated from potential beneficiaries; a social division that was permanent; and advantages that accrued not only to the artisans but also to the upper and middle classes themselves, in the form of enhanced status.[177] The opposite was true in America. The Franklin Institute and the institutes in Boston and Maryland all had constitutional provisions that at least three-quarters of the members of their boards of directors should be practical mechanics.[178] More fundamentally, in contrast to the position in Britain, for the great majority of American mechanics' institutes, reform consisted of eliminating class distinctions rather than their solidification; to broaden the avenues of opportunity rather than to close class ranks;[179] and 'by instructing the labouring part of the community, to elevate them to their proper rank in a republican society'.[180]

Class division was viewed not simply in social terms but also in intellectual terms. As Francis Jeffrey, who was a subscriber to the Edinburgh School of Arts, argued:

> We allude now to the rapid and remarkable progress which the lower orders are making in [political economy] and in all other branches of knowledge. . . . [O]f all the derangements that can take place in a civilised community, one of the most embarrassing and discreditable would be that which arose from the working classes becoming *more intelligent* than their employers. It . . . could not fail, in the meantime, to give rise to great and unseemly disorders. To avoid this, however, there seems to be nothing left to the richer classes but to endeavour to maintain their intellectual superiority by improving their understandings.[181]

It is clear that the upper middle-class literary Whig intellectuals who pioneered the mechanics' institute movement in Scotland and Britain subscribed not to a conflict model of society but to one of conservative ameliorative action. The issue of parliamentary reform, regularly debated in the *Edinburgh Review*, illuminates the political thinking of these philanthropic gentlemen. Some of what Jeffrey and Brougham wrote can be put down to ambition, the frustration of opposition, the high opinion in which they held their own abilities, and to a natural tendency on the part of opposition to criticise those in power.[182] Writing on parliamentary reform, Jeffrey emphasised the key role of the aristocracy in parliament:

> The most perfect representative legislature must be that which reunited in itself the greatest proportion of the effective aristocracy of the country. . . . That country is happiest in which the aristocracy is most numerous and most

diversified as to the sources of its influence; that government the most suitable, secure and beneficial, which is exercised most directly by the mediation of this aristocracy.[183]

This line of argument led Jeffery to favour a balance of the three great national classes in the community: the sovereign, those with hereditary property, and the people.[184] Jeffrey also wanted the pecuniary qualification for the franchise to be raised and estimated on all kinds of property, not merely land, but the landed interest would have a lower qualification because of their 'superior weight and respectability'.[185] The Whig royalists, backbone of the mechanics' institute movement, argued that the rights of the people were best protected by a regulated hereditary monarchy and a large, open aristocracy.

The modest political reforms suggested by Jeffrey, Brougham and other Scots Whigs harmonised with a theocratic objection to interference by a secular state with the liberties of the Christian individual. Presbyterianism, however, had as its historical base a strong democratic element whereby the equality of man before God was asserted, and which held that every man was entitled to his voice, and that wisdom might be found in everyone.[186] But this notion was qualified by the idea that wisdom had to be carefully directed. The ideal of universal education and further education for the working classes was linked with the belief that by proper instruction and regulation a godly society could be created.[187]

Francis, Lord Jeffrey. By Colvin Smith, Scottish National Portrait Gallery

Mechanics' Institutes: Response of the Working-Class Movement

The middle- and upper-class advocates of mechanics' institutes had it in mind to provide scientific education for discrete occupational subcategories of 'artisans', 'operatives' or 'mechanics' and not for the working class as a whole.[188] The economic rationale of the mechanics' institutes was to permit the economy to function without skill bottlenecks, to allow a small degree of social mobility, to help preserve the social order by overt social control over institute membership, and to promote social cohesion between worker and manufacturer. The middle classes were well aware that the mechanics' institute movement was one method, along with others, of moulding society in their own image. The mechanics' institute movement was a clear attempt to modify working-class culture and behaviour and impose the accepted value system of respectable society, although it is difficult to understand the concern that popular education, without powerful safeguards, would be 'destructive to the nation'. Sponsors of mechanics' institutes were determined to ensure they remained under the influence of Radical–Whig ideas, if not personalities, and their middle-class patrons worked hard (not always successfully) to steer them clear of political discussion and religious controversy.

It was not lost on intelligent working-class men that much socio-educational effort by the middle class was inspired by an element of apprehension, at times deep fear, of independent working-class action. The education provided by the mechanics' institutes, inspired by a desire for social control, was effective in suffusing middle-class ideals and precepts to some of the 'lower orders'. For some the need to promote adult education for the working classes appeared as a moral duty, which fortunately also coincided with self-interest. The net result was a powerful and sustained propagation of the ideology of the middle classes,[189] while providing opportunities for some of the working class to better themselves. The Whig educationalists did not adopt a value-free perspective; they were drumming pro-capitalist, pro-machinery, anti-trade-union, self-help messages into working minds.

The movement, although related to the needs of a section of the working classes, was not initiated by them and was not popular with certain working-class leaders. Cobbett foresaw that with the advent of philanthropists such as Brougham and Birkbeck, control of the institutes, as at Edinburgh but not Glasgow, would be wrested from the mechanics and he expounded sarcastically over the 'brilliant enterprise to make us "a enlightened" and to fill us with "intellect", brought, ready bottled up, from the north of the Tweed'.[190] When Brougham, in his *Practical Observations* had warned that it might be wise to allow workers a considerable degree of control, even including political discussion, his advice was not heeded in many institutes. When the reaction came, it was in the form of a challenge to the very concept that the middle class should monopolise and control the workers' education in their own interests. The working class came to see through the pretensions, to understand the motives of aristocratic Whigs and Radical educationists as they found expression in the mechanics' institutes and the SDUK. The National Union of the Working Class declared:

> We will read nothing of which the Diffusion Society meddles with. They call the members of it Whigs, and the word Whig with them, means a treacherous rascal, a bitter implacable enemy.[191]

Was the knowledge offered by the SDUK and its *Penny Magazine* of any real use to the working class, asked James Watson:

> Had it any tendency to improve their condition, by giving them more of the fruits of their own labour? Would it lead them any better to understand their rights, to comprehend and act upon the principles of co-operation? No.[192]

Frederick Engels also regarded mechanics' institutes as

> organs for the dissemination of the sciences useful to bourgeoisie. Here the natural sciences are now taught, which may draw the working-man away from opposition to the bourgeoisie. ... Here all education is tame, flabby, subservient to the ruling politics and religion, so that for the working-man it is merely a constant sermon upon quiet obedience, passivity, and resignation to his fate. The mass of the working-men naturally have nothing to do with these institutes, and betake themselves to the proletarian reading-rooms and to the discussion of matters which directly concern their own interests.[193]

Throughout the Enlightenment and down to 1832, Scotland had been ruled by the Tories. By the 1830s, however, an increasing proportion of the intelligentsia was moving in the Whig direction and Scottish Whigs were successful in the Reform Bill of 1832; the formerly excluded middle class could now participate in Parliament by the extension of the franchise, increasing the Scottish electorate from 4,500 to 65,000. By insisting on a property qualification, however, it swept away such working-class rights to vote as existed, and thereby excluded the working class from any part in electing representatives to Parliament. The workers who lent support to the middle class in the campaign for parliamentary reform were rapidly disillusioned by their exclusion from the franchise in 1832 and began to understand what government by the middle class implied.[194] After the Reform Act of 1832, Radicals, while allegedly supporting the need to extend the franchise and promote education, connived at policies in the industrial field which made increased education for the workers and their children impossible. While opposing the limitation of adult hours of labour, they supported the new Poor Law which swept away old practices and safeguards in the interests of efficiency.[195] So the struggle for economic demands, for the Ten Hours Bill, for repeal of the Poor Law, for freedom of speech and the extension of the franchise fused together in the Chartist movement. Chartists recognised that the days of relying on upper-class educational patronage were over:

> The working men of this nation have passed the Rubicon, they have their own movement – their own circulating libraries – a newspaper press they claim as their own.[196]

As it became clear that the Whigs, for whom Brougham was again Lord Chancellor, had no intention of extending the franchise any further, working-class agitation for reform found its voice through the Chartists, believing, in the tradition of the Enlightenment, that the gross inequality of the 1832 Act could be overthrown by moral pressure and reason. The Chartist petition was presented to Parliament on three occasions: 1839, 1842 and 1843. The movement was dealt a mortal blow in 1842 by the rejection of its petition to the Westminster Parliament. The disorganised and divided state of Chartism resulted in the withering away of most local associations by 1843,[197] and the skilled working class (men only) had to wait until Disraeli's Second Reform Act of 1867 before receiving the vote.

Plain weavers in the west of Scotland earned only 4s 8d to 5s in 1833, and hand-loom weavers 3s weekly; even children at the New Lanark mills earned only 3d per day.[198] Such miserable wages drove workers in weaving areas to desperate measures: employers were shot at, mills set on fire, blacklegs mutilated or burned with vitriol.[199] Even in 1841 the average weekly wage in the west of Scotland for female power weavers was 7s for a working week of 69 hours.[200] Little wonder that Chartist doctrines spread through the factory population like a bush fire. After the failure of the Chartist petition, however, the working class realised that in order to achieve political power they must acquire political knowledge, and they could only gain that knowledge in educational centres under their own control. The prime mover behind the establishment of Independent Mechanics' Institutes in Lancashire – in Hulme, Salford and Manchester – was Rowland Detrosier who,

inspired by Robert Owen's vision of the good society, believed workers must found and administer their own educational centres:

> How can the working men of this country become intelligent, submitted as they are to an education which is the veriest mockery that ever insulted the human understanding? When shall they find time to devote themselves to study, who have scarcely time to swallow their food from one week's end to another? To the first enquiry I answer, become yourselves the founders and supporters of Institutions where the governing principle shall be the greatest possible knowledge of each, that all may enjoy the greatest possible happiness. Where the business of youthful education shall be to form the character of the future man; ... where, in short, education shall be rationally conducted.[201]

Detrosier's initiative was supported by John Doherty, leader of the Lancashire cotton operatives and most prominent trade unionist of his time. Doherty observed ironically in a leader in his journal, *The Poor Man's Advocate and People's Library*, that teachers in mechanics' institutes

> professing to be for the exclusive use of the working class ... seem to imagine that it is of much more consequence to the working man to understand the theory of winds, which it is impossible he can control, than the theory of government, which can render him either happy or miserable. ... Let the huxtering owners of the misnamed Mechanics' Institutions, and the would-be

rulers of mechanics' minds, see that the day is gone by when the millions will be satisfied with the puny morsel of mental food which aristocratic pride and pampered cunning have been wont to deal out to them.[202]

Robert Owen attended the annual delegate meeting of the independent mechanics' institute in Manchester in 1833. Owen, born the son of a saddler, started work at the age of 10 but by 1800 had become manager of a large textile concern in Scotland, the New Lanark Mills, where he implemented his radical educational ideas. He argued that industry could be rendered efficient and profitable by humane treatment of the workers and by an education designed to develop potentialities of all kinds.[203] Owen's ideas diffused through the country.

A school opened in Salford in 1831 was the intellectual, social and propaganda centre for the Owenite movement in the Manchester district.[204] When, in the late 1830s, it was transformed into one of the first Owenite Halls of Science, a new phase of educational activity had begun.[205] From 1839, Halls of Science, inspired by Owen and controlled by socialists, started to proliferate, especially in the north of England, and they were supplemented by more numerous socialist Sunday schools and Chartist Halls.[206] By 1841 no less than £32,000 had been invested by the Society of Rational Religionists in building Halls of Science, which could hold a total of 22,000.[207] The new Halls of Science were opposed by employers and the clergy and there was considerable intimidation. There was even a violent assault on Owen himself when he visited the Bristol hall in 1841.[208] The workers' disillusion

Robert Owen. By Mary Ann Knight, Scottish National Portrait Gallery

with the mechanics' institutes was the background against which the Halls of Science were supported. Mechanics' institutes, proclaimed the *New Moral World* in 1840, were willing to educate the working people in so far as the instruction given squared with the 'interests of the clergy and the wealthy classes';[209] by contrast, Owenites were concerned to produce not capable machine operators, but fully developed men and women exposed not only to physical and natural science, but also to social and political science.

The extent to which such sentiments, and the relative strength of the natural theology and value-free science perspectives, influenced the thinking and policies of the directors of the nascent Edinburgh School of Arts, as it evolved from 1821, will be an important theme of the next two chapters.

The Influence of the Edinburgh School of Arts on the Mechanics' Institute Movement

Many of the policies implemented by the directors of the School of Arts, as the pioneering mechanics' institute, were advocated and adopted by other institutes in Britain. The founders of the Leeds Institute received advice from Leonard Horner and Lord Brougham before drafting their own rules.[210] When the Manchester Institution was founded in 1824, it followed the Edinburgh model by entrusting the management of the institute solely to honorary members, a move deplored by Brougham,[211] as did Leeds under the influence of Horner's advice 'to avoid falling into the error of giving too much of the direction of the establishment to the Mechanics themselves'.[212] Their aim was to use their powers to instil their own doctrines of the freedom of industry and the security of property, and to ensure this they banned all political and religious controversy and any form of free discussion, normally not even allowing newspapers on the premises. The aim of the Manchester Mechanics' Institution was inspired by that of the Edinburgh School:

> The Institute is formed for the purpose of enabling mechanics and artisans, of whatever trade they may be, to become acquainted with such branches of science as are of practical application in the exercise of that trade.[213]

Indeed, Benjamin Heywood, the public-spirited banker and Unitarian (he became an Anglican in 1840) who founded the Manchester Institution, referred to the Edinburgh School in his address of 30 March 1825 as 'an institution for which we are all indebted for the ground work of our regulations'.[214] Again, at the annual general meeting of members on 28 February 1838, Heywood suggested that meritorious students should be awarded a certificate of proficiency:

> I am indebted for this suggestion to a conversation on the subject with my friend Mr. Horner; his indefatigable and judicious exertions in the establishment of the Edinburgh School of Arts, which formed the ground work of our own Institution are known to you and the great cause of popular education has not a more zealous advocate. It is with no common pleasure that I witness his presence here this evening.[215]

The Manchester founders also looked to the Edinburgh School as a model for their educational policy. A major defect of many mechanics' institutes as centres of learning was the failure to provide a progressive system of graduated instruction. The Edinburgh School pioneered this idea, and at the annual Christmas party in 1838 Heywood did not confine his remarks to seasonal greetings but spoke of his desire to develop the subject teaching into two or three years of progressive study 'by following the example which has worked so well in the Edinburgh School of Arts'. [216]

The influence of the School of Arts became global, extending to Australia as early as the 1830s. The Reverend J. D. Lang, a graduate of Glasgow University, arrived in Sydney from Scotland in 1823 and, as a member of the Legislative Council, was intimately concerned with every colonial enactment.[217] He was the first Presbyterian minister to officiate in New South Wales and his violently expressed prejudices against Irish Catholics motivated him to organise four shipments of emigrants from Scotland as contributions to permanent colonisation. The ethnic and religious sentiments that underlay his immigration schemes were not universally popular in the colony; he was constantly at odds with government officials and the Colonial Office and, at the age of 60, was horsewhipped in the street.[218] He chartered a ship, the *Stirling Castle*, in 1831 and filled it with 52 Scottish mechanics and their families to take them to Sydney to build a secondary school, the Australian College.[219] In keeping with the Calvinistic tone of the initiative, it was decided to devote the months at sea to the moral and intellectual enlightenment of the mechanics: five days per week of the four-month voyage were devoted to the study of arithmetic and geometry, taught by the Reverend Henry Carmichael. Although lack of previous education condemned the majority of mechanics to the role of onlookers only, some five or six who had previously attended the Edinburgh School of Arts finished six books of Euclid and even mastered logarithms before the ship had reached Port Jackson. After departure from the Cape of Good Hope, twice weekly instruction in political economy was offered, and before long some thirty mechanics had worked through the first two books of the *Wealth of Nations*.[220]

Two ingredients were necessary to produce a mechanics' institute in Sydney: initiative from the state and moral revolutionaries. The moral revolutionaries arrived in October 1831 on the *Stirling Castle*. The Reverend Henry Carmichael was invited by Governor Bourke of New South Wales to found a mechanics' institute in the colony.[221] The venture was an immediate success and with a membership of 812 by 1841, 1 in every 14 Sydney male adults was a member.[222] The *Stirling Castle* immigrants were an elite among workmen: one-third of them joined the new Sydney Mechanics' Institute, several started Scottish horticultural and similar societies, and obtained positions on Sydney City Council.[223]

Notes

[1] Magnusson, M. (1974) *The Clacken and the Slate: The Story of the Edinburgh Academy 1824–1974*, London, p. 15.

[2] Cruft, K. and Fraser, A. (1995) *James Craig 1744–1795*, Edinburgh, p. 13.

[3] Shapin, S. (1983) Nibbling at the teats of science: Edinburgh and the diffusion of science in the 1830s. In Inkster, I. and Morrell, J. (eds) *Metropolis and Province: Science in British Culture 1780–1850*, London, p. 152.

[4] Checkland, S. and Checkland, O. (1984) *Industry and Ethos in Scotland 1832–1914*, London, p. 36.

[5] Saunders, L. J. (1950) *Scottish Democracy 1815–1840*, Edinburgh, p. 88.

[6] Checkland and Checkland, *op. cit.*, p. 36.

[7] *Ibid.*, p. 37.

[8] Smout, T. C. (1986) *A Century of the Scottish People 1830–1950*, London, p. 34.

[9] Magnusson, *op. cit.*, p. 22.

[10] Handley, J. E. (1943) *The Irish in Scotland, 1798–1845*, Cork, p. 133. The Edinburgh to Glasgow railway line was opened in 1842 and the route south to Berwick-upon-Tweed followed in 1846.

[11] Gray, R. (1976) *The Labour Aristocracy in Victorian Edinburgh*, Oxford, p. 11.

[12] Daiches, D. (1978) *Edinburgh*, Hamish Hamilton, London, p. 223.

[13] *Reports on the Sanitary Conditions of the Labouring Population of Scotland* (House of Lords Papers, 1842, v. 28) p. 156.

[14] Engels, F. (1844) *The Condition of the Working Class in England* (1983 edition), Oxford, p. 47.

[15] Quoted in MacGregor, F. (1981) *The Story of Greyfriars Bobby*, Edinburgh, p. 42. I am grateful to Prof. R. J. Knops for drawing this to my attention.

[16] Magnusson, *op. cit.*, p. 20.

[17] Daiches, *op. cit.*, p. 224.

[18] In 1831 the number of capitalists, bankers, professional men 'and other liberally educated persons' was estimated at 7,463 in a population of 161,909 (including Leith). Glasgow was reported to have only 2,723 in a population of 202,426. The Edinburgh figure explains the presence in the city of 1,400 male servants and 12,500 female servants. Census of 1831.

[19] Lythe, S. G. E. and Butt, J. (1975) Population and economic growth 1707–1871. In Lythe, S. G. E. and Butt, J., *An Economic History of Scotland 1100–1939*, Glasgow and London, p. 106.

[20] Checkland and Checkland *op. cit.*, p. 37.

[21] Knox, J. (1905) *The History of the Reformation of Religion in Scotland*, London. This contains the Book of Discipline.

[22] Letter from Prof. Alex Tyrrell to Prof. P. N. O'Farrell, 10 November 2002.

[23] *Ibid.*, p. 382.

[24] Smout, T. C. (1969) *A History of the Scottish People 1560–1830*, London, p. 96.

[25] *Ibid.*, p. 454.

[26] Letter from Prof. Alex Tyrrell to Prof. P. N. O'Farrell, 10 November 2002.

[27] Wilson, A. (1970) *The Chartist Movement in Scotland*, London, p. 10.

[28] Checkland, O. (1980) *Philanthropy in Victorian Scotland*, Edinburgh, p. 104.

[29] Saunders, L. J. (1950) *Scottish Democracy 1815–1840*, Edinburgh, p. 275.

[30] *Ibid.*, p. 242.

[31] Smout (1986), *op. cit.*, p. 209. The Scottish attitude, which was destined in the course of the nineteenth century to become the norm in Britain as a whole, was articulated by Adam Smith in *The Wealth of Nations*.

[32] Wilson, *op. cit.*, p. 12.

[33] Anderson, R. D. (1983) *Education and Opportunity in Victorian Scotland: Schools and Universities*, Oxford, pp. 8–9.

[34] Smout (1986), *op. cit.*, p. 211.

[35] Smout (1986), *op. cit.*, p. 214.

[36] Saunders, *op. cit.*, p. 274.

[37] Anderson, *op. cit.*, p. 15.

[38] *Ibid.*, p. 187.

[39] Curtis, S. J. (1967) *History of Education in Great Britain*, 7th edn, London, p. 533.

[40] Smout (1986), *op. cit.*, p. 213.

[41] Scotland, J. (1969) *The History of Scottish Education*, London, Vol. 2, p. 266.

[42] Anderson, *op. cit.*, p. 336.

[43] From 1583, with the founding of Marischal College, there were two universities in Aberdeen.

[44] Scotland, *op. cit.*, Vol. 1, p. 263.

[45] Anderson, *op. cit.*, pp. 3–4.

[46] Bagehot, W. (1879) The First Edinburgh Reviewers, *Literary Studies*, Hutton, R. H. (ed.) 2 vols.

[47] Chitnis, A. C. (1976) *The Scottish Enlightenment: A Social History*, London, p. 142.

[48] Letters chiefly connected with the Affairs of Scotland from Henry Cockburn to Thomas Francis Kennedy MP (1874) pp. 137–38.

[49] Checkland, *op. cit.*, p. 126.

[50] Scotland, *op. cit.*, Vol. 2, p. 274.

[51] Hansard, cccxxxvii, HC 20 June 1889, col. 381.

[52] Quoted in Anderson, *op. cit.*, p. 32.

[53] What students sought was to gain the learning and testimonials of the masters, and it was only those who required the degree for specific purposes (such as the ministry) who actually bothered to obtain it. I am grateful to Dr Norman Reid, former Heriot-Watt University archivist, for clarifying this point.

[54] Inkster, I. (1985) Hypotheses: patterns in the economic and social history of steam intellect prior to 1914. In Inkster, I. (ed.) *The Steam Intellect Societies: Essays on Culture, Education, and Industry, circa 1820–1914*, London, p. 193.

[55] Cosh, Mary (2003) *Edinburgh: The Golden Age*, Edinburgh, p. 807.

[56] Podmore, F. (1906) *Robert Owen*, London, p. 357.

[57] Simon, B. (1960) *Studies in the History of Education 1780–1870*, London, *op. cit.*, p. 198.

[58] Shapin, S. (1983) Nibbling at the teats of science: Edinburgh and the diffusion of science in the 1830s. In Inkster and Morrell, *op. cit.*, p. 154.

[59] Gibbon, C. (1878) *The Life of George Combe*, London, Vol. 1, p. 177.

[60] *Ibid.*, p. 154.

[61] Popular Education. Address to the public by the directors of the Edinburgh Philosophical Association, Edinburgh 1835, p. 8. Quoted in Shapin, *op. cit.*, p. 155.

[62] *Ibid.*, p. 155.

[63] *Ibid.*, p. 162.

[64] *Ibid.*, p. 169.

[65] Cosh, *op. cit.*, p. 756.

[66] Chambers, W. (1882) *Story of a Long & Busy Life*, Edinburgh, p. 30. Quoted in Tyrrell, A. (1969) Political economy, Whiggism and the education of working class adults in Scotland 1817–1840. *Scottish Historical Review*, Vol. XLVIII, no. 2, p. 159.

[67] Webb, R. K. (1955) *The British Working Class Reader*, London, p. 77.

[68] Simon, *op. cit.*, p. 144.

[69] *Ibid.*, p. 45.

[70] *Ibid.*, p. 46.

[71] Cavanagh, F. A. (1931) *James and John Stuart Mill on Education*, p. 15.

[72] Mill, J. S. (1923) *Autobiography*, London, p. 108.

[73] Cavanagh, *op. cit.*, p. xi.

[74] Simon, *op. cit.*, p. 146.

[75] *Ibid.*, p. 75.

[76] *Ibid.*, p. 144.

[77] *Ibid.*, p. 75.

[78] Cavanagh, *op. cit.*, p. 58.

[79] Simon, *op. cit.*, p. 147.

[80] Butt, J. (1996) *John Anderson's Legacy: The University of Strathclyde and Its Antecedents 1796–1996*, East Linton, p. 31.

[81] *Mechanics Magazine* (1823) Vol. 1, no. 12, 15 November, pp. 178–91.

[82] Cable, J. (1973) Early Scottish science: the vocational provision, *Annals of Science*, p. 194.

[83] Hudson, J. W. (1851) p. 36. A nominal fee of 1s was charged for the second course, raised to 5s for the third, and then reduced to 2s 6d after representations by Birkbeck.

[84] Kelly, T. (1952) The origin of mechanics' institutes, *British Journal of Education Studies*, November, p. 23.

[85] Kelly, T. (1957) *George Birkbeck: Pioneer of Adult Education*, Liverpool, p. 20.

[86] Scotland, *op. cit.*, Vol. 1, p. 167.

[87] *Ibid.*, p. 167.

[88] Cable, *op. cit.*, pp. 181–94.

[89] Read, J. (1950) Joseph Black MD: the teacher and the man. In Kent, A. (ed.) *An Eighteenth Century Lectureship in Chemistry*, Glasgow, p. 84.

[90] Considerable confusion has arisen from the use of the term 'mechanics' institute'. Most institutes were intended for skilled artisans rather than labourers. As the movement spread, however, 'mechanics' was commonly used more loosely, to include ordinary machine tenders, and other semi-skilled or even unskilled labourers.

[91] Kelly, (1957) *op. cit.*, p. 56.

[92] *Ibid.*, p. 56.

[93] *Munimenta Alme Universitatis Glasguensis*, Vol. 11, p. 578, cf. Kelly (1957), *op. cit.*, p. 20.

[94] Smith, A. (1776) *The Wealth of Nations*, Book V, Part III, Art. II.

[95] *Edinburgh Review*, August 1825, Vol. XI, p. 499.

[96] Verse quoted by Dr O. Gregory in a speech at Deptford and reported in *Mechanics Magazine*, 18 November 1826.

[97] Cotgrove, S. T. (1958) *Technical Education and Social Change*, London, p. 17.

[98] Quoted in Hammond, J. L. and Hammond, B. (1949) *The Town Labourer*, 2nd edn, Vol. 1, London, p. 66.

[99] Cotgrove, *op. cit.*, pp. 16–17.

[100] Scotland, *op. cit.*, Vol. 1, p. 264.

[101] Kelly (1957), *op. cit.*, p. 63.

[102] *Ibid.*, p. 66.

[103] Dick, Thomas (1814) Letter to the editor of the *Monthly Magazine*, Vol. 37, p. 219.

[104] *Monthly Magazine*, Vol. 37, pp. 219–21, cf. Kelly (1952) *op. cit.*

[105] Kelly (1957), *op. cit.*, p. 74.

[106] *Ibid.*, p. 209.

[107] *Ibid.*, p. 209.

[108] Sinclair, B. (1974) *Philadelphia's Philosopher Mechanics: A History of the Franklin Institute, 1824–1865*, Baltimore, pp. 7–8.

[109] Silver, H. (1964) *The Concept of Popular Education*, London, p. 52.

[110] The *Edinburgh Review* became a leading organ in the formation of critical opinion throughout Britain, adopting an avowedly Whig perspective.

[111] Kelly (1957), *op. cit.*, p. 64.

[112] Smout (1986), *op. cit.*, p. 211.

[113] See Mr Brougham's correspondence concerning mechanics' institutes in SDUK Papers (University College London).

[114] Brougham, H. (1825) *Practical Observations on the Education of the People Addressed to the Working Classes and Their Employers*, 15th edn (reprinted 1979) London. The substance of the pamphlet first appeared in the *Edinburgh Review*, Vol. XLI, pp. 96–122 (1824) under the pen-name of William Davis.

[115] Brougham, H. (1825) Supposed dangers of knowledge, *Edinburgh Review*, Vol. XLIII, pp. 243–45.

[116] Brougham, H. (1825) *Practical Observations ...*, *op. cit.* p. 12.

[117] *Ibid.*, p. 15.

[118] *Speeches of Henry Lord Brougham*, Vol. 3, p. 103, Inaugural Discourse on Being Installed Lord Rector of the University of Glasgow, 6 April 1825.

[119] Hays, J. N. (1964) Science and Brougham's Society, *Annals of Science*, Vol. 20, p. 227.

[120] Webb, R. K. (1955) *The British Working Class Reader 1780–1848*, London, p. 89.

[121] *Consequences of a Scientific Education to the Working Classes*. Reviewed in *Edinburgh Review*, Vol. XLV, pp. 189–99 (1826).

[122] Shapin, S. and Barnes, B. (1977) Science, nature and control: interpreting mechanics' institutes, *Social Studies of Science*, Vol. 7, p. 43.

[123] Quoted in Tylecote, M. (1957) *The Mechanics Institutes of Lancashire and Yorkshire Before 1851*, Manchester, p. 43.

[124] *Blackwood's Edinburgh Magazine*, Vol. XVII, no. C, May 1825, p. 535.

[125] *Ibid.*, pp. 534–35.

[126] *Ibid.*, p. 535.

[127] *Ibid.*, p. 549.

[128] Price, R. H. (1971) The working men's club movement and Victorian social reform ideology, *Victorian Studies*, Vol. XV, no. 2, p. 117.

[129] Grinfield, E. W. (1825) *A Reply to Mr. Brougham's Practical Observations. . . .* Quoted in Tylecote, *op. cit.*, p. 21.

[130] Bellot, H. H. (1929) *University College London, 1826–1926*, pp. 69–71. Quoting *John Bull*, 18 December 1825.

[131] Kelly, T. (1952) *op. cit.*, p. 25.

[132] Hudson, *op. cit.*, p. 213.

[133] Saunders, L. J. (1950) *Scottish Democracy: 1815–1840*, Edinburgh.

[134] Smith, J. V. (1983) Manners, morals and mentalities: reflections on the popular enlightenment of early nineteenth century Scotland. In Humes, W. M. and Peterson, H. M. (eds) *Scottish Culture and Scottish Education 1800–1880*, Edinburgh, p. 126. Much of the discussion of the two perspectives is informed by Smith's paper.

[135] Smith, J. V. (1983) *op. cit.*, p. 41.

[136] Dick, T. (1846) *The Christian Philosopher*, Glasgow, Vol. 2, p. 9.

[137] *Dundee, Perth and Cupar Advertiser*, 17 December 1829, cf. Smith (1983) *op. cit.*, p. 39.

[138] Shapin and Barnes, *op. cit.*, p. 46.

[139] *Ibid.*, p. 216.

[140] Smith, J. V. (1978) *The Watt Institution Dundee 1824–49*, Abertay Historical Society, Publication 19, Dundee, p. 5.

[141] Altick, R. D. (1957) *The English Common Reader*, Chicago, p. 191.

[142] Kelly (1957), *op. cit.*, p. 217.

[143] *Edinburgh Review*, 1826, p. 193.

[144] *Ibid.*, p. 48.

[145] Brougham, H. (1825) *Practical Observations . . .*, *op. cit.*, p. 11.

[146] *Blackwood's Edinburgh Magazine*, *op. cit.*, p. 545.

[147] Cotgrove, *op. cit.*, p. 18.

[148] Holyoake, G. J. (1893) *The History of the Rochdale Pioneers, 1844–1892*, London, p. 23. Quoted in Silver, *op. cit.*, pp. 215–16.

[149] Shuttleworth, p. 17. Quoted in Tylecote, *op. cit.*, p. 50.

[150] Brougham, H. (1825) *Practical Observations . . .*, *op. cit.*, p. 32.

[151] *Ibid.*, p. 5.

[152] Tyrrell, A. (1969) Political economy, Whiggism and the education of working class adults in Scotland, 1817–1840, *Scottish Historical Review*, Vol. XLVIII, note 78, pp. 161 and 165.

[153] Workers' self-education enterprises set up in opposition to middle-class-controlled institutes often included novels, newspapers and political literature. See, for example, details of the Edinburgh Mechanics' Subscription Library, *The Scotsman*, 16 April 1825; cf. Shapin and Barnes, *op. cit.*, p. 67.

[154] *Blackwood's Edinburgh Magazine*, *op. cit.*, p. 547.

[155] Smith, J. V. (1978) *op. cit.*, p. 4.

[156] Shapin and Barnes, *op. cit.*, p. 49.

[157] Hanna, T. (1851) *Memoirs of the Life and Writings of Thomas Chalmers*, Edinburgh, Vol. III, p. 26.

[158] Brougham, H. (1825) *Practical Observations . . ., op. cit.*, p. 9.

[159] On the general question of whether the labouring classes ought to be educated and to what extent, *Edinburgh Christian Instructor*, Vol. 2, pp. 519–20 (1833).

[160] Davie, G. E. (1964) *The Democratic Intellect in Scotland and Her Universities in the Nineteenth Century*, 2nd edn, Edinburgh, Ch. 8.

[161] Brougham, H. (1838) Address to the members of the Manchester Mechanics' Institution. *Speeches*, Vol. III, p. 164.

[162] See Tyrrell, *op. cit.*, pp. 151–65, and Shapin and Barnes, *op. cit.*, p. 32.

[163] Smith, J. V. (1983) *op. cit.*, p. 245.

[164] *Ibid.*, p. 45.

[165] Address by Captain Basil Hall, RN at Dunbar Mechanics' Institute, *Fraser's Magazine*, 1830, p. 41.

[166] Quoted in Tylecote, *op. cit.*, p. 42.

[167] Detrosier, an address delivered at the new Mechanics' Institution . . . Manchester, December 30, 1829, pp. 14–15. Quoted in Tylecote, *op. cit.*, p. 42.

[168] *The Wigan Mirror*, 17 June 1825, pp. 26–27.

[169] Hudson, *op. cit.*, p. i.

[170] Smith, J. V. (1983) *op. cit.*, p. 28.

[171] Tylecote, *op. cit.*, p. 48.

[172] Inkster, I. (1997) The social context of an educational movement: a revisionist approach to the English mechanics' institutes, 1820–1850. In Inkster, I. *Scientific Culture and Urbanisation in Industrialising Britain*, Aldershot, p. 285.

[173] Engels, F. (1892) *The Condition of the Working Class in England in 1844*, p. 239.

[174] Dick, T. (1870) *The Philosophy of Religion*, Glasgow, p. 99.

[175] Briggs, A. (1979) *The Age of Improvement*, London, p. 71.

[176] *Inauguration of the Rev. J. Ackworth*, pp. 7–8 (speech by Rev. Walter Scott). Quoted in Tylecote, *op. cit.*, p. 46.

[177] Smith, J. V. (1983) *op. cit.*, p. 28.

[178] Sinclair, *op. cit.*, p. 12.

[179] *Ibid.*, p. 12.

[180] Letter from the corresponding secretary of the Franklin Institute of the state of Pennsylvania, for the promotion of the mechanic arts, Philadelphia, 15 December 1824, p. 14. Quoted by Sinclair, *op. cit.*, p. 12.

[181] Jeffrey, F. (1825) Political economy. *Edinburgh Review*, Vol. XLIII, p. 11.

[182] Chitnis, A. (1986) *The Scottish Enlightenment and Victorian English Society*, London, p. 102.

[183] Jeffrey, F. (1807) Cobbett's political register. *Edinburgh Review*, Vol. X, pp. 407–8.

[184] *Ibid.*, pp. 409–11.

[185] Chitnis, A. (1986) *op. cit.*, p. 107.

[186] Checkland and Checkland *op. cit.*, p. 83.

[187] *Ibid.*, p. 83.

[188] Shapin and Barnes, *op. cit.*, p. 34.

[189] Harrison, J. F. C. (1961) *Learning and Living 1790–1960*: A *Study in History of the English Adult Education Movement*, London, p. 89.

[190] Cole, G. D. H. (1924) *The Life of William Cobbett*, London, pp. 264–65.

[191] Quoted by Webb, R. K. (1955) *The British Working Class Reader*, New York, p. 144.

[192] *Proceedings of the Third Co-operative Congress*, April 23, 1832, W. Carpenter (ed.) pp. 70–71.

[193] Engels, F. (1844) *The Condition of the Working Class in England in 1844* (1983 edition), Oxford, pp. 245–46.

[194] Simon, B. (1960) *Studies in the History of Education 1780–1870*, London, p. 128.

[195] *Ibid.*, p. 224.

[196] Chartist Circular, 15 May 1841, quoted by Tyrrell, A. (1969) Political economy, Whiggism and the education of working class adults in Scotland 1817–1840, *Scottish Historical Review*, Vol. XLVIII, no. 2, p. 164.

[197] Wilson, A. (1970) *The Chartist Movement in Scotland*, London, pp. 195–97.

[198] Johnston, T. (1929) *The History of the Working Classes in Scotland*, Glasgow, p. 306.

[199] *Ibid.*, p. 305.

[200] *Ibid.*, p. 309.

[201] Detrosier, R. (1831) An address on the advantages for the intended Mechanics' Hall of Science, delivered at the New Mechanics' Institution, 31 December 1831. Quoted by Simon, *op. cit.*, p. 218.

[202] Doherty, J. (1832) *The Poor Man's Advocate and People's Library*, no. 6, 25 February 1832, pp. 43–44. Quoted by Simon, *op. cit.*, p. 218.

[203] Simon, *op. cit.*, p. 194.

[204] *Ibid.*, p. 215.

[205] *Proceedings of the Third Co-operative Congress*; *Proceedings of the Fourth Co-operative Congress*; *The Crisis*, Vol. 111, nos 7/8, pp. 58–59, 19 October 1833.

[206] Simon, *op. cit.*, p. 235.

[207] Black, A. (1955) Education before Rochdale, *Cooperative Review*, Edinburgh, p. 42.

[208] *Ibid.*, p. 44.

[209] *New Moral World*, Series 3, Vol. 1. no. 23, 5 December 1840, p. 60. Quoted in Simon, *op. cit.*, p. 239.

[210] Letter to Lord Brougham from J. Marshall Jr, 12 January 1825. Quoted in Tylecote, M. (1957) *The Mechanics Institutes of Lancashire and Yorkshire Before 1851*, Manchester, p. 61.

[211] Brougham, H. (1825) *Practical Observations . . .*, *op. cit.*

[212] Letter to Lord Brougham from J. Marshall Jr. See Tylecote, *op. cit.*, pp. 61–62.

[213] Heywood, B. (1843) *Addresses Delivered at the Manchester Mechanics' Institute*, London, p. 3.

214 *Ibid.*, Address of 30 March 1825, p. 11.

215 *Ibid.*, Address of 28 February 1838, p. 109.

216 *Ibid.*, Address of 3 January 1840, p. 111.

217 Nadel, G. (1957) *Australia's Colonial Culture*, Melbourne, p. 37.

218 *Ibid.*, p. 39.

219 *Ibid.*, p. 39.

220 *Ibid.*, pp. 114.

221 Todd, J. (1985) Colonial adoption: the case of Australia and the Sydney Mechanics School of Arts. In Inkster, I. (ed.) *The Steam Intellect Societies: Essays on Culture, Education and Industry, circa 1820–1914*, London, pp. 108–09.

222 *Ibid.*, p. 109.

223 Nadel, *op. cit.*, p. 116.

Chapter Two

Leonard Horner and his Scheme for the Edinburgh School of Arts

If mechanics' institutes succeed, and I firmly hope they may, the ancient aristocracy of England will be secure for ages to come. The most useful and numerous body of people in the nation will then judge for themselves, and when properly informed, will judge correctly.

Lord Byron

Leonard Horner, founder of the Edinburgh School of Arts. Print from crayon drawing by Samuel Lawrence

Horner's Education and Early Life

In order to understand the kind of educational visionary and entrepreneur that Leonard Horner became, it is useful to know something of his origins, something of the kind of Scotsman he was and was not, and of the kind of politician and churchman he was and was not. To read of his upbringing, education and his circle of friends is to see the most striking features of his character develop, and his own gift of being able to translate his idea of providing education for the working class into the reality of the School of Arts.

Horner was born in Edinburgh on 17 January 1785, the third son (there were three daughters) of John Horner, a prosperous linen bleacher and merchant, living at the time in the elegant setting of George Square.[1] John Horner was a prominent member of the Whig upper middle class of Edinburgh and his children were introduced into this highly educated and politically active elite. Leonard and his brilliant brother Francis were educated at the High School and the University of Edinburgh. It appears that there was a certain parental indifference to Leonard's day-to-day activities and his progress as a boy. He wrote later in life, 'I do not remember that, at home or anywhere else, anyone ever enquired what I'd been

This view from Craigleith, 1829, would have been familiar to Leonard Horner

about, what I had learned or was learning.'[2] Although his brother Francis was seven years older, their relationship was close and through it Leonard became intimate with a remarkable group of Whigs including Henry, later Lord Brougham, with whom Leonard was to be associated in the new University of London and who subsequently became Lord Chancellor, Francis Jeffrey and Henry Cockburn, who as Lord Advocate and Solicitor General, respectively, realised their potential in the Whig administration of 1830–34, presenting the first Scottish Reform Bill of 1832. The focus of intellectual and cultural life in Edinburgh was centred on the halls of justice; the elite in education, in talent of oratory and letters, in metaphysics, philosophy and political economy, were the men of the law.[3]

When he entered Edinburgh University in 1799 at the age of 14, Leonard Horner, in a somewhat desultory way, began to attend classes in Greek, Latin, moral philosophy and mathematics, but these evinced little interest.[4] In November 1802, however, he enrolled in Thomas Charles Hope's class in chemistry, which included some lectures on mineralogy, and this sparked his enthusiasm for geology. From this and from his family's friendship with James Hutton, whose *Theory of the Earth* in 1795 laid the foundations of modern geology, Leonard began to explore the volcanic slopes of Arthur's Seat and developed a lifelong passion for geology. His brother Francis embarked on a career as a Whig politician in London but he and Leonard corresponded frequently. Francis had an important influence on his younger brother and on one occasion he advised Leonard to concentrate on political economy while he could take advantage of the lectures in Edinburgh, since such a course would not be available in London.[5] Francis suffered poor health and in the autumn of 1816 Leonard accompanied him to Italy in the hope that it would cure Francis, but he died in Pisa from tuberculosis in 1817 at the age of 39. The bond between the two brothers was such that when Horner revisited Pisa as a 76-year-old man in 1861, 45 years after Francis's death, he wrote, 'This place is associated in my mind with the greatest calamity of my life.'[6]

The family moved to a large house on the north side of York Place in the New Town in 1799, where one of their neighbours was Alexander Nasmyth the painter, whose son James was destined to become an engineering alumnus of the Edinburgh School of Arts. Leonard left university in 1803 at the age of 19, and since he was going into partnership with his father and not a profession, he did not take a degree. John Horner decided to move his family to London as much of his business was with London merchants, and in 1804 they relocated to Hampstead.[7] Leonard soon became romantically attached to Anne Lloyd, also from a Whig family, and they were married in Hampstead Church in June 1806.[8]

James Hutton, pioneering geologist

The linen trade was entering a state of decline and Horner, with his family's approval, became an insurance underwriter at Lloyd's. He was unhappy with the risks involved in this type of speculation and in 1813, after some serious losses which his father redeemed for him,[9] he gave up his post and returned to the family business in Edinburgh. Francis regarded his action as overly cautious but accepted that his brother's conscientious temperament could not cope with the strain of financial anxiety.[10] Horner spent a quarter of a century as a linen merchant, travelling extensively in Britain and Europe, corresponding widely with economists, politicians, lawyers, scientists, churchmen as well as family, friends and business contacts. In this way he maintained the intellectual and political interests which he had developed under his brother's influence as a boy and he remained a scholar all his life.

Horner's Philosophy and Interests

Horner's Presbyterian and upper middle-class Whig background led him to value independence and a strong sense of public duty.[11] From the Enlightenment he inherited a tradition of broad scholarship and the assumption that the objective of learning was to pursue truth; his independence of thought may have been derived from the influence of the Church of Scotland;[12] and he belonged to the Utilitarian school of political economy, respecting what was useful, practical and likely to improve the quality of life for any social group.[13] The principle of liberty was important to him but he was also part of a paternalistic Whig tradition which was sympathetic with the collectivist aspect of utilitarian thinking. As an experienced businessman, he was not inimical to the desire of textile manufacturers to maximise profits, but he was convinced of the necessity and ultimately of the profitability of good working conditions, of education of the working classes, and that children needed state protection. Horner's judgements were carefully reasoned; his opinions were expressed fearlessly, irrespective of popular opinion, and his intellectual honesty is revealed in a letter to his daughter Frances on 15 November 1857:

I suppose it is a rare quality, the possession of that candour which would be as ready to admit *a fact* against as in favour of a preconceived opinion. I believe that the cultivation of such a frame of mind is as necessary in science as in politics or religion.[14]

Leonard Horner, founder of the Edinburgh School of Arts. Print from crayon drawing by Samuel Lawrence

Horner's major private interest, apart from his family, was geology, not yet a laboratory subject, which at this time attracted many gentlemen with private means, and the opportunity to walk in the country armed with a hammer. True to his character, Horner was no dilettante and, although lacking a formal training in the nascent discipline, he achieved a scientific reputation of some distinction. His interest was serious both for the intellectual challenge posed and for the practical value which its discoveries might bring, and so it was entirely in character that he was one of the initiators in 1835 of the Geological Survey of Great Britain.[15]

Horner became a fellow of the Geological Society of London in the second year of its existence in 1808, was its secretary in 1810–14, and its president in 1845–46 and again in 1860–61. In 1811 his first paper to the society, 'On the Mineralogy of the Malvern Hills', reveals the key characteristics of his research: careful observation and open-mindedness. He made some important contributions to the subject but no discovery of note. In obituary addresses for Horner, W. J. Hamilton, president of the Geological Society, admired the 'cautious manner in which he avoids a too hasty generalisation'[16] and Archibald Geikie described Horner as 'ever ready to receive and sympathise with new developments of truth'.[17] Hamilton concluded that Horner helped to 'lay the foundations of those principles which – chiefly by the labours of Murchison and Sedgwick – have been so successfully applied to the history of the Paleozoic rocks'.[18] The fine critical quality of his mind was exhibited in his contributions to discussion and his deliberate and carefully reasoned assessments of current work. Election to a fellowship of the Royal Society in 1813 at the age of 28 is testimony to his quality as a geologist, as judged by his peers;[19] and his influence was manifest in his patronage of the young geologist Charles Lyell, who married his daughter Mary.[20]

In a spirit of wider dissemination of knowledge, during his second presidency of the Geological Society between 1860 and 1862, Horner 'made strong efforts to render the meetings of the Society more popular and attractive to the general public by the admission of ladies to the meetings'.[21] Such a radical idea was disliked by many members and, unfortunately for Horner, was not a success. There was a notable lack of enthusiasm among the older generation of ladies and only three or four appeared, but among them 'Lady Lyell and the Misses Horner were constant attendants'.[22] As an indication of the extent to which Horner's initiative was ahead of its time, the rule was reversed immediately following his presidency at a special general meeting on 8 January 1863 and women were not admitted again to meetings until 1904.[23] Horner's open-mindedness to new concepts led him into another controversy. Much of his presidential address of 1861 was devoted to defending his friend Charles Darwin's *Origin of Species* and to a critical review of the inadequacy of Archbishop Usher's Bible chronology of creation.[24] His opinions were expressed cogently and courageously whether they ran with or counter to popular opinion. Afterwards he received an appreciative letter from Darwin, and more cautious thanks from W. E. Gladstone and Archbishop Sumner of Canterbury.[25]

Horner displayed a lifelong devotion to the museum of the Geological Society and when he retired from 25 years' service as a factory inspector at the age of 74 in 1859, he spent much of his time reorganising the contents of the museum and preparing extensive catalogues, with illustrative notes. Even in the year of his death in 1864, at 79 years of age, Horner 'spent several hours almost daily in the museum' and worked at arranging and cataloguing the collections in a manner which Hamilton judged had 'never been equalled by any other member of the Society'.[26]

Although Horner adhered to the tenets of the Church of Scotland, he was also friendly with many Anglican ecclesiastics and, in one of his last letters, refers to attending the 'Free Christian Church'.[27] Horner's liberalism gave him trouble with Catholicism; in 1829 it led him to support the emancipation of Catholics from their legal disabilities, but in 1850 it made him hostile to the restoration of the hierarchy and diocesan structure of a church that he saw as intolerant and obscurantist.[28] Horner equated religion not with rituals or authority but with intellectual rigour and deep thought on serious issues;[29] it was the keeper of his conscience. His attitude to the Sabbath was exemplified in a letter to his wife on 9 September 1843:

[on Sunday] I did not go to Church, but read *three* sermons of Robert Hall, and a part of Cicero's disquisition on the immortality of the soul, in his Tusculan Questions, so I was not without any serious reflections on my day of rest. I had Madame de Staël's 'Allemagne' for another part of the day, and when candles came, I took to the larger print of Humboldt ['Asie Centrale'].[30]

Hard work and independence of thought are illustrated in the same letter, written while touring Lancashire factories: 'I was in a comfortable little fly and I read the first two books of "The Paradise Lost" by the way; such majesty of diction is not to be found in any other work in our tongue.'[31] Both the practice of employing usefully every minute of the day, even while travelling between cotton mills, and the admiration for the puritan Milton are characteristics of Horner. He always rose between 5 A.M. and 6 A.M. and used the period before breakfast for reading and writing; he would return to his private studies again at the end of the working day.[32] In addition to his interest in geology, politics and political economy and his knowledge of classical languages, Horner taught himself French, German and Italian; and at the age of 77, to occupy himself after the death of his wife, he translated Professor Villarí of Pisa's biography of Savonarola.[33] His letters to his wife and daughters are sprinkled with references to Scott, the Brontës, Dante and Schiller, indicating the mind of a true scholar.

Horner's Educational Initiatives

Horner enjoyed a lifelong friendship with Henry, later Lord Cockburn, an Edinburgh advocate, Whig, wit, sage and reformer whose *Memorials of his Time* paint a colourful portrait of Edinburgh life and society in the first half of the nineteenth century. From this friendship evolved the idea of founding in Edinburgh an institution, Edinburgh Academy, at the opposite end of the social and academic spectrum from the School of Arts, a new school for the middle and upper classes.

Cockburn wrote in his *Memorials*:

Leonard Horner and I had often discussed the causes and remedies of the decline of classical education in Scotland; and we were at last satisfied that no adequate improvement could be effected so long as there was only one great classical

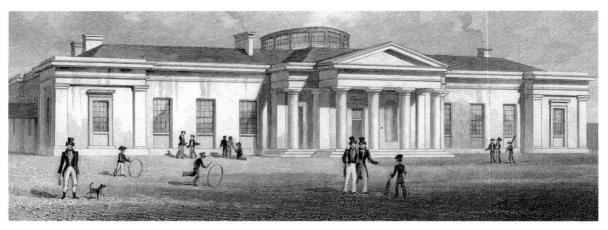

Education for the social elite: Edinburgh Academy, co-founded by Leonard Horner and Lord Cockburn

school in Edinburgh, and this one placed under the Town Council, and lowered, perhaps necessarily, so as to suit the wants of a class of boys to more than two-thirds of whom classical accomplishment is foreseen to be useless.[34]

Cockburn and Horner made their decision to found the Edinburgh Academy while walking over the summit of one of the Pentlands (the precise hill is not named), emblematic as Cockburn wrote 'of the solidity of our foundation and of the extent of our prospects'.[35] Clearly for two gentlemen in early middle age (Cockburn was 43 and Horner 37) prospering in their own careers, comfortably housed in the New Town, and prominent members of the elite of Edinburgh, this was a courageous decision made in the knowledge that, as Whigs, there would be powerful opposition from the Tory establishment.[36] Edinburgh Academy was designed for the sons of gentlemen, and Henry Brougham, fellow Whig and former High School pupil, criticised the socially divisive nature of the new school at a dinner in 1825.[37] Horner never equated liberty with simple egalitarianism as did some of the Radicals, but always held the view that the good state needed an enlightened and educated people and an elite who could protect the liberties of all, a combination characteristic of both Whig and Enlightenment thinking.[38]

Indeed the two Edinburgh educational projects, the School of Arts and Edinburgh Academy, founded in 1824, three years after the School of Arts, reveal the two objectives which Horner also pursued in the Geological Society: the preservation of the highest academic standards for an elite while at the same time extending useful knowledge to the working class. Horner and Cockburn realised that if their scheme was to succeed, Tories must be allowed to take a prominent part in the management of the academy.[39] In the opinion of the board of

Edinburgh Academy, it was Leonard Horner to whom the major credit was due for the successful launch of the new school:

> He has uniformly evinced the most signal talents for such a task, insomuch as they ascribe the complete success which has attended their new and very difficult undertaking principally to his unwearied zeal, literary tastes, bland manners, good sense and great powers of method.[40]

The appointment of a rector of the academy revealed another aspect of Horner's character. Sir Walter Scott campaigned zealously for the Reverend John Williams and fired off letters in all directions vilifying Horner and suggesting a vicious Whig plot to discredit an able Tory candidate. Nothing in Horner's voluminous correspondence, however, suggests anything but devotion to duty and fair-mindedness in his interviewing of candidates. After Williams' appointment – Horner and Cockburn had voted unsuccessfully for another candidate – Horner displayed his true nature in a letter: 'The more I saw Williams the more I liked him. He appears to be thoroughly master of the duties of a schoolmaster.'[41] Horner was clearly an educational entrepreneur with a combination of principles, energy, fair-mindedness and organisational ability so necessary to translate a vision into reality. His next educational challenge was to take him to London, and was to reveal other aspects of his character.

The University of London was established by a group of Scots, Dissenters and Jews, of whom the Scots Whigs, especially Henry Brougham, were the most influential group among the proprietors and council. On 30 May 1827, on behalf of the council, Brougham invited Horner to be warden of the new university. From the start there were two major sources of trouble destined to make Horner's task difficult. The university was a joint-stock company and this entailed first the exclusion of all teaching staff, including professors, from corporate representation, and second the remuneration of professors from the fees of such students as they had the power to attract to their classes.[42] Brougham had predicted a professorial income of £1,200 from fees but the typical income, even with guarantees, was around £300 with some professors struggling to live as 'gentlemen' on as little as £100.[43] In negotiations over salary, Horner refused to accept less than £1,200, which was unlikely to have endeared him to the professoriate. Horner and the council also took a view of the office of warden as conferring 'that authority over the Professors, which is usually vested in the Principal . . . of other Academical Institutions'.[44] Horner was effectively both principal and secretary of the new university.

To some extent, Horner was a victim of the council's policy to exercise a considerable measure of control over the activities of the professoriate; but in exercising it, he made it clear that the council's word was to be obeyed. It appears that despite his humanitarian views, Horner was less than sensitive in implementing these unusual powers; at times he was autocratic, tactless and high-handed over petty administrative and financial matters and on academic appointments.[45] Horner was also punctilious and a strict observer of the proprieties: he annoyed professors by setting up beadles to record their students' attendance at lectures that he might report it to the council;[46] he interfered with the purchase of apparatus; and he stood between the professors and the council and forwarded or withheld their communications at his discretion.[47] He also exercised academic patronage in appointments; in 1828 he invited Charles Lyell to the chair of mineralogy at King's College, London.[48]

A medical academic, Professor Pattison, refused to teach the most modern theories of anatomy, and was the object of complaints by students and colleagues who considered that his lectures were ill-prepared and lacked scientific content.[49] At the beginning of the Autumn term in 1830, Horner permitted a student leader, Alexander Thompson, to harangue Pattison's students on the incompetence of their professor.[50] Horner's action was repudiated by the council and Thompson was expelled, but the students prevented Pattison from lecturing for over a month.[51] In February 1831 Pattison openly charged Horner before the council with complicity in the cabal which had been got up against him. Thenceforth Horner ceased to attend meetings of the council and he resigned on 26 March 1831, largely on grounds of ill health. The ill-conceived constitution of the college demanded reform, and the events which led to Horner's resignation prompted changes in college government. The professoriate was given a part in university government, and the warden was replaced by a secretary with restricted powers. The university controversy displays a less attractive aspect of Horner's independent spirit; he considered independence and authority to be inseparable and he was uncomfortable with having limited authority.[52] This terminated the least successful episode of his life and it reveals that Horner seemed to have taken himself very seriously, to have been lacking in a sense of humour and to have found compromise difficult.

After his resignation as warden, Horner travelled in Europe with his family to restore his health and spent two years studying the geology of the Rhineland. After returning to Britain in 1833 at the age of 48, Horner wrote to Brougham (then Lord Chancellor in the Whig administration) seeking employment. His plea was successful and Horner was appointed to a commission of inquiry into the employment of children in factories. In November 1833, after the Factory Act had become law, he was offered a post as one of the four inspectors of factories by the notable Whig Francis Jeffrey, an old friend of Horner's, in whose gift Lord Melbourne had placed the post. Horner therefore acquired his two most prestigious appointments, as warden of the University of London and as a factory inspector, via a system of patronage through Whig connections.

Inspector of Factories

U nder the Factory Act of 1833, Horner was appointed to inspect a district covering Scotland, Northern Ireland and the far northern counties of England.[53] Later, in 1836, he took over the inspectorship of Lancashire and Yorkshire, cradle of the textile industry. Horner was moved by the injustices inflicted on the working classes and was ready to support realistic measures which could produce genuine improvements, and prepared to work unremittingly towards that end:

> I hail the Factory Act as the first legislative steps in this country towards that to which, under some modification or other we must sooner or later come – a compulsory education for all classes.[54]

Horner inspected factories and mills; made rules and regulations to enforce the Act; performed the judicial function of deciding factory cases; ensured that schools were established and maintained for the education of factory children; and reported to the Home Secretary twice a year. He was the most active and uncompromising of the early inspectors and each Home Secretary consulted Horner in advance of his colleagues whenever legislation was contemplated.[55] This is not entirely explained by the fact that Horner was a social equal of the ministers; he was in effect *primus inter pares* and the Home Secretary Sir James Graham in 1842 referred to him as 'the Inspector General of Factories'.[56]

Certificate presented to Horner by factory operatives on his retirement. Photograph: Douglas McBride

Horner's attention to detail was also legendary. When facilitating the establishment of factory schools, he did not merely suggest general grants for books and equipment but sometimes specified the precise books he thought a school should have.[57] There are examples of his liberal views on the curriculum: one is a grant of £50 for 'terrestrial globes' and the other an even more unusual grant of £10 to Manchester Normal School in 1849 for 'the cultivation of Music'.[58] Heriot-Watt was to wait another 150 years, until 1998, for an equivalent Musician-in-Residence initiative by Principal John Archer. The success of the Factory Act owed much to Horner's intelligence, honesty and diligence and this was even recognised by the Lancashire operatives who paid tribute to him on his retirement.[59] Horner was the major innovative administrator behind the Factory Act. Although as a civil servant his contribution remains somewhat anonymous, he confronted the major social and human problems of the Industrial Revolution, was always open to new ideas, courageously influenced politicians and public opinion, and introduced reforming measures to humanise factory-based capitalism in the interests of social justice and economic efficiency.

Horner's reforming work was even admired by Karl Marx who, in discussing manufacturers' attempts to falsify working hours, described Horner as 'the tireless censor of the manufacturers'[60] and observed that 'the ruthless factory inspector was again on the spot'.[61] Marx eulogised that 'his services to the English working classes will never be forgotten. He carried on a life-long contest, not only with the embittered manufacturers, but also with the cabinet.'[62] In a life of domestic happiness, Horner worked unremittingly, serving his day and generation. A life ordinarily and extraordinarily spent, in the pains and pleasures of his family and friends, with the humblest and most powerful people. A life spent in civic work, business, scholarship and philanthropy, but above all, much time expended serving the needs of others ranging from oppressed factory operatives to the working class eager for education. Until his death in 1865, he retained a strength of interest in the School of Arts, by whose members he was revered; his original and specific ideas in its founding remain the university's guiding light to this day.

Horner and Bryson: A Mechanics' Institute in Edinburgh

Although Horner was aware of John Anderson's classes for the mechanics of Glasgow and he laid 'no claim to any originality of invention',[63] the immediate stimulus to the foundation of the Edinburgh School of Arts arose from a conversation between Horner and Robert Bryson. Horner, the upper middle-class Whig gentleman, called into Bryson's clock and watchmaking shop at 8 South Bridge, now occupied by a cut-price department store, in Edinburgh's Old Town and inquired whether young men in the watchmaking trade received

Robert Bryson, watch and clockmaker, Horner's ally in the scheme to found the School of Arts

any mathematical education. Bryson confirmed that his workmen were unable to attend the classes due to the expense and the time at which mathematics was usually taught.[64] As a result, Horner, although he probably did not realise it at the time, conceived the idea for the world's first mechanics' institute.

Robert Bryson (1778–1852) founded the family watch and clockmaking business in 1810 with an address in the High Street, although he had practised as a clockmaker before this date. He moved to South Bridge in 1815 where the business remained until 1840 when the firm relocated to 66 Princes Street.[65] Bryson's reputation as a horologist was such that he was included among the first 24 councillors of David Brewster's Society for the Promotion of Useful Arts in Scotland, which was set up in 1821.[66] He was not only an inventive improver of watches and clocks, but was also interested in scientific instruments which incorporated timepieces, exhibiting an ingenious self-registering barometer to the Society of Arts in 1844.[67]

While Leonard Horner conceived the original idea and is the recognised prime mover in the foundation of the school, Robert Bryson, no esoteric philanthropist, seems to have been motivated by practical concerns; he pursued the idea of an institution to teach mechanics, not because of any egalitarian ideals, but because he

This fine long-case clock made by Robert Bryson, was purchased for the university in 1972 by Principal R. A. Smith with funding from Dr Arthur G. B. Metcalf. Photograph: Douglas McBride

recognised that the economy had developed to a stage where technical education and skill were required of people for whom previously it had not been attainable.[68] Bryson's pragmatic enthusiasm for Horner's concept – he even arranged for students to register in his shop – helped make the school a reality. He displayed his strong commitment to the school, acting as a director from 1821 to 1836 (vice-president 1837) and again from 1840 until 1851 (vice-president 1846). As almost two centuries have passed, society's needs have changed, and Heriot-Watt University has evolved to remain in tune with the society which generates the demand for its educational and research services, but Robert Bryson's applied science perspective continues to influence the ethos of the university up to the present day.

When Bryson informed Horner that it was not possible for his watchmakers to attend mathematics classes – there were no day release schemes in 1821 – Horner outlined his idea that a means might be devised of providing such education for the working class. Bryson was in no doubt that if given the opportunity, it would be taken up with alacrity. Following their conversation, Horner 'set to work to supply this deficiency';[69] a preliminary plan was drawn up and circulated among 'the most considerable master mechanics' to identify 'the names of their workmen who expressed a desire to obtain instruction of the kind proposed'.[70] Bryson had been correct; within a fortnight of the conversation in his shop, between 70 and 80 names were put down.[71] Encouraged by this evidence, 'several gentlemen' met within a month on 19 April 1821 and resolved to publish a prospectus to be circulated among the mechanics of Edinburgh.[72] Philanthropy and civic duty were the responses of the Whig social elite to a community and its problems; they were private forms of social citizenship.[73] The meeting constituted itself into a committee to bring the plan to fruition under the name of the School of Arts, and Horner agreed to act as secretary. Horner is acknowledged as the prime mover in the foundation of the school and his friend Lord Henry Cockburn asserted that 'the whole merit, both of its conception and of its first three or four years' management, is due exclusively to Leonard Horner'.[74] Bryson became a director and was acknowledged by Horner as 'my right-hand man in starting the School of Arts'.[75]

When drafting the first annual report for 1821–22, Horner was unable to find the piece of paper outlining his first scheme; he discovered it on 12 December 1825 and noted that he had 'sought for it in vain during my controversy with Dr Brewster, and that according to the best of my recollection it was drawn up in the summer or autumn of 1820'.[76] Horner's original ideas were more tentative, more experimental and more modest than those outlined for the School of Arts in the prospectus approved on 19 April 1821. The latter articulated narrowly utilitarian curricular objectives 'for the purpose of enabling industrious Tradesmen to become acquainted with such of the principles of Mechanics, Chemistry and other branches of Science as are of practical application in their several trades'.[77] Horner's original idea had been for 'the establishment of a mathematical class only';[78] ironically there was no maths tuition during the first year of the school. His draft scheme of 1820 proposed to teach 'such parts of Practical Science as are of most extensive application in the Arts', that the fees 'shall be 6/- per quarter for each pupil'.[79] It is clear that Horner's thinking evolved and was modified as a result of discussions with employers and middle-class subscribers.

The syllabus outlined in the prospectus of April 1821 was largely Horner's original concept, as communicated in a letter on 10 April 1821 to his intimate correspondent Dr Marcet,[80] and it was frequently reiterated publicly in almost identical language. Education was not to be provided free and the artisans were expected to 'lay aside ... such a portion of their earnings as they can reasonably spare'.[81] The prospectus expressed confidence that the 'more opulent classes of Edinburgh [would] ... come forward in support of so laudable and beneficial a scheme; nor is there any way in which it can be so effactually promoted as with the advice and co-operation of the better educated part of the community'.[82] Both an economic rationale and social control agendas were articulated clearly in the prospectus: 'Workmen ... would derive the greatest advantage ... not only from the increased skill, but from the sober habits it would encourage.'[83] Indeed the social and moral improvement to be expected from better education was constantly stressed: 'It would fill up the leisure hours of the Tradesman with a useful and honourable employment, and would save him from the dissipation and evil consequences of the public house.'[84] For the school's first two sessions from 1 October, the fee was 15 shillings, payable at one time or in two successive quarters, which entitled students to attend all lectures and to borrow books from the library.[85] Registration and the sale of tickets for the first year of the school took place at Bryson's shop in South Bridge.

On 21 September 1821 the committee, satisfied that the prospectus had met with the cordial approbation of the higher classes in Edinburgh, published an address in which they outlined key elements of their educational strategy, emphasising that

> it is not intended to teach the trade of the Carpenter, the Mason, the Dyer, or other particular businesses; but there is no trade that does not depend, more or less, upon scientific principles, ... [but it was] not possible during the first year, to do more ... than to teach the more general principles of Chemistry and Mechanical Philosophy, together with a brief notice of their practical application in some of the principal arts.[86]

A utilitarian philosophy infused with Calvinism, reflecting a cautious and limited approach, permeated the mission statement of the scholarly Whig founder:

> The School of Arts has been established for the purpose of giving you real and substantial instruction, not to amuse a vacant hour, or excite your wonder, by exhibiting some curious and showy experiments; that it is intended, in a word, to enable you to carry away information that will be of solid advantage to you in the exercise of your trade.[87]

When the School of Arts was founded in 1821, the state had barely intervened on the terrain of the philanthropic elite in providing education and other welfare provision for the working classes. Voluntary bodies continued to play an important role in the improvement of life for Edinburgh's poor throughout the nineteenth century, despite a gradual retreat before increasing state control.

The problem of finding suitable premises was solved when the officers of the Grand Lodge of Scotland granted the use of the Freemasons' Hall, Niddry Street. This building, St Cecilia's Hall – named after the Roman virgin, the patron saint of music, who suffered martyrdom in the third century – was built for the Edinburgh Musical Society and is the oldest purpose-built concert hall in Scotland. The architect, Robert Mylne (1733–1811), is alleged to have designed it on the model of an Italian opera house, the Teatro Farnese of Parma.[88] It was completed in 1762 at a cost of £1,328 and formed the east side of a courtyard of older houses set back from the medieval Niddry's Wynd in the heart of the Old Town.[89] All of this, with the exception of the hall, was demolished in 1785 during the

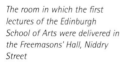

The room in which the first lectures of the Edinburgh School of Arts were delivered in the Freemasons' Hall, Niddry Street

*South Bridge, Edinburgh, 1829.
Engraving by Thomas Shepherd*

construction of the South Bridge which spanned the Cowgate valley south of the North Bridge and was opened to foot passengers in July 1788.[90] Deprived of its courtyard, overshadowed by the bridge, and now opening directly onto the new and narrow Niddry Street, further east than the line of Niddry's Wynd, the amenity value of the hall was greatly reduced.

The last concert was held in St Cecilia's Hall in 1798; the venue for recitals followed the middle classes to the New Town and relocated to the Assembly Rooms on George Street. After becoming the property of the Baptist community in 1802, St Cecilia's Hall was purchased for £1,400 by the Grand Lodge of Scotland in 1809 for the purposes of converting it into the Freemasons' Hall of Scotland.[91] The Freemasons constructed an additional hall adjoining the original in 1812, on the Cowgate side of which 'Free Masons Hall 1812' is clearly visible today, carved on a stone tablet. Above the vestibule, accessed by two splendid stone staircases, lay the beautiful elliptical concert hall with its concave ceiling and cyclopean cupola. Between 1809 and 1810 the Freemasons had 'altered and handsomely fitted up' the interior of the concert hall by removing the inner walls and converting it into a rectangle.[92]

The enlarged St Cecilia's Hall formed the home of the Grand Lodge of Freemasons of Scotland from 1809 to 1844 and it was during this period that the Edinburgh School of Arts rented a lecture room and adjoining rooms for a library and apparatus. The worthy artisans who enrolled for the first classes in October 1821 would have passed through the fine entrance, with its lintel and ornamental supports, into the vestibule where a few years earlier the ladies attending concerts alighted in comfort from their sedan chairs without the risk of having their finery or satin shoes soiled. The restructured concert hall, adorned by its glorious cupola, was the room where the School of Arts was due to be launched.

The success of Horner's scheme, with the enthusiastic cooperation of Bryson, now depended entirely on the response of a particular section of the working class of Edinburgh, their willingness to attend night classes after a hard day of labour and to pay fees to cover part of their tuition costs.

Notes

[1] Greig, J. (1982) *Leonard Horner 1785–1864, Scottish Men of Letters*, History of Medicine and Science Unit, University of Edinburgh, p. 1.

[2] Horner manuscripts, Kinnordy House. Quoted in Greig, *op. cit.*, p. 1.

[3] Magnusson, A. (1974) *The Clacken and the Slate: The Story of the Edinburgh Academy 1824–1974*, London, p. 16.

[4] Greig, *op. cit.*, p. 1.

[5] Lyell, K. (1890) *A Memoir of Leonard Horner*, London, Vol. 1, pp. 5–6, 6 June 1803, Frances Horner to Leonard Horner. The memoirs were compiled by Leonard's daughter, Katherine, and are more concerned with Horner's private and scientific pursuits than with his public career.

[6] Lyell, *op. cit.*, Vol. 1, p. 135.

[7] Greig, *op. cit.*, p. 2.

[8] *Ibid.*, p. 2.

[9] Lyell, *op. cit.*, Vol. 1, p. 24, 11 November 1813, and p. 26, 10 November 1813.

[10] Greig, *op. cit.*, p. 3.

[11] Martin, B. (1969) Leonard Horner: a portrait of an inspector of factories, *International Review of Social History*, Vol. XIV, no. 4, p. 415. Many of the insights into the intellectual influences on Horner are derived from Martin's excellent paper.

[12] *Ibid.*, p. 418.

[13] *Ibid.*, p. 415.

[14] Lyell, *op. cit.*, Vol. 2, pp. 279–80, 15 November 1857, Leonard Horner to his daughter Frances.

[15] Martin, *op. cit.*, p. 416, from information supplied from the archives of the Geological Society by Dr W. Bishop, Bedford College, University of London.

[16] Hamilton, W. J. (1864) The anniversary address of the president, *Proceedings of the Geological Society*, Vol. 21, p. xxxiii.

[17] *Proceedings of the Royal Society*, Vol. XIV, p. 5 (1865).

[18] Hamilton, *op. cit.*, p. xxxiii.

[19] Horner was elected to a fellowship of the Royal Society of Edinburgh in 1816.

[20] Martin, *op. cit.*, p. 416 states that Horner virtually ensured the post of director of the Geological Survey to Geikie. This is erroneous since Horner died in 1864 and Geikie did not become director general of the survey until 1882, having been director in Scotland since 1867. See Bailey, E. (1952) *Geological Survey of Great Britain*, London, p. 100.

[21] Woodward, H. B. (1907) *The History of the Geological Society*, London, p. 242. Quoted in Martin, *op. cit.*, p. 417.

[22] *Ibid.*, p. 243.

[23] *Ibid.*, p. 244.

[24] Martin, *op. cit.*, p. 417.

[25] Lyell, *op. cit.*, Vol. 2, p. 300, 20 March, 1861 and p. 303, 26 March and 1 April 1861.

[26] Hamilton, *op. cit.*, p. xxxviii.

[27] Lyell, *op. cit.*, Vol. 2, p. 366, Leonard Horner to his daughter Frances.

[28] Lyell, *op. cit.*, Vol. 2, p. 175, 27 December 1850, Leonard Horner to his sister Mrs Byrne, and Vol. 1, p. 243, 7 February 1829, Francis Jeffrey to Leonard Horner.

[29] Martin, *op. cit.*, pp. 418–19.

[30] Lyell, *op. cit.*, Vol. 2, p. 63, 9 September 1843, Leonard Horner to his wife.

[31] *Ibid.*, Vol. 2, p. 64, 9 September 1843, Leonard Horner to his wife.

[32] Martin, *op. cit.*, p. 418.

[33] Hamilton, *op. cit.*, p. xxxix.

[34] Cockburn, H. (1856) *Memorials of His Time*, Edinburgh, p. 414.

[35] *Ibid.*, p. 415.

[36] *Ibid.*, pp. 29–30.

[37] *Ibid.*, p. 52.

[38] Martin, *op. cit.*, p. 420.

[39] Magnusson, *op. cit.*, p. 34.

[40] Quoted in Magnusson, *op. cit.*, p. 60.

[41] *Ibid.*, p. 75.

[42] Martin, *op. cit.*, pp. 423–24.

[43] Bellot, H. H. (1929) *University College London 1826–1926*, London, p. 175.

[44] Lyell, *op. cit.*, Vol. 1, pp. 233–34, Leonard Horner to Lord Auckland, president of the council.

[45] Martin, *op. cit.*, p. 424.

[46] Bellot, *op. cit.*, p. 200.

[47] *Ibid.*, p. 200.

[48] Lyell married Horner's daughter Mary in 1832 but there was no question of Horner having foreseen this in 1828; he was surprised by news of this engagement in 1831. Lyell, *op. cit.*, Vol. 1, pp. 251–52, 20 July 1831, Leonard Horner to his daughter Mary.

[49] Admitted both in letters to the council; see Martin, *op. cit.*, p. 425.

[50] Bellot, *op. cit.*, pp. 206–7.

[51] *Ibid.*, pp. 207–8.

[52] Martin, *op. cit.*, p. 426.

[53] Djang, T. K. (1942) *Factory Inspection in Great Britain*, London, p. 33.

[54] Nassau, W. Sr (1837) *Letters on the Factory Act*, p. 37.

[55] Manuscript minutes were kept from 1833 to 1867 and are now in the Public Record Office, London; see Martin, *op. cit.*, p. 428.

[56] Letter from Graham to the Bishop of London dated 27 December 1842. From Parker, C. S. (1907) *Life and Letters of Sir James Graham*, London, Vol. 1, p. 343.

[57] Inspectors' Letter Books, 14 February 1853 and 17 February 1858, No. 87, Vols 3 and 4, respectively, quoted in Martin, *op. cit.*, p. 434.

[58] Inspectors' Letter Books, 17 December 1853 and 9 November 1849, No. 87, Vols 3 and 2, respectively, quoted in Martin, *op. cit.*, p. 434.

[59] Lyell, *op. cit.*, Vol. 2, p. 291, 16 September 1860, Leonard Horner to Lady Bunbury.

[60] Marx, K. (1976) *Capital: A Critique of Political Economy*, Vol. 1, London, p. 538. Translated by Ben Fowkes.

[61] *Ibid.*, p. 397.

[62] *Ibid.*, p. 334.

[63] University College London Library, Brougham Papers, 8651, 7 January 1824, Horner to Lord Brougham.

[64] Heriot-Watt University Archive (hereafter HWUA), SA 1/1/1 *Annual Report of the Board of Directors*, 1821–22, p. 1.

[65] Smith, J. (1921) *Old Scottish Clockmakers*, 2nd edn, Edinburgh, p. 69.

[66] National Library of Scotland, Royal Scottish Society of Arts Archives, Dep 23011, Minute Book, Vol. 1, entry for 9 July 1822.

[67] Bryson, Robert (1851) Description of new self-registering barometer, *Transactions of the Royal Scottish Society of Arts*, Vol. 3, Appendix 6, pp. 11–39.

[68] Notes on Robert Bryson compiled by Dr Norman Reid, former Heriot-Watt University archivist.

[69] Lyell, K, *op. cit.*, Vol. 1, p. 194.

[70] HWUA, SA 1/1/1, *op. cit.*, p. 1.

[71] *Ibid.*, p. 1.

[72] *Ibid.*, p. 1.

[73] Meller, H. E. (1976) *Leisure & the Changing City, 1870–1914*, London, p. 74.

[74] Quoted in Lyell, *op. cit.*, Vol. 1, p. 196.

[75] *Ibid.*, Vol. 2, p. 152.

[76] HWUA, University Papers 72, A. Anderson's Papers: Leonard Horner 'First Sketch of the School of Arts', Autumn 1820.

[77] HWUA, SA 1/1/1, *op. cit.*, p. 2.

[78] University College London, Brougham Papers, 8651, 7 January 1824, Horner to Lord Brougham.

[79] HWUA, University Papers 71, *op. cit.*

[80] Lyell, *op. cit.*, Vol. 1, p. 192.

[81] HWUA, SA 1/1/1, *op. cit.*, p. 2.

[82] *Ibid.*, p. 2.

[83] *Ibid.*, p. 4.

[84] *Ibid.*, p. 4.

[85] *Ibid.*, p. 3.

[86] *Ibid.*, p. 6.

[87] *Ibid.*, p. 13.

[88] Fraser Harris, D. (1898) *St Cecilia's Hall in Niddry Wynd*, Edinburgh and London, p. 2. I am indebted to Jane Blackie for information on St Cecilia's Hall.

[89] *Ibid.*, p. 249.

[90] Youngson, A. J. (1966) *The Making of Classical Edinburgh*, Edinburgh, p. 112.

[91] In 1844, after the School of Arts had moved to Adam Square, the town council purchased the hall for £1,800 to convert it into a school. After a somewhat chequered history, including functioning as a palais de danse (the Excelsior Ballroom) during the 1940s and 1950s, when it was decorated in art deco style, the hall became part of the music faculty of the University of Edinburgh in 1959. Mylne's original elliptical concert hall was reconstructed and baroque chamber concerts are now held once more, two centuries after the last concert in 1798.

[92] Laurie, W. A. (1859) *The History of Freemasonry and the Grand Lodge of Scotland*, Edinburgh, p. 184.

Chapter Three

The Edinburgh School of Arts, 1821–1852

Education makes a people easy to
lead, but difficult to drive; easy to
govern but impossible to enslave.
Lord Brougham

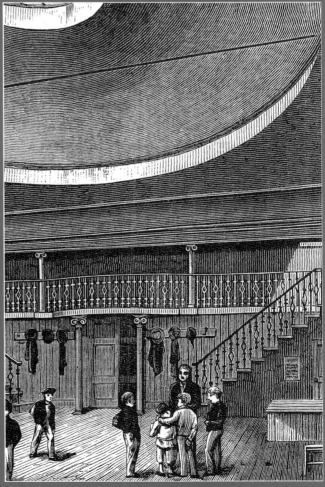

The room in which the first lectures of the Edinburgh School of Arts were delivered
in the Freemasons' Hall, Niddry Street

The Foundation and Early Years of the First Mechanics' Institute

Edinburgh during the early nineteenth century displayed many examples of Enlightenment reforming zeal. The new Royal Botanical Gardens were opened in 1824; in 1829 moves were made to found infant schools in the city; and frequent public meetings were held to agitate over issues such as slavery, trade unionism, temperance, electoral reform, the Corn Laws, the Chartist Movement and Poor Law reform. The School of Arts, therefore, was but one manifestation of Edinburgh's involvement with the burning issues of this reforming age.

The school owed its foundation to an initiative by enlightened Edinburgh 'gentlemen' of the Whig upper middle classes – guaranteeing both the respectable

List of subscribers to the School of Arts, 1821, including Robert Craig and James Gibson (later Gibson-Craig) of Riccarton

44

	L.		
Robert Craig, Esq. of Riccarton, Prince's Street	L. 1	1	0
George Cranstoun, Esq. Advocate, George Street	1	1	0
Archibald Craufurd, Esq. W. S. Picardy Place	0	10	6
William Craufurd, Esq. of Cartsburn	1	1	0
Lord Cringletie, Charlotte Square	1	1	0
David Constable, Esq. Advocate, Prince's Street	1	1	0
A. Cowan, Esq. Penuicuik	1	1	0
David Cowan, Esq.	1	1	0
Convener Crombie, Lauriston Place	0	10	6
The Hon. General Lesslie Cumming, Queen Street	1	1	0
John Cuninghame, Esq. Advocate, Great King Street	1	1	0
Mr William Cushnie, Lothian Street	0	10	6
Mr William Cusine, Bank Street	1	1	0
Prince Adam Czartoryski	1	1	0
Rev. Dr Davidson, Hanover Street	1	1	0
Dr J. H. Davidson, York Place	1	1	0
William Davidson, Esq. younger of Muirhouse	1	1	0
Mr Dick, Drawing-master, South Bridge	1	1	0
Mr John Dick, Graham Street	1	1	0
Andrew Dickson, Esq. Waterloo Place	1	1	0
Rev. David Dickson, St Cuthbert's	0	10	6
Mr Robert Dods, Builder	1	1	0
Edward Douglas, Esq. Abercrombie Place	1	1	0
Sir James Douglas, Coates Crescent	1	1	0
Robert Downie, M. P. Charlotte Square	1	1	0
Henry Home Drummond, Esq. Prince's Street	1	1	0
Adam Duff, Esq. Advocate, Charlotte Square	1	1	0
Dr Duncan, senior, Adam's Square	1	1	0
Dr Duncan, junior, York Place	1	1	0
Sir Robert Dundas, Bart. Heriot Row	1	1	0
Right Hon. W. Dundas, M. P.	5	0	0
James Dundas, Esq of Dundas	1	1	0
Alexander Dunlop, Esq. George Street	1	1	0
George Dunlop, Esq. W. S. Great King Street	1	1	0
The City of Edinburgh	5	5	0
J. F. Erskine of Mar, Esq. Shandwick Place	1	1	0
David Falconar, Esq. of Carlowrie	1	1	0
Mr A. Falkner, South Bridge	1	1	0
Robert Ferguson of Raith, Esq.	1	1	0
John Ferrier, Esq. York Place	1	1	0
L. H. Ferrier, Esq. Queen Street	1	1	0
Sir William Fettes, Bart. Charlotte Square	1	1	0
The Hon. Admiral Fleming	1	1	0
Archibald Fletcher, Esq. Advocate, Castle Street	1	1	0
Sir William Forbes, Bart. George Street	1	1	0

45

	L.		
George Forbes, Esq. Coates Crescent	L. 1	1	0
Mr George Forrest, Nicholson Street	1	1	0
Mr John Forsyth, Builder, Charlotte Place	1	1	0
Robert Forsyth, Esq. Advocate, Mound Place	1	1	0
Frederick Fotheringham, Esq. Abercrombie Place	1	1	0
Mr P. S. Fraser, Graham Street	1	1	0
John Fullerton, Esq. Advocate, Charlotte Square	1	1	0
William Fullerton, Esq. of Skeldon	1	1	0
A. Fyfe, Esq. Surgeon, Adam's Square	1	1	0
Dr John Gairdner, Hanover Street	1	1	0
Thomas Gairdner, Esq. W. S. Hanover Street	0	10	6
Mr Alexander Gelkie	1	1	0
Messrs Gibb and Macdonald, South Bridge Street	2	2	0
James Gibson, Esq. W. S. Picardy Place	1	1	0
A. C. Maitland Gibson, Esq. Queen Street	1	1	0
Ebenezer Gilchrist, Esq. St Andrew's Square	1	1	0
Mr Giles, Painter, Horse Wynd	1	1	0
Alexander Gillespie, Esq. York Place	1	1	0
Lord Gillies, York Place	1	1	0
Lord Glenlee, Brown Square	1	1	0
Incorporation of Goldsmiths	10	10	0
Alexander Gordon, Esq. Great King Street	1	1	0
Rev. Robert Gordon, Buccleugh Place	0	10	6
Messrs Graham and Anderson, Jewellers, Potter-Row	1	1	0
Dr Graham, Professor of Botany, St Andrew's Square	1	1	0
Mr James Grant, Hunter's Square	1	1	0
The Rev. Dr Grant, James' Square	0	10	6
Mr George Gray	1	1	0
Deacon R. Gray, Grassmarket	1	1	0
Mr Gray, Gorgie Mains	1	1	0
Mr W. Grinton	1	1	0
Mr John Grant	1	1	0
Mr Alexander Hamilton, Shoemaker, Charles Street	1	1	0
Sir William Hamilton, Bart. Howe Street	1	1	0
Mr Robert Hamilton, Parliament Stairs	0	10	6
Dr R. Hamilton, Northumberland Street	1	1	0
Mr Thomas Hamilton, junior, Architect, Albany Lane	1	1	0
Adam Hay, Esq. Drumsheugh	1	1	0
Mr George Hay, Catherine Street	1	1	0
Sir John Hay, Bart. Drumsheugh	1	1	0
Sir John Hay, Bart. Advocate, Pitt Street	1	1	0
Alexander Henderson, Esq. Warriston	1	1	0
Alexander Henderson, Esq.	1	1	0
Mr John Henderson, Builder, Tobago Place	1	1	0
William Henderson, Esq. London Street	1	1	0
William Henderson, Esq. South Bridge	1	1	0

Sir Walter Scott, the most prominent Tory supporter of the School of Arts. By William Allan, Scottish National Portrait Gallery

and law-abiding character of the new institution and financial support. The first report lists those luminaries who supported the school financially; over 350 of Edinburgh's middle and upper classes and trade associations made donations ranging from 5 shillings to 10 guineas. A few names from the list attract attention: Lord Henry Cockburn, Francis Jeffrey, William Playfair, Henry Raeburn, Robert Stevenson (famous for his designs of Scottish lighthouses), Robert Craig of Riccarton, Alexander Nasmyth, William Burn the architect (who later designed the new Riccarton house), and Sir Walter Scott. The City of Edinburgh also supported the new institution with a contribution of 5 guineas. The appearance of Scott's name as a subscriber – he was a dedicated Tory and ardent supporter of the British monarchy – indicates a consensus in support of the school which was not confined to Whigs.[1] Indeed, Scott addressing the third AGM on 1 June 1824 'warmly approved of the institution' and 'considered it as great a crime to hide knowledge from the people as it would be to hide the sun from them if they had that power'.[2]

An analysis of the curriculum offered to the artisans of Edinburgh needs to be informed by an understanding of the thinking of the directors concerning the effectiveness of science in achieving social control of the working class by transforming their values, behaviour and morals. The annual reports indicate that directors revisited regularly the social control agenda in their perorations. On the opening night, Horner stressed to the new students that

by occupying your leisure hours in the cultivation and improvement of your mind, you will elevate your character to a higher scale; and, in proportion as you withdraw from frivolous and useless occupations, to say nothing of those that are injurious to your health and your morals, you will add respectability to your station as members of society and you will have far happier and more contented minds. It will lead you, moreover, to the contemplation of those beautiful contrivances, by which the Almighty has adapted the whole system of the universe ... and which display the infinite wisdom and goodness of an all-perfect Being.[3]

At the end of the first academic session on 24 April 1822 and having been presented with an inscribed silver inkstand, Horner gave a valedictory address to 400 students and 50 'gentlemen' reminding his working-class audience of their debt to the upper-class philanthropists for 'there had been no backwardness in the higher ranks of your fellow citizens to come forward on your behalf, no jealousy of imparting knowledge to the less elevated ranks'.[4]

Two years later, Robert Forsyth, an advocate, asserted the link between science and behaviour: 'While students were engaged in scientific pursuits their morals were improved.'[5] This fundamental rationale was proclaimed regularly at the annual general meetings of the school. The Reverend Thomas Chalmers, at the same meeting in June 1824 – when moving the adoption of Leonard Horner's report – also maintained that attending the school would reduce social class conflict:

Next to the general elevation of plebeian habits, and of the plebeian understanding ... there is not a more pleasing result than the mutual kindliness which it is fitted, and that immediately to engender between the upper and lower classes of society.[6]

Chalmers stated that 'there is nought more delightful than when an individual such as Watt, whose original lot was cast among the multitude – than to see him struggle through all the impediments of his birth, and ... at length attain a place of honour ... and equal companionship among the nobles of our land'.[7] Chalmers, however, did not hold out the same enticing prospect of social mobility for the mass of workers, reaffirming both the permanence and necessity of a rigid class structure:

The capitalists and the land-owners and much more the original inventors of our community, must still be the few, and that to the end of time its artizans and its labourers must compose the vast multitude of our species – that there is positively as little room for them all in the high places of our own society, as there is among the clerkships of India for all members of the Hindoo population. . . . You may as well try to change the geography of a whole people. . . . Theirs is no Quixotic or hopeless adventure, such as to loosen the platform of the social edifice, and then raise it to the pinnacle; but leaving both the platform and the pinnacle untouched, their main, and indeed only design, is to let down upon humble life the lights of philosophy.[8]

The Reverend Andrew Thompson, editor of the *Edinburgh Christian Instructor* and a director of the School of Arts, averred in his address on 7 June 1825 that the lower orders were 'necessarily so much occupied by objects of sense, and so little accustomed to purely mental exercises, when they seek for recreation, they are apt to seek it in the indulgence of mere appetite; and to this cause . . . is to be attributed a very large proportion of the vice and dissipation which prevails amongst them'.[9] It was the business of the Edinburgh School of Arts to

The Old Town from the New Town: vegetable and fish market beneath the North Bridge, Edinburgh, 1829. Engraving by E. Stalker from drawing by T. H. Shepherd

rescue them from the power of these temptations . . . by providing them with occupations, which elevate them far above the grossness of sensuality, which decidedly indispose them for its grovelling pleasures; [and which would] train them . . . to habits of purity, sobriety, and correct deportment.[10]

The Lawnmarket in the heart of Edinburgh's Old Town, 1825

Intellectual development is seen to be inseparable from parallel improvements in manners and morals. Dr Thompson did not omit, however, the link to economic efficiency, suggesting that the 'fruit of their exertions is to be found in the increased wealth, and strength, and prosperity of the empire at large'.[11]

The directors of the new Edinburgh School of Arts and its philanthropic subscribers were not radicals; the stark social divisions of Edinburgh society, with its gross income inequalities and disparities in housing, health and employment opportunities, were not questioned by them. Few would have shared the concern of R. L. Stevenson as he roamed the city as a young man in the 1860s observing that

> social inequality is nowhere more ostentatious than at Edinburgh. . . . To look over the South Bridge and see the Cowgate below full of crying hawkers is to view one rank of society from another in the twinkling of an eye.[12]

The worthwhile zeal of the Edinburgh philanthropists was directed to filling a gap in educational provision for the working class which was not met by the market, to enhance the enskilling of workers so necessary to a successful economy, while simultaneously exercising social control and improving the morals and behaviour of artisans. They did not seek to promote social mobility as a general principle, but rather to maintain the existing rigidity of the class structure, while justifying the system by the few who could fight their way through to moderate prosperity. The desire to better oneself was described as a mean motive for study 'connected with the low ambition of being above other people'.[13] Mechanics' institutes reflected a growing sense of class consciousness, which involved awareness by working men that they would always be working men.

Harrison has suggested that 'the development of a literate section of the working classes opened the way to the spread of radical and unorthodox opinions, and a good deal of adult educational effort stemmed from the middle class desire to check this'.[14] This attitude flavoured the speeches and writings of leading Whigs and their middle-class supporters – men who were prepared to adjust gradually to changing circumstances, but who, unlike Radicals, also zealous advocates of education for the working class, 'had no intention of countenancing any reform movement which could be turned into a major attack on the existing political, social and economic structure'.[15]

The directors offered the working class of Edinburgh a very spartan educational diet during the first year. On Tuesdays, Dr Andrew Fyfe delivered lectures on the general principles of chemistry, 'clear in exposition and providing useful experiments for a crowded class, with great competition for front seats'.[16] Mr Galbraith taught mechanical philosophy on Fridays between 8.30 and 9.30 P.M.[17] These gentlemen showed the 'utmost disinterestedness' in negotiation with the directors.[18] In addition, during the first winter, courses of lectures on architecture and farriery were delivered gratis by Mr James Milne and Mr Dick. The school was organised on university lines, with sessions from October to May, lectures and examinations.

It is interesting that lectures on architecture and farriery were accepted by the directors but that other courses were turned down. There were also proposals for lectures on astronomy and geography but

> to the class of persons who attend the School of Arts, the answer of the Directors has been, that it is not within the objects of the Institution; and they conceive that if they were to deviate from this rule, they would act in opposition to the opinion of many who now give the School of Arts their patronage and support.[19]

Why the directors should have rejected offers of classes on geography and astronomy, subjects not in any way tainted by political controversy, is difficult to comprehend, especially as they demonstrate the glories of God's creation and were likely to appeal to those patrons with natural theological sympathies. Their exclusion suggests an unimaginative and rigid utilitarian concept of what was deemed appropriate for the minds of working-class artisans. The directors justified their decision in patronising terms:

> those who have already acquired a knowledge of the principles of Chemistry and Mechanical Philosophy may enter upon other subjects of science: they certainly may, but if they do so, another institution must be created ... a smattering of science too generally engenders conceit and confirms ignorance. ... It would be very easy to introduce many parts of science which would attract by striking phenomena, and, by contributing to their amusement, would draw together a very crowded audience; but this could not be done without sacrificing subjects of far higher value.[20]

No subject was more popular, and none was of more doubtful educational value in the mid nineteenth century than phrenology, popularised across Britain from Edinburgh by George Combe. Combe founded the Phrenological Society in 1820 and in 1823 launched the *Phrenological Journal*. The claim of phrenologists was that the shape of the skull determined, or at least demonstrated, mental and emotional characteristics. None of the principles on which phrenology was based has proved true, with the result that the whole of phrenological theory was in fact erroneous.[21] When Combe offered a free course in phrenology in 1825–26, the directors declined, stating that it 'would be most unwise ever to deviate, from the original object for which the School of Arts was founded',[22] Natural science, because of its alleged objectivity and value neutrality – free of disturbing political implications – was thought to be particularly appropriate since it did not divide the middle and upper classes; and Whigs and Tories, hopefully, could collaborate in institutionalising its provision. The curriculum of the later mechanics' institutes seemed superficial by comparison.

Dr Andrew Fyfe, first lecturer in chemistry. Image: Aberdeen University

With regard to teaching methods, the issue of whether instruction for artisans should have been communicated in an academic style was seldom a matter of dispute and the majority of institutes used lectures as the mode of teaching. In terms of a serious mission to enhance technical education, lectures had their limitations, creating a tension between objectives and learning outcomes. Horner realised this and warned the students that 'it is by *reading* that you will make what you have heard in the lectures your own',[23] a comment which presupposes the generality of literacy among the working classes in Scotland. The real problem undermining the educational aspirations of the Edinburgh working classes was lack of time. The mechanic

Table 3.1 Syllabus of Dr Fyfe's chemistry lectures, 1821–22

HEAT	METALS	ACIDS, ALKALIS AND SALTS
Expansion	Iron	Nitrous acid
Fluidity	Copper	Muriatic acid and aqua regia (sulphuric acid)
Evaporation	Lead	Potassa
Communication of heat	Tin	Soda
Radiation of heat	Zinc	Ammonia
Sources of heat	Mercury	Nitre
Sources of cold	Gold	Potashes and soda
	Silver	Muriate of soda
	Platinum	Muriate of ammonia
ATMOSPHERE, GASES AND INFLAMMABLES	Cobalt	Super oxymuriate of potassa
Air	Arsenic	
Oxygen	Bismuth	**ANIMAL BODIES**
Nitrogen	Antimony	Gelatin
Hydrogen	Manganese	Albumin
Charcoal		Milk
Carburetted hydrogen		Bile
Oil and gas	**VEGETABLE BODIES**	Colouring mater
Oxymuriatic acid	Sugar	
	Gum	
EARTH	Starch and gluten	**ELECTRICITY**
Lime	Wax	
Alumina	Oils	**GALVANISM**
Silica	Volatile oils	
	Resins	**CHEMICAL ATTRACTION**

must be in his workshop from six in the morning to seven o'clock in the evening. . . . As he must go home to take some refreshment after work, . . . he cannot conveniently reach the lecture-room sooner than half past eight o'clock. . . . No lecture can be less than an hour long, so that it will be nearly ten o'clock before he can reach home. . . . Then it is evident, that supposing a workman to devote the whole of his leisure time to this object, an hour and a half in the day is the utmost he has at his disposal.[24]

Under such circumstances it was remarkable that the artisans patronised the mechanics' institute at all. How were mechanics to devote themselves to assiduous scientific study without neglecting the interests of their families? It clearly required unusual levels of commitment and stamina to complete such an arduous schedule and yet many students enrolled for more than one year of study.

The syllabus of Dr Fyfe's chemistry course evolved over time from the first year's programme outlined in Table 3.1. In response to a decision by the directors

Table 3.2 Syllabus of Mr Galbraith's mechanical philosophy lectures, 1821–22

Introduction	Mechanical agents	Hydrostatics
General properties of matter	Motion of machines	Hydrodynamics
Statics	Mill work	Acrostatics
Centre of gravity	Clock work	Pneumatics
Dynamics	Architecture	Acoustics
Mechanics	Smithery	Optics
Machines	Strength of materials	Magnetism
Friction	Wheel carriages	Electricity

to place greater emphasis on practical science, he added specific gravity, brewing and distilling, vinegar making, baking, tanning and dyeing, soap making and candles, all more closely reflecting Edinburgh's industries.[25] Fyfe also initiated examinations for the first time, on a voluntary basis, and some 50 students, including three from the blind asylum, presented themselves and all 'evinced a knowledge beyond what the most sanguine had anticipated'.[26]

In mechanical philosophy, Mr Galbraith presented the syllabus illustrated in Table 3.2 for only the 1821–22 academic session, to be succeeded for two years by a civil engineer, Mr George Buchanan. Mr George Lees, a graduate of St Andrews University, was appointed in 1824 and lectured in mechanical philosophy for 30 years before returning to a post at St Andrews in 1854; he also taught mathematics until 1831. Lees further developed the mechanical philosophy syllabus, introducing gravity, the motion of bodies down inclined planes, the theory of the pendulum, the principles of hydrostatics, pneumatics, the causes of winds, the theory of hydraulics, and the principles of the steam engine. Lees stated that his aim was to show 'the application of Mathematics to the various subjects which fell under our notice; first, by deducing formulae from fundamental principles, and then showing the application of these formulae to the solution of practical examples';[27] in short, goals which would not be out of place in an applied mathematics or a mechanics syllabus today.

William Dick obtained a diploma in veterinary surgery in London and returned to Edinburgh in 1818. When the prospectus for the School of Arts was published in 1821, Dick offered to give a course of lectures gratis. The directors had doubts as to the advisability of accepting the offers of lectures on architecture by James Milne and farriery by Dick 'from the danger of distracting the attention of the students'; they were convinced that they would do most good by confining themselves to 'that instruction which is of more general application'.[28] The first session of Dick's course, predominantly concerned with equine treatments, was attended by 17 farriers, one of whom travelled in 10 miles from the country.[29]

Although Dick was permitted to deliver the course during the second year – the directors 'being anxious to contribute to Mr Dick's views of establishing a veterinary school in Edinburgh' – he was cautioned about 'the objectives of the School not admitting the practicality of that subject being adopted as a permanent branch of instruction in the School of Arts',[30] the first of several poor decisions by the management. Lecturing at the school allowed Dick to systematise his teaching and was the seed from which flowered the Highland Society's Veterinary School in 1823, later to become the Edinburgh Veterinary College (1839) before eventually being incorporated into the University of Edinburgh in 1951.

Surprisingly mathematics, the subject first mentioned in Horner's discussions with Bryson, was not offered; but some 30 students, realising that their knowledge of mathematics was insufficient to understand Galbraith's mechanical philosophy lectures (by 1829 described as natural philosophy), challenged the excessively narrow curriculum by forming themselves into a class under a joiner, James Yule, who agreed to teach gratuitously one session per week in the elements of geometry and another in arithmetic.[31] Having obtained the approval of the directors, the class met in a house on Castlehill and, to carry out the principle of mutual instruction, students were arranged in five divisions, each under the best scholar as a monitor, revising on one evening the previous lesson before proceeding further.[32] The number of this class being limited to 30, other students who were excluded formed another under a cabinetmaker, David Dewar. Following the clear evidence of enthusiasm for mathematical instruction revealed by this Mathematical Academy of Tradesmen, the directors introduced formal mathematics teaching during the second session and hired the Reverend Andrew Wilson to provide it. The syllabus offered was designed to meet the aim that

> artizans should at least be initiated in the science of calculation and of mensuration ... that Algebra ... may easily be taught as far as Quadratic equations; ... that the elements of Geometry form a study of even higher importance; ... [but] it would be injudicious to attempt the more diffuse and elaborate system of an academical course ... in Geometry.[33]

Wilson's mathematics course included, among other things, simple and quadratic equations, logarithms, the first four books of Euclid 'in a condensed form', and elements of plane trigonometry.[34] Although no textbook was used, a brief synopsis of each lecture was sold to the students; twelve sheets were printed in total at a cost which did 'not exceed 2s 6d'.[35] The mathematics class commanded 'an audience of above 150 students in regular attendance' and the students were also requested to attend a session 'every Saturday evening to examine them on the work they had gone over'.[36] How many of today's students or staff would be willing to participate in *viva voce* maths examinations every Saturday night? Since some students who enrolled for mathematics in the school's third session had attended during the previous year, a special class of one hour per week was organised during which Mr Wilson taught 30–50 students trigonometry, logarithms and surveying using the institution's previously acquired theodolite.[37]

Having reviewed the curricula of the mechanics' institutes, Shapin and Barnes concluded that the science was factual rather than theoretical or speculative, pure rather than applied, and simplified in presentation.[38] The central notion was to show 'how things really are in nature', rather than allude to the provisional nature of scientific knowledge. The science delivered to the mechanics was differentiated from that of the middle classes at university in being hard, descriptive and factual; it was not theoretically informed, in contrast to the metaphysical science of the Scottish universities.[39] The evidence of the School of Arts curricula suggests that this conclusion was only partly valid; although emphasis was placed on actual demonstrations, machines, chemical substances and geometrical diagrams, there were elements of the chemistry and mechanical philosophy courses which addressed theory and deduced formulae from basic principles. Moreover, at the universities, much of the chemistry teaching was delivered to medical students and was unlikely to have been metaphysical.

Horner realised that it was not practical to 'support such institutions from the fees of the students and keep that fee sufficiently low' so that 'there must be another source of revenue besides the students' fees'.[40] The statement of accounts for the first year records the income as £737 19s 2d, of which £295 (40 per cent) was derived from students' fees and £430 (58 per cent) from subscriptions, thereby underlining the importance of the 'great and the good' of Edinburgh to the viability of the institution.[41] The middle and upper classes were firmly in control of the school, providing essential financial support and dominating the management. The directors sanctioned £151 spending on apparatus, £76 on furniture, £148 on books and binding and £49 rent for the Freemasons' Hall. Total remuneration of lecturers, assistants and other attendants was only £81 and, although individual salaries were not published, payments to Dr Fyfe and Mr Galbraith were unlikely to have exceeded £32 each for the academic year. The directors were sufficiently confident of the future to look forward to the acquisition of a building for the School of Arts. To that end, they established a separate fund and deposited £100 with the city chamberlain, to which a further £200 was added the following year.[42] Horner's original proposal had been for a one-year experiment on a limited scale but such was the success of the first year that, so far as Horner and his friends were concerned, continuation was in no doubt. However, storm clouds of a political nature were brewing during the summer of 1822, threatening to wrest control of

Dr David Brewster. His interest in early photography is reflected in this Calotype image by pioneer photographers D. O. Hill and Robert Adamson. Scottish National Portrait Gallery

the school from Horner and his Whig associates and place it under the Tory leadership of Dr David Brewster and Professor Thomas Charles Hope.

A Takeover Bid

D r Brewster (1781–1868), a leading physicist who later became principal of the United Colleges of St Salvator and St Leonard at St Andrews, was the first chairman of the board of directors of the School of Arts. Early in the first session, however, Brewster dissociated himself from the school and began what in effect amounted to a campaign of sabotage against it by establishing the Scottish Society of Arts to encourage invention and improvement. Brewster envisaged that if Horner's scheme was successful, it could lead to the establishment of similar schools elsewhere in Scotland. Such schools could be set up or organised under the aegis of his own Society of Arts. He viewed Horner's scheme as complementing his, and perhaps as offering the possibility of enlarging the society's activities in the educational sphere. Thomas Charles Hope (1766–1844) became professor of chemistry at Edinburgh in 1795, and although he had no

James Gibson-Craig, radical lawyer and laird of Riccarton. Caricature by Crombie

direct association with the School of Arts, he had considerable influence on Horner and early lecturers, notably Fyfe (who served as Hope's assistant for many years).[43] Brewster and Hope made a clumsy attempt to gain control of the School of Arts under the auspices of the Society of Arts for Scotland.

At a meeting of the subscribers in September 1822 in the Waterloo Tavern, Leonard Horner addressed the gathering of 300 people, referring to

> a printed circular he had received that morning . . . entitled 'Edinburgh School of Arts, under the direction and patronage of the Society of Arts for Scotland' . . . announcing lectures by Dr Fyfe on the Chemical Arts to commence on 15th October.[44]

The circular, dated 30 August, had been sent around without any communication with himself or any other director of the School of Arts.[45] Dr Fyfe confirmed that Dr Brewster had asked him to lecture for the Society of Arts, to which he agreed, provided it did not interfere with his commitments to the School of Arts. Fyfe was surprised, therefore, to find advertised in the circular distributed by Dr Brewster the day and hours fixed on which it was intended he should lecture at the School of Arts; and Horner had 'waited on Dr Fyfe that morning for an explanation, and he was authorised by him to state to the meeting, that he [Brewster] had been given no authority whatsoever for the announcement in the circular'.[46]

Mr John Shank More, an advocate, then addressed the meeting and argued that the Society of Arts 'contained within it the greater part of the rank, science and opulence of Scotland, and . . . he thought the smaller society [the School of Arts] would derive the greatest benefit from a union with the larger, and in being taken under its wing and patronage'.[47] Mr More then read part of a private letter from Horner to Brewster; James Gibson (who became Gibson-Craig when he inherited the Riccarton estate a year later) interrupted and requested More to explain how he became acquainted with such a confidential letter. More replied that he regretted the absence of Dr Brewster, which 'he believed to be owing to Dr Brewster having gone to the country'.[48] The redoubtable Henry Cockburn, who was sitting next to Mr More, intervened to inform the gathering, to the accompaniment of cheers and a laugh, that he had seen Dr Brewster in the street ten minutes before the hour of the meeting. Mr More, ignoring this comment, pressed his case that there was not room for two institutions of this kind; that dissensions had developed among the directors of the School of Arts; and moved that the school should be placed under the control of the Society of Arts.[49]

Horner rose to the challenge and addressed the assertion that it had always been the intention to place the school under the control of the society. He read out both

Henry Cockburn, Lord Cockburn, eminent Whig advocate, man of letters and supporter of the School of Arts. Caricature by Crombie

the minutes of the first meeting of the School of Arts in April 1821, at which Dr Brewster was present, 'where there is not the most remote allusion to the Society of Arts', and the subsequent prospectus, which was drawn up with the assistance of Dr Brewster, in which 'not a word is said about the Society of Arts'.[50] He stated that Dr Brewster 'showed great coldness and indifference to the School of Arts . . . never attending one meeting of the directors'.[51] Horner also informed the meeting that it 'has been most injuriously circulated . . . that he [Mr Horner] had the School of Arts for a political purpose. At such an imputation he naturally felt indignant.'[52]

Henry Cockburn intervened again and robustly defended the school, strongly denying that there had been any dissension among the directors, apart from Dr Brewster. Cockburn ascribed the problem that had arisen to the personal ambitions of Dr Brewster 'to make every scientific institution in the country subordinate to it [the Society of Arts]'.[53] He went on to argue that the society, embracing as it did the whole country, 'made it unfit for the daily government of an institution purely local'.[54] Following Cockburn's speech, the meeting rejected More's motion that the school should be placed under the direction of the Society of Arts, and the 10 or 12 people who favoured it (of the 300 attending) left the room.[55] The meeting then elected directors for the ensuing year and on Dr Brewster being proposed to continue as a director 'there was a loud cry of *No, No*, from every part of the room'.[56] Cockburn then delivered one of his many eulogies to Horner, a motion seconded by Professor Pillans, who stated that the success of the school was 'due solely to Mr Horner . . . the very soul and spirit of the institution'. The *Scotsman* concurred, describing Horner as 'bland in his manners, tolerant in his spirit, and honourable in his principles, no guarantee could have been stronger that no partiality of feeling, no bias from politics, would be yielded to', while it argued that Dr Brewster 'has been scattering brands where he should have planted the olive'.[57] Later, on 14 September 1822, in a letter to his friend Dr Marcet, Horner gave vent to his feelings:

> Brewster's iniquities have been fully exposed, and that he has met with a complete defeat. . . . In order to neutralise Hope we made him a director but happily he has declined acting, so that we shall not be annoyed with him.[58]

Relations between Horner and Brewster, unsurprisingly, remained distant for many years.

Waterloo Palace and Calton Hill, Edinburgh, 1829

Governance of the School of Arts

Horner was sufficiently astute to realise, as in the case of Edinburgh Academy, that Tories should be part of the management and he had 'found the greatest advantage in the School of Arts from having the countenance of a few of these gentlemen'.[59] In a letter to his sister in April 1822, Horner wrote:

> I took some pains to get a pretty full attendance of the friends of the Institution, and had the magistrates present, with a strong band of Tories. They have supported the School of Arts with great heartiness and liberality, and considering that I have taken so great an interest in it, shows that they have here many good opinions which are not to be found among the Tories of England.[60]

Having survived this takeover bid, the directors limited numbers in the second year to 400 because of the size of the lecture room; in practice 430 enrolled, of whom 250 were students who had attended during the previous year.[61] Copies of busts of Watt, Rennie and Dr Franklin were presented to the school by the sculptor Sir Francis Chantrey and were placed in the lecture room so that the students may 'see before them those eminent men who raised themselves to opulence and distraction from the humbler stations of life, by the mere force of their genius . . . these busts may serve a higher purpose than that of mere decoration'.[62]

At the general meeting of subscribers on 3 September 1822 it was agreed that

> all who contribute not less than one guinea annually shall be considered as Subscribers, entitled to vote at all meetings, and shall be eligible to serve as Directors. The management of the affairs of the institution shall be entrusted to eighteen Directors, to be chosen from among the Subscribers, of whom the Lord Provost of the City of Edinburgh, and the Deacon Convener of the Trades shall, *ex officio*, always be two. The remaining sixteen Directors shall be chosen annually by the Subscribers, at a General Meeting. . . . Two of the elected Directors . . . shall go out annually by rotation, and shall not be re-eligible for one year.[63]

The directors were also empowered 'to appoint the Teachers and shall have the whole management of the affairs of the Institution, with the power of making by-laws for the due regulation thereof'.[64] This system of governance, with no representation of the mechanics, was strongly supported by the middle-class supporters of the school. The Reverend Dr Thomas Chalmers justified this regime as facilitating the mixing of the classes:

> The rich and the poor will love each other more . . . and so highly indeed do I prize the blessedness which must ensue from their mingling frequently together that I fondly trust no such change will ever take place in the constitution of this seminary, as shall discover them in the management of its affairs.[65]

In 1824–25 George Lees, a St Andrews graduate, took over both the mechanics and mathematics classes; Lees was to become a mainstay of the school, and his son maintained the dynasty into the twentieth century. Meanwhile Lord Brougham expressed his reservations concerning the exclusion of the mechanics from the management of the institution, commenting in 1825 that 'it seems, according to the most obvious principles, inconsistent with the prosperity and permanence of the plan'.[66] The system of governance was partially reformed in 1835 when the directors recognised the need to receive advice from people who are 'brought by their occupations into constant and free intercourse with the working classes of the Community' and particularly from former pupils of the school.[67] Three new directors were duly appointed: Mr Slater, a die-caster; Mr Black, a surveyor; and Mr Ritchie, a machinist. Horner, as secretary, administered the school more or less single-handed with the minimum necessary involvement of the directors, attending there most evenings. The annual reports of the Edinburgh School of Arts then settled down into serious if somewhat smug accounts of the good work accomplished during the previous year; seldom did the breath of controversy stir through the pages.

Broadening the Curriculum

T otal student attendances in the early years of the school reflected closely the trade cycle, rising when the city's economy was prosperous and falling during depressions, as in 1826–27 (Figure 3.1). The directors reduced the

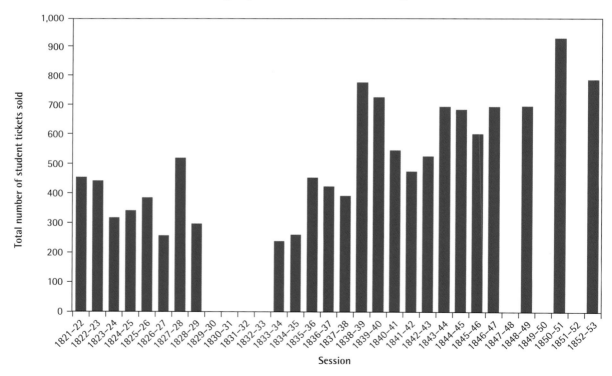

Figure 3.1 Total student tickets sold, 1821–53. No annual reports were published between 1829 and 1833 and in 1847–48, 1849–50 and 1851–52

Source: Annual Reports of Directors, Edinburgh School of Arts, and Watt Institution and School of Arts

SCHOOL OF ARTS

FOR THE

Instruction of Mechanics, &c.

LIBRARY ROOMS, No. 2, DRUMMOND STREET.

LECTURES during the WINTER SESSION 1835 and 1836, beginning Thursday 1st of October, and continuing to the end of April.

MECHANICAL PHILOSOPHY, *Thursday.* By GEORGE LEES, A. M.   CHEMISTRY, *Tuesday.* By DAVID B. REID, M. D.

MATHEMATICS, { JUNIOR CLASS,—*Monday* and *Friday.* } By MR. JAMES JOHNSTONE, Teacher in the Southern Academy.
{ SENIOR CLASS,—*Wednesday.* }

The Fee for *each* of the above four Classes, the Junior Mathematics, the Senior Mathematics, the Natural Philosophy, and the Chemistry, is FIVE SHILLINGS.

A Ticket, which gives admission to all the Lectures, (except that on Practical Chemistry,) is TWELVE SHILLINGS. The privileges of the Library are extended to all Students, whether attending one or more Classes.

The Directors earnestly recommend to those who desire fully to avail themselves of the benefits of the School of Arts, to pursue their Studies on the following plan :—

During the *First* Year, to attend the Junior Mathematics alone.
During the *Second* Year, to attend the Senior Mathematics, and the Chemistry Classes ; and,
During the *Third* Year, to attend the Natural Philosophy and the Chemistry Classes.

In consequence of the great numbers who have for several Sessions past, on the Opening Nights of the Season, crowded the Lecture-Room, to the exclusion of those who ought to have been present, the Directors have this year resolved to issue Tickets of Admission to the Two Introductory Lectures, *price Sixpence,* which sum will be deducted, should the Person afterwards take out a Season Ticket. These Tickets to be had by applying to Mr. MACDONALD, at the Library, or at the Shops of Mr. BRYSON and Messrs. SCLATER and SON, South Bridge, on and after Monday next, the 21st of September.

In consequence of the great success of the Class of Practical Chemistry last year, it is very desirable that it should be continued during the ensuing Winter Session ; and, therefore, should a sufficient number of Students come forward, so as to cover the increased expense which must necessarily attend such a course, the Directors will make arrangements with Dr. REID for its commencement as early in the Session as possible. Those, therefore, who are anxious to avail themselves of this opportunity of acquiring a thorough acquaintance with the Practical Details of this most useful Science, will be so good as leave their names with Mr. MACDONALD, when they apply for their other Tickets. The Fee for this Course will be FIVE SHILLINGS.

The Hour of Lecture is half-past Eight o'Clock in the Evening.

Applications for Tickets to be made to the Librarian, at the Library, on Monday the 21st instant, and every subsequent Evening, from Eight to Ten o'Clock.

LIBRARY ROOMS,
2, Drummond Street, 19th September 1835.

WM. THOMSON, M. D. } Secretaries.
GEORGE M. SINCLAIR, }

ALEX. LAWRIE & CO. Printers.

The limited curriculum offered by the School of Arts, 1835 to 1836

fees from 15s to 7s 6d and this helped to raise numbers from 384 to 515 in 1827–28 (Figure 3.1). Leonard Horner departed for London in 1827 to take up his ill-fated wardenship of the University of London, and Dr David MacLagan and Mr William Thompson were appointed joint secretaries. Student numbers continued to fluctuate; the session 1833–34 marked a low point, as did 1841–42, but the long-term trend was upwards.

The institution experienced financial difficulties in the late 1830s when for several years expenditure exceeded income and the fund laid aside for building was exhausted to meet the shortfall. Income from subscriptions, which had averaged over £400 per annum from 1821–22 to 1825–26, had fallen to only £166, and fee income from upwards of £200 annually to £105. The early days of plenty were indeed over and there were to be many lean years. The decade of the 1840s, however, witnessed steady expansion in numbers to reach a peak of 927 in 1850–51 (Figure 3.1). The increasing enrolments were also related, at least in part, to the introduction of new subjects into the restricted curriculum offered during the 1820s. The first hint of a relaxation in the narrow curriculum of the school surfaced at the AGM of subscribers on 10 July 1829, perhaps reflecting a diminution of Horner's personal influence after his move to London:

It is highly important to guard against the possibility of mischief from a too exclusive study of the physical sciences; to connect the phenomena of nature with the existence and character of its Author, and to show that the cultivation of science has other and more exalted effects than to make a man more skilful in his vocation. With these objects in view it is proposed that a series of Lectures shall be delivered 'Upon the Manifestations of a Divine Agency in the

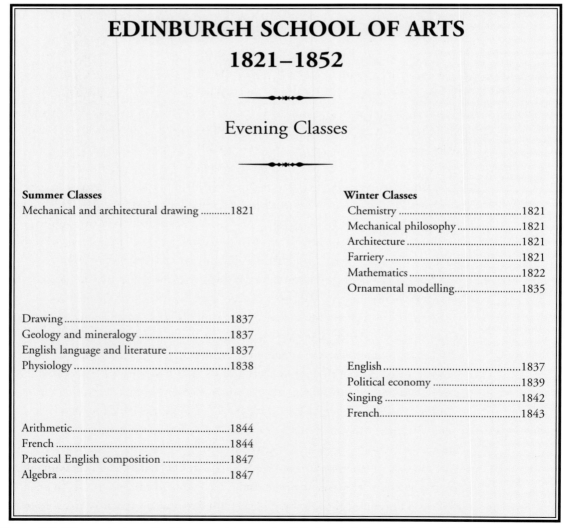

EDINBURGH SCHOOL OF ARTS
1821–1852

Evening Classes

Summer Classes

Mechanical and architectural drawing 1821

Drawing..1837
Geology and mineralogy 1837
English language and literature 1837
Physiology...1838

Arithmetic..1844
French 1844
Practical English composition 1847
Algebra 1847

Winter Classes

Chemistry 1821
Mechanical philosophy 1821
Architecture 1821
Farriery..1821
Mathematics 1822
Ornamental modelling........................1835

English..1837
Political economy 1839
Singing 1842
French..1843

Figure 3.2 The evolution of subject provision at the Edinburgh School of Arts, 1821–52. Some courses survived for only a short period but only the date of introduction is shown

Structure of the Universe, and the Intimations of the Will of the Author of Nature afforded by the Study of Physical Science'.[68]

A new subject, ornamental modelling, was introduced during the 1835–36 session so that workmen could be taught the art of acquiring 'a classic chasteness of expression in the designs of articles passing through their hands'.[69] However, consistent with the narrow utilitarian ethos of the school, the directors emphasised that 'it is not the object ... to open up a nursery for artists, but to teach those engaged in all trades where ornament is in the least concerned, such as silver-chasers, jewellers ... and others ... to enable them ... to contemplate and imitate acknowledged excellence'.[70] This winter course proved popular, with attendances ranging from 30–50 students throughout the 1840s (Table 3.3). As the curriculum continued to expand during the 1830s, the directors resolved to confine the winter course of study to what they described as 'the leading and more generally applicable subjects of Chemical, Mechanical and Mathematical Science, reserving the summer for any courses of a lighter and more recreative kind'.[71] Hence a committee of the directors initiated lecture courses during summer 1837 on natural history, geology and mineralogy and in 1838 on physiology; but the major new development was the introduction of a class on the structure of the English language, with an especial reference to its Greek and Latin roots which 'will enable the students more thoroughly to understand these numerous phrases which so unavoidably and frequently occur in the illustration of a scientific course'[72] (Figure 3.2). By 1839–40 the directors decided that too many subjects were being taught on the same evening and so provision was rationalised, with the winter programme restricted to the core disciplines: mathematics, natural philosophy and chemistry. Courses for English, modelling and drawing were planned for the summer.[73] This scheme was never implemented (Table 3.3).

Edinburgh Whigs realised earlier than their English counterparts the need to promote the learning of political economy[74] but had no intention of countenancing any reform movement which could threaten the stability of society at a time when the political activities of the working classes seemed to presage the outbreak of social strife. Most institutes reflected the views of the Haddington School of Arts Committee, which in 1826 asserted that the introduction of political economy would help in 'reconciling the lower orders to their circumstances, and promoting the peace and welfare of the community at large'.[75] This apologia is an example of using adult education as a means of containing the search for solid improvement within limits acceptable to employers. Dr Thomas Murray, a director of the Edinburgh School of Arts and a staunch Whig, delivered the first session of lectures on public and private economy during the 1839–40 session. Murray associated the accumulation of capital with virtue and religion,

Table 3.3 Student numbers by subject, 1838–53

	WINTER COURSES											SUMMER COURSES				
	Natural philosophy	Chemistry	Mathematics	Junior mathematics	Senior mathematics	English	Natural history	Political economy	Modelling	French	Singing	Drawing	Arithmetic	Algebra	English composition	French
1838–39	183	179	222			49	31		49			64				
1839–40	142	186	194			59		27	52			64				
1840–41	94	87		127	10	46			53			64				
1841–42	85	76		114	16	30			53			65				
1842–43	70	84		88	15	32			45			67				
1843–44	96	94		73	15	35			39	141		58	46			29
1844–45	102	106		96	10	43			29	117		65	39			26
1845–46	99	87		76	11	33			36	85		65	38			18
1846–47	104	83		91	10	62			56	85	74	68	29	9	12	24
1847–48																
1848–49	81	59		84	7	40			34	78		68		15	4	13
1849–50																
1850–51	104	95		105	13	46			42	124		55	27	17		22
1851–52																
1852–53	60	85		89	20	51			47	111		64	22	9		32

Note: There were no reports in 1847–48, 1849–50 and 1851–52
Source: Annual Reports of Directors, Edinburgh School of Arts, and Watt Institute and School of Arts

'both of which it has a direct and powerful tendency to promote', and asserted that it 'teaches all the nature of their relative position; ... and proved that the greatness of the nation depended on the unfettered commercial pursuits of "a middle class of men" who were diligently accumulating capital'.[76] The number that attended Murray's course was disappointingly small (27) and the initiative was abandoned. The lack of support was not perhaps surprising for, by the end of the 1830s, working-class spokesmen were increasingly frustrated by the limited reform agenda being articulated by the philanthropic Whigs; the days of relying on middle- and upper-class patronage were numbered.

New techniques of teaching choral singing were popularised in this era – the Mainzer and Hullah systems – which were associated with attempts to civilise the working classes. A class in singing and the elements of music was introduced in 1842–43, but despite an enrolment of 74 students, the directors judged that it was 'not so well attended as to warrant its extension to a second session' and it was discontinued after one year.[77] During the 1843–44 session, the directors 'in consequence of an urgent desire for a French class made by the students' engaged a Frenchman, Monsieur Cornillon, to teach it.[78] Demand was buoyant and 141 students enrolled for the winter session and an additional 29 for the summer one. A summer class in arithmetic was added in 1844 and one in algebra three years later. The broadening of the curriculum into cultural subjects such as singing, English and French reflected not only the concessions to the varied interests of the members and a desire to spread middle-class gentility to the lower orders, but a lack of strategic direction in responding to low enrolments. In 1844 the directors felt moved to re-emphasise their utilitarian credentials in that they

> have not, in the least degree, interfered with the constitutional classes established at the commencement of the School, namely, Chemistry, Natural Philosophy, and Mathematics ... which they regard as of paramount importance, they have always given preference as the standard and characteristic features of the institution. Nor do they wish these ever to be modified or changed.[79]

This view of the pre-eminence of science and engineering disciplines relative to social sciences and humanities, an unfashionable opinion in 1844, is one which permeates the thinking of some staff of the university even to this day. Hence, although some diversification of the curriculum occurred during the 1830s and 1840s, the predominant emphasis on teaching science to the working classes remained, prompting Hudson to declare in 1851 that

> the Edinburgh School of Arts is the only establishment in Britain deserving the title of 'People's College'. For twenty-eight years it has continued to supply to

Table 3.4 Percentage of total students by socio-economic group

	Professional (%)	Managers, lower professional (%)	Intermediate non-manual (%)	Skilled manual (%)	Semi-skilled manual (%)	Unskilled manual (%)	Total Students
1821–22	0	0.7	12.1	82.6	4.5	0	452
1839–40	4	4.5	25.0	62.5	3.5	0.3	724

Source: Annual Directors' Reports, Edinburgh School of Arts

one class of society in the Scottish capital the training which the University has to another.[80]

The issue of the social mix attending the institutes prompted Altick to assert that it was not long before the mechanics were pushed out to be replaced by business and professional men and their families.[81] The proportion of 'mechanics' in attendance at different institutes cannot be determined with accuracy due to deficient statistics and the lack of an agreed definition of the term.[82] The number of mechanics, however, is merely a technical point; the crucial issue is to determine how far the membership was working class as defined by skilled, semi-skilled and unskilled manual occupations. The occupational distribution of students enrolled for the first year of the School of Arts in 1821–22 was heavily skewed towards those trades for which the institution was established. The largest group, representing 82.6 per cent of students, was skilled manual workers comprising predominantly cabinetmakers, joiners and wrights; smiths and iron machine makers; masons and marble cutters. By 1839–40 the socio-economic mix of students had broadened but the skilled artisans were still the largest group and had not deserted the institution, as elsewhere in the UK (Table 3.4). The school had become more attractive to intermediate non-manual workers of whom the largest groups were clerks (44), shopkeepers (24) and drapers (18). Among higher-status occupations there were teachers, writers, veterinary surgeons, architects, accountants, dentists and solicitors. By contrast, manual workers constituted only 38 per cent of the membership of the Manchester Mechanics' Institute in 1840, falling to 26 per cent by 1844,[83] whereas the manual proportion at the Edinburgh School of Arts was 66 per cent in 1840. Hence the clientele at the School of Arts was predominantly drawn from the skilled working class and, to a lesser extent, the lower middle class, mirroring the original aims of the institute. The existence of the Edinburgh Philosophical Association from 1832 – catering specifically for the additional needs of the Edinburgh lower middles classes – was clearly a factor in the maintenance of the working-class profile of students at the Edinburgh School of Arts.

In 1828 the directors proposed developing the syllabus into a two-year course of study. The first year's programme would be the elements of mathematics and chemistry, and the second year's programme would be higher mathematics and mechanical philosophy. Separate tickets at 7s 6d were to be issued for each course, although students would have the option to purchase both tickets.[84] Horner returned to live in Edinburgh from November 1833 to September 1836. He did not resume office in the school, but there can be little doubt that his influence was felt, especially behind the directors' decision in 1834 of the need for 'young men . . . to follow a systematic and well organised course of study'. A radical reform of the syllabus was implemented as follows:

1 A junior class in mathematics, meeting twice per week with the following syllabus: arithmetic, including vulgar and decimal fractions; algebra, including simple and quadratic equations; geometry, first and second books of Euclid.

2 A senior class in mathematics, with one session a week incorporating geometry, the remaining books of Euclid; logarithms; mensuration and trigonometry.

3 Natural philosophy, illustrated by experiments, meeting once per week, and covering the following topics: mechanics, including statics and dynamics; hydrostatics, hydraulics, pneumatics and optics.

4 Chemistry, meeting once per week, in which the 'principles of the science shall be taught, together with the application in the chief arts and manufactures in the processes of which chemical principles are involved'.[85]

The directors recommended, but did not insist, that students during their first year should attend only the junior mathematics class; that they should enrol in the second year for the senior mathematics and chemistry classes; and during the third year attend the natural philosophy and chemistry classes.[86] To encourage students to pursue this course of study, the directors decided that students who adopted it 'shall be eligible to be admitted as Members of the School of Arts, and to have the privilege of free admission to the lectures for the remainder of their lives' provided that the student satisfied the examiners 'in the presence of at least two Directors' at the end of each session when they 'shall receive an *Attestation of Proficiency*'.[87] Every student who at the end of three years' study had accumulated attestations of proficiency for all subjects – indicating a 'competent knowledge of the subjects taught' – received a certificate (later called a diploma of life membership) granting them free admission to the lectures for life and use of the library for two shillings annually and which would also be a 'powerful recommendation . . . [in] applying for a situation in business'.[88] Hence, for the first time, the school provided a certification of the learning outcomes after three years of study. Subsequently, in 1842, the directors extended the chemistry and natural philosophy courses over two years.[89] The diploma never proved very popular; around four per year were awarded from

1834–35 to 1875–76. Its introduction, however, demonstrated the desire of the school's authorities to encourage students to undertake a systematic course of study.

Innovations in teaching were not confined to the introduction of a systematic programme of study; Dr David Reid, a lecturer in chemistry, informed the directors in 1834–35 that 'from the want of proper furnace-apparatus in the hall of meeting'[90] he was prevented from conducting several experiments. Permission was granted to deliver half the chemistry lectures in Dr Reid's own classroom; more fundamentally, practical classes – attended by 100 students which also attracted a 'considerable number of visitors' – were introduced and Dr Reid 'personally defrayed the expense of the materials employed'.[91] Within two years Dr Reid introduced new arrangements for the practical class since, under the previous regime, the class met from 9.00 P.M. till 10.30 P.M. and some pupils had to walk 'two miles after attending the class before they reached their respective abodes'.[92] Reid solved the problem by introducing a basic kit of portable chemical apparatus which the students were expected to use at home,[93] a pioneering idea introduced some 130 years before the Open University.

By 1833–34 student numbers were low (239) and the level of subscriptions from the public had decreased to such an extent that the school's income did not match its essential expenditure. Attempts were made in 1840–41 to obtain grant aid from the government and, although the support of Robert Peel (the leader of the Opposition) was forthcoming, the proposal was not successful.[94] In their annual reports the directors aimed most of their criticisms not at the working men for failure to attend en masse, but at the middle and upper classes of Edinburgh whose financial support they considered to be inadequate.

This recurrent financial crisis prompted a letter from Horner in London on 19 November 1846 expressing concern about the drop in subscriptions to £126 in 1845–46, suggesting that

> the funds collection for the Free Kirk have reduced other subscriptions. . . . I am quite willing to double my subscription [at the time it was one guinea] if others will do the same; which last condition I only make because I do not wish to appear ostentatious.[95]

Horner's assertion concerning the Disruption reducing subscriptions cannot have been a major factor since the decline had started before 1843 and may reflect more of Horner's attitude to the Free Kirk than of the school's financial health. His appeal had little effect and subscriptions fell to a low of £99 in 1848–49 which, even without adjusting for inflation, was derisory compared with the £466 received in 1822–23.

Some relief from the difficult financial circumstances of the institution followed

Dr Thomas Murray, who presided over the School of Arts from 1844 to 1866. Posthumous image by J. Horsburgh, 1898. Photograph: Douglas McBride

in 1853 when the school was recognised by the Department of Science and Art (recently founded by the Board of Trade) and, as a consequence, qualified for one or more scholarships to the Metropolitan School of Science Applied to Mining and the Arts in London; and apparatus and diagrams were made available at a reduced rate.[96] The government did not intend to make schools dependent on public money, a policy endorsed by the directors who argued that 'a money grant – and the more literal the worse – would have had a tendency to paralyse or destroy local liberality, and to make schools of art and mechanical institutions dependent seminaries, devoid of life and energy'.[97]

Dr Andrew Fyfe's long association with the school ended in 1844. He had applied unsuccessfully for the chairs of materia medica (1832) and chemistry (1844) at Edinburgh University, but was appointed to the chair of medicine (but de facto and later de jure of chemistry) in King's College and University, Aberdeen.[98] When Fyfe resigned as both lecturer in chemistry and secretary, Dr Thomas Murray, the political economist, commenced his long tenure 'as autocrat of the school – presiding genius of the place'.[99] Murray (1792–1872), born the son of a crofter in Kircudbrightshire, was a friend of Thomas Carlyle with whom he walked from Galloway to Edinburgh each session during their university career.[100] In 1841 he obtained the printing business of Murray and Gibb, enabling him to 'crown a youth of labour with an age of ease'[101] and to devote time to the School of Arts. Dr Pryde complimented him as 'one of the kindest of men', of 'unfailing tact and knowledge of the world', and as the 'embodiment of quality and benevolence'.[102] Pryde qualified his praise, however, adding that 'the Doctor with all his kindliness and suavity, was an ugly customer to meddle with; and he could retort with the most biting satire'.[103] His old room mate, Thomas Carlyle, recalled him as 'worldly, egoistic, small and vain'.[104]

By the middle of the nineteenth century, the nation was in the grip of industrial fever and the most impressive celebration of this national mood was the Great Exhibition of 1851. The School of Arts was caught up in the excitement. A scheme was devised to reward the eight best students in chemistry, natural philosophy and mathematics by sending them to the exhibition. A fund was raised by friends at the school to enable the students to spend a fortnight at the exhibition.

Library Provision

In an era when fewer working-class households could afford to purchase books, the directors, with considerable foresight, realised that provision of a library was critical to the success of the educational programme. The prospectus reveals a restricted vision concerning the scope of the library and its contents: 'books on Mechanics and Chemistry, and their application to the Arts, and on all branches of Natural and Physical Sciences'[105] and 'the Directors shall have the entire control of the books that are to be admitted'.[106] Concern about the possibility of unsuitable reading corrupting the minds of the Edinburgh working classes led the directors, suspicious of the influence of newspapers, to introduce 'an indispensable rule, that no newspapers shall be brought to this room nor any other books read in it than such as relate to the objects of the Institution'.[107] The management of the library was delegated to the librarian, Mr James Cochrane, and a committee of 12 students, significantly not elected, but chosen by the directors.

By the opening date, the library was stocked with between 300 and 400 volumes; books were taken in on Thursdays and issued on Fridays from seven in the evening and could be borrowed for a fortnight with a penalty of sixpence for every additional fortnight.[108] The directors were aware that many mechanics faced domestic circumstances 'very unfavourable for reading' and opened the library from eight to ten o'clock on those evenings when there was no lecture, and provided 'both fire and light'.[109] The fortnightly issue of books was 270; 30 to 50 men were found each evening in the reading room studying 'with silence and attention'.[110] The first report of the directors published a catalogue of the library's holdings, and this reveals that all the works listed were of a scientific and practical nature, varying from publications on bees, brewing, clockmaking and farriery to a report of the Parliamentary Commissioners appointed to inquire into the nature and extent of the bogs of Ireland.

By the end of the second year, the number of volumes in the library had increased to 691. A year later the directors confirmed: 'We have adhered strictly to the exclusion of all works that do not relate to science and art, having declined several donations of books because they were not connected with the purpose for which the School of Arts was founded.'[111] Eventually a major advance occurred on 3 May 1842 when the directors received a letter from the Library Committee 'requesting permission to introduce into the library works on Biography – Poetry – History etc – as works of that nature were much in request by the pupils'.[112] This plea was granted, but the directors did not relax their censorship, conceding to the request 'on condition that before any work is admitted the consent of the Directors be obtained'.[113]

The annual reports reveal that no particular provision had been made for the funds necessary to support the library, an oversight that was to lead to difficulties throughout the nineteenth century. Over the first decade of its existence, the directors allocated between 8 per cent and 10 per cent of the total financial outlay of the school to the library, ranging from £50 to £90 per annum, but subsequently they found it necessary to spend ever increasing amounts on maintenance and other commitments, largely at the expense of the library, which came to rely heavily on donations of books. By the 1840–41 session, the number of books in circulation from the library amounted to 2,937 volumes, but expenditure on the library and apparatus had slumped to £18 3s 9d.[114]

In 1844 another problem arose in the shape of Mr John Austin Weir, the librarian, who appears to have been supplementing his income with the proceeds of the library. At a meeting of the directors on 18 October 1844, the treasurer reported that

he had failed, after repeated applications, to effect a settlement with Mr. Weir, the Librarian, for the proceeds of the Summer Session – the balance due being

James Watt. By Sir William Beechey. Purchased with grant in aid from the Heritage Lottery Fund, the National Fund for Acquisitions and a donation from the Watt Club Council. Photograph: Douglas McBride

very considerable, the meeting, after discussion, was unanimously of opinion that some new and more definite arrangements must be made as to the office and duties of Librarian.[115]

Mr Weir subsequently tendered his resignation; the library was then audited and its accounts were found to be in a 'confused and unsatisfactory state; . . . they cannot in any respect be relied on'.[116] The audit also discovered that although over 500 new volumes had been acquired, the committee could not ascertain 'how many volumes are a-missing'.[117] The Library Committee continued to be concerned by the inability of students to consult books which were not held, and the directors responded to this problem in 1846 by permitting students who had attended the school for at least two years, even if not life members or currently enrolled, to be granted admittance to the library at a fee of 3s annually; that the sum paid by life members, 2s annually, be devoted to the library; and that library fines be hypothecated for the use of the library.[118]

The Search for a Permanent Building

The renowned inventor and engineer James Watt (1736–1819) has no direct connection with the School of Arts, which was founded two years after his death. Yet a fund established in his memory was to have a defining influence on the school's development. Watt, the son of a Greenock carpenter, left school to become an instrument maker at 15, was appointed to Glasgow University in this capacity, and was able to use the knowledge gained from discussions with the eminent chemist Joseph Black and others in solving the initial problems of the steam engine. From 1775 Watt and his business partner, the Birmingham ironmaster Matthew Boulton, had a monopoly on steam engine construction. By Watt's retirement in 1800 the engines were the driving force behind the Industrial Revolution.[119] From the School of Art's inaugural meeting, the example of Watt's life and achievements had been held up as an inspiration to students.[120] However, the notion of associating James Watt's name and reputation with the school was first proposed by Henry, Lord Cockburn at a meeting in the Waterloo Hotel on 21 July 1824. Lord Cockburn moved the resolution, seconded by Mr Solicitor-General Hope, that

> an architectural edifice should be erected in the capital of Scotland, in such a style as to be within reach of our probable funds. . . . That . . . it shall be employed for the accommodation of the Edinburgh School of Arts; whereby the memory of Watt may forever be connected with the promotion, among a class of men to which he himself originally belonged, of those mechanical arts from which his own usefulness and glory arose.[121]

The directors hailed this resolution and resolved to add their accumulated savings of £500 to the subscription. The proposal was not unopposed, however, for a Mr Craig argued that

> Edinburgh did not appear to him to be in any respect a proper place for a monument of Mr. Watt. . . . The School of Arts was really a monument to a different person [Mr Horner] and could be a monument to no other person.[122]

This plea to honour Horner in an appropriate manner fell on deaf ears, as it has done ever since.

At a meeting of the directors on Thursday, 12 January 1837, a committee was appointed for the purpose of identifying a suitable site for the erection of a building for the School of Arts, or a building which could be altered, the directors being convinced that 'one of the great causes of the falling off in attendance was the present disunited state of the school'.[123] The aggregate sum available was £1,590, including the Watt Monument Fund.[124] In the early 1760s Robert Adam had built two handsome houses with large bay windows – the design suggesting both strength and simplicity – which being recessed back and having the new university buildings (now Old College) on the south, formed Adam Square, later demolished to make way for Chambers Street.[125] One option considered by the Building Committee of the school on 1 February 1837 was the upper half of the central house in Adam Square, formerly Lord President Dundas's property, containing a large hall (45 ft by 22 ft) with a gallery, capable of seating around 350 students; also four other rooms (each 22 ft by 17 ft) and a range of attics consisting of five rooms.[126] This was available for £1,600 and alterations and fitting out were estimated at an additional £300. At a special meeting of directors on 4 April 1837, Mr Sinclair, secretary, was authorised to conclude a lease and to incur the necessary expense to fit out the hall of the Adam Square house as a lecture room.[127] Sinclair negotiated a lease for 10 years and also suggested 'the propriety of having an official seal cut for the institution' and that 'the officer should be provided with a hat and gold band, to be worn when on duty'.[128]

For the first time, the school occupied 'a building fitted up for the accommodation, and devoted exclusively to the purposes of the institution' and each class 'has now an apartment for its special use'.[129] Dr Pryde, who had to teach there, was less flattering, finding it 'dingy, cramped and not well suited for educational purposes'.[130] The school had also been in consultation with Mr Steele, a sculptor, on the subject of a statue of James Watt to be placed on the front wall of the house 'in bold relief against the sky, to be about 8 or 9 feet in height, and executed in freestone'.[131] However, at a joint meeting of the managers of the Edinburgh School of Arts and the Committee of Subscribers to James Watt's Monument on 10 February 1837, it was agreed that it would be impossible to erect any statue on the front of the Adam Square house 'in a style worthy of the subject which the Watt subscription was set on foot to commemorate'.[132]

The curriculum was broadened for the first but not the last time. In 1836–37 summer classes in English language were begun at the request of students; and English, under George MacDonald, became a winter class from 1837–38, attracting annually some 30–60 students. This was the first permanent extension to the original trivium. In the four summer sessions of 1836–37 to 1838–40, a series of single courses was given in geology, physiology, natural history and political economy; the next permanent addition was French in 1843–44, added like English at the request of the students, which succeeded in attracting over 100 students annually.

Although the directors spent £226 2s 4½d on fitting up the Adam Square premises,[133] the financial situation was sustainable; the school had broken even over the session, although the long-standing 'building fund' had seen no increase since 1826. This financial stability did not last and over the two sessions 1838–40 expenditure exceeded income by £153 and fears were expressed that unless an 'addition can be made to the annual income, the school cannot long continue to exist'.[134] The committee of the Watt Fund agreed that the school should receive the interest on the capital for the two years 1840–42.[135] At the general meeting of subscribers on 25 October 1841, the directors appealed to patrons and friends for subscriptions to the building fund, and £300 was donated. By 1846 this building fund stood at £500 and, following a meeting between the directors of the school and the Watt Fund Subscription Committee, the two funds were amalgamated, amounting to £1,856 15s 0d. A joint committee was appointed under the chairmanship of Alexander Bryson (son of Robert Bryson) and it purchased the Adam Square building for £2,500 in 1851,[136] whereupon the school adopted the title of the Watt Institution and School of Arts.

Robert Adam's distinguished building from the 1760s which became the home of Edinburgh School of Arts from 1837. The statue of James Watt in the foreground was unveiled in 1854

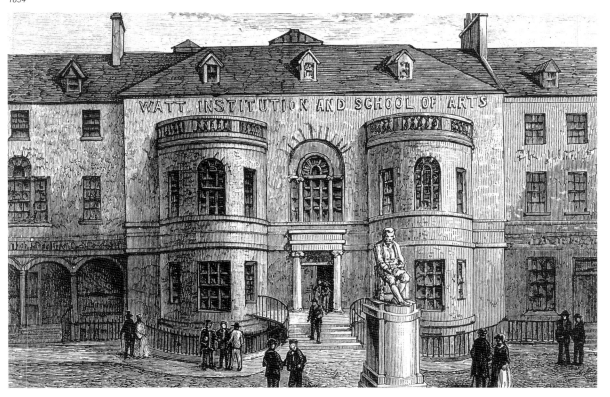

James Nasmyth and the Edinburgh School of Arts

There are very few first-hand accounts written by staff or students of their experiences at the School of Arts during its infancy. The only record of the school and its lectures from its inception is that of James Nasmyth (1808–1890), youngest surviving child of the landscape painter Alexander Nasmyth. Nasmyth, the greatest engineer to have attended the institution, combined to a marked degree both the artistic and practical attributes of the family. He was clearly inspired on returning from the High School one day, at the age of 9, to see James Watt leaving his father's house and 'his buoyant countenance and his tall but bent figure made an impression on my mind that I can never forget'.[137] Nasmyth became famous at the High School for producing tops on his father's foot-lathe – for which the boys would pay any price – centred so accurately that they could spin twice as long as a shop-bought toy; he also made kites and balloons of tissue paper, which they flew on Calton Hill.[138] He left school at age 12 and continued to acquire his education in a desultory way, much of it in his father's workshop. He designed and produced various inventions, including small brass cannon, popular for the loud noise they made, and beginning with a small steam engine for the purpose of grinding the oil colours used by his father.[139] Nasmyth then 'contrived a sectional model of a condensing steam-engine of the beam and parallel motion construction'.[140] The first of these models was made for the Edinburgh School of Arts (currently on display in the School of Engineering and Physical Sciences) and he subsequently sold others to mechanics' institutes for £10 each; 'and with the pecuniary results I made over one-third to my father, as a sort of help to remunerate him for my "keep", and with the rest I purchased tickets to certain classes in the University'.[141]

James Nasmyth, inventor of the steam hammer and one of the first students of the Edinburgh School of Arts

James Nasmyth's model
demonstrated Watt's
revolutionary improvements to
Newcomen's steam engine

Nasmyth turned his bedroom into a miniature brass foundry (much to the chagrin of his father), bricking up the fireplace, taking up the carpet and installing a furnace fuelled by gas coke and cinders from the kitchen, the heat was 'sufficient to melt in a crucible six or eight pounds of brass'.[142] With this he could raise a white heat which would melt several pounds of brass in the crucible. His brass foundry was over the bedroom of his father, who had forbidden the young Nasmyth to work late at night, which he did 'occasionally on the sly'. Sometimes when 'detected by the sound of the ramming of the sand on the moulding boxes ... my father let me know that I was disobeying his orders by rapping on the ceiling of his bedroom with a slight wooden rod of ten feet', but James, inventive as ever, overcame detection 'by placing a bit of old carpet under my moulding boxes as a non-conductor of sound, so that no ramming could afterwards be heard'.[143] Decades later in 1864 Nasmyth, replying to Mr Robert Wilson who had sent him a planing machine, wrote 'I would like to have ... the ratchet wheel.'[144] It had sentimental associations for the 56-year-old inventor for the 'wheel I cast myself' from 'a pair of old candlesticks that I begged of my Father', they 'being the first pair he and my Mother set up house with and that they had held the candle to many a crack with Burns'.[145]

James Nasmyth's steam carriage

Nasmyth enrolled as a student at the School of Arts aged 13 in 1821 and was impressed by Dr Fyfe's chemistry course, praising him as

an excellent man. His clearness of style, his successful experiments, and the careful and graphic method by which he carried his students from the first fundamental principles to the highest points of chemical science, attracted a crowded and attentive audience.[146]

Nasmyth described the lecture room in the Freemasons' Hall as containing 'a noble lecture table, with accommodation for any amount of apparatus. . . . The seats were arranged in concentric segments, with the lecture table as their centre.'[147] The social control agenda of the Whig founders was symbolised by an alcove opposite the lecturer where 'might often be seen the directors of the institution – Jeffrey, Horner, Murray and others – who took every opportunity of dignifying by their presence this noble gathering of earnest and intelligent working men'.[148] Nasmyth also recalled the enthusiasm of his fellow students to borrow from the library:

Standing . . . amidst a number of applicants awaiting the opening of the . . . library . . . as crowded as if I had been . . . at the gallery door of the theatre . . .

James Nasmyth's steam hammer

when some distinguished star from London was about to make his appearance. There was the same eagerness to get a good place in the lecture room, as near to the lecture table as possible, especially on the Chemistry nights.[149]

Of the School of Arts, the great inventor acknowledged, 'I owe a deep debt of gratitude to it, and because of the instructive and intellectually enjoyable evenings which I spent there, in fitting myself for entering upon the practical work of my life.'[150] Indeed only one year after completing his studies at the School of Arts in 1827, at the age of 19, Nasmyth displayed his inventive flair by constructing a road steam carriage. After exhibiting a working model to the Society of Arts, successful trials were held along 4–5 miles of the Queensferry Road, carrying eight passengers on benches 4 feet above ground. This was some two years before Stephenson's Rocket was tested at the Rainhill trials; but Dr Brewster's Society of Arts for Scotland saw the carriage as only an interesting experiment and did not realise its commercial potential. Nasmyth therefore broke it up and sold its two high-pressure engines and their boiler for £67.[151]

James Nasmyth was one of the most able and versatile engineers of his generation, introducing a host of improvements in the production and design of locomotives, steam engines and foundry equipment. He founded the Bridgewater Foundry at Patricroft, Lancashire, in 1836 to manufacture industrial machinery. It was here that Nasmyth played a central role in the invention of the steam hammer,[152] the crowning achievement of his genius. He was stimulated by a letter from the Great Western Company on 24 November 1839 informing him that 'there was not a forge hammer in England or Scotland powerful enough to forge the intermediate paddle-shaft of the engines for Isambard Kingdom Brunel's steamship the SS *Great Britain*, then under construction in Bristol'.[153] Nasmyth then posed the question: how was it that existing hammers were incapable of forging a wrought-iron shaft of 30 inches diameter? He set to work and in little more than half an hour after receiving the letter, 'I had the whole contrivance in all its executant details before me in a page of my Scheme Book'.[154] While Nasmyth conceived some notion of a steam hammer in 1839 and was aware of its commercial potential, the design of the hammer changed substantially between November 1839 and 1842.[155] Nasmyth did not realise the significance of his invention since the steamship project did not mature, and the drawings were relegated to the files. The first steam hammer was built by Schneider at the Le Creusot works in France from the drawings he was shown on a visit to Patricroft in Nasmyth's absence. Nasmyth saw this hammer in 1842 and, realising that he might lose the benefits of his invention, he returned to Britain and secured the patent within two months in June 1842.[156] Looking back some years later, Nasmyth felt no small gratification:

> When I look over my rude and hasty first sketch, to find that I hit the mark so exactly, not only in the general structure but in the details; and that the invention that I then conceived ... still retains its form and arrangements intact in the thousands of steam hammers ... throughout the civilised world.[157]

Nasmyth had managed to invent a hammer of great power and delicacy which weighed 6 tons; in a demonstration at Devonport he made it 'break an eggshell in a wine glass without injuring the glass; whilst the next blow would shake the parish, or be instantly arrested in its descent mid-way'.[158] Leonard Horner visited the Patricroft factory of 'my young friend Nasmyth' on 21 February 1838, describing him as 'an old pupil of the School of Arts, and a most ingenious and meritorious person'.[159] On a subsequent visit in October 1846, Horner observed several steam hammers in production and again lauded the Scot as having

> an unpretending simplicity about him and an enthusiasm that are very agreeable to find. ... He is full of genius in a variety of ways. ... He lives with great simplicity in a very small house near his works; ... he has made two very large telescopes which stand in his garden, with which he has been for years observing the moon.[160]

The fame of Nasmyth's great invention has tended to obscure his merits as a contriver of machine tools; he also developed his steam hammer into a steam hammer pile-driving machine to facilitate the construction of harbours, and he was the first to suggest the use of submerged chains for towing boats on rivers and canals. His fortune secured through the success of the Bridgewater foundry, Nasmyth retired to Kent at the age of 48 to pursue his keen interest in astronomy, which had captured his imagination since he constructed his own reflective telescope at the age of 19 in 1827. During his retirement, he won the Prize Medal at the Great Exhibition of 1851 for his relief map of the Moon's surface and he wrote a number of publications on the subject.[161]

Two Accounts of the School of Arts

After Dr Fyfe's departure for Aberdeen, the directors appointed George Wilson, who had attended chemistry classes at the school and at the university under Dr Thomas Hope, as lecturer in chemistry. Like many able teachers at the time, Wilson was engaged to teach numerous classes, commenting in 1834:

> I have twenty students at my 10.00am medical class; forty at my twelve o'clock (three days a week) veterinary class; some hundred young ladies at the Scottish institution; and some two hundred stout fellows at the School of Arts.[162]

This was a punishing schedule for one who had recently endured the amputation of a foot, without the benefit of anaesthetic. Wilson recorded the only first-hand account of lecturing at the school in the 1840s:

> I shall never forget the first sight of the sea of faces at the introductory lecture at the School of Arts, rising tier above tier, piled to the very ceiling. I cast my eye around for a familiar face, and lighted on uncle's white head, like the foam on the crest of a billow. A dragoon soldier likewise attracted me with his red coat and his moustache, and I now look instinctively for him. . . . He takes notes, and is very attentive. . . . This class is rapidly increasing under my care over its former numbers, and is my favourite class. My great pleasure is in lecturing to the working people, to whom I may do intellectual and moral service.[163]

Wilson's sister, in her *Memoir,* lauded him:

He could not give a lecture without taking much more trouble than was necessary in preparing for its illustration, and in the School of Arts this was most evident. ... At one of the introductory lectures, he requested the crowd outside to permit him to pass in. But they, looking around and seeing only a little man in a pea-coat and cap, indignantly declined, to his great amusement. A laughing assurance that in that case they should have no lecture, soon cleared a passage for him. A grateful expression of the pleasure received was left each evening ... by one pupil, a gardener, in the shape of a bouquet of the most choice greenhouse flowers. ... It would have gratified them to see the intense pleasure with which, on his return, jaded from the lecture, he lay on the sofa and drank in their beauty.[164]

This Tuesday evening lecture at the School of Arts was his most exhausting duty of the week and he often remarked on throwing off his outer coat on return, 'Well there's another nail put into my coffin.'[165]

One of Wilson's students, William Lauder Lindsay, later to become a botanist and expert on lichens, wrote of the class:

The students were chiefly artisans, self-educated, though there was a sprinkling of youths of higher ranks in society. They [the latter] were generally very young, I myself only fourteen, and attending the High School classes. The same qualities of head and heart which have subsequently distinguished Prof. Wilson[166], then distinguished him among the teachers of the School of Arts. There was the same power of riveting the attention of the audience, nay, almost fascinating them; the same playful fancy and practical prose in his prelections;

... the genial sympathy with the pursuit of knowledge under difficulties; the same familiar homely mode of illustration; the same aptitude in experiment; the same affability to his most humble and obscure student. The qualities combined to render him at once the greatest favourite and the most efficient teacher among his colleagues at the School of Arts. I well remember the enthusiasm which his prelections and experiments stimulated in myself ... leading, at the close of the second session, to a 'Chemical Association' where a fund was raised for apparatus, papers were read, discussions held, and experiments conducted.[167]

The Evolution of the Mechanics' Institute Movement

The successes of the first experiments in Scotland and the London Mechanics' Institution were misleading. In general, the survival of mechanics' institutes was directly related to the degree to which they abandoned their original purpose. They were a typical product of the utilitarian social philosophy; but subsequent success tended to occur only as the utilitarian motive was diluted.[168] In England, two major assumptions on which the movement was based were invalid. Neither the method of instruction (the lecture) nor the subjects of study were generally acceptable, and the process of disillusionment was rapid.[169] The use of lectures continued to be urged even when it had become generally accepted that the main teaching work should be conducted in classes.[170] The audience which faced a lecturer at many mechanics' institutes was not the compact body of skilled mechanics, like-minded in pursuit of knowledge, inspired by a wholesome sense of self-improvement as envisaged by the founders, but a collection of individuals differing in occupation (many lower middle-class non-manual workers), varying in prior knowledge, and similar in suffering from limited previous education. The larger Scottish institutes, however, at Glasgow, Edinburgh and Aberdeen made few concessions to the desire for general culture and entertainment and the lecture course continued as the major teaching mode.

The second major error made by the pioneers of the movement was the assumption that the working man was interested in receiving tuition related directly to his trade. The institutes had been founded on the assumption that education could begin at the age of 30 or 40. Most men for whom they were intended, especially in England, were totally unequipped to deal with the scientific topics of the lectures. It took a special zeal for self-improvement to attract working men to the classes after a long, hard day's work. Sooner or later the mechanics departed from the great majority of institutes and they became increasingly petit bourgeois in character; clerks, shopkeepers and men from the higher branches of handicrafts replaced the artisans and mechanics.[171] When a failure of the policy of science for artisans became apparent – usually about five years after the foundation of the institute (although longer in Scotland) – a remedy was sought in the introduction of subjects such as literature, political economy and travel into the curriculum. The price of respectability in some of the institutes, especially in rural areas, was the abandonment of any pretence to being a mechanics' institute.[172] The demand for serious science melted away, especially in England as the revolution of increasing leisure followed on the heels of the Industrial Revolution.[173] There was an explosion in the 1840s of a popular culture based on the entertainment provided by the mysteries of science, rather than science itself. Showpiece lectures on topics such as the 'Wonders of Creation' attracted large audiences. When such diversions as musical evenings and billiards replaced the talks later in the century, the lecture was left with a much smaller number of supporters. Lectures were given by outside paid speakers or by unpaid people recruited locally. A popular speaker could deliver the same lecture in different places for a nightly fee of between £5 and £10, plus expenses, during the 1840s and 1850s.[174] There were attempts to titillate audiences with lecture performances such as the following in Cornwall:

> Mr. Potts announced that next Tuesday he shall deliver a lecture on Galvanism, and though he might not have an executed criminal to operate upon, yet he hoped to be able to procure some animal of sufficient size to exhibit distinctly the extraordinary effects of this powerful agent.[175]

Similarly, in 1840, the Stourbridge Mechanics' Institute advertised the appearance of Mr Newman, the celebrated ventriloquist, whose imitations included 'the full cry of a pack of hounds and a gang of eight or ten smugglers landing their cargo'.[176] Clearly an element of pure entertainment was now creeping into the programmes; it was but a short step from Shakespearean readings to ventriloquists. Hence by the 1840s, except in the larger Scottish institutes, the systematic science courses which had been the raison d'être of the early institutes gave way to a miscellaneous programme embracing popular science, literature, music, history, travel and phrenology, which attracted a largely lower middle-class rather than a working-class audience.[177]

Interest in general rather than technical knowledge, and the demand for recreational activities, was illustrated also by the development of concerts, dramatic readings, excursions and tea parties which came to fill an ever more important place in institutes' programmes. Benjamin Heywood's addresses delivered at the Manchester Mechanics' Institution between 1825 and 1840 reveal how, although modelled closely on Edinburgh, a new tune was animating the English institutes. Heywood introduced a number of exciting innovations: a gymnastic class in 1832, the first excursion in 1833 (a trip by rail to Liverpool), the first Christmas party in 1833, the first season of the cricket club in 1834, the first concert in 1837, and the first exhibition in 1838.[178] Exhibitions were especially popular in the north of England; in Manchester alone, four exhibitions were held between 1837 and 1842 which attracted more than 300,000 visitors.[179] The notion of moral improvement was a keynote of such exhibitions. They were good money-spinners and they gave an outreach into the wider community. Religion and politics were still excluded and political economy, because of its controversial nature, made but a rare appearance, as at Edinburgh. It is apparent that the majority of the students who enrolled in mechanics' institutes, especially in England, were more intent on sampling general culture and entertainment than improving themselves in the principles of the arts they practised. Charles Dickens referred to the alleged frivolity of the lecture and library provision. In his description of Dullborough Mechanics' Institute in *The Uncommercial Traveller* (1861), he comments on the sense of guilt that still afflicted the managers of many institutes when they offered entertainment as part of their programmes:

> I observed that it was necessary for the members to be knocked on the head with Gas, Air, Water, Food, the Solar System, the Geological Periods, criticism on Milton, the Steam-Engine, John Bunyan, and Arrow-Headed Inscriptions, before they might be tickled by those unaccountable choristers … or brought-to by a Miscellaneous Concert.[180]

This broader educational and cultural curriculum – far removed from the original mission to educate the skilled artisan in scientific principles – helped the movement to develop during the 1840s. Sponsored by coteries of Unitarians, Whigs, Utilitarians, Radicals of various hues, and reform-minded civic leaders, institutes had appeared in almost every sizeable British town by the 1840s. In 1841 there were some 300 mechanics' institutes; by 1851 this had expanded to 698, with the peak of the growth reached about 1860.[181] Yorkshire, Lancashire, Cheshire, the North-east and South Wales were the areas of most rapid growth during the 1840s. The total membership in 1851 was of the order of 110,000: 97,000 in England, 10,000 in Scotland and 3,000 in Wales.[182] When institutes first sprang up, their most formidable competitors – indeed the resorts from which they were designed to attract patrons – were the public houses, coffee houses, and radical newsrooms where newspapers were freely available, and where political discussion was carried on. Although by the 1850s most institutes had newsrooms, a narrow scientific curriculum was unattractive to most working men; what they sought was relaxation from the daily toil – a place to air their opinions, a spirit of fellowship, a pint, a pipe, and a selection of papers with working-class sympathies.

As evangelical hostility to fiction wore off and the Utilitarians began to concede that the reading of imaginative literature in moderation could contribute to the health of society, the advocates of a more liberal policy in the institute libraries gained ground. Demand for works of literature, travel and general knowledge was clearly expressed. At some institutes there was a long resistance by managers to the introduction of fiction and everywhere efforts were made to ensure that only 'reputable' authors were represented on the shelves. Some promoters of mechanics' institutes were of the opinion that sensational reading 'quenches the desire for more substantial nutriment'. At Sheffield, while the works of Shakespeare 'were cast out and sold by auction', Byron's tragedies were admitted, and so were the works of Thackeray, while those of Scott and Disraeli were not.[183] In the libraries, scientific textbooks came to be outnumbered by works of fiction and travel, and reference rooms began to be converted into newsrooms. The extension of the library collections into the arts and humanities, miscellaneous lectures, concerts and excursions all provided much general cultural education in an age without cinema, radio, public art galleries or museums. Although they frequently departed from the original aims of their patrons, the institutes contributed to the intellectual – and thereby political – emancipation of working men, and to a much lesser extent, women.

The continued expansion of the mechanics' institute movement did little to disarm the suspicions of its opponents, for the Whig–Nonconformist ideology which infused the management of the institutes during the 1820s continued to dominate for several decades. There were those who shared the views expressed by the Duke of Newcastle in 1832 that education uncontrolled by religious precepts was bound to be evil, and that mechanics' institutes had become 'the debating societies for radicals, republicans and anarchists of various species; for atheists, and for dissenters of every description'.[184] From about 1835 onwards the more progressive Church of England clergy began to establish rival institutes for their own church members so that by the mid nineteenth century the opposition to institutes appears to have softened. The mechanics' institute movement foreshadowed the end of the old religious-utilitarian monopoly on adult education and asserted the common man's right to share in a culture that did not end with a knowledge of the principles of the steam engine and the Christian theory of social subordination. Even though they laid the foundation of a small set of institutions that grew in time from technical to technological, from institutes to colleges and universities, 'in their own generation they did not bring technology within the pale of the formal education system'.[185] By the middle of the nineteenth century, the permanence and utility of the Edinburgh School of Arts, despite its austere programme, seemed a settled issue; its influence on the development of other institutes was profound; and ownership of its own building ratified the past and signalled renewed confidence in the future.

Notes

1 Lord Liverpool, a Tory with liberal views, led the government from 1812 to 1826 and it became possible for men such as Scott to express progressive views on education.

2 HWUA, SA 1/1/1, *Annual Report of the Directors*, 1823–24, p. 8.

3 HWUA, SA 1/1/1, *Annual Report of the Directors*, 1821–22, *op. cit.*, pp. 14–15.

4 *Ibid.*, p. 25.

5 HWUA, SA 1/1/1, *Annual Report of the Directors*, 1823–24, p. 11.

6 *Ibid.*, p. 7.

7 *Ibid.*, pp. 4–5.

8 *Ibid.*, p. 5.

9 HWUA, SA 1/1/1, *Annual Report of the Directors*, 1824–25, p. 5.

10 *Ibid.*, pp. 5–6.

11 *Ibid.*, pp. 6–7.

12 Stevenson, R. L. (1925) *Edinburgh: Picturesque Notes*, London, p. 16.

13 Kelly, T. (1952) The origin of mechanics' institutes, *British Journal of Education Studies*, November, p. 23.

14 Harrison, J. F. C. (1961) *Learning and Living*, London, p. 43.

15 Tyrrell, A. (1969) Political economy, Whiggism and the education of working-class adults in Scotland 1817–40, *Scottish Historical Review*, Vol. XLVIII (no. 2), p. 154.

16 Cosh, M. (2003) *Edinburgh: The Golden Age*, Edinburgh, p. 807.

17 Employment in the early nineteenth century involved extremely long hours of work: bricklayers had a 60 hour week until 1864 whereas engineers, pattern makers, boilermakers, tinplate workers and printers worked 54 hours. Shopworkers ranged from a 69½ hour week in china shops to 83½ in bakers' shops. Shops had a normal 8 P.M. closing in Edinburgh during the 1830s with a one-hour extension on Saturday. See Marwick, W. H. (1930) *Economic Developments in Victorian Scotland*, London, pp. 154–55; Smout, T. C. (1986) *A Century of the Scottish People 1830–1950*, London, p. 102.

18 HWUA, SA 1/1/1, 1821–22, *op. cit.*, p. 6.

19 *Ibid.*, p. 17.

20 HWUA, SA 1/1/1, *op. cit.*, 1823–24, pp. 14–15.

21 Harrison, *op. cit.*, p. 115.

22 HWUA, SA 1/1/1, *Annual Report of the Directors*, 1825–26, p. 20.

23 HWUA, SA 1/1/1, 1821–22, *op. cit.*, pp. 21 and 14.

24 HWUA, SA 1/1/1, 1823–24, *op. cit.*, p. 14.

25 Anderson, A. and Gowenlock, B. G. (1998) *Chemistry in Heriot-Watt 1821–1991*, Edinburgh, p. 12.

26 HWUA, SA 1/1/1, *Annual Report of the Directors*, 1822–23, p. 12.

[27] HWUA, SA 1/1/1, 1824–25, *op. cit.*, p. 18.

[28] HWUA, SA 1/1/1, 1821–22, *op. cit.*, p. 17.

[29] *Ibid.*, p. 15.

[30] HWUA, SA 1/1/1, 1822–23, *op. cit.*, p. 26.

[31] HWUA, SA 1/1/1, 1821–22, *op. cit.*, p. 18.

[32] Hudson, J. W. (1851) *The History of Adult Education*, London, p. 40; HWUA, SA 1/1/1, 1821–22, *op. cit.*, pp. 18–19.

[33] HWUA, SA 1/1/1, 1822–23, *op. cit.*, p. 10.

[34] *Ibid.*, pp. 15–16.

[35] *Ibid.*, p. 16.

[36] *Ibid.*, p. 11.

[37] HWUA, SA 1/1/1, 1823–24, *op. cit.*, p. 19. The Reverend Mr Wilson resigned in 1824 to take up an appointment as a Presbyterian minister in Liverpool.

[38] Shapin, S. and Barnes, B. (1977) Science, nature and control: interpreting mechanics' institutes, *Social Studies of Science*, Vol. 7, p. 48.

[39] Davie, G. E. (1964) *The Democratic Intellect in Scotland and the Universities in the Nineteenth Century*, 2nd edn, Edinburgh, Ch. 8.

[40] University College London Library, Brougham Papers, 2 January 1825, Horner to Lord Brougham.

[41] *Ibid.*, p. 41.

[42] *Ibid.*, p. 41.

[43] Although not a productive researcher, Hope proved that a mineral from Strontian in Ardnamurchan contained a new element, strontium, and he also showed in 1805 that water reaches a maximum density at 4°C.

[44] *The Scotsman*, 4–10 September 1822.

[45] Another part of the circular announced, again without consent, that tickets would be sold henceforth at the shop of a Mr Marshall.

[46] *The Scotsman*, 4–10 September 1822.

[47] *Ibid.*

[48] *Ibid.*

[49] *Ibid.*

[50] *Ibid.*

[51] *Ibid.*

[52] *Ibid.*

[53] *Ibid.*

[54] *Ibid.*

[55] *Ibid.*

[56] *Ibid.*

[57] *Ibid.*

58 Lyell, K. (1890) *A Memoir of Leonard Horner*, London, Vol. 1, p. 204, 14 September 1822, Leonard Horner to Dr Marcet.

59 Combe, G. and Murray, William, 30 December 1835, quoted in Shapin, S. (1983) Nibbling at the teats of science: Edinburgh and the diffusion of science in the 1830s. In Inkster, I. and Morrell, J. (eds) *Metropolis and Province: Science in the British Culture, 1780–1850*, London, p. 163.

60 HWUA, SA 14/1/1/17, Mary Lyell, *Francis Horner and Leonard Horner*, Edinburgh. Letter from Leonard Horner to his sister, 25 April 1822.

61 HWUA, SA 1/1/1, 1822–23, *op. cit.*, p. 27.

62 *Ibid.*, p. 29.

63 *Ibid.*, p. 31.

64 *Ibid.*, p. 31.

65 HWUA, SA 1/1/1, 1824–25, *op. cit.*, p. 7.

66 Brougham, H. (1825) *Practical Observations on the Education of the People Addressed to the Working Classes and Their Employers*, 15 edn (reprinted 1979), London, p. 20.

67 HWUA, SA 1/1/4, *Annual Report of the Directors*, 1834–35, p. 18.

68 HWUA, SA 1/1/2, *Annual Report of the Directors*, 1828–29, p. 15. No reports were published between 1830 and 1834 and when they reappeared in 1834–35 there were no further references to this course.

69 HWUA, SA 1/1/5, *Annual Report of the Directors*, 1835–36, p. 16.

70 *Ibid.*, p. 17.

71 HWUA, SA 1/1/6, *Annual Report of the Directors*, 1836–37, p. 17.

72 *Ibid.*, p. 17. The syllabus included the principles of English grammar, the derivation from Greek and Latin roots, and principles of literary criticism applicable to English composition.

73 HWUA, SA 1/1/8, *Annual Report of the Directors*, 1839–40, p. 11.

74 Southgate, D. (1962) *The Passing of the Whigs*, London, pp. 20–21.

75 *Third Report of the Committee of the School of Arts in Haddington for 1825–26*, p. 13.

76 Summary of lectures on political economy, as published in the *Edinburgh Weekly Chronicle*, Edinburgh, p. 151 (1837).

77 HWUA, SA 1/1/12, *Annual Report of the Directors*, 1843–44, p. 8.

78 *Ibid.*, p. 7.

79 *Ibid.*, pp. 7–8.

80 Hudson, J. W. (1851) *The History of Adult Education*, Longman, London, p. 75.

81 Altick, R. D. (1957) *The English Common Reader*, Chicago, p. 191.

82 Some sources refer to mechanics as machine operatives as opposed to craftworkers, while others have used a more restrictive definition of those concerned with the repair and maintenance of machinery.

83 Tylecote, M. (1957) *The Mechanics Institutes of Lancashire and Yorkshire Before 1851*, Manchester, p. 139.

84 HWUA, SA 1/1/2, *Annual Report of the Directors*, 1827–28, p. 11.

[85] HWUA, SA 1/1/3, *Annual Report of the Directors*, 1833–34, p. 6.

[86] *Ibid.*, p. 7.

[87] *Ibid.*, p. 7. Exams governed by regulations were first introduced in 1826.

[88] *Ibid.*, p. 7.

[89] In the first-year natural philosophy syllabus, Mr Lees covered acoustics, mechanics, dynamics, optics and astronomy, moving on in the second year to consider the properties of matter, hydrostatics and hydraulics. In the first year of chemistry, Dr Fyfe's curriculum was confined to heat, light and electricity, leaving until the following year the chemistry of inorganic and organic bodies. See HWUA, SA 1/1/10, *Annual Report of the Directors*, 1841–42, p. 6 and HWUA, SA 1/1/11, *Annual Report of the Directors*, 1842–43, pp. 11–12.

[90] HWUA, SA 1/1/4, 1834–35, *op. cit.*, p. 12.

[91] *Ibid.*, pp. 12–13.

[92] HWUA, SA 1/1/7, *Annual Report of the Directors*, 1837–38, p. 15.

[93] Reid introduced this also to his university students. See Anderson and Gowenlock, *op. cit.*, p. 16.

[94] HWUA, SA 1/1/9, *Annual Report of the Directors*, 1840–41, p. 7.

[95] HWUA, SA 1/3/1, *Minute Books of the Directors*, 1836–1850, p. 130.

[96] HWUA, SA 1/1/18, *Annual Report of the Directors*, 1852–53, pp. 13–14.

[97] *Ibid.*, p. 15.

[98] Anderson and Gowenlock, *op. cit.*, p. 18.

[99] Pryde, D. (1883) *Pleasant Memories of a Happy Life*, Edinburgh, p. 90. Murray was a sleeping partner in a printing firm and sat on the town council as a Whig from 1845 to 1860.

[100] HWUA, SA 14/2/2, Thomas Murray (1792–1872) article in Stephen, Sir L. and Lee, Sir S. *The Dictionary of National Biography from the earliest times to 1900*, Vol. XIII, pp. 1302–03; reprinted by Oxford University Press, 1967–68.

[101] *The Scotsman*, 16 April 1872.

[102] *Ibid.*, pp. 90–91.

[103] *Ibid.*, p. 94.

[104] *Ibid.*, p. 93.

[105] HWUA, SA 1/1/1, 1821–22, *op. cit.*, p. 2.

[106] *Ibid.*, p. 7.

[107] *Ibid.*, p. 8.

[108] *Ibid.*, p. 7.

[109] *Ibid.*, p. 8.

[110] Lyell, *op. cit.*, Vol. 1, p. 197.

[111] HWUA, SA 1/1/1, 1823–24, *op. cit.*, p. 15.

[112] HWUA, SA 1/3/1, *Minute Book of the Directors*, 1836–1850, meeting of the directors 3 May 1842.

[113] *Ibid.*

114 HWUA, SA 1/1/9, *Annual Report of the Directors*, 1840–41, p. 10.

115 HWUA, SA 1/3/1, *Minute Book of the Directors*, 1836–1850, meeting of the directors, 26 April 1844.

116 *Ibid.*, meeting of the directors, 18 October 1844.

117 *Ibid.*

118 *Ibid.*, meeting of directors, 19 February 1846.

119 Herman, A. *(2001) The Scottish Enlightenment*, London.

120 Leonard Horner's address on the opening night of the school eulogises Watt and Rennie; HWUA, SA 1/1/1, 1821–22, *op. cit.*, p. 10.

121 HWUA, SA 1/1/1, 1824–25, *op. cit.*, p. 22.

122 *The Scotsman*, 24 July 1824.

123 HWUA, SA 1/2/1, 1836–50, *op. cit.*, pp. 5–6.

124 *Ibid.*, p. 7.

125 Horner was pleased with the Adam Square location: 'its proximity to the College having an indirect good effect – a sort of Academic Alliance'. HWUA, SA 1/2/1, 1834–50, *op. cit.*, p. 130.

126 *Ibid.*, p. 8.

127 *Ibid.*, pp. 16–17.

128 *Ibid.*, p. 21. The 'officer' was the doorman or janitor.

129 HWUA, SA 1/1/6, 1836–37, *op. cit.*, p. 21.

130 Pryde, *op. cit.*, p. 84.

131 HWUA, SA 1/2/1, 1834–50, *op. cit.*, p. 8.

132 *Ibid.*, p. 12.

133 HWUA, SA 1/1/7, 1837–38, *op. cit.*, p. 24.

134 HWUA, SA 1/1/8, 1839–40, *op. cit.*, p. 11.

135 *Ibid.*, p. 12.

136 HWUA, SA 1/1/17, *Annual Report of the Directors*, 1850–51, p. 9.

137 Smiles, S. (1897) (ed.) *James Nasmyth: An Autobiography*, London, p. 87.

138 Cosh, M. (2003) *Edinburgh: The Golden Age*, Edinburgh, p. 497.

139 Smiles, *op. cit.*, p. 108.

140 *Ibid.*, p. 108.

141 *Ibid.*, p. 112.

142 *Ibid.*, p. 112.

143 *Ibid.*, p. 112.

144 Institute of Mechanical Engineers Library, IMS 99, 9 February 1864, James Nasmyth to Mr Robert Wilson.

145 *Ibid.*

146 *Ibid.*, p. 110.

147 *Ibid.*, p. 111.

148 *Ibid.*, p. 111.

[149] *Ibid.*, p. 111.

[150] *Ibid.*, p. 111.

[151] Cosh, *op. cit.*, p. 864.

[152] In 1784 James Watt anticipated Nasmyth by more than half a century in considering the possibility of attaching a 'hammer or stamper … directly to the piston or piston rod of the engine'. Also the French engineer François Bourdon had developed his own design before visiting and seeing Nasmyth's scheme in Patricroft in 1840, so he had the advantage of viewing Nasmyth's ideas before building his machine. See Cantrell, T. A. (1985) James Nasmyth and the steam hammer. *The Newcomen Society for the Study of the History of Engineering and Technology Transactions*, Vol. 56, p. 136.

[153] *Ibid.*, p. 230.

[154] *Ibid.*, p. 231. The hammer block was attached to the piston rod, and the piston and hammer were raised by steam and allowed to fall by gravity; the whole machine tool was controlled through a hand-operated slide valve.

[155] Cantrell, *op. cit.*, p. 136.

[156] Smiles, *op. cit.*, p. 239.

[157] *Ibid.*, p. 233.

[158] *Ibid.*, pp. 239–40. Nasmyth failed to acknowledge that Robert Wilson, works manager at the foundry, designed the self-acting apparatus which enabled the valves to operate satisfactorily. See also Cantrell, *op. cit.*, p. 136.

[159] Lyell, K. (1890) *A Memoir of Leonard Horner*, London, Vol. 1, p. 354, 22 February 1838, Leonard Horner to his daughter Leonora.

[160] Lyell, *op. cit.*, Vol. 2, p. 106, 25 October 1846, Leonard Horner to his wife.

[161] Smiles, *op. cit.*, p. 332.

[162] Wilson, Jesse Aitken (1860) *Memoir of George Wilson*, Edinburgh, p. 307.

[163] *Ibid.*, p. 308.

[164] *Ibid.*, p. 308.

[165] *Ibid.*, p. 309.

[166] In 1855 Wilson was appointed as first director of the Industrial Museum of Scotland and soon after as professor of technology at the University of Edinburgh.

[167] Wilson, *op. cit.*, p. 309.

[168] Altick, R. D. (1957) *The English Common Reader*, Chicago, p. 188.

[169] Tylecote, *op. cit.*, p. 87.

[170] *Ibid.*, p. 96.

[171] Altick, *op. cit.*, p. 172.

[172] Harrison, J. F. C. (1961) *Learning & Living 1790–1960: A Study in the History of the English Adult Education Movement*, London, p. 179.

[173] Roderick, G. W. and Stephens, M. D. (1985) Steam intellect created: the educational roles of mechanics' institutes. In Inkster, I. (ed.) *The Steam Intellect Societies*, Nottingham, p. 21.

[174] *Ibid.*, p. 24.

[175] *Royal Cornwall Gazette*, 27 February 1819. Quoted by Roderick and Stephens, *op. cit.*, p. 28.

[176] Palfray, H. E. (1948) *Stourbridge Institute*, pp. 6–7. Quoted in Kelly, *op. cit.*, p. 234.

[177] Tylecote, *op. cit.*, p. 111.

[178] Kelly, *op. cit.*, p. 237.

[179] Kusamitsu, T. (1985) Mechanics institutes and working class culture: exhibition movement, 1830–1840s. In Inkster, I. (ed.) *op. cit.*, p. 34.

[180] Dickens, C. (1861) *The Uncommercial Traveller*, London, Ch. XII.

[181] Kelly, *op. cit.*, p. 259.

[182] *Ibid.*, p. 265.

[183] Tylecote, *op. cit.*, p. 109.

[184] Duke of Newcastle (1832) Address to all classes, p. 11. Quoted in Kelly, *op. cit.*, p. 251.

[185] Ashby, E. (1958) *Technology and the Academics: An Essay on Universities and the Scientific Revolution*, New York, p. 53.

Chapter Four

Penury and Progress: 1852–1885

You apprehend that knowledge must
be hurtful to the sex, because it will be
the means of their acquiring power ...
the manners of society must totally
change before women can mingle in
the busy and public scenes of life.
Maria Edgeworth

Robert Adam's distinguished building from the 1760s which became the home of Edinburgh School of Arts, 1837

The Curriculum Diversifies

By the mid nineteenth century, the tide of the Industrial Revolution had receded, the engineer and operative were rapidly replacing the craftsman, and the demand for technical education, attuned to the needs of industry, increased. The major impetus for technical education came from the government Department of Science and Art set up in 1853 at South Kensington,[1] but during the second half of the nineteenth century, it failed to establish an overall system of technical education for the country. Meanwhile in Europe the competition had already begun: by 1831 Germany had six Technische Hochschulen, while France developed the École Polytechnique. In Britain chairs in science subjects were introduced before engineering and little was done to integrate applied sciences and technology within the curriculum, although modern theoretical sciences had begun to acquire a proper status in some of the existing universities.[2] The idea of technical universities and colleges made scant headway due to lack of support from the state and industrialists; trade unions were equally unenthusiastic about scientific training for their members.[3] Supporters of a broader curriculum embracing science and engineering had to convince industrialists, politicians and trade unionists that their ideas – although contrary to the prevailing political and economic orthodoxy of self-help – were valid and beneficial to society.[4] The social and living conditions of the population were changing in the mid nineteenth century: the postal service and telegraph had been introduced; the railway had brought country and town closer together; the streets were lit with gas; Macadam had revolutionised road construction; the Factory Acts, implemented partly by the ever vigilant Leonard Horner, had made the lot of the ordinary worker somewhat easier; the Reform Act of 1867 gave thousands of workmen the vote for the first time; and friendly societies and trade unions had made them socially more secure. The attitudes of the people at all levels to education were changing. The fear that the educated workman would be a threat to society had passed, while working people regarded with suspicion education which was offered by philanthropists.

The governing oligarchy of enlightened and self-willed Edinburgh Whigs of business and the law was forced on occasion by popular demand or the pressure of circumstances to broaden the educational provision at the Watt Institution and School of Arts. The 1870s witnessed the peak period for the introduction of new subjects into the curriculum and by the end of the decade the institution had developed a large portfolio of science, social science and humanities subjects, much broader than its founders had ever contemplated and indeed more diverse than exists today (Figure 4.1). The criterion of direct utility in the workplace had been relaxed, although the directors were clearly sensitive about this changing mission, asserting in 1878–79 that they had only introduced new classes 'in which there is a systematic course of teaching on subjects of real practical interest'.[5] Quite how subjects such as life and nature painting, draped life model, Hebrew, Sanskrit, Hindustani and the theory of music, which were sanctioned by the directors, satisfied this utilitarian criterion was not explained. The directors conceptualised two types of provision: 'general education on subjects of wide interest . . . and special education in those

WATT INSTITUTION AND SCHOOL OF ARTS

Evening Classes

Winter and Summer Sessions	Winter Classes Only	Summer Classes Only
German 1866		
Botany 1870		
Geology 1872		
Pitman's Shorthand...............1873	Hebrew..................................1873	
	Physiology............................1873	
	Practical chemistry...............1873	
Latin 1874		
Greek...1875	Zoology 1875	
	Engineering...........................1875	
	Sanskrit and Hindustani.....1876	
Biology 1877	Sanitation 1877	
Freehand drawing..................1877	History 1877	
Theory of music.....................1877	Economic science.................1877	
Life and nature painting........1877		
Draped life model..................1878		
Bookkeeping and writing 1879	Harmonium...........................1879	
	Agriculture...........................1881	
		Elocution 1882

Figure 4.1 Date of introduction of new subjects at the Watt Institution and School of Arts, 1852–85

principles of science, which are of daily application to the work of all classes of artisans'.[6] They reaffirmed, however, their view of the primacy of science:

> However great may be the advantages which the School is able to offer in general education, they believe that care should be taken that what have been called the fundamental classes of the Institution should not only be especially cherished and promoted, but that every exertion should be made to induce those for whom these classes were designed to take the benefit of them. ... The fundamental classes Mathematics, Chemistry and Natural Philosophy to the Artisan or mechanic ... are all important.[7]

This diversification of the subject range, however, was not entirely inconsistent with the philosophy of the institution. The strict interpretation of its intentions may have been relaxed, but fundamentally the school had been founded in order that the demands of the working class for education could be satisfied. In the second half of the nineteenth century those needs were broader than they had been in the 1820s. The flowering of new subjects at the school reflected the rapid growth in student numbers, the enrolment of women students (see next section), the decline in the proportion of manual workers attending, the changing demands of the Edinburgh labour market, and the rising standards of education and its consequent effects on students' aspirations. The directors also took advantage of buoyant recruitment to

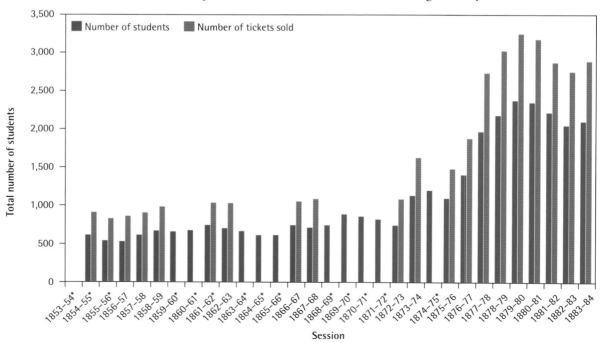

Figure 4.2 Total number of students and class tickets sold, 1853–84. An asterisk indicates a year when no annual report was published

impose a matriculation fee of one shilling in October 1869 – estimated to yield £30 annually – and to request teachers to keep a roll of students' attendance.[8] Although student numbers fluctuated as a consequence of the economic cycle and the difficulty of finding fees, the number of students in 1872–73 (747) was only 21 per cent greater than in 1854–55. The diversification of the subject mix, however, heralded a secular trend of sustained growth from 1,108 students in 1875–76 to a peak of 2,375 in 1879–80 (Figure 4.2). That the institution escaped the worst effects of the industrial depression reflected both the variety of occupations among the membership, and the increasing number of men who lived above the level of those who suffered want and destitution in the back streets and wynds of the city.

The new classes under the directors' classification of 'General Education' fell into two categories: those which developed 'useful skills' and those of a more 'cultural' nature. Among the former, the English language and literature course had evolved by 1878–79 'to give the student a knowledge of the chief English authors, and at the same time the power of speaking and writing the English language correctly';[9] it attracted a regular attendance of over 200 students (Table 4.1). The introduction of shorthand in 1873, bookkeeping and writing in 1879 and elocution (1882) reflected an acknowledgement of the changing mix of students and the need for such skills as 'an accomplishment by applicants as clerks in the legal profession, and in the business of merchants, bankers and others'.[10] Among subjects of a more cultural nature, history and the theory of music were introduced in 1877; French, which had been launched originally in 1843, commanded attendances in excess of 200 during the 1870s; a German class was offered in 1866; and Latin, Greek, Sanskrit and Hindustani were added between 1874 and 1876, although tuition in Sanskrit and Hindustani was soon terminated (Table 4.1).

The 1870s also witnessed expansion of the science base with a new course in botany, following a petition signed by 84 chemists and druggists, an early example of how the institution responded positively to the needs of the market. Other new programmes in geology, biology, zoology, physiology and practical chemistry were also introduced, but none except physiology attracted significant numbers (Table 4.1). The first engineering class was initiated in 1875 and sanitation (1877) generated attendances of 35 to 40 during the 1870s. Growth in attendance at summer courses was less buoyant than at those offered during the dark winter months when there were fewer alternative recreational attractions to tempt the artisan bent on self-improvement (Table 4.2).

By 1855–56 the socio-economic mix of male students had broadened from that of 1839–40 but the skilled manual group, for whom Horner founded the institution, was still the largest, accounting for 52 per cent of students. Skilled workers had not deserted the institution as elsewhere in Britain, but change was afoot. Among higher-status occupations represented were teachers, architects,

Table 4.1 Student numbers by subject, winter courses, 1856–84

	Natural Philosophy	Chemistry	Practical chemistry	Junior mathematics	Mathematics	Senior mathematics	English	Modelling	French	German	Botany	Geology	Drawing	Physiology	Shorthand	Hebrew and Hindustani	Latin	Arithmetic	Zoology	Greek	Engineering	Sanitation
1856-57	53	91		78		12	42	36	126													
1857-58	72	94		84		18	49	56	131													
1858-59	68	79		102		17	62	57	148													
1861-62	97	104		115		17	100	33	144													
1862-63	70	127		96		22	91	25	174													
1866-67	73	112		135		15	126		194	30												
1867-68	79	104	25	117		13	112		167	45												
1872-73	60	86		114		18	142		167	59	14	35										
1873-74	76	129	34	148		31	188		209	99												
1875-76	100	81	10		137		152		163	74	21	14	66	88	76	3	68	108	17			
1876-77	111	99	8		148		215		191	63	16	18	157	39	80		68	144	17	11	29	
1877-78	111	89	10		208		224		226	54	16	13	206	53	111		93	269		25	54	24
1878-79	104	116	21		215		251		268	71	27	11	162	48	120		91	259		32	50	30
1879-80	93	99	17		259		255		230	104	29	14	212	77	154		91	274		35	54	41
1880-81	94	143	12		230		251		222	95		22	229	68	159		96	259		31	35	49
1881-82	86	137	14		220		186		244	72			147	39	142		79	195		39	34	22
1882-83	80	141	24		187		186		203	79	32		135	49	154		72	208		21	36	14
1883-84	72	161	22		195		197		208	61			190	34	130		112	202		34	41	

Note: There are no reports for 1853–54, 1854–55, 1855–56, 1860–61, 1861–62, 1863–64, 1864–65, 1865–66, 1868–69, 1869–70, 1870–71, 1871–72, 1874–75

Source: Annual Reports of Directors, Edinburgh School of Arts, and Watt Institution and School of Arts

Table 4.2 Student numbers by subject, summer courses, 1856–84

	Drawing	Arithmetic	Mathematics	Algebra	French	English	German	Botany	Geology	Shorthand	Hebrew	Hindustani	Latin	Freehand drawing	Biology	Greek	Life and nature painting	Theory of music	Draped life model	Bookkeeping and writing	Elocution
1856–57	43	18		8	33	55															
1857–58	70	40		11	48																
1858–59	66	26		12	22	20															
1861–62	60		42		67																
1862–63	59		40		52																
1866–67	42		47		19	20	14														
1867–68	64		25		29	34	9														
1872–73	22		41		19	30	19	40	17												
1873–74	34		55		37	32	20	41	12	28											
1875–76	21		46		25	31	26	41		22	2	2	22								
1876–77	20		64		39	52	14	57	20	32			41	10							
1877–78	39	52		41	84	57	19	18		16			42	21	6	20	19	33			
1878–79	23	45		49	65	56	28	23		38			48	35		15	42	35	7		
1879–80	23	48		32	58	57	30	15		31			33	24		23	23	35	5	33	
1880–81	20	41		26	76	43	36	19		20			35	24		14	20	29	15	36	
1881–82	18	36		30	53	42	33	37		27			27	35	7	16	16	39	6	47	31
1882–83	22	52		32	42	46	20	34	16	36			21	32		9	10	28		41	17
1883–84	30	32		33	64	47	28	30	11	29			40	23		18	20	36		44	28

Note: There were no reports in 1853–54, 1854–55, 1855–56, 1860–61, 1863–64, 1864–66, 1869–70, 1870–71, 1871–72, 1874–75

Source: Annual Reports of Directors, Edinburgh School of Art, and Watt Institution and School of Arts

Table 4.3 Percentage of total male students by socio-economic group

	Professional (%)	Managers, lower professional (%)	Intermediate non-manual (%)	Skilled manual (%)	Semi-skilled manual (%)	Unskilled manual (%)	Total students
1855–56	4.2	11.1	19.4	51.6	13.5	0.2	513
1884–85	5.1	7.2	49.1	32.7	3.8	2.1	1,625

Source: Annual Directors Reports and Calendars, Watt Institution and School of Arts

artists and dentists. By 1884–85 the intermediate non-manual group, constituting 49 per cent of all students, had replaced skilled manuals as the largest category; clerks, of whom there were 390, were the largest occupational group, reflecting the changing service-based employment structure of Edinburgh (Table 4.3). This shift in the composition of the student body occurred half a century later than at the Manchester Institution, where clerks, warehousemen and others made up two-thirds of the membership by the late 1830s.[11]

The Watt Institution was no longer educating primarily mechanics and artisans, a change reinforced by the occupational mix of female students. Of the 284 female students in 1884–85, the largest occupational groups enrolled were teachers and assistants (38), dressmakers (27), shopkeepers and saleswomen (17), and compositors (17), further underlining the change in the profile of the students towards lower middle-class intermediate non-manual service employees.

The Admission of Women

Apart from the Mechanics' Institute and the Edinburgh Philosophical Association, a plethora of book clubs, debating societies and literary societies rose and fell in Edinburgh, catering to every state and interest; a few were even open to artisans. The assumption that men would occupy the position of power and leadership within them was rarely challenged. The world was divided into 'separate spheres' for men and women, with women confined to the domestic sphere and excluded from the public world.[12] Some divisions between men and women were enshrined in bricks and mortar, some in custom and practice and others in association rules and regulations; but few were so rigid as not to be open to negotiation. Women also faced contradictions. Their religion recognised their spiritual equality yet defended social and sexual subordination.[13] The struggle for the emancipation of women in the nineteenth century was conducted over a very broad front. The women's movement embraced the campaign for the vote, agitation for a Married Women's Property Act, the fight to enter the medical profession, and the struggle to be admitted to higher education and adult education classes.

The admission of women became a topic of much discussion at directors' meetings by 1869, and, reading between the lines, may have been the cause of some acrimony. Not that women were in themselves an innovation of the 1860s but at the Watt Institution they certainly were. In the context of the mechanics' institute movement, the Watt Institution, a pioneer in so many respects, lagged behind in the provision of educational opportunities for women. In general, the early institutes were exclusively a male preserve, but by the 1830s some began to admit women to lectures: the London Mechanics' Institution permitted female relatives and friends of members to attend lectures in 1830;[14] at Manchester, women members are recorded as early as 1835;[15] while at Huddersfield and Keighley, separate female institutes were established under the wing of the mechanics' institute.[16] The objectives of the directors of the Manchester Mechanics' Institution in establishing separate classes for females were partly to enable them 'to learn what would make them better wives, sisters, mothers'.[17] There were no courses designed to educate men to become better husbands. The idea that women had a claim to enjoy a similar education to men was combined with a particular desire 'to prepare them to sustain the high responsibilities which devolved upon them'.[18] The department was placed in the charge of a 'lady superintendent' and the women's classes were usually held in the afternoon in rooms 'perfectly distinct from those used in the ordinary day business of the Institution'.[19] Developments at Anderson's College in Glasgow were foreseen by a codicil to John Anderson's will in 1796 where he expressed the view that the professor of natural philosophy would deliver two courses, the 'mathematical' and the 'ladies course' in which no mathematical reasoning was to be used.[20] Eventually the ladies course was to be open to men and women 'with the idea of making the ladies of Glasgow the most accomplished in Europe'.[21] Entry to those lectures was by ticket: 'No men may be admitted who are disorderly, talkative, ill-bred or intoxicated; and no women that are giddy or incorrect in their manners.'[22] The University of Edinburgh was also the focus of a long and bitterly fought campaign for female access from the late 1860s.[23]

The key figure in the campaign to secure female entry to the Watt Institution was the redoubtable Mary Burton (1819–1909), born in Aberdeen, the youngest of four children.[24] She moved to Edinburgh in 1832 and, although she never married, family responsibilities kept her there, first to care for her mother and then to raise orphaned nephews and nieces 'and to see that they were trained on the intellectual and practical side of life'.[25] She gained a formidable reputation as an educational and

Mary Burton, redoubtable leader of the campaign to admit women to the Watt Institution and School of Arts. Photograph by Tunny, Trustees of the National Library of Scotland

social reformer and made trailblazing inroads into public life at a time when prevailing notions of social respectability decreed that a lady's place was in the drawing room.[26] Her commitment to practical as well as academic attainment was characteristic of her contribution to education and politics in Edinburgh,[27] where she was also among the first to advocate the enfranchisement of women and Irish home rule. Girls, she argued on election hustings, should learn to use a sewing machine and boys the use of a saw and plane, adding that 'she herself could work with these tools and she had mended a floor before now'.[28] As a member of the Edinburgh School Board, she advocated that boys and girls should be taught to knit and sew. A kindly, spare figure with 'fresh bright face and Quaker like garb' of large bonnet and cloak, Mary Burton was often seen driving her pony and cart to meetings. She was an energetic landlord of tenement properties in the Old Town,[29] encouraging her tenants to embrace thrift and often taking a bucket and brush to wash down a dirty flight of stairs as a lesson in cleanliness to her tenants,[30] whom she entertained to parties at her home, Liberton Bank, during the summer months.

At a directors' meeting on 8 October 1869, a letter from Mary Burton seeking access for women to the Watt Institution's courses was discussed. The directors initially deferred making a decision on this potentially thorny issue by remitting the case to a committee 'to wait on the Lecturers and get their views on the subject'.[31] This committee formed the opinion that

Director's Meeting
1 Novem 1869

Female Students

School of Arts, Nov 1869

At a meeting of the Directors held here this day Present Dr. Gray in the chair, Dr. Donaldson, Dr. Ferguson, Dr. Bedford, Mr. Robertson, Mr. Crichton, Mr. Dymock, Mr. Crombie, Mr. Henderson, and Convener Field—

The report of the Committee in regard to the admission of young women to the classes of the Watt Institution and School of Arts was read and considered— The Directors approved of the Report of the Committee and agreed that young women should be admitted to the classes, with the Concurrence of the Lecturers & Teachers on the same terms as other Students, the Directors reserving power to themselves to reconsider this resolution should circumstances occur, and authorise the Secretary to communicate the same to the Lecturers & Teachers.

The fateful decision to admit women students in 1869

tho' it was not the intention of the Founders to have young women as scholars, there is nothing in the original rules or in any regulations afterwards made positively to exclude them, and they recommended that the Directors should allow female scholars to be admitted to any of the classes they may wish to attend, provided Teachers and Lecturers do not object to the arrangement.[32]

This somewhat grudging acceptance of female students was endorsed by the directors on 1 November 1869, a relatively liberal position when compared with

Scottish universities who did not permit women to graduate until 1892. The directors, however, conceded lecturers the right to veto the attendance of females – a democratic concession which was never applied to the admission of males – although there is no record of anyone ever exercising the veto. The directors also reserved 'the power to themselves to reconsider this resolution should circumstances occur'.[33] Miss Burton, ever vigilant on behalf of female students, wrote to the directors in April 1870 requesting that tickets be issued to 'girls of the artisan class at the same rate as they were given to other students when more than one class was taken, that is at half price'.[34] The request was refused. However, the educational equality that Plato had recommended more than two thousand years before was now won.

In the following year, Mary Burton's attempt to persuade her colleagues in the Edinburgh Ladies Educational Association to sponsor 'deserving girls' to attend classes at the Watt Institution revealed some telling fault lines within the women's movement.[35] Despite her bid to forestall criticism by insisting that candidates should be 'staid in their dress and manner' and 'produce from their employer a character for diligence in their occupation and high moral and intellectual worth',[36] her proposal was roundly condemned. Although members who debated the issue were at pains to stress that their views were in no way 'tantamount to an expression of disapproval of the work Miss Burton had done in procuring the classes to women ... of the lower classes', some certainly disapproved of 'gratuitous education for that class'. But it was the concept of mixed classes that aroused the most forceful criticism. Even Mary Burton's sister-in-law, Katherine, 'was of the opinion that advantage would be taken of the fixed hours and evenings of the classes for the making of appointments and that great evils would thus arise'.[37]

Women did not flock to the institution in large numbers, and the enrolment of 67 in 1872–73, the first year for which there is published data on gender, represented 10 per cent of all students. This proportion was not exceeded until the end of the decade, when total numbers had grown to 2,348 (1880–81), of whom 17 per cent (343) were women. Thereafter, until the mid 1880s, women usually made up around 15 per cent of the student intake. Although women gained access to the courses in 1869, they were not accorded full equality of status. On the laying of the foundation stone for the new building in Chambers Street three years later in 1872, an anonymous lady observed tartly:

Although many ladies were present in the open air, without any covering ... not one was invited to the banquet – surely very strange and inconsistent conduct.[38]

At the dinner the Reverend Dr Gray, vice-president, in a self-congratulatory tone, declared:

To meet the cry of women's rights they had opened the door of the School of Arts (Voice 'Not the School of hearts'; laughter) – to the ladies, and he was bound to say as a director with the very best results.[39]

The following year a letter from a Miss Stevenson, signed by 26 ladies and gentlemen, 'praying the Directors to put Miss Burton on the Board', was placed before the directors' meeting on 3 November 1873.[40] The directors considered it too late for them to take action, 'the arrangements having been completed for this year's meeting'.[41] This did not prevent them from appointing new (male) directors, but Miss Burton became the first woman elected to the board of directors in November 1874. When the institution merged with George Heriot's Trust to form Heriot-Watt College in 1885, she became a life governor of the college until her death in 1909.

Some institutes taught women separately from men, and Glasgow University introduced an unusual arrangement for segregation in the form of a wooden partition in the humanities classroom which permitted only the professor to see both sexes at once.[42] The Watt Institution, however, although admitting women later than many institutes, never taught them in segregated classes or provided special tuition in subjects such as needlework or dressmaking. Lord Shand revealed in 1877:

> There were some who doubted the expediency of this step but experience has shown that doubts or fears were groundless. The earnestness of work in every class has been unabated, the greatest decorum prevails, and the teachers have every reason to be satisfied with the arrangement for having mixed classes.[43]

Hence women had to adapt to a curriculum largely developed for the needs of male mechanics, although the rapid introduction of new humanities subjects during the 1870s is likely to have been related, in part at least, to the different demands and aspirations of female students. In a period where many mechanics' institutes were closing, the broadening of the curriculum at the Watt Institution was undoubtedly one of the factors influencing its wider reputation and which therefore contributed to its long-term survival.

The Atmosphere of Teaching and Learning

Looking beyond the statistics of student recruitment and the admission of women, what can we glimpse of teaching and student life at this time? Dr David Pryde, born in Kinghorn, Fife, in 1834, lectured in English at the Watt Institution and School of Arts from 1863 to 1886 and he recorded his impressions of teaching a class of artisans:

I was to attempt to introduce them to the lives and works of the great authors. ... I then took up his chief works, gave an account of their contents, ... illustrating my remarks by choice extracts, ... pointing out the beauties or the defects, as the case may be. ... I told the students that, unless they could write shorthand, they should not attempt to take notes while I was speaking. They should simply listen attentively, and at the end of each division I would dictate notes so carefully framed that they would recall all that I had said. ... Friday

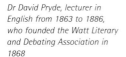

Dr David Pryde, lecturer in English from 1863 to 1886, who founded the Watt Literary and Debating Association in 1868

evening, the time for meeting my class, was to me the brightest part of the week. I found the large lecture-hall filled with a crowd of young men and young women the most intelligent of their class, all eager for information.[44]

Preparation of the lecture notes was

my most congenial task, occupying for several years all my leisure. . . . I carried a small notebook with me, and whenever, in the course of my reading, or in my walks, an appropriate fact, thought, or illustration occurred, it was jotted down. . . . Every afternoon I frequented the Botanic Garden and the Arboretum. On Saturdays, with a sandwich and a play of Shakespeare in my pocket, I set out to pursue my peripatetic studies. My favourite walk was on the shady heights and bypaths of Corstorphine Hill. But sometimes I crossed in the ferryboat to Fife, to the scenes where I first loved nature and poetry.[45]

Dr Pryde was also an acerbic critic of the Edinburgh elite and their lack of support for the institution:

At the opening and closing of the session, eminent citizens appeared on the platform and eulogized its usefulness. But their goodwill went no further than words; the flowers of speech never developed into fruit; the praise was unaccompanied by the smallest bit of solid pudding. . . . The Directors were still obliged to keep up the institution with the paltry subscriptions levied with difficulty from an indifferent public.[46]

Hugh Robert Mill, born in Thurso in 1861, was a student at the Watt Institution and School of Arts between 1878 and 1880 and described William Lees, the natural philosophy lecturer, as 'an elderly man, who aroused no enthusiasm'. However, the overall experience of the Watt Institution was of 'the greatest value to me, not only by the orderly acquisition of knowledge, but also by introducing me to a new class of society'.[47] Mill subsequently lectured in geography and physiography at the institution from 1887–1892 and was somewhat less flattering about the students in his class:

I am fairly claimed here with a class of Industrial and Commercial Geography, at the Heriot-Watt College. It is a small class and not enthusiastic, presenting a horrendous contrast to a course of lectures on Physiography which I am about concluding at Perth.[48]

Dr Stevenson Macadam (1829–1901), a previous assistant of George Wilson's, succeeded him as lecturer in chemistry in 1855. He practised a form of continuous assessment by conducting oral examinations on the topic of the previous lecture before his weekly class; and he revived practical classes after a lapse of three decades, taking these initially in the laboratory at Surgeon's Hall with about 20 students participating.[49] He presented oral evidence to the Select Committee on Scientific Instruction in 1868 and reported that the institution had no chemical or physical laboratories; and that the level of fees was 5s for a single class, 7s 6d for two, and 10s if a student enrolled for the four subjects of chemistry, natural philosophy, mathematics and English.[50] When the institution moved to the new premises in Chambers Street in 1873, Macadam was able to conduct practicals in a laboratory for the first time, but the room provided was described by Macadam as small, low and thus inadequately ventilated, 'and deficient in appliances'.[51] In his evidence to the select committee, Macadam reported that the catchment area of the school was expanding and that some students travelled eight miles and walked back in the evening, and others 'also came from Leith, Portobello and Musselburgh', the third-class return rail ticket from Leith to Edinburgh being 3d in 1868.[52]

During this period, the dominant figure at the Watt Institution was the secretary, Dr Thomas Murray. On the concluding night of the winter session, it was customary for Dr Murray to invite the lecturers and directors to a frugal supper in the boardroom in Adam Square and he became 'the breathing embodiment of geniality and benevolence'. He 'revelled in reminiscences and anecdotes, called for jovial songs'.[53] Dr Murray, despite his bonhomie, was a demanding employer who could be highly critical of the lecturing staff:

I heard that lecture, sir. . . . You mispronounced a word. You're an excellent man, sir, but no lecturer: you want *cadence*.[54]

Dr Murray resigned his post as secretary in 1866 after more than two decades of service, accepting a position as honorary secretary until his death in 1872. After his death, the *Scotsman's* obituary reported that he was 'decidedly liberal in theology' while his biographer, John Fairley, spoke of his 'self-complacency and sense of his own importance' and concluded that he was a 'useful writer rather than a profound scholar'; his literary efforts 'lack originality and power, and are of no permanent value'.[55] After Murray's retirement, his assistant R. T. Scott became secretary but the predominant figure was Thomas Knox, honorary treasurer and ex-master of the Merchant Company, a person of 'big manly form, expressive features, face of character . . . and commanding voice who was never happier than when he was haranguing on the platform, writing a letter to *The Scotsman*, encouraging the lecturers or addressing the students'.[56]

Of considerable concern to the special interests of those sponsors of mechanics' institutes was the extent of their effect on the attitude of labour towards capital. Specifically it was intended that certain principles, the foundation of the economic faith of the middle class, would be spread among the workers through classes in political economy. Some insight into the ideology of the political economy taught by Dr Hodgson, an academic at Edinburgh University, may be gleaned from notes taken by a student, Mr Kemp, during the 1878–79 session:

> The employer is only a middleman, the consumer being the real employer. (Lecture, 27 February 1879)

> The interests of the capitalists and labourers in any one line are identical and opposed to all other. ... It is the interests of both that the profits should be as large as possible. (Lecture, 27 February 1879)

> Trade unions are shameful in blending their charitable and dispute funds. (Lecture, 27 March 1879)

> Trade unions don't encourage innovations. (Lecture, 3 April 1879)[57]

It was not that political economy was ignored at the Watt Institution but rather that an attempt was made, as Kemp's notes suggest, to ensure, by employing the philosophy of 'jug to mug education', that the working man's conception of it was the same as his master's.

John Thomson, pioneering photographer, gained a life diploma at the Watt Institution and School of Arts in 1858

Senior Mathematics.

James Symons, Cabinetmaker.
Alex. Innes, Bookbinder.
John Purdie, Millwright.
John Bayne, Engineer.
John M'Taggart, Pupil Teacher.
James Dick, Clerk.
William Bruce, Engineer.
William Hall, Blacksmith.

Natural Philosophy.

James Reekie, Brassfounder.
William Goldie, Architect.
John Purdie, Millwright.
William Johnstone, Pupil Teacher.
Alex. Innes, Bookbinder.

Sinclair Robertson, Engineer.
Robert Davies, Engineer.

Chemistry.

William Rattray, Clerk.
Robert M'Gregor, Tobacconist.
William Goldie, Architect.
James Halden, Stationer.
Archd. C. Seton, Clerk.
William F. Vernon, Dentist.
James Dick, Clerk.
John Thomson, Optician.
George Bonnalie, Dentist.
John Purdie, Millwright.
Stewart Robertson, Engineer.
John Tod, Cabinetmaker.
John Sanderson, Coachbuilder.
Peter Baxter, Shopman.

The Students who obtained "Life Diplomas,"—the result of three years' attendance, and of passing a strict examination in Mathematics, Natural Philosophy, and Chemistry—are six in number.

Alexander Innes.
William Bruce.
John Thomson.

William Goldie.
William Bain.
James Symons.

It was stated, in last *Report*, that Leonard Horner, Esq., the founder of the School, was in the way of taking steps to found a perpetual Prize of the annual value of Three Guineas, to be given successively, to the best Student in the Classes of Junior Mathematics, Natural Philosophy, and Chemistry, respectively.

One student who attended the institution in the mid nineteenth century, John Thomson, went on to become one of the great pioneers of the photographic art. Thomson, born in Edinburgh on 14 June 1837, was the son of a tobacco spinner who later became a tobacconist, and the family occupied a flat in the Old Town.[58] Thomson, a man of strong religious faith, was not born into the right social background to be guaranteed an education at Edinburgh University and by the age of 13, in 1851, he had become apprenticed to James Mackay Bryson, son of the cofounder of the Edinburgh School of Arts, at his optician's business on Princes Street, Edinburgh. In common with most scientifically minded men in the mid nineteenth century, the Brysons all held a keen interest in photography (his business also traded in photographic supplies) and James Mackay Bryson may have sparked Thomson's interest in the subject.[59] After serving six years of his apprenticeship, Thomson, as a 19 year old, attended the sessions 1856–57 and 1857–58 at the School of Arts, gaining the attestation of proficiency in natural philosophy, junior mathematics and chemistry, and thereby qualifying for the life diploma in 1858. He was also awarded a Watt Club prize for English in 1857.[60] At the school, Thomson had access, probably for the first time in his life, to a library, including Nicolas-Marie-Paymal Lerebour's *Treatise on Photography*, a possible source of inspiration for his life's work, and H. Murray's *Historical Account of China*, which may have given him a taste for the Orient.[61]

Although the dates of Thomson's travels are hard to determine with precision, we know that he left Edinburgh on 29 April 1862 and arrived in Singapore on 12 June.[62] He continued his services as a photographer while he and his brother also jointly operated a business making chronometers, optical and nautical instruments.[63] The majority of Thomson's photographs were created using the wet collodion process, which was very cumbersome in operation, requiring a considerable quantity of chemicals and expertise in their handling.[64] Coating, sensitising and developing plates were activities which had to be performed inside a dark tent, a simple temporary structure of Thomson's own design and construction.[65] Working in such conditions was arduous: 'I have felt, after day's work in a tent so thoroughly saturated with chemicals, that I might almost be used for coating a plate or printing upon.'[66]

Thomson sought to use the publishing industry to disseminate his photographs in printed books with the accompanying text written by him, and this aspect of his work was as important in shaping contemporary opinion of his oeuvre as the photographs. Thomson's publications stood at the forefront of the development of the technology in reproducing text and images in printed publications.[67] By the time of his death in 1921, John Thomson's life had coincided with almost the entire history of photography up to that point, and he had embraced many of its crucial developments in the creation and reproduction of photographs. Always

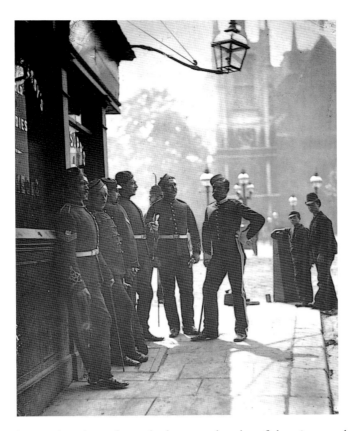

innovating throughout the last two decades of the nineteenth century (the range of his photography was breathtaking), he experimented with new photographic printing technologies such as the platinum print and the gelatin-silver print.[68] Thomson absorbed the nature of the landscape, the quality of the light, and was always focused on the individual, the essential element in any society, be it Chinese, Cypriot, Siamese or British.[69] Sir David Puttnam has suggested that his work is

> marked by an immediacy and a democracy of outlook . . . [his] photographs not only circumvented the stifling formalities of Victorian Britain, thereby allowing us to meet, face-to-face, some of the individuals whom the respectable reading-public would normally have crossed the street to avoid.[70]

Thomson opened up parts of the world to a western audience for the first time; to him the major purpose of his art was education, perhaps stimulated by his experiences at the School of Arts. One of the art's great pioneers, he was brilliantly successful in forming the critical genres of photography for the next century and in establishing photography as an essential aspect of book illustration.[71]

Development of Student Societies and Clubs

The 1870s was the formative period of student societies in Scottish universities and the various literary, athletic, social and religious groups were sufficiently numerous to form the basis for the student representative committees, whose establishment was in turn closely linked with the building of unions, the founding of student magazines, and similar activities.[72] The late nineteenth century also witnessed the political awakening of students as a body. Modern patterns of student life were established within quite a short period but the first expression of the spirit of this new movement at the Watt Institution arose in conjunction with the public unveiling of the statue of James Watt (executed by Peter Slater) on 12 May 1854. The statue, which now graces the Riccarton campus standing beside a noble Hungarian oak on the piazza outside the main entrance, was carved from a block of freestone presented by the Duke of Buccleuch and hewn from his quarry at Granton. There was an impressive inauguration ceremony outside the Watt Institution and School of Arts in Adam Square:

> Evergreens were profusely arranged in decorative wreaths over the whole front of the building. From the centre dormer window, on the roof, floated the Union Jack; lower down, ... the silver set cross of St Andrew, and ... the red cross of St George were displayed; while on the front of the whole, elevated over the doorway, 'James Watt' was inscribed in flowered letters of surpassing delicacy and beauty. A section of a steam engine, ... worked with considerable spirit, on the front of the tenement. ... Crowds of interested spectators thronged the scene. ... A little after two o'clock, Mr Slater gave the signal, and the flags were removed from the statue ... and the spectators ... expressed their delight and admiration by long continued and reiterated cheers.[73]

A party of about 50 gentlemen – the directors and their male guests – dined in the evening, in honour of the occasion, at the London Hotel, St Andrew's Square, while the students attended a much livelier dinner in the Guildford Arms, Register Street. At 11 P.M. several directors joined the students at the Guildford Arms and 'the meeting which was enlivened by the vocal powers of several gentlemen present broke up about two o'clock'. It was on this occasion that Mr J. E. Vernon, a jeweller, proposed that a club should be formed 'whose object would be to sup together on the anniversary of the birth of James Watt ... and also to promote the

A souvenir of the unveiling of Peter Slater's iconic statue of James Watt on 12 May 1854. Staff and students were inspired by this event to found the Watt Club

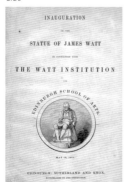

Mr J. E. Vernon, the jeweller who proposed the formation of the Watt Club during a dinner at the Guildford Arms on 12 May 1854

A classic example of Victorian students' initiative: the magazine of the Excelsior Association for Mutual Improvement

interests of the School, by raising a Fund each year to provide prizes'.[74] The Watt Club Medals are still awarded today to the top first-class graduate in each discipline, and the club, now the university's alumni association, flourishes with branches all over the world.[75] The initial annual subscription was set at one shilling, or ten shillings for life membership.[76] The first celebration of the birthday of Watt took place on 20 January 1855 at a dinner in the Café Royal attended by 50 members, costing 2s and 3d each, at which the president of the club presented 'a very chaste and handsome baton'.[77] This function became an annual event and the entertainment was not confined to music; in 1862 the highlights were a solar microscope and an 'exhibition of a series of dissolving views' which brought forth 'hearty marks of approbation from the audience'.[78] At the AGM of the club on 31 October 1870, a motion was passed to 'allow ladies to compete for the prizes along with the gentlemen on the same terms'[79] and in 1871 it was agreed that ladies should be admitted to the annual dinner.[80]

The first magazine edited and produced by the students, the *Excelsior*, appeared in the early 1860s with the aim of improving their literary and debating skills,[81] and it was entirely the result of students' initiative. Students prepared an essay on a topic of their choice, frequently illustrated by pen and ink drawings, and other members honed their analytical skills by writing a critique of it. The magazine was circulated among members to enable them to comment on the latest essay but they were required to 'leave the magazine at the abode of the person whose name follows yours on the list'. If anyone kept it for longer than two days, there was a penalty of 1d per day, subsequently raised to 2d.[82] Of the membership in 1870, some 25 per cent were female, although they constituted only 8 per cent of the study body; indeed the editor wrote that 'special thanks is due to those of the gentle sex who have favoured us with their writings'.[83] Although only three issues survive – 1864, 1869 and 1870 – it is clear that the imaginations of the students roamed over a wide range of issues, including Edgar Allan Poe, King David of Israel, the triumph of falsehood, whether offensive or defensive war is according to Bible principles, an explanation of supposed contradictions in the Bible, Robespierre's public career; literary immorality (plagiarism); and Negro emancipation in America. The last topic, addressed by the editor in November 1864, was an apologia for slavery – 'emancipation in America would be a curse rather than a blessing' – which provoked a mixed reaction, mostly supportive, among the members.[84]

The Watt Literary and Debating Association, by contrast, was instituted in 1868 by Dr David Pryde, lecturer in English literature, who was honorary president for 39 years.[85] The objects of the association were

the moral and intellectual improvement of its members, and the facilitating of social intercourse among them. . . . The means by which these objects shall be promoted are – Essays, Readings, Recitations and Debates.[86]

The society was initially highly successful, recruiting 150 members for the second session 'with an additional impetus given to its progress by the admission of ladies'.[87] The ablest lady during the formative years of the association was Miss Ella Burton, who lived with her aunt, Mary Burton, and wrote essays, led debates, and prepared original recitations and plays for the annual soirée.[88] The soirée was a major social occasion first held in 1870, but no records are available until the event of 13 March 1873, which commenced at 6.30 P.M. in the New Waverley Hall, Waterloo Place. The programme, which 'was particularly well rendered in all its parts', incorporated a service of tea, an interval with a service of fruit, and included music by Beethoven, Mozart, Weber and Mendelssohn, preceded by a recitation, songs and a play. The assembly which followed was attended by about 140 people and belied the decorous programme: dancing was kept up 'with great spirit until 5.30am'.[89]

Despite the attractions of the soirée, annual membership fluctuated during the 1870s from a maximum of 132 in 1876–77 to 77 in 1878–79; concern was

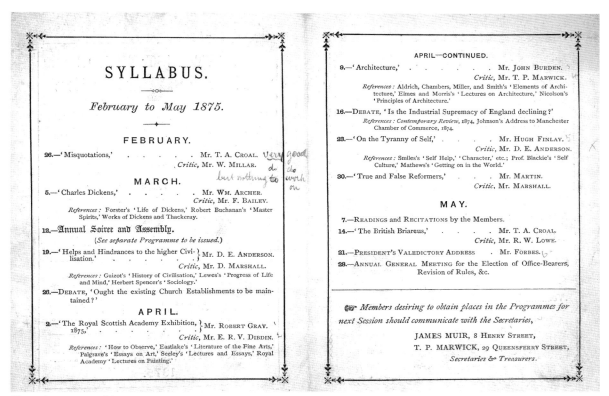

SYLLABUS.

February to May 1875.

FEBRUARY.

26.—'Misquotations,' . . . . . Mr. T. A. CROAL. *Very good*
Critic, Mr. W. MILLAR. *du do but nothing to work on*

MARCH.

5.—'Charles Dickens,' . . . . . Mr. WM. ARCHER.
Critic, Mr. F. BAILEY.
References : Forster's 'Life of Dickens,' Robert Buchanan's 'Master Spirits,' Works of Dickens and Thackeray.

12.—**Annual Soiree and Assembly.**
(*See separate Programme to be issued.*)

19.—'Helps and Hindrances to the higher Civi- } Mr. D. E. ANDERSON.
lisation.' }
Critic, Mr. D. MARSHALL.
References : Guizot's 'History of Civilisation,' Lewes's 'Progress of Life and Mind,' Herbert Spencer's 'Sociology.'

26.—DEBATE, 'Ought the existing Church Establishments to be maintained ?'

APRIL.

2.—'The Royal Scottish Academy Exhibition, } Mr. ROBERT GRAY.
1875,' . . . . . }
Critic, Mr. E. R. V. DIBDIN.
References : 'How to Observe,' Eastlake's 'Literature of the Fine Arts,' Palgrave's 'Essays on Art,' Seeley's 'Lectures and Essays,' Royal Academy 'Lectures on Painting.'

APRIL—CONTINUED.

9.—'Architecture,' . . . . . Mr. JOHN BURDEN.
Critic, Mr. T. P. MARWICK.
References : Aldrich, Chambers, Miller, and Smith's 'Elements of Architecture,' Elmes and Morris's 'Lectures on Architecture,' Nicolson's 'Principles of Architecture.'

16.—DEBATE, 'Is the Industrial Supremacy of England declining ?'
References : Contemporary Review, 1874, Johnson's Address to Manchester Chamber of Commerce, 1874.

23.—'On the Tyranny of Self,' . . . Mr. HUGH FINLAY.
Critic, Mr. D. E. ANDERSON.
References : Smiles's 'Self Help,' 'Character,' etc.; Prof. Blackie's 'Self Culture,' Mathews's 'Getting on in the World.'

30.—'True and False Reformers,' . . . Mr. MARTIN.
Critic, Mr. MARSHALL.

MAY.

7.—READINGS and RECITATIONS by the Members.

14.—'The British Briareus,' . . . . Mr. T. A. CROAL.
Critic, Mr. R. W. LOWE.

21.—PRESIDENT'S VALEDICTORY ADDRESS . Mr. FORBES.

28.—ANNUAL GENERAL MEETING for the Election of Office-Bearers, Revision of Rules, &c.

☞ *Members desiring to obtain places in the Programmes for next Session should communicate with the Secretaries,*

JAMES MUIR, 8 HENRY STREET,
T. P. MARWICK, 29 QUEENSFERRY STREET,
Secretaries & Treasurers.

This worthy programme of the Watt Literary and Debating Association 1875 illustrates how the ethics of moral and intellectual improvement influenced even the students' social life

expressed that falling attendance was due to a 'lack of cordiality amongst members especially of older members to newcomers',[90] rather than the level of the annual subscription, 1s 6d in 1878. Meetings of the association were held following the English literature class at 9.30 P.M. on Friday evenings and seldom ended before 11 o'clock. At first, only current students were admitted to membership, but in 1870 the rule was amended to include all who may have been in any way connected with the institution. One of the first to take advantage of this change was Mary Burton, who became an honorary president of the association in 1883, having been vice-president in 1874–75.[91]

The general political tone of the society during the late nineteenth century was Liberal. From 1879 there was an annual political debate 'that the present Government is unworthy of the support of the country', and for 12 years the Liberals were victorious, but in 1891–92 the Unionists succeeded for the first time. Debates and voting on other issues reflected a volatile period in politics and revealed a membership displaying alternating Liberal and Conservative positions. The rights of women and their changing role in society, for example, commanded the attention of the debaters on a number of occasions. In 1869–70 the result of the debate 'Should spinsters and widows possess the political franchise?' was not recorded, but in 1882–83 the society carried the motion that 'women householders ought not to have the franchise'. By the following year a more enlightened mood prevailed with support for the notion that 'women should be admitted to our Scotch universities'.[92] In 1884–85 the members concluded that 'the higher education of women is not injurious to society', but the following year a Conservative majority asserted itself in determining that 'women should not be admitted to the learned professions'.[93] Similar swings in political sentiment between Liberalism and Conservatism are revealed by the debates on more general political issues: in 1877–78 students supported the motion that 'Britain will be benefited by retaining her colonies' whereas the following year, by a majority of 4 to 1, trade unions were judged as 'not beneficial to the community'.[94] Conservative and imperialist sentiments still prevailed in 1878–79 with support for the Conservative government and the motion that 'emigration to our colonies ought to be encouraged by State aid'. The Darwinian position on evolution was endorsed in 1880–81 and, unsurprisingly, members also decided that a 'limited monarchy is preferable to a republic'.[95]

A more radical mood began to prevail among the members in the 1880s with motions passed supporting legislation to 'prevent summary evictions in the Highlands' (1881–82); 'to abolish the House of Lords', 'to nationalise land' (1883–84), and 'in support of government intervention in the economy' (1884–85).[96] Liberal sentiments on domestic policy, however, did not extend far from Britain's shores and in 1882–83 a majority supported the somewhat patronising motion that 'our colonies should yet remain under the protecting care of the mother country'.[97] The dedication of these students and their willingness to debate serious issues at 9.30 P.M. on a Friday night after a long day's work and lectures is a glowing testimony to their zeal for self-improvement. Students had started to debate and articulate their own opinions, later harnessed to exert more overt pressure on the providers of education.

The Chambers Street Building

A City Improvement Act of 1866 cleared the way for widespread changes in the Old Town of Edinburgh. The Improvement Trustees developed extensive plans for redevelopment of much of the area in the Cowgate and its environs; this had major repercussions for the Watt Institution since Adam

The demolition of Adam Square in 1871 forced the institution to seek a new home. Watercolour by J. Horsburgh. Photograph: Douglas McBride

Square was one of the areas threatened with demolition. On 28 October 1867, in moving the adoption of the annual report, Provost William Chambers, having praised the school as 'the earliest institution of the kind in Great Britain' in which 'the City of Edinburgh had reason to be proud',[98] warned

> this was probably the last time they would meet in the same place, as . . . it was proposed to widen North College Street, and . . . it would carry away the Watt Institution entirely, leaving a broad street to the south.[99]

Demolition began in 1868 and the following year the directors entered negotiations with the Improvements Trustees for the sale of the Adam Square building, a process which was to prove abortive. Given that the improvements were definitely going ahead, the directors were somewhat unrealistic about these negotiations and their refusal to settle with the trustees was tantamount to sticking their heads in the sand and hoping the problem would go away.[100] After two years' notice of the problem, it can hardly have been a surprise when on 11 September 1871 the directors were informed at an emergency meeting that the Improvements Trustees, without having bought it, had sold the building and the purchaser had already started to demolish it.[101] This, however, gave the directors a strong hand in subsequent negotiations which led to the granting of a site on the newly widened College Street, later renamed in honour of the Lord Provost, William Chambers. Meanwhile, temporary accommodation was secured in St Peter's Church in Roxburgh Place (the lower two floors of the tenement on the west side) and in little more than a year the foundation stone of the new building had been laid.[102]

The contract for the new building was awarded to Messrs D. Sutherland and Sons on 6 May 1872 based on an estimate of £7,234. It was resolved to lay the foundation stone, after the custom of the times, with full Masonic honours.[103] Although attitudes today are wary of the secrecy involved in freemasonry, in nineteenth-century Scotland it was central to the life of many working men. The lodges had their origins in the medieval guilds and by the nineteenth century these male associations – in which dining, drinking, toasts and proceedings all played a part – had become an accepted feature of British life. Freemasonry was perceived as an organisation that promulgated egalitarian views – 'a man's a man for a' that', as the Freemason Robert Burns said – and in an era without radio, TV or cinema, the social and ritual functions that lay at the heart of the lodges were a source of fellowship and reassurance for working men. Masons viewed processing through the streets in full regalia as a way of signalling their position in society and their willingness to participate in its affairs; it also contributed to the creation of an oligarchy of social dominance and deference so that Masonic processions became symbols of institutional power.[104]

The city of Edinburgh, on the 9 October 1872, was 'favoured with the most propitious weather ... bright and sunny' as some 1,100 members of 74 Masonic lodges assembled in Charlotte Square – the North British Caledonian, Glasgow and South Western Railways having permitted the Masonic brethren to travel to and from the event for a single fare.[105] The brightly coloured sashes of the brethren, their banners, and their mystic insignia 'afforded matter of wondering speculation to the crowd who surrounded the place of rendezvous'.[106] It was a few minutes past two when the huge procession headed by an artillery volunteer band commenced its march along George Street. The leading band had reached the head of the Mound, while the last carriage of the cortège was turning the corner of Princes Street and South Andrew Street.[107] A platform had been erected in Chambers Street capable of accommodating 500 people, mostly reserved for the Freemasons, the Lord Provost, magistrates and town councillors, the directors and teachers of the Watt Institution:

The centre of the platform was laid with crimson cloth, and the sides were covered with pink and white calico. Numerous flags and banners fluttered gaily from all parts of the building, including Masonic flags.[108]

All gave way to the grand master on the platform, and the grand jewels were laid on the table in front of him.[109] The inscription on the foundation stone read:

> At Edinburgh, in the 36th year of the reign of Her Most Gracious Majesty Queen Victoria, and on the 9th day of October of the Christian era 1872, and of the Masonic Epoch 5876, the Foundation Stone of this, the Watt Institution and School of Arts, was publicly laid with full Masonic honours, by the Right Honourable Earl of Rosslyn, Most Worshipful Grand Master Mason of Scotland.[110]

The grand master then gave the stone three taps with the mallet saying, 'May the Almighty Architect of the Universe look down with benignity upon our present undertaking, and crown the edifice, of which we have now laid the foundation with every success.' The band played 'On! On! My Dear Brethren' and then 'a cornucopia of vases with oil and wine were handed to the Grand Master who, in accordance with ancient custom, threw their contents upon the stone'.[111] Finally, a horn containing a sheaf of corn was emptied on the stone and the band struck up the 'Mason's Anthem' and 'Rule Britannia'.[112]

The celebration continued in appropriate style with a banquet, attended by over 200 people, at the Freemasons' Hall, George Street. The chair for the occasion was Lord Ardmillan, who emphasised unambiguously the importance of the links between the school and freemasonry:

> They had now, therefore, the ancient and glorious tradition, the high distinction, the popular acceptance, the mystic power and the singular cohesiveness of Freemasonry, as a fresh and potent guarantee for the prosperity and stability of the Watt Institution (cheers) – and he was sure that an institution could not fail to succeed which had at once the power of Masonic influence and the power of popular confidence.[113]

The elaborate celebrations were appropriate since, more than anyone yet realised, it was the beginning of a new era for the institution.

The original design of the building was by one of Edinburgh's most prominent Victorian architects, David Cousins, but the directors were not entirely satisfied with his work and employed their own architect, David Rhind, to make alterations. It was on these altered plans that the building was constructed and the

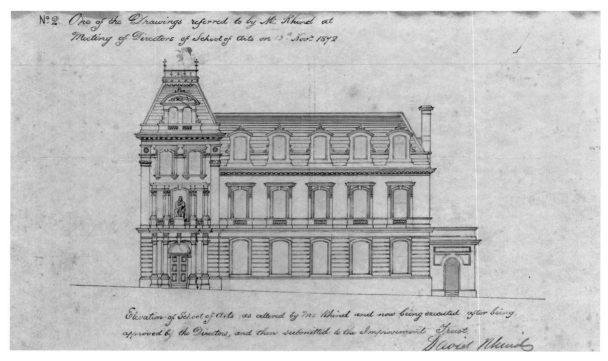

No 2. *One of the Drawings referred to by Mr Rhind at Meeting of Directors of School of Arts on 13th Novr 1872*

Elevation of School of Arts as altered by Mr Rhind and now being executed after being approved by the Directors, and then submitted to the Improvement Trust.

David Rhind

David Rhind's alterations to the original plan for the Watt Institution and School of Arts new building, Chambers Street, Edinburgh, 1872

public attribution of the building to Rhind became the subject of a dispute between the two architects. On 10 October 1872 the directors received a letter from Cousins protesting that Rhind was described as the architect when he had only laid out the interior.[114] Mr Rhind subsequently argued convincingly that he had also altered Cousin's external designs; and it required considerable tact and diplomacy on the part of the directors to assuage Mr Cousins' ire.

The building was completed in time for the opening of the 1873–74 session and was in the mixed Italian style, the eastern portion being fenestral and the west part of the front, incorporating the entrance, being columnar in its main features. The windows were ornamented with cornices and trusses on the ground and first floors. The west portion of the building was higher, forming a French roofed pavilion with large dormer windows and a mansard roof. There was a lecture room on the ground floor capable of accommodating 150 students; a 'noble hall' on the first floor with seating for 500 people, a library, two other classrooms – one 'adapted for the exhibition of specimens in geology or natural history' – and a large chemistry laboratory in the basement.[115] Slater's statue of James Watt was moved from Adam Square and positioned above the main entrance. In 1874 the directors entered into an agreement for the purchase of the site to the west with a view to the erection of a building whose ground floor – with its distinctive external decoration of carved heads – would belong to the Henderson Trust for a Phrenological Museum, and whose upper floors would form an addition to the institution.[116] This building was completed in 1875–76 at a cost of over £2,600. Since the institution was plagued by continuing financial problems, with falling annual subscriptions and no endowments, and was more than £500 in debt, it was necessary to borrow £2,600 from the Henderson Trust; the total debt of the institution in 1875–76 amounted to £3,000.[117] The erection of the building jeopardised the whole future of the institution.

It was clear that the library had not kept pace with the expanding curriculum and the broadening of the student intake. After the opening of the Chambers Street building, the directors announced on 1 December 1873 that the library would be closed during the coming session so that a thorough weeding out could take place and additions could be made to the stock. Five years later there were still problems and a committee was appointed 'to consider what steps should now be taken with a view to having the Library placed on a satisfactory footing'.[118] This committee suggested that 'they might successfully appeal to publishers and others for donations of books' and by March 1878, the upgrading having been completed, books began to arrive from Messrs Macmillan, Black, Longman and others.[119] Moreover, in June a letter from the Trustees of the Gilchrist Education Fund indicated that they were 'prepared to give a grant of £200 for the purchase of books for the Library and apparatus'.[120] In October 1878 Mr James Cameron was appointed assistant secretary and librarian, at a salary of £60 per annum, although at this time 'the reading room was still being fitted up with chairs and tables for the use of students, and in the meantime the Library was to be used only as a "consulting one" '.[121]

By the 1878–79 session, the library contained 2,500 volumes consisting 'almost entirely of scientific works ... and a number of works of Biography, Travel, Essays, Poetry and Fiction'.[122] The size of the collection was paltry: the Manchester Mechanics' Institution possessed no fewer than 12,000 volumes as early as 1850.[123] Since the attendance at the non-science courses at the Watt Institution had grown rapidly – in 1878–79 there were 268 studying French and 251 studying English literature – the library was clearly inadequate.[124] With some 1,500 students attending during the winter session, and a collection of 2,500 volumes only, the directors restricted the library entirely for reference; each student was charged 6d for the use of the library to defray the expense of printing a catalogue.[125] Expenditure on the library, as on other departments, was most uneven, varying with the state of the finances. During the 1878–79 session, spending on books, apparatus and school furnishings amounted to £105 2s 1d,[126] but by 1883–84 the total amount spent on the library and school furnishings dropped drastically to £6 18s 0d,[127] underlining further the pressing need to place the finances of the institution on a firmer footing.

From Watt Institution and School of Arts to Heriot-Watt College

In the mid nineteenth century, major resources were tied up in educational endowments bound by their founding statutes to provide education for limited classes of children. Scotland had many such 'hospitals' – endowed institutions providing board, lodging and education of a rather primitive character for orphans or children whose parents had come down in the world.[128] Of those in Edinburgh, the most notable were George Heriot's Hospital and the several hospitals administered by the Company of Merchants of the City of Edinburgh. There was a campaign in the interests of the professional middle classes of Edinburgh to capture for their own purposes the funds of endowed schools, especially the Merchant Company schools and those of the Heriot's Trust.[129] The Endowed Institutions (Scotland) Act of 1869 was largely drafted by officers of the Edinburgh Merchant Company and they exploited it by obtaining an order permitting the reorganisation of their 'hospitals' into fee-paying day schools for the middle class which the working class could not afford, a total rejection of the philosophy of everyone starting from common ground.[130] The Trades Council of Edinburgh and the Free Church Presbytery opposed this change, arguing that the intention of the seventeenth-century founder had been 'to raise up a respectable, thinking, able class of artisans or citizens', not to 'favour an elite'.[131] Their view did not prevail and the Edinburgh School Board later found it difficult to develop good quality secondary education in its own publicly financed schools.[132] A hierarchy of schools thus emerged in the city in the late nineteenth century as provision became anglicised and began to evolve on class lines – a feature of the Edinburgh educational scene which has persisted to this day – giving the lie to the constant assertion that Scottish education was inclusive.[133] The major achievement of these schools was to put secondary education of guaranteed quality within reach of the lower ranges of the middle class; the working class, however, were much less well served.[134]

George Heriot's trustees acted less expeditiously than the Merchant Company. Since the reign of James VI, the name of that king's goldsmith and banker, George Heriot 'Jingling Geordie' (1563–1634), had been commemorated in the school which was founded from the fortune Heriot had accumulated as James's financier. He bequeathed £23,625 to establish a hospital school for the 'faitherless bairns' of the City of Edinburgh. In 1870 the trustees sought to take advantage of the Act by applying for an order empowering them to reform the hospital into a boys school,

George Heriot, jeweller and moneylender to the Royal Family. Portrait by George Scougall

to retain their day schools, and make a moderate allowance to the Watt Institution. Their application was refused as beyond the powers conferred by the Act, which was now proving unworkable.

The Disruption of 1843 and the subsequent fragmentation of Scottish elementary education, with many small-scale institutions competing, intensified the conviction that a thorough reorganisation of national education on the basis of state aid and secular control was the only solution. This was articulated in the Education (Scotland) Act of 1872. The Act made education compulsory for children from 5 to 13 (although small fees were payable) and was the only type to be funded from the education rate.[135] The 1872 Act, with its requirement to provide elementary education as a charge on the local rates, quickly changed the favourable attitude of George Heriot's trustees. The majority were town councillors who realised that the more the trust's day schools could be used in preference to board schools, the less would be the burden on the rates.[136] Their priority was to retain the day schools and this delayed for over a decade the allocation of funds to the School of Arts by George Heriot's Trust.

Meanwhile the financial needs of the Watt Institution were becoming still more urgent. Since moving to the Chambers Street building, the institution was now attracting rapidly increasing numbers of students to an ever wider range of

Heriot's Hospital, from the Calton Hill, Edinburgh, 1829

classes; but student fees fell far short of the cost of the additional staff and the burgeoning enrolments were not accompanied by any increase in income from subscribers. In 1873 David Cousins, original architect of the Chambers Street building, persuaded the Lord Provost to convene a meeting of influential citizens to which he put a proposal for a major new technical institution in the city.[137] Cousins favoured a wholly new institution separate from the School of Arts, which he observed condescendingly 'had done good service in its day'.[138] Professor Fleeming Jenkin, who had become a director in 1873, responded vigorously, asserting that 'the School of Arts ... gave the right kind of technical education and the only kind worth having to the workman (Hear hear) ... and the right way to give additional education was to extend the institution in its present form'.[139] The meeting moved to a vote and Cousins' concept was rejected in favour of a motion of Bailie Lewis that a technical institution should be based on the existing school.[140] The directors of the Watt – prompted by their laudable drive to introduce more subjects, extend the library, add a reading room, initiate courses during the day, fully equip the laboratories and, above all, pay the lecturers better – turned for support to the Heriot's Trust.[141]

It was propitious for the Watt Institution that the late Lord Neaves was succeeded as president in 1876 by Alexander Burns Shand, Lord Shand. Charles Neaves, an eminent judge and man of letters, formed a link with the generation of Cockburn, Jeffrey and Brougham, all of whom he had known, but he had taken

Alexander, Lord Shand, dynamic president of the institution from 1876 to 1890. Portrait by George Paul Chalmers. Photograph: Douglas McBride

little part in the affairs of the institution, and the de facto leadership had been supplied by the Reverend W. H. Gray.[142] Lord Shand (1824–1904) had studied at Glasgow University and Edinburgh University before being called to the Scottish Bar in 1853. After serving for 18 years as a judge, he moved to London at the age of 62 in 1890, where he became a member of the Privy Council.[143] Of unusually small stature with a round cherubic face, Shand, like Neaves before him, was a liberal and when on the bench showed 'singular adroitness and tact' and a 'seemingly instinctive faculty to hitting the real points of a case'.[144] Despite judicial and other commitments, Shand proved to be an energetic and effective president of the institution; he personally wrote the first calendar in 1877–78; and he played the major role in negotiating the eventual union with the Heriot's Trust.

While the 1869 Act had proved unhelpful, subsequent legislation, the Endowed Institution (Scotland) Act 1878, revived the hopes of the institution's directors. They estimated that 'endowments of at least £1,000 to £1,500 a year were required to maintain the school in a state of efficiency'.[145] Mr W. S. B. McLaren, in a lecture at the institution in December 1878, presented his report on technical education based on visits to a number of continental trade schools in Belgium, France and Switzerland. He declared that 'there was not one of them with such a complete range of subjects and of evening studies offered for the working classes as in the Watt School of Arts'.[146] The directors of the Watt Institution at their meeting on 22 November 1878 requested Lord Shand 'to draw up a Memorial to the Trustees of Heriot's Hospital and [of] the Merchant Company soliciting a yearly grant to the funds of the Institution'. Lord Shand submitted the memorial, emphasising that the school had educated over 32,000 students in its 58 years, but the Merchant Company, having already reorganised its schools, did not take up Shand's proposal. The Heriot's Trust, however, responded positively, proposing to insert in their draft provisional order under the new Act a clause giving them powers to take over the institution.[147] The way forward now seemed clear. The Endowed School Commissioners recommended acceptance of the order and ministerial opinion was believed to favour it. For reasons which remain somewhat obscure, the order failed to secure parliamentary approval. Each year from 1879 onwards the institution confidently expected that it would be taken over and financed by the Heriot's Trust within months and, partly as a consequence, subscribers failed to respond to appeals, however urgent. Efforts by the Watt Club and the directors fell on deaf ears and the financial position deteriorated.[148]

The new Endowed Institutions (Scotland) Act was passed in 1882 and gave the commissioners far-reaching responsibilities, including the power to submit their own schemes for the reorganisation of endowments to the Scotch Education Department, which had been established in 1872 and existed for many years 'only as a name printed on a door in Whitehall'. At the hearings of the commission chaired by Lord Balfour of Burleigh (and with Lord Shand as one of its most prominent members), Professor Fleeming Jenkin (a director) and Dr Stevenson Macadam (a senior lecturer in chemistry who had already proved an eloquent advocate for the institution) recommended the improvements outlined in Shand's memorial of 1879. Fleeming Jenkin (1833–1885), who had been the first professor of engineering at the University of Edinburgh since 1868, had worked with Lord Kelvin on the insulation of electric cables.[149] Dr Stevenson Macadam (1829–1901) had studied chemistry at the Anderson Institution in his native Glasgow, took his PhD at Giessen, conducted research on vulcanology, iodine and water supply, and succeeded Wilson as lecturer in chemistry in 1855.[150]

The commission heard the grim evidence that in 1881–82 external income, not arising from fees, was a mere £174; that from this meagre sum the institution was providing 25 classes in winter, 17 in summer – for which 3,000 class tickets had been issued – and that the average salary of the 17 lecturers was £50 9s 4d.[151] Macadam informed the commission that in 1881–82 he received £36 10s 0d for teaching chemistry and £15 5s for the practical class; that Mr Lees was paid £31 5s for his six-month course on natural philosophy while Dr Pryde delivered the English course for £43 10s.[152]

Macadam's evidence also revealed how far the lecturers effectively subsidised the teaching and, even more, the provision of apparatus and equipment, from their own pockets; their net earnings were clearly negligible or even negative:

> The School possesses absolutely nothing in the way of chemical apparatus. . . . The lecturer must supply everything – all the apparatus and chemicals he uses; and he must also . . . have his own assistants. . . . The apparatus for the single course of lectures in chemistry will amount to about £300 in all; . . . and the Directors of the School supply no part of it. Even the use and waste of chemicals . . . must be borne by the lecturers.[153]

Such derisory levels of payment had prompted a letter from Mr James Pryde in March 1872, after 33 years lecturing on mathematics, indicating his intention to retire. When first appointed in 1839 he was paid 15 guineas annually and this was raised eventually to £41 10s 0d. However, Pryde argued that during his three decades in the post he had 'received £25 per annum less than my fair proportion of salary . . . a sum amounting to £1,882'.[154] Alleging that he had raised this concern on numerous occasions with Dr Murray, he was informed that 'we gain by your classes and lose by the others'.[155] The directors 'were unanimously of the opinion that Pryde had no claim against the Institution', whereupon Pryde conceded meekly and agreed to 'continue to conduct the classes as usual'.[156] The directors' response was to add the sum of £5 to his salary the following winter.

Fleeming Jenkin performed many duties on behalf of the school, including checking accommodation and teaching standards in a number of classes and soliciting books for the library,[157] but he did not want radical change. He articulated a limited vision for the school in his testimony, while protecting the interests of engineering at the University of Edinburgh, where he was professor of engineering:

> I feel that it is of importance that this large technical college which we are contemplating should grow up by degrees . . . rather than that any attempt should be made to found with a large capital some new school which would tend, in my opinion, to aim much too high and would be a sort of small rival to the university. . . . The teaching goes as high as is required in evening classes. . . . It is not desirable that the Watt Institution should overlap the university teaching.[158]

Fleeming Jenkin did not advocate technical classes in the daytime in Edinburgh not, he asserted, because it would interfere with the university, but because the 'technical school would become another college for the upper classes'.[159] To protect

Professor Fleeming Jenkin, director of the Watt Institution and School of Arts and professor of engineering at the University of Edinburgh from 1868. Engraving by William Hole

the interests of the university, Fleeming Jenkin resorted to the argument used by the founders in the 1820s that the instruction intended for workmen and foremen should be of a 'different kind from the scientific instruction for the professional classes, and that the two should not clash'.[160] He did approve, however, of successful students moving on to degree programmes. A somewhat different perspective was articulated by Dr Macadam, who considered that 'evening classes should look forward to being feeders for day classes where intelligent apprentices and artisans with bursaries or scholarships may ... pursue their studies'.[161] Disagreeing with Fleeming Jenkin, he 'did not think it would interfere with the usefulness of the university' but 'would act as a great spur to the university for increased exertions on the part of the university's professors'.[162]

Whatever their differences on the question of daytime classes, Fleeming Jenkin and Macadam agreed on the priority of technical subjects relative to what they disparagingly described as 'literary subjects'. Fleeming Jenkin 'would rather sacrifice some of those literary subjects than depart from the teaching in the purely technical branches'.[163] Macadam regarded the literary department as at best unimportant and at worst a threat to recruitment into the technical subjects, so he advocated that either it should be in a separate building or it could be taken over by other institutions in Edinburgh.[164]

The testimony of witnesses, skilfully elicited by Lord Shand, was that £2,000 was the minimum annual sum necessary to maintain and improve existing teaching provision; any expansion would require double that amount.[165] The commissioners rejected the trustees' proposals to retain their day schools and put forward their own scheme for a governing body on which town councillors would be in a bare majority and required that the trust pay not less than £4,000 a year to the institution, hereafter to be called Heriot-Watt College.[166] The trustees then piloted the scheme through the Scotch Education Department, the Privy Council Committee for Education in Scotland, and Parliament; it was finally approved by Queen Victoria in Council on 12 August 1885 when the name of the new institution, Heriot-Watt College, became effective.

The college was to be governed through a committee of the Heriot's Trust consisting of not more than 21 members, of whom initially 7 were life members nominated by the directors of the School of Arts (these were Shand; Fleeming Jenkin; Robert Bryson; John Milne, brass founder; William Raeburn, brewer; John Marshall, rector of the High School; and Miss Mary Burton). The other members were to be governors of the Heriot's Trust, whose number would increase from 14 as the life members died. As the governors now included, in addition to councillors, members of the school board, ministers, two members of the *senatus* of Edinburgh University and one member each from the Royal Society of Edinburgh and the Edinburgh Chamber of Commerce, a reasonable spread of interest among the committee was likely.

The aims of the new college, as defined by the Endowments Commissioners, implied a rejection of the views of Macadam and Fleeming Jenkin and a belated recognition of an existing reality:

A College for providing technical and general education for the industrial classes of both sexes on a scale suitable to the great and increasing wants of these classes.[167]

Moreover, the governors of George Heriot's Trust also envisaged establishing classes during the day and the provision of new laboratories and special classes for boys leaving George Heriot's School who were to be granted preference in admissions.[168]

New College, New Leadership

The first ever principal was to be appointed 'at a fixed yearly salary of not less than £500 plus such payment as the governors may think fit for teaching any of the classes'.[169] The range of powers and responsibilities vested in the principal were extensive:

> The Principal shall exercise a general supervision over the teaching of the college, and shall have under his control . . . the whole organisation, discipline, and management of the college including the power of expelling pupils from the college or suspending their attendance thereat, subject to an appeal to the governors.[170]

The governors, after consultation with the principal, had the 'power of appointing and dismissing all professors, lecturers and teachers'.[171] In this way the college became, with the Royal Technical College, Glasgow (now the University of Strathclyde) and the Manchester College of Science and Technology (now UMIST), one of only three non-university institutions in the United Kingdom with the privilege of appointing professors, a sign of the status which the commissioners conferred on it.

The scheme represented a change in the mission of the institution and was much more far-reaching than anything that had been proposed by the directors of the Watt Institution, let alone by the Heriot's Trust. It proposed a college whose core was to be in an extended range of the basic scientific and technical subjects and implied that these might be taught to a level comparable with that of universities, thus prefiguring the central institutions. By obliging the trustees of the Heriot's Trust to hand over their day schools to the school board, it ensured that the funds necessary for the Watt Institution's development would be available, and thus gave the Watt Institution the financial foundation it had so long needed, but on a far more generous scale than it had ever expected. The dynamic, fast-growing but impecunious phase of the Watt Institution was over, to be resurrected and baptised to a new life as a fully-fledged technical college. There was no great celebration as there had been in 1872 when the Chambers Street building was opened; the new enhanced status of the institution was unheralded. The investment by the Heriot's Trust was conditional on the name Heriot being incorporated in the baptismal ceremony. This did not meet with the approval of Leonard Horner's family and on 4 April 1879 his daughter Mary wrote to Sir James Gibson-Craig, third baronet of Riccarton, concerning the proposed name change:

that *his name* connected with it should go down to posterity. ... My Father was the sole originator and founder of it, as had been repeatedly acknowledged. To call it the Heriot-Watt College for the industrial classes would be most unjust, if it must have a compound name, I hope it may be called the *Heriot, Watt and Horner College*. I know my Father never thought of self in any of his good deeds, but for his fellow citizens to omit such a tribute to his memory would, I think, be very unjust.[172]

This plea did not meet with a positive response so that Horner remains to this day the unsung hero of the institution.

The Decline of the Mechanics' Institute Movement

At a time when the Watt Institution was on the threshold of the new era, what were the fortunes of the mechanics' institute movement? Up to about 1875 it was still vigorous, especially in Scotland and northern England, but by 1900 many mechanics' institutes, perhaps the majority, had perished and many others maintained an attenuated existence.[173] As we have seen, the mechanics' institutes, as originally developed, embodied four elements which are clearly distinguishable: technical education by lectures and classes, a library element, art galleries and museums, and a social dimension which forced its way in against the wishes of many founding fathers (especially in Scotland) and which found expression in concerts, soirées, excursions and other recreational activities. The social and general education provision emerged much later and was less dominant at the Watt Institution than at the English institutes. Their functions as libraries, art galleries and museums were taken over by local authorities after mid-century; it was this role in technical education that was most enduring. The institutes were in essence the beginnings of the British technical education system.

The mechanics' institutes were helped in many areas by the creation of the Department of Science and Art in 1853, which made government funds available for technical education for the first time. The aid took the form of 'payment by results' to teachers.[174] The mechanics' institutes (including the Edinburgh School of Art) were ready to work in alliance with the department by arranging science classes, which were able to find a new role at a time when it seemed they had lost working-class support. There were 70 mechanics' institutes which ran such classes in 1878 – the most popular subjects being mathematics and chemistry – and the number of students in attendance was 6,670.[175] A further timely development helped the survival of the institutes: the Society of Arts introduced an examination system from 1857. The philosophy underlying the formation of the Department of Science and Art was that of local initiative based on the belief that the government should not do for people what they ought to do for themselves. The consequence of this policy was a gross inequality of provision between one part of the country and another.[176] In the final quarter of the century, the Victorians moved gradually along the spectrum from laissez-faire non-intervention to ever greater degrees of support and education, motivated in part by Britain's relative industrial decline vis-à-vis Germany. But had the founders of mechanics' institutes succeeded in persuading governments to take up the cause of mechanics' institutes earlier, the history of nineteenth-century technical education and indeed of Britain's industrial progress might have been very different.[177] The late and stunted growth of technical and scientific education, due to industrialists' suspicion of education, the mystique of practical experience, and unattractive job and promotion opportunities for science graduates, explained much of Britain's industrial retardation.[178]

During the second half of the nineteenth century, the provision of technical education was gradually taken over by the local authorities so that the scope of the institutes became restricted, until eventually they survived, if at all, as social clubs.[179] Continuity was maintained as many of the people managing the new technical institutes were the same people who had formerly been responsible for the mechanics' institute. After two Royal Commissions and a select committee on the subject of technical education,[180] the government passed the Technical Instruction Act of 1889 and the new system was operated through technical instruction committees appointed by county and borough councils. Few institutes, however, were transformed into technical colleges (e.g. Heriot-Watt College, Glasgow Royal Technical College, Leeds College of Technology and Manchester College of Technology) and even within these there was a failure to develop (or even seriously to plan for) actual technical research, unlike the Franklin Institute in Boston. Many other institutes simply disappeared or were transformed into art schools, day schools, libraries or museums.

Even in the nineteenth century, commentators were acutely aware that mechanics' institutes had failed to attract large numbers of working-class students: 'The banquet was prepared for guests who did not come,'[181] wrote Robert Elliott in 1861. J. W. Hudson, Samuel Smiles and others echoed this theme and later historians, notably E. P. Thompson, agreed that 'after the mid-twenties the tendency was general for the custom of artisans to give way to that of the lower middle class'.[182] The rapid growth in clerical occupations after about 1870 created a demand for an educated body of clerks and stimulated a need for further education, both in general subjects and vocational topics such as bookkeeping and shorthand. The presence of a growing lower middle-class element may have tended to deter working-class students, conscious of their different manners, dress and speech.

While weariness after work, scanty leisure time and a lack of basic education were important reasons for the failure of mechanics' institutes to realise their original objectives, and periods of economic recession influenced the rise and fall of their fortunes, there was another factor – the lack of a sense of fellowship – which also hastened the demise of many institutes. While directors regularly deplored the competition provided by the public house, they generally ignored the comparison which could also be made with the experience of trade unions, friendly societies and Chartist clubs;[183] and the growing popularity of the pleasure garden, the dancing saloon, and the music hall. In the saloon or political club, working men met their own class and shared their interests in a convivial atmosphere. At the mechanics' institutes there was the strain of mixing with middle-class employers combined with the effort to be mentally alert. Pursuit of knowledge in the mechanics' institute was usually a means to an end; it had an individualistic purpose and the numerous class prizes helped to promote an ethos of competition rather than cooperation: the Dick Whittington motive was the predominant reaction. Working people for the most part, after ten or more hours' labour each day would not flog their intellects till bedtime through manuals of chemistry or political economy. The vision of Dick Whittington gradually faded, for it became apparent that opportunity as well as inherent ability was required if the highly stratified British social pyramid was to be scaled. The able industrial worker turned his attention more to organising through trade unions, seeking a sense of fellowship and common purpose which mechanics' institutes did not supply.[184] To the economic and social aspirations of the workers, the middle-class directors were largely indifferent, while applauding the upward climb of the few Watts and Rennies.

The mechanics' institutes of England and Wales failed in a limited sense to become all that they might have been, to be what they were thought to have been, and they failed to live up to the expectations of their patrons.[185] They did not attract a majority of working men or teach much science, unlike the institutes in the larger Scottish towns.[186] Royle argues:

Engels' charge that the institutes were, or became, nothing more than instruments of the bourgeoisie, is at best only partly true. ... Behind the appearance of institutes with a large middle-class, hearing middle-class lectures, lies solid achievement – an achievement which helped other, more ostensibly working-class, movements to improve the conditions of working men.[187]

One obvious area of achievement was in greatly boosting the library movement. For much of the nineteenth century a neighbourhood's most accessible book supply was to be found within the institutes. They made a similar contribution to the creation of many local museums.[188] Even their survival, albeit in a modified form, is testimony to the power of the idea that leisure should be devoted to self-improvement, not self-indulgence. At a conference on technical education in Edinburgh in 1868, Mr George Harrison, chairman of the Chamber of Commerce, observed:

> A large proportion of the mechanics' institutes have degenerated into a mere means of amusement, or at best, content themselves with the production of popular and desultory lectures. . . . In Edinburgh, . . . they still adhere very closely to the curriculum which they started.[189]

Mr James Mitchell, a brass finisher, representing the School of Arts, also presented oral evidence:

> Mechanics' institutes require to be remodelled. If you study the programmes of these institutes you will find a lecture on Charles Dickens; another on paper-making; a third on 'A Race through Spain'; and a fourth on Chemistry. Now that kind of popular lecture will never do. (Hear hear) What we want is that the pupils commence from the first and go through a process of daily training. . . . The Edinburgh School of Arts is a model to a great extent of what real mechanics' institutions ought to be.[190]

Horner and Bryson had created an institution that served as a role model for others elsewhere, that had succeeded despite severe financial constraints, and finally, with the investment of Heriot's endowment, had a secure basis on which to develop the college to meet the complex demands for technical education at the end of the nineteenth century.

Notes

1 From 1857 it came under the Education Department.

2 Butt, J. (1996) *John Anderson's Legacy: The University of Strathclyde and Its Antecedents, 1796–1996*, East Linton, p. 70.

3 *Ibid.*, pp. 70–71.

4 *Ibid.*, p. 70.

5 HWUA, SA 4/3, *Calendar and Syllabus of Lectures of the Watt Institution and School of Arts*, 1878–79, p. 20.

6 *Ibid.*, p. 20.

7 *Ibid.*, p. 20.

8 HWUA, SA 1/3/2, *Minute Book of the Directors*, 1869–1885.

9 *Ibid.*, p. 30.

10 *Ibid.*, p. 37.

11 Tylecote, M. (1957) *The Mechanics' Institutes of Lancashire and Yorkshire Before 1851*, Manchester, p. 139.

12 Davidoff, L. and Hall, C. (2002) *Family Fortunes*, 2nd edn, London, pp. XV–XVI.

13 *Ibid.*, p. 451.

14 Kelly, T. (1957) *George Birkbeck: Pioneer of Adult Education*, Liverpool, p. 126.

15 Hudson, J. W. (1851) *The History of Adult Education*, London, p. 131.

16 Tylecote, *op. cit.*, p. 264.

17 *Annual Report of the Manchester Mechanics' Institution*, 1847, p. 44. Quoted in Tylecote, *op. cit.*, p. 186.

18 *Ibid.*, p. 186.

19 *Ibid.*, p. 187.

20 Butt, *op. cit.*, p. 22.

21 *Ibid.*, p. 22.

22 *Ibid.*, p. 22.

23 The unsuccessful struggle of an Englishwoman, Sophia Jex-Blake, to train as a doctor at Edinburgh University marshalled support for the cause of women's university education in Scotland. Miss Jex-Blake won the first round in the struggle when women were permitted to matriculate and attend classes in 1869. There then occurred the famous Surgeon's Hall riot of 1870 when male students revealed their prejudices and opposition by hustling and impeding women from attending an anatomy lecture. See Hamilton, S. (1983) The first generations of university women, 1869–1930. In Donaldson, G. (ed.) *Four Centuries of Edinburgh University Life*, Edinburgh, pp. 100–103.

24 Jones, A. (forthcoming) Mary Burton. In Harrison, B. (ed.) *New Dictionary of National*

Biography, Oxford. Jones, A. (2000) Rescued from oblivion? The case of Mary Burton and Liberton Bank House, *Scottish Archives*, Vol. 6, p. 50.

[25] *The Scotsman*, 22 March 1909.

[26] Jones (2000) *op. cit.*, p. 49.

[27] In 1889 she unsuccessfully urged the Edinburgh School Board to petition Parliament to enable country or town councils to provide schools free of charge; see Jones, *op. cit.*

[28] *Edinburgh Evening News*, 24 March 1885; quoted in Jones (forthcoming) *op. cit.*

[29] Jones (forthcoming) *op. cit.*

[30] Tooley, Sarah A. (1932) Notable Victorians, some recollections of Edinburgh's foremost women. Third article: Miss Louisa Stevenson, Miss Flora Stevenson, Miss Hill-Burton. *The Weekly Scotsman*, 20 February 1932.

[31] HWUA, SA 1/3/2, *Minute Book of the Directors*, 1869–1885, meeting of the directors 8 October 1869.

[32] *Ibid.*, Committee on the Admission of Female Students, 1 November 1869.

[33] *Ibid.*, meeting of the directors, 1 November 1869.

[34] *Ibid.*, meeting of the directors, 14 April 1870.

[35] Jones (2000), *op. cit.*, p. 52.

[36] Edinburgh University Library EUL Gen. 1877/15.3. Letter from Mary Burton to Mary Crudelius, 31 March 1870. Quoted by Jones, A. (2000) *op. cit.*, p. 52.

[37] Edinburgh University Library EUL Gen. 1877/5, Minutes of Fifteenth Meeting (General) 13 April 1870.

[38] HWUA SA 2/3/1, Press cuttings relating to laying of foundation stone, Watt Institution.

[39] *Ibid.*, *Daily Review*.

[40] HWUA, SA 1/3/2, *Minute Book of the Directors*, 1869–1885, meeting of the directors 3 November 1873. The author of the letter would almost certainly have been either Flora or Louise Stevenson, both renowned campaigners for women's rights to education and the vote. Flora Stevenson served on the Edinburgh School Board from 1873; in 1885 she was joined by Mary Burton. Both Stevensons were subscribers to the Watt Institution and School of Arts by 1875–76. Jones, A. (2000) *op. cit.*, p. 53; HWUA, SA 1/1/27, p. 19.

[41] *Ibid.*

[42] Scotland, J. (1969) *The History of Scottish Education*, London, Vol. 2, p. 159.

[43] HWUA, SA 5/3, Address by Lord Shand, 1 November 1877.

[44] Pryde, D. (1893) *Pleasant Memories of a Busy Life*, Edinburgh, pp. 86–87, p. 97.

[45] *Ibid.*, pp. 87–88.

[46] *Ibid.*, p. 84.

[47] Mill, H. R. (1951) *An Autobiography*, London, pp. 20–21.

[48] HWUA, SA 14/3/2, Letter from H. R. Mill to Mr Bates, 30 November 1887.

[49] Anderson, A. and Gowenlock, B. G. (1998) *Chemistry at Heriot-Watt, 1821–1991*, Edinburgh, p. 23.

[50] HWUA, SA 13/4/3, Minutes of evidence taken before the Select Committee on Scientific Instruction (1868) p. 372.

[51] Anderson and Gowenlock, *op. cit.*, p. 24.

[52] HWUA, SA 13/4/3, *op. cit.*, p. 375.

[53] Pryde, *op. cit.*, p. 91.

[54] *Ibid.*, p. 93.

[55] Marwick, W. M. (1933) Adult educationalists in Victorian Scotland, *Journal of Adult Education*, Vol. 6, April, p. 134.

[56] Pryde, *op. cit.*, pp. 96–97.

[57] HWUA, SA 6/1/1, Mr Kemp's Notes on Economic Science.

[58] Ovenden, R. (1997) *John Thomson, 1837–1921, Photographer*, Edinburgh, p. 1. Much of the discussion of Thomson's career is drawn from this source.

[59] *Ibid.*, p. 5.

[60] HWUA, SA 1/1/19, pp. 7, 9; SA/1/20, pp. 7–8.

[61] See *Catalogue of the Library of the Edinburgh School of Arts*, Edinburgh, pp. 22, 29. Quoted in Ovenden, *op. cit.*, pp. 4, 6.

[62] Ovenden, *op. cit.*, p. 6.

[63] *Ibid.*, p. 6.

[64] *Ibid.*, p. 167.

[65] Thomson, J. (1886) Practical photography in tropical regions, *British Journal of Photography*, 10 August 1886, p. 404.

[66] *Ibid.*, p. 404.

[67] Ovenden, *op. cit*, p. 176.

[68] *Ibid.*, footnote 69, p. 203.

[69] Puttnam, D. (1997) Foreword in Ovenden, *op.cit*, p. vii.

[70] *Ibid.*, p. vii.

[71] Royal Geographical Society Archives, Letter, Thomson & Mr Hinks, 10 February 1921. Quoted in Ovenden, *op. cit.*, p. 184.

[72] Anderson, R. D. (1983) *Education and Opportunity in Victorian Scotland*, Oxford, p. 330.

[73] HWUA, SA/11/1, *Inauguration of the James Watt Statue*, 1854, pp. 5–6.

[74] *Ibid.*, p. 23.

[75] Leonard Horner wrote on 1 January 1855 approving the objects of this club but requesting that it should be called the School of Arts Watt Club. This was agreed. See HWUA, JWC1/1, Minutes of the Meetings of the Watt Institution Club.

[76] *Ibid.*

[77] *Ibid.*, HWA JWC1/1, pp. 11–12. A description of the dinner on 20 January follows the minutes of the meeting on 8 January 1855.

[78] *Ibid.*, p. 93.

[79] *Ibid.*, p. 147, AGM of the Watt Club, 31 October 1870.

[80] This was at Mary Burton's suggestion. *Ibid.*, p. 151, AGM of the Watt Club, 30 October 1871.

[81] HWUA, SA 8/2/1/1, *Excelsior Magazine.*

[82] *Ibid.*

[83] *Ibid.*

[84] HWUA, SA 8/2/1/1, *op. cit.*, Part 1, Vol. 3, November 1864.

[85] Pryde, *op. cit.*, pp. 89–90.

[86] HWUA, HWC 4/1/1, *The Watt Literary and Debating Association, Minutes of the Committee and Special Business Meetings*, 1872–1891.

[87] *The British Controversialist*, 1870.

[88] Moir, D. G. (ed.) (1929) *A History of the Heriot-Watt College Literary Society: 1868–1928*, Edinburgh, p. 11.

[89] HWUA, HWC 4/1/1, *op. cit.*

[90] *Ibid.*

[91] Moir, *op. cit.*, p. 11.

[92] HWUA, HWC 4/1/1, *op. cit.*, Secretary's Annual Report, April 1884.

[93] *Ibid.*, April 1885.

[94] *Ibid.*, 31 May 1878 and 30 May 1879.

[95] *Ibid.*, 8 April 1881.

[96] *Ibid.*, 6 April 1882, April 1884, April 1885.

[97] *Ibid.*, April 1884.

[98] HWUA, SA 1/1/23, *Annual Report of the Directors*, 1866–67, pp. 8–9.

[99] *Ibid.*, p. 12.

[100] I am grateful to Dr Norman Reid for drawing my attention to this point.

[101] HWUA, SA 1/3/2, *Minute Book of the Directors*, 1869–1885, meeting of the directors 11 September 1871.

[102] Reid, N. (1984) Heriot-Watt: An Edinburgh Institution. Mimeo.

[103] HWUA, SA 1/3/2, *Minute Book of the Directors*, 1869–1885, meeting of the directors 6 May 1872.

[104] Stewart, T. (1998) Masonic processions reconsidered. A lecture delivered on 7 November 1998, Edinburgh Castle Lodge, No. 1764, pp. 11, 12.

[105] *The Scotsman*, 10 October 1872.

[106] *Ibid.*

[107] *Ibid.*

[108] *Ibid.*

[109] HWUA, SA 2/3/1, *The Edinburgh Courant*, October 1872.

[110] *The Scotsman*, 10 October 1872.

[111] *Ibid.*

[112] HWUA, SA 2/3/1, *The Edinburgh Courant*, October 1872.

[113] *The Scotsman*, 10 October 1872.

[114] HWUA, SA 1/3/2, *Minute Book of the Directors*, 1869–1885.

[115] *The Scotsman*, 1 November 1873.

[116] HWUA, SA 1/1/26, *Annual Report of the Directors*, 1873–74, p. 9.

[117] HWUA, SA 1/1/27, *Annual Report of the Directors*, 1875–76, p. 9.

[118] HWUA, SA 1/3/2, *Minute Book of the Directors*, 1869–1885.

[119] *Ibid.*, meeting of the directors 7 December 1877.

[120] *Ibid.*, meeting of the directors 14 June 1878.

[121] *Ibid.*, meeting of the directors 18 October 1878.

[122] HWUA, SA 4/3, *Calendar*, 1878–79, *op. cit.*, p. 52.

[123] Tylecote, *op. cit.*, p. 153.

[124] At the Manchester Mechanics' Institution, works on general literature came to outnumber those on scientific subjects by the 1830s, and by 1849 the largest section in the library was 'Novels, Romances and Tales'; see Tylecote, *op. cit.*, p. 133.

[125] HWUA, SA 4/3, *Calendar*, 1878–79, p. 53.

[126] HWUA, SA 1/1/27, *Report of the Directors of the Watt Institution and School of Arts*, 1883–84, p. 8.

[127] HWUA, SA 1/1/27, *Report of the Directors of the Watt Institution and School of Arts*, 1878–79, p. 15.

[128] Anderson and Gowenlock, *op. cit.*, p. 28.

[129] Smout, T.C. (1986) *A Century of the Scottish People 1850–1950*, London, p. 221.

[130] *Ibid.*, p. 221.

[131] Anderson, *op. cit.*, p. 183.

[132] Smout, *op. cit.*, p. 222.

[133] Anderson, *op. cit.*, p. 26.

[134] *Ibid.*, p. 200.

[135] The state took over statutory parochial schools, replaced the old managers (usually the minister) by a democratically elected school board, thereby making the schools independent of church control, and thus established a complete network of schools over the whole country. Some success resulted: within 30 years, illiteracy for both sexes had been virtually eliminated. See Smout, *op. cit.*, p. 219.

[136] Anderson and Gowenlock, *op. cit.*, p. 29.

[137] *The Scotsman*, 23 June 1873.

[138] *Ibid.*

[139] *Ibid.*

[140] *Ibid.*

[141] HWUA, SA 1/1/27, *Annual Report of the Directors*, 1881–82, pp. 11, 15.

[142] Anderson and Gowenlock, *op. cit.*, p. 30.

[143] *Dictionary of National Biography*, 1901–1911, Oxford, p. 295.

[144] Anderson and Gowenlock, *op. cit.*, p. 30.

[145] HWUA, SA 1/1/27, *Annual Report of the Directors*, 1877–78, p. 15.

[146] *Ibid.*, p. 15.

[147] Anderson and Gowenlock, *op. cit.*, p. 31.

[148] *Ibid.*, p. 32.

[149] *Concise Dictionary of National Biography* (1930), Oxford, p. 686.

[150] Anderson and Gowenlock, *op. cit.*, p. 23.

[151] HWUA, SA 13/2/1, *First Report of the Educational Endowed Institutions (Scotland) Commission 1884*, pp. 776–77.

[152] *Ibid.*, p. 793.

[153] *Ibid.*, pp. 792–93.

[154] HWUA, SA 1/3/2, *Minute Book of the Directors of the School of Arts*, 1869–85, *op. cit.* Letter from James Pryde to Dr William H. Gray, March 1872.

[155] *Ibid.*

[156] *Ibid.*

[157] *Ibid.*, 2 August 1875; 4 May 1877; 15 November 1877; April 1878.

[158] HWUA, SA 13/2/1, *op. cit.*, pp. 780–81.

[159] *Ibid.*, p. 782.

[160] *Ibid.*, p. 782.

[161] *Ibid.*, p. 796.

[162] *Ibid.*, p. 796.

[163] *Ibid.*, p. 783.

[164] *Ibid.*, p. 795.

[165] Anderson and Gowenlock, *op. cit.*, pp. 32–33.

[166] *Heriot-Watt University: From Mechanics Institute to Technological University 1821–1973*, Edinburgh, pp. 12–14.

[167] HWUA, SA 3/1/4, *Calendar of the Watt Institution and School of Arts*, 1884–85, p. 28.

[168] *Ibid.*, p. 31.

[169] *Ibid.*, p. 31.

[170] *Ibid.*, p. 32.

[171] *Ibid.*, p. 32.

[172] HWUA, SA 14/1/1/10, 4 April 1879, Mary Lyell to Mr Gibson Craig.

[173] Kelly, *op. cit.*, Liverpool, p. 271.

[174] Roderick, G. W. and Stephens, M. D. (1985) Steam intellect created – the educational roles of mechanics' institutes. In Inkster, I. (ed.) *The Steam Intellect Societies: Essays on Culture, Education and Industry, circa 1820–1914*, Nottingham, p. 28.

[175] *Ibid.*, p. 29.

[176] Roderick, G. W. and Stephens, M. D. (1985) Mechanics' institutes and the state. In Inkster, I. (ed.) *op. cit.*, p. 67.

[177] *Ibid.*, p. 71.

[178] Landes, D. (1968) *The Unbound Prometheus*, Cambridge, p. 344.

[179] Kelly, *op. cit.*, p. 271.

[180] Select Committee on Instruction in Science for the Industrial Classes 1868; Royal Commission on Scientific Instruction 1872–75; Royal Commission on Technical Instruction 1882–84.

[181] Elliott, R. (1861) On the working men's reading rooms, as established in 1848 at Carlisle. *Transactions of the National Association for the Promotion of Social Science*, p. 676.

[182] Thompson, E. P. (1963) *The Making of the English Working Class*, London, p. 745.

[183] Tylecote, *op. cit.*, pp. 111–12.

[184] *Ibid.*, p. 119.

[185] Royle, E. (1971) Mechanics' institutes and the working classes, 1840–1860, *Historical Journal*, Vol. XIV, no. 2, p. 320.

[186] At the Manchester Mechanics' Institute, lectures in science declined from 235 in 1835–39 to 68 in 1845–49. See Cotgrove, S. F. (1958) *Technical Education and Social Change*, London, p. 47.

[187] Royle, E. (1971) *op. cit.*, pp. 320–21.

[188] *The Glasgow Mechanics Magazine and Annals of Philosophy*, 1838, 1, p. 80.

[189] HWUA, SA 13/4/2, Conference on technical education. *Transactions of the Royal Society of Arts*, Vol. VII, no. iv, p. 447 (1868).

[190] *Ibid.*, pp. 452–53.

Chapter Five

Changing Times: 1885–1928

Education ... has produced a vast
population able to read but unable to
distinguish what is worth reading.
G. M. Trevelyan

*Heriot-Watt College in the early 20th century, showing busts of Horner and Heriot
above the main entrance and the statue of James Watt*

A Safe Pair of Hands: Francis Grant Ogilvie

The Paris exhibitions of 1867 and 1878 had revealed the extent of the British shortfall in technical education, and the government of Gladstone, thoroughly perturbed, established the Samuelson Commission on Technical Instruction. It spent four years investigating arrangements in Britain and on the continent, where it found systematic instruction, better equipment, state aid and a higher quality of teaching.[1] The commission paid a brief visit to Edinburgh and singled out the Watt Institution as being 'one of the most important evening schools in the United Kingdom'.[2] The commission's recommendations, issued in 1884, set the pattern for British technical education for many years. Stung by the implications of this report, the government passed the Technical Schools (Scotland) Act of 1887, which allowed certain funds held by local authorities to be applied to technical education. The Act, however, was not very effective and defined technical education as 'instruction in the branches of Science and Art with respect to which grants are for the time being paid'.[3] The pursuit of a consistent policy with respect to technical education was hindered by lack of political stability: in the 50 years between the fall of Lord Rosebury's government in 1895 and the election of a Labour government under Clement Attlee in 1945, there were to be only two periods of normal majority government by a single party: the Liberals after 1906 and the Conservatives after 1924.

In the dying years of the nineteenth century, however, the Heriot endowment held out the alluring prospect of transforming the college from a struggling voluntary body that survived on meagre students' fees and declining subscription income – and where grossly underpaid lecturers provided their own apparatus to teach large classes in cramped premises – into a fully-fledged technical college with new buildings and laboratories, headed by a principal. Nevertheless, the new Heriot's Trust trustees proceeded cautiously and left the existing programme to run for two years while they sought advice. Meanwhile the period between midsummer 1885 and the beginning of the administration of the Heriot-Watt College Committee early in 1886 saw the departure of three important figures: Professor Fleeming Jenkin died in June 1885; and early in 1886, two more of the seven newly nominated life-governors – sons of original directors of the School of Arts, Robert Bryson and John Milne – both died. With their deaths, representation of master mechanics on the College Committee ended, although this does not appear to have affected subsequent college strategy.

The new Heriot-Watt College Committee appointed a subcommittee which invited Mr, later Sir, Philip Magnus, director of the City and Guilds of London Institute and an authority on technical education, to make proposals for the future direction of the institution. Magnus visited Edinburgh and reported on 18 January 1886. He envisaged the college as a place where

> artisans, clerks and others occupied in trade or commerce may supplement their previous education by evening instruction, and in which youths leaving school about 15 years may continue their education during the day for two or three years before entering some industrial occupation. Because of numbers the Evening Department would be more important.[4]

He also emphasised that the scientific tuition should be strongly laboratory based; and he recommended that there should be a principal, preferably a scientist, who would double as a professor in one of the departments (either physics or mechanics). Magnus went on to specify in detail the accommodation needs of departments, library and administrative offices, and concluded that 'the present building in Chambers Street is defective in every respect. ... I cannot recommend that money be expended to adapt [it]'; he therefore proposed totally rebuilding, preferably on a new but nearby site.[5] The College Committee accepted Magnus's academic recommendations without qualification but, as to buildings, John Chesser, superintendent of works to the Heriot's Trust, argued that the cheapest alternative (a characteristic emphasis) was to gut the existing Chambers Street building and extend it at both ends. The committee agreed. This was a fortunate decision, for adjacent land soon became available.[6]

On 7 May 1886 the committee interviewed two candidates for the post of principal and agreed to recommend to the governors, in order of preference, Henry Dyer and Francis Grant Ogilvie. Dyer, aged 38, was a Glasgow-trained engineer who had for 10 years been principal of the Tokyo Engineering College. Ogilvie was young, only 28, and inexperienced but he was the governors' choice. Their decision was a wise one and in 1887 he also became the first professor of physics and electrical engineering. Francis Grant Ogilvie was born at Moneymusk in 1858 and came from an Aberdeenshire family of distinction in education. His father, Alexander Ogilvie, headmaster of Robert Gordon's College, Aberdeen, was one of six brothers, five of whom became heads of famous schools or colleges; one of these, George, was headmaster of George Watson's College in Edinburgh from 1870 to 1898, and may have influenced the governors in Francis's favour. Francis, after taking an arts degree (but specialising in physics) at Aberdeen, came to Edinburgh University, where he devoted himself to science. A favourite pupil of the geologist Sir Archibald Geikie and a friend of Sir John Murray of Challenger

Francis Grant Ogilvie, first principal, 1886–1900

Voyage fame, he developed a lifelong interest in geology. He became assistant to the professor of natural philosophy at Aberdeen University in 1880–81, and the following year he was appointed the first science master at his father's school, Robert Gordon's College, Aberdeen.[7] There he first displayed a flair for administrative work.

Ogilvie took up his appointment almost immediately and went with Chesser to London to discuss with Magnus the plans for the rebuilding. Wisely he postponed the appointment of professors and the beginning of day classes until the building was complete. In his inaugural address, Ogilvie stressed his fundamental doctrine – in which he followed Horner – that technical education must have a firm base in the sciences. He departed, however, from earlier policy in proposing the introduction of trade classes and day classes, and in widening considerably the spectrum of subjects taught. His development plan, on the line of Magnus's report, proposed

- a technical department offering evening courses in physics, chemistry mechanics and engineering, mathematics, other science subjects (botany, physiology and hygiene), art, and the technology of trades such as masonry and brickwork and carpentry and joinery; the evening classes 'ought to be arranged as far as possible, in conformity with the schemes of the Science and Art Department and City & Guilds of London Institute, so that full benefit may be derived from the grants offered by these';[8]
- a day college offering subjects from the technical curriculum with some commercial classes (shorthand, practice of business, geography and modern languages);

- the continuation in the literary department of evening classes in Latin, French, English literature and bookkeeping, and the addition to them of classes in commercial geography and history, practice of business and further foreign languages;
- the continuance of the award of diplomas to students passing examinations in groups of subjects;
- the discontinuance in time of all classes which 'ought not properly to fall to the college', a category which later brought to an end the long-established course on the harmonium, among others;
- the provision of popular lectures.

The evening class programme continued in sessions 1886–87 and 1887–88 with few changes. Although doing only a moderate amount of lecturing himself, Ogilvie took part in some classes in physics and mechanics, and kept in close touch with the work of every lecturer. He also dealt tactfully with one or two long-serving lecturers whose arrangements had to be changed.[9] The rebuilding programme went ahead, alternative accommodation for classes being found in Brown Square School (a former Heriot's Day School of which the college gained and retained possession) and in the Church of Scotland Training College at the foot of Chambers Street.

The Phrenological Museum (which by then was in decline, and whose collections had been transferred to the Royal College of Surgeons) was purchased for £1,816 in 1888 and incorporated into the college building. The entrance pavilion was rebuilt on a more opulent scale 'with columns at the rope-moulded door and first floor bow window, a hammering cherub in the scrolly broken pediment and a wrought iron crown on the French pavilion roof'.[10] As part of this remodelling, the iron cresting was carried the full length of the building to create cohesion between the old and new sections. The busts of Horner and Heriot, which now grace the entrance at the Riccarton Campus, also date from this period. The bust of Horner – like that of Heriot carved from blonde sandstone – was commissioned from J. S. Rhind in 1888 at a cost of £19.[11]

Leading Lights

Thomas Hudson Beare, first professor of mechanics and engineering, 1887–1889

William Henry Perkin Junior, first professor of chemistry, who with his assistant, F. Stanley Kipping, wrote a classic textbook on organic chemistry

The time had come to appoint the first professors. Ardent, sincere, painstaking and an able administrator,[12] Ogilvie showed by the appointments made in 1887 that he was also a first-rate judge of talent. The initial salary offered to the new professors (the principal's salary was £650) attracted a fine quality of applicant.[13] A young Australian, Thomas Hudson Beare – who had come to University College London in 1879 after a spell in the Department of Public Works in South Australia – was appointed to the chair of mechanics and engineering. William Henry Perkin Junior, son of a distinguished British chemist, came from private research work after research in Germany to be professor of chemistry at the tender age of 27. Both were to become, in time, leaders in their respective fields. Ogilvie himself, in accordance with Magnus's suggestion, took the chair of physics and electrical engineering. In 1890, however, he found that combining the duties of principal with those of the chair was too much even for his abundant energy and Robert Mullineux Walmsley was appointed to the chair. Walmsley was a genial and humorous man with a handsome presence and beard who always wore a frock coat, with long tails and spats, and when outside, a top hat.[14] An astute diplomat, he had an extraordinary capacity for work, finding time not only to undertake a heavy teaching load (though he was not an outstanding lecturer), but also to act as a consulting electrical engineer and to publish two widely used textbooks during his five years at the college. Professors were permitted to supplement their salaries by consultancy work, although the governors were concerned to recover a share of the earnings on behalf of the institution where college equipment was involved:

> On any profits which may accrue to any of the Professors or Lecturers for Commercial Testing involving the use of the permanent appliances of the College, ten per cent shall be handed over to the College in recognition of the uses of such appliances.[15]

Bright young men tend to move on quickly, and these were no exceptions. Ogilvie himself moved across the road in 1900, following his appointment as director of the Royal Scottish Museum; and in 1903 he became principal assistant secretary (technology and higher education in science and arts) at the Board of Education (London). A self-effacing person – 'I never knew a man who having done so much did it so quietly or was so careless of recognition'[16] – Ogilvie's major achievement had been to establish the college as an efficient and well-administered evening and day technical and commercial institution predicated on the belief that technical education should be based in physical and chemical science.[17]

Beare, whose main contribution was the design of his laboratories and workshops, returned to a chair at University College London in 1889. He was appointed to the chair at Edinburgh University in 1891 and became effectively the doyen of British academic engineers and, as a governor from 1919 to 1938, an important influence on the Heriot-Watt College. Perkin, having in five years laid the foundations of a teaching and research school in chemistry with the help of F. Stanley Kipping, his assistant professor from 1888 to 1891, went on to chairs in Owens College Manchester and subsequently to Oxford University. He became arguably the most distinguished British organic chemist of his time. Generations of chemistry students were bred on the textbook *Organic Chemistry* by himself and Kipping, published in 1884, and based largely on their lecture courses at the college. Although undertaking a programme of evening classes, Perkin kept one evening per week free to indulge his love of chamber music; a pianist of almost professional standard, he would rise at 5.00 A.M. to practise.[18] Kipping left in 1891 and subsequently occupied the chair of chemistry at Nottingham University College. Walmsley also remained for five years before becoming in 1895 the first principal of Northampton College, London, now City University.

The second generation of professors lacked the brilliance of the first but stayed longer and, building on their predecessors' foundations, established a reputation for effective and relevant teaching that has endured to this day. Beare's successor in engineering was Richard Stanfield, a Manchester-trained engineer who had been on the staff of the Royal Mint Laboratory until he was appointed to the chair at the age of 25 in 1889. He held it for 40 years. In effect, the founder of his department as a teaching entity, he was an extremely able lecturer: clear in exposition, precise in wording and master of demonstration, he gained the confidence and affection of day and evening students, staff and colleagues alike.[19] A great success as the head of the largest department in the college, he was also an able administrator, a fact recognised by his being the regular choice to act as interim principal from 1900 onwards.

Perkin was succeeded in the chair of chemistry by John Gibson, an Edinburgh man who, like Macadam and Perkin, had studied in Germany, taking his PhD under Bunsen at Heidelberg, before working for 16 years at Edinburgh University. Primarily an analyst, he had published on the composition of sea water (a strong aversion to sea voyages compelled others to collect his samples) but published little after joining the college.[20] Though not to be compared with Perkin as a scientist, he maintained a tradition of sound teaching and laboratory work with a modicum of research and several lecturers of considerable ability were appointed to his department. He was not, however, an easy man and played less part in college life than Stanfield.

Francis Gibson Baily, the third of the new professors, studied at Cambridge and spent some years in industry before lecturing at University College, Liverpool. He succeeded to a department (physics and electrical engineering) already well established under Ogilvie and Walmsley. So began a period of 37 years' conscientious service, during which he enhanced the department's reputation for thorough training in what was still an infant subject. Personal recollections of Baily depict a perfect gentleman who, from the time of his appointment, published little [21] but encouraged research students, who remembered him with gratitude and affection.

The leading scholar among the teachers of the period was Patrick Geddes, who lectured in botany from 1886 to 1890. He taught one class per week, for which he received an annual salary of £30. To Geddes goes the credit of being the founder

Patrick Geddes in 1898, aged 44

of the summer school movement that was to change the educational world of the twentieth century; he brought to Edinburgh the first summer school in Europe in 1887.[22] Geddes had received an unconventional education, refusing to submit himself to examinations on the grounds that they stifled real learning. Nevertheless, he obtained his professorial appointment on the strength of research and publications.[23] Geddes became committed to the evolutionary view of life and used it as a basis for his work in an astonishingly wide range of fields: town planning, sociology, Celtic publishing, cultural exhibitions, as well as academic and social reform. His internationalist outlook was combined with a deep concern for the future of Scotland and he wrote scornfully of those Scots who compromised their nationality in the pursuit of 'political honours from the other side of the Tweed'.[24] An iconoclast, it is easy to see why he was unpopular with the Scottish establishment; his caustic references to the 'decaying educational mandarinate'[25] were not calculated to persuade by sweet reason. Geddes is recognised today not only as the seminal influence on sociology and planning, but also as the father of environmentalism. Ironically, when Geddes died in 1932 there was no evidence that any of his ideas on urban life, especially avoidance of social segregation and of the integration of housing and recreational space, had influenced city planning in his native Scotland. For Geddes the besetting sin of Edinburgh was respectability; it was a culture, he said in *The Evergreen*, 'frozen as if in an icepack'.[26] Like Rennie

Ramsay Garden. Photograph: Gordon Wright

Mackintosh, Geddes was a prophet unsung in his own homeland. His imperishable monument to the city that spurned him was Ramsay Garden – a unique collection of houses with distinctive red and white turn-of-the-century architecture – an indispensable part of the skyline, which forms a rousing finale to the Royal Mile as it enters the Castle Esplanade. The flats were to house artists and intellectuals dedicated to his local republic of letters.[27] Unfortunately, the college could not retain a person of this calibre for long and he subsequently became professor of botany at University College, Dundee.

Geddes' successor in botany, who also taught zoology from 1893, was J. Arthur Thomson, a prolific writer of both academic and popular works who left Edinburgh in 1899 for the chair of natural history at Aberdeen. (Sir) John S. Flett, lecturer in geology from 1895, later became director of the Geological Survey and thus a colleague of Ogilvie's in his later career. Hugh Robert Mill was persuaded by Geddes to undertake the lectureship in commercial geography in 1887, later adding physiography to his teaching. Mill, an outstanding lecturer, found his work at the college 'not much of a pleasure, as the classes were small, and the few students who developed a real interest drifted away after a single session'.[28] During his time at the college, Mill wrote some of the first and most successful elementary

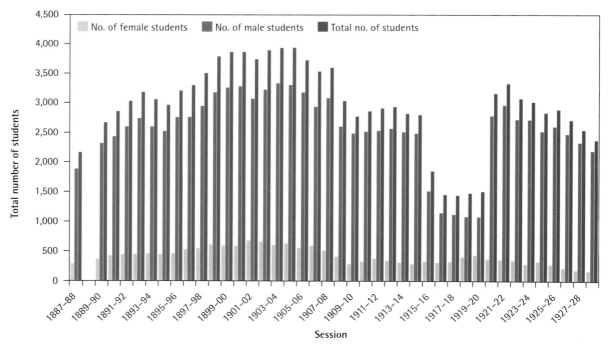

Figure 5.1 Total number of evening class students, 1887–1929. Between 1887 and 1892 the evening class total may include a small number of day class students

Source: George Heriot's Trust, Minutes of Meetings of Governors, 1887–1928

Table 5.1 Number of students and subjects in 1886–87 and 1900–01

Evening classes	1886–87	1900–01
Technical Department		
Enrolments	1,800	4,200
Subjects	27	53
Literary and Commercial Department		
Enrolments	1,300	1,800
Subjects	14	21
Individual students registered	2,000	3,750
Day students	43 (1889–90)	165

geographical textbooks. In 1892 he became librarian to the Royal Geographical Society and, later, was director of the British Rainfall Organisation. In commerce, Robert Cockburn Miller (practice of commerce, 1886–1908) and George Lisle (accountancy, 1896–1903) were notable figures in their profession and important contributors to its literature. Lisle's *Accountancy in Theory and Practice* became a classic.

The new staff were by no means underemployed. Under Ogilvie the college effectively doubled in size in terms of evening class student numbers and subjects offered (Figure 5.1 and Table 5.1). In evening classes much of this growth resulted from the provision of more advanced and specialised courses in the basic subjects of physics (with mathematics), chemistry and engineering, and engineering began to divide into electrical, mechanical and (from 1887–88) civil.

Perhaps the most significant development of Ogilvie's principalship, however, was the addition of further classes to broaden the curriculum and to enhance traditional strengths. In 1887–88 and 1888–89, Ogilvie initiated six trade classes (eschewed under the old regime), including the first courses in printing, later to become a major speciality. By 1900–01 there were 10 trade classes, including joinery, cabinetmaking, printing, masonry and brickwork, plumbing, painters' work, and watch and clockmaking. In agricultural subjects – first offered in one class from the early 1880s – a rapid development took place and by 1900–01 eight agricultural evening classes and a day course were offered. These continued until transferred to the new Edinburgh and East of Scotland College of Agriculture in the next decade. A number of classes in art were established or revived. Mining, after an earlier false start, began in 1898–99, and architecture was revived in 1896–97. In humanities eight new commercial classes were introduced and language teaching was expanded by the addition of Spanish and Dano-Norwegian in 1893.

By no means all the day students were full-time; the majority took one to three classes for one year only, and concentrated on taking City and Guilds or Science and Art Department examinations rather than the college ones. Of the full-time two-year courses first offered in 1889–90, mechanical and electrical engineering flourished but others were less successful; a course in science lasted until 1896–97 and the course in general and commercial subjects only until 1892–93. Nevertheless, by 1900 a day college in engineering was firmly established, gaining a considerable reputation for the quality of its diplomates. Its courses in this and other subjects suffered, however, from the absence of any national system of recognition of either colleges or their courses. Day class student numbers were only recorded separately from 1893–94 and, under Ogilvie, they reached 141 by 1899–1900 (Figure 5.2).

A systematic departmental structure began to emerge in the 1890s. Mathematics, physics and electrical engineering came under Walmsley (later Baily); chemistry under Gibson; Stanfield, at the head of engineering and constructive arts, was responsible for all engineering other than electrical, building subjects, and for all the trade classes. Art formed a separate division under James Riddel and the 'natural sciences', mainly agriculture and related subjects including physiology, botany and zoology, another. The Literary and Commercial Department (see Table 5.1) embraced English, foreign languages (which still

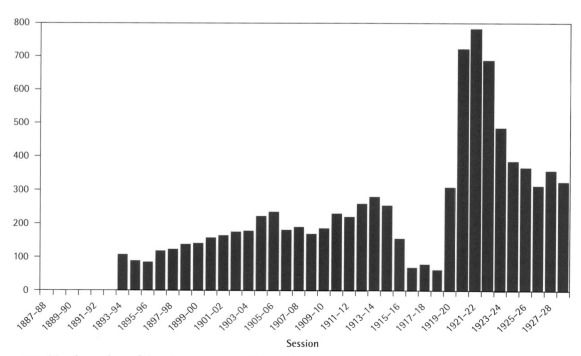

Figure 5.2 Total number of day class students, 1887–1929

included Latin and Greek), history and economics, and commercial classes. These latter were taught entirely (as were many of the technical and all the trade classes) by part-time evening staff, although a few day classes in commerce and languages were offered.

The majority of the students, especially at evening classes, were local but a few came from further afield to take day courses. Ogilvie and the governors, however, clearly regarded the college as an institution of national status or at least aspirations, and its courses were widely advertised throughout Scotland and, to a lesser extent, elsewhere in the United Kingdom. Little is known of the subsequent careers of most of the earlier students. William Graham Griffith (diploma 1899) became professor of electrical engineering in University College Galway. James Cameron Smail received the diploma in 1899 after a successful career as a student, and following rapid progress in educational administration in Ireland and London, returned to the college as principal in 1929. Another former student who later joined the college staff was Alexander R. Horne (diploma 1902, professor of mechanical engineering 1930–46). Thomas Rowatt (diploma 1903) spent his life in the Royal Scottish Museum, becoming director in 1934, and a number who went into industry attained high positions at home and abroad.

The government of the college was carried on – in so far as can be judged from the sparse record of the Heriot's Trust minutes – with a minimum of fuss by the Heriot-Watt College Committee and the trustees. The outstanding member of the committee and its convener from 1885 until 1891 was Lord Shand. Shand had been the first to draw up an outline scheme for the college as early as 1879 and his strategy was largely followed by Magnus and Ogilvie, in turn. He had been a most industrious and imaginative chairman who more than anyone was the architect of the new regime under the Heriot's Trust. If Horner was the founder of the institution, Shand can be claimed as the second founder, with Ogilvie as the architect of its academic form. Shand retired from the bench after a severe illness in 1890 and from the convenership of the Heriot-Watt Committee in 1891, having served for 15 years as the chairman of the governing body. He expressed the hope that the college would aim at 'bringing the commercial part of the college up to the same high standard of utility which the technical department has now reached'.[29] He retired to London, remaining a life member of the College Committee but taking no further part in its activities until his death in 1904.[30]

A New Style of Leader: Arthur Pillans Laurie

Arthur Pillans Laurie succeeded Ogilvie as principal and resembled him in coming from a distinguished Scottish academic background, but in little else. His father, Simon Somerville Laurie, had risen from humble origins to become the first professor of the theory, history and practice of education at the University of Edinburgh and a philosopher of high if short-lived repute. Brought up near Portobello, baptised into the Episcopalian church (his mother was Church of England), Arthur Laurie attended Edinburgh Academy, Leonard Horner's foundation, which he disliked, in part because of the overwhelming emphasis on Classics.[31] Young Laurie grew up in a cultured, high-thinking household in which John Stuart Blackie, John Hill Burton (historiographer royal for Scotland and Mary Burton's brother), Fleeming Jenkin, who gave Laurie his first piece of chemical apparatus,[32] Archibald Geikie and James Lorimer were frequent visitors; later he studied under several of these as a student at Edinburgh University.

Arthur's father, a philosopher and classicist, had no time for science and made no secret of his belief that neither Arthur nor his younger brother Malcolm (later a lecturer in biology at the college and at Surgeon's Hall) – both of whom showed

Arthur Pillans Laurie, who enjoyed a lengthy and colourful reign of 28 years as principal

early inclinations towards the sciences – would ever amount to anything by his own exacting standards. After an indifferent performance at Edinburgh Academy and the University of Edinburgh, where he neglected his classical curriculum in favour of science and engineering (BSc 1881), Arthur went to King's College, Cambridge. Devoting himself to electrochemistry, he took a first in the natural sciences tripos in three years instead of the then customary four. His Cambridge experience, however, was not entirely a fulfilling one: 'I came into Cambridge a fanatic for science: I left bored by the whole subject.'[33]

Laurie was something of a rolling stone during the years between Cambridge and his appointment to Heriot-Watt College. A man of boundless energy and considerable versatility, his interests embraced science, education, art, social conditions and politics. After completing his DSc at home in Edinburgh in 1895 for a thesis on the constitution of alloys, he then joined (Sir) Thomas Thorpe at South Kensington, where, at the Royal Mint, he worked on the atomic weight of gold and undertook some university extension lecturing, thus strengthening his interests in adult and continuing education. He was also concerned to study the social conditions in the East End of London. Laurie joined the University Extension Movement and became Gilchrist lecturer at Toynbee Hall. Building a village theatre for folk dancing, art schools in Whitechapel and agitating for better industrial conditions were activities towards which he directed his immense energy.[34] He also purchased a cottage at Loughton in Epping Forest, where he set up a colony for East End boys and artists and shared in organising the famous dockers' strike in which Cardinal Manning acted as an arbitrator.

Laurie then made the acquaintance of Holman Hunt, the pre-Raphaelite master, who laid out before him the theme of his lifetime's research – the investigation of methods of painting and dating pictures.[35] After returning to Edinburgh, Laurie worked on electrochemistry but soon medieval painters and their methods exercised an irresistible fascination.[36] Laurie published the first in a series of papers in the *Society of Arts Journal* in 1891 entitled 'On the Durability of Pictures Painted with Oils and Resins'.[37] It is difficult nowadays to envisage that it was considered eccentric to apply the tools of the scientist to the problems of the artist but it was at a time when there were no laboratories, or groups of research chemists at the National Gallery, the Louvre or the Courtauld Institute. These and their counterparts elsewhere owe much to the pioneering research of Arthur Pillans Laurie. Although he specialised in the materials employed in painting and the graphic arts and became an accepted authority on the technical methods of the old masters, his interests extended to other crafts. He wrote a book on building materials which takes an honourable place beside his more famous works: *Processes, Pigments and Vehicles* (1895), *The Pigments and Mediums of the Old Master* (1914), *The Painter's Methods and Materials* (1926), *The Brushwork of Rembrandt and His School* (1932), *Pictures and Politics* (1934), *New Light on Old Masters* (1935).[38] Laurie developed many ingenious methods of investigating pigments and media at a time when microchemistry had not yet become an orthodox technique, and he figured prominently in many *causes célèbres* on the authenticity of old master paintings, frequently disagreeing with gallery officials and art experts. He was a pioneer in the application of scientific method to connoisseurship, which became a science in its own right. He was interested in how the refractive index of paint media in pictures might serve as an indication of the picture's age. His duties at Heriot-Watt College did not exhaust his remarkable vitality and in 1912 he accepted an appointment as professor of chemistry at the Royal Academy of Art, where he delivered a course of six lectures per annum for 24 years:[39]

> Generations of students at the Academy Schools will remember his jovial presence at the lecture table, whether conducting experiments dressed in a farmer's smock or expatiating in his inimitable way on the materials of the painters' craft.[40]

A chemist of the old school, he was accustomed to solve all problems where possible at the bench or at the easel.[41]

Laurie was frustrated in an attempt to become a Fellow of the Royal Society (FRS). In a letter to Sir Arthur Church on 18 March 1915, Laurie wrote:

> I can only hope to have better luck next time. . . . I believe the trouble is that I am neither 'fish, flesh nor good red herring' and so get pushed out by stronger claims. I should have made my original application when you were on the Council.[42]

It is clear that an old boy network operated in 1915, as is still the position even today when women, for example, constitute fewer than 4 per cent of the fellows. Laurie had been an unsuccessful candidate for the chair of chemistry at Heriot-Watt when Perkin was appointed in 1887. At his father's insistence, he applied for the principalship, the low parental opinion of the son's abilities having apparently been revised. Young Laurie demurred, having seen the Chambers Street building, saying that he could not apply for a post whose duties would involve 'entering that architectural horror every day';[43] his sensitivity to this was apparently a new development since 1887. His scruples overcome, he was appointed by twelve votes (including that of his father, a governor of the Heriot's Trust since 1888) against six for the runner-up, Professor J. C. Beattie of the South African College, Cape Town.

Laurie's gifts, though considerable, were of a very different character from Ogilvie's. No enthusiast for administration and impatient of bureaucracy, he was a visionary and an idealist, whose ideas on educational and social matters were far in advance of his time. His great aim was to transform the college into an institution of teaching and research of university standard in the fields of applied science, technology and industrial design, while maintaining and developing to a higher standard its part-time sub-degree-level work. From the beginning he threw himself wholeheartedly into the work of the college, but delegated an increasing amount of routine administration to the clerk, who from 1901 was Alexander M. B. Cullen. He was active to a greater degree than Ogilvie had been in national bodies concerned with technical education and other matters, and his Cambridge and London background provided the basis for a large circle of influential contacts in scientific, artistic and governmental circles. He maintained regular and close relations with Sir John Struthers, secretary of the Scotch Education Department (SED) from 1903. Soon after his arrival in Edinburgh, Laurie married one of the two daughters of Professor Gibson and his German wife, and an only daughter, Caroline, was born. Not long afterwards, Mrs Laurie fell ill with meningitis which left her permanently incapacitated; she died later after many years in a nursing home. Laurie reverted to the life of a somewhat eccentric bachelor in a flat in Buccleuch Place while his daughter was brought up by his sister and joined her father only for holidays.[44]

Laurie was a character: straightforward, forthright, honest to a fault; burly in figure, brusque and gruff in manner, versatile, scholarly, humanitarian, lover of the arts; pugnacious, full of vitality, stubborn and argumentative, generous and kindly; a good talker on any topic, but most of all on pictures; a good friend and a stimulating antagonist; a man intensely individual and unorthodox, authoritarian yet himself impatient of authority. A letter he wrote on 15 January 1909 enclosing a cheque for 43 shillings for 1,000 Turkish cigarettes indicates that he was a heavy smoker and a pungent aroma followed him throughout the corridors of the college.[45] On his favourite topic he wrote as he talked – rapidly, staccato with confident authority and little inclination to revise, prune and polish – but his topic was of such novelty and interest that, as Ritchie testified, 'it was easy to forgive the brilliant *non sequitur* which now and again delighted the reader'.[46] He established close official and social relations with his staff, to whom he gave far greater freedom in the running of their departments than had Ogilvie; his ability to do so was a tribute to the effectiveness of the framework Ogilvie had established. The students saw little of the principal who, unlike his predecessor, never did any regular teaching. He was a great wheeler and dealer, promoting projects in the college and elsewhere, and his extensive connections enabled him at times to bring influence to bear where it mattered; but he did not always succeed in bringing it to bear at the right time, or pay enough attention to the detail and practicality of his projects, and the patient diplomacy they needed was not in his character. He lacked a sense of discipline and responsibility and, as a result, he achieved less than he had hoped and than his gifts might have made possible.[47]

Laurie's period as principal falls into two halves, separated by the First World War of 1914–1918; the first of these was a period of rapid change and, for the most part, progress; the war period showed Laurie at the height of his powers and achievement, but not in the service of the college. One suspects that after the war he aspired to a senior post in the reconstruction of education and of scientific research; instead he found himself back in his old position surrounded by an ageing staff and inadequate buildings, without the resources to resume the rapid development of earlier years. The latter part of his principalship amounted in effect to 10 years of stalemate – though the same period was that of his greatest achievement as an art expert. A fervent Liberal, he contested unsuccessfully the South Edinburgh seat in 1929. It caused, perhaps, less surprise than distress to the friends of this robust and authoritarian old scholar when, in his seventies, he took up the cudgels on behalf of the Nazi philosophy, even to the extent of publishing a defence thereof, *The Case for Nazi Germany*. The book was the outcome of two years studying conditions in Nazi Germany and was accepted by a Berlin publishing company after being rejected in London. Laurie denied the imputation that he had been paid to write propaganda for Germany. Since it was published just before the outbreak of the Second World War, it lost him friends; characteristically, however, he did not deviate from views honestly held, however unpalatable.[48]

Scarcely had Laurie taken office when a disagreement arose with Peter McNaughton, clerk to the Heriot's Trust. At this time, and for many years afterwards, communication with the SED – then in London – over matters major and trivial alike was necessary and extremely frequent; for example, the transfer of one student from one examination centre to another required written approval of the department. McNaughton, perhaps seeking to impress on the new principal the dependence of the college on the Heriot's Trust, proposed to control all communication with the SED. Laurie was equally anxious to assert his own authority and the autonomy of the college and insisted vehemently that such a change would paralyse the college's work. A compromise was reached and routine dealings with the department were handled by George Brand, the college clerk. In June 1901, however, Brand was found guilty of irregularities in the conduct of some City and Guilds examinations and was asked to resign; his successor, A. M. B. Cullen, a member of the trust's staff, was the real founder of the college administration and remained in office until 1935. Henceforward, Laurie and McNaughton worked together well enough, while jealously guarding their respective prerogatives. The governance and administration of the college remained firmly with the Heriot's Trust until it was reconstituted just before Laurie's retirement in 1928. All financial business was handled at the trust's offices in York Place, even to the extent that the staff had to report there to collect their salaries.

When Ogilvie was succeeded as principal by Laurie in 1900, the number of students attending evening classes was 3,886 (of which, thanks to Mary Burton, 590 were females) whereas only 157 attended day classes (Figures 5.1 and 5.2). Consequently, Laurie's first academic task was to promote the growth and to raise the academic standard of the still small day department. To this end, an entrance examination for day class students intending to take full courses and obtain the college diploma was introduced in 1901. Formal course structures extending over three years were introduced in mechanical and electrical engineering in place of the earlier two-year 'recommended course of study', and a similar structure was brought in for chemistry; all would lead to the diploma of the college, and a fourth year in chemistry would prepare for the examinations of the Institute of Chemistry. It was the intention of the SED that such diplomas should correspond, in so far as the specialised training was concerned, to university degrees. This represented the first flowering of Heriot-Watt's future mission. Hitherto the diploma had been obtainable by evening students on rather easy terms; now such students had to undertake a curriculum equivalent to the day students, and the

Students in chemistry laboratory, 1900

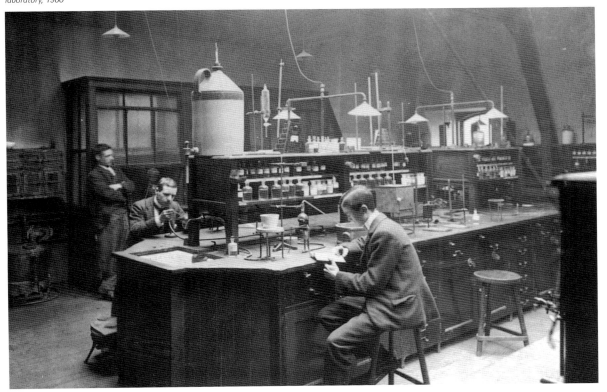

normal award for evening students would be a certificate. In ensuing years it became the norm – as a new subject came into the college curriculum – for a diploma course to be set up. Consequently, further diplomas were introduced in mining (1911) and technical mycology (1912).

Central Institution Status

In the next few years national developments had a far-reaching effect on the college's work and status. The SED was reorganised in 1885 under its new permanent secretary, Henry Craik (1846–1927), who was to dominate educational policy making until 1904. Craik was a 'London-Scot': the son of a Glasgow minister, he was educated at Glasgow University and Balliol College, Oxford; the whole of his subsequent career was on the Education Department's London staff.[49] He held strongly Unionist views, gave voice to imperialist sentiments[50] and, after his retirement, became a Conservative MP for the Glasgow and Aberdeen university seat. Craik's authority was absolute and Scottish Secretaries, who had many other responsibilities, tended to follow his advice, including the encouragement of new and extended ventures in technical education.[51] Much of the responsibility for the nature of Scottish education in the twentieth century can be fairly laid at the feet of the SED under Craik, an unflagging educational reformer, and his successor, John Struthers, who ruled the department from 1905 to 1921.

The administration of the Kensington-based Science and Art Department's grants in Scotland had been transferred to the SED in 1897. The Scotch Department, however, remained in London, described disparagingly by the Duke of Richmond as 'simply a room in Whitehall with the word Scotland painted on the door'.[52] There was little prospect of a transfer to Edinburgh. The explanation given by Lord Balfour of Burleigh in 1884 was not agreeable to Scottish *amour propre*:

> I very much doubt whether it is possible for the government to allow such a large spending department as the Education Department has become to have an office away from London.[53]

The department eventually opened a branch office in Edinburgh early in the twentieth century but the headquarters did not transfer until January 1921.

Scottish sensitivities were assuaged in the Act of 1918 when the title of the department was changed from 'Scotch' to 'Scottish'.

The Scottish Continuation Class Code of 1901, the brainchild of Craik, set up a pyramidal structure for further education. Continuing education in schools throughout Scotland was organised into four regions based on Glasgow, Edinburgh, Dundee and Aberdeen. The local school boards would provide elementary further education, the courses and syllabuses being drawn up in consultation with one or more central institutions in each region (the name suggested a penitentiary to some observers), to whose advanced courses the schools would act as feeders. This distinctive feature of the educational landscape, a Scottish animal never visible to the Sassenach, was in effect the predecessor of the colleges of advanced technology established south of the border half a century later. Considerable government intervention was involved in setting up such institutions and Craik was the mastermind in devising and implementing the change. He envisaged that they would adopt a polytechnic role acting as centres of advanced instruction serving specific geographical areas.[54] The central institutions were designed to offer courses up to degree and diploma levels in technology, applied science, art, music, drama, commercial and other studies. The Continuation Classes Code of 1901 gave permission to the SED to exempt certain regional colleges from the code's provisions, to deal with them under special minutes and to pay grants according to the number of students attending and the nature of the courses.[55] Ten, including Heriot-Watt College, were granted special status as central institutions between 1901 and 1909 under Article 87 of the code and five others were controlled by the Department of Agriculture. The SED initiated payment of an annual grant of £1,900 to Heriot-Watt College for five years from 31 July 1901.[56] The new institutions were clearly envisaged as more than simply providing technical education:

> It is from such institutions and the opportunities for research and discovery which they will naturally afford, that decisive advantage to the industries of the country ... is to be looked for.[57]

The central institutions were viewed by the SED as 'technical universities' (a rather pretentious term but in the light of subsequent developments it displayed some prescience) and capable of doing work of that standard:

> But no system of technical education is complete which does not provide for work at the University level. ... Such Technical Universities, as they may be called, will form the crown of the Continuation Class system, as the older Universities form the crown of the Day School system.[58]

Some central institutions, notably West of Scotland College and Heriot-Watt College, were also pursuing higher engineering courses which were not generally available at other universities.[59]

Heriot-Watt College became the central institution for south-east Scotland in 1902, in part a tribute to Laurie's high personal profile, political connections and reputation. The college was granted a supervisory role for the commercial and technical education by the school boards throughout the Lothians, Fife, Clackmannan, Kinross, Stirling, the Border counties including (surprisingly) Dumfriesshire;[60] and this new status contributed to the accelerated development of day classes. The effect of this development was as great as, if not greater than, the advent of college status in 1885. The code altered completely the former position of Heriot-Watt College as an isolated centre of evening instruction. From being a college whose academic results could only be judged by successes obtained in external examinations over whose syllabuses it had no control, it became one of four large officially recognised institutions with defined catchment areas, entrance standards, and the ability to regulate to a large extent its own academic policies and to grant diplomas and awards by its own examinations but with some national standing. The institution would, or at least should, be able to concentrate most of its evening work on higher-level instruction, the elementary teaching being undertaken in the local schools whose syllabuses it could inspect and monitor to ensure that the students admitted to its own classes were adequately prepared. Conditions were implemented for the first time governing entry into a large number of evening classes:

> a merit certificate from an elementary day school; a certificate of sufficient attainment from an evening continuation school; at least one year's attendance at a senior class at a recognised seconding school; or to be over 20 years of age.[61]

Up to 1900 the college had been financed by the funds of the Heriot's Trust, the fees of the students, and grants from the Science and Art Department and from Midlothian County Council under the Local Taxation (Customs and Excise) Act 1890. Under the 1901 Continuation Classes Code, Article 87, the funds formerly administered in Scotland by the Science and Art Department were handed over to the SED and grants were no longer given as payments on results in the Science and Art Department's examinations (which many academics had found too constraining). The town council of Edinburgh paid a grant of £1,017 10s in 1903, in addition to £150 from Midlothian; and in 1907 the SED and the governors of the Heriot's Trust arranged that the trust should contribute to the maintenance of Heriot-Watt College a sum equivalent to not less than one-sixth of the fee income subject to a minimum of £5,248.[62] Total maintenance expenditure reached £13,000 in 1913 and an agreement was reached whereby 25 per cent of any expenditure beyond this amount would be funded by the trust and 75 per cent by the SED.[63]

The ambitious structure set up by the 1901 code failed to realise many of its objectives, either in the short or the long term. Inevitably, it took some time for the various school boards to set up their continuation classes and there was much variation between them. Liaison with them was far from easy, especially as the college was not able for many years to appoint a full-time liaison officer; the region covered was too large, and very few students could be expected to attend evening classes in Edinburgh from Dumfries, Berwickshire or the remoter parts of Fife and Stirlingshire. Neither did the college succeed for a long time, if indeed ever, in discontinuing elementary classes. Edinburgh Corporation, in particular, accustomed to keeping down the city's rates, was slow to make any financial contribution to the new central institution (though other less well-endowed authorities did so) and showed no particular enthusiasm for setting up elementary continuation classes to replace those which the college already provided without any charge on the rates. Of 260 pupils in the school board's continuation classes in 1905–06, only 25 proceeded to the college. This low rate of progression led to a new agreement with the school board of Edinburgh in June 1907 to improve articulation arrangements.[64] Nevertheless, within the immediate catchment area of Edinburgh – including the southern part of Fife which shared with Lothian a strong interest in the mining industry – the scheme did work to a reasonable degree and undoubtedly contributed to the development of the college by providing a natural progression through local classes to the college's evening classes and thence, in some cases, to day courses. The day classes so developed that in 1904 approval was given for the introduction of the associateship of the Heriot-Watt College (AH-WC). This qualification, awarded on successful completion of a three- or four-year full-time course in certain technical departments, rapidly gained recognition by educational and professional bodies as being of university degree standard. Indeed, following the granting to the college of university status in 1966, the associateship became capable of conversion to the degree of bachelor of science of the university.[65]

By April 1902, thinking about the need for larger laboratories and lecture rooms for the day classes had advanced far enough for plans to be drawn up for an extension on part of the former brewery site at the back of the college. On the rest of the site, roughly corresponding to the later second extension, it was proposed to erect a five-storey building of some 20,000 square feet to house chemistry and mechanical engineering; the remainder of the site would provide single-storey accommodation for engineering workshops and laboratories. An appeal was issued to some 500 potential donors asking for £50,000 and pointing out that the

Glasgow and West of Scotland College had recently raised £173,000 for its building fund. Despite this invocation of the perennial Edinburgh–Glasgow rivalry, the college's plea fell on deaf ears and seems to have been abandoned after the initial unsuccessful circulation.

In the shorter term (but with significant long-term effects), discussions took place with the SED about substantial developments in the advanced work of the college. These had the tangible result of a grant of £2,035 in 1903–04 which made possible four appointments; these were assistant professors in mechanical engineering (W. C. Houston), physics and electrical engineering (W. M. Varley), chemistry (B. D. Steele) and a chief lecturer in mathematics (Roderick M. Shearer who, though only 25, came as senior colleague to Firth, aged 35 and already nine years in post).

Laurie's Failure to Capture Art Education

The new structure set up by the 1901 code had not so far provided for art education. The Edinburgh School of Arts almost from its earliest days had provided classes in ornamental modelling, and after various vicissitudes an art school had developed devoted predominantly to the industrial and craft aspects of art and including trade classes for house painters; the college also provided tuition in printing, bookbinding, architecture and the building trades. There were also several other art schools in Edinburgh. Painting, drawing and sculpture were taught at the Trustees' Academy on the Mound. Closely associated with it were the advanced classes of the Royal Scottish Academy, while Sir Rowand Anderson had initiated classes in architecture. In 1901 approaches were made to the college as to its willingness to take over these three schools. With Laurie's interest in art went a strong conviction that industrial design should form part of the education of the engineer, and that designers with a training in art should be employed widely in industry. Laurie greeted the approach with enthusiasm, for his aim was to transform the Heriot-Watt College Art School into a school for the crafts of printing, bookbinding, furniture making, and the building trade, leaving the Mound School to be organised by the Royal Scottish Academy for the production of painters and sculptors.[66]

The college had just taken possession of the former Raeburn's brewery at the back of the Chambers Street building. This consisted of a four-storey grain store at the south end of the site and other lower buildings beyond. The college's expensive needs for accommodation for engineering could only be met in the lower buildings; the high building, Laurie reasoned, could form an art school. He persuaded the governors to convert it into premises for 400 art students in such a manner that it would be 'readily adaptable to any teaching purpose'. This tall building had crow-stepped gables into which longer windows were inserted to give the necessary light. The work was complete and opened in October 1902 at a cost of £13,022.[67]

Laurie, however, had been carried away and acted too quickly. A report in February 1901 had been highly critical of art education at the college:

> The accommodation is already inadequate ... the rooms ... besides being small and ill furnished, are gloomy by day and badly lighted by night. The equipment of examples is of the poorest description. ... The designing work done at present is very limited in scope. ... The whole question of Art and Craft Education in Edinburgh needs serious attention ... it needs

All-female art class, 1900

consideration whether the College can provide fully for education in the artistic crafts.[68]

J. R. Findlay, editor of *The Scotsman* and chairman of the Board of Manufacturers, was strongly committed to the establishment of a large, new separate art school[69] and an editorial in *The Scotsman* on 23 September 1902 was scathing both about the college's lack of strategic focus and its ambitions in art education:

> The Heriot-Watt College is a queer and unfortunate combination. In many matters it gives elementary instruction, it is also a sort of people's university at popular prices, and recently it has been endeavouring to raise itself to the position of a technical college. . . . But the College will have to make up its mind to what it is to devote itself. Is it to be an elementary school, a people's university, or a technical college? If it tries to be all three it will fail to get a reputation beyond the narrow limits of Edinburgh.
>
> It is clear that the Heriot's Trust is trying to force the pace and secure to its control the Art School which the Education Department want to see established. . . . It seems at present a singularly unsuitable institution to which to entrust the higher art education of Scotland. . . . A school controlled by a body representative of the Government, the Town Council, and any other persons who might give it support would be much more likely to attain national importance than one conducted by Heriot's Trust.[70]

This severe blow to Laurie's ambitions was reinforced in another report by Pittendrigh MacGilivray in June 1905 which was 'generally disappointed' with the modelling class, and the bookbinding tuition was described as 'very unsatisfactory and imperfect'.[71]

The SED favoured the establishment of one comprehensive art school with the status of a central institution in each of the four cities. Thus, the Edinburgh College of Art was established in 1908 on a site in Lauriston which, if Laurie is to be believed, he had suggested to its promoters. Ironically, on 2 October 1908 the governors of Heriot-Watt College granted permission to the Edinburgh College of Art to use the college's premises since their buildings were not yet ready. The relevant college classes were transferred to the new institution, although Heriot-Watt College continued to provide instruction in such subjects as engineering for its architectural students. Attempting to turn humiliation to his advantage, Laurie accepted that this 'proposal to remove the Art and Artistic Trade classes to the new Municipal Art School' would 'enable the College to make use of the present Art School for improved accommodation for the Chemistry and Applied Chemistry departments'.[72] During this period the college operated in dingy, cramped and overcrowded facilities. A report in 1906 by Dr J. J. Dobbie had been very critical of the chemistry accommodation:

> There is only one laboratory capable of holding any considerable number of students. ... There is, for example, no combustion room, no room for rough and dangerous operations, and no gas analysis room ... the fume chambers being specially defective judged by present day standards. ... The lecture room accommodation is also insufficient.[73]

The rooms formerly devoted to art were converted at a cost of £5,773 for the chemistry department and the old chemistry laboratories were handed over to technical mycology.[74] There were long delays in the reconversion of the building and it was not opened until October 1913. In 1908, spacious and well-lit new

The opening of the new engineering laboratories, 16 September 1908

laboratories and workshops for mechanical engineering were created in the remaining parts of the former brewery (between the chemistry building and the Cowgate), and electrical engineering took over the space vacated in the basement of the main building where the department was to remain, not wholly to its satisfaction, until 1967. The classes in agriculture went to the College of Agriculture in George Square in 1905. Considerable progress had been made in a short time, and the college was now equipped with buildings which, though in some cases conversions, were on the whole not much over 20 years old and were adequate for its immediate needs.

As certain manufacturing industries and services required a scientific basis, so new classes and disciplines took root. Both day and evening classes in brewing were provided from 1904–05 offering complete combined courses for brewers, distillers, maltsters and margarine manufacturers of eight months' duration full-time, or part-time during two winter sessions. With financial support of the Brewers' Association of Scotland, a department of technical mycology, the precursor of the department of brewing and biological sciences, was set up in 1906–07. A new chair was created for its head, Dr Emil Westergaard, a talented but unpredictable Dane. The decision to make mycology a separate department rather than including it in chemistry may well have been due to the difficult personalities of both Gibson and Westergaard.[75] Student numbers were never large and in the summer of 1918 the College Committee became concerned about the extent of Westergaard's involvement with a margarine company, a commodity he had done much to develop. In May 1918 the convener of the College Committee (Harrison) was invited to investigate Westergaard's connection with the Caledonian Creamery Company. Westergaard was at first evasive, but then abruptly resigned in July 1918.[76] The department of technical mycology ceased to exist and the vacant laboratories were taken over by chemistry. The Brewers' Association of Scotland made a grant to support a lectureship in biochemistry in the department of chemistry, thereby enabling brewing classes to continue. Pharmacy was also taught in the chemistry department and attracted large numbers of female students who attended the same botany classes as the brewers, allegedly leading to the creation of many interesting friendships while sharing a microscope.[77] Pharmacy eventually became an independent department in 1947.

As early as 1873, at the meeting convened by David Cousin to discuss technical education in Edinburgh, Sir William Chambers (the publisher after whom Chambers Street was named) had advocated the inclusion of a printing school in the proposed technical school. Evening classes in printing had been provided since the late 1880s, and in 1908 – with the provision of new rooms for areas of the work which required substantial equipment – the nucleus of a printing school began to emerge. Its development owed much to Edinburgh printers, both masters

Printing class

and men; in particular, Robert Wilson, a member of the firm of Pillans & Wilson and later vice-chairman of the governors, and W. G. Hampson, secretary of the Edinburgh Typographia (the compositors' union) played a large part in the development of the department and of the college.

The annual report of 1907 contained a lengthy paper by the principal on the present and future work of the college, arguing that in order to develop fully as a technical college, it should confine itself to a more limited range of work; thus, just as art had been transferred to the new art college, commercial education should be hived off to a new commercial college. Although this was then accepted as policy, and so remained, the teaching of commercial subjects continued at the college until its elevation to university status in 1966; but it was not until the 1950s that any full-time staff were employed. There was, said Laurie, overlap between the college's classes and those of the school board's evening classes, although some of this was inevitable. He indicated the main lines for future development as being principally in[78]

1 mechanical and electrical engineering and coal mining;
2 applied chemistry, especially as relating to pharmacy, brewing, paraffin oil manufacture, papermaking, rubber and celluloid manufacture;
3 printing;
4 building.

Overleaf: Heriot-Watt College in the early twentieth century, showing busts of Horner and Heriot above the main entrance. Professor David Manners collection. Photograph: M. Wane and Co.

Laurie also articulated his vision of the college's research mission, suggesting a highly applied focus in connection with shale distillation, paper manufacture, drug

manufacture, technical mycology and mining.[79] He recognised the crucial future role of the institution in providing research and consultancy for private companies, involving the payment of fees for consulting services;[80] and he called for the establishment of postgraduate research scholarships available not only to British students but also to those from the 'Universities of the Allies'.[81]

On the whole, the developments during the remainder of Laurie's principalship were in accordance with these proposals, although of the branches of applied chemistry mentioned, only pharmacy (after the 1914–18 war) and brewing (from 1905) were successful. The decline of the West Lothian shale oil industry rendered the development of the study of paraffin oil manufacture irrelevant, and papermaking never developed into a subject in its own right, although classes were held in the printing department.

Laurie had problems dealing with the higher civil servants of the SED in London who were highly intelligent, systematic individuals with an attention to detail and procedure that was alien to Laurie's character. Laurie and Professor Darroch visited the SED in May 1910 and the permanent secretary, John Struthers, wrote in his minute that they drew his attention to

> the extreme difficulty of getting the present Committee of the Heriot-Watt College to take anything in the nature of a forward step, unless they were positively assured that it was going to pay, or at least not going to cost the Trust anything.[82]

Struthers, however, also opined that

> Principal Laurie is one of the most unbusiness-like of mortals, and his committee have no end of trouble in getting him to keep the everyday accounts of the College straight, or indeed to keep accounts at all.[83]

Relations with the SED deteriorated further in 1913 when, in relation to the SED policy of dealing with each central institution according to its circumstances, Struthers wrote:

> It would appear from the circular letter which Principal Laurie seems to have addressed to various central institutions that he is organising a campaign against us. . . . It was probably clear that Principal Laurie was heading for a fall.[84]

Later, in 1916, after Laurie provided what an official described as a 'disingenuous reply' concerning engineering courses, Struthers responded to his subordinate official:

I am half inclined to suggest that you should reply – not that I think an answer will do Laurie any good, but because he has not sufficient sense to understand what would be meant by leaving him alone.[85]

Several days later, following further letters and telegrams from Laurie, Struthers was clearly angered and replied:

Your double barrelled correspondence of the past few days has been positively bewildering and I am afraid that when we meet I shall have some unpleasant things to say about your … unbusiness-like way of doing business.[86]

Laurie's restless brain continued, nevertheless, to develop far-reaching schemes. The most ambitious of these was for the creation of an educational precinct covering the area bounded, from north to south, by the Cowgate and the Meadows, and from east to west by Nicholson Street and George IV Bridge. This was to be created by the purchase and demolition of the substandard property in the area and the gradual erection of buildings for the expansion of the university, the college, the teacher training college, the veterinary college and the agricultural college. Laurie 'implored [Principal] Turner [of Edinburgh University], [Professor] Darroch [of the Training College], Lord Provost Brown and Findlay of the *Scotsman* to approach Andrew Carnegie. They one and all refused. 'It was useless for me to approach him. I was a nobody.'[87] Nobody or no, he did appeal to Carnegie to aid in the purchase of the property, but Carnegie – at this time very fully committed in other directions – replied in one sentence that he was not currently prepared to take up the matter of 'High Education' in Scotland.

Undoubtedly Laurie's plan was too far ahead of its time, and its practical difficulties were probably insurmountable. Yet it was basically sound and far-sighted. Had it been implemented, the development of Edinburgh University would have been immensely eased, and the major split of the university between the city and the King's Buildings site, if not avoided, might at least have been postponed until a more propitious period, architecturally, than the 1920s and 1930s. Laurie lived long enough to write in 1934, 'Today the slums remain, and the University is being forced out of the city.'[88] He did not survive to see his college become a university and subsequently relocate, though it is doubtful whether that eventuality would have been averted even had his dream been realised.

Collaboration with the University of Edinburgh

At a meeting of the governors of George Heriot's Trust on 2 October 1888, the clerk was instructed to apply to the senatus of the University of Edinburgh to have the college recognised and approved by the university as one of the institutions whereby attendance at its science classes would qualify in part for the degree of bachelor of science. This initial approach was rebuffed, but the first tangible evidence of agreed collaboration between the college and the university came in the form of a letter of 1 November 1895 from Sir Ludovic J. Grant, interim secretary to the senatus of the university, intimating the conditions on which certain classes at the college would be recognised by the University Court for the purposes of graduation in science (Figure 5.3).[89]

UNIVERSITY OF EDINBURGH,
1st November 1895.

DEAR SIR,

Referring to your letters of 17th May and 12th July 1894 I am directed to inform you that the University Court have resolved to recognise, for the purposes of graduation in Science, both by men and by women, the following courses in the Heriot-Watt College - Mechanics and Physics, as equivalent to the course in Natural Philosophy in the University qualifying for the first B.Sc. examination in Pure Science; Advanced Chemistry as qualifying for the final B.Sc. examination; Electricity, pure and applied, Engineering, Laboratory Practice, Mechanical or Electrical as qualifying for the degree of B.Sc. in Engineering.

The Court make it a condition of recognition that the authorities of the Heriot-Watt College should submit annually to the University Court a report setting forth the character and extent of the instruction given, and specifying any changes proposed to be made in the courses,

I am, Yours faithfully,

(Sgd.) L. J. GRANT, Intm. Sec.

P. Macnaughton, Esq., S.S.C.

Figure 5.3 Letter from Sir Ludovic J. Grant

The major thrust of joint working between the two institutions, however, was to develop in the teaching of engineering. The story of the Edinburgh University engineering department[90] was written by Professor Hudson Beare (former professor at Heriot-Watt College) who, either by accident or design, discreetly ignored all references to the part played by Heriot-Watt College in the development of the university department.[91] The degree in engineering at the University of Edinburgh, as established by Ordinance 21 under the Universities (Scotland) Act 1889, contained a clause which enabled a working relationship to be developed between the university and Heriot-Watt College.[92] After a conference between the University Court and the governors of George Heriot's Trust in 1901, a minute of agreement was drawn up, the major provisions of which were

1 the establishment of a joint advisory committee consisting of the dean of the Faculty of Science and four professors of the university, four governors of George Heriot's Trust, and the principal of Heriot-Watt College;
2 to charge the advisory committee with drawing up a programme each year for a joint curriculum of study and examination for a degree in engineering;
3 appointment of examiners who shall be the professors and lecturers and, 'in order to keep the teaching in the Heriot-Watt College in touch with the range and standard of examinations, the University Court shall appoint additional examiners . . . from Heriot-Watt College whose courses have been recognised as qualifying for a degree in Engineering'.[93]

Both institutions sought to retain a degree of independence while recognising the mutual benefits of arranging an effective system of academic collaboration. Appropriate standards had to be assured; examiners in the two institutions worked together and there had to be a degree of mutual trust in organising curricula. The agreement was approved by the governors of the college at a meeting on 29 March 1901.[94]

Heriot-Watt students attended the second-year civil engineering course in strength of materials at the university; university students following courses in electrical and mechanical engineering attended the college in their second and third years for classes in mechanical engineering delivered by Professor Stanfield, and in electrical by Professor Baily.[95] There was also an 'unwritten understanding between Heriot-Watt College and the Engineering Department of the University that before any capital expenditure was undertaken, the proposal should be carefully considered by the Professor of Engineering in the University and the staff of the Heriot-Watt College, with a view to making any extensions complementary to each other or avoiding overlapping'.[96] Such a degree of enlightened rational cooperation appears to be more difficult to achieve in the contemporary British

Henry Briggs (front row, second from right) and students. Briggs was the first lecturer, and subsequently, professor of mining

university system. The relationship between the two institutions continued to evolve and the next important development was the decision of the University Court in 1912 to take advantage of the ordinance to include specialisation in the subjects of mechanical and electrical engineering as well as in civil engineering. This heralded an era of unprecedented cooperation. From 1912 students of the Heriot-Watt College were enabled to obtain a degree in civil, mechanical or electrical engineering; the first year of study was at Edinburgh University, the second year partly at Edinburgh and partly at Heriot-Watt, and in the third year the greater part of the courses in mechanical and electrical engineering were at Heriot-Watt whereas the whole of the civil engineering course was at Edinburgh.[97] These joint courses were regulated by the Joint Advisory Committee.

The major flowering of this spirit of cooperation between the two institutions was the development of a degree programme in mining. In 1907 the governors of George Heriot's Trust decided to establish a lectureship in mining at the college, and Henry Briggs (1883–1935), a Lancashire man and formerly a lecturer at the University of Birmingham, was appointed. Under Dr Briggs, teaching in mining developed rapidly; on 3 July 1908 the principal submitted the syllabus for a full course in mining over four years, the first of which would be taken by students in the continuation classes, and the subsequent years at the college on Saturdays between 4.30 P.M. and 6.30 P.M.[98] Local centres for the first year of the course were sanctioned at West Calder, Dalkeith, Lasswade, Gorebridge, Inveresk, Tranent, Prestonpans, Ormiston and Pencaitland. A full department of mining was established in 1913. In a related development, the first mine rescue stations in Scotland were opened at Coatbridge in 1910 and at Heriot-Watt College in 1915, where the Rescue Research Centre for Scotland was established under Briggs. The mine rescue station, maintained by local colliery companies, was intended to train brigades belonging to local mines; mining students preparing for the diploma of the college were given the opportunity of training in rescue work.

Briggs was an able lecturer and indefatigable investigator, although severely hampered by lack of laboratory accommodation.[99] He was promoted to a professorship of the college in 1919;[100] his burgeoning reputation contributed to enhancing the climate of cooperation with Edinburgh University[101] and in 1921 an ordinance of the University Court was approved giving power to confer the degree of BSc in mining and metallurgy.[102] Since at that time there was no course at the university, the ordinance made provision for candidates to attend approved programmes in these subjects at Heriot-Watt College.[103] In effect, the programme combined the engineering and geological departments of the university with the mining, metallurgical and engineering departments at the college.[104] In 1923 James A. Hood, a Midlothian colliery owner, offered the university £15,000 to establish a chair in mining; he also expressed the hope that the 'University would secure the co-operation of the governors of the George Heriot's Trust in the teaching of mining'.[105] An agreement was reached in July 1928 under which the university professor of mining would also be the professor of mining at Heriot-Watt College, the salary to be provided jointly; the college was responsible for finding accommodation for the professor and staff, the necessary equipment, and for meeting the current expenditure of £700 per annum.[106] Under this agreement, Henry Briggs was appointed and the new chair and the mining school developed rapidly; a substantial grant of £8,000 from the Miners' Welfare Committee enabled the university and college to reconstruct a building in the Grassmarket, opened on 23 November 1928 by Viscount Chelmsford, to house the joint department.[107] The professor's room had a unique feature in that Professor Briggs enjoyed the benefit of a coal fire, the coal being supplied by local collieries.[108] Although complete coordination was established between the teaching of mining in the two institutions, demand for the joint course did not meet expectations and student numbers were not large; the industry never regained the importance it enjoyed up to 1920. Nonetheless, the rationalisation of the industry into larger units stimulated the demand for highly trained mining managers; and the problems posed by increased mechanisation and deeper mines added to the need to apply science to production.[109] The joint course in mining continued until 1966 when the college became a university and all such collaboration in engineering ceased.

An ordinance came into force at the university in 1922 creating the degree of BSc in technical chemistry. Some of the special courses in technical chemistry could be taken either at Edinburgh University or Heriot-Watt College, but metallurgy, biochemistry, oil technology, paper, foods and drugs were available only at Heriot-Watt College.[110] As with the course in mining, collaboration between the two institutions continued at various levels in technical chemistry (renamed chemical technology in 1955 and chemical engineering in 1960) until 1966, but the rest of that story belongs to a later chapter.

The most eminent alumnus from the period of collaboration between Edinburgh University and Heriot-Watt College was Eric Liddell. He embarked on a science degree in 1920 and in the first year he studied physics, mathematics and inorganic chemistry at Heriot-Watt College; in each of the following three years Liddell took at least two courses per year at the college in organic, physical and inorganic chemistry. At the Olympic Games in Paris in July 1924, Eric Liddell won the 400 metres in a world record time of 47.6 seconds, a distance he had rarely run competitively. Liddell, who had also played rugby for Scotland, earlier refused to run in his strongest event, the 100 metres, because the heats were run on a Sunday. His athletic triumphs – he also won a bronze medal in the 200 metres at the Paris Olympics – were immortalised in the film *Chariots of Fire*. At his graduation ceremony in 1924, the principal of Edinburgh University capped him and declared, 'Mr Liddell you have shown that none can pass you but your examiners.'[111] After the Olympics and his graduation, Eric Liddell served as a missionary in China, where he died of a brain tumour and typhoid fever, aged 43, in 1945, after two years imprisoned in a Japanese internment camp.

The professoriate had remained unchanged since 1900, save for the addition of Westergaard to the triumvirate of Stanfield, Baily and Gibson. In the latter part of 1913, however, Gibson fell ill and he died on 1 January 1914. The college was particularly concerned to obtain recognition of its courses in applied chemistry for degree purposes by the University of Edinburgh and it was therefore agreed to defer the appointment to the vacant chair until discussion had been completed with the university and within the college on the possible development of the chemistry department. War broke out, however, in August 1914 and it was agreed to leave the chair unfilled, Laurie nominally undertaking the duties of departmental head while A. A. Boon became the effective active head of department. William Watson, who had a classical education before turning to natural science, became head of physics in 1912. He remained in this post until 1944 and did not publish during his career at Heriot-Watt.

By 1913–14, just prior to the Great War, the day department provided courses over three or four years, leading to diplomas in mechanical engineering, electrical engineering, mining engineering, chemistry (four years) and technical mycology (four years). The total number of students enrolled on these courses in 1913–14 amounted to only 100; there were also 36 Edinburgh University engineering students attending courses at the college.[112] Evening class provision was highly diverse in both subject mix and standard, ranging from technical subjects such as applied mechanics, strength of materials, electrical engineering, chemistry and physics to basic training for tradesmen in, for example, painting, bookbinding, plumbing, brickwork, watchmaking and joinery; to commercial classes including bookkeeping, accounting, banking, actuarial science and languages; to 'general' subjects such as vocal physiology, music and elocution; and to sciences such as geology, botany and physiology. The number of students attending evening classes in 1913–14 totalled 2,837, a fall of 28 per cent compared with the peak year of 1903–04 (Figure 5.1).[113] It is evident that the college was performing functions which on the continent were divided among several institutions – from day programmes of university standard to training for tradesmen and elementary instruction in commercial subjects. Little had changed since the scathing *Scotsman* editorial of 23 September 1902.

The College during the Great War and its Aftermath

During the 1914–18 war, Scottish industry became a vast military arsenal for the great conflict; the Clyde Valley was the single most important concentration of munitions production in the whole of the UK. The demands of the war and the advent of a depression which devastated the international economy greatly tested the resilience of the institution, which did not stand aloof from the war effort. Laurie, a fervent patriot, led the college into a key involvement in the prosecution of the war:

The various departments of the College are principally occupied in devoting such technical knowledge as they possess to assisting the Government in pursuing the one supreme object before us at present – the defeat of the enemy.[114]

Laurie was in constant demand, largely on account of his acquaintance with Lloyd George, who appreciated his capacity for swift experimentation and technical expertise.

The immediate effect of the outbreak of war was a substantial drop in student numbers as men went off to the forces, and several members of staff enlisted as well. Day students dropped immediately from 282 to 67 in 1916–17; in effect, only the first-year engineering classes continued throughout the war, the second- and third-year students going into the forces or to munitions production (Figure 5.2). Similarly, evening class student numbers dropped immediately from 2,837 to stabilise from 1916–17 at between 1,400 and 1,500;[115] the technical classes, largely attended by males, suffered most and a number of classes were combined, though only 10 were suspended. Fee income dropped dramatically from its pre-war total of some £3,000 to £1,800 and then to £1,100 and rigorous economies were imposed. Nevertheless, numbers increased after the war so that by 1920–21 evening class student numbers had recovered to 3,171 and the day students to over 700, of whom only 8 per cent came from outside Scotland.[116] Day student numbers then fell to around 320 by 1926–27 (Figure 5.2), while evening class numbers declined steadily from 3,300 in 1921–22 to 2,189 by 1928–29 (Figure 5.1).

In the first year of the war, Laurie and Briggs worked for the Board of Trade identifying sources for chemical manufactures formerly obtained from Germany. The major 'war effort' of the college, however, developed in 1915. Under the direction of Stanfield, the entire staff of the engineering department organised and supervised the manufacture of shells and other munitions in the south-east of Scotland, while the teaching of first-year engineering students was undertaken by members of physics and mining staff. Little teaching was going on in the college, and the engineering laboratory 'was soon piled from floor to ceiling with thousands of shells'.[117] The mechanical engineering department provided training courses for munitions workers and disabled soldiers, run on lines subsequently followed by the Ministry of Munitions throughout the country; the electrical engineering department trained women from Rosyth Dockyard. Classes were also open to officers undergoing medical treatment at Craiglockart War Hospital; Laurie modified the first-year engineering course 'to make it a suitable training for the future officer under modern war conditions'.[118]

The college conducted extensive research in support of the war effort. Professor Boon in chemistry investigated the purification of wool fat, the electrical insulation of steel wire, the analysis of oils collected from the surface of the sea from sunken German U-boats (the first of these being at the island of Fidra in the Firth of Forth), and on the composition of German flares.[119] The mining department, at the request of the Trench Warfare Committee, also carried out research on mine

The First World War heralded an unprecedented influx of women into the Mechanical Engineering Department – as munitions workers

breathing apparatus, mine detectors and on the preparation of poisonous substances; the technical mycology department conducted experiments in connection with the treatment of dysentery; Professor Briggs also invented rescue apparatus and, with Laurie, prepared a report on the problem of Zeppelin rangefinders;[120] Professor Baily developed a sensitive microphone to detect the approach of enemy submarines and also tunnelling activities in trench warfare.[121] Principal Laurie, through his acquaintance with Lloyd George, was appointed chairman of the Chemical Section of the Scientific Advisory Panel of the Munitions Inventions Department in 1915; these duties took up an increasing proportion of his time until, in spring 1918, they became full-time and he was granted leave of absence from the college. Stanfield became acting principal until Laurie's return a year later.

After the war ended in November 1918, men began to return from their military service and for some of them special courses were provided in the latter part of the 1918–19 session. Returned servicemen of several past years whose courses had been interrupted had to be accommodated, in addition to the normal student intake.[122] A variety of special day and evening courses were arranged for discharged soldiers: British, American and Australian. Not surprisingly, the war service students did not accept unquestioningly what was put before them. In 1922 a petition from 257 students asked for a common room and a reading room; the College Committee expressed sympathy but professed itself unable to find accommodation. Furthermore, two new academic areas were developed: biochemistry, effectively the continuation of the former technical mycology department, and classes for the Pharmaceutical Society's examinations were instituted. The teaching of chemistry to pharmacy students was entrusted in 1921 to a college alumnus, Hugh H. Campbell; he was to remain in the department until his appointment as the head of an independent pharmacy department in 1947, becoming first professor of pharmacy in 1965 before his retirement in 1966.[123]

Christina C. Miller, a student contemporary of Campbell, became an eminent researcher in chemistry. Born in 1899 at Coatbridge, Lanarkshire, Miller showed an early aptitude for mathematics; at that time, teaching was the probable career for a female mathematician but her deafness, the legacy of childhood measles, was an obstacle to this.[124] Chrissie Miller won an entrance bursary to Edinburgh University but was advised that Heriot-Watt College was the place to go to for would-be industrial chemists and she eventually combined a four-year diploma at the college with a three-year degree course at the university. In her final year at the college, she worked as a demonstrator at £20 per annum, carried out research on organic arsenicals and mercurials, and taught herself German while commuting between Kirkcaldy and Edinburgh.[125] Completing her PhD in 1924, Chrissie Miller was one of the few people to have her first paper accepted by the *Proceedings*

Christina Miller and colleagues, 1919–20. Miller, a student and demonstrator in chemistry, became the first woman chemist to be elected a Fellow of the Royal Society of Edinburgh

of the Royal Society of London. She produced the first ever sample of pure phosphorus trioxide in 1928 and gave the definitive explanation of the glow given by this material.[126] This work led to a DSc when Chrissie Miller was only 29, and she became a member of staff at Edinburgh University. At a time when analytical chemistry was practically non-existent in British universities, her versatility in research, whether in chemistry – organic, physical, inorganic and analytical – topic or technique, was outstanding.[127] Her energy and persistence in overcoming difficulties were proverbial; she obtained a key to the department by letting it be known to the professor that she had to return to work one night by climbing in through a window she had left open for the purpose.[128] In 1949 she became the first woman chemist to be elected a Fellow of the Royal Society of Edinburgh.

A new departure in day class provision was the beginning of once-a-week day release classes for printers' apprentices in 1918–19. Laurie was a strong advocate of such classes for apprentices in many trades, and these were the first of their kind under the Education (Scotland) Act of 1918. Unfortunately, however, they were not supported after the first two years and their establishment on a permanent basis had to wait until the Smail era. It would not be accurate, however, to regard the period after the Great War between 1918 and 1928 as one of complete stagnation although Laurie, after his lengthy tenure in office, was a less proactive principal. Unless colleges had considerable endowments or other sources of finance, they relied partly on the generosity of local industry and on grants from the SED, and since the SED would only give grants in proportion to the contributions of industry and endowments, resources were not forthcoming whenever there was a trade recession or where local industrialists were especially parsimonious.[129] Student numbers were at the mercy of local firms who were largely reluctant to grant day release or even encourage attendance at evening classes. This problem was a national one echoed in a report of 1918 under the chairmanship of J. J. Thompson, the physicist, which showed that only 7 per cent of the UK's male population was receiving any trade instruction, and most of this was in scientific principles rather than technical education.[130] A similar cry was heard north of the border from the Scottish Education Reform Committee, which emphasised the need to improve the *general* education of the average worker and alleged that a purely utilitarian training would detrimentally affect workers' morale.[131] The committee were of the opinion that

> each university should recognise and utilise by affiliation the work done within its area by Technical College … insofar as it is on a University level.[132]

The Robbins Committee raised the same issue four decades later, implying that such developments were difficult to seed and nurture.

Fluctuating Fortunes of Student Societies

Throughout this period from 1885 to 1928 a minority of the students strove to keep the flame of social and cultural life alight, although their various initiatives met with mixed success. The Watt Literary and Debating Society, which became the Heriot-Watt College Literary Society in 1886, was an innovative organisation: its first joint debate was with Greyfriars Literary Association in 1885–86; a night for readings and recitations was initiated in the same year; the parliamentary election was introduced in 1895–96; a cycling club in 1903; dramatic evenings and performances in 1909–10; and in 1927–28 a lecture with gramophone selections. Membership of the Literary Society had fallen to 74 in 1890–91[133] and, to promote the social life of the society, a 'smoking concert' was suggested, but the idea was abandoned because 'ladies don't smoke in public yet ... and the non-smoking gentleman is not yet extinct'.[134] By 1892–93 motions supporting Scottish home rule and female suffrage secured majorities in debates but liberal sentiments did not extend far. In 1894–95 the society approved the motion that 'the working classes should not form for themselves a political party' and that 'the secularist attitude towards Christianity was unreasonable'.[135] A more enlightened attitude to domestic political and social issues, however, was not applied to countries within the British Empire: in 1896–97 a majority supported the motion that 'Britain should retain Egypt'; and the following session members decided that 'the annexation of foreign territory is beneficial to civilisation'.[136] The secretary expressed the view in 1904 that 'there is a feeling among a large section of the society that it is fast becoming a medium for the propagation of socialism'.[137] One joint debate with the Edinburgh Indian Association in 1908–09 addressed the subject of British rule in India:

> The Indian who led off ... pulled a revolver from his pocket. He began an excited tirade against British Rule in India and punctuated all his remarks by waving his revolver and tapping it on the desk in front of him. The atmosphere became electrical. ... Finally he sat down and lay the revolver on the counter beside him. Mr. H. M. McLeod, who was in the chair, stretched quietly across and took it away.[138]

At least three members of the society served subsequently in government: William Graham, president of the Board of Trade, Dr T. Drummond Shiels,

Heriot-Watt College Literary Society, ticket for picnic at Roslin, June 1903

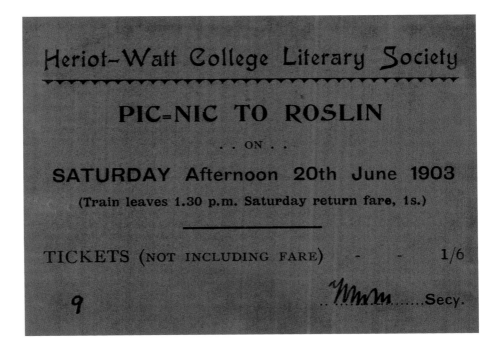

undersecretary for India, and Mr J. C. Watson, solicitor-general for Scotland. The society grew and by 1913–14 women (157) outnumbered men (129) among the membership for the first time.[139]

From 1879 there was also an annual party political debate that 'the present Government is unworthy of the support of the country'. For 12 years in succession the Liberals were victorious; while from 1895–96 onwards, instead of the usual debate, there was an election with candidates subjected to 'severe heckling' before the vote.[140] There was some excitement in 1903–04 when a socialist was elected for the first time, although the result was unlikely to have caused concern among the crowned heads of Europe.

A picnic to Roslin was organised in June 1903 when members spent a pleasant afternoon in the glen participating in a game of rounders, 100 and 200 yard races for men, 50 and 100 yards for ladies, and a tug of war. Tea cost 9d and was taken in the Roslin restaurant at 4.30 P.M.; the party then adjourned to Brown's Hall at 7.45 P.M. for songs, recitations and dancing.[141] The picnic evolved into rambles in 1907; the first took place on 15 June to Cramond, where tea was obtained, and the ramblers walked home by Granton.[142] On 6 July 1907, after walking from Aberdour to Burntisland, the members boarded a train for Edinburgh. They had not reckoned, however, on the vagaries of the rolling stock of the North British Railways: 'The pungent aroma of Kirkcaldy was perceptible at midnight, the Channel Fleet as viewed from the Forth Bridge looked picturesque at 1.15, but

FIXTURES.

DATE.	DESTINATION.	MEETING PLACE.	TIME.	L'ght'ng UpTime	READINGS ETC.
Saturday, Apr. 4	*Musselburgh	Melville Drive	3.30 p.m.	7.54	Reading, "Midsummer Night's Dream."
,, ,, 11	Hawthornden			8.8	Discussion on ,,
,, ,, 18	Dalkeith			8.23	Reading—"Omar Khayyam."
,, ,, 25	Kirkliston	Maule's		8.37	,, " The Golden Butterfly."
,, May 2	Balerno	Melville Drive		8.51	,, " The Roadmender."
Tuesday ,, 5	Swanston	.. ..	7.30	8.57	
Saturday ,, 9	Leadburn	.. ..	3.30	9.4	Reading from "Idle Thoughts of an Idle Fellow."
Tuesday ,, 12	Cramond	Maule's	7.30	9.10	
Saturday ,, 16	Aberlady	Melville Drive	3.30	9.18	Discussion, "Poetry."
Tuesday ,, 19				9.23	
Saturday ,, 23	Ormiston	.. ..	3.30	9.30	Essay, "On the Alleged Obscurity of Mr Browning's Poetry, from "Obiter Dicta."
Tuesday ,, 26	Carlowrie	Maule's	7.30	9.35	
Saturday ,, 30	Loganlea	Melville Drive	3.30	9.41	Selection from Browning's Poetry.
Tuesday, June 2	Exhibition	Maule's	7.30	9.45	
Saturday ,, 6	aEdgelaw	Melville Drive	3.30	9.49	" The Egoist."
Tuesday ,, 9	Currie	.. ..	7.30	9.52	
Saturday ,, 13	Carlops	.. ..	3.30	9.56	Reading, "As You Like It."
Tuesday ,, 16	Queensferry	Maule's	7.30	9.58	
Saturday ,, 20	Gifford	Melville Drive	3.30	10	Discussion on ,, ,,
Tuesday ,, 23	Kirknewton	Maule's	7.30	10	
Saturday ,, 27	Linlithgow		3.30	10	Extract from Maeterlinck's 'Life of the Bee.
Tuesday ,, 30	Rallion Green	Melville Drive	7.30	9.59	
Saturday, July 4	aCauld Stane Slap	.. ..	3.30	9.57	Discussion, "Music."
Tuesday ,, 7	Glencorse	.. ..	7.30	9.55	
Saturday ,, 11	Hangingshaw	.. ..	3.30	9.51	Essay, "The Mutability of Literature," from Washington Irving's Sketch Book.
Tuesday ,, 14	Cramond	Maule's	7.30	9.48	Reading—Arnold's "Scholar Gypsy."
Saturday ,, 18	Blackness		3.30	9.42	
Tuesday ,, 21	Roslin	Melville Drive	7.30	9.38	
Saturday ,, 25	Dirleton	.. ..	3.30	9.32	,, Lamb's "Popular Fallacies."
Tuesday ,, 28	Craigmillar Castle	.. ..	7.30	9.26	
Saturday, Aug. 1	Almond Dell	Maule's	3.30	9.18	" David Elginbrod."
Tuesday ,, 4	Juniper Green	Melville Drive	7.30	9.12	
Saturday ,, 8	Borthwick Castle, via Arniston	.. ..	3.30	9.4	Reading—Wendell Holmes, "Latter-Day Warnings," etc.
Tuesday ,, 11	Dreghorn	.. ..	7.30	8.58	Reading—"Conformity," a Reading from " Friends in Council."
Saturday ,, 15	Habbie's Howe	.. ..	3.30	8.48	
Tuesday ,, 18	Ratho	Maule's	7.30	8.41	Reading—" Bonnie Kilmeny."
Saturday ,, 22	Pathhead	Melville Drive	3.30	8.32	
Tuesday ,, 25	Exhibition	Maule's	7.30	8.24	
Saturday ,, 29	Musselburgh via Roslin ..	Melville Drive	3.30	8.14	Humorous Reading " Dombey and Son."
,, Sept. 5	Livingstone	Maule's	3.30	7.56	Reading, " Othello."
,, ,, 12	Loganlea	Melville Drive	3.30	7.38	Discussion on ,,
,, ,, 19	Abercorn	Maule's	..	7.19	Reading from Edward Lear's Works.
,, ,, 26	Balerno	Melville Drive	..	7	Social

Meet at East End Melville Drive.   ***If wet, meet train at 5.45**   a **Picnic.**

*Exercising body and mind: the
Melville Cycling Club
programme for 1908*

that Waverley Station was decidedly chilly at 2.00am.'[143] By 1913 the programme had expanded to eight rambles, including one over the Pentlands in the moonlight.

The Melville Cycling Club originated in a motion at the annual business meeting of the Literary Society on 13 March 1903 and the first run to Cramond was held on 18 April 1903. The membership for the first season was 16 (the annual subscription was 1s 6d) and a series of runs on the Saturdays and Tuesdays of alternate weeks were held between June and September 1903, commencing at the east end of Melville Drive. Destinations on Saturday included Aberlady, Carlops, Hopetoun, and Penicuik whereas on Tuesdays shorter trips, starting at 7.30 P.M., were made to places such as Ratho, Balerno, Roslin and Fairmilehead.[144] Prizes were awarded to the lady and gentleman who completed the most runs, and picnics were introduced in 1905. The season was extended from April to October in 1906 and the connection with the Literary Society was underlined when it introduced the feature of having a prescribed subject or book, preferably one associated with the place visited, for discussion during the cycle run. The yearning for self-improvement of these students embraced simultaneously physical, intellectual and cultural dimensions of personal development, to an extent that would be remarkable today. The literary fare discussed on these excursions was a serious one. The prescribed works in 1906 included Macbeth, Julius Caesar, Wordsworth, Hazlitt's essay 'On Cant and Hypocrisy', Bacon's essay 'Of Fortune', and Ruskin's 'King's Treasuries'.[145] Literary education on two wheels may have been more feasible in an era of negligible motor traffic but the club, which displayed every indication of being better organised than the college itself, was constantly innovating. In 1911 six joint rambles were held with the Literary Society on the first Saturday of each month; and in 1915 the redoubtable Miss Louisa Burton (niece of Mary Burton) also organised a programme of winter rambles. Membership, seldom more than around 36, sadly dwindled and the club was wound up on 8 February 1922. One of the founders of the cycling club, James Albert Thompson – who attended classes in history and economic science between 1899 and 1904 – went on to a highly successful business career and covenanted over £30,000 to the college between 1939 and 1941. The governors decided to create a lasting memorial to his munificence by associating a future assembly hall with his name.[146]

The proposal for a magazine was revived in 1904 and, with the support of Principal Laurie, the *College Quarterly* appeared in November 1904 selling at 3d.[147] The second and last number was published in March 1905, the venture being a financial failure. In October 1913 a new magazine, the *Heriot-Watt College Magazine*, was published and monthly numbers continued until February 1914, when it too failed for financial reasons.[148] The magazine sold for 2d and was worthy and serious, with articles on public speaking, the black arts, college societies and sports. It provided the first reference to organised sport in the college: a hockey club, which practised on the shinty ground at Inverleith Park, was formed by Professor Baily, a canny half-back, but it languished after three seasons through an insufficient fixture list.[149] A couple of years later an attempt was made to organise a rugby team, but the club became defunct after two seasons.

The Dramatic Study Club, set up in 1909 in connection with the Literary Society, met fortnightly on Wednesdays between 8.00 P.M. and 10.00 P.M. in the Oddfellows Hall.[150] The procedure was to read and discuss a Shakespearean play for the first hour and then a modern play for the second hour. The 1909–10 session witnessed the club's first performance in the Causwayside Lads' Institute when scenes from *The Tempest* were enacted. Sophisticated modern plays were selected with a heavy emphasis, surprisingly, on Irish authors, especially Goldsmith, Sheridan, Shaw, Synge, Wilde, Lady Gregory and Yeats. The club, however, only managed to stage four public performances during the first 19 years of its existence.[151]

During this period only one record survives which captures the experiences of a student at the college. William Anderson, born in 1875, lived in the Fountainbridge area of the city and was employed as a coalman by St Cuthbert's Co-operative Society. After rising at 5.00 A.M. each morning to work a 54 hour week delivering coal (Co-op carters earned only 28 shillings per week in 1911), Bill Anderson, an active socialist, was determined to improve himself by attending evening classes, reading widely and writing poetry and prose which were published in local magazines.[152] He attended lectures at Heriot-Watt College in English literature and composition and other classes elsewhere in bookkeeping, arithmetic, economics and French.

On Wednesday, 5 October 1904, Anderson paid his fee of 8s 6d to Heriot-Watt College and the following evening attended his first English literature class on Geoffrey Chaucer.[153] By 30 January 1905 the lecturer was discussing 'at some length' Pope's satirical poem *The Dunciad*.[154] Anderson entered a poetry competition at the college in April 1905, by which time the class was also tasked with writing an essay on Goldsmith's *Deserted Village*. He won the poetry competition for which the prize was *Choice Essays* and *Virgil's Works* translated by John Dryden. Later that week, on Thursday, 13 April, after a hard day's work delivering coal, Anderson retired to his sitting room and 'read part of Goldsmith's *She Stoops to Conquer*'.[155] The following year in 1906 he emigrated to Canada.

A Devastating Appraisal

Acedemic developments prior to 1916 had been primarily responses to a prevailing situation rather than part of a coherent strategy. In 1916, however, the governors appointed a special committee to consider the college's post-war development. The committee approached its task with no great sense of urgency but after a sharp reminder from the governors, brought two reports to them in November 1917, one from Principal Laurie and the other from Alexander Darroch, professor of education at Edinburgh University and one of its representatives on the Heriot's Trust. Laurie, after reviewing uncritically the existing situation, urged the hiving off of the commercial classes to a separate college, more adequate provision for trade classes, and for an extended range of subjects in engineering and chemistry, with recognition by Edinburgh University.

Professor Darroch delivered his report on 19 October and was forthright and devastating in his criticisms:[156]

The College has attempted and still attempts to do too many things, to be a kind of educational omnibus, and as a consequence of this spread of energy over too wide a field nothing has been done adequately and well.[157]

Turning to the provision of trade education, Darroch was equally critical:

In no one department is there adequate provision made for this kind of education at the present time. . . . Adequate and efficient provision for the teaching of no one trade, with the possible exception of engineering, exists at present.[158]

Darroch was also concerned with low rates of progression from the continuation classes of the school board to the trade courses of the college: only 16 per cent of the students qualified at the evening and continuation commercial classes in 1912–13, for example, actually enrolled in the college in the succeeding year.[159] With respect to the education of the technical expert, Darroch considered that the day department was unsatisfactory in terms of 'the number and quality of students attracted' and 'the adequacy of the provision made for the training'.[160] Furthermore, 'the equipment and accommodation for teaching mechanical engineering are still inadequate; . . . in mining, no laboratory has yet been provided, while technical mycology can hardly be said to have been the success it was expected to be'.[161] The subject advisory committees met only once a year and failed to inspire confidence in industrialists.

Professor Darroch, with the advantage of being a member of the governors and an academic at Edinburgh University, was uniquely qualified to comment on the relationship between the college and the university and his conclusions were characteristically unequivocal:

The College stands in no close and organic connection with the University. It is true . . . that since 1901 . . . certain classes taken at the College are counted *pro tanto* as qualifying for the degree in Engineering. . . . But the arrangement is merely a working arrangement, which may be dissolved at any time. . . . The real remedy lies in a closer union of the two bodies. . . . Every technical college in the country has some scheme of union with its local university. Edinburgh alone stands as an exception.[162]

Professor Darroch was severely critical of the lack of strategic direction of the college, a clear indictment of Laurie's management style:

The unsatisfactory position of the College has been and is still largely due to the want of any consistent plan or scheme of development. ... Lecturers (e.g. Mining) have been appointed, and no adequate laboratory provision has been made in advance, or since, for the teaching of the subject. Instead of proceeding by stages and securing that adequate provision has first been made for the teaching of one trade, or of one profession, it has been attempted to carry on all together, with the consequent result of failure to achieve anything satisfactorily. This is due to some extent to the lack of money, but is also due to the want of any clearly defined policy – any clearly defined idea as to the particular function in an educational system of a technical college.[163]

Darroch made several clear recommendations for the future of the college: 'the functions performed ... must be circumscribed and definitely limited'; it should restrict itself to technological and technical education, handing over commercial education to some other body; in trade education it should limit provision to the 'higher stages of those particular trades which require either highly specialised machinery, or extensive laboratory accommodation'; for technical and scientific examination 'the College should be brought into closer union with the University'.[164] Professor Darroch also addressed the management of the college, arguing that the Heriot's Trust neither could nor should be expected to manage, let alone finance, the college, and a new governing body should be created on which local industry and university teachers of science should be represented.[165] He also proposed an increase in the authority of heads of departments who should be brought into closer touch than at present with the governors.[166] Darroch urged that the problems were 'pressing and urgent, and demand immediate solution'.[167] Discussions were held with the SED and Edinburgh University and centred on the composition of the new governing body, but in July 1918 the governors decided to delay further consideration until the Education Bill, then before Parliament, became law. Although the Education Act was passed in 1918, the whole matter remained in abeyance until 13 July 1925 when Robert Wilson urged that the governors give consideration to the formation of a new governing body.[168]

It was becoming increasingly clear that the continued expansion of the college to meet the growing demand for technological education was increasingly circumscribing the financial resources of the Heriot's Trust; the cost of its future development would make it impossible for them adequately to discharge their obligations under the terms of their original endowment.[169] Under Section 9 of the Education (Scotland) Act 1918, the education authorities of Fife, Midlothian and West Lothian agreed to contribute from 1925 £1 per 100 student hours for each student from their areas. But Edinburgh Education Authority, parsimonious as ever, declined to help the college.[170] An independent board of governors was established and the severance of the college from the trust was effected by the promotion of the Heriot-Watt College and George Heriot's Trust Confirmation Act of 1927. Under this Act the trust would continue to provide the college with a fixed annual payment of £8,000, exactly twice the minimum figure to which they were bound by the 1885 scheme. And the college government was entrusted to a body of not less than 25 governors.[171] Financial support from the Heriot's Trust was to continue until the college came under the control of the University Grants Committee in 1965. Then the trust's contribution was reduced, by agreement, to a nominal level of 100 guineas. In all, the Heriot-Watt College benefited from the munificence of the Heriot's Trust to the extent of over £300,000.[172]

The first meeting of the new governing body of Heriot-Watt College was held on 16 January 1928, the Heriot-Watt College and George Heriot's Trust Order 1927 having become law from 1 January. The composition of the new board of governors was rather a revision than a complete reformation of its predecessors. It comprised, as elected governors, the Lord Provost, the principal of Edinburgh University and the chairman of Edinburgh Education Authority, with three additional representatives from each of these bodies,[173] three members elected by George Heriot's Trust governors, and one each by the Royal Society of Edinburgh and the Chamber of Commerce. In addition, under Section 10 of the order, certain trade associations and unions nominated one governor each, thereby doubling industry representation:

- Edinburgh Printing and Kindred Trades' Association;
- Engineering and Allied Employers' East of Scotland Association;
- The Lothian Coal Owners' Association;
- Edinburgh, Leith, and District Building Trades' Association;
- Edinburgh Typographical Association;
- Amalgamated Engineering Union;
- The Mid and East Lothian Miners' Association;
- Edinburgh and District Trades and Labour Council.

Provision was made for up to three further governors to be appointed by the elected ones, and contributing education authorities could also elect one member each. In view of the similarity of their constitutions, it is not surprising that there was a large overlap between the old and new governing bodies. Thirteen of the 28 initial members of the college governors had served either on the Heriot's Trust or as additional members of the trust's College Committee. The Lord Provost was nominally, and occasionally in fact, chairman of the governors, but the effective head for all practical purposes was the vice-chairman. At the first meeting of the new governors, the unanimous choice for vice-chairman was Robert Wilson, since

1922 the representative on the old College Committee of the Printing and Kindred Trades Federation, and one of those most involved in the drafting of the new constitution. Wilson remained vice-chairman until his death in 1953 and his influence on the college's development was profound.

As Laurie's three decades of directing the institution through a world war and a major depression drew to a close in 1928, with most of Professor Darroch's key recommendations of 1917 not having been implemented, this burly, forthright, and stimulating authoritarian scholar moved into a retirement marked by the controversy created by his pro-Nazi sentiments. After a decade of stalemate, the college clearly required new leadership to provide strategic direction and administrative competence.

Notes

[1] Scotland, J. (1969) *The History of Scottish Education*, London, Vol. 2, p. 136.

[2] Quoted in Cowper, H. E. (1970) The Scottish Central Institutions. Master of Education thesis, University of Edinburgh, p. 32.

[3] Checkland, O. (1980) *Philanthropy in Victorian Scotland*, Edinburgh, p. 121.

[4] Anderson, A., Heriot-Watt College: Francis Ogilvie's Principalship, 1885–1900. Mimeo.

[5] Anderson, A. and Gowenlock, B. G. (1998) *Chemistry in Heriot-Watt 1821–1991*, p. 34.

[6] *Ibid.*, p. 34.

[7] HWUA, HWC 3/1A, *The Scotsman*, Obituary, 15 December 1930.

[8] HWUA, HWC 1/2/1, *Minutes of the Meetings of the Governors of George Heriot's Trust*, 9 May 1887, p. 67.

[9] HWUA, HWC 3/1A, Sir Francis Grant Ogilvie: An Appreciation. By Hudson Beare.

[10] Gifford, J., McWilliam, C. and Walker, D. (1984) *The Buildings of Scotland: Edinburgh*, London, p. 182.

[11] Anderson, *op. cit.*

[12] HWUA, HWC 3/1A, Obituary notice, *Proceedings of the Royal Society of Edinburgh*, 1931, Vol. 51, p. 214.

[13] HWUA, HWC 1/2/2, *Minutes of the Meetings of the Governors of George Heriot's Trust*, 1888, pp. 126–27. The janitor's salary in 1888 was £100 with an allowance of £30 to meet house rent, coal and gas; and five cleaners were also engaged at 8s 6d per week.

[14] HWUA, HWC 3/1A, Biographical information relating to governors, staff and students, *Journal of the Institute of Electrical Engineers*, Vol. 62, p. 987 (1924).

[15] HWUA, HWC 1/2/2, *op. cit.*, p. 145.

[16] HWUA, HWC 3/1A, Letter from H. Frank Heath to Lady Ogilvie, 16 December 1930.

[17] In 1920 Ogilvie became principal assistant secretary for the newly created Department of Scientific and Industrial Research and chairman of the Geological Survey Board. He died in December 1930.

[18] Anderson and Gowenlock, *op. cit.*, p. 37.

[19] HWUA, HWC 3/1A, Obituary notice. *Year Book of the Royal Society of Edinburgh*, 1949–50, p. 57.

[20] Anderson and Gowenlock, *op. cit.*, p. 40.

[21] Letter from Mr R. G. Roberts to A. Anderson, 20 January 1982.

[22] Barclay, J. B. (1960) Adult Education in South East Scotland. PhD thesis, University of Edinburgh, p. 126.

[23] Humes, W. M. (1983) Science, religion and education: a study in cultural interaction. In Humes, W. M. and Paterson, H. M. (eds) *Scottish Culture and Scottish Education 1800–1980*, Edinburgh, p. 130.

[24] Geddes, P. (1890) *Scottish University Needs and Aims*, Dundee, p. 3.

[25] Boardman, P. (1944) *Patrick Geddes: Maker of the Future*, North Carolina, p. 85. Quoted in Humes, *op. cit.*, p. 131.

[26] HWUA, HWC 3/1/A, Cuthbert, M. (1982) *Patrick Geddes 1854–1932*, Edinburgh, p. 3.

[27] *Ibid.*, p. 7.

[28] HWUA, SA 14/3/2, Mill, H. R. (1951) *An Autobiography*, London, p. 65.

[29] HWUA, HWC 1/2/5, *Minutes of the Meetings of the Governors of George Heriot's Trust*, 1891, p. 101.

[30] Shand became a member of the Judicial Committee of the Privy Council from 1890 and, having been raised to the peerage in 1892, he was an active judge in the House of Lords; he was taking part in the appeal in the celebrated *Free Kirk* case at the time of his death.

[31] Laurie, A. P. (1934) *Pictures and Politics: A Book of Reminiscences*, London, p. 20.

[32] *Ibid.*, p. 27.

[33] *Ibid.*, pp. 47–48.

[34] HWUA, HWC 3/1/A, Unpublished mimeo.

[35] Laurie, *op. cit.*, p. 98.

[36] *Ibid.*, p. 102.

[37] HWUA, HWC 3/1/A, Obituary notice.

[38] HWUA, HWC 3/1/A, Obituary, *Nature*, 10 December 1949, p. 988.

[39] Laurie, *op. cit.*, p. 117.

[40] HWUA, HWC 3/1/A, Obituary, *The Times*, 15 October 1949.

[41] *Ibid.*

[42] HWUA, HWC 3/1/9, Letter Box Number 8: A. P. Laurie Correspondence.

[43] Laurie, *op. cit.*, p. 120.

[44] Anderson, A., Heriot-Watt: An Edinburgh Institution. Mimeo.

[45] HWUA, HWC 3/1/4, Letter Box Number 3: A. P. Laurie Correspondence.

[46] HWUA, HWC 3/1/A, Ritchie, P. D., Obituary, *Nature*, 10 December 1949.

[47] HWUA, HWC 3/1/A, Alex Anderson interview with Mr Peter Kilpatrick, governor.

[48] HWUA, HWC 3/1/A, Obituary, *Nature*, 10 December 1949.

[49] Anderson, R. D. (1983) *Education and Opportunity in Victorian Scotland*, Oxford, p. 206.

[50] Craik was a strong supporter of the idea of military training in schools. See Humes, W. M. (1983) Science, religion and education: a study in cultural interaction. In Humes, W. M. and Paterson, H. M. (eds) *Scottish Culture and Scottish Education 1800–1980*, Edinburgh, pp. 115–36.

[51] Anderson, R. D., *op. cit.*, p. 206.

[52] Quoted in Scotland, *op. cit.*, Vol. 2, p. 5.

[53] *Ibid.*, p. 24.

[54] Cowper, *op. cit.*, p. 54.

[55] Scotland, *op. cit.*, p. 137.

[56] HWUA, HWC 1/2/16, *Minutes of the Meetings of the Governors of George Heriot's Trust*, 1902, p. 4.

[57] *Report of the Committee of Council on Education in Scotland*, 1903–4. Cmnd 1973, Appendix 1, p. 205.

[58] *A Selection of the Circular Letters of the Scottish Education Department 1898–1904*, (Cmnd 4077 1904) with explanatory memorandum, p. 17.

[59] Cowper, *op. cit.*, pp. 56–57.

[60] HWUA, HWC 1/2/31, *Minutes of the Meetings of the Governors of George Heriot's Trust*, 1917, p. 251.

[61] HWUA, HWC 1/2/16, *Minutes of the Meetings of the Governors of George Heriot's Trust*, 1902, pp. 96–97.

[62] HWUA, HWC 1/2/31, *Minutes of the Meetings of the Governors of George Heriot's Trust*, 1917, p. 258.

[63] *Ibid.*, p. 259.

[64] HWUA, HWC 1/2/21, *Minutes of the Meetings of the Governors of George Heriot's Trust*, 1907, p. 167.

[65] Boyle, J. S. (1973) *Heriot–Watt University: From Mechanics Institute to Technological University, 1821–1973*, Edinburgh, p. 16.

[66] Laurie, *op. cit.*, p. 123.

[67] HWUA, HWC 1/2/31, *Minutes of the Meetings of the Governors of George Heriot's Trust*, 1917, p. 252.

[68] HWUA, HWC 1/2/15, *Minutes of the Meetings of the Governors of George Heriot's Trust*, 1901, pp. 79 and 81.

[69] Laurie, *op. cit.*, p. 125.

[70] *The Scotsman*, 23 September 1902.

[71] HWUA, HWC 1/2/19, *Minutes of the Meetings of the Governors of George Heriot's Trust*, 1905, pp. 206–7.

[72] HWUA, HWC 1/2/21, *Minutes of the Meetings of the Governors of George Heriot's Trust*, 1907, p. 52.

[73] HWUA, HWC 1/2/20, *Minutes of the Meetings of the Governors of George Heriot's Trust*, 1906, p. 87.

[74] HWUA, HWC 1/2/31, *Minutes of the Meetings of the Governors of George Heriot's Trust*, 1917, p. 253.

[75] Anderson and Gowenlock, *op. cit.*, p. 45.

[76] *Ibid.*, p. 53.

[77] Manners, D. S. (2001) *Brewing and Biological Sciences at Heriot-Watt University, 1904–1989*, Edinburgh, pp. 5–6.

[78] HWUA, HWC 1/2/21, *Minutes of the Meetings of the Governors of George Heriot's Trust*, 1907, p. 65.

[79] *Ibid.*, p. 277.

[80] *Ibid.*, p. 278.

[81] *Ibid.*, p. 278.

[82] The National Archives of Scotland, ED 26/293, Memo by John Struthers, May 1910.

[83] *Ibid.*

[84] The National Archives of Scotland, ED 26/293, Memo by John Struthers, 21 February 1913.

[85] The National Archives of Scotland, ED 26/294, Memo by John Struthers, 1 July 1916.

[86] *Ibid.* Letter from John Struthers to Principal Laurie, 7 July 1916.

[87] Laurie, *op. cit.*, p. 124.

[88] *Ibid.*, p. 124.

[89] HWUA, HWC 1/2/9, *Minutes of the Meetings of the Governors of George Heriot's Trust*, 1895.

[90] Turner, A. L. (ed.) (1933) *History of the University of Edinburgh, 1883–1933*, Edinburgh.

[91] Birse, R. M. (1983) *Engineering at Edinburgh University: A Short History, 1673–1983*, Edinburgh, p. 108.

[92] HWUA, HWC 1/2/31, *Minutes of the Meetings of the Governors of George Heriot's Trust*, 1917, pp. 254–55.

[93] *Ibid.*, p. 256. The 1901 agreement is printed in full in the 1917 minutes.

[94] HWUA, HWC 1/2/15, *Minutes of the Meetings of the Governors of George Heriot's Trust*, 1901, p. 67.

[95] HWUA, HWC 1/2/31, *op. cit.*, pp. 256–7.

[96] HWUA, HWC 1/2/23, *Minutes of the Meetings of the Governors of George Heriot's Trust*, 1909, p. 290.

[97] Birse, *op. cit.*, p. 113.

[98] HWUA, HWC 1/2/22, *Minutes of the Meetings of the Governors of George Heriot's Trust*, 3 July 1908.

[99] HWUA, HWC 3/1/A, Obituary, *University of Edinburgh Journal*, Vol. 7, p. 284 (1935).

[100] Evening classes in mining had been given since 1913.

[101] Beare, T. H. (1935) Henry Briggs: an appreciation, *University of Edinburgh Journal*, Vol. VII, no. 3, p. 284.

[102] Birse, *op. cit.*, pp. 113–14.

[103] *Ibid.*, p. 114.

[104] HWUA, HWC 1/2/35, *Minutes of the Meetings of the Governors of George Heriot's Trust*, 1921, p. 122.

[105] Beare, *op. cit.*, p. 284.

[106] Birse, *op. cit.*, p. 114.

[107] *Ibid.*, pp. 114–15.

[108] I am grateful to Prof. Brian G. Gowenlock for informing me of this.

[109] Butt, J. (1996) *John Anderson's Legacy: The University of Strathclyde and Its Antecedents, 1796–1996*, East Linton, p. 135.

[110] Birse, *op. cit.*, p. 115.

[111] Edinburgh University Library, Gallery of Benefactors.

[112] HWUA, HWC 1/2/28, *Minutes of the Meetings of the Governors of George Heriot's Trust*, 1914, p. 261.

[113] I am grateful to Rachael Vincent who so thoroughly researched the complex issue of defining an accurate time series of student numbers.

[114] HWUA, HWC 1/2/41, *Minutes of the Meetings of the Governors of George Heriot's Trust*, 1918, p. 278.

[115] *Ibid.*, p. 270.

[116] HWUA, HWC 1/2/36, *Minutes of the Meetings of the Governors of George Heriot's Trust*, 1922, p. 177.

[117] Laurie, *op. cit.*, p. 134.

[118] HWUA, HWC 1/2/30, *George Heriot's Trust, Heriot-Watt College Committee*, 1916, p. 123.

[119] Anderson and Gowenlock, *op. cit.*, p. 51.

[120] HWUA, HWC 1/2/30, *Minutes of the Meetings of the Governors of George Heriot's Trust*, 1916, pp. 210–11.

[121] HWUA, HWC 3/1/A, Obituary, *Year Book of the Royal Society of Edinburgh*, 1944–45, p. 13.

[122] Anderson and Gowenlock, *op. cit.*, p. 53.

[123] *Ibid.*, p. 53.

[124] Chalmers, R. A. (1993) A mastery of microanalysis. *Chemistry in Britain*, Vol. 29, no. 6, p. 492.

[125] *Ibid.*, p. 492.

[126] Obituary, *The Guardian*, 30 July 2001.

[127] *Ibid.*, p. 494.

[128] *Ibid.*

[129] Cowper, *op. cit.*, p. 76.

[130] *National Science in Education: Being the Report of a Committee on the Position of National Science in the Educational System of Great Britain*, HMSO, 1918.

[131] *Reform in Scottish Education, Report of the Scottish Education Reform Committee (1917)*, Edinburgh.

[132] *Ibid.*

[133] HWUA, HWC 4/1/2, *Heriot-Watt College Literary Society, Minutes of the Committee and Special Business Meetings*, 1891–1904.

[134] HWUA, HWC 4/1/2, *op. cit.*, 1892–93.

[135] *Ibid.*, 1894–95.

[136] *Ibid.*, 1896–97 and 1897–98.

[137] HWUA, HWC 4/1/3, *Heriot-Watt College Literary Society, Minutes of the Committee and Special Business Meetings*, 1904–5.

[138] Reminiscences of Mr D. B. Mackay, secretary, 1902–03; Moir, D. G. (1929) Heriot-Watt College Literary Society Diamond Jubilee Booklet, Edinburgh, p. 30.

[139] HWUA, HWC 4/1/4, *Heriot-Watt College Literary Society, Minutes of the Committee and Special Business Meetings*, 1913–14.

[140] HWUA, HWC 4/1/23, Moir, *op. cit.*, p. 21.

[141] HWUA, HWC 4/1/2, *op. cit.*, p. 24.

[142] Moir, *op. cit.*, p. 24.

[143] *Ibid.*, p. 25.

[144] *Ibid.*, p. 31.

[145] HWUA, HWC 4/1/20, *Melville Cycling Club Minute Book*.

[146] HWUA, HWC 3/3/2, *Biographical Information Relating to College Students*, James Albert Thompson.

[147] Moir, *op. cit.*, p. 22.

[148] *Ibid.*, p. 22.

[149] HWUA, HWC 4/4/1, *The Heriot-Watt College Magazine*, Vol. 1, no. 1, October 1913, p. 10.

[150] Moir, *op. cit.*, p. 34.

[151] *Ibid.*, p. 37.

[152] Anderson, W. (1990) *No Ordinary Man: William Anderson's Edinburgh Journal, 1903–1906*, City of Edinburgh District Council, Libraries Division, Edinburgh, pp. vi–vii.

[153] *Ibid.*, p. 91.

[154] *Ibid.*, p. 101.

[155] *Ibid.*, p. 117.

[156] H-WU 1/2/31A, *Minutes of the Meetings of the Governors of George Heriot's Trust*, 1917, p. 287.

[157] *Ibid.*, pp. 294.

[158] *Ibid.*, p. 288.

[159] *Ibid.*, p. 289.

[160] *Ibid.*, pp. 290–91.

[161] *Ibid.*, p. 291.

[162] *Ibid.*, pp. 292–93.

[163] *Ibid.*, p. 294.

[164] *Ibid.*, pp. 295–96.

[165] *Ibid.*, pp. 297–98.

[166] *Ibid.*, p. 298.

[167] *Ibid.*, p. 299.

[168] H-WU 1/2/39A, *Minutes of the Meetings of the Governors of George Heriot's Trust*, 1925, p. 213.

[169] Boyle, *op. cit.*, p. 17.

[170] HWUA, HWC 1/2/39, *Minutes of the Meetings of the Governors of George Heriot's Trust*, 1925, p. 235.

[171] Boyle, *op. cit.*, p. 18.

[172] *Ibid.*, p. 18.

[173] HWUA, HWC 1/2/42, *Minutes of the Meetings of the Governors of George Heriot's Trust*, 1928, pp. 2–4.

Chapter Six

New Beginnings: 1928–1966

Tis well enough for a servant to be
bred at an university: but education is
a little too pedantic for a gentleman.
William Congreve

A room with a view: pharmacy laboratory in the Grassmarket, 1960s.
Photograph: © The Scotsman Publications Ltd

A Change of Style: James Cameron Smail

The late 1920s witnessed an emerging crisis in the coal, iron and steel, engineering and shipbuilding industries, most dramatically manifested in the General Strike of 1926. The Scottish economy, because of its dependence on a small number of exporting industries, was more vulnerable than the rest of the UK when the world slumped into depression between 1929 and 1933. Unemployment in Scotland was 27.7 per cent in 1932, compared with a UK figure of 22.1 per cent. Foreign competition, protective tariffs elsewhere, and the failure of the international economy to grow, all undermined the British economy. National unemployment stood at 2 million people; industry seemed unable to recover from the slump; and the Ramsay McDonald government was all but bankrupt. The 1930s was a deeply unhappy period when politics encroached on the lives of individuals and institutions virtually all the time. A dismal financial environment embraced the college in an ever darkening gloom as day student numbers declined (Figure 6.1).

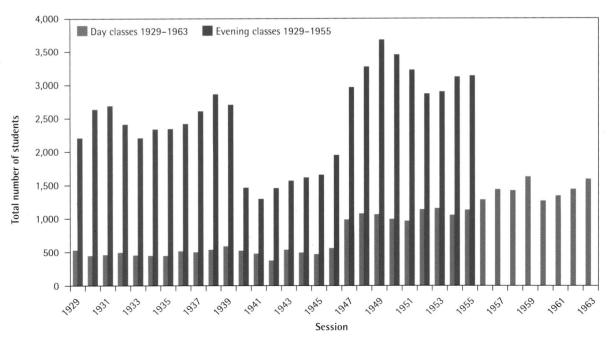

Figure 6.1 Number of students enrolled, 1929–63

All these factors represented a major challenge to the newly constituted board of governors of the college. At their first meeting on 16 January 1928 the board appointed an Interim Committee on whose recommendation they soon resolved that business should be handled by a College Committee of 19 members and a Finance Committee of 11, whose functions were academic policy and matters of finance and fabric, respectively. No representation of the staff – other than through the attendance of the principal at meetings – was deemed necessary even in the case of the College Committee, though years before Laurie and Darroch had urged the establishment of a senate. The professors, however, wrote to the governors, suggesting the formation of a 'consultative board' consisting of the principal, themselves and the head of mathematics and physics. After their long experience of Laurie's easy regime, they were naturally apprehensive of any invasion of their freedom by his successor. Subsequently, a board of studies was established consisting of the heads of departments which, however, wielded no real power. Any business it wished to progress came via the principal to the College Committee, which was concerned simply with whether a proposal was educationally desirable, in which case it would be referred to the Finance Committee.

An Appointments Committee, chaired by Robert Wilson, was established. The governors, on its recommendation, agreed on 11 May 1928 to offer the post of principal at £1,500 per annum to James Cameron Smail, principal assistant to the education officer of the London County Council. Smail (1880–1970) was the

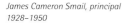

James Cameron Smail, principal 1928–1950

Robert Wilson, printer and influential vice-chairman of the college governors.
Portrait by Stanley Cursiter.
Photograph: Douglas McBride

second of the three sons of Adam Smail of Edinburgh. Educated at Daniel Stewart's College, he then attended Heriot-Watt College, where he acquitted himself with credit rather than distinction, taking the diploma in mechanical engineering in 1902. He later studied briefly at the Royal College of Science and the London School of Economics, becoming a Whitworth exhibitioner and a royal exhibitioner but never taking a degree. After two short spells in industry, he became an inspector in the Department of Agriculture and Technical Instruction in Ireland in 1902 under Robert Blair, who adopted him as one of several disciples who later attained some distinction. When Blair became education officer to the London County Council, Smail followed him in 1911, first as organiser of trade schools, and later as head of the technology branch in charge of some 50 technical schools and 200 evening institutes. Smail was no philistine; he was an omnivorous reader who read books on every subject from 11 o'clock at night to 2 o'clock in the morning; and a man of wide culture, with a particular interest (appropriate to the college) in fine printing and the physical aspects of the book.

Smail was to prove himself a leader and able administrator rather than a scholar (though an erudite man), a devourer of work who yet had time for people, a discreet and kind man of resolute personality who, once determined on a course of action, pursued it vigorously.[1] Mr John White worked with Smail for 22 years as clerk to the governors and had a high regard for the new principal, who was 'expert at picking a hole in any argument and first class at writing a difficult letter'.[2] His warm-heartedness endeared him to a wide circle of colleagues and friends for he 'always had time for everyone'; his leadership was an 'unfailing source of confidence and encouragement';[3] a charming man, he was, nevertheless, somewhat distant with some professorial colleagues, aware of the disparity in academic qualifications.[4] Alan Shaw, who studied electrical engineering at the college in the 1930s, remembered Smail as 'an unobtrusive but benign figure. You always felt he was there and could go and see him if you wanted.'[5] Smail took over the helm of the college at a difficult time after a period of decline and then strove to develop it during the severe economic recession of the 1930s. Against this background, he succeeded in revitalising the institution and in realising the first two stages of his building plan, only to suffer the frustration of the completion being deferred by the Second World War, although he lived to see the opening of the final (third) extension in 1958.

The situation to which Smail came on 1 September 1928 was far from encouraging. On the credit side, there was a new governing body with an enthusiastic, energetic and influential vice-chairman in Robert Wilson, who was de facto chair as the Lord Provost of Edinburgh seldom attended, and who formed a favourable partnership with Smail. Governors' meetings were held at the City Chambers, symbolising the remoteness which many academic staff felt from their executive authority. Money was very tight and the budget during Smail's first year in 1928–29 was a mere £32,000.[6] There had also been little development of any kind in the previous decade. According to his daughter Betty Macpherson, his first impression of the college building was of its dirt and gloom and he personally brightened these surroundings by wearing a new rose in his buttonhole each day, symbolising the freshness of his alert mind.[7] Smail felt strongly that people coming to work and study must do so in pleasant surroundings. Among his first actions was to bring in bright colours with light curtains and a cork floor in the principal's room; somehow he found money to lighten the drab interiors elsewhere and to set about improving the social climate, with more civilised amenities for students and staff.

Prior to Smail's arrival there were no student facilities and 'people used to stand on the front doorstep and smoke between classes'.[8] The conversion of a room to form a students' common room for day and evening students, equipped with a table and a coffee urn, was approved in December 1928. Talks with the students led to the formation of a Students' Representative Council (SRC) in January 1929.[9] Soon afterwards a canteen was established, first for Saturday and evening students and later for all. There was a demand for playing fields, but until 1958 nothing could be done other than to seek the occasional use of public playing fields or those of other institutions. A letter from the SRC in March 1931 requested the governors to allocate funds in aid of athletics; a grant of £10 was made, reflecting the parsimony of the committee and the financial constraints during the recession.[10]

New buildings were badly needed. On the main site, even the most recent additions, the engineering laboratories and workshops of 1908, were seriously cramped. Chemistry was divided between the former brewery/art block (on the site of the later third extension) and the main building, eventually linked by a bridge; while electrical engineering was even more inadequately housed. Extensive repairs to the external stonework of the Chambers Street building were urgently needed and were carried out in Smail's first year. The exception to this gloomy picture was the department of mining, whose building at 79 The Grassmarket (another converted brewery which was not the *dernier cri* in modern design and planning) was opened on 23 October 1928 by Lord Chelmsford, a former Viceroy of India, chosen for the task perhaps because many mining students went to posts there. The inauguration of the £21,590 building, attended by about 260 guests, was doubtless an important public relations exercise; the coal owners at this stage were reducing their previously significant contributions to the costs of the department to nominal levels. Thus, news of a gift of £1,000 from W. A. Tait, CE, the governor appointed by the Royal Society of Edinburgh, as the nucleus of a fund for research, especially in mine safety, was particularly welcome. The professor, Henry Briggs, was active alike in research, teaching and the industry. As head of a joint university/college department, however, Briggs seemed to have remained somewhat aloof from college affairs, and the department, located in the Grassmarket and therefore physically as well as administratively separate, was less an integral part of the college than the others.

Under Smail's leadership, ambitions for the physical expansion of the college were more than matched by academic developments. On the academic side (and still in Smail's first year) advisory committees for the courses in the various departments were revived and interested members of industry were recruited to serve on them. Developments in courses included new classes for Stock Exchange apprentices and clerks, and classes in advertising and salesmanship. While the revival of advisory committees was a reversion to Laurie's policy (if not latterly his practice), the new commercial classes represented a complete reversal of Laurie's avowed desire to hive off commercial subjects; this side of the non-scientific work continued to grow through the remaining years of the college's history.

New salary scales for teaching staff were agreed in 1929: lecturers, £300 rising by increments of £15 to £500; senior lecturers, £500 increasing by £20 increments to £600; and professors, £1,000 with increments of £50 to £1,200.[11] Subsequently, as a consequence of the severe impact of the depression on the Scottish economy, the salaries and wages of all staff were cut by 7.5 per cent in October 1931, and they were not restored to previous levels until 1 July 1935.[12] To relieve Cullen, clerk to

the governors, a senior clerk was appointed, Mr John Y. White; he was destined to become Cullen's successor as clerk to the governors in 1935 and served for 30 years, forming a third member of the triumvirate of Smail, Wilson and White.

The principal was soon busy with new schemes. A committee was set up to consider the provision of a college library, the former library having slowly withered away until its remnants were sold for wastepaper by Laurie. A central library was established in January 1931 on the first floor of the main building in Chambers Street. The opening hours were 11 A.M. to 2 P.M., and 6.30 P.M. to 9.30 P.M.[13] This appears to mark a turning point in the history of the library and some effort was made to develop it; by degrees the departmental libraries were absorbed. The acquisition policy was less restrictive than previously and works of a more general nature were now encouraged in the interest of a liberal education. The library, however, never had a prominent place in college priorities.

A New Building Programme

The most important of all Smail's early efforts was decisiveness over future building plans, something on which Wilson had no doubt been poised to act as soon as the new principal arrived. The town clerk, the city architect (E. J. MacRae) and Smail produced a report with remarkable speed in January

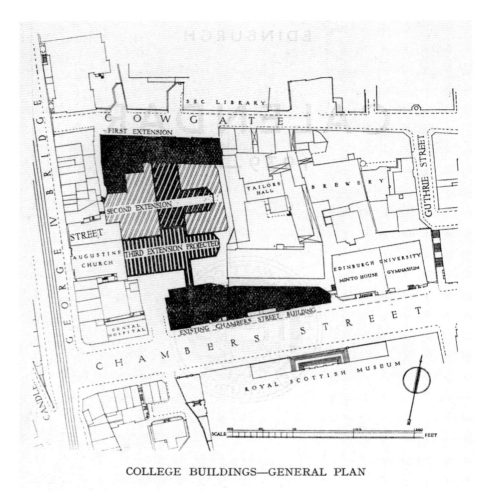

COLLEGE BUILDINGS—GENERAL PLAN

1929 which – rejecting both the options of disposing of existing buildings to move elsewhere and of erecting further accommodation on other sites (following the example of mining) – firmly recommended extension to the north of the existing building on a 3½ acre site extending to the Cowgate. The decision to develop northwards coincided with (and no doubt resulted from) the adoption by Edinburgh Corporation of plans to clear slum property on the south side of the Cowgate and widen the street.[14] Hitherto, development of the former brewery site acquired some 30 years earlier had been impeded because the area was intensively occupied by the engineering and (adapted) chemistry buildings; these departments, heavily dependent on workshop and laboratory accommodation, could not function during rebuilding. The availability of extra space on the Cowgate frontage permitted phasing of the building programme so as to decant departments in a logical sequence as accommodation was completed. It was for this reason that the development began at the Cowgate end farthest from the existing main building

The gymnasium within the first extension, 1935

The dining room within the first extension, 1935

and that subsequent extensions gradually filled in the gap between. That completion of this infilling process occupied over 20 years was not the fault of Wilson, Smail and other colleagues, but of a short Austrian painter of posters whose Nazi aspirations had scarcely been heard of in Edinburgh in 1929.

The first delay on progress, however, was because the Lord Provost, Thomas B. Whitson, proposed a grandiose town planning scheme for the central area of the

HERIOT WATT COLLEGE

CHAMBERS STREET
EDINBURGH
TELEPHONE Nᵒˢ 23271 & 23272

PRINCIPAL. J. CAMERON SMAIL O.B.E. F.R.S.E.

HERIOT-WATT COLLEGE EXTENSION

COWGATE FRONT

1935

Calendar

Departments

MECHANICAL
ENGINEERING

ELECTRICAL
ENGINEERING

MINING
ENGINEERING

CHEMISTRY

PHARMACY

Departments

BUILDING

PRINTING

PHYSICS

MATHEMATICS

COMMERCE

LANGUAGES

MUSIC

SALESMANSHIP

city under which the college would be relocated in the Pleasance (a step which, in the long run, might have proved propitious and perhaps enabled the university eventually to have developed in a pleasant valley below Arthur's Seat). The governors, however, continued to develop the plans for the Chambers Street–Cowgate site which were approved by the Scottish Education Department in July 1931. The Carnegie Trust allocated a grant of £2,000 for equipment and £3,000 towards the extension of the college buildings.[15] By now public funds were under very severe pressure as a result of the depression and this delayed the start of work until January 1933. Smail always considered that Edinburgh Corporation was less than enthusiastic in supporting Heriot-Watt.[16]

The lecturers and students who came to the college in the 1930s certainly heard and remembered the hammering sound of construction work. The Heriot-Watt College Extension Scheme, as approved, and as made the subject of successive appeals for funding, was for a development in three phases. The first extension, a three-storey block occupying the cleared site fronting the Cowgate, provided space for the printing department, mechanical engineering, a gymnasium and a dining hall. The front of the building facing the Cowgate was designed with hammer-dressed coursers of pink Duddingston stone from Northumberland and it was roofed with West Highland slates from Ballachulish; the extension cost £38,000.[17] It was opened on 22 January 1935 by Sir Geoffrey Collins, Secretary of State for Scotland, wearing a grey suit and spats. At the opening ceremony, Mr Robert Wilson, vice-chairman of the governors, launched an appeal for £100,000 as a Jubilee Fund.[18] Work on the six-storey second extension commenced immediately, and following delays caused by a firm going into liquidation, was formally inaugurated by John Colville, Secretary of State for Scotland, on 18 October 1938. This added improved accommodation for physics, optics, engineering and printing, a library, and separate common rooms for men and women. It also provided laboratories for chemistry, a staff room and a room for the professor of chemistry, complete with the ultimate symbol of academic prestige at the time, a personal lavatory – a similar facility being available only to the principal.[19]

The old chemistry building, the last relic of the much adapted brewery, was then to be cleared for the third extension (approved by the SED in 1938), a five-storey block which would provide an assembly hall, a boardroom, rooms for pharmacy and, showing great prescience, an air-raid shelter which could ultimately be used as a cycle store. The steep fall in the ground from south to north enabled the first extension to have two high-ceilinged floors below the level of the Chambers Street ground floor, with ample scope for the second and third extensions being carried to considerable height to compensate for the restriction in width imposed by the need to admit daylight and air on a site almost entirely enclosed by existing high buildings.

The Second World War delayed the completion of the third extension until 2 July 1958. Despite this, the entire development was carried out to the basic plan evolved in 1929 by Wilson, Smail and MacRae, and proved singularly well adapted to the requirements of the college. The third extension, a five-storey block with a floor area of 63,000 square feet, was to provide accommodation for chemical engineering, physics, optics, organic chemistry, lecture rooms, staff rooms, a boardroom, and the Albert Thompson Memorial Hall, with a seating capacity of 603. The financing of the extensions was far from simple. It was made clear from the outset that the SED would not fund the entire building costs, and in 1933 the department announced provision of £5,000 a year in each of 1932/33, 1933/34 and 1934/35. In the event, of the £102,000 cost of the two pre-war extensions, £57,000 came from the department, £20,500 from the college's own reserves, and £20,500 from donations in response to appeals (including a cheque for £21 from the Irish writer George Bernard Shaw);[20] £7,000 from the Carnegie Trust for the Universities of Scotland; £5,000 from the Miners' Welfare Fund; and £5,050 from the estate of Edward Clark, an Edinburgh printer who was a notable benefactor of the printing department. A further development of considerable technical difficulty was the construction in 1961 of an additional storey above the first extension building on the Cowgate to accommodate the department of brewing and biological sciences.[21] The post-war college was better housed, better equipped and, eventually, better staffed than it had been in the dreary days between the wars.

The sight testing laboratory, 1938. Photograph: McLagan and Cumming

The Old Order Changeth

The institution Smail inherited from Laurie was one where the ageing professoriate had been allowed to run their departments with a minimum of interference or coordination. Principal Smail started to intervene and some heads did not like it. The holders of the three foundation chairs were, however, all approaching retirement: Stanfield, who had several times served as acting principal, retired in 1929 having been professor of mechanics and engineering since 1889. At the close of the 1930–31 session, Professor Boon retired from the chair of chemistry, which he had held since 1919. He had been responsible for establishing chemistry as a subject for the college associateship, and for seizing the opportunity to add pharmacy and biochemistry to the department's activities; distinction in research, however, never matched the Perkin–Kipping era, largely as a consequence of heavy teaching loads, both day and evening, mainly at an elementary level for engineers and pharmacists.[22]

Boon's successor, Professor Slater Price, a London graduate of distinction, arrived from Birmingham Technical College, where he had published some 40 papers between 1903 and 1920.[23] Slater Price clearly hoped that under his leadership the department might regain the reputation it held under Perkin, but he soon realised that it was necessary to emphasise teaching at the expense of research because of the wide subject spread, embracing not only chemistry but also pharmacy, biochemistry, brewing and applied chemistry. Furthermore, the dedicated teaching staff, with a couple of exceptions, were not research-minded by inclination or habit.[24] Slater Price retired in 1940 and his valedictory report reveals a disappointed man, especially with the difficulties of promoting research. A motorcycle accident before he joined the college had left him lame though still able to play the departmental sport of golf, but his health was not robust.[25] This may have also affected his research, for after early years of major scientific output, his time at Heriot-Watt yielded only one paper.[26] Nevertheless, he inspired others, notably William Watt, who graduated with an associateship in 1935 and pursued a career at RAF Farnborough, where he was the major pioneer in the development of high-strength carbon fibres, for which he was made a Fellow of the Royal Society (FRS) in 1976.[27]

Day classes in pharmacy which had been introduced in 1921 under the auspices of the department of chemistry were boosted by an agreement in 1935 between the college and the Royal Dispensary School of Pharmacy (where pharmacy had been taught since 1776) whereby the Royal School was incorporated into the college.[28] A separate department of pharmacy was eventually created in 1949. Even before amalgamation, the largest number of students in the chemistry department were those taking one-year courses in pharmacy: from 1931–32 to 1934–35 these totalled some 70 each year, whereas chemistry students amounted to only 11–16 per session.[29] The amalgamation became effective in 1935, the Royal School contributing Eric Knott to the staff (though he continued to serve the school as an apothecary) plus some equipment and the sum of £1,000 (the college had requested £5,000) towards the new accommodation for pharmacy.[30] The teaching of pharmacy was shared among Campbell (for chemistry), Henderson and Knott (for all other areas). Knott, son of a Girvan weekly newspaper editor, had been an apprentice at Graham's Pharmacy in Girvan, where he made chilly outings to the quay during the cod season to collect livers in order to prepare cod-liver oil.[31] Knott remained a loyal member of staff until 1960. Following absorption of the Royal Dispensary School in 1935, pharmacy numbers rose to about 140 a year, often outnumbering chemistry diploma students by 10 to 1.[32]

The revival of the Scottish economy following the depression was faltering and inconsistent. Electrical engineering, however, remained buoyant throughout the interwar period because of its widespread applications and the capital investment in supply companies, the National Grid, railway electrification and new consumer industries such as cars, radios and white electrical goods. Professor Baily retired from the chair of electrical engineering in 1933, having served the college for 37 years, to be succeeded by Dr Maurice G. Say from the Royal Technical College, Glasgow, where he had conducted research related to railway electrification. He found few industrial contacts in Scotland, however, since British railway companies' experiments with electrification were conducted south of Hadrian's Wall.[33] Say, an inspiring and exacting teacher who published a number of standard books on electrical machines, was to occupy the chair of electrical engineering for 30 years until 1963. Other key departments also witnessed changes in leadership during the 1930s. During 1933–34, Frank Restall was appointed as head of the printing department and Thomas Brown as head of building; following the death of Professor Henry Briggs in 1935, Professor W. H. McMillan, professor of mining at University College Nottingham, was appointed to the joint chair of mining in 1936.

Alan Shaw, who graduated with an associateship in electrical engineering in 1938, studied at the college under Professor Say while employed as a student apprentice by the Edinburgh manufacturer Bruce Peebles. According to his testimony, 'Heriot-Watt College was a hard-working place'. A culture of overteaching students prevailed:

> The idea of free periods or having an afternoon off to study . . . was absolutely unheard of. . . . We were a fairly serious lot actually. We had a lot of fun . . . out of class but you knew your place – the lecturer was boss.[34]

Students of brewing at Heriot-Watt College combined academic lectures with hands-on experience at the nearby Argyll brewery of Campbell, Hope and King. This photograph from the 1960s shows the company fleet of delivery lorries lined up along Chambers Street. Heriot-Watt College can be seen top-left of image. Photograph: Scottish Brewing Archive

Despite the new building programme, safety standards in laboratories and workshops would never have complied with modern regulations:

> There were no safety precautions whatsoever. It was quite common for turners to get metal swarfs in their eye.[35]

During the 1930s and 1940s the education of a brewer was still a part-time affair. The student brewer spent two days each week in a brewery and attended classes on the other days; lectures never started before 10.00 A.M. so that the student, if required, could put in an early morning mash before turning his thoughts to scientific matters.[36] Four groups were being trained at the college after the war: men (there were no women) took the two-year certificate course; others studied for a three-year associateship; some engaged on a short postgraduate course; and yet others attended evening classes over five or six years.[37] When Dr I. A. Preece arrived from Birmingham as a lecturer in 1931, staffing was minimal due to the depression and he was responsible until after the war for the teaching of biochemistry, botany, malting and brewing to both day and evening students. The staff complement was doubled in 1945 by the appointment of Dr Anna MacLeod to teach the biological aspects of brewers' studies.

Professor Patrick N. O'Farrell, Dame Muriel Spark, Principal Alistair MacFarlane, Professor Claus Moser and Professor John H. McCutcheon at the honorary degree ceremony, July 1995

Although William Watt FRS was the most distinguished scientific graduate of the college in the interwar period, it is ironical that the most celebrated alumnus of all from this time was not a male engineer or scientist but Scotland's greatest living author, Dame Muriel Spark. At the age of 11, Muriel Spark and her classmates fell into the hands of a remarkable schoolteacher, Miss Christina Kay, or as Muriel Spark was later to say, Miss Kay was a character in search of an author. She became the inspiration for *The Prime of Miss Jean Brodie*, but in 1929 Miss Kay's little girls were the *crème de la crème*. The options were limited for a girl of slender means on leaving James Gillespie's Senior School in 1934 at the age of 16. Her elder brother Philip had already studied for the HNC in chemistry at Heriot-Watt College so, as Dame Muriel records:

> I inscribed myself at the Heriot-Watt College (now a university) to complete my education in English prose. I was particularly interested in précis-writing, and took a course in that. I love economical prose, and would always try to find the briefest way to express a meaning. Heriot-Watt College had a reputation for practical and businesslike teaching.[38]

Each Monday evening in the autumn chill of 1934 she travelled by the yellow and green number 23 tram down from Bruntsfield to Tollcross and up Lauriston to

Forrest Road. The class, from 7 P.M. to 8 P.M. in the college building on Chambers Street, was conducted by a Mr Douglas Heath. The course was 12s 6d and the prescribed textbook, Robeson's *Précis Writing*, was half a crown.[39]

Muriel Spark, not for the only time in her life, had eschewed the conventional:

> My friends thought Heriot-Watt a strange choice for me. But in fact it offered something I wanted and needed. The use of language in the daily life of commerce, of trade, banking and even politics, was plainly more genuinely based in proportion as it was less rhetorical. I found that the work I put in, and the knowledge I absorbed at Heriot-Watt College was useful – for instance, later in my life. . . . I find 'managerial' speech unpretentious, direct, quite expressive enough.[40]

Dame Muriel is a writer of universal rather than particular location, but she is Edinburgh by formation, influenced by Heriot-Watt, and shaped by the city's antitheses, its social divisions, its contrasts between 'grim and guid', of gothic Old Town and classical New Town, of Jekyll and Hyde or Deacon Brodie, of evil and enlightenment. Although the settings of her novels include London, Jerusalem, New York and Rome, she has firmed up rather than softened the hyper-Edinburgh

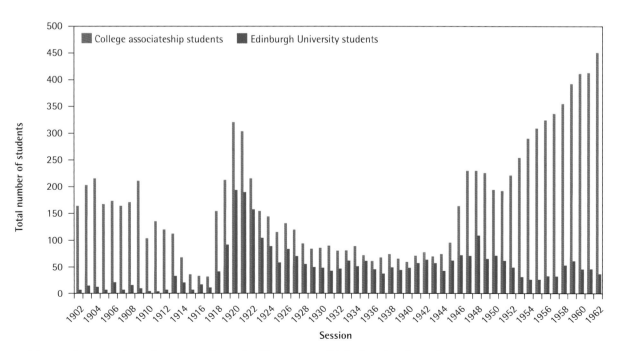

Figure 6.2 Number of students from the University of Edinburgh taking degree courses at Heriot-Watt College, 1902–62

style for which she was early recognised: tart, exegetic, teasingly proleptic, prone to deflation, perfectly turned out. The nosiness and the partiality for just deserts are also pure Edinburgh. Happily she returned to the city of her childhood and her alma mater to be conferred with an honorary doctorate of the university in 1995.

Neighbourly Relations

The University Grants Committee (UGC) visited the college on 29 May 1929 and agreed to make a grant of £2,000 in 1929–30 to the college via Edinburgh University to support university work at the college.[41] The governors then resolved that 'the time was now suitable for consideration by the University Court and the governors for a scheme to affiliate the Heriot-Watt College to the University of Edinburgh'.[42] Following negotiations, the university authorities agreed in May 1931 to draft an ordinance under which a joint Board of Technological Studies would be constituted.[43] This ordinance received the royal assent in February 1933, from when the college was affiliated to the university.[44] Under the scheme the University Court continued to recognise courses for degrees in science, engineering, technical chemistry and mining: 'Such recognised College courses shall be deemed to be courses taken in the University.'[45] During the first decade after the Second World War, with large numbers seeking admission to university courses, a further measure of cooperation under the ordinance took place and college classes in mathematics, physics, chemistry and engineering subjects were recognised for degree purposes. Even as late as 30 June 1958, Principal Appleton of the university was writing to Principal Nisbet suggesting that the university would consider instituting degrees in pharmacy and applied biochemistry and the recognition of suitable college classes for the purpose of graduation in those subjects.[46] By 1960, however, the number of Edinburgh University students attending degree courses at Heriot-Watt College had fallen to below 50 (Figure 6.2).[47] Some tensions in the relationship between the college and the university had emerged by 1950 and these will be explored later.

War Again

When Hitler's invasion of Poland brought Britain once again into military conflict with Germany in September 1939, there was little of the surprise that had surrounded the events of August 1914 or of the subsequent jingoism and war fever that had gripped the staff from Principal Laurie down. The first immediate casualties of the war for the college were 73 evening courses, but 144 survived, including those for National Certificate,[48] and evening classes were conducted without interruption despite difficult travelling conditions and the blackout. Arrangements for blacking out the buildings so that evening classes could proceed were completed in September 1939. To provide air-raid shelters adequate for the number of students, basements below the lithographic machine room were adapted and a shelter was built in the mechanics laboratory.[49] Further shelters were erected by September 1940. Bricking up the basement windows in Chambers Street cost £93 6s 4d.[50] A night patrol of members of staff and some students (males only) was arranged; some 70 staff and students were engaged on this duty, while students were also involved with the Home Guard and Senior Training Corps.[51] Staff were also organised in sections for firefighting, first aid and other emergencies. Nine full-time and six evening part-time staff enrolled for war service at the outbreak of hostilities, and five more followed later.[52] Military conscription had been slow in inception and, when begun, left large parts of the student body exempt from immediate service.

The number of students enrolled in the college evening classes in 1939–40 fell dramatically from 2,698 to 1,453. This decline of 46 per cent was higher than the 35 per cent drop in the First World War. Day class numbers declined less steeply (Figure 6.1). The commercial evening courses were more severely affected than the technical ones, with the fall in enrolment of clerks being especially marked.[53] Transport difficulties reduced severely the numbers attending from Fife, West Lothian and other outlying areas. By the early summer of 1940, however, the military situation had taken a turn for the worse, and by July 1941 the age of call-up for males had been reduced to 18. Both evening class and day class numbers fell substantially (Figure 6.1). The social and educational background of day class students during the war years was highly polarised: approximately half the class in electrical engineering in 1942 was drawn from Edinburgh University – mainly products of the Merchant Company Schools – whereas the college intake was largely composed of students who had completed National Certificates.[54]

The college was called on to respond to a wide variety of wartime needs. College staff and volunteers were manufacturing munitions in the mechanical engineering workshops, with production continuing throughout the summer vacations.[55] The electrical engineering department did not stand aloof from the war effort; it repaired voltmeters and ammeters for ship installations and assisted the Admiralty in degaussing ships in local waters in order to neutralise their magnetic fields and protect them against mines. In 1940–41 the training programmes introduced at the request of the army were extended to electricians, turners, fitters and instrument mechanics, and courses were run on behalf of the RAF to train radio and wireless mechanics.[56]

Professor Say of electrical engineering records that on the day war broke out (3 September 1939) he was asked 'to take a batch of soldiers for training in a new defence weapon [radar] which could track the position of enemy aircraft'.[57] The training of RAF aircraftmen (and later women) became a major commitment: groups of 50 enrolled every four weeks for six months' training in radio and radar.[58] The electrical engineering staff had to deliver lectures to the RAF and the college students from eight in the morning to five in the evening, in addition to Saturday and evening classes. Professor Say even taught RAF cadets on Christmas Day during wartime.[59] The physics department trained groups of instrument mechanics and radar mechanics for the RAF and the Royal Navy. William Watson retired as head of physics in 1944 after 32 years, during which time he never published a paper.[60] Professor McMillan of the mining department was granted leave of absence to undertake war service as district supplies officer for Scotland under the Mines Department Directorate of Mining Supplies;[61] Dr Hugh Nisbet (chemistry) provided special courses in fuels for Royal Engineers cadets and also served as a member of the Scottish Fuel Efficiency Committee.[62]

A communication from the War Office indicating that training was expected to continue during 'alerts' led to arrangements to obtain the services of some non-commissioned officers (NCOs) to act as roof spotters.[63] Certain female members of staff were permitted to assist in firefighting duties, but only during the hours of daylight. By 1942, however, when the 'necessary provision had been made', six female members of staff and one student were permitted to undertake overnight firewatching duties.[64] As a wartime expedient, the college instituted a vacation term between July and September 1944 to accelerate training. A semblance of humour and social life was preserved even during the darkest days of war. The SRC bulletin of 25 October 1940 advertised a dance:

> To be held – Goering permitting – on Saturday 2nd November, from 7.30pm to 11.00pm. Tickets, price 1/6 each. HM Forces in uniform are cordially invited at a reduced rate of 9d each – would they kindly bring shoes.[65]

The commitment to the war effort absorbed much of the energy and creativity of the college between 1939 and 1945 and Principal Smail, clearly wearied by the burden of managing an under-resourced institution in wartime, submitted his resignation in 1944. He was persuaded to remain in office until 1950 and to continue the task of rescuing the institution from its past and preparing it for its future.[66]

The Second World War helped to destroy the retrenchment philosophy of British financial policy. The war budget of 1941 is usually regarded as marking the adoption of a Keynesian approach to demand management and public finance.[67] The reformist Labour government of 1945 was intent on creating a comprehensive welfare state through policy interventions in health, housing, pensions and education, and by transforming the prospects of a flagging British economy through the nationalisation of key industries and institutions, the use of economic planning and the pursuit of full employment. The raising of the school-leaving age from 14 to 15, and the 1944 Education Act (although leaving the grammar schools intact), facilitated the passage of many able working-class children into higher education. Attlee's successors, Churchill, Eden and Macmillan, led administrations dominated by pragmatic conciliatory Conservatives who made no attempt to dismantle the welfare state. Throughout the years 1945–67 unemployment rarely exceeded 3 per cent; inflation was on average 4 per cent per annum throughout the 1950s and 1960s and, by comparison with the mass unemployment of the 1930s, this was an era of comparative prosperity. The rising living standards of the 1950s and 1960s were not fully justified, however, by the performance of the UK economy. Rates of economic growth only averaged around 2.2 per cent, less than half those enjoyed by France and Germany, and the mid 1950s witnessed the Butler budget of 1955, which heralded the start of the depressing stop/go cycles in the economy.[68] The level of strikes, survival of restrictive practices, and wage-driven inflation seriously impaired the competitiveness of British industry. Demand for skilled and educated people, however, was buoyant in a fully employed society: industry, commerce, public utilities and social services required more graduates and thus higher education entered more centrally into government policy.[69] The war had also given a valuable stimulus to innovation in agriculture, chemicals, electronics, aircraft, and the motor industry due to developments in radar, jet propulsion, antibiotics and atomic power. This greatly strengthened science-based industry after 1945 and boosted demand for Heriot-Watt College graduates.

The news of victory in Europe on 7 May 1945 and the celebrations that surrounded it, followed by the Japanese surrender on 2 September, came in time for the staff and students to start the new academic year with a sense of relief and expectations for the future. Students whose courses were interrupted by war service returned and were eligible for assistance from the Edinburgh Research and Welfare

Fund, administered by the principal. Numbers recovered rapidly from 1,658 evening and 468 day class enrolments in 1945–46 to over 3,600 evening and 1,000 day class students by 1949–50 as ex-service personnel took advantage of educational opportunities and school-leavers sought training for a society committed to Beveridge's notion of full employment (Figure 6.1). Evening numbers then declined steadily to 3,128 by 1955–56 (Figure 6.1). The precise trend is impossible to discern after 1955 since, for reasons unexplained, part-time day classes were then aggregated with evening class student totals. Total day class students doubled between 1945 and 1952 to be followed by a slow growth to 1,587 by 1963 (Figure 6.1).

After the cessation of hostilities, three key appointments were made: Dr W. G. Green, from the Municipal College Portsmouth, became professor of mechanical engineering in 1945; Hugh Nisbet was promoted to the chair of chemistry in September 1946; and Dr W. H. J. Childs, principal scientific officer of the Ministry of Supply, was appointed to the first chair in physics in 1947. Childs, an expert in spectroscopy, later described the situation when he arrived:

> The workshop was a narrow little room off the mechanics laboratory and contained one lathe and one drill press and little else. . . . I had a small office off the Optical Laboratory, which I shared with Milne.[70]

*Professor Hugh Nisbet,
principal 1950–1967.
Portrait, Alan Sutherland.
Photograph: Douglas McBride*

He was at once beset by problems of a department which was underfunded, understaffed (three lecturers) and overcrowded; it remained a concern for him almost until his retirement in 1969. A very heavy teaching load, day and evening (Childs and his colleagues taught two evening sessions per week from 6.00 P.M. to 9.00 P.M.) and departmental administration without even secretarial assistance made serious research almost impossible. With much to offer in research, he was at times depressed and disappointed by the lack of support for his efforts to enhance the status of his department and to further the role of physics. Yet he was still able to make a number of valuable contributions to the college and university, especially the introduction of an associateship programme in physics in 1954–55, years after chemistry and engineering. He was in every sense a gentleman of the old school, well liked by his colleagues despite a reserved nature. A sprightly, dapper figure – complete with bow tie and Breton-style beret – combined with his natural talents to make him a highly respected and well-kent figure in the college.[71]

Staying at Home: Hugh Bryan Nisbet

Hugh Bryan Nisbet was born in Edinburgh on 31 March 1902 and received his early education at George Heriot's School. Nisbet entered Heriot-Watt College as a student in 1918 and at the end of his first year he was invited to become an evening class demonstrator in organic chemistry for two evenings per week at a salary of £10 per annum. After completing an associateship and a BSc from Edinburgh University, Nisbet was appointed to the staff of the college as a full-time demonstrator in chemistry in 1921. He was to remain in the college until his retirement some 46 years later in September 1967. Nisbet threw himself into research but could hope for little support. He realised the significance of the microanalytical techniques developed over many years by Pregl and travelled to the laboratory in Graz for a course of instruction; this was supplemented by a course in Feigl's laboratory in Vienna.[72] A number of research papers in organic chemistry followed, mainly dealing with pyridine bases in shale oil, and in 1938 he presented a thesis on pyrazoline local anaesthetics for the degree of DSc (Edinburgh), having previously been awarded a PhD. At the onset of war, he perceived the need to develop the study of fuels; later he investigated the bases present in Scottish shale oil and coal tar.[73]

Nisbet, whose great relaxation was fishing, was clearly very ambitious; his

This laboratory in the department of brewing and biochemistry commanded an impressive view of the Edinburgh skyline. Photograph: © The Scotsman Publications Ltd

private papers contain a large number of testimonials supplied to him for the numerous posts for which he applied outside the college. The earliest of these applications dates from 1925 when Nisbet sought to become a schoolteacher; over the next decade he applied, apparently unsuccessfully, for positions in the Department of Health, Scotland, and for inspectorships at the Board of Education, London, and the SED.[74] At the age of 33 in 1935, he began applying for university chairs in Exeter, Bangor and Leeds, to none of which he was appointed.[75] By the outbreak of the Second World War it had probably dawned on him that the only avenues to promotion lay within the walls of his own institution.

The references supplied on behalf of Nisbet for his numerous sorties into the job market provide some insights into the character of the man who became the university's first vice-chancellor. Professor J. W. Cook of Glasgow University described him as 'a careful and methodical teacher and an enthusiastic chemist'; Kermack of the Royal College of Physicians, Edinburgh, was impressed by his 'tact and good sense' and regarded him as a 'careful, diligent and fruitful researcher'.[76] Principal Laurie, in a reference of 1 October 1929, damned him with faint praise: 'Mr. Nisbet has proved himself a competent teacher and lecturer, a sound student and a capable researcher.'[77] Similarly, a testimonial written by Professor C. G. Barkla of Edinburgh University, stated that he attended the 'Intermediate Honours Classes and did quite creditable work'.[78] These judgements, combined with Nisbet's failure to be awarded a chair in open competition outside the college, indicate that he was a dedicated, conscientious and methodical scholar producing research in very difficult circumstances, but that he was not especially gifted, a verdict corroborated by reading some of his speeches which reveal a kindly, competent and caring person who did not display a great breadth of learning or the ability to move an audience with a carefully crafted rhetorical flourish.

The vacant chair of chemistry was filled in 1946; from a field of 38 applicants a shortlist was drawn up which, apart from a future holder of the chair, Frank Bell, contained some talented academics, including R. M. Barrer, who became professor at Aberdeen in 1948, followed by Imperial College, London, in 1954, and Wesley Cocker who became professor at Trinity College, Dublin. Although Nisbet had striven heroically to develop his research at the college, he was not the intellectual equal of those applicants, but as Bell opined, 'Nisbet had spent his whole life time there, and he was the natural choice.'[79] Four years later when the post of college principal fell vacant, Nisbet did not apply. The governors displayed an extraordinarily parochial attitude in being reluctant to offer the principalship to their first-choice candidate, an Englishman, ironically called Scott, because they were anxious to appoint a Scot.[80] Consequently, they considered two internal candidates, Say and Nisbet, and the latter was appointed from 1 April 1950 at a salary of £1,750. Hence the committee preferred someone who had spent his whole life in the institution and had never worked in a university.

Nisbet was very active in establishing new departments and developing existing ones. A separate pharmacy department had been created in January 1949 under the leadership of Hugh Campbell and it moved to a new building in the Grassmarket in 1951. Further fragmentation of the department of chemistry took place in 1950 after Nisbet had become principal when Arthur Preece, a Birmingham graduate, was appointed to the chair and headship of a new department of brewing and fermentation, with Anna MacLeod (a botanist), a demonstrator, and a technician.[81] The title of the department was changed in 1957 to brewing and applied biochemistry. With around one-third of its undergraduates sponsored by breweries, more staff were hired.[82] Principal Nisbet won financial support from the brewing industry and the SED and new lecture rooms and laboratories were built and occupied in 1962.[83]

The growth of research students in chemistry, largely supervised by Nisbet and

Preece, led to the award of several PhDs under the long-established arrangements between the college and the university. When Frank Bell, formerly professor of chemistry at Belfast College of Technology, arrived at the college to assume the chair of chemistry on 1 September 1950, two major changes had occurred since his interview: brewing and fermentation had become a separate department, and the University of Edinburgh had given notice that it would insist henceforth on the precise interpretation of certain regulations – which had been honoured in the breach – so that Heriot-Watt College would no longer be accepted as a suitable locus for research students to carry out their studies for an Edinburgh PhD, thereby making it more difficult to create a viable research school.[84] Bell eventually persuaded a somewhat reluctant Nisbet to create a research award, the fellowship of the college (FH-WC), intended to be the equivalent of a doctorate, but not surprisingly it failed to compete against the established PhD and did not prevent the best college diplomates from seeking their research training elsewhere.[85] Only 20 such fellowships were awarded between 1954 and their termination in 1963.[86]

The Advisory Council on Education in Scotland floated the idea of a Federal University of Technology in April 1950; the proposed constituents were the five central institutions.[87] This proposal did not bear fruit but higher technological education was placed firmly on the national agenda as concern about the relatively poor technical performance of the British economy, especially the manufacturing sector, became apparent. Lord Woolton, Lord President of the Council in Churchill's government, suggested to the Cabinet in 1952 that a new group of three free-standing higher technological institutions of university rank should be created: Imperial College, London, Manchester Institute of Technology and the Royal Technical College, Glasgow.[88] Heriot-Watt College, therefore, was not selected as the Scottish technological university. Lord Woolton's proposal was accepted and from 1952–53 the UGC became the major source of funds for the Royal Technical College, which was designated as the University of Strathclyde in June 1964.[89]

Meanwhile further course development was being undertaken in Heriot-Watt College. A new associateship course in civil engineering was introduced in 1953 by the department of mechanical engineering. Subsequent developments led to the creation of a separate department of civil engineering in 1962 and a chair to which Dr Arthur Bolton, senior lecturer in civil engineering at the University of Liverpool, was recruited. Courses in management studies were first introduced in 1950 with students studying for the Intermediate Certificate of the British Institute of Management and the Institute of Bankers exams. The college established a department of industrial administration and commerce in 1955 to which Mr Joseph Gloag was appointed head. Also, after Norman Sidwell was made head of building in 1950, courses were upgraded to associateship level; an associateship was introduced in applied biochemistry during 1961. In 1955 Principal Nisbet, whose own research work generated a network of contacts in the petrochemical industry, was instrumental in obtaining support from the industry for the endowment, jointly with Edinburgh University, for a chair of chemical engineering (called chemical technology by the university). This department functioned initially under Professor Kenneth Denbigh at Kings Buildings, but was rehoused in the college's third extension in 1958. Edinburgh University transferred equipment to the college without charge. Denbigh moved to Imperial College in 1960 and was replaced by Professor P. H. Calderbank.

A report on the coordination of evening classes in Edinburgh in 1946–47 indicated that students who had been admitted to the college on transfer certificates direct from local schools had achieved poor results. Principal Smail suggested to the city that it should place 'a larger share of the elementary work in the Corporation Centres'.[90] Was this the first sign of the college reconsidering its role as a provider of elementary classes as part of a strategy to focus more on higher education? It appears that this was not the case; rather the college was apparently responding to events. Evening class numbers had remained fairly constant between

Architect's vision of the third extension, by Esme Gordon, 1956. Photograph: Douglas McBride

2,500 and 3,000 (apart from the world wars) when the policy to devolve these courses became effective. It was planned to transfer first-year National Certificate courses in mechanics and electrical engineering to Bristo Technical Institute from September 1949.[91] However, Edinburgh Corporation could not provide accommodation, but did take over maths classes and the first-year part-time mining course; the first-year National Certificate building courses transferred to the School of Building and Crafts, New Street.[92] By 1950–51 the total number of student hours on evening courses was 290,193, down 9 per cent from 1949–50, reflecting the transfer of S1 to S2 courses to Bristo Technical Institute and the School of Building and Crafts.[93] In 1956–57 the city education officer suggested that all printing classes be transferred with equipment to the newly planned Napier College.[94] The only National Certificate courses being conducted in the college by 1961 were limited to the S3 years of programmes in chemistry and applied physics. Thereafter, the process of decanting elementary work to local authority colleges accelerated and Higher National courses in chemistry and in mechanical, production and electrical engineering were taken over by Napier College.

Although the achievement of university status was to be the apotheosis of Dr Nisbet's career, he also masterminded a number of important building developments. Premises for the department of pharmacy in the Grassmarket were formally opened by the Earl of Home, minister of state at the Scottish Office in 1951; celebrations to mark a new £20,000 extension to the mine rescue station were presided over by Robert Wilson in June 1953; and the third extension, the brainchild of Principal Smail, was opened in 1958 by the Duke of Edinburgh. One of Principal Nisbet's most important contributions to the expansion of the college, however, was the construction (at a cost of £650,000) of the Mountbatten Building in the Grassmarket, on the site of the old corn exchange. Although not opened until January 1968, after Nisbet's retirement, he had been intimately involved in planning this accommodation for electrical and electronic engineering, the TV centre and the departments of accountancy and finance, business organisation, economics, and languages.[95]

The College Community: Staff and Student Life

A t this time college staff lacked empowerment as there was a long-standing practice of the management residing with the board of governors. There was also a board of studies, consisting of departmental heads, which met monthly to consider an agenda prepared by the principal. The results of these deliberations were presented by the principal to the board of governors; no member of the board of studies other than the principal was present at governors' meetings. The organisation of a staff association reflected the demand for more open and democratic procedures and participation in decision-making. Yet academic staff exerted scant influence over the goals and policies of the institution. The governors were reluctant to relinquish control and change was slow to come. The staff association was a toothless body whose major function was to prepare and submit to the governors' proposals for the annual salary review to be communicated to the SED. This was done via the principal since the association had no direct representation on the board of governors. The minutes of the meetings of the governors were not even made available to the members of the staff association, except to heads of department.

In submitting recommendations about salaries on 26 October 1950, Professor Childs made the extraordinary concession that he 'was prepared to accept the superiority of the Royal Technical College [Glasgow] – but he wished to remain separate from the other technical institutions'.[96] Gender discrimination in pay was also explicit in the salary structure, an issue which was opposed by Professor Preece (perhaps motivated by the presence of Anna MacLeod in his department) on 13 September 1954 when, for example, the Lecturer II(b) scale for men was £640 rising by £30 increments to £840; while for women it was £575 rising by £25 increments to £725.[97] Most agenda items at staff association meetings were innocuous: design of the college Christmas card, organisation of the annual social event, or requests for coffee in the common room in the mornings. Mr Leslie Wallace (physics) on 11 February 1954 raised the issue that 'an electric plug in the Staff Common Room had been diverted for outside use';[98] on 7 October 1957 Dr Sidwell (building) opined that the 'situation at the canteen counter was still a source of embarrassment as there was no means of distinguishing between students and staff'.[99]

During the 1950s the social life of staff focused on a golf club, badminton, an angling club (which organised two outings per year) and a dramatic circle. The

The college magazine, 1939

The college magazine, 1959

Separate common rooms for men and women in the second extension, opened in 1938

Separate common rooms for men and women in the second extension, opened in 1938

pinnacle of the social calendar in those days of rationing was the annual social; on 25 March 1950 it consisted of a play by the Dramatic Circle, *The Amazed Evangelist* by James Bridie, supper, a diversion with rewards, presentation to the principal, and ballroom and Scottish country dancing. The evening ended promptly at the bewitching hour of 10.00 P.M.[100]

The interwar period and even up to the early 1960s witnessed little sporting, social and cultural life at the college. The opening of the first extension in 1935 heralded the enticing opportunity for holding student dances in the newly built gymnasium. Alan Shaw and his friends decided to enhance their prospects of impressing female students at the weekend dances by enrolling for lessons at Miss Glendenning's School of Ballroom Dancing in Chalmers Crescent, Marchmont.[101] However, several other cultural activities had started to falter through lack of support. By 1936 the meetings and productions of the Dramatic Study Club, which presented readings to the Literary Society and performed a play each year, were 'severely handicapped by lack of members'.[102] The subscription was cut to 2s 6d in 1936 but to no avail as the average attendance was around five.[103] At a meeting on 12 May 1939, as storm clouds gathered over Europe, the club was wound up. Later even the Literary Society was plagued by falling attendances and membership; the membership declined from 107 in 1951–52 to 64 in 1959–60. At a committee meeting on 18 March 1960, Dr Sandilands (chemistry) moved that the society should cease to exist and this motion was carried by 10 votes to 5,[104] a sad end after a century of valiantly maintaining a spark of corporate cultural life in a somewhat indifferent technological environment. Following the demise of the Literary Society, the major student recreational pastimes, apart from watching TV, were sport and dancing. The college did not acquire its own playing fields until May 1958, grounds of 8.58 acres at Paties Road, Colinton.[105]

Students had little scope to exercise independence over their facilities and recreational activities. The college implemented a highly paternalistic regime. In

Youthful glamour at the student ball, 1953

1954, for example, Principal Nisbet decided that 'the Common Room should not be for both men and women'.[106] During an SRC debate on 7 February 1957 – concerning a proposal for a mixed common room – one member argued that it would 'cut out loitering in the corridors'; another thought that 'female company would distract him from his work'.[107] Female students were treated in a patronising manner and had been attending courses at the college for almost 70 years before the management recognised that they had a responsibility to make some provision for their welfare. On 1 October 1937 Mrs C. M. Adam was appointed superintendent in the college canteen and 'regarding the supervision of women students, the Committee recommended that Mrs. Adam be authorised to deal with any questions arising'.[108] Quite what supervision of women students actually entailed was not defined, but Mrs Adam was paid an extra £10 for such duties. There does not appear to have been a parallel arrangement for male students. In 1961 the SRC was authorised to hold dances outwith the college 'subject to the location and other necessary information being submitted to the Principal for approval in advance'.[109] The principal had the 'authority to discontinue the concession if he was not satisfied with the manner in which the dances were being conducted'.[110] So even in 1961 autocracy prevailed at the college; the tide of late 1960s student radicalism was yet to wash over the paternalistic walls of Chambers Street.

Student facilities were rudimentary: a common room for men on the ground floor in Chambers Street, a separate small common room for women and a small meeting room. By the late 1950s women could use the male common room but this was an infrequent occurrence as most male students indulged in smoking and playing cards.[111] College students were also permitted to use the Edinburgh University canteen in Chambers Street. The college had acquired a Georgian building in Brown Square in 1887 to teach elementary arithmetic and writing,[112] and the SRC, forerunner of the students' association, persuaded the principal to refurbish the vacant building as a student house. This reopened in February 1965 and, although described as 'quite inadequate' for the student population of 900, the student house nevertheless boasted 'lounge facilities with coffee and music on tap, a non-smokers lounge and a TV lounge ... with darts, table tennis facilities (at sixpence the half hour) and chess'.[113] Nightlife included folk singing and regular discotheques but incredibly there was no bar, although beer could be brought in for a function. This basic SRC building, with an overflow into an adjacent rented shop, had no refectory; the only one, already under severe pressure, was in Chambers Street. The provision of a Students' Union building symbolised the way in which the needs of students were now recognised. The ambition and confidence of the SRC blossomed as evidenced by dances organised in the Palais and featuring major bands, including the Dutch Swing College Band and the Kenny Ball Jazz

Band. The students did not confine themselves entirely to sport and dancing, although there was 'no cultural life whatsoever'.[114]

The debates in the SRC were conducted in an apparently exemplary manner, adopting a rigid set of procedures; the issues discussed, however, were unlikely to have ruffled the calm waters of the autocratic regime in Chambers Street. At an SRC Meeting on 17 November 1964, a motion was passed that 'the authorities should be asked why nothing had been done about the synchronising of the College clocks'; and a further motion by Mr Treat proposed that the 'Librarian be asked to whisper when speaking in the Library'.[115] The union moved to a larger home in Grindlay Street in 1970, leaving Brown Square School to enjoy relative calm as a library reading room. The building was subsequently demolished and the New Museum of Scotland now commands the site.

Who were the Heriot-Watt students at this time, from where did they come, and did their profile differ from those attending during the 1930s? The home addresses of the 211 diploma, university, pharmacy and brewing day students attending the college in 1933 provide a fascinating glimpse into the geographical origins of the student body in the interwar period. Some 186 (88 per cent) of the students lived in Scotland, only 10 (5 per cent) were domiciled in England and 15 (7 per cent) came from overseas. The institution, therefore, was overwhelmingly Scottish and of the 15 overseas students, 11 of whom lived in India, over half had British surnames implying that they were offspring of British citizens working in the colonies. Of the Scottish contingent, 56 per cent were resident in Edinburgh and the Lothians, 20 per cent in Fife, 11 per cent in the Highlands and Islands, 9 per cent in the Borders, Dumfries and Galloway but only 3 per cent in Glasgow and the Strathclyde region, where there has always been a pronounced preference to attend a local university. By 1964 the number attending associateship and diploma courses had grown to 816 but the spatial patterns of recruitment had not changed greatly in three decades. The 643 Scots (79 per cent) represented a small proportionate decline as overseas numbers had risen to 120, 15 per cent of the student body. A total of 73 Norwegians, even outnumbering the English, made up 9 per cent of the students; the balance of the overseas intake came predominantly from British colonies or former colonies such as Nigeria (12), India (7), Kenya (3), Pakistan (3), Tanganyika (3) and Uganda (2). In contrast to 1933, however, almost all of the overseas students from these colonial countries were from the indigenous populations; there were few sons (and no daughters) of the Raj as decolonisation proceeded. One unusual aspect of the English intake was the predominance of students from public schools such as Harrow, Uppingham, Ampleforth and Sedbergh on the brewing course. Of the Scottish students in 1964, the proportions resident in Edinburgh and the Lothians, Fife and the Borders, Dumfries and Galloway were identical to 1933. The only significant change after three decades was a fall in the proportion from the Highlands to 6 per cent. Recruitment from Glasgow and the West remained very low; Oslo accents were much more common in the corridors of Chambers Street than those from the west of Scotland. What is even more striking about Scottish recruitment in both 1933 and 1964 is how similar it was in its geographical pattern to that of today.

Research in the College

Those who did manage to sustain a research programme in the post-war period did so despite obstacles that staff in universities never had to face, nourished as they were by the dual support system of research funding and the availability of PhD students. Heavy teaching loads and inadequate laboratories were further handicaps. In chemistry, for example, staff delivered 14 or 15 lectures a week plus substantial laboratory teaching, and each person taught two evenings per week from 6.30 P.M. to 9.00 P.M.[116] To maintain a research programme under such unfavourable circumstances demanded a degree of self-motivation and commitment rare even in the academic world. Staff were appointed as teachers and there was no contractual obligation to conduct research. It is no surprise, therefore, that the level of research output during the 1950s was so low. Between 1954 and 1959, 14 students of the college were awarded PhDs by Edinburgh University and 4 gained fellowships. Throughout the decade from September 1949 to August 1959, a mere 108 research papers were published by around 70 full-time college academic staff, an average of less than two papers per staff member in 10 years. The memorandum on the work of the college submitted to the Robbins Committee in 1961 presented scant evidence of externally funded research. There was a project on Scottish shale oil supported by BP in the chemistry department; sponsored research on mass transfer coefficients in distillation processes in chemical engineering; and several funded projects in brewing and applied biochemistry ranging from the biochemistry of barley to continuous cultivation of micro-organisms, supported by Distillers Co. Ltd.[117]

With no institutional encouragement to engage in research and little leadership, the research effort was largely confined to around 10 staff, the most productive of whom were Professor Bell and Dr Mackie in chemistry, Professor Denbigh in chemical engineering, and Professor Preece and Dr MacLeod in brewing and applied biochemistry. These five staff alone published 80 per cent of all the research papers from the college between 1954 and 1959.[118] The work of Professor Preece and Dr MacLeod was principally concerned with the carbohydrate composition and metabolism of grass seeds; Preece and colleagues studied the enzymic breakdown of cereal β-glucans and pentosans during malting while Anna MacLeod surveyed the sugars and water-soluble polysaccharides of British grass seeds.[119] Sadly Arthur Preece died suddenly in 1964 at the age of 57 before seeing his department achieve university status. Frank Bell observed when he arrived in the chemistry department in 1950 that the older members of staff – Sandilands, Dakers and Webster – were not only unproductive in research but 'they were opposed to it'.[120] Bell, despite the burdens of teaching and administration, pursued research at the bench from a small laboratory adjoining his office throughout his 16 year tenure of the chair, publishing some 30 papers on stereochemistry and aromatic substitution reactions.[121] His colleague Alex Mackie, with the support of the Agricultural Research Council, studied anthelmintics (substances inimical to parasitic worms in the bodies of animals). Research by the dedicated few was pursued on a shoestring, for no item costing more than £5 could be ordered without the permission of the principal.[122] Hence, with no contractual research requirement and no culture of scholarship, it is no surprise that some 90 per cent of the staff were not active in research as the college entered the 1960s, indicating the scale of the problem facing the institution in transforming itself from a worthy technical college into a research-based university. It was to be another 40 years (in 2001) before the university reached a position of having over 80 per cent of its academic staff research-active at appropriate levels of quality and volume to be returned in the Research Assessment Exercise (RAE).

A Parting of the Ways

The affiliation agreement with the University of Edinburgh never commanded the unquestioning endorsement of both institutions and the one action which was ultimately to sound the death knell for the relationship occurred in 1946 when the university appointed the energetic and research-minded Ronald N. Arnold to the professorship of engineering. He was effectively in charge of the mechanical engineering course, could exercise a degree of control over civil engineering, but had virtually no influence over the teaching of electrical engineering at Heriot-Watt College.[123] He quickly decided that this devolution of responsibility for what he regarded as an area of teaching and research essential to the future development of engineering in Edinburgh University and vital to his personal research interests was unacceptable.[124] This prompted him to initiate a phasing out of the arrangements for joint courses with Heriot-Watt College and to take steps to establish electrical engineering teaching in the university. A lecturer in applied electricity was appointed and this allowed the teaching of electrical technology and electricity (a second-year course) to be internalised in Edinburgh University for the first time in 1949–50.[125] In the following session, the third-year electrical course was also taken over from Heriot-Watt, but the college continued to provide the teaching and the laboratory facilities for the course in electrical machinery and power until 1956.[126]

The issue of collaboration in the teaching of electrical engineering was not the only occasion on which Professor Arnold attempted to undermine cooperation between the two institutions. In a letter to the secretary of the university of 11 July 1950 he asserted:

> I have great doubt if the staff at the Heriot-Watt College are capable of doing justice to our Final Year work together with their heavy teaching commitments. ... For myself I find that collaboration with the College throughout the session ... adds considerably to my duties. ... I strongly resent unnecessary work which has only as its object the enhancement of the College status. ... It is possible in the future that the number taking Mechanical and Electrical Engineering at the Heriot-Watt College may even outnumber those at the University – a situation which would be quite untenable. ... The implications of this Affiliation are becoming serious.[127]

A year later Arnold, then dean of science, was clearly concerned at the climate of increasing cooperation between the institutions and expressed his concerns in a letter to the secretary on 30 May 1951:

> It would appear that certain discussions have already taken place on this matter within the University. ... I consider it somewhat irregular, however, that a matter of vital importance not only to my Faculty but to my Department should have been discussed without my knowledge and have reached a state which, if my interpretation is correct, has already put the University in a compromising position.[128]

Despite this protestation, Professor Sir Edward Appleton, principal of Edinburgh University, wrote to Sir Arthur Trueman of the UGC in February 1952 proposing that the university create a Faculty of Technology embracing engineering subjects, chemical technology and possibly mining and with relevant Heriot-Watt courses recognised as qualifying for degrees:

> My own thoughts run in the way of making the principal of the College (Nisbet), an excellent fellow, Dean of the Faculty; but, of course, there are many other views. I might be Dean myself with the principal Vice-Dean.[129]

Had Arnold been marginalised deliberately by the principal because of his well-known hostility to the collaboration? His attitude contrasted starkly with that of Professors Edmund Hirst and Kendall of chemistry on 23 May 1951:

> The logical centre to provide some extension is the Heriot-Watt College, rather than the University, and we recommend that the University give its strongest support to the scheme outlined in the memorandum, in order to bring it into operation as soon as possible.[130]

Hence there was a strong difference of opinion within the science faculty of Edinburgh University which cannot have enhanced the process of collaboration. Professor Arnold's attitudes ranged from outright hostility to the affiliation agreement – which he clearly viewed as a threat to the expansion of engineering in Edinburgh University – to a genuine concern to ensure university standards in the joint degree programmes taught by college staff.

A memo drafted in December 1959 expressed concern at the gradual drift of work from the college to the university in mechanical and electrical engineering:

> The College authorities are perturbed at the general trend of events in University relations. Although the Affiliation Order allows us to train mechanical, electrical and chemical engineering students for the BSc degree from first year studies right through to the final year this in fact, has gone into desuetude. Is the University policy to discontinue this recognition and discard Affiliation?[131]

The University of Edinburgh had an interest in protecting its own plans for development; these occasionally clashed with the aspirations of the college. The turning point in the long association between the two institutions was the sudden decision by the university during the 1959–60 session to create a chair of electrical engineering. As a consequence, the facilities provided by the college were no longer required, bringing to a close a collaboration which had operated since the beginning of the twentieth century.[132] Principal Nisbet was clearly aggrieved and this surfaced publicly, when presenting oral evidence to the Robbins Committee on 11 December 1961:

We had no intimation from the University that they were going to appoint a Professor of Electrical Engineering. I immediately raised the question with my governors and my governors sought an interview with the University authorities pointing out that there had been some neglect in informing us that they were in fact going to start a degree in electrical engineering. We tried to persuade them against that. ... The Professor of Electrical Engineering had been appointed in the University and the classes have been taken away from us. ... We had no information about this and had been carrying the classes from the beginning of the century and we thought it was rather hard that we had no previous intimation.[133]

Three years later Nisbet wrote to Professor J. Grieg of King's College London and gave vent to his frustration: 'Our association with Edinburgh University has not been a terribly happy one over the long years we have "enjoyed" an Affiliation Order.'[134] It is clear that Edinburgh University assumed complete autonomy to take decisions without consulting or raising the issue with a long-standing partner where local and national needs could be considered.

The functioning of the joint department of chemical engineering was fraught with problems; the differences in attitude and opinion came to a head in 1965 when preparations were being made for the college to attain independent university status. It was apparent that the two institutions were no longer thinking of a joint department. The premises belonged to Heriot-Watt but the ownership of the equipment was disputed. Mr Clayton, bursar of the college, reminded the UGC on 9 June 1965 that 'the equipment had been bought with the proceeds of a joint appeal so there should be some payment to Heriot-Watt College, or else half the equipment should be left to them'.[135] Sir John Wolfenden, chair of the UGC, clearly perturbed, wrote to Professor Michael Swann, acting principal of Edinburgh University on 30 September 1965:

I think you would agree that to have two such departments, separately staffed and equipped, in the University and in Heriot-Watt, would be indefensible from the point of view of economical deployment of resources in manpower and materials. ... Nisbet, I may say, entirely accepts the reasonableness of this position.[136]

Events north of the border, however, had developed an unstoppable momentum fuelled by distrust, and Nisbet and Swann in a joint response to Sir John Wolfenden's letter concluded that 'as the building situation eases at Edinburgh University and as the Heriot-Watt expands ... we see no sensible solution but to split apart'.[137] Joint provision was doomed and Edinburgh

A room with a view: a laboratory in the Grassmarket, 1960s. Photograph: © The Scotsman Publications Ltd

University lost no time in obtaining approval from the UGC for a separate chemical engineering building and the senatus sanctioned its construction at a cost not exceeding £60,000.[138] The two departments separated from 1 August 1967. This left some difficult issues to be resolved between the institutions: the division of the fund which had been subscribed by industry on the creation of the joint department in 1955, and the position in regard to equipment which, in the main, had been installed by the University of Edinburgh.

This brought to an end a long era of collaboration between the two institutions. The quality and level of informal cooperation, depending inevitably on mutual respect and reciprocity, was frequently fruitful at departmental level; difficulties were more likely to arise with more senior staff.[139] Collaboration, as is so often the case, depended on the goodwill of personalities keen to make it successful rather than on formal affiliation agreements. For example, when Frank Bell was head of chemistry, relations with the university department under Professor Sir Edmund Hirst were harmonious and productive.[140] Mutual suspicion, competing aims, incipient rivalry and the consistent opposition of one key member of the Edinburgh University staff resulted in the demise of an agreement which, had it continued, would probably have yielded major benefits to Scottish higher education and may even have led to a different institutional outcome in the city of Edinburgh.

The Robbins Report

The Technical Education Subcommittee of the Advisory Council on Education in Scotland investigated the state of technical education, and its report in 1946 was highly prescient, anticipating many of the Robbins Committee recommendations two decades later. It suggested, among other things, that elementary work should be devolved to local education authorities; that central institutions should have more staff to enable evening work, day work and research to be carried out without undue pressure; that it was not possible to draw a clear frontier between the work of the universities and that of technical colleges in the field of applied science; and that in the allocation of new work there should be collaboration and mutual understanding between central institutions and university. Since post-war reconstruction moved at a slow pace in the realm of technical education, it was several years before any of the report's major recommendations were implemented.

Lionel Robbins, professor of economics at the London School of Economics (LSE), was reluctant to accept the chairmanship of the Committee on Higher Education offered to him by R. A. Butler, the Home Secretary. He wished to write a book on economic theory, and changed his mind only when an old friend pointed out to him, a little unkindly perhaps, that the Committee on Higher Education might have a longer-term effect than the book he was planning to write.[141] The appointment of the committee in 1961 meant that the position and status of the Scottish central institutions would be closely examined. The reasons for setting up the Robbins Committee were many and various. New academic institutions in advanced technology and teacher training, whose status was unclear, had sprung up; the general penchant of the 1960s for planning had reached education, but above all there was the problem of the 'bulge': a generation of school-leavers were about to arrive at the doors of universities.

During 1961 the committee collected evidence, and members, including Robbins himself, visited Heriot-Watt on the afternoon of 15 December 1961. Principal Nisbet submitted a memorandum summarising the position of the college at that time.[142] Annual expenditure for 1960–61 was £250,000, mostly funded by the SED, but including £7,500 from the UGC (through Edinburgh University), £8,000 from George Heriot's Trust and £6,000 from Edinburgh Corporation.[143] Associateship (with honours) courses of four years' duration were available in mechanical engineering, chemical engineering, electrical engineering, civil engineering, building technology, applied chemistry, applied physics and applied mathematics. In addition, three-year associateships were available in mining and brewing. The college associateships in engineering were recognised by the various professional institutions in Britain as granting exemption from the exams for graduate membership; the Universities of Edinburgh, Birmingham and Aberdeen accepted the associateship for postgraduate entry for PhD studies.

Nisbet argued that degree-awarding powers could be conferred by

- an extension of the orders of affiliation with the university, or
- by creating university faculties of technology within the Royal College of Science and Technology and the Heriot-Watt College, or
- by establishing the two technical colleges as independent university colleges of technology.

The college made clear that the third option was the preferred one; it would give the greatest boost to technological education in Scotland.

The failure of Edinburgh University to consult the college about the decision to create a chair in electrical engineering was clearly a factor in the college's decision to seek independent technological university status rather than amalgamation with Edinburgh, and the asymmetric power balance between the institutions was further underlined by the fact that the university had representation on the college's governing body but no governors sat on the University Court. The SED in its memorandum submitted to the Robbins Committee was openly critical of Edinburgh and Glasgow Universities stating that they

> have shown themselves desirous of discontinuing where they could, or at least not extending affiliation arrangements whereby their degrees could be taken in courses wholly pursued at the Royal College of Science and Technology and at the Heriot-Watt College. Some of the Universities have also taken decisions, without prior consultation with their partner institution, to depart from arrangements made jointly with an art college or a technical college under which degree courses have been pursued partly in the University, and partly in the central institution.[144]

Under cross-examination Principal Nisbet revealed he had hoped that when the special ordinance was approved by Edinburgh University for the BSc in technological science,

> this would be an umbrella under which all the departments could eventually come, but so far the umbrella has only covered one department. We hope by 1970 good feeling will be aroused and there may be a possibility of doing

something in that way. If that does not come, we would hope we might have degree-granting powers of our own.[145]

After further questioning, Principal Nisbet betrayed a degree of uncertainty:

We might become a faculty of technology within the University on the Manchester pattern ... [which] seems to be nearest the one which could work. Complete independence would be easier because then we would be standing on our own feet, but I am not sure whether we are big enough for that.[146]

Principal Nisbet's response appears to contradict the college's stated preference. It is apparent that he did not have a clearly articulated vision of the appropriate strategic direction for the college in moving to university status, while simultaneously betraying anxiety about its relationship with Edinburgh University.

The Scottish Union of Students in its submission to the Robbins Committee urged that the Royal College of Science and Technology in Glasgow be given the status of a technological university and that 'at least one other such establishment in another centre would be necessary' but it did not advocate that Heriot-Watt College should be the other university.[147] Similarly, the Association of Directors of Education in Scotland argued that the Royal College be granted degree-awarding powers but also made no reference to Heriot-Watt College.[148]

The Robbins Report, published on 23 October 1963, was accepted by the government the very next day with the despatch appropriate to an election year. Nationally student numbers had already risen by about 40 per cent in the six years preceding the Robbins Report; new plans were made to raise them by another 50 per cent within four years. Projecting that student numbers at Scottish universities would rise from some 19,550 in 1961 to 61,610 in 1985, Robbins' figures were challenged by the SED, which estimated a more realistic increase to 44,000 students.[149] Robbins recommended a 'varied pattern of development' for the Scottish central institutions and that the 'future of the Central Institutions must be worked out in detail in Scotland in the light of national needs and local circumstances'.[150] Strathclyde University, formerly the Royal College of Science and Technology, had already admitted its first students in October 1962 and Robbins also recommended the erection of an entirely new university (Stirling) and two other 'conversion' universities: Heriot-Watt, announced in January 1964, and Dundee, by separation from its parent institution, St Andrews. Although the dominant theme of Robbins was the need for expansion of the system, the subsequent growth was remarkably superficial. By 1980 the age participation index for Scots entrants to Scottish universities stood at only 8.9 per cent.[151] It scarcely touched school-leavers whose parents had not participated in higher education and

The white heat of technology.
Mr J. Landon in the mechanical
engineering department in the
second extension, Chambers
Street, 1960s

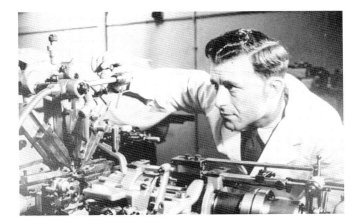

it did little to eradicate the poverty of expectation among the lower socio-economic groups.

Representatives of Heriot-Watt College met Sir William Arbuckle, secretary of the SED, on 27 November 1963 to inform him that, after a careful review of the relations with Edinburgh University, they had a clear preference for the college to become an independent technological university. The governors planned to increase numbers from 830 to 1,600 by 1967 and to 3,000 by 1975–80. A group representing the college met with Sir Edward Appleton and representatives of the Edinburgh University Court on 20 December 1963. Principal Appleton stated that the university had no strong views on continued association and indeed 'welcomed the idea of the College developing as an independent degree-granting technological university'.[152] Principal Appleton also indicated that the university would wish to take over the 'scientific aspects of chemical engineering' while raising no objections to the college continuing to provide for the 'technological aspects of the subject', and that the college should take over all the work in mining.[153]

The AAC: A Broader Vision Unrealised

The governors of the college, with the consent of the UGC, appointed seven men (no women were invited) in March 1964 to act as the Academic Advisory Committee (AAC) under the chairmanship of

Sir Edmund Hudson, former managing director of Scottish Agricultural Industries Ltd, who had been educated at Marlborough College and King's College, Cambridge. It included a chemical engineer, Professor J. M. Coulson (University of Newcastle-upon-Tyne); an electrical engineer, Professor E. G. Cullwick (University of St Andrews), a physicist, Professor H. J. Lipson (Manchester College of Science and Technology), a political scientist, Professor D. D. Raphael (University of Glasgow), together with Principal E. M. Wright of the University of Aberdeen and Principal Nisbet. Mr Peter Kilpatrick, a governor of the college, hosted a dinner party for members of the AAC on the eve of its first meeting at the New Club, Edinburgh. Both Kilpatrick and Sir Edmund Hudson were members of the New Club and had been undergraduates together at King's College, Cambridge.[154] The AAC met on 11 occasions and consulted widely, inviting members of staff to submit memoranda communicating their views on the future development of the institution as a university. Many responded and their thoughts reveal the nature and scale of the problems inherent in transforming a technical college into a university when located in proximity to an ancient university of repute. The submissions also disclose, unsurprisingly, some undercurrents of disagreement among staff about future directions and policy.

Some staff members were sufficiently perceptive to realise that modes of teaching and course content would need to change. Professor Lipson argued that timetables were overcrowded and that lectures were 'overfull of factual detail';[155] Mr H. F. Black (mechanical engineering) concurred, suggesting that staff of technical colleges were 'servants of the governing body' while overteaching produced graduates 'with little capacity for original thought or initiative'.[156] Professor R. A. Silver, an expert on desalination of sea water who had been appointed to the headship of mechanical engineering in 1962, recommended that all science and technology undergraduates should be required to study English prose, logic and the theory of knowledge, and a modern language.[157] This reflected Silver's thinking as a polymath, for he also wrote poetry, newspaper articles and plays, one of which, *The Bruce: Hert o Scotland*, was performed at the Edinburgh Festival in 1991. Many staff expressed anxiety about the entrance qualifications set by the Scottish Universities Entrance Board, especially the requirement, not imposed by Heriot-Watt College, to possess a pass in 'one language other than English'. The belief that school-leaving qualifications apparently mattered more than later qualifications, a position that would be ridiculed today, was endemic in the older Scottish and English universities. Heriot-Watt College, conversely, articulated an enlightened concern to maintain some semblance of a wider access agenda by retaining an entry route for students holding National Certificates.

Professor Silver posed the key issue of what purposes the new university would fulfil which the University of Edinburgh did not serve. He concluded that we must 'frankly recognise that we are in competition'.[158] Silver also asserted that in order to compete for students, the top priority was to improve social facilities for staff and students, including the provision of a Students' Union and the liberalisation of regulations in the college; even in 1964 it was impossible, even for staff, to have wine or beer with meals.[159] Silver also recognised that a complementary aspect of the enforced competition for students was that staff in all departments needed to develop a reputation for the quality of their research. Dr Anna MacLeod was even more candid:

> Heriot-Watt College is essentially a 9–5, term-time teaching establishment, with a rather poor research record. Many of my colleagues consider that the future University should be mainly a teaching University. I think that to adopt such a policy would be fatal. . . . Research should not be an optional extra.[160]

Dr Anna MacLeod was also concerned that a University should be governed not as a dictatorship, however benevolent, but by representatives of all members of the university. During her years on the staff, she had 'never been told officially of any aims or aspirations of the College . . . indeed, I have more knowledge of Edinburgh University ambitions than I have of those of my own College'.[161]

Having considered the submissions, the AAC sought initially to articulate a vision of the 'kind of institution which it considered should be established':

> The successful development of technology (and of the education and training of technologists) will depend on the joint contributions of physical and biological sciences, of economists and other social scientists, engineers, architects, builders, historians and philosophers. In erecting a technological university, the framework should be such as to provide a range of interests, a common ground for the exchange of ideas, a forum for discussion for scholars who draw on arts and humanities as well as on science and technology.[162]

The committee recognised that 'much of the structure of the Faculties of Engineering and Science is already established' and therefore only recommended one new department, materials science. They expressed concern, however, that 'only the nucleus of the Faculty of Humanities yet exists, namely the Department of Industrial Administration and Commerce'.[163] The AAC concluded:

> The main activities in the Faculty of Humanities should comprise courses in industrial administration, applied economics, politics and sociology . . .

philosophy including history and philosophy of science ... economic history and geography and languages.[164]

New departments were proposed in languages, applied economics, politics and sociology, philosophy and communication.[165] These ideas clearly did not meet with the approval of Nisbet and the governors. Six months earlier, on 28 June 1965, at a meeting with the chairman of the UGC, Professor John Wolfenden, Nisbet was asked whether it was the intention to institute honours degrees not only in industrial administration and economics but also in history, geography, philosophy and modern languages? Nisbet opined that the governors, having already deferred the creation of chairs in history, geography and modern languages, were likely to take the view that 'studies in humanities should in the main be ancillary to other subjects'.[166] This view was confirmed in a letter to the UGC on 3 September 1965 in which Nisbet reported that the governors 'do not consider, however, that there is an immediate need in a technological university for the establishment of a wide range of studies in the Faculty of Humanities, each leading to a degree award therein'.[167] To Nisbet and the governors it was occupational need that provided the justification for the social sciences, specifically industrial administration and management studies. Ultimately only two of the departments proposed by the AAC, languages and economics, were ever established so that its aim of creating a faculty embracing humanities and social science disciplines, as at Strathclyde University, was never pursued by the new university, thereby ensuring that their vision, with technological students incorporating 'arts and humanities' in their studies, was not realised.

The failure to expand the humanities faculty, as envisaged by the AAC, led to other consequences inimical to the development of a university: few opportunities to develop interdisciplinary courses on the interfaces between technological subjects and social sciences; a low proportion of female students; a lack of cultural activities; and an unbalanced subject portfolio with a marked preponderance of those science and engineering disciplines suffering from a secular decline in demand in the closing decades of the twentieth century. This resulted in a constant struggle to fill funded places in some subjects each year while the university, because of its extremely restricted subject mix, could not take advantage of the more popular social science and humanities disciplines.

The AAC considered the problems of the department of chemical engineering and concluded, 'It is essential that Heriot-Watt University, as a technological university, should continue to have a Department of Chemical Engineering.'[168] It was very short-sighted to sanction two departments of chemical engineering, a specialised and expensive subject in limited demand, in a city of only 400,000 population dominated by the finance sector, law and education. Neither has become a leading centre of excellence in the subject, and supporting a larger joint department with Edinburgh might have been more successful.

Throughout the post-war period, the Royal Institute of British Architects (RIBA) exerted mounting pressure on art colleges to surrender their architecture courses to the university sector.[169] The Edinburgh College of Art had little option but to arrange a joint degree course with either the University of Edinburgh or Heriot-Watt University (discussions having been sanctioned by the AAC in June 1965). The response from Edinburgh proposed that the university would establish a new Faculty of Art to absorb all the existing schools of the college of art.[170] Conversely, Heriot-Watt envisaged an association whereby students would receive a degree, but the course would remain under the control of the college, recognising its independence and separate identity. This option was more palatable to the governors of the Art College, and the Schools of Architecture and Town and Country Planning formed the new Faculty of Environmental Studies of Heriot-Watt University from October 1968, with the respective heads becoming members of the senate, in addition to elected members of staff in a protected ratio.

Turning to academic standards, the AAC accepted that full-time courses for the associateship of the college equated fully to university degrees but noted that entry did not require a pass in a language additional to English. The AAC accepted a college recommendation that students without a foreign language at entry should pass an exam in one before entering the third year of their studies.[171] This proposal was implemented initially but the advent of a degree course in languages made such demands that the condition had to be dropped. In reviewing the first degree courses planned for 1965–66, the AAC expressed concern regarding

- the hours of formal instruction which seemed rather high;
- the low degree of utilisation of the resources of the humanities faculty in the course structures in the science and engineering faculties;
- the lengths of courses and the styles of degrees, and in particular the introduction of degree courses of only three years' duration.[172]

The AAC was extremely prescient since the problems of high student contact hours and negligible humanities and social science content in science and engineering courses, and vice versa, still exist almost four decades later.

The AAC expressed a somewhat utilitarian perspective on research:

Research in areas which are at or near the frontiers of present knowledge is an essential part of the academic activities of the new university. Research nourishes and stimulates teaching ... acts directly as an inspiration to all students, both undergraduate and postgraduate. ... The concept of research must be far removed from the traditional 'Ivory Tower' ideal of the pursuit of new knowledge for its own sake, regardless of consideration of utility. . . . Research should . . . be inspired by a knowledge of, and feeling for, the practical problems and needs of the working community of which the University forms an integral part.[173]

The committee reviewed the research activities in the various departments of the college which, 'in spite of the difficulty of access to higher degrees and the heavy teaching load carried by the staff, have been maintained at a volume which, while moderate, is commensurate with the opportunities available to the staff'.[174] By 1965 the number of research students in the college was growing and this caused some difficulties with the janitorial staff who closed the building at 6.00 P.M. each weekday evening and all weekend, and who could not understand why access was necessary outwith these hours.[175] After representations the buildings remained open on weekdays until 10.00 P.M. and on Saturdays until 1.00 P.M. from October 1965.

Jobs for the Boys

The staff of the college were now on their way to being university teachers, with time built into their schedules for research. Many were unable to effect the transformation. It would have been inhumane to halt teachers in mid-career because their institution was to be designated a university and they then, after years of loyal and dedicated service, did not pass an unlooked-for test. The issue of whether such staff should be considered for research leadership roles as professors is one that was addressed by the AAC. Under the Acts of 1885 and 1928, the governors of the college were given the power to appoint professors, a privilege enjoyed by only two other non-university institutions – the Royal Technical College Glasgow and Manchester College of Science and Technology. The chairs already established in the college were chemistry (1887), mechanical engineering (1887), electrical engineering and physics (1890–95), electrical engineering separately (1895), mining (1924) jointly with Edinburgh University, brewing and applied biochemistry (1950), physics (1946), mathematics (1961), chemical engineering (1955) jointly with Edinburgh University, and civil engineering (1962). To these the governors, advised by the AAC, added chairs in pharmacy, building and industrial administration and commerce, to which the existing heads of department were appointed from 1 April 1965, without having to face external competition. H. H. Campbell, who had been on the staff for 44 years without being active in research, was promoted to a chair in pharmacy; Dr N. C. Sidwell, in post since 1950, was appointed to the professorship in building; and Mr Joseph Gloag, who joined the college in 1952, took the new chair in industrial administration. These appointments followed the previous promotion to a chair of mathematics of Mr Raymond Smart in 1961. Raymond Smart, a St Andrews graduate, was appointed as a lecturer in 1938 and became head of mathematics at the college in 1943. When elected to become the first professor of mathematics in 1961, he had published little research 'other than notes in the *Mathematical Gazette*'.[176] Professor Frank Bell (chemistry) realised that some of these professors were 'not of a calibre needed for a university'.[177]

The procedures adopted in 1965 involved the AAC in examining the qualifications, experience and records of the heads of department, and interviewing them to determine if they were deemed suitable for assimilation as a professor, even if it was by no means certain or even likely that among a field specially assembled they would necessarily secure the post or even reach the shortlist. The UGC recognised that in some cases this might involve some temporary lowering of standards, especially regarding eminence in research. The consequence of this well-meaning but questionable policy of the AAC, combined with the fact that most of the senior hierarchy of Heriot-Watt College had little or no research experience and were therefore likely to favour the appointment of people who replicated their own approach, was to delay the emergence of Heriot-Watt as a research-based university. This policy decision by the AAC deprived the fledgling university of the all-important oxygen of new ideas which would have breathed life into its departments. There were two exceptions to this trend. First, David Manners, reader in chemistry at Edinburgh University, was appointed to the chair of brewing and applied biochemistry in 1965, following the sudden death of Professor Preece at the age of 57 in August 1964. Second, on the afternoon of Monday, 13 June 1966, Brian Gowenlock, senior lecturer in chemistry at the University of Birmingham, was interviewed for the chair in chemistry. He had the foresight to pack a waistcoat as Edinburgh was enveloped in a haar, a cold sea mist, out of the east.[178] This reveals two characteristics of Brian Gowenlock that were to be of inestimable value to Heriot-Watt over the next 25 years: a prodigious memory and a legendary attention to detail. Professor Gowenlock was also destined to make his mark at national level being a member of the UGC from 1975 to 1984 and acting as vice-chairman for 1983 and 1984. Also in 1966, however, A. R. Rogers, who was not an active researcher, was appointed to the chair in pharmacy, indicating that there was a transition period before normal university practices became universally adopted.

The committee made recommendations for the new chairs to be instituted over the five years from 1967 to 1972:[179]

- chemistry, a second chair;
- applied economics;
- materials science;
- politics and sociology;
- biology;
- philosophy;
- mathematics, a second chair;
- communication;
- electrical engineering, a second chair.

They also proposed chairs in mining and chemical engineering, following negotiations with Edinburgh University. The new university did not create the chairs in communication, philosophy or politics and sociology in the period 1967–72, or indeed thereafter, an unsurprising if unimaginative outcome in a senate dominated by scientists and engineers. It was to deprive the university of a fully developed social science faculty to complement science and engineering.

The staff/student ratio in January 1966 was 1:10.3, a level at which the committee judged that the present staff were 'seriously over-extended' relative to other universities at the time.[180] The AAC suggested a target of 1:8 as a 'reasonable (and by no means extreme) figure';[181] by 2001 it had become 1:16. To achieve a 1:8 ratio by 1971–72, when the AAC assumed there would be 2,495 students, would have required increasing academic staff numbers from 109 in 1965–66 to

Principal Nisbet, Lord Provost Sir Duncan Weatherstone, chairman of the board of governors, and Stefan Kay, SRC president, raise a toast to the new University

EXTRACT of MATRICULATION of the Arms of HERIOT-WATT UNIVERSITY

Whereas the Governors of Heriot-Watt College, for and on behalf of the said College, now the HERIOT-WATT UNIVERSITY, having by Petition unto the Lord Lyon King of Arms of date 9 December 1965 Shewn THAT the "School of Arts and Mechanics Institute" was established in Edinburgh in the year 1821 but that the name of the said Institution was changed to the "Watt Institution and School of Arts" in 1854; THAT the name of the said Institution was further changed to the "Heriot-Watt College" in the year 1885 when the Governors of George Heriot's Trust (whose Arms are recorded of date 3 January 1917 in the Public Register of All Arms and Bearings in Scotland, Vol. 23, folio 13) took over its administration; THAT Ensigns Armorial were recorded in the said Public Register of Arms, Volume 41, folio 99, of date 8 August 1958 in name of the said Heriot-Watt College; THAT a Petition having been presented in April 1965 to Her Majesty in Council praying for the grant of a Charter of Incorporation to the said Heriot-Watt College, Edinburgh, under the name and style of "Heriot-Watt University", which said Charter was approved on 31 January 1966, and passed under the Seal on 23 March 1966; AND the Petitioners having prayed that the foresaid Ensigns Armorial might be matriculated of new in name of the Heriot-Watt University in manner conform to the academic status and dignity of the said University, The Lord Lyon King of Arms by Interlocutor of date 16 May 1966 Granted Warrant to the Lyon Clerk to matriculate in the Public Register of All Arms and Bearings in Scotland in name of the Heriot-Watt University the following Ensigns Armorial, videlicet:— Per pale, two coats both demidiated; dexter, Barry of six Or and Azure, an oak-tree eradicated Vert; sinister, Argent, on a fess Azure between an open book undemidiated, binding Gules, in chief proper, and a mullet in base of the Second, three cinquefoils of the First.

Matriculated the 20th day of July 1966.
Extracted furth of the 8th page of the 50th Volume of the Public Register of All Arms and Bearings in Scotland this 20th day of July 1966.

N.W.N. Lawson.
Rothesay Herald.
Lyon Clerk Keeper of the Records.

Heriot-Watt University updated its shield of arms to reflect its new status in 1966

312 by 1971–72.[182] Proposals for administrative staff were also made, including 'three assistants (male)' for the bursar to deal with accounting, salaries and cash.[183] Quite why such posts should have been reserved for men by the all-male committee was never justified.

The UGC wrote to the principal on 18 August 1965 responding to the AAC report and the comments of the governors thereon:

- It suggested that humanities should 'concentrate upon studies closely related to the teaching of technological subjects'.
- It did not commit itself to the extent and timescale of the expansion in student numbers suggested by the AAC.
- It also suggested reconsideration of the proposal to break the link with Edinburgh University in relation to the joint department of chemical engineering.[184]

The college governors accepted the UGC view on humanities, agreeing to make new appointments in languages, economics, management and social studies, but rejected the suggestion to reconsider the decision to develop a separate chemical engineering department; they also queried comments on student numbers, pointing out that the increase was in accordance with the Robbins Report.[185] This issue of student numbers bedevilled the infant university.

The drafting of a charter of statutes for the new university was to represent a radical change in governance, the final stage in the move away from a paternalistic autocracy. The AAC agreed that in general outline the Heriot-Watt charter and statutes should mirror those recently promulgated for Strathclyde University.[186] The committee consulted widely when drafting the charter and, although differing views were expressed, there was consensus over the objective of producing a charter which would function in the interests of all members of the university. The draft was circulated for comment to the College Board of Studies, the staff association and the Association of University Teachers (AUT). In addition, Sir Edmund Hudson consulted with the SRC; its president at the time, Stefan Kay, was highly impressed: 'one of the smartest, brightest and nicest men I have ever met'.[187] In stark contrast to the college era, this was an enlightened approach to students who under the new charter would be represented both on court and senate. The staff association commented that the charter and statutes of the University of Newcastle were the most desirable model and it rejected the draft charter of Strathclyde University mainly because of provisions for non-professorial staff representation, which were regarded as 'largely ineffectual'.[188] The arguments of the non-professorial staff were ultimately conceded: one-third of the academic members of the senate are drawn from the ranks of the non-professoriate so that, unlike ancient Greece, democracy extends to the lowest levels – the considerable body of persons engaged in teaching.

The 1966 charter provided for the creation of the corporate body, the university, and prescribed in general terms its objects, powers and functions. It also specified the principal elements of its constitutional structure, organs of government and methods of organisation and operation. The charter enshrined rights of democratic assembly and free expressions of opinion for academic staff. Departmental committees, established under the charter and statutes, were an important and necessary innovation. The General Convocation, which meets annually to receive a report on the working of the university, was conceptualised as a collection of influential citizens drawn from the community of which the university is an integral part.[189]

There was a clear division of functions between the University Court and the senate. The court is composed of lay people, an elected group of senate members and a token presence of non-academic staff with, among other things, custody and disposition of all property and a remit to control the finances of the university. The senate is the executive body responsible for the academic work of the university, both teaching and research. The senate is therefore the prime source of decisions on such academic matters as the form and content of degrees, methods of teaching, quality assurance, and selection of students and staff. Significant power and influence, however, is exercised by the chairs of the University Court and the Finance Committee (both lay people) and other active lay members of court, especially on issues of finance and buildings; the advice of the senate is normally accepted on appointments which are formally the responsibility of court. The presence of lay court members, many with invaluable business experience, guarantees prudent administration of the large sums of money entrusted to universities. A draft charter was formally submitted by the governors to the UGC and the Privy Council on 31 March 1965. The AAC continued to provide advice and guidance to the university until 1971 when it was dissolved.

What's in a Name?

The AAC invited debate on whether the name of the institution should be altered to reflect the granting of university status. There was a difference of opinion between the minority of research-active academics and the rest. Professor Silver (mechanical engineering) strongly disagreed with the view that the Heriot-Watt name should be retained, arguing that a new name would 'indicate a complete break with our past functions … a considerable part of these past functions having been transferred to Napier College'.[190] Silver suggested several alternatives, including Queen's University of Scotland, Queen Elizabeth University of Technology, St Giles University and Saltire University. Dr Anna MacLeod (brewing and applied biochemistry) also sought change to 'rise, phoenix-like from the ashes of a rather parochial establishment to become the Technological University of the Lothians',[191] a name also endorsed by Professor Preece from the same department.[192] Later, at a meeting of the AAC on 16 November 1964, it was decided that the new university should not be qualified by 'technology' or 'technological'.[193] The place or district names suggested did not prove sufficiently attractive to the AAC and they agreed to recommend to the governors to adopt the title Heriot-Watt University. The staff association conducted a referendum in January 1965 to identify the preferences of staff on a suitable name for the university. Only 19 people voted to retain the name Heriot-Watt, 34 objected to retention and 10 were indifferent.[194] The association, in true academic style, decided to hold another referendum. Consequently, on 2 February 1965 a special

Principal Hugh Nisbet, second from the left, inspecting the new university mace, 1966. Photograph: The Herald

meeting of the association was held at which the results of the second referendum were announced. The pattern of voting, unsurprisingly, was similar with 24 favouring Heriot-Watt, 36 opposing the name and 10 indifferent.[195] Other suggestions included the University of the Lothians (13), Midlothian (6), Dunedin (6), James Watt (3), Strathforth (2), and one vote each for Forth, Queen's, Prince's, Laudonia, Duke and Greyfriars.[196] It seems scarcely credible that no one suggested incorporating the name of Scotland's beautiful capital city into the title or recognised the pre-eminent role of Leonard Horner in founding the institution. An amendment that 'the name Heriot-Watt should not be retained' was carried by 20 votes to 16.[197] The executive committee was charged with conducting a third referendum, which does not appear to have taken place; and the views of the association were clearly ignored when it was finally agreed not to alter the name.

University Status

News that the institution had been granted its royal charter was announced in the House of Commons by the Secretary of State for Scotland, Mr William Ross, on 1 February 1966. The elevation to university status was a cause of major celebrations but was not welcomed by all Scottish universities. Sir Malcolm Knox, vice-chancellor of St Andrews University, told the Carnegie trust that 'no institution which did not possess the four traditional faculties – Divinity, Arts, Law and Medicine – could properly be called a university. . . . It remained to be seen whether Stirling and Dundee would be universities in the true sense; Strathclyde and Heriot-Watt, he added, were not.'[198] This view decrying the award of university status to technological institutions was strongly criticised by Lord Robbins on 15 April 1966.[199]

The City of Edinburgh presented the university with a mace manufactured in the George Street workshop of gold- and silversmiths Messrs Hamilton and Inches Ltd. The mace was designed by Ian Davidson of the Edinburgh College of Art and is worked in gold and silver with a head incorporating 12 straps, each representing a department of the university at that time, beneath which the boss bears the coats of arms of the city and the university chased in gold.[200] The mace made its first public appearance at the installation of the new chancellor, Sir Alec Douglas-Home, on 20 April 1966. This was performed with all due ceremony (leavened by some undergraduate humour) at the Usher Hall immediately following a service of thanksgiving and dedication in St Giles' Cathedral.[201] Lord Balerno was appointed the first chairman of court.

The sense of exhilaration, amounting almost to euphoria, did not last long and was soon affected by uncertainties, not least as to how the institution would fare under the UGC. New responsibilities were reflected in changing roles: the professoriate, deans and other officers, and not least the subtle change of role from central institution principal to that of vice-chancellor, an uncertain change involving loss of power for a gain in influence. There is some evidence to suggest that Nisbet was uncomfortable in dealing with the UGC and the difficult transition to university status. John White, who 'worked well with Nisbet', stated that Nisbet 'found it a strain' as he was 'pressured by Sir Edmund Hudson, a demanding man, as Chair of the Academic Advisory Committee'.[202] Also Mr Alex Anderson, the scholarly librarian, appointed in 1967 and responsible for trying to create a true university library from a base collection of only 20,000 volumes stated:

> I've always been particularly annoyed about the first quinquennial submission ... to the UGC ... the Principal [Nisbet] who in the last few years has been sitting on a UGC committee on libraries ... put in a couple of sentences that said that, although small, the library was adequate for the work being done at the moment.[203]

Principal Nisbet was unfamiliar with the university system, having never worked in one, and Neill Campbell, former professor of chemistry at Edinburgh University and member of Heriot-Watt Court 1968–76, was not convinced that Nisbet 'had the vision or a clear idea what to do but Lord Balerno, Chairman of Governors, certainly did; it was through Balerno's prompt action that Hermiston House was purchased'.[204] Campbell did not think it was the happiest period of Nisbet's life. For a conscientious, generous-spirited and decent gentleman, it was clearly difficult to cope daily with the absurd situation in the college days, whereby even if the chemistry department required a dozen test tubes, the decision ended up with the principal.[205] Mr R. D. N. Clayton, former bursar, echoed Professor Campbell's view:

> Instead of growing into the job Nisbet almost contracted; that somehow he felt the constraints of it more than the opportunities. ... [He] never really got away from being a Professor of Chemistry.[206]

Stefan Kay, however, as president of the SRC in 1965–66, recalled that 'it was a bit of an event to get to see Principal Nisbet ... a very austere rather distant man, well disposed towards students, who always listened with great courtesy'.[207]

The people running the college and the university in its infancy had no real research motivation and did not regard it as an essential dimension of a university; they lacked understanding of the resources needed and the change in outlook required to develop research.[208] Their idea of what constituted criteria for academic promotion was also defective.[209] Mr Clayton also commented, that 'Mr. John White also found the transition of the UGC very difficult indeed', which cannot have helped since initially nobody ever communicated with the UGC except the principal or secretary.[210] The parsimonious attitude to expenditure (lecturing staff even had to apply for chalk[211]) was a consequence of a policy implemented by Nisbet and White, although the principal appears to have been 'under the influence of White', a strong personality, for there was a 'very significant change as soon as [Duncan] Cameron came and replaced White'.[212] Prior to the award of university status, the accounts at the college were kept at City Chambers and everything had to be requisitioned from there. Even petty cash accounts (with all relevant receipts) had to be submitted before the total reached £5,[213] and nothing

Duncan Cameron, secretary of the university, carries the royal charter in procession at the installation of Chancellor Alec Douglas-Home, 1966. Photograph: The Herald

could be ordered costing more than £5 without the prior approval of the principal. Even after gaining university status, all order forms had to be taken to the bursar's office for approval and signature, a practice which continued until 1967.[214]

The equipment budget was held by the principal, who simply informed heads of departments of their allocation after they had submitted their bids and had them pared down.[215] The attitude of Principal Nisbet and J. Y. White was to minimise costs; between 1955 and 1965, for example, the chemistry department received a total of only £10,000 for equipment.[216] Moreover, Nisbet and White were the sole link between the staff and governors before the institution became a university. There was at least one member of the professoriate who considered that Nisbet should have made stronger representations about underfunding, but 'his attitude was to keep in, as far as possible, with the SED'.[217] The Nisbet and White era drew to a close on 31 August 1965 when John White retired to be succeeded by Duncan I. Cameron, who became the first secretary of Heriot-Watt University and ipso facto of the Academic Advisory Committee. Stefan Kay considered that this change made a profound difference:

> White was always rather dismissive actually of student affairs. Duncan Cameron wasn't like that at all ... and in fact we formed a very good relationship. ... He was always business like and constructive. ... I was never turned away empty handed.[218]

Duncan Cameron's performance as secretary over 25 years was characterised by professional competence, excellent judgement and an acute memory, earning him the respect of all with whom he worked; a man of authority, he had an unusual ability to see solutions to problems. Donald MacDonald, who joined the university as public relations officer in 1968 and was himself to make a major contribution to the cultural life of the university and its students, regarded Duncan Cameron as a 'perfect person to work with ... he would always share information'.[219] Duncan Cameron also benefited from having David Sturgeon as registrar and deputy secretary; he was a 'tower of strength'.[220] A conscientious, meticulous, very approachable and loyal person, David Sturgeon – a lawyer with a highly idiosyncratic golf swing – always sought what was best for the university; he and Duncan Cameron were a formidable team.

The installation of those support services regarded as essential to the functioning of a university in the 1960s proceeded apace. When the governors decided in May 1966 to appoint a chaplain, they did not stipulate a specific denomination, 'but the chaplain would be of the Protestant faith, as most of the students were Protestants'.[221] The Reverend Tom Scott was appointed from October 1966, and although every chaplain since has been recruited from the ranks of the Church of Scotland, clergy from other denominations have been on subsequent shortlists.[222] The Magdalen Chapel (a sixteenth-century guild hospice of the Incorporation of Hammermen), the home of the first General Assembly of the Church of Scotland, attended by John Knox in 1560, was used as the university's chaplaincy centre. Principal Nisbet, 'a very straight and ethical man'[223] with the interests of the university at heart, eventually retired aged 65 on 30 September 1967, having witnessed the fruits of his many years of dedicated service to the college in its achievement of university status.

The new university was a minnow in the pool of Scottish universities. It had 1,200 students, tiny compared with Edinburgh's 10,000; Glasgow's had just under 8,000, and St Andrews, Aberdeen and Strathclyde had over 4,000 each. The fledgling university now required a new type of leadership with strategic vision to formulate the policies that would be required to transform a worthy technical college into a fully-fledged research institution able to compete globally for students and research funding.

Notes

[1] Obituary, *Year Book of the Royal Society of Edinburgh*, 1971–72.

[2] HWUA, Box 72, *A. Anderson's Papers*, Interview with Mr J. Y. White, 1980.

[3] HWUA, HWC 3/1/53, R. Smart, *James Cameron Smail, The Commemoration Address*.

[4] HWUA, HWC 3/1/A, A. Anderson, Interview with Prof. H. H. Campbell, 11 November 1986.

[5] HWUA, A. Jones, Interview with Alan L. Shaw, 25 July 2003.

[6] HWUA, Box 72, *A. Anderson's Papers*, Interview with Mr J. Y. White, 1980.

[7] HWUA, Box 72, *A. Anderson's Papers*, Interview with Mrs G. P. S. MacPherson, 7 May 1981.

[8] HWUA, HWC 3/1/A, A. Anderson, Interview with Dr R. C. Howie, undated.

[9] HWUA, HWC 1/2/43A, *Minutes of the Meetings of the Governors of the Heriot-Watt College*, 1929, p. 17.

[10] HWUA, HWC 1/2/45A, *Minutes of the Meetings of the Governors of the Heriot-Watt College*, 1931.

[11] HWUA, HWC 1/2/43A, *Minutes of the Meetings of the Governors of the Heriot-Watt College*, 1929.

[12] HWUA, HWC 1/2/45A, *Minutes of the Meetings of the Governors of the Heriot-Watt College*, 1931, p. 104.

[13] Payne, J. F. (1969) *A History of the Heriot-Watt University Library*, Edinburgh, p. 23.

[14] HWUA, HWC 1/2/47A, *Minutes of the Meetings of the Governors of the Heriot-Watt College*, 1933, p. 2.

[15] HWUA, HWC 1/2/44A, *Minutes of the Meetings of the Governors of the Heriot-Watt College*, 1930, p. 3.

[16] HWUA, HWC 8/7/1, A. Anderson, Interview with Mrs G. P. S. MacPherson, 7 May 1981.

[17] HWUA, HWC 1/6/16A, *Heriot-Watt College Extension Scheme*, p. 34.

[18] HWUA, HWC 1/2/49A, *Minutes of the Meetings of the Governors of the Heriot-Watt College*, 1935, p. 9.

[19] Anderson, A. and Gowenlock, B. G. (1998) *Chemistry in Heriot-Watt 1821–1991*, p. 60.

[20] HWUA, HWC 1/6/23.

[21] *Heriot-Watt University Bulletin*, Vol. 22, no. 116, 26 July 1989.

[22] Anderson and Gowenlock, *op. cit.*, p. 56.

[23] *Ibid.*, p. 57.

[24] *Ibid.*, p. 58.

[25] *Ibid.*, p. 63.

[26] *Ibid.*, p. 64.

[27] HWUA, *Heriot-Watt University Bulletin*, Vol. 18, no. 95, 15 August 1985.

[28] Boyle, J. S. (1973) *Heriot-Watt University: From Mechanics Institute to Technological University*, Edinburgh, p. 21.

[29] Anderson and Gowenlock, *op. cit.*, pp. 59–61.

[30] *Ibid.*, p. 59.

[31] Figures in the pharmaceutical world, *Chemist and Druggist*, 2 August 1958, p. 119.

[32] Anderson and Gowenlock, *op. cit.*, p. 61.

[33] Butt, J. (1996) *John Anderson's Legacy: The University of Strathclyde and Its Antecedents 1796–1996*, East Linton, p. 134.

[34] HWUA, A. Jones, Interview with Alan L. Shaw, *op. cit.*

[35] *Ibid.*

[36] MacLeod, A. (1965) The history of the Heriot-Watt brewing school, *Brewers' Journal Centenary Number*, p. 241.

[37] *Ibid.*, p. 241.

[38] Spark, Muriel (1993) *Curriculum Vitae*, London, p. 102.

[39] O'Farrell, P. N. (1995) *Laureation for Dame Muriel Spark*, Heriot-Watt University, 11 July 1995.

[40] Spark, *op. cit.*, p. 103.

[41] HWUA, HWC 1/2/43A, *Minutes of the Meetings of the Governors of the Heriot-Watt College*, 1929.

[42] HWUA, HWC 1/2/43A, *Minutes of the Meetings of the Governors of the Heriot-Watt College*, 1929, p. 95.

[43] HWUA, HWC 1/2/45A, *Minutes of the Meetings of the Governors of the Heriot-Watt College*, 1931, p. 46.

[44] HWUA, HWC 1/2/47A, *Minutes of the Meetings of the Governors of the Heriot-Watt College*, 1933, p. 23.

[45] HWUA, HWC 1/2/46A, *Minutes of the Meetings of the Governors of the Heriot-Watt College*, 1932, p. 17.

[46] HWUA, HWC 1/5/6, *Relations with Edinburgh University*.

[47] HWUA, HWC 1/5/6, Memorandum on the Structure of the University of Edinburgh and the Relationship with Heriot-Watt College.

[48] HWUA, HWC 1/1/13, *Minutes of the Meetings of the Governors of the Heriot-Watt College*, 1939–40, p. 1.

[49] *Ibid.*, p. 2.

50 HWUA, HWC 1/2/54A, *Minutes of the Meetings of the Governors of the Heriot-Watt College*, 1940, p. 35.

51 HWUA, HC 1/1/14, *Heriot-Watt College Annual Report*, 1940–41, p. 2.

52 *Ibid.*, p. 2.

53 HWUA, HWC 1/1/13, *op. cit.*, p. 2.

54 HWUA, Box 72, *A. Anderson's Papers*, Interview with Mr J. Lawrence, 17 December 1979.

55 HWUA, HWC 1/1/13, *op. cit.*, p. 3.

56 HWUA, HWC 1/1/14, *op. cit.*, p. 2.

57 HWUA, HWC 3/1/A, Prof. M. G. Say, Reminiscences of the Heriot-Watt College.

58 *Ibid.*

59 HWUA, Box 72, *A. Anderson's Papers*, Interview with Prof. E. Taylor, September 1979.

60 Wallace, L. A. (1993) *A History of Physics at Heriot-Watt University 1821–1992*, Edinburgh, p. 23

61 HWUA, HWC 1/1/15, *op. cit.*, p. 8.

62 Anderson and Gowenlock, *op. cit.*, p. 66.

63 HWUA, HWC 1/2/55A, *Minutes of the Meetings of the Governors of the Heriot-Watt College*, 1941, p. 17.

64 HWUA, HWC 1/2/56A, *Minutes of the Meetings of the Governors of the Heriot-Watt College*, 1942, p. 95.

65 HWUA, HWC 4/4/34, *SRC Bulletin*, No. 2, Friday 25 October 1940.

66 HWUA, HWC 1/2/63A, *Minutes of the Meetings of the Governors of the Heriot-Watt College*, 1949.

67 Pugh, M. (1999) *The State and Society: A Social and Political History of Britain*, 2nd edn, London, pp. 280–81.

68 Butt, *op. cit.*, p. 140.

69 HWUA, HWC 1/2/61A, *Minutes of the Meetings of the Governors of the Heriot-Watt College*, 1947, p. 27.

70 Wallace, *op. cit.*, p. 28.

71 Obituary, W. H. J. Childs, *Yearbook, Royal Society of Edinburgh*, 1984, p. 17.

72 Obituary, H. B. Nisbet, *Yearbook, Royal Society of Edinburgh*, 1971–72, p. 67.

73 *Ibid.*, p. 67.

74 HWUA, HWC 3/1/59, H. B. Nisbet, Correspondence.

75 *Ibid.*

76 *Ibid.*

77 *Ibid.*

78 *Ibid.*

79 HWUA, HWC 3/1/A, A. Anderson, Interview with Prof. F. Bell, 9 August 1979.

80 HWUA, HWC 8/7/1, *A. Anderson's Papers*, Interview with J. Y. White, 1980.

81 Anderson, A. and Gowenlock, B. G. (1998) *op. cit.*, p. 69.

82 MacLeod, A. (1965) *op. cit*, p. 242.

[83] Manners, David J. (2001) *Brewing and Biological Sciences at Heriot-Watt University 1904–1980*, Edinburgh, p. 12.

[84] Anderson and Gowenlock, *op. cit.*, p. 71.

[85] HWUA, HWC 3/1/A, A. Anderson, Interview with Dr A. Mackie, 4 November 1981.

[86] Anderson and Gowenlock, *op. cit.*, p. 72.

[87] Butt, *op. cit.*, p. 158.

[88] *Ibid.*, p. 158.

[89] *Ibid.*, p. 159.

[90] HWUA, HWC 1/2/61A, *Minutes of the Meetings of the Governors of the Heriot-Watt College*, 1947, p. 103.

[91] HWUA, HWC 1/2/61A, *Ibid.*, 1947, p. 2.

[92] *Ibid.*, p. 62.

[93] HWUA, HWC 1/2/65A, *Annual Report on the Work of Heriot-Watt College*, 1950–51, p. 9.

[94] HWUA, HWC 1/1/43, *Ibid.*, 1956–57, p. 32.

[95] *Ibid.*, p. 27.

[96] HWUA, HWC 4/3/7, Heriot-Watt Staff Association, Special General Meeting, 26 October 1950.

[97] *Ibid.*

[98] *Ibid.*

[99] HWUA, HWC 4/3/4, Heriot-Watt Staff Association, Minutes of Committee Meetings.

[100] HWUA, HWC 4/3/7, *op. cit.*

[101] HWUA, A. Jones, Interview with Alan L. Shaw, *op. cit.*

[102] HWUA, HWC 4/1/29, *Drama Study Club 1935–39*.

[103] *Ibid.*

[104] HWUA, HWC 4/1/14, *Heriot-Watt College Literary Society, Minutes of the Committee and Special Business Meetings*, 18 March 1960.

[105] HWUA, HWC 1/1/32, *Annual Report*, 1958, p. 48.

[106] HWUA, HWUSA, *Student Representative Council Minute Books*, January 1953 to November 1963.

[107] *Ibid.*

[108] HWUA, HWC 1/2/51A, *Minutes of the Meetings of the Governors of the Heriot-Watt College*, 1937, p. 69.

[109] HWUA, HWC 1/2/75A, *Minutes of the Meetings of the Governors of Heriot-Watt College*, 1961, p. 144.

[110] *Ibid.*, p. 144.

[111] HWUA, Prof. P. N. O'Farrell, Interview with Mr Stefan Kay, 7 June 2001.

[112] HWUA, HWC 1/2/1, *Minutes of the Meetings of the Governors of George Heriot's Trust*, 1887, p. 55.

[113] HWUA, HWC 4/4/35, *Heriot Watt College Students Handbook*, 1965–66, p. 15.

[114] HWUA, Prof. P. N. O'Farrell, Interview with Mr Stefan Kay, 7 June 2001.

[115] HWUA, SRC, *Minutes of the Meetings of Heriot-Watt College SRC*, 17 November 1964.

[116] Anderson and Gowenlock, *op. cit.*, p. 73.

[117] *Report of the Committee on Higher Education* (Robbins Report), Evidence Part 1, Cmnd 2154, 1963.

[118] HWUA, HWC 9/2/5, *Bulletin of Publications*, No. 2.

[119] Manners, D. J. (2001) *op. cit.*, p. 9.

[120] HWUA, HWC 3/1/A, A. Anderson, Interview with Prof. F. Bell, 9 August 1979.

[121] Anderson and Gowenlock, *op. cit.*, p. 75.

[122] *Ibid.*, p. 75.

[123] Birse, R. M. (1983) *Engineering at Edinburgh University: A Short History 1673–1983*, Edinburgh p. 130.

[124] *Ibid.*, p. 130.

[125] *Ibid.*, p. 131.

[126] *Ibid.*, p. 131.

[127] University of Edinburgh Archives, Box 196/UF, Letter from Prof. R. N. Arnold to the Secretary, 11 July 1950.

[128] *Ibid.*, Letter from Prof. R. N. Arnold to the Secretary, 30 May 1951.

[129] *Ibid.*, Letter from Appleton to Sir Arthur Trueman, 15 February 1952.

[130] *Ibid.*, Letter from Prof. E. Hearst and Kendall to the Secretary, 23 May 1951.

[131] HWUA, HWC 1/5/6, *Relations with Edinburgh University*.

[132] HWUA, HWC 1/1/33, *Heriot-Watt College Annual Report*, 1959–60, p. 27.

[133] *Report of the Committee on Higher Education* (Robbins Report), Evidence Part 1, Cmnd 2154, 1963, London, p. 931.

[134] HWUA, HWC 1/5/11, Letter from Prof. R. Nisbet to Prof. J. Grieg, King's College, London, 3 February 1964.

[135] *Public Record Office*, UGC, 7/535, Meeting between Heriot-Watt College and University Grants Committee, 9 June 1965.

[136] *Public Record Office*, UGC, 7/535, Letter from Sir John Wolfenden to Prof. Michael Swann, Acting Principal, University of Edinburgh, 30 September 1965.

[137] *Public Record Office*, UGC 7/535.

[138] University of Edinburgh Archives, Senatus Academicus, *Printed Minutes 1966–67*, Vol. XIX Pt 2, p. 1613.

[139] HWUA, HWC 8/7/1, A. Anderson, Interview with Dr Blair Maxwell, 5 October 1979.

[140] *Ibid.*, A. Anderson, Interview with Prof. Neil Campbell.

[141] Dahrendorf, R. (1995) *A History of the London School of Economics and Political Science, 1895–1985*, London, p. 428.

[142] *Report of the Committee on Higher Education* (Robbins Report), Evidence Part 1, Cmnd 2154, 1963, London, p. 915.

[143] *Ibid.*, p. 918.

[144] *Ibid.*, Evidence Part 1, Vol. F, p. 1841.

[145] *Ibid.*, pp. 928–29.

[146] *Ibid.*, p. 930.

[147] *Ibid.*, p. 891.

[148] *Ibid.*, p. 1060.

[149] Moss, M., Forbes Munro, J. and Trainor, R. H. (2000) *The University City and State: The University of Glasgow Since 1870*, Edinburgh, p. 280, and SED Circular, 1963.

[150] *Ibid.*, p. 133.

[151] Scottish Tertiary Education Advisory Council (1985) *Future Strategy for Higher Education in Scotland*, Edinburgh, HMSO (Cmnd 9676).

[152] HWUA, HWC 1/5/10.

[153] *Ibid.*

[154] HWUA, HWC 3/1/A, A. Anderson, Interview with Mr Peter Kilpatrick, 10 August 1979.

[155] HWUA, HWC 2/2/7, *Academic Advisory Committee*, Memorandum by Prof. H. Lipson, 9 June 1964.

[156] *Ibid.*, Mr H. F. Black, 9 June 1964.

[157] *Ibid.*, Prof. R. S. Silver, 9 June 1964.

[158] *Ibid.*

[159] *Ibid.*

[160] *Ibid.*, Dr Anna MacLeod, 9 June 1964.

[161] *Ibid.*

[162] HWUA, HWC 2/2/11, *Report of the Academic Advisory Committee*, 31 January 1966, p. 3.

[163] *Ibid.*, p. 4.

[164] *Ibid.*, p. 5.

[165] The committee also endorsed the negotiations to affiliate the departments of architecture and town and country planning of the Edinburgh College of Art with the new university. *Ibid.*, p. 12.

[166] *Public Record Office*, UGC 7/535, Meeting 28 June 1965.

[167] HWUA, HWC 1/2/81, Letter from Principal Nisbet to the University Grants Committee, 3 September 1965.

[168] HWUA, HWC 2/2/11, *Report of the Academic Advisory Committee*, *op. cit.*, p. 13.

[169] Lawrie, S. J. (1996) The Edinburgh College of Art 1904–1969: A Study in Institutional History. MPhil thesis, Heriot-Watt University, p. 106.

[170] HWUA, HWC 2/2/11, *Report of the Academic Advisory Committee*, *op. cit.*, p. 13.

[171] *Ibid.*, p. 11.

[172] *Ibid.*, p. 13.

[173] *Ibid.*, p. 14.

[174] *Ibid.*, p. 14.

[175] Manners, *op. cit.*, p. 20.

[176] *The Scotsman*, 13 May 1961.

[177] HWUA, HWC 3/1/A, A. Anderson, Interview with Prof. Frank Bell, 9 August 1979.

[178] HWUA, Prof. P. N. O'Farrell and Ms A. E. Jones, Interview with Prof. B. Gowenlock, 15 October 2002.

[179] HWUA, HWC 2/2/11, *Report of the Academic Advisory Committee*, *op. cit.*, p. 16.

[180] *Ibid.*, p. 17.

[181] *Ibid.*, p. 17.

[182] *Ibid.*, p. 17.

[183] *Ibid.*, p. 18.

[184] HWUA, HWC 2/2/11, Letter from UGC to Principal Nisbet, 18 August 1965.

[185] HWUA, UGC Files, Letter from Principal Nisbet to UGC, 3 September 1965.

[186] HWUA, *Academic Advisory Committee*, Papers and Supporting Correspondence, 1963 to June 1966, Explanatory Note by Sir Edmund Hudson, 26 October 1964.

[187] HWUA, Prof. P. N. O'Farrell, Interview with Mr Stefan Kay, 7 June 2001.

[188] HWUA, *Academic Advisory Committee*, Staff Submissions and Memoranda, Staff Association, 1 June 1964.

[189] HWUA, *Academic Advisory Committee*, Papers and Supporting Correspondence, 1963 to June 1966, Explanatory Note by Sir Edmund Hudson, 26 October 1964.

[190] HWUA, HWC 2/2/7, *Academic Advisory Committee*, Memorandum by Prof. R. S. Silver, 9 June 1964.

[191] *Ibid.*, Memoranda by Prof. I. A. Preece and Dr A. M. MacLeod, 9 June 1964.

[192] *Ibid.*

[193] HWUA, HWC AAC 3, Academic Advisory Committee.

[194] HWUA, HWC 4/3/4, Heriot-Watt Staff Association, 12 January 1965.

[195] *Ibid.*, 2 February 1965.

[196] *Ibid.*

[197] *Ibid.*

[198] *The Scotsman*, 1 March 1966.

[199] *The Glasgow Herald*, 16 April 1966.

[200] Boyle, *op. cit.*, p. 33.

[201] *Ibid.*, p. 33.

[202] HWUA, HWC 8/7/1, *A. Anderson's Papers*, Interview with J. Y. White, 1980.

[203] HWUA, Box 72, *A. Anderson's Papers*, Interview with R. D. N. Clayton, 25 February 1980.

[204] HWUA, HWC 8/7/1, *A. Anderson's Papers*, Interview with Prof. Neil Campbell, 10 October 1986.

[205] *Ibid.*

[206] HWUA, Box 72, *A. Anderson's Papers*, Interview with R. D. N. Clayton, 25 February 1980.

[207] HWUA, Prof. P. N. O'Farrell, Interview with S. Kay, President of the SRC, 1965–66, 7 June 2001.

[208] HWUA, Prof. P. N. O'Farrell and Ms A. E. Jones, Interview with Prof. B. G. Gowenlock, 15 October 2002.

[209] *Ibid.*

[210] HWUA, Box 72, *A. Anderson's Papers*, Interview with R. D. N. Clayton, 25 February 1980.

[211] Letter from Prof. B. G. Gowenlock to Prof. P. N. O'Farrell, 5 November 2001.

[212] HWUA, Box 72, *A. Anderson's Papers*, Interview with Prof. E. Taylor, September 1979.

[213] HWUA, HWC 3/1/A, Reminiscences of Prof. F. Bell, August 1977.

[214] Letter from Prof. B. G. Gowenlock to Prof. P. N. O'Farrell, 5 November 2001.

[215] HWUA, Box 72, *A. Anderson's Papers*, Interview with R. D. N. Clayton , 25 February 1980.

[216] HWUA, Prof. P. N. O'Farrell and Ms A. E. Jones, Interview with Prof. B. G. Gowenlock, 15 October 2002.

[217] HWUA, HWC 3/1/A, A. Anderson, Interview with Prof. Frank Bell, 9 August 1979.

[218] HWUA, Prof. P. N. O'Farrell, Interview with Mr Stefan Kay, 7 June 2001.

[219] Prof. P. N. O'Farrell and Ms A. E. Jones, Interview with Mr Donald MacDonald, 22 January 2002.

[220] HWUA, Prof. P. N. O'Farrell, Interview with Dr David Cameron, 26 June 2001.

[221] *The Glasgow Herald*, 19 May 1966.

[222] Letter from Prof. B. G. Gowenlock to Prof. P. N. O'Farrell, 5 November 2001.

[223] HWUA, Prof. P. N. O'Farrell and Mrs P. McIntyre, Interview with Prof. Jim Murray, 17 June 2002.

Chapter Seven

A Troubled Childhood:
The University from 1966 to 1988

The whole of modern education is radically unsound. Fortunately, in England, at any rate, education produces no effect whatsoever. If it did, it would prove a serious danger to the upper classes, and probably lead to acts of violence in Grosvenor Square.
Oscar Wilde

Student dining room in the Leonard Horner Hall. Photograph: John Dewar Studies

Skirmishes with the UGC

The university system in Britain altered more rapidly during the 1960s than at any time since the medieval period. The call was for more universities. Some 40 towns across the UK, including Perth and Inverness, had launched university promotion committees.[1] Country houses with ample parks were everywhere on offer. The mid 1960s witnessed the creation of a crop of new universities – glass and concrete inspired piles in architectural free-form with a dramatic centrepiece that often turned out to be a cumbersome disappointment. They sprawled across the cities and countryside from the wetlands of Essex to the braes of Stirlingshire. The campus became a little modern state with a pub, bookshop, supermarket and a crèche, while dining halls with perspex domes resembling sun umbrellas sprung up by plastic-bottomed artificial lakes beside which ambled the first students, who, it was hoped, had all the makings of a modern intelligentsia.

The route early chosen by Heriot-Watt College was not one of classical learning and dreaming spires but of useful training for the Edinburgh working

Student common room in the Mountbatten Building, late 1960s. Photograph: John Dewar Studios

Student dining room in the Leonard Horner Hall, c.1968. Photograph: John Dewar Studios

classes. No attempt was made to imitate the posture of the ancient Scottish universities nor even to clone a nineteenth-century British civic university. Instead the first ever mechanics' institute evolved into a technical college that eventually became a technological university. Development took place along a relatively low-status pathway, one that for 150 years left the institution outside the mainstream of the British university system. Writing during the period when Heriot-Watt was awarded university status, Ashby noted:

> It was difficult enough for British universities to adapt themselves to scientific thought … it is proving much more difficult for them to adapt themselves to technological thought. … [T]he crude engineer, the mere technologist (the very adjectives are symptoms of the attitude) are tolerated in universities because the state and industry are willing to finance them. Tolerated, but not assimilated: for the traditional don is not yet willing to admit that technologists may have anything intrinsic to contribute to academic life.[2]

Hence the technology routeway – from mechanics' institute to university – gave Heriot-Watt a distinctive place in a small subsector of British university education, thus placing the institution in a niche that lacked status among British universities generally. Humanities and most social sciences were absent; it did not devote itself primarily to basic research; indeed it was proudly utilitarian.

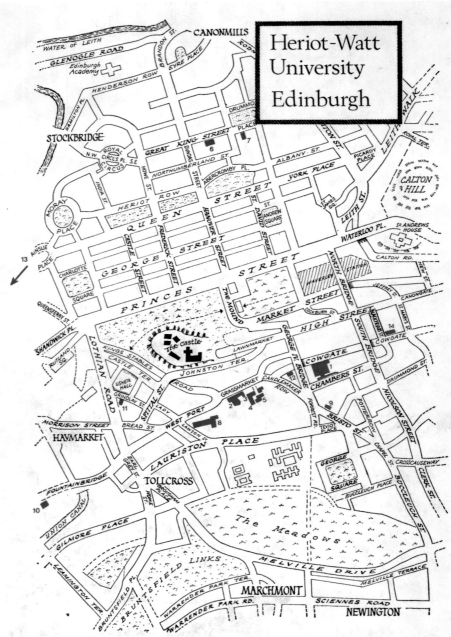

Heriot-Watt
University
Edinburgh

1. Chambers Street Buildings.
2. Mountbatten Building—Faculty of Humanities and Department of Electrical and Electronic Engineering.
3. Department of Computer Science.
4. Department of Mining Engineering.
5. Department of Pharmacy.
6. Leonard Horner Hall.
7. Bryson House.
8. Edinburgh College of Art.
9. Darien Building — Department of Civil Engineering.
10. Fountainbridge Building.
11. Students' Union.
12. Magdalen Chapel.
13. To Palmerston Place — Department of Town and Country Planning.
14. St Ann's Building.

Opposite: Multi-site working: in addition to its new campus at Riccarton, the university maintained a strong presence in the city centre as shown on this map from the 1972–73 prospectus

The university was confined to its original cramped college buildings in the Old Town of Edinburgh. The newly emerging university experienced some teething problems as although the UGC agreed the purchase of the Riccarton site in 1966, it quickly became evident that during the years up to 1973 any space required to accommodate additional student numbers or new developments would have to be found within the existing city-centre buildings, or by the short-term acquisition, with minimal conversion, of property close to them. Indoor physical recreation relied on the hospitality of Edinburgh University's centre in the Pleasance and later on that of the Commonwealth Games Stadium at Meadowbank. Outdoor sports were limited by the continuing impossibility of improving the ground at Paties Road to a tolerable or even safe standard. Residential accommodation for men only was provided from 1967 after the purchase and modification of two properties at Drummond Place and Great King Street in the New Town. A former Territorial Drill Hall, not conveniently located, in Grindlay Street was converted to form a Students' Union building. The conversion proved much more costly than anticipated since the Drill Hall was Crown property, thereby exempting it from fire regulations. Although the costs were met by the UGC, the episode did not enhance the university's reputation with the funding body.

The handling of building projects, the administration of students and academic staff, involvement in trade union negotiations, health, safety and public relations was to lead to a growing bureaucracy. Once the charter had been received, the university began to make provision for chaplaincy, accommodation, welfare services and a careers advisory service. An accommodation and welfare officer, Ann Trotman, was appointed in September 1968. A woman of great commitment and determination, she is greatly admired and respected by former students. She worked closely for over a decade with a much loved chaplain, Tom Scott, to provide a professional welfare service for students in Chambers Street and at Riccarton. The library, however, was in grave difficulties of accommodation and finance. Despite its identification by the Academic Advisory Committee as an area requiring priority of attention, the college and the university displayed a paucity of vision regarding library provision. The college and later the university authorities had so far been unable to add to the original library rooms in Chambers Street anything more than a purely local provision in the Mountbatten Building; a little more foresight on the part of the college authorities could have ensured that an adequate library was provided as part of that building project, but the opportunity was missed. The UGC proclaimed that a bookstock of 80,000 volumes was the minimum necessary for any university library, and proceeded to hand out a once-for-all grant of £26,000 to supplement the university's normal library allocation; this would have sufficed to raise the stock to the prescribed figure had it been possible in 1968 to stock a university library at around 30p per volume.

The library is not typical of British technological university libraries in the timing of its development; for whereas the libraries of the former colleges of advanced technology (CATs) began their expansion from 1956 onwards, the Heriot-Watt library followed suit only in the late 1960s. The new university had inherited from its predecessor college a library staff of four and only 20,000 volumes; there were only 40 reading places for almost 1,500 students.[3] The decision in 1966 to continue as a technological university set a limit to the subject content of the library, while the move to Riccarton implied that the library had to become more self-sufficient than it had been. The history of the library since chartering has been one of expansion under severe constraint; the university was financed for its library during the first decade on a scale much lower than the English CATs. Despite financial pressures, primarily due to the tendency for journal prices to rise much faster than inflation, the library under its capable librarians – Mr Alex Anderson from 1967 to 1985 and Mr Michael Breaks from 1985 – has consistently provided a highly effective and friendly service to staff and students and now has 136,000 volumes (excluding journals) at Riccarton, seating for 596 readers and 100 additional places at PC terminals. This is complemented by the Martindale Library at the Scottish Borders campus.

The UGC was a committee appointed by the government to assess and advise on the distribution of finances to universities. An ad hoc decision had located the UGC under the Treasury in 1919 until it was transferred to the Department of Education and Science (DES) in 1964. It was not a quango, had no income or revenue-producing capacity, but acted as a buffer between government and universities. The committee met 10 times a year and every financial decision or formal communication with the universities had to receive the approval of the committee itself.[4] At no time did the UGC adopt an overriding formula for the distribution of its grant to different universities. Although appointed by government, the UGC never lent itself to direct political intervention by government in decisions which lie with universities, nor was its advice on the distribution of grants between institutions ever overruled or even questioned by government.[5] The allocation of the recurrent grant required judgement at the margins and was distributed to universities with advice, admonition and diplomacy, but the money once given was at the disposal of the universities. It was through the decisions on buildings that the UGC exerted direct power over each university; it was for the UGC alone – as Heriot-Watt was to discover – to decide which building proposals to select in the light of its general overview and its opinion of the university concerned, and to fix limits of cost within which each should be built.[6]

During its first decade, the university suffered by comparison with other universities through receiving a very low level of grant per student from the UGC.

Heriot-Watt University entrance, Chambers Street, 1960s. Photograph: © The Scotsman Publications Ltd

In 1972–73 the recurrent grant per student, at £780, was 35 per cent below the national average of £1,200.[7] The resourcing of the Heriot-Watt College had also been on a modest scale by comparison with existing universities or with the colleges of advanced technology in England. Initially the UGC had based the Heriot-Watt University grant on the parsimonious funding levels the college had received from the SED. To some degree this was a self-inflicted wound as the college administration had not pressed the SED for improvement.[8] This funding squeeze at the crucial time of its infancy lasted a decade and significantly impeded the university's development. Despite this, the university was spared the violent student protests of the late 1960s, and the students' desire for improvements in their facilities was expressed with moderation remarkable by comparison with that in some of the old universities and institutions of the Robbins generation. The Heriot-Watt authorities, aware as they were of the shortcomings of the university in these areas, did not seek to conceal from the students their concern or their difficulty in improving matters under the prevailing financial situation.

One response to chronic underfunding was to try to expand student numbers. At a meeting of the senate in December 1967, it was agreed that the university should plan to achieve a student population of 3,000 by the mid 1970s. What alarmed the senate, however, was that the target number of 1,495 quoted by the UGC in 1967 for the end of the five-year period in 1972 was actually lower than the 1967 population of 1,500 students. The AAC had envisaged growth to 2,275 by 1971–72. The UGC allocations for 1971–72 were as follows.

Science-based subjects (undergraduate)	1,330
Other subjects	125
Postgraduate	40
Total	**1,495**

To achieve a student population of 1,495 in 1971–72, implied reducing annual intake from 640 to only 500.[9] The UGC also planned to cut postgraduate numbers by 50 per cent, which would have resulted in the university's proportion of postgraduate students falling to less than 3 per cent, whereas the proportion in other comparable institutions was at least 10 per cent.[10] This UGC policy was completely at variance with the desire to develop the research base of the new university. Acting Principal Smart, a rotund and jovial figure, popular with students, who was used to swaying so many college meetings by the sheer force of his ebullient personality, made representations to the UGC. The recurrent grant was raised by a mere £50,000 per annum (approximately 5.5 per cent) over the period 1967–1972.[11] The university chose to ignore the UGC student number allocations, believing that if they expanded more rapidly the increased grants would be forthcoming, as they had been previously, to some degree, under the Scottish Education Department during the college era.[12] Accordingly, recruitment was increased, especially in the engineering faculty, until a population of 2,590 UGC-supported students was reached by 1972, some 1,100 above the UGC target (Table 7.1). The recruitment drive was aided by the creation in 1969 of the part-time post of schools liaison officer, for which Charlie Wood from mathematics was paid an honorarium of £150 per annum.[13] The UGC grants, however, were maintained at a level set for only 1,495 students and the committee's refusal – in the face of continued pressure from the university – to bridge the gap led to a serious (if in the end temporary) problem with resources, staff and services. Principal Robin Smith arrived in June 1968 and despite his persistent advocacy of the university's case, the UGC under Wolfenden refused to make more than token increases in the projected grant, which consequently remained at an exceptionally low level throughout the period 1967–72. This chronic level of underfunding constrained for many years the extent to which the university could improve its infrastructure and recruit more new staff to develop the research profile and introduce new courses. It was not until well into the succeeding five-year period that Heriot-Watt's grant per capita approached the national norm.

Table 7.1 Full-time student numbers, 1971–72

Undergraduate intake					Total undergrads	Total postgrads	Total
1967–68	1968–69	1969–70	1970–71	1971–72	1971–72	1971–72	1971–72
596	768	946	810	824	2,415	175	2,590

Source: HWUA, Senate Minutes, 7 December 1971

Inflation rose rapidly in the early 1970s, and apart from statutory increases (usually covered), Heriot-Watt, like other universities, was at risk for up to 50 per cent of whatever increases accrued in a given year. Worse was to follow. In 1972–73, the start of a new five-year period, the UGC imposed a provisional year in which all universities had to make short-term plans without knowledge of their recurrent grants and their student number targets for that five-year period.[14] When the allocations were finally announced, it was clear that the era of rapid expansion was over. A 2 per cent reduction in grant per student was built in, and inflation adjustments would be provided by ad hoc supplementary grants given, as a rule, one year in arrears.[15]

The university was invited by the UGC in June 1973 to determine its planned size in 1981–82 and the faculty mix of students within that total (Table 7.2). The university sought to expand rapidly from 2,931 in 1976–77 to 5,000 by 1981–82. Tom Patten, professor of mechanical engineering, opposed the recommendations on the grounds that the numbers proposed for the Faculty of Engineering in 1981 were inadequate.[16] The senate agreed to reduce the target number of social science students from 1,490 to 1,385 and increase correspondingly the number of science-based students from 3,510 to 3,605. The following year (1973–74), however, the university failed to achieve its agreed undergraduate intake quotas due largely to a significant shortfall in engineering.[17] A letter from the UGC on 6 November 1973 designated a higher rate of growth in social science numbers than the figure proposed by the university (and much greater than Professor Patten's suggestion) and a correspondingly lower rate of growth in science-based numbers (Table 7.2).

Table 7.2 Planned student growth, 1976–77 to 1981–82

	Heriot-Watt targets			UGC targets	
	1976–77	1981–82	Growth	1981–82	Growth
Humanities and social science students	716	1,490	108%	1,600	127.3%
Science-based students	2,215	3,510	58%	3,400	53.5%
Total	2,931	5,000	71%	5,000	71.3%

The UGC wrote on 24 April 1975 indicating 'there is no evidence to suggest that the swing in student preference away from science is being reversed'.[18] Recruitment problems continued in science and engineering; between 1976 and 1978 they failed by 278 to reach their student intake quotas. Despite this, the UGC responded inconsistently in July by announcing that the financial allocations for the three years from 1978–80 to 1981–82 would be based on a total of only 3,000 students, 2,160 science and engineering based, and 840 social science students.[19] Hence the planned target numbers of the UGC announced in 1978 represented an increase in the proportion of science and engineering students over the 1973 targets, despite the recruitment problems. The tendency of the UGC to change planned target numbers several times over a five-year period reflected harsh economic and political realities but was not conducive to stability.

A New Vice-Chancellor

A key figure in the university's development during this challenging period was Principal R. A. Smith. Robin Allan Smith, the son of a tailor, was born in Kelso in 1909, the older of two boys. He was educated at Kelso High School and Edinburgh University, where he graduated with first-class honours in physics and mathematics in 1930. He subsequently completed the mathematical tripos at Cambridge University in 1932. After he won a prize at Cambridge, the pupils at Kelso High School were awarded a holiday because, as one boy informed Robin Smith's mother, 'Ye ken, yer son, he's cleverer than the Heid Maister.'[20] After the award of his PhD in 1935, brief spells at the Universities of St Andrews and Reading were interrupted by wartime service. Smith joined a group of scientists working on the development of radar. During the Battle of Britain, Smith was involved in bringing into use mobile radar equipment in difficult conditions to fill gaps caused by German dive-bombing attacks on the British radar chain.[21]

After the war, Smith directed the physics department at the Royal Radar Establishment, Malvern. His group led the world on infrared detectors, and the balance he kept between basic and applied research 'led to a series of very important contributions, both to the defence capability, basic science and device development in the U.K.'.[22] Robin Smith was a stimulating, approachable and inspiring leader who showed great consideration for his staff.[23] His breadth of

Robin Allan Smith, principal, 1968–74. Portrait by H. Raeburn Dobson. Photograph: Douglas McBride

outlook from basic research to the very practical was indicative of his vision and clearly matched perfectly the needs of Heriot-Watt University. After only a year at Sheffield University and election as a Fellow of the Royal Society in 1962, Robin Smith migrated westwards to the Massachusetts Institute of Technology (MIT) to become director of the Materials Science Centre. He remained until 1968. Smith's main contribution was to bring together groups of people and to create conditions in which collaborative research could flourish. When Hugh Nisbet retired on grounds of ill health in September 1967 – he had been unable to resume duties after his sudden illness in September 1966 – the chairman of court, Lord Balerno, had the perspicacity to realise that a new university needed an internationally respected academic who would be able to attract good quality staff.[24] Lord Balerno hosted a lunch at the Houses of Parliament at which Robin Smith was introduced to the chancellor of the university, Sir Alec Douglas-Home.[25] Robin Smith was duly appointed principal, taking office on 1 June 1968.

Prior to the granting of the university charter in 1966, the infrastructure

Principal Smith, Principal Nisbet, Principal Smail, J. Gibson-Watt MP and Professor E. O. Taylor examine a letter copying press patented by James Watt, at an exhibition to mark the bicentenary of James Watt's separate condenser patent, 1968. Photograph: The Herald

necessary for research did not exist; nevertheless, there were significant research programmes in brewing and biochemistry and in chemistry. Unlike most newly established 1960s universities, Heriot-Watt did not have the advantages of new staff and large equipment budgets. SED funding had contained no research component; staff inherited from the college days had not originally been engaged to conduct research, and many were unable to adjust to new expectations. Principal Smith, a true academic, was not a great administrator;[26] this was left in the capable hands of Duncan Cameron, but Smith made the first attempt to instil a research culture in the university by using his reputation to recruit professors. He had a talent for spotting intellectual leaders. In the Faculty of Science, the retirement of Smart and Childs created an opportunity to bring to the departments of mathematics and physics new professors whose appointments were to transform these departments, hitherto almost exclusively concerned with service teaching, into ones in which research and honours courses became at least as significant as in any of the existing departments. Professor S. Desmond Smith, an able, energetic and mercurial person, took up the chair of physics in September

1970, bringing with him from Reading a large project in the field of non-linear optics, including Nimbus satellite radiometers and tunable spin-flip Raman lasers. Des Smith was largely responsible for developing a physics department of international repute. To accommodate this development, a temporary laboratory (the first academic building on the site) was erected at Riccarton, where a theoretical physics group was later added under Professor Philip C. Harper in 1972. The other beacon of hope in an otherwise largely barren research landscape was to be the department of mathematics, where Robin Knops, who moved from Newcastle University on 1 October 1971, initiated the transformation of the department into a world-class centre of research in applied mathematics. A man of great rigour and attention to detail who set very high standards and who was destined to make a major contribution to the development of the university at all levels, including vice-principal, he acknowledges that the physics department was 'a great source of encouragement and support in those early days'.[27] Professor Gordon Nicoll, a previous colleague of R. A. Smith at Malvern, was also recruited from Cambridge University to the chair in electrical engineering in 1968.

Mathematics had already given birth to a separate department of computer science; a chair created in 1971 was filled by Alec Balfour, head of the department from its foundation. Its course in computer science, approved by the AAC in 1969, was the first to be offered in a Scottish university. On Professor Smart's retirement, appointments were made not only to the chair of mathematics but also to a new chair of actuarial mathematics and statistics (James R. Gray from St Andrews), the establishment of which was made possible by the generosity of the life assurance offices with head offices in Edinburgh. A year later two separate departments were constituted. Actuarial mathematics introduced the first honours degree in actuarial science in a British university in 1972 as well as developing postgraduate studies in operational research. Actuarial mathematics has consistently recruited high-quality students, whereas mathematics has been more innovative in research.

Elsewhere in the Faculty of Science, a chair in organic chemistry was filled from October 1969 by Professor J. G. Buchanan, who brought with him research interests in carbohydrate chemistry. This complemented those already existing in the department of brewing and biological sciences, hitherto known as brewing and applied biochemistry. Industrial microbiology developed and marine biology was introduced in 1972, presaging a later involvement with the university's general research interests in matters marine.

In the engineering faculty there was not initially the same transformation to an emphasis on research, though significant development soon took place. The faculty continued to fulfil its mission for local industry in which the departments were involved with developmental activity such as practical problem solving, testing and

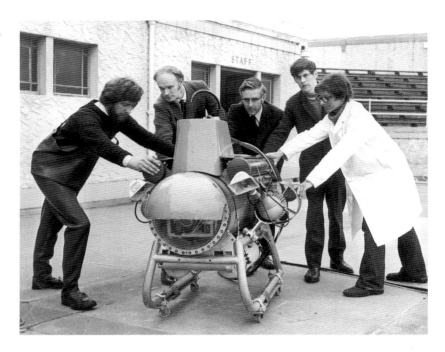

ANGUS submersible vehicle, the brainchild of the Department of Electrical and Electronic Engineering's Robin Dunbar and Robin Holmes (centre). Photograph: The Herald

stress analysis. Tom Patten, previously senior lecturer at Edinburgh University, was appointed as head of mechanical engineering in April 1967 and students found him 'immensely approachable'.[28] A build-up of research activity began, especially in thermofluids; the department's links with industry, always strong, developed further with the appointment of Jim Murray to a lectureship in 1966. Murray, a person of infectious enthusiasm, was strongly committed to building links with industry. Later he initiated an MSc programme in technology management in collaboration with Strathclyde University, and he founded the Institute of Technology Management in 1991 to provide a range of services at the university–industry interface.

The pace at which departments changed to become research-led, usually with an emphasis on applied problems, was dictated primarily by new professorial appointments. Professor Arthur Bolton (civil engineering), for example, had immediately made a positive impact. Other staff enabled the breadth of the university's research strength to be extended as small groups of people in most departments participated in the build-up of research. In 1969–70 a programme of research into small submarine vessels was initiated in electric and electronic engineering under Professor Gordon Nicoll. Nicoll had to raise £50 to buy a torpedo body from the Royal Navy for the first underwater submersible, which led to the successful development of ANGUS (a navigable guided underwater system).[29] A chair was advertised in chemical engineering in order to provide leadership following the division of the department with Edinburgh University.

Professor John Coulson of the University of Newcastle, who was a member of the Academic Advisory Committee and an assessor for the chair, was unimpressed by the quality of the applicants.[30] Coulson suggested to Acting Principal Smart that he would be prepared to take leave of absence from Newcastle and spend the academic year 1968–69 at Heriot-Watt. As one of the founding fathers of the academic discipline of chemical engineering, he proved to be a quiet but profound influence on the development of the department.[31] There were also disappointments: a UGC letter noted that there was overprovision nationally in mining engineering, that the Heriot-Watt department 'had recently attracted few students', and that its existing resources and accommodation were inadequate.[32] The undergraduate intake to the department of mining engineering in February 1970 was to be the last.

The work of the Faculty of Humanities, renamed Economic and Social Studies in 1972, was at an embryonic state in the late 1960s. Under Professor Joseph Gloag, the parent department of industrial administration and commerce continued to cover for BA degrees and service teaching to science and engineering students, a wide range of subjects which in more established universities or business schools would be taught in separate departments. The university decided in June 1971 that the name of the department should become 'business organisation', that it should concentrate on behavioural science and marketing, but that law and production management would continue to be offered.[33]

The department of economics, to which Dr Tom L. Johnston from Edinburgh University was appointed professor and head of department in 1966, offered a BA degree course (honours or ordinary) from October 1967, as well as providing service teaching for all faculties. Research in manpower studies and industrial economics was soon established. A second chair in the economics of government was funded from 1977 with a £7,500 per annum grant for 10 years from the Immanuel Charitable Foundation. The chair was occupied by Dr Alan C. Thompson, previously of Edinburgh University, who had been a Member of Parliament for the Dunfermline burghs from 1959 to 1964. The Esmée Fairbairn Research Centre was also established in economics under Professor Keith Lumsden to conduct pioneering research into the methodology of economics teaching. The difficulty of embedding a universal research culture in the faculty is demonstrated by a letter from the head of the department of business organisation, Professor Leslie Rodger, on 18 March 1976 arguing that 'appropriate business consultancy activity should be equated with research and scholarship as a criterion for promotion'.[34] The Principal and Deans Committee responded that it was unreasonable for staff who chose to undertake paid consultancy work to expect the research criterion to be waived in their case.[35]

The long-standing arrangement was discontinued whereby the University of

Professor Henry Prais, pioneer of languages in translation

Edinburgh provided a year's full-time course for candidates seeking the qualification of the Scottish Institute of Chartered Accountants. Thanks largely to the initiative of the new secretary of the university, Duncan Cameron, himself a chartered accountant and a lawyer, Heriot-Watt created a chair in accountancy and finance. This was filled from September 1967 by John R. Small, previously senior lecturer at the University of Glasgow, and a department was established that at first provided the 'academic year' for trainee accountants, and then developed a degree of BA in accountancy and finance, the profession moving, like many others, to graduate entry.

Under Principal Smith the university rejected firmly the merely fashionable in educational trends but maintained its educational commitment to develop applied areas of industrial and social relevance. A good example of this was the way in which languages – located in the department of industrial administration and providing classes in French, German and Russian to second- and third-year science and engineering students – was developed after its establishment as a separate department in October 1967. Henry Prais, a man who had survived Buchenwald concentration camp and fled to the UK as a refugee in 1939 and who worked for a spell as a toolroom turner in a Glasgow engineering firm, joined Heriot-Watt as a lecturer in languages in 1966. He became head of the new department of languages in 1967 and was instrumental in the design and introduction of the new languages degree (French, German, Spanish and Russian) for interpreting and translating in 1970, a departure from traditional literature-based university language teaching, unique in Scotland. The degree attracted a high calibre of applicant from its inception and gained the university an enviable reputation in this area of study. Much of this was due to the enormous energy and enthusiasm of Henry Prais. He was a fine scholar, an outstanding public speaker and debater and a highly effective administrator; but above all, he was warm, outgoing and liberal, with a mischievous sense of humour.[36]

Equally significant was the growth in quality and quantity of students and staff. In the year 1967–68, on Principal Smith's arrival, there were 1,493 undergraduate and postgraduate students, dominated by some 768 engineers and only just over half as many scientists. By the time of his departure in 1974 there were 2,574 students, of whom postgraduates had risen from 65 to 229 and science numbers to within 10 per cent of the engineering complement. Degrees awarded rose from 226 in 1968 to 629 in 1974. The subsequent growth of research under R. A. Smith's influence was also significant for the future of the university. The annual number of publications trebled and research grants, which totalled £46,000 in 1968, increased to £260,000 in 1974.[37] This compares with the rise in total income to the university from about £1 million in 1968 to £3.5 million on Robin's retirement in 1974.

Principal Smith crucially perceived that the university needed to broaden its provision. In 1968 the Edinburgh College of Art and the university, therefore, agreed to the establishment of a formal link between the two institutions whereby the Schools of Architecture and of Town and Country Planning became joint departments of the college and the university within a new Faculty of Environmental Studies. From 1978 the university validated diploma courses in art and design offered by the college and in July 1986 these courses were placed on the same footing as those pertaining in environmental studies by the establishment of a Faculty of Art and Design.

One day in 1971 Professor Tom Johnston was chatting to R. A. Smith in his office and suggested to the principal that the university should take an initiative on North Sea oil.[38] Both men recognised the interdisciplinary implications of the exploitation of North Sea oil resources, including the environmental aspects of land and marine resources conservation. Gordon Nicoll and Tom Patten were brought into the informal group and Patten prepared a proposal for the Wolfson Foundation. The university was awarded a grant of £177,780 in 1972 to establish the Institute of Offshore Engineering (IOE) in a building on the research park and to meet its staff and operational needs for a four-year period.[39] Appointed acting director of IOE in 1972, Tom Patten had resigned as dean of engineering after one year because he considered that he was not being supported sufficiently from the top.[40] He became director of IOE in March 1974, continuing in post until 1979 when he was succeeded by Cliff Johnston, a biologist with interests in environmental pollution. A programme of work commenced involving research, consultancy, the organisation of conferences and seminars, and provision of an information service. The institute developed a portfolio of major clients, including BP, Conoco, Marathon, Esso, Occidental, Statoil and Shell. Shell UK awarded an annual grant of £100,000 to IOE in 1978 for a five-year period. The declared aim of the institute was 'to meet speedily and effectively the needs of the ancillary industries in oil exploration by establishing a source of specialised knowledge in offshore engineering to the advantage of the participating companies and the primary industry'.[41] IOE was an administrative anomaly and attempts to create a cross-faculty, interdepartmental administration for IOE were not successful.[42]

Environmental studies, incorporating environmental impact assessment and oil-spill behaviour, including use of the institute's oil-slick drift prediction model, were a major focus of the institute's activity by the early 1980s, together with topics as diverse as survival techniques, offshore accidents, abandonment of offshore installations, hydraulic modelling and bioresource development, including seaweed harvesting, shrimp cultivation and shellfish husbandry. The institute was also marine environmental consultant for the Eurotunnel project. The first graduates from the undergraduate degree programme in offshore engineering completed their degrees in 1976, and in 1985 an MSc in marine resource development and protection was launched.

Having distinguished the largest waves in the tide that the university vessel harnessed so successfully at the time, it is important to note there were tensions among the crew. Professor Patten had argued in the late 1960s that Heriot-Watt was 'in danger of moving towards a more conventional university'.[43] His vision of a technological university, led by engineering, differed from that of Principal Smith, whom he perceived was prioritising the development of science.[44] The depth of this division emerged on 17 June 1973, when Principal Smith was due to attend a social gathering of senior staff at Hermiston House but was prevented from going by a virus infection. He sent a handwritten message to the participants that revealed the depth of division within the institution and his own disillusionment with factional, small-minded behaviour:

> I had for a long time been looking forward to tonight as an opportunity of meeting with those directly concerned with the healthy progress of the University ... and of discussing with them what best can be done to cure the University of the malaise from which it is suffering – largely, I believe fear and envy. These have been generated by the situation of poverty and adversity in which we had been thrown through having developed more rapidly than we have been able with the money at our disposal and have been given quite

inadequate funds to continue this rate of development so far as recurrent grant is concerned. ... The engineering departments at the Heriot-Watt have always so far been predominant and are now seeing pure science departments growing in strength and some of them don't like it – they fear that pure science will take over the leadership. But this is foolish – leadership falls to the leaders and engineering will never in my view flourish in a rapidly changing world without the strongest backing from pure science – and that backing will never come while the engineers have this defensive thinking. The same can be said about the common fear of the growth of the arts-based side. So long as we avoid the traditional 'arts faculty' style both engineering and science have lots to gain from a strengthening of the 'arts' side and indeed this is bound to come. Wouldn't it be better to accept it with good grace and together get the right kind of growth rather than each faculty thinking only of its own development in competition with the others.

I have been frequently accused of favouring the scientists at the expense of the engineers. Naturally I see the need for a strong physics department and helped where I could help – what a waste of time and talent if I'd been got here and forbidden to use *any* of my past experience – goodness knows I've used very little of it. When I think of all the effort I put into making myself really familiar with a whole range of subject areas in materials, some right outside my own original expertise, so that I could work with engineers I feel very sad to think how little I have used it since being at Heriot-Watt. I *have* gone out of my way to help the engineers. I've tried to arrange contacts and I went out of my way to bring in friends in high places over the Wolfson grant.[45]

Principal Smith was clearly profoundly distressed by the short-sighted narrow conservatism that persisted in many parts of the institution in the early 1970s.

A 1973 report for government, *Education and Training for Offshore Development*, predicted a growing demand for graduates in the oil and gas industry. It recommended there should be two UK centres for higher education in petroleum engineering, Imperial College in London and one Scottish institution. The University of Aberdeen was invited to discuss this possibility with Imperial College.[46] Principal Burnett, then professor of chemistry at Aberdeen, tried to persuade the principal of Aberdeen to take up this option but he was reluctant, reasoning that the prosperity of the oil industry would be short-lived.[47] Professor Tom Patten, as director of IOE, realised this was a golden opportunity for Heriot-Watt. The UGC designated Heriot-Watt as the second UK centre for petroleum engineering in 1974. The UGC provided a grant towards the relevant costs of up to £15,000 for the first year from August 1974 for advance recruitment of staff, £50,000 per annum for the subsequent two years, and thereafter funding would continue through the five-yearly block grant.[48] The UGC rejected a claim by the university for capital resources of £200,000, £125,000 of which was for a new building, arguing that these costs should be sought from industry.[49] Professor Patten negotiated a grant of £300,000 for the building from the Department of Energy.[50]

Principal Smith retired in September 1974 indicating that he had no desire to seek an extension to his seventieth birthday.[51] He was somewhat disillusioned as he had been sold a vision of a promised land at Riccarton to persuade him to return from MIT. As Lord Balerno put it:

Robin was a very private person. Though with very great patience, he used to conceal his irritation when colleagues were difficult and needless difficulties were raised, he would remain silent, but as soon as possible disappeared to his room and continued with a bit of research or writing that he always had on hand.[52]

George Burnett, principal
1974–80. Portrait by Peter
Collins. Photograph: Douglas
McBride

Although to some he was a somewhat remote figure and staff seldom saw him,[53] those who knew him well remember his integrity, the warmth of his personality and the zeal with which he would embark on any new undertaking. By contrast, he was a shy person who was less at ease in a public role where perhaps he felt awkward although, whatever the occasion, his sincerity always shone through.[54] On his retirement in 1974, Professor Smith became president of the Royal Society of Edinburgh between 1976 and 1979. He revived his research, initially in the University of Edinburgh, but later returning to physics at Heriot-Watt where he published several papers on lasers and molecules, remaining active until his death in 1980.

The End of Normality

George Burnett took up his appointment as principal on 1 October 1974. He was born in South Africa, where his parents, both from Aberdeenshire, were farming. To benefit from a Scottish education, he returned with his mother to Aberdeen in 1927 and attended Robert Gordon's College and the University of Aberdeen. He graduated in 1943 with first-class honours in chemistry and gained a PhD in 1947 for a study on the kinetics of the polymerisation of vinyl acetate. He became a lecturer at the University of Birmingham in 1949, where he remained until 1954 when, aged 34, he returned to Aberdeen as professor and head of the department of chemistry. His research, characterised by elegant yet fundamentally simple experimental techniques supplemented by rigorous application of his detailed mathematical insight, contributed significantly to the developing discipline of polymer chemistry.[55] In planning the growth of his department, his ability to delegate as well as direct enabled him to give further of his time and energy to the wider aspects of university administration. He was vice-principal of Aberdeen from 1966 to 1969 and was also a member of the Physical Sciences Subcommittee of the UGC between 1971 and 1974, where his contribution – as in the exposition of his work as a frequent guest lecturer to scientific societies – was notable for its clarity and gentle good humour. A man of organisational ability, he was 'clear thinking, even-handed and knew how to cope with difficulties'.[56]

A shrewd, pleasant and humorous man, George Burnett's realism, foresight and absence of pretension, and his natural desire to persuade rather than confront, tempered with caution and combined with an ability to maintain and project a 'calm sough' (to hold one's tongue), suited the traditions of Heriot-Watt ideally. A popular and warm-hearted person, who knew the university scene well, George Burnett had the respect of his staff and the Association of University Teachers (AUT) and he gave Heriot-Watt a feeling of trust in the management. He had a unique gift for persuading other people that they had thought of a good idea even though he had implanted it in the first place.[57] He deployed these skills to minimise the frustrations felt by staff in the severe inflationary climate of the times, and at the action of the UGC in shelving the university's plans for further development on the Riccarton campus, by redirecting energy to important new areas of academic growth, encouraging young staff, and fostering postgraduate post-experience courses and research. He also bought more cohesiveness to the institution by seeking to reduce some of the funding disparities between departments.

The beginning of George Burnett's tenure of office was blighted by grim financial news. With rampant inflation, the UGC's five-yearly system broke down, never to be restored, and funding for 1975–76 was only made public after Easter 1975. The last year of the final five-year period ended on 31 July 1977. What followed were 'planning figures' of diminishing firmness for five years ahead,

Anna MacLeod, first woman professor at Heriot-Watt University. Photograph: John Dewar Studios

revised each year. Inflation had destroyed five-yearly planning and reduced management at every level to a condition of perpetual crisis. Fortunately, at this time of severe financial stringency, the university benefited by having Professor John Small of the department of accountancy and finance as vice-principal from August 1974 to 1978. By 1979, however, the financial constraint was eased and the UGC unit of resource per student was close to the average for all universities.[58]

A further broadening of the university's portfolio of degree courses occurred in 1976–77 with the first intake of students to the degree programmes in government and modern history, and business law. During George Burnett's principalship there was a major flowering of new undergraduate degree programmes in actuarial mathematics, statistics, marine biology and structural engineering; and postgraduate MSc courses in microbiology, computer science, pharmacy, soil mechanics and environmental construction.

The UGC also implemented a moratorium on new building starts that was to greatly delay the move to Riccarton. This prompted the purchase of Lorne House in 1977 for £216,000 to provide more student accommodation in the city centre. The appointment of the ebullient Lord Thomson of Monifieth as chancellor, a former government minister, European Commissioner and editor of the *Beano* comic, seemed appropriate in such difficult times. Despite the financial chill, several talented professors were appointed in 1975, including Henry Black (mechanical engineering) and John McCutcheon (actuarial mathematics and statistics), while Anna MacLeod (brewing and biological sciences) became the university's first woman professor when promoted to a personal chair. Although inflation was rampant, recurrent finances were maintained in equilibrium, but on the capital side there was a debt arising from the overspend on phase 1 at Riccarton. During George Burnett's principalship, income from research grants and contracts grew from 7.4 per cent of total income in 1974–75 to 13.6 per cent of income, over £900,000, in 1978–79. The whole infrastructure necessary to optimise university–industry collaboration was now in place, including Unilink, the research park, the Institute of Offshore Engineering, and Teaching Company schemes.

Following the UGC's decision to fund the university as the UK's second centre in petroleum engineering, the court established a chair in 1975 and Professor Jim Brown was appointed first head of department, following a distinguished career with Shell. Jim Brown had participated in Operation Chariot on 17 and 28 March 1942, the most spectacular seaborne raid carried out in the Second World War against the German naval base at St Nazaire in Brittany. He recalled the experience of lying down in pitch darkness on the deck of the converted ship which was used as a battering ram against the gates of the largest dry dock in the world: 'I had the runs – it wasn't very pleasant to know you were surrounded by cannon. I think we

Principal George Burnett (left), Professor Jim Brown (second right) and colleagues in the department of petroleum engineering, 1978

all knew we were expendable.'[59] In trying to fight their way through and out of the dock area and of the old town, over 50 per cent of the commandos were wounded, including Stuart Chant-Sempil, author of a book on the St Nazaire raid. He recalls:

> There was no way I could continue to run, or walk even, and I collapsed. . . . 'Ron' Butler, one of my sergeants, would have none of this and with young Jimmy Brown . . . they carried me until I realised that I was a hindrance to their own chances of escape and I ordered them to leave me. . . . I watched them run alongside the dock basin with the others until they reached the main bridge which connected the docks with the town. Despite the German's defensive fire . . . and the noise of ricocheting bullets and the explosion of grenades, the Commandos fought their way through the town.[60]

Jim Brown was captured by the Germans and sent to a prison camp in Germany from where he and two other commandos escaped 'in one of the most dramatic and audacious escapes of the war'.[61] Having been recaptured after three escape attempts, they were despatched to Gross-Zeidel prison camp in Poland. From there, on his fourth attempt, Brown succeeded in reaching Switzerland and freedom.[62] He was awarded the Military Medal. When Jim Brown came to Heriot-Watt as the first professor of petroleum engineering in 1975, the department had an initial complement of only five staff, including Dr Adrian Todd and Dr George Stewart, who moved from chemical engineering. An MSc in petroleum engineering was launched in October 1975; the focus of the course was determined by the needs of industry, especially Shell, from where Professor Brown had been recruited.[63] Research was launched through funding from two initiatives: the department obtained the first grant through the Science Research Council's marine technology programme, and the Advisory Committee on Enhanced Oil Recovery, a government committee established by energy minister Tony Benn, awarded a grant for research on water injection. Such were the modest beginnings of what was to become the jewel in the university's research crown in the 1990s. The university established a School of Offshore Engineering embracing all staff from the departments of offshore and petroleum engineering with two boards of studies. Tom Patten, who was given strong support and encouragement from Principal Burnett, was adamant that petroleum engineering had to be a stand-alone activity and consequently the senate approved the creation of two separate departments in 1975: offshore engineering, under Professor Roy Halliwell, and petroleum engineering.[64]

Professor Patten played a major role in persuading the Science Research Council (SRC) to fund a programme of research on marine technology.[65] In August 1976 Heriot-Watt was designated by the SRC as one of four academic centres to concentrate on marine technology with designated themes in the areas of safety, instrumentation, underwater vehicles and environmental protection. The university established the Marine Technology Centre and secured five grants totalling £100,000 initially. A second grant of £658,000 was awarded in September 1977 for a programme embracing techniques relating to offshore oil recovery, developments of unmanned submersibles, environmental protection, economic monitoring, safety analysis, and problems of marine instrumentation. Two years later the university won a further grant of £1,138,000, followed by £2.3 million in 1981. The latter grant was for a programme of 30 research projects in four major areas: surface systems (including fluid dynamics), petroleum engineering, environmental and bioresource studies, and underwater engineering. The programme involved approximately 40 academics and 60 research staff.[66] At this high water mark of the marine technology initiative, staff were involved from petroleum engineering, chemical and process engineering, mechanical engineering, civil engineering, offshore engineering, electrical and electronic engineering, IOE, biological sciences, chemistry, physics and economics. This represented an unprecedented degree of interdepartmental collaboration never to be repeated on such a scale.

The Science and Engineering Research Council (SERC) introduced two important changes to the programme in 1985: a reduction in the overall level of funding available and a requirement, as a condition of awards, that SERC funding sought should be matched pound for pound with support from other sources.[67]

Heriot-Watt adapted well to this new funding regime. The level of SERC funding for the period 1985–1987 was around £1 million, with over £400,000 in direct industrial sponsorship and support in kind from industry (i.e. provision of equipment, material, use of facilities, data and manpower) of a similar order.[68]

The university's involvement in Orkney dates from 1974 when Cliff Johnston and Roy Halliwell carried out consultancy for Occidental. IOE staff started to develop a research presence on the islands in 1980. The research programme was strengthened in March 1987 with the establishment by the university – with £2 million support from Conoco (UK) and the Occidental Consortium – of the Orkney Water Test Centre at the Flotta terminal. The centre provided a facility where oil companies or equipment vendors could bring equipment used to process water on North Sea oil platforms in order to improve their efficiency and environmental standards. A new £500,000 marine culture research unit was added to this Orkney Water Test Centre in August 1991. These investments consolidated the university's presence in Orkney. The diving unit was relocated to the campus in Stromness in 1991, enabling both undergraduate and postgraduate students to use its wide variety of dive locations, especially Scapa Flow with its battleships and cruisers of the scuttled First World War German High Seas Fleet, and spectacular underwater wildlife. The university created a campus in the former buildings of Stromness Academy in 1991 and part of two MSc courses – marine resource development and protection, and marine resource management – were taught there. There are currently six academic staff at the Orkney campus teaching around 20 MSc students and supervising seven doctoral students.

A Chill Wind from the Right

At the end of the 1970s there was a more hopeful university system: around 50 institutions each expecting to grow, five research councils sure of their responsibilities, a UGC prepared to confront government, a dual support system that had not yet failed, a binary divide that had some degree of logic other than academic elitism, and underpinning all an implicit assumption of the importance of Newman's and Robbins' ideals of the value of independence of mind and of knowledge as an end in itself. All this was about to change. It was the failed attempt of the Callaghan Labour government to restrain the growth of wages and the response of the unions to that aspect of monetarism during the

Professor Tom Patten

'winter of discontent' that led to Mrs Thatcher's electoral success in May 1979. Mrs Thatcher initiated a novel brand of Conservative ideology that largely ignored the influence of 'one nation' Tory grandees and introduced major changes in economic policy. The cult of individualism, a distaste for the public sector, and a self-conscious populist radicalism were central to her philosophy of self-help 'Victorian values'. This involved a rigid commitment to Friedmanite supply-side economics – privatisation, tight monetary controls via interest rate management, lower taxes, lower public expenditure and deregulated markets.[69] This new ideology of the supremacy of markets began to pervade all institutions and to replace the ethic of public goods and public service.

A series of policy decisions over the next decade were about to shake the foundations of the university system. Thatcherism for a university implied behaving like an efficient business, providing value for money, satisfying customers (students) and employers, and demonstrating a teaching and research capability that could be assessed.[70] Students should be prepared to contribute to the cost of their education, so value for money implied a reduction in the unit of resource provided by the state. Whereas the cuts imposed by previous Labour and Conservative governments had been pragmatic reactions to economic difficulties, the Thatcher government articulated a doctrinaire commitment to roll back the corporate state and to improve efficiency in all areas of public spending. Sir Keith Joseph, Secretary of State for Education and Mrs Thatcher's guru, a free-market conservative, believed paradoxically that higher education was an area where government could interfere without betraying its principles. The new government instantly imposed strict cash limits on universities and refused to give any guarantees about future funding. The subsequent decades increasingly saw the university having to respond to challenges from outside. The story which has to be told is therefore one of how Heriot-Watt fared in the face of the demands of the time: cuts in funding, external assessments of teaching and research, the needs of diverse groups of students, the widening access agenda, the continuing decline in demand for science and engineering, and the commitment to both Edinburgh and the world.

Principal Burnett died on 4 September 1980 at the age of 59. Universally liked and respected by his staff, this was a severe blow to the university at a most difficult time. His contribution had been outstanding and he would have made a huge impact had he lived. Professor Tom Patten, who had been vice-principal since August 1978, became acting principal (Professor Alan Rogers was appointed vice-principal) until Tom Johnston took office as principal on 1 October 1981. The government decided in October 1980, without consulting the UGC, to withdraw over three years the component of the UGC grant that supported the education of overseas students, who would now be required to pay full tuition fees. The fee story was not yet over because in 1981–82 the government proceeded to halve the home student fee. The UGC, which had acted as a buffer between universities and government in the 1960s, had now become an arm of the state; it advised universities to charge a minimum of £2,000 per annum for arts courses and £3,000 for science.[71] This impacted heavily on Heriot-Watt, which consistently recruited some 15 per cent of its students from overseas outwith the European Union, the highest proportion in Scotland. Other painful reductions were announced. Even apart from the overseas element, university grants would not keep pace with inflation. Academic salaries were set to fall in relative terms; by 2002 salaries of dons had risen only 6 per cent in real terms since 1980, lower than any other group, compared with 44 per cent for all public sector employees. Dr Edward Parkes, chairman of the UGC, made clear that he would not let 'a mulish opposition to any form of change based upon sterile application of a concept of academic freedom' stand in his way.[72]

The overall policy thrust of the government was informed by a determination to cut public spending. In the university sector this was to be achieved by concentrating and selecting overall research priorities; increasing accountability by, among other things, assuming control over fees and the salary settlement; improving the perceived 'relevance' of academic research; increasing reliance on directive programmes by the research councils, with fewer resources for responsive mode projects; and improving academic–industrial collaboration. Indeed Sir Keith Joseph warned in a letter to Dr Edward Parkes that it was appropriate for ministers 'to take more responsibility than they have hitherto for determining priorities affecting the broad character of the allocation of resources to the universities'.[73] Creativity, while not extinguished, had its wings clipped. These changes barely affected the public mood; as public expenditure came under pressure for all kinds of reasons, there was no outcry from public opinion against making life more difficult for the universities and their students. The wider public seemed unaware that some of the greatest assets of the UK – that had lost popularity during the disturbances of the late 1960s – were under sustained assault. As Dahrendorf opined, 'When has there ever been such a wave of destruction of successful institutions, with the authors of the destruction gleefully viewing their work?'[74] There was, however, a fundamental contradiction in the Conservatives' logic, a conflict between more emphasis on private funding from fees, industry, conference business and other sources with the greater degree of autonomy that it would give to university managers, and the desire of the government to manage the system in the pursuit of narrowly conceived micro-objectives such as prescribing how many pharmacy students should be recruited each year.

The government informed the UGC in 1981 that it should plan on the basis that the recurrent grant for home students would be reduced by 1983–84 to a level 8.5 per cent below that given in the 1980 public expenditure White Paper.[75] This policy change, together with the decision to withdraw the subsidy from overseas students, produced a reduction in total resources for universities of 11–15 per cent between 1980–81 and 1983–84.[76] When the blow fell in July 1981, the recurrent grant was ruthlessly and selectively cut; three technological universities (Aston, Bradford and Salford) received reductions in grants of more than 30 per cent. Heriot-Watt faced a cut of £800,000 (11 per cent) in its recurrent grant.[77] The UGC letter of 1 July 1981 proposed a 12.8 per cent reduction in the number of home/European Union students from 2,430 in 1979–80 to 2,120 in 1984–85. The cuts were designed to impact much more severely on economic and social studies (an area not favoured by the Conservatives) with a scheduled reduction of 36.5 per cent from 630 to 400 students by 1984–85. Science and engineering numbers were scheduled to fall by a modest 4.4 per cent from 1,800 to 1,720.[78] The severe cuts in arts subjects were to be achieved by discontinuing Russian, substantially reducing numbers in economics (associated with a request to consider collaboration with Edinburgh University) and discontinuing the separate degree courses in government and modern history, and business law.[79] In science and engineering the UGC recommended an increase in physical science numbers, a substantial reduction in pharmacy numbers, and invited the university to explore the possibility of integrating activities in chemical engineering with Edinburgh University.

The university reacted by freezing all vacant posts, increasing non-pay allocations at below the rate of inflation, and by opting into the UGC early

Tom Johnston, principal 1981–1988. Portrait by Victoria Crowe. Photograph: Douglas McBride

retirement scheme. The new principal, Tom Johnston, met the UGC on 2 December 1981. At this meeting the UGC confirmed its advice of July 1981 to discontinue separate degree courses in business law, and government and modern history, and that there was no possibility of a full-time population of more than 400 in economic and social studies unless courses were structured around existing strengths in business and management studies, accountancy and finance, and economics.[80] The original proposal to discontinue the teaching of Russian was successfully resisted but the senate accepted the recommendation to phase out business law, and government and modern history. Although there was little choice but to accept the UGC's overall strategy of rationalisation, discussions with Edinburgh University with the aim of reuniting the two departments of chemical engineering broke down in May 1982 and the UGC permitted separate provision to continue. The government made it clear that because of the system of student support (a public expenditure item) it expected tight control of numbers. To protect the unit of resource available for each student, the UGC therefore imposed limits on future intake and universities that exceeded their targets faced penalties. This decision was described by Alwyn Williams, principal of Glasgow University, as 'easily the nastiest piece of bureaucratic fatuity to emerge from the UGC'.[81] Heriot-Watt was promptly fined £20,000 for overshooting the entry targets for October 1982.[82] At the same time as imposing penalties, the UGC for the first time specifically encouraged universities to attract additional income from external sources and any income so raised would not lead to a consequential reduction in grant. The whole system was now in crisis and the ideals of Robbins were but a dream.

Professor Johnston became principal and vice-chancellor on 1 October 1981, the first and only social scientist to be head of the institution in 180 years. Thomas Lothian Johnston was born in 1927 in Whitburn, West Lothian, the son of a railway signalman. When Tom was 3, the family moved to Newcastleton in the Borders, where he grew up in that lovely landscape embraced by the Cheviot Hills to the south and the Lammermuirs to the north, an area vibrant with the hidden pulse of history, where the muses smiled on James Hogg and Sir Walter Scott. After schooling at Hawick High School as a weekly boarder, he joined the Royal Naval Volunteer Reserve, during which time he spent six months at Edinburgh University and was exposed for the first time to political economy. He entered the University of Edinburgh in 1947 – the first person in his family to pursue higher education – and gained an MA with first-class honours in 1951, but probably of equal importance to the young Borderer steeped in the great rugby traditions of the region, he won a rugby blue at Edinburgh University. He was awarded a scholarship to conduct research at the University of Stockholm, returning to Edinburgh University in 1953 to teach political economy.

Tom Johnston embarked on the first of his three careers at Heriot-Watt University in 1955. He became the part-time evening lecturer in economics at Heriot-Watt College from 1955 to 1960, teaching for one hour every Friday night from September to March for a total fee of £48.[83] Later the hours were doubled but the fee only rose to £84. The finance office clearly believed in declining marginal productivity and that the lecturer would be less productive in the second hour than the first. After 12 years at Edinburgh University he resigned on a point of principle. He was appointed to the new chair of economics at Heriot-Watt University in 1966. While serving as dean of the Faculty of Humanities (now Economic and Social Studies), Professor Johnston, together with Professor Tom Patten and Principal R. A. Smith, was closely involved in establishing the university's Institute of Offshore Engineering, recognising the multidisciplinary implications arising from the exploitation of North Sea oil resources. He also chaired the committee responsible for establishing the research park in 1971, and he was involved in setting up the university's industrial liaison unit, Unilink. He resigned from the university in 1976 to work freelance as an economist and to continue his involvement in industrial relations arbitration; he was replaced as professor of economics by Donald McKay

from Aberdeen University. From 1977 to 1980 Tom Johnston was the highly regarded first chairman of the Manpower Services Committee of Scotland.

On the evening when Tom Johnston was interviewed for the post as principal by a committee chaired by Sir Douglas Haddow, his wife was also invited to the dinner beforehand 'for inspection'.[84] This extraordinary practice continued for the appointment of Principal MacFarlane; one wonders what would have happened if there had been a female candidate. When he returned for his third career as principal in October 1981, an unpleasant baptism awaited – the first round of UGC cuts had been announced three months earlier. Tom Johnston regarded the 1981 cuts as a salutary shock, obliging the universities to take stock:

> Having been out of academic life was the best thing I did, because when I came back, I didn't have this curious notion that the world owed us a living. . . . I didn't think universities saying their world was falling apart was a very sensible reaction, because other people's worlds had been falling apart for some time, and universities were seen as rather comfortable bailiwicks.[85]

By June 1982 Principal Johnston had done much to restore the battered morale of the institution; after a UGC visit, the chairman, Sir Edward Parkes, found Heriot-Watt 'in good heart, and confident we know where we were going'. Tom Johnston's academic prowess was concealed by a pawky Borders humour and self-effacing manner. A person of principle and integrity, his strength of purpose was complemented by tact, kindness and a strong commitment to the well-being of staff and students. Typically he never moved into the principal's residence at Hermiston House and eschewed the use of a chauffeur-driven car. He and his wife, Joan, created a caring family atmosphere on campus and he could be seen on occasions 'walking into the canteen to talk to the women washing the dishes'.[86]

Following the landslide victory for Mrs Thatcher's government at the polls in May 1983, Sir Keith Joseph invited universities to take more students with no increase in funds. The government was now targeting the universities' unit of resource that, in its view, compared very favourably with that of the polytechnics that were expanding rapidly. Sir Keith Joseph underlined his criticisms of the university sector in 1984 by imposing an 'efficiency saving' (cut) of 1 per cent in the following financial year and 2 per cent in the next. The government clearly remained determined to force universities to seek an even greater proportion of

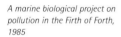

A marine biological project on pollution in the Firth of Forth, 1985

funds from private sources. The most pervasive influence on policy change in higher education during the 1980s and 1990s was the growth in student numbers, coupled with the dynamic between that growth and the drive to cut public expenditure.[87] The university system had passed the point at which such cuts began to hurt and to impact on quality. The only relaxation in this period of gloom was the decision to make new money available on a competitive basis to fund new lectureships for young researchers, so-called new blood posts. Heriot-Watt responded with a series of interesting bids and was rewarded in 1982 with two new blood posts in optoelectronics and languages and two IT lectureships in physics and electrical engineering. Further new blood appointments were secured in mathematics, petroleum engineering, brewing and biological sciences, and chemistry.

Despite the severity of the 1981 cuts, the deficit in 1981–82 was a mere £151,000 and the institution moved back to a small surplus of £630,000 in 1982–83, while also eliminating the debts on the capital account. Once the government had embarked on its cutting agenda, it was clear that the university needed to reduce its dependence on public funding. This was highlighted by the UGC letter of 26 May 1986 which increased the recurrent grant by only 0.4 per cent, a cut of 4.5 per cent in real terms, while the university had been asked to assume a 2 per cent cut per annum.[88] After several years of enduring cuts in the unit of teaching resource, the university recorded a deficit of £867,000 in 1987–88 as it incurred substantial expenditures in the rundown of the pharmacy department while new programmes in optoelectronics and IT were being developed.[89] By the following year, 1988–89, the cumulative deficit in catering and residences (including the conference centre) totalled £365,000. The university was also experiencing great difficulty in coping with the underfunding for inflation and pay awards that had been a feature of government policy for a decade. The objective of becoming more independent of direct government funding was achieved surprisingly quickly; this policy was a cause and an effect of Heriot-Watt becoming a more outward-looking and entrepreneurial institution. Whereas in 1980–81 the UGC provided 60.7 per cent of income, by 1985–86 its share had fallen to 53 per cent, and it fell further to 37 per cent by 1990–91. Government support had been reduced to the bare bones of institutional livelihood. Tuition fee income rose from 14 per cent of total income in 1980–81 to 20 per cent by 1990–91. Similarly, research grant income rose rapidly from £3.682 million in 1981–82 (at 2001 prices), 13.7 per cent of total income, to £13.065 million by 1990–91, 21.8 per cent of total income. Heriot-Watt's traditional willingness to work with industry, along with other sources of income such as conference business and overseas students, had become crucial elements in institutional viability. Meanwhile, however, storm clouds were gathering over the department of pharmacy.

No Cure for Pharmacy

The post-1979 period greatly strengthened the UGC's position vis-à-vis the universities. Dr Edward Parkes, chairman, warned the universities in unambiguous terms:

> There is going to be in the future a somewhat greater degree of direct intervention by the UGC in the affairs of individual universities than has been customary or necessary in the past.[90]

In the early 1980s, the UGC sought to plan the level of specific subject provision across the UK on the dubious assumption that the demand for certain skills could be predicted accurately, even in the medium term. In the spirit of this policy, the UGC reconstituted its Panel on Studies Allied to Medicine and charged it to report on the provision for pharmacy in the UK. There was more justification for attempting to plan pharmacy numbers, given that only members of the Pharmaceutical Society can deliver prescribed medicines. The panel, chaired by Professor C. T. Dollery, – a member of the UGC and the Royal Postgraduate Medical School, Hammersmith – and containing among its membership a person who had been an unsuccessful applicant for the chair at Heriot-Watt in 1966, visited the university on 12 November 1982. The note of the final meeting was an ominous one:

> The Panel did however foresee problems related to the minimum viable size of a Pharmacy Department; and, although Prof. Gilbert was trying to motivate the staff to undertake research, there was a problem in translating this effort into publications in refereed journals and research grants from harder sources, such as Research Councils. The Panel were not sure it could be done.[91]

The arrival of a new chairman of the UGC, Sir Peter Swinnerton-Dyer, in 1982, produced a marked change in attitude.[92] Under his guidance the UGC embarked on large-scale subject rationalisations. The difficult position at Heriot-Watt was made considerably worse on 12 September 1983 by the tragic death in a car accident of Professor John Gilbert, a pharmacologist and the leading researcher in the department, who had held the chair of pharmacology since 1975–76. This was soon followed by a grim if predictable message despatched from the UGC on 2 December 1983:

The Committee came to the conclusion that Pharmacy teaching at Heriot-Watt ought to be discontinued.[93]

Two reasons were advanced by Sir Peter Swinnerton-Dyer to justify closure of the department: the annual undergraduate intake of 45 students (the 1981 cuts reduced the intake to 30) was below the critical number of 60 regarded as the minimum satisfactory size for a pharmacy school, so Heriot-Watt had recorded the highest unit costs of the British university departments of pharmacy;[94] and 'considerable capital expenditure would be required to re-house it at Riccarton'.[95] The UGC did not feel that this expenditure of around £800,000 could be justified.

The university's case was presented to the UGC at a meeting on 2 February 1984 by Principal Johnston, Professor Des Smith (dean of science), Dr Gordon Jefferson (acting head of pharmacy), and Mr Duncan Cameron (secretary). The university argued that it had acted responsibly throughout the 1970s in restraining its annual intake in keeping with the manpower requirements of the profession. Moreover, the figure of 60 as the minimum size intake was an arbitrary number. The argument that the university was placed at risk by implementing a responsible admissions policy is convincing given that applications totalled 598 in 1982 and 620 in 1983.[96] Furthermore, the course maintained a 100 per cent placement in employment after graduation for the period 1978–83, although a one-year pre-registration was a statutory requirement for any pharmacy graduate who wanted to secure employment as a pharmacist. In a subsequent letter on 21 February 1984, Swinnerton-Dyer observed that the research of the department 'has been for some time well below the minimum standard that ought to be expected in a University department'.[97] The UGC decided, however, to refer the closure recommendation back to the Panel on Studies Allied to Medicine for further advice before coming to a final conclusion. The campaign to save the department reached the House of Commons in March 1984 when an all-party group of MPs, led by Martin O'Neill MP, a Heriot-Watt graduate, met the chairman of the UGC. This was followed by a debate on the adjournment motion in the House of Commons on 20 March 1984.[98]

A subsequent proposal to introduce a specialist degree in industrial pharmacy and to organise pharmacy teaching within a School of Pharmaceutical, Chemical and Biological Sciences did not persuade the UGC

that the proposed course would be sufficiently different from the existing course to justify them in changing their view that the 1985 entry to the Department ... should be the last.[99]

The annex to this letter from Sir Peter Swinnerton-Dyer of 27 July 1984 illustrated how difficult it was for the university to mount a credible defence of the department's research record:

> The staff, with one or two exceptions, were not, and had not in recent years, been engaged upon the sort of research which the Committee would have expected. . . . The Department at Heriot-Watt was not receiving grants from any Research Council when the Panel visited the University, and only one or two of its members were publishing articles in refereed journals. . . . On the research side the Heriot-Watt Department was below the minimum standard to be expected of a university department of pharmacy.[100]

Indeed the university, in advance of the meeting with the UGC on 2 February 1984, had conceded that 'some acknowledgement has to be made of this low research standing of the department' where grant income had averaged only £83,000 for the five years prior to 1984.[101] Prior to the UGC panel's visit to pharmacy in November 1982, the department had been led by Professor Alan Rogers between 1966 and 1980. Professor Rogers was a methodical and authoritarian head but he did not encourage research and locked the department at 5.15 P.M. every evening.[102]

Principal Johnston, Mr Cameron and Dr Jefferson, together with six representatives of the Pharmaceutical Society, met the UGC on 19 December 1984. The Pharmaceutical Society proposed that the UGC should allow the department a five-year period of grace.[103] The UGC, however, concluded that 'the new arguments which had been put forward were not sufficient to lead it to alter its previous decision'.[104] The clear research weaknesses in the Heriot-Watt department of pharmacy and the saving of £800,000 on a new building at Riccarton enabled the UGC to fulfil its agenda of offering up a sacrificial lamb to place on a funeral pyre composed of spurious manpower forecasts and the application of a rigid policy to cut public expenditure in universities, and the political imperative of being seen to close a department.

The closure of the pharmacy department was a major crisis for the university yet, throughout, Professor Johnston showed tenacity and dignity in his dealings with the UGC. He was instrumental in persuading the UGC to allow the university to retain all the pharmacy student numbers following the closure of the department,[105] and a promise that the UGC would provide some £30 million to fund the final phase of the move to Riccarton.[106] The university emerged from this sad episode better than it might otherwise have done. Tom Johnston ensured that the UGC delivered on this commitment and a number of new buildings were opened during his tenure, including the administration block (Lord Balerno Building), the Leonard Horner

Hall, the Esmée Fairbairn Research Centre, an extension to the library, television centre and buildings for the departments of building, languages and chemical and process engineering. In December 1985 the senate approved a reallocation of the pharmacy numbers to introduce a degree course in optoelectronics within physics and to admit a number of students to a degree in information technology in electrical engineering and computer science, later modified to information systems engineering.[107] Professor Denis Hall and Professor Brian Cavenett, both of whom were destined to make major contributions to the research of the university, were recruited from Hull to lead this new initiative. Throughout this difficult period, Principal Johnston benefited from the advice and sound judgement of Duncan Cameron, an outstanding secretary for a quarter of a century.

A Surfeit of Planning

As the devolution debate gathered momentum in the late 1970s, the Scottish Central Institutions saw the process as an opportunity to end the autonomy of the universities through the creation of a Council for Higher Education in Scotland, responsible for managing the whole higher education system in Scotland. The Scottish universities were not enthusiastic about this proposal but they were unable to agree among themselves about the future shape of higher education under a devolved government.[108] Staff were concerned to remain integrated within the UK system, and the issue was shelved as the devolution proposals were defeated in a referendum in March 1979.

In 1983 the Secretary of State for Scotland established the Scottish Tertiary Education Advisory Council (STEAC), the members of which included only one representative of Scottish universities, Sir Alwyn Williams, principal of Glasgow, and a UGC observer, Professor Brian Gowenlock. The chairman of STEAC, Donald McCallum, a businessman, requested information on the relationship between the universities and other higher education institutions in Scotland.[109] STEAC reported in December 1985 arguing that the declining population of school-leavers in the 1990s should be used as an opportunity to improve wider access to higher education in Scotland. The council also recommended the establishment of a joint funding and planning body, the Scottish Higher Education Planning and Funding Council, responsible for universities and central institutions. STEAC was proposing the blurring, if not the ending, of the binary divide.

The UGC operated for most of its existence on the basis of trust and mutual respect – a shared set of values and beliefs – and strong personal connections between members of elites. By the early 1980s, however, under increasing pressure from the government, the UGC had become a full-blooded planning organisation that called for statements of overall objectives for the planning period, detailed research plans, and forecasts of student numbers and finance.[110] When replying to the UGC's circular letter of 1 November 1983, which asked a series of questions 'towards the development of a strategy for higher education into the 1990s', Principal Johnston responded:

> First, it is simply farcical to pretend that the straitjacket on resources and student numbers within which the questions have been posed can provide a positive climate for strategic thinking. The questions are not about higher education at all, but about methods of cutting public expenditure. This is a deplorable way to treat the Parable of the Talents.[111]

There was growing concern that the dual support system for teaching and research, as envisaged by Robbins, was under threat, and that proposals for the selective funding of research would prevent staff working in non-selected areas from conducting research. The UGC published its advice to the government in *A Strategy for Higher Education into the 1990s* in September 1984. By early 1985 it became apparent that the government had not accepted the UGC plea for level funding to the end of the decade; indeed a reduction in income of 3 per cent per annum was planned for the next three years.

When the government finally published the Green Paper *The Development of Higher Education into the 1990s* in May 1985, Peter Swinnerton-Dyer wrote to the universities with the grim news that the recurrent grant for the next three years was to be reduced by a further 1.5 per cent below the government's estimates of inflation, which were to be consistently overshot. This implied a total reduction of at least 5 per cent per annum in real terms.[112] Research selectivity between and within institutions was an inevitable consequence of such severe cuts. All universities were asked to submit plans by 30 November 1985 showing how they intended to accommodate the cuts and selectively support research across 37 subject groups. A detailed research statement and a forecast of student numbers had also to be submitted. The UGC would then use a system of peer review to assess the research of the whole sector.

A Research Subcommittee was established as an advisory body to the Principal and Deans Committee. Although the Research Subcommittee under the convenership of Professor Des Smith argued for a direct role in the distribution of 30 per cent of the annual recurrent grant on research grounds, the university awarded it no executive powers other than the authority to allocate research scholarships. A systematic effort was made to ensure that research performance and potential were recognised in departmental allocations. The basis of the allocation system included a funding element related to research income, research load and research innovation.[113] The Research Subcommittee was charged with responding to the UGC requests for plans.

After some robust internal debate, research priorities were agreed for the UGC submission, with optoelectronics, marine technology and oil-related topics given the top priority. The results of the research selectivity exercise were announced in May 1986. Heriot-Watt had five subjects that were judged to be better than average within the UK: mathematics, electrical and electronic engineering, mechanical engineering, petroleum engineering and other technologies. Applied mathematics was rated as outstanding. Three departments were graded average: physics, computer science and modern languages. And five departments were assessed as below average: biological sciences, chemistry, chemical engineering, civil engineering, economics, business management and accountancy. The press immediately translated the ratings into league tables comparing all universities. This destroyed any cosy illusion of uniform excellence in research.

The UGC informed universities in December 1986 that the additional funding for 'rationalisation and change' announced by the DES would be dependent on the preparation of yet another academic plan by 11 February 1987. The Conservative government published the White Paper *Higher Education: Meeting the Challenge* in April 1987.[114] Most of its recommendations had been signalled in advance: expansion was to be resumed at a rate similar to that proposed by Robbins; in defiance of all previous trends in demand, the government was to continue trying to engineer a shift towards science and technology; there was scope for greater efficiency throughout the system which would permit higher participation at no extra cost; and yet more resources were to be found from the private sector. The White Paper proposed the concentration of control of higher education in the hands of the Secretary of State through the establishment of the Polytechnic and Colleges Funding Council (PCFC) and the Universities Funding Council (UFC) to replace the UGC in 1988. The UFC did not have a planning role, in contrast to the UGC, and neither did it have the responsibility of offering advice to government. The White Paper rejected STEAC's proposal for a Scottish Higher Education Planning and Funding Council in favour of a Scottish Committee of the new UFC. Although the binary divide was to be preserved, there was no explanation as to how the constituent parties were to work together.[115] In May 1987 the UGC, presumably at the behest of the Treasury, requested financial forecasts to 1991 within a fortnight. The university planned to achieve savings of some £500,000 in 1987–88 through retirals and non-replacement of staff. After another comfortable Conservative election victory, Kenneth Baker implemented the White Paper in the Education Reform Act of 1988.

There was surprise when Tom Johnston announced that he was retiring on 31 December 1988, at the age of 61. Few recalled that when he took up his post in 1981 he had said seven years was an appropriate term:

> In a job like this, you have to be fresh, vigorous, and full of new ideas and I think after seven years or so, there is a tendency to get a little stale. My feeling is that it's bad to appoint to a Chief Executive's post someone who could expect to do the job for 15 years.[116]

Principal Johnston, in the traditional style of vice-chancellor, had administered rather than managed the university. This enabled certain strong personalities to become more powerful than perhaps was healthy for the university as a whole. During the 1980s, because of severe financial constraints and the problems of pharmacy, Principal Johnston was more concerned with defending the institution than developing a forward vision. Tom Johnston was a well-loved principal, popular with staff and students, who always strove to achieve consensus, but like most people, he did not relish taking unpleasant decisions. Staff trusted him so that even when he made a decision which was disagreeable, no one ever believed that it was taken other than because he thought it was in the best interests of the university. This lack of self-seeking was typical of the man, who always declined to use graduation addresses as vehicles for his views on the state of universities, on the grounds that it was the graduates' day. He also initiated the university's art collection and unobtrusively spent some £40,000 of his own money purchasing paintings to enhance it. He instigated the university's collection of paintings by the Edinburgh artists who taught or studied at the Edinburgh College of Art between the end of the First World War and the late 1960s. Professor Johnston was president of the Royal Society of Edinburgh between 1993 and 1996.

The University Community

The new university in the 1960s experienced some difficult problems, including a wholly inadequate library, lack of good sports facilities, high contact hours on courses and large failure rates. Student participation in the governance of the university was initially very limited. Principal Smith 'did not believe that membership by students of the Senate is the best way to achieve student participation'.[117] It was 1981 before the students' association had three representatives on the University Court and three on the senate. A culture of paternalism, a hangover from the college era, still pervaded the institution and its attitude towards students. Tariq Ali was booked to speak at the Albert Thompson Hall on 13 May 1968. When the university authorities realised that he would be addressing the meeting, permission to use the hall was retracted. The university management later relented on the understanding that only Heriot-Watt students were admitted.

Archie Kirkwood, a pharmacy student (now a Liberal Democrat MP) became the first ever sabbatical president of the students' association in 1968. Two major issues dominated debates at the Students' Representative Council (SRC) meetings in the late 1960s: apartheid in South Africa and whether to install a contraceptive vending machine in the men's toilets. At a meeting on 16 January 1968, a pro-contraceptive proposal was defeated by 22 votes to 13;[118] the issue re-emerged in 1970 after the move to Grindlay Street Union and contraceptive machines were installed. Both the content of the student magazine, *Omega*, and the recreational facilities in the union reflected the male-dominated culture. *Omega* introduced pin-ups in 1968 and on 27 November of that year it advertised a competition to find Miss Heriot-Watt 1969. An independent panel under the chairmanship of Tom Scott, the university chaplain, 'will be judging the personality of the entrant as well as the more obvious points'.[119] The union bar opened on 5 October 1971 and 4,000 pints were consumed in the first weekend.[120] A sauna was available by 1974 at 20p per session, with mixed sessions on Tuesdays only. Its other facilities and services included pin tables, table football machines, pool tables, dartboards, and a gaming machine. Although the halls of residence in Drummond Place and Great King Street accommodated 124 students from May 1967, the University Court did not sanction the admission of women to the halls until 1975.[121]

It was the policy of the students' association to allow strip shows in the union and the first of these was held on 2 November 1971. On 18 February 1975 the council of the students' association passed a motion by 19 to 17 to further

Maureen Mair, Miss Heriot-Watt, 1969. Photograph: The Herald

women's rights and thereby, in effect, to ban strippers from the union.[122] But David Brew, president, argued that 'to ban strippers from the Union would be a form of censorship'.[123] The practice therefore continued. Student hecklers disrupted the first strip show of the year in 1976, bombarding the stage with flour bombs and eggs. Two students were removed and the show continued before an audience of 300. The policy of continuing to book striptease artists incurred the wrath of the Christian Union, some women's rights demonstrations and counter demonstrations, the inevitable interest of the *Daily Record* and, in the end, occupied the morning of an admonishing justice.[124] On 27 February 1980 a strip show was again interrupted by a group of 30 protesters invading the stage, including past president Bruce Heil and past honorary president Jon Side; police were called before order was restored and the show proceeded. The policy on stripping was endorsed by the council after a debate on 9 November 1982, although a motion that 'this particular function would ban female students' was lost.[125]

*Musical group in Chaplaincy,
Magdalen Chapel*

Some students were active in the anti-apartheid movement during the 1960s.
An extraordinary meeting of the SRC on 4 December 1969 passed a motion tabled
by Martin O'Neill, who was to become president of the Scottish Union of
Students in 1970 and is currently chairman of the House of Commons Trade and
Industry Committee:

> That this students' Council instructs the Honorary Treasurer to provide bail
> for any student of the Heriot-Watt University who may be charged after any
> incidents following protests against the visit of the South African Rugby
> team.[126]

The focus of the anti-apartheid campaign then shifted to target the university's
chancellor, Sir Alex Douglas-Home, British Foreign Secretary, on the issue of arms
sales to South Africa. A lecture given by Sir Alec Douglas-Home at the university
on 12 February 1971 was drowned out by a constant stream of abusive language.[127]
There was a gap between the necessary freedom of speech characteristic of
university education and the attitudes of some totalitarians in student circles who
had their own agenda. A motion condemning this action was defeated by 23 votes

to 4 on 23 February 1971.[128] The following year, the council of the students' association called for the removal of Sir Alec as chancellor because of 'the proposed settlement with the illegal Rhodesian Front regime'.[129]

In general, conventional types of student activity struggled to generate sufficient support. The Drama Society performed Harold Pinter's *The Lover* in May 1967 and 'the main disappointment was the lack of our own students at the otherwise reasonably attended performances'.[130] In February 1968 the club performed *Cross Purpose* by Albert Camus, but by autumn of the same year a cast could not be raised among the student body. There was also an attempt to form a debating society in May 1973 after a lapse of some years. Two decades later, in May 1994, the association tried again to revive debating. The general mass of the student body was untouched by any semblance of culture and intellectual pursuits. From time to time the students' association was able to attract major folk groups to perform in the union: Lindisfarne appeared in October 1983 and a full house enjoyed Runrig in November 1986.

The Music Society, founded in 1973, was the major social activity of academic and administrative staff, along with the Staff Golf Club. The Music Society formed sections for singers, musical appreciation and chamber music; established a record library; founded a brass and wind band, a Norwegian promenade orchestra, a jazz society, and a folk group; started a series of informal concerts by members and guest artistes; and organised excursions to musical events. Over 120 members, drawn almost equally from staff and students, joined in the first year.[131] This extremely ambitious programme of activities was largely the responsibility of Donald MacDonald, the university press officer, who made a great contribution in supporting the Watt Club and Norwegian students; Roger Gray, an enthusiastic music lover and statistician; and Ralph Parkinson, a fine tenor who provided invaluable advice to academics for three decades and organised memorable graduation ceremonies.[132] The Music Society had some influence on the corporate life of the university by allowing the well of musical talent to express itself and by uniting students, academics and administrative staff for a common purpose. The society was thriving by 1978 with a membership of 350, but Donald MacDonald admonished the university for its lack of interest in the arts: 'total expenditure annually is £260 paid to hire pictures on loan from the Scottish Arts Council'.[133] The university did not even permit the hire of the Albert Thompson Hall for the Edinburgh Festival Fringe performances, although the Grindlay Street Union was a fringe venue for some years. The Music Society never became student focused and interest waned somewhat when, in the 1980s, staff and students were split between Riccarton and the city centre.[134] The Chambers Street building, unlike Riccarton, had a staff common room that facilitated social interaction between the departments in that building. When staff moved to Riccarton, social life became largely balkanised within departments, which was inimical to the flowering of friendships and research collaboration. There was less sense of community than in the restricted confines of Chambers Street, and the Music Society gradually declined as departments relocated.

Notes

[1] Carswell, John (1985) *Government and the Universities in Britain*, Cambridge, p. 57.

[2] Ashby, E. (1958, 1966) *Technology and the Academics: An Essay on Universities and the Scientific Revolution*, New York, p. 66. Quoted in Clark, B. R. (1998) *Creating Entrepreneurial Universities: Organizational Pathways of Transformation*, Oxford, p. 64.

[3] HWUA, Box 31, Heriot-Watt University Library.

[4] Carswell, *op. cit.*, p. 83.

[5] *Ibid.*, p. 88.

[6] *Ibid.*, pp. 93–94.

[7] HWUA, *Senate Minutes*, 8 May 1973.

[8] Letter from Prof. B. G. Gowenlock to Prof. P. N. O'Farrell, 25 April 2003.

[9] HWUA, *Senate Minutes*, 5 December 1967.

[10] *Ibid.*, p. 6.

[11] HWUA, *Court Minutes*, 2 April 1968.

[12] HWUA Box 72, Alex Anderson's Papers.

[13] HWUA, *Court Minutes*, 18 November 1969.

[14] Dahrendorf, R. (1995) *A History of the London School of Economics and Political Science, 1985–1995*, London, p. 476.

[15] *Ibid.*, p. 476.

[16] HWUA, *Senate Minutes*, 5 June 1973.

[17] HWUA, *Senate Minutes*, 6 November 1973.

[18] HWUA, *Senate Minutes*, 3 June 1975.

[19] HWUA, *Court Minutes*, 30 October 1978.

[20] Smith S. D. (1982) Robert Alan Smith. In *Biographical Memoirs of Fellows of the Royal Society*, Vol. 28, p. 481.

[21] *Ibid.*, p. 483.

[22] *Ibid.*, p. 487.

[23] Obituary Notice, *Year Book, Royal Society of Edinburgh*, 1982, p. 69.

[24] HWUA, Prof. P. N. O'Farrell, Interview with Mr D. I. Cameron, 26 June 2001.

25 *Ibid.*, p. 491.

26 HWUA, Prof. P. N. O'Farrell, Interview with Prof. J. R. Small, 28 June 2001.

27 HWUA, Prof. P. N. O'Farrell, Interview with Prof. R. J. Knops, 5 July 2001.

28 HWUA, Prof. P. N. O'Farrell, Interview with Mr Stefan Kay, 17 June 2001.

29 HWUA, Mrs P. McIntyre, Interview with Prof. Gordon Nicoll, 4 June 2002.

30 Letter from Prof. B. G. Gowenlock to Prof. P. N. O'Farrell, 25 April 2003.

31 *Ibid.*

32 HWUA, *Court Minutes*, 17 June 1969.

33 HWUA, *Senate Minutes*, 1 June 1971.

34 HWUA, *Principal and Deans Committee Minutes*, 18 March 1976.

35 *Ibid.*

36 *The Scotsman*, 16 February 1996.

37 Smith. S. D., *op. cit.*, p. 432.

38 HWUA, Prof. P. N. O'Farrell and Ms A. E. Jones, Interview with Prof. T. L. Johnston, 29 July 2002.

39 HWUA, Heriot-Watt University, *Annual Report*, 1972–73, p. 29.

40 HWUA, Prof. P. N. O'Farrell, Ms A. E. Jones, Interview with Prof. B. G. Gowenlock, 15 October 2002.

41 HWUA, Principal Smith's Papers, Box 3, Institute of Offshore Engineering, Paper B.

42 HWUA, Box 72, Alex Anderson's Papers.

43 HWUA, Box 71, Alex Anderson's Papers.

44 *Ibid.*

45 HWUA, Box 12, Prof. R. A. Smith's Papers.

46 HWUA, Mrs P. McIntyre, Interview with Prof. Adrian Todd, 17 December 2001.

47 *Ibid.*

48 HWUA, *Senate Minutes*, 7 May 1974.

49 HWUA, *Senate Minutes*, 7 May 1974.

50 HWUA, Mrs P. McIntyre, Interview with Prof. Adrian Todd, 17 December 2001.

51 Letter from Prof. B. G. Gowenlock to Prof. P. N. O'Farrell, 25 April 2003.

52 Smith, S. D. *op. cit.*, p. 501.

53 HWUA, Mrs P. McIntyre, Interview with Prof. Colin Davidson, 9 July 2002.

54 Smith, S. D. *op. cit.*, p. 501.

55 *Heriot-Watt University Bulletin*, Vol. 14, no. 2, 4 September 1980.

56 HWUA, Prof. P. N. O'Farrell, Interview with Prof. R. J. Knops, 5 July 2001.

57 HWUA, Prof. P. N. O'Farrell and Ms A. E. Jones, Interview with Mr Donald MacDonald, 22 January 2002.

58 HWUA, *Heriot-Watt University Papers*, No. 49, Commentary on UGC letter of 3 May 1979.

59 Grant, C. (1988) L'evolution de la Resistance à St Nazaire 1939–1943. Undergraduate dissertation, Heriot-Watt University.

60 Chant-Sempil, S. (1985) *St Nazaire Commando*, London, p. 49.

[61] *Ibid.*, p. 70.

[62] *Ibid.*, p. 70.

[63] HWUA, Mrs P. McIntyre, Interview with Prof. A. Todd, 17 December 2001.

[64] HWUA, *Senate Minutes*, 3 June 1975.

[65] HWUA, Mrs P. McIntyre, Interview with Prof. Adrian Todd, 17 December 2001.

[66] HWUA, *Heriot-Watt University, Annual Report*, 1980–81.

[67] HWUA, *Heriot-Watt University, Annual Report*, 1984–85, p. 44.

[68] *Ibid.*, p. 45.

[69] Butt, J. A. (1996) *John Anderson's Legacy: The University of Strathclyde and Its Antecedents 1776–1996*, East Linton, p. 197.

[70] *Ibid.*, p. 197.

[71] HWUA, *Senate Minutes*, 27 November 1979.

[72] Sir Edward Parkes, Speech at the Meeting of the Committee of Vice-Chancellors and Principals, 24 October 1980. Cited in Moss, M., Forbes Munro, J. and Trainor, Z. H. (2000) *The University, City and State: The University of Glasgow since 1870*, Edinburgh, p. 301.

[73] *University Grants Committee Annual Survey 1981–82*, London, p. 35.

[74] Dahrendorf, A., *op. cit.*, p. 501.

[75] *University Grants Committee Annual Survey 1980–81*, London, p. 5.

[76] *Ibid.*, p. 24.

[77] HWUA, *Court Minutes*, 13 July 1981.

[78] HWUA, *Bulletin*, Vol. 14, no. 78, 2 July 1981.

[79] *Ibid.*

[80] HWUA, *Senate Minutes*, 14 December 1981.

[81] *Newsletter, University of Glasgow*, No. 44, 8 October 1981. Quoted in Moss *et al., op. cit.,* p. 302.

[82] HWUA, *Senate Minutes*, 8 March 1982.

[83] HWUA, Prof. P. N. O'Farrell and Ms A. E. Jones, Interview with Prof. T. L. Johnston, 29 July 2002.

[84] *Ibid.*

[85] *Times Higher Education Supplement*, 13 January 1989.

[86] HWUA, Prof. P. N. O'Farrell and Mrs P. McIntyre, Interview with Prof. Jim Murray, 17 June 2002.

[87] Henkel, Macy (2000) *Academia: Identities & Policy Change in Higher Education*, London, p. 36.

[88] HWUA, *Court Minutes*, 30 June 1986.

[89] HWUA, *Heriot-Watt Reports and Accounts*, 1987–88.

[90] UGC (1980) *Planning for 1980–81*, Letter to Universities, 18 May 1980.

[91] HWUA, Box 69, Visit of Panel on Studies Allied to Medicine to Heriot-Watt University, 12 November 1982.

[92] Shattock, M. (1984) *The UGC & the Management of British Universities*, Buckingham, p. 26.

[93] HWUA, Box 69, Letter from Sir Peter Swinnerton-Dyer to Principal Johnston, 2 December 1983.

[94] Letter from Prof. B. G. Gowenlock to Prof. P. N. O'Farrell, 25 April 2003.

[95] *Ibid.*

[96] HWUA, Heriot-Watt University, Press Information, 13 December 1983.

[97] HWUA, Box 69, Letter from Sir Peter Swinnerton-Dyer to Principal Johnston, 21 February 1984.

[98] HWUA, *Heriot-Watt University Bulletin*, Vol. 17, no. 55, 27 March 1984.

[99] HWUA, Box 69, Letter from Sir Peter Swinnerton-Dyer to Principal Johnston, 27 July 1984.

[100] HWUA Box 69, Annex to Letter from Sir Peter Swinnerton-Dyer, 27 July 1984.

[101] HWUA, *Heriot-Watt University Papers*, Box 48, Pharmacy Teaching.

[102] HWUA, Prof. P. N. O'Farrell and Ms A. E. Jones, Interview with Prof. B. G. Gowenlock, 16 October 2002.

[103] HWUA, *Heriot-Watt University Bulletin*, Vol. 18, no. 33, 21 December 1984.

[104] HWUA, Box 69, Letter from Sir Peter Swinnerton-Dyer to Principal Johnston.

[105] HWUA, Prof. P. N. O'Farrell, Interview with Mr Duncan Cameron, 26 June 2001.

[106] HWUA, Box 69, Letter from Sir Peter Swinnerton-Dyer to Principal Johnston.

[107] HWUA, *Senate Minutes*, 3 December 1985.

[108] Moss *et al.*, *op. cit.*, p. 299.

[109] *Ibid.*, p. 368.

[110] Henkel, *op. cit.*, p. 38.

[111] *Heriot-Watt University Bulletin*, Vol. 17, no. 57, 4 April 1984.

[112] *Ibid.*, p. 314.

[113] HWUA, File 2/2 Box 67, *UGC Return*, Annex 1, Part 2, 4 November 1985.

[114] *Higher Education: Meeting the Challenge*, April 1987.

[115] Moss *et al.*, *op. cit.*, p. 320.

[116] *Times Higher Education Supplement*, 13 January 1989.

[117] HWUA, *Omega*, 26 February 1969.

[118] HWUA, *Heriot-Watt University Students Association Council Minutes*, 16 January 1968.

[119] HWUA, *Omega*, 27 November 1968.

[120] HWUA, *Omega*, 5 October 1971.

[121] HWUA, *Omega*, 3 March 1975.

[122] HWUA, *Omega*, 18 February 1975.

[123] HWUA, *Omega*, 4 February 1976.

[124] *Ibid.*

[125] HWUA, *Omega*, 9 November 1982.

[126] HWUA, *Students' Representative Council Minutes*, 4 December 1969.

[127] Letter from Prof. B. G. Gowenlock to Prof. P. N. O'Farrell, 25 April 2003.

Heriot-Watt University: An Illustrated History

128 HWUA, *Omega*, 23 February 1971.

129 HWUA, *Omega*, 7 March 1972.

130 HWUA, *Omega*, May 1967.

131 HWUA, *University Papers*, Box 42.

132 Ralph Parkinson inherited the tradition of the graduation ceremonies from Gordon Jamieson.

133 HWUA, *Watt Now*, March 1978.

134 HWUA, Prof. P. N. O'Farrell and Mrs P. McIntyre, Interview with Mr R. V. Parkinson, 10 June 2002.

Chapter Eight

Realising a Vision: The Move to Riccarton

Education has for its object the
foundation of Character.
Herbert Spencer

Riccarton House in the early twentieth century

The Search for a Campus

The elevation of Heriot-Watt College to university status brought into sharp focus the problem of providing much-needed additional accommodation for the new university. Principal Nisbet explored the possibility of expanding into the Grassmarket area of the Old Town. At a meeting with Edinburgh Corporation in February 1965, officials had indicated that portions of the Grassmarket, West Port and Cowgate areas might be zoned for educational purposes. It was agreed that alternative proposals to find and develop a different site were not justified, although the deciding factor would have to be whether the UGC would sanction development in the Grassmarket and make available the necessary finances. Mining engineering and pharmacy were already in the Grassmarket and expansion into this area continued when electrical engineering and industrial administration eventually moved to the new £650,000 Mountbatten Building in January 1968.

The governors decided on 5 November 1965 that 'because of lack of space for further expansion . . . immediate steps should be taken to obtain a suitable peripheral site'.[1] The UGC responded by inviting the Academic Advisory Committee (AAC) to comment on whether the new university should develop in the Grassmarket area or at a new site on the outskirts of Edinburgh. Messrs Walls & Partners, consultant architects, argued that by a policy of costly acquisition the whole Grassmarket site would accommodate ultimately only 3,000 students, excluding residential accommodation.[2] Moreover, technological research could not be located in the Grassmarket for amenity reasons, thereby implying divided working, with teaching in the city centre and research and residences at a distant site on the periphery of the city.[3] The cost of implementing the Grassmarket development, based on February 1966 prices, was estimated at £15.1 million.[4] The AAC endorsed the view of the governors and expressed a strong preference to the UGC for a suitable peripheral site for the institution where it might be possible to develop in the long run an 'industrial park' in close association with the university.[5] The chairman of the AAC, Sir Edmund Hudson, argued that if the expansion was carried into the Grassmarket area of the city, it would lead inevitably to integration of working and ultimately to some form of federation or even merger with the University of Edinburgh.[6]

The possibility of relocation as a solution to the problem of the college had been under consideration for some time. A year earlier, in July 1964, the East Stirlingshire University Committee invited the governors of Heriot-Watt College to consider relocating to a 500 acre site at Callandar Estate near Falkirk. Sir Edmund Hudson firmly rejected the offer:

On the face of it, this is a suggestion to remove from Edinburgh something that was intended to be of and for Edinburgh. The Government made their decision on the basis that Heriot-Watt had a central location in Edinburgh.[7]

On 26 November 1965 the Building Extension Committee of the college visited four prospective sites in Edinburgh at Cammo, Southfield Farm, Mortonhall Estate and Silverknowes.[8] The committee eliminated Cammo and Southfield Farm from further consideration on the grounds that it would be impossible to build an electronics laboratory on either site since they were in line with the proposed second runway at Turnhouse Airport and the navigational equipment of a low-flying aircraft could be seriously affected.[9] The Mortonhall Estate, to the south of the city, was their preferred option. The secretary was instructed to seek the views of the Planning Committee of the city as relocating to Mortonhall would include a section of the Alnwickhill housing development area. Meanwhile, in a letter to the UGC on 21 January 1966, one month after the AAC had indicated their preference for a peripheral site, the secretary, referring to their request for the views of the governors of the college on the advisability of expanding in the Grassmarket or seeking a peripheral site, replied that as yet no

Aerial view of Riccarton, 1969

decision had been reached. This appeared to contradict the view expressed by the governors only two months before, an inconsistency not lost on the mandarins at the UGC. A handwritten note on the letter by a UGC official indicated some exasperation in London: 'They seem to have made no progress at all since the occasion when we visited them twelve months ago.'[10] On 18 February 1966 Edinburgh City Council determined, by 28 votes to 27, to re-zone 235 acres of land at Alnwickhill for possible development by Heriot-Watt University, although it did not indicate whether the site would be a free gift.[11] Alnwickhill is approximately 3 miles south of the City centre and lies 400–600 feet above sea level. At a meeting with Mr A. E. L. Parnis, assistant secretary, on 25 March 1966, Mr Cameron was reminded that it was for the government to decide whether or not the university would move and that there would be little money around for building during the next few years.[12] The Labour government wished to expand the system but not to fund it adequately; the universities were always an easy target when failings in the economic management of the UK economy demanded cuts in public expenditure.

Edinburgh was not the only council keen to offer a location for the new university. On 10 May 1966 Midlothian County Council submitted a plan showing a proposed site for the university at Riccarton Mains, six miles south-west of the city centre. The 248 acre estate, standing 300–350 feet above sea level, was well landscaped with extensive mature tree belts.[13] Edinburgh Corporation and Midlothian County Council were both asked on 19 May 1966 if they were prepared to make a gift of a site of approximately 200 acres to the university or to give financial assistance towards the purchase of a site.[14] Edinburgh Corporation decided to continue consideration of the university's request until the Secretary of State's decision about rezoning Alnwickhill for cultural and university purposes was known. Mr Stronach of the UGC visited the two potential sites at Alnwickhill and Riccarton in June 1966. Of Alnwickhill, Stronach observed:

> This site overlooking the City from the South East has drawbacks. Although it is reasonably flat the high position (400′–525′) is exposed to the weather and during the winter months the snow is slow to clear.[15]

Global warming had not then made an impact on Edinburgh's winter weather. In a letter of 30 June 1966, Midlothian County Council offered to make the Riccarton site 'available to the University without payment or on nominal terms'.[16] This led later to an honorary degree for the then convener of Midlothian County Council, Mr J. G. Methven, who was instrumental in persuading his Labour colleagues to agree. This letter coincided with Stronach's visit to the Riccarton site, with which he was clearly impressed:

Conveniently placed for liaison with local industry and is also near to a good class residential area which could afford facilities for accommodating staff. . . . In my view the Riccarton site is much the better. It is practically flat, and I understand that there are no development problems. . . . It was quite obvious as I toured the Grassmarket area that the decision to abandon any idea of developing Heriot-Watt there was the right one.[17]

Stronach failed to appreciate that university liaison with industry is a global phenomenon, so that proximity of Riccarton to the airport was probably more relevant.

In July 1966 the University Senate unanimously recommended a move to Riccarton because 'a Research Park could be developed more easily there than at Alnwickhill'.[18] The following month, on 12 August 1966, a group from the UGC visited Edinburgh. Having examined the two sites, the UGC endorsed the move to Riccarton:

There is no doubt that the site at Riccarton Mains is far superior in every way. . . . Development *in situ* is to be preferred only if the long term aim is to contrive an amalgamation between the two institutions [Heriot-Watt University and the University of Edinburgh]. . . . It would be unrealistic to decide the issue in a way which would only make sense if Heriot-Watt is to be conceived as a future part of the University of Edinburgh. . . . The timing and nature of the development at Riccarton . . . could be such as to allow a building up of consultative arrangements between the two institutions to secure a measure of rationalisation and complementarity.[19]

A letter from Sir John Wolfenden to Sir Herbert Andrews, permanent undersecretary at the Department of Education and Science (DES), on 10 October 1966 reveals the UGC attitude at the time:

A fairly substantial increase in student numbers will be necessary in the long term in order that the University may achieve a satisfactory development and contribute to the required expansion of Scottish University places . . . but the Committee believe that some figure well above 2,000 is a desirable objective. . . . The situation of the Riccarton site . . . does not preclude the possibility of a phased development extending over 10 years or so. This would make it easier to fit building developments into the university building programme, and allow for the building up of consultative arrangements between the two universities. Our conclusion therefore is that the University should be authorised to accept the Midlothian offer.[20]

Hence the former city-based college had found its greenfield site, although it did not seek green courses to go with it.

Origins of the Riccarton Estate

After almost 150 years of continuous educational service to the citizens of Edinburgh from sites within the historic Old Town, the new university had decided to look westwards to solve its space problem. The Riccarton estate, as we shall see, had connections with the original foundation of the School of Arts and Leonard Horner himself had enjoyed its serene setting. [21]

King Edward I of England destroyed a Scottish army at Dunbar in 1296 and swept his victorious armies across Scotland, subjecting the country to military occupation. This was the most comprehensive victory that any English king had ever achieved in Scotland and to secure it Edward demanded that all Scottish landowners should come to Berwick and swear allegiance to him.[22] Among those who obeyed this command was one Mariorie de Ricardestone – the first written reference to Riccarton, on which estate, over 700 years later, the university now stands.[23] Robert Bruce, who had a dynastic claim to the throne, rose up against the English hegemony and, after his famous victory at Bannockburn in 1314, regained much of the land in the south of Scotland. In 1315 Riccarton was granted by King Robert I (Robert the Bruce) to his daughter Marjory and her new husband, Walter Stewart. Their marriage was cut short a year later when Marjory died after falling from her horse, but the posthumous birth of their son, Robert, established the Stewart dynasty.[24]

Sir Thomas Craig, first of a long line of lawyers and lairds of Riccarton. Sudlow collection

Riccarton did not reappear on the stage of history until the end of the fourteenth century and we must assume that the estate passed through the hands of a branch of the Stewarts, and from them, perhaps by marriage, eventually to one Mariota (Marion) Wardlaw who owned the land in 1392.[25] Riccarton remained in the possession of the Wardlaw family for over two centuries and a tower house was built by them during the fifteenth century. This 'tower and manner place' at Riccarton is first mentioned in a legal document in 1508, when James Wardlaw leased the estate to Alexander Hepburn and his wife Isobel Napier.[26] The Hepburns lived at Riccarton for the next hundred years while the Wardlaws lived nearby at Curriehill. Some of the Wardlaws played a prominent role in church and state. Walter Wardlaw, secretary to David II, was Archdeacon of Midlothian and signed a document at Currie Kirk in 1359. He went on to become Bishop of Glasgow and later a cardinal. His nephew, Bishop Henry Wardlaw, tutor and adviser to James I, founded Scotland's first university at St Andrews in 1411.[27]

The Wardlaws and the Hepburns were embroiled in the turbulent politics of Mary Queen of Scots' reign. Alexander Wardlaw was involved in the murder of Mary's secretary, David Riccio, at Holyrood in March 1565. The Hepburns were related to the fourth earl of Bothwell, who married Mary after conspiring to kill her husband, Lord Darnley. In 1568 Alexander Hepburn, laird of Riccarton, helped her escape from Loch Leven Castle, where she had been imprisoned by the Earl of Moray, regent to the future King James VI. In 1593 the minister of Currie Kirk excommunicated Patrick and Thomas Hepburn for leading a violent night-time raid on the neighbouring estate of Baberton in which two Borthwick brothers were killed and a woman injured. The Borthwicks murdered Patrick, Laird of Riccarton, in a revenge killing in 1599.[28] In 1605 the owner of the estate, William Wardlaw, perhaps in financial difficulties, sold the Mains of Riccarton to Thomas Craig, a well-known advocate and jurist. He founded a long line of lawyers and judges who were to have a major impact on Riccarton over the next two centuries. Thomas wrote *Ius Fudale*, a key work on feudal law, which was reprinted many times. Such was his reputation that King James VI, who had inherited the English throne in 1603, appointed him as a commissioner to consider the possible union of Scotland and England. After Thomas Craig died in 1608, his son Lewis bought the rest of the estate from William Wardlaw.[29] As a gift to his wife, Beatrix Chirnside, Sir Lewis Craig built a new house on the estate in 1621 incorporating the original tower at its west end.[30] This transformation from fortress to luxury home may have reflected their hopes for a more law-abiding era.

However, Scotland and the Craig family were soon drawn into political and religious conflict. In 1638 nobles, lairds, lawyers, burgesses and ministers signed the National Covenant in protest against Charles I's autocratic rule and his attempts to impose the Episcopalian form of church government on the Scottish

Left: Artist's impression of the first tower house at Riccarton in the fifteenth century, by George Reid, University Fabric Officer

Right: From fortress to family home, artist's impression by George Reid of Lewis Craig's extensions to Riccarton house, 1621

church. Civil war in Scotland and England led to the execution of Charles I, Cromwell's republic and ultimately the revolution of 1688–89 when his daughter Mary and her husband King James VII lost his throne to William of Orange.[31] Thomas Craig II, laird of Riccarton at this time, was a devout man who gifted two communion cups to Currie Kirk. He was also a Covenanter. He led a troop of horse in the Army of the Covenant and helped muster local men and horses to join an army to repel Cromwell's invasion in 1650. In 1662 he was fined 2,400 Scots pounds, roughly £16,000 in today's money, for covenanting. Thomas escaped lightly in comparison with his cousin, Archibald Johnston, Lord Warriston, co-author of the National Covenant, who was executed in 1663. Thomas's son and successor, Lewis, shared his father's Presbyterian faith. He fell foul of the government by attending forbidden religious meetings, conventicles, at Cramond.[32]

Despite this turmoil, the Craigs held on to Riccarton and even managed to enlarge the estate, buying Currie, Longhermiston, and Hermiston House, which was to become the estate dower house. From 1691 to 1823 just three men owned Riccarton: uncle (Robert Craig), nephew (Thomas Craig) and his brother (Robert Craig). None ever married. Robert Craig was one of the last members of the Scottish Parliament before it voted itself out of existence with the Act of Union in

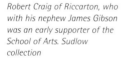

Robert Craig of Riccarton, who with his nephew James Gibson was an early supporter of the School of Arts. Sudlow collection

1707. He brought prosperity to Currie by holding a market and fair there and gave land to build the village's first school.[33]

By the early eighteenth century the lands of Riccarton were farmed by nine principal tenants but accounts show that relatively little produce was ever sold; the estate survived on a subsistence economy.[34] Later during the eighteenth century, agricultural reform gripped the country and the land at Riccarton was enclosed into fields; new land was brought under the plough, trees were planted to reduce soil erosion, drainage ditches were dug, and the shelter-belt plantation of the estate[35] was carried out, dividing the land into squares, still visible today.[36] Maps of the Riccarton area drawn in 1772 indicate that by the last quarter of the eighteenth century, the total acreage of range pasture was small in relation to the extent of arable land; as little as 70 acres of uncultivable land lay interspersed amid 1,000 acres of arable land, nearly half of which was continuously cultivated infield.[37] Moreover, the improvements were almost complete and the field boundaries on the maps are very similar to those visible on modern aerial photographs.[38] Another sign of increasing prosperity as early as the 1760s was the large set of new stable buildings erected by the laird (the demolition of these eighteenth-century stables was one of the more controversial aspects of the university development at Riccarton). The instigator of these agricultural reforms was Robert Craig's nephew Thomas, who inherited the estate in 1748. Thomas was an eccentric man who dressed like a pauper despite his wealth. Known as the 'improving laird', he was a popular landlord who enjoyed hosting dances for his tenants and neighbours. When Thomas died in 1814, the estate passed to his brother Robert, a senior advocate.[39] Agricultural improvement continued well into the nineteenth century. A report on Hermiston Farm in 1825 suggests a crop rotation regime: year 1, potatoes with 30 tons of police dung per acre; year 2, wheat; year 3 barley with 12 tons of police dung per acre; year 4, hay; and year 5, oats.[40] Police dung was the dung removed from the streets of Edinburgh and sold to farmers in order to raise funds for the city's policing.[41]

The last direct descendant of the original Thomas Craig who bought Riccarton Mains in 1605, Robert Craig, died unmarried at the age of 92 in 1823. The estate passed into the hands of the Gibsons, a prominent family of lawyers and politicians. James Gibson's grandmother was the granddaughter of Thomas Craig III, the laird from 1681 until 1691.[42] When James Gibson succeeded to the estate, he adopted the name of Gibson-Craig and was created a baronet in 1831.[43] Sir James, a lawyer, was a formidable political opponent – leader of the radical wing of the Scottish Whigs – who was nonetheless an amicable and good-natured man.[44] Bold adherence to the Whig cause was not without certain dangers. He helped to organise a dinner in Fortune's Tavern in 1789 attended by a party of 24 to celebrate the fall of the Bastille.[45] The guests had their names taken by the police as

The dining room, Riccarton House from article published in The Scotsman, Saturday, 21 August 1937

they entered, while the sheriff of the county was subsequently discovered in an adjoining room noting down as much of the proceedings as could be heard through the partition.[46] Sir James campaigned for the passing of the first Reform Act in 1832, after which his political activity abated. 'Prompt able and vigorous, with a decisive and resolute manner, his whole life was spent in fearless usefulness.'[47] A friend of Leonard Horner, his philanthropic nature led him to give financial support to the foundation of the Edinburgh School of Arts in 1821. How pleasing, therefore, that Horner himself visited Riccarton on at least one occasion and recalled one day in June 1841:

> On Thursday the Gibson-Craigs pressed me so kindly to come out to see them … and went out this morning to breakfast. … It is a most glorious day, and the country is in the greatest beauty, and most especially Riccarton. Sir James took me into the garden before breakfast … they walked about the gardens and grounds with me till twelve, when I left them, very much gratified with my visit.[48]

The great change which took place at the instigation of James Gibson-Craig was the construction of a new mansion house. Sir James commissioned the architect William Burn to design a large extension to the 1621 house which resulted in a fashionable neo-Jacobean-style mansion, completed in 1827, that occupied the site of the present university library until the 1950s. Guests including the prime minister, Lord Palmerston, and the king of Siam enjoyed lavish banquets in the house's grand dining room. An imposing portrait gallery of Riccarton lairds and ladies, past and present, gazed down from the walls. Among

Portraits by Sir Henry Raeburn of Sir James Gibson-Craig, 1st Baronet Riccarton, his wife, Lady Anne, and their son, Sir William, 2nd Baronet. Purchased for the university with a grant from the Heritage Lottery Fund and a donation by Mrs Lesley Archer, 2001

Riccarton House in the early twentieth century, showing William Burn's grand enhancements, commissioned by Sir James Gibson-Craig in the 1820s

them were three fine paintings by Sir Henry Raeburn depicting James, Anne and their son, Sir William, second baronet. These works have since returned to Riccarton having been purchased for the University Museum collection.[49]

The verdant parkland environment that the university enjoys owes much to the foresight and dedication of Sir James, who was an ardent collector of plants and specimen trees. His son, Sir William, introduced many exotic trees from north-west USA that still grace the campus today. Unusual species include the small Tasmanian cedar, wellingtonia, Corsican pine, the cucumber tree, the cedar of Lebanon, and the Riccarton sweet chestnut. The formal gardens to the north had already been laid out during the eighteenth century, but Sir James probably constructed the walled garden and the artificial lake.[50] The family graveyard to the west of the lawn was also laid out by him. One of the earliest gardeners at Riccarton was James Young. He earned lasting renown in around 1830 by developing a new fuchsia, named *F. m. riccartonii* after the estate. It remains a versatile feature of borders around the campus.[51]

After Sir James died in 1850, he was succeeded by his son, Sir William, second baronet (1787–1878), who served as MP for Edinburgh, MP for Lothian, a Lord of the Treasury and Keeper of the Signet in Scotland. The third baronet, James, who succeeded in 1878, also played a great part in the enhancement of the

Riccarton estate through further improvement of the grounds. As prominent landowners, the Gibson-Craigs took an active part in community life. They were benefactors of Currie Kirk and gifted land to Baberton golf club and Currie bowling green. Above all, they were keenly competitive curlers, hosting tournaments at Riccarton. The outline of a curling pond in the sunken garden can still be seen today, striking evidence of much colder winters in the nineteenth century.

Behind the glamour and elegance of Riccarton and its high-society gatherings, the smooth running of house and estate depended on the labours of a small army of servants. Most have vanished from the historical record. A few references in the archives give us a tantalising glimpse of these otherwise invisible residents. Census records from the height of Riccarton's prosperity in 1891 provide evidence of the number of people who worked on the estate and the variety of their occupations. James Gibson-Craig, his wife Julia and their seven children had 18 servants, including two governesses, a cook, coachman, footmen, and an assortment of scullery, kitchen, laundry and lady's maids. A butler was also normally resident. The lodges and other estate buildings at various times housed the forester, gamekeeper and so many gardeners that they needed their own servant to cook and clean for them.[52]

One member of the family whose contribution to community life has become a

Riccarton at war. Servicemen and women outside Riccarton house in the early 1940s

matter of folklore was Miss Annie Gibson-Craig, a daughter of Sir William, second baronet. She lived at Hermiston at the end of the nineteenth century. She donated and endowed Balerno village hall, was a very active mission worker, and could always be relied on to have handy tracts with titles such as 'Moral Living', 'Beware of the Demon Drink' and 'Kindness to Animals'. A great supporter of Band of Hope meetings in Currie temperance hall, Annie Gibson-Craig thought nothing of walking there alone from Hermiston 'on a wild, stormy night' because, as she said, 'it was no night for coachmen or horses'.[53]

The Gibson-Craig Memorial Hall at Currie is a poignant legacy of the family's close links with the community. The hall is named after Robert, heir to Riccarton, who died in the Boer War in 1900 at the age of 18.[54] Sir James, third baronet, died in 1908 and, as was so often the case throughout its history, the fortunes of war continued to influence the destiny of Riccarton. Archibald, fourth baronet, died at the battle of Aisne only a few months after the outbreak of the First World War.[55] Following his death, the title passed to a younger brother, Henry, who lived until 1926. On his death, the estate was disentailed, the land parting company with the title. The estates were left to Henry's nephew, Julian Cumming, who adopted the surname Gibson-Craig, although he did not live regularly on the estate; the house was usually rented out. In 1930 the estate passed to Julian's sister Hermione. Her daughter, Mrs Josephine Sudlow, inherited Riccarton in 1945.[56]

Miss Annie Gibson-Craig outside Hermiston House, c. 1900

The demolition of Riccarton House, 1956. Photograph by local historian John Tweedie

The Second World War marked the end of an era for Riccarton. The army requisitioned the house and estate, which became the headquarters of Scottish Command, a tenancy that left its mark even on the trees, some of which contain embedded shrapnel from training exercises. Riccarton house was reinforced heavily with concrete bunkers. Although Riccarton's role in the war effort is still shrouded in some mystery, evidence suggests that it was the command headquarters for the liberation of Norway.[57] Donald MacDonald met the crown prince of Norway during his visit to the Riccarton Campus on 16 November 1979 and took him to the library where the future king suddenly remembered that he had visited Riccarton during the Second World War.[58] At the time, the crown prince served as a chief of defence in the Norwegian government in exile. King Harald and Queen Sonja of Norway unveiled plaques in the university library commemorating this wartime connection during their visit to Riccarton in July 1994.[59] After the war, Riccarton became a resettlement camp for ex prisoners of war, and from 1947 to 1954 was headquarters of the Royal Artillery's Third Anti-Aircraft Group.[60] It was equipped with radar and searchlights and was linked by telephone to all gun batteries in Scotland and Northern Ireland. At the height of its use as a military base, Riccarton was almost as busy as today's campus. Hundreds of servicemen and women lived there in Nissen huts and dormitory blocks. Foundations of some of the huts can still be seen in the woodland above the sunken garden. The Navy, Army and Air Force Institutes (NAAFI) provided a canteen, bar and social facilities for the troops. There was even a cinema on the base.[61]

When the army finally relinquished the estate, the house was in a state of extensive disrepair. Reluctantly, the decision was taken to demolish it in 1956. The house gone, the owners could no longer use the estate even as an occasional home, so the residence of the lairds of Riccarton finally came to an end. Mrs Sudlow, however, still owned the estate and the adjoining farms.

You heard it here first … Omega, the Edinburgh student newspaper, announces the university's plans to move to Riccarton, January 1967

Developing the Campus: UGC Battles

On 12 August 1966, the same day as the UGC visit to Riccarton, a letter was despatched to Midlothian County Council from Dundas & Wilson, solicitors, acting on behalf of Mrs Sudlow, owner of Riccarton, indicating that Mrs Sudlow 'was not at all anxious to sell her land'.[62] Subsequent correspondence from Sir John Wolfenden of the UGC to Principal Nisbet in December 1966 confirmed the move to Riccarton but expressed ominous reservations about timing and the rate of building development:

> For the next few years the Committee's capital allocations are already stretched to the limit, and I cannot at the moment say when it will be possible to make even minimal provision for work on the site. ... The move makes possible and should involve a thorough re-appraisal of the relationship between the two Universities, of the division of responsibility for particular lines of work, and of the forms and methods of co-operation. The Government's approval, in principle, of the move has indeed been secured on the understanding that the possibility of further co-operation will be actively explored.[63]

There is no evidence that such cooperation was ever thoroughly investigated.

Sir Herbert Andrews of the DES wrote to Sir John Wolfenden on 13 December 1966 indicating that the DES

> did not expect any claim to be made for building work for Heriot-Watt University or the new site to be started in any building programme down to and including that for 1971–72.[64]

Wolfenden, after his Christmas break, responded decisively on 30 December:

> I feel sure that the UGC would wish to feel free to allocate to the University, out of the total starts programme, such amounts, in such years, as they might judge to be appropriate. ... They will, I think, find it difficult to understand the basis on which you say that you would not expect any claim to be made for building work to be started in any year up to and including 1971–72. ... This is not the foundation of a new university – which would be subject to the Secretary of State's 10 year ban – but the move of an existing university.[65]

This power struggle resulted in a victory for the UGC when the DES conceded in a reply of 19 January 1967 that

> It was within the Committee's discretion to make allocations to Heriot-Watt as they thought fit. . . . So the Committee will feel it reasonable (not to move Heriot-Watt to the top of Ben Nevis) but to make some modest provision for starting on the development of the new site for which Government approval has been given.[66]

This assertion of autonomy from the DES did not herald a softening of attitudes within the UGC towards Heriot-Watt's capital starvation, for on 15 February 1967, Mr A. E. L. Parnis, who was to prove a thorn in the university's ambitions on several occasions, wrote:

> Though we *could* help Heriot-Watt to the tune of £50,000 from this year's reserve, I am rather reluctant to do this, as it encourages the ex-CATS in the belief they have only to ask in order to get.[67]

Apart from the patronising tone of this comment, Parnis clearly did not realise that Heriot-Watt was not an ex college of advanced technology, a flower only visible in England, something apparently not appreciated in the higher echelons of the UGC.

The acting principal of Heriot-Watt, Professor Raymond Smart, wrote to Sir John Wolfenden on 23 February 1967 (in advance of a meeting on 1 March) requesting £80,000 for each of the years 1967–68, 1968–69, and 1969–70 plus a grant of £250,000 for site works at Riccarton in 1968–69 and £1 million for 1969–70 as a grant for the first year of the major building programme. A handwritten note on this letter from a UGC official commented:

> I think there is nothing unexpected about this particular bunch. I only hope that the Acting Principal of Heriot-Watt is a bit more accommodating in person than his letter would indicate – otherwise we are going to have a troublesome time on Wednesday.[68]

It is clear that the UGC envisaged a lengthy relocation process leading to a small-sized institution of between 2,000 and 3,000 students. Neither the scale nor the timing satisfied the university's aspirations. A group of four – Lord Balerno (chairman of court), Acting Principal Smart, Mr Cameron and Mr Clayton

A shadow of the past: aerial view showing cleared site of Riccarton House, prior to library development, c. 1970

(bursar) – met the UGC on 1 March 1967 to present their plan for the development of the Riccarton campus. This envisaged facilities for 1,000 students by October 1971, 2,000 by 1972, and 3,000 by 1975, following the transfer of all departments to Riccarton. This scheme, involving expenditure of £9 million by 1975 (compared with £15 million to expand in the Grassmarket), including £1.25 million on residences, was regarded by the UGC as 'quite impracticable', one official commenting:

> I do not really see why Heriot-Watt should expand to 3,000 students until such time as it suits the national need for them to do so.[69]

The university was invited to frame its development plan so that it could be adjusted flexibly to the flow of capital.[70] How prophetic this statement proved to be could not even have been envisaged by the mandarins at the UGC since it was to be more than two decades later before the university was completely relocated. The UGC's building expenditures were fully allocated until 1970–71. Hence, although the UGC agreed the acquisition of Riccarton in 1966, it was to be 1970–71 (two years earlier than the DES had recommended) before the first building allocation was received. Meanwhile the university opened the Mountbatten Building in the Grassmarket in January 1968 to house the Faculty of Humanities and the department of electrical engineering.

Midlothian County Council applied to the Secretary of State for Scotland requesting 242 acres of agricultural land at Riccarton Estate to be re-zoned as a site for the university. In a letter to the Scottish Development Department on 16 February 1968, Dundas & Wilson, on behalf of the owner, Mrs A. J. Sudlow, argued that the county council had not shown that the site was necessary for university purposes; it was against sound planning in that it lay within an area designated as of landscape value in the green belt; it consisted of good agricultural land; and moreover, the need to designate the whole 242 acres for compulsory acquisition had not been shown.[71] These objections to amending the development plan for Midlothian were the subject of a public local inquiry on 22–24 July 1968, presided over by Mr C. E. Jauncey QC. James Mackay QC, current chancellor of the university, was retained to appear on behalf of the council, while Donald Ross QC, later chairman of court, represented Mrs Sudlow. On 17 December 1968 the Secretary of State accepted Mr Jauncey's recommendation that the proposed alteration to the development plan should be approved, subject to the exclusion of the four westmost fields from the area designated for compulsory purchase.[72] It had not been established that they would be required until the university expanded beyond 3,000 students. With these four fields excluded, the site was limited to 190 acres (78 of which were amenity land) leaving 110 developable acres. This was much smaller than the UGC recommendation that the site for a new university should include 200 acres of developable land. The other ten 1960s greenfield universities had an average of 257 acres of developable land, varying from Warwick (380) to York (155).[73]

After only two weeks in post, Principal Smith, Professor Nisbet's successor, received a most unwelcome letter on 11 June 1968 from Sir John Wolfenden, chairman of the UGC, stating that 'the UGC is unlikely to be able to give any priority at this stage to starting a major development on the Riccarton site'.[74] Funds to enable work to commence at Riccarton would not be available before 1972–73, some six years after the approval was granted to the university to accept the offer of the site. Wolfenden adopted the same date that he had objected to when proposed by the DES in December 1966, suggesting that the argument with the DES was a Whitehall power struggle and not a disagreement over policy.

Principal Smith wrote to Sir John Wolfenden on 21 June 1968 arguing that such a delay would rule out the opportunity to establish a research park in association with the university.[75] Principal Smith met Sir John Wolfenden on 2 July 1968. Smith was clearly persuasive and the fruits of his representations ripened six months later in a letter from the UGC of 31 January 1969; this allocated £0.95 million for the period 1970–71 and 1971–72 which, together with an allocation of £225,000 from UGC reserves, would finally enable site development at Riccarton to commence.[76]

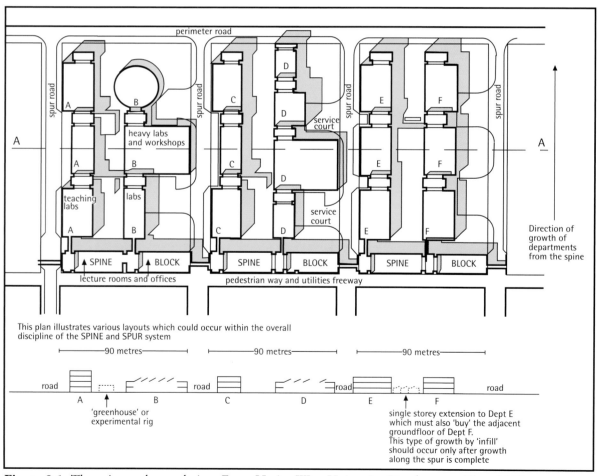

Figure 8.1 The spine and spur design. From Heriot-Watt University Development Plan, 1968

A Brown–Brick University

Following the UGC announcement in December 1966 that the university would transfer to Riccarton, a development officer, Mr Peter Smith, formerly of the University of Liverpool, was appointed. Smith contracted consultant architects Alan Reiach, Eric Hall & Partners, and Professor Arnold Weddle as landscape consultant to prepare a development plan. This was approved by the court in 1968.

Each academic zone was planned on a spine and spur system, with a continuous first-floor spine route for circulation within and between buildings housing non-specialist spaces such as offices and lecture rooms (Figure 8.1). This facilitated the expansion of faculties by the addition of new departmental units at the open ends of the spine; departments could grow by adding units at right angles to the spine.[77] The separate buildings of the academic departments are therefore continuously and seamlessly linked with one another, with the social areas which intersperse them, and with the main central facilities and concourses. It was intended to be an arrangement fertile in academic interchange and supportive of identity and community; in practice the interior design was inflexible and

The best laid plans ...? An early model for campus development, thwarted by government funding cuts in the mid 1970s

unimaginative and tends to confuse and deter visitors and staff. Irrespective of the rate of growth, the three components – residence, core and academic – were planned to expand in tandem so that the university would be complete and compact at each stage. The original plan was for a university of 3,000 students, with 5,000 by the 1980s. Cores of communal buildings containing lecture theatres, central dining and shops were designed to take advantage of the leafy landscape, although few windows afforded vistas of the splendid woodland. The *Architects' Journal* described the development plan as

> a mature no nonsense scheme in which the better features of our universities development plans have been absorbed. ... The designers have not attempted to break new ground but have concentrated on developing ideas already tried in other schemes. There is, therefore, a clear lineage from such development plans as those for Leeds, Essex, Lancaster, Bath and Surrey.[78]

After Professor R. A. Smith had been appointed principal, Peter Smith, the new development officer, visited him at the MIT campus. The two Smiths were in agreement concerning the overall building design concept. After taking up the principalship, R. A. Smith adopted a benign attitude to the building programme, concentrating on developing the nascent research profile of the university, while Lord Balerno, chairman of court, was involved actively in the development of Riccarton.[79] Lord Balerno, an astute man of gravitas who was totally dedicated to the success of the university, was the 'real driving force' behind the campus development with a clear view about what he wanted, including the desirability, given the capriciousness of the Scottish climate, of linking all the buildings.[80]

From the outset of development of the Riccarton campus, the university recognised the special challenge of building within a mature parkland estate. A line running west and east is the natural heart of the old Riccarton estate – mature and attractive woodland surrounding sloping lawns – and to the east of this, a loch tightly enclosed by trees. This central belt of landscape – the lawn, the loch and the surrounding woodland – was a barrier to the integration of the north and south sections of the site; it was also an enviable asset to be conserved and enhanced. The challenge for the architects was to pierce this barrier to permit easy passage across the campus without destroying the amenity of the magnificent woodland landscape. It was decided, therefore, to locate the core here, drawing the woodlands into the recreational areas where possible, and to carry the link to the south at first-floor level, thereby affording vistas of the loch and mature woodland. Seen from a distance on the rising ground to the south of the A71, the appearance has the look of a technological university: 'massive blank verticals for physical work, windowed horizontals for thought'.[81]

After much debate – Professor Smart favoured red brick[82] – it was agreed to build an unobtrusive brown, rustic brick university, varied with exposed aggregate panels where a change was required; the brown bricks would blend into the specimen trees to minimise the visual intrusion on their aesthetic value. A scheme of natural-toned, brown brick finishes are much in evidence, and while some buildings explore adventurous uses and styling of novel building materials, the general impression remains discreet, if somewhat bland. None of the buildings is individually outstanding as the university decided wisely not to build any shiny academic monuments. There was no attempt to create a focus of maximum architectural eminence on campus, a substitute for a spire or campanile. The leafy landscape was the central feature with the effects of woodland carried into the building areas by planting associated with the pedestrian ways. The planning authority also restricted the height of the buildings to a maximum of four storeys because of the proximity to Edinburgh airport where, at that time, the runway was aligned north-west to south-east.[83] Restricting the buildings to four storeys enabled much of the campus to be screened behind the trees, thereby minimising the visual impact of a university development in the green belt. The consultant architects not only faced the challenge of designing a university in a mature parkland setting but they were also constrained by the strict space norms specified by the UGC. As

A blank canvas? A view across Riccarton campus c. 1970. Photograph: John Dewar Studios

Sir Alec Douglas-Home, chancellor, Principal R. A. Smith and Lord Balerno, chairman of court, preside over the unveiling of a plaque commemorating gift of Riccarton by Midlothian Council to Heriot-Watt University, 10 November 1969. Photograph: The Herald

Colin McWilliam concluded, the campus offers 'an excellent discipline of layout and materials, made interesting by the site, which has a general slope towards the south and by the established trees'.[84] Cost constraints are often mentioned as a reason for the monastic rigour of the buildings, 'but whatever the truth of this, the money has been well spent'.[85]

The Vision Realised

The first two buildings erected were temporary structures, one for Peter Smith and his team and the other for a physics research group under Professor S. D. (Des) Smith, who had moved north from Reading. Buildings for mathematics, physics and dining accommodation were started. The UGC, however, did not provide sufficient resources to incorporate the department of chemistry in the first phase.[86] Lord Balerno, tenacious as ever, simply insisted that chemistry be included.[87] The university sought to accommodate 40 per cent of the students on site, but the UGC would no longer make available 100 per cent grants to any institution for student residences. The first residences providing 397 places in three separate blocks, each of three stories, were located close to central catering facilities and the amenity of the loch. These were catered halls, and therefore the small kitchenette facilities were limited to the production of beverages and snacks. Appeal funds of £100,000 towards the provision of playing fields and £155,000 for the construction of a sports centre were also made available.[88]

A ceremony was held at Riccarton on 10 November 1969 to commemorate the start of work on the new site. A team of cross-country runners carried the university standard through a snowstorm from Chambers Street to Riccarton where it was hoisted in a burst of sunshine. The chancellor, Sir Alec Douglas-Home, unveiled the plaque on a boulder excavated from the playing fields. The first phase of general site works started in spring 1970. This included the provision of roads, footpaths, sewerage, water and electric distribution systems, telephone services and improvements to the loch. In addition, the UGC financed 150 car parking spaces in phase 1. On a matter of such passionate concern to academics, about which they rarely disagree, the court approved with alacrity the sum of £27,000 to provide an additional 450 free parking spaces.[89]

The erection of the sports centre and the development of the playing fields (at a cost of £110,000) – including football pitches, an all-weather surface in the walled garden, the provision of floodlights and the construction of tennis courts – enabled the university to offer much better facilities than were available previously at Craiglockhart.[90] The sports centre, the first completed new building on site, was opened by Lord Killanin, president of the International Olympic Committee, on 10 November 1973, a cold and windy autumn day. The centre was an incentive to students to become familiar with the campus on which many (because of their discipline) might not have occasion otherwise to visit.

In January 1970 the senate agreed to achieve a student population of 3,000 at Riccarton by 1976, expanding to 5,000 by 1980–81 (including the environmental

Procession including Principal Smith, Chancellor Sir Alec Douglas-Home and mace bearer prepare to lay the foundation stone of the Riccarton campus, 1971

studies faculty).[91] It was not long, however, before the university had to alter the sequencing of the development at Riccarton in response to the inability of the UGC to deliver its future capital spending commitments, subject as it was to the caprice of central government's public spending cuts. A letter of 30 October 1970 from the UGC indicated that it would only provide £1 million each year for building starts in 1973–74 and 1974–75.[92] Consequently, in order to achieve 1,500 students at Riccarton by 1976–77, the UGC proposed that phase 2 should include civil engineering and an additional spine for a temporary library instead of biological sciences and chemical engineering. Phase 3 would include the library for 3,000 students, biological sciences, chemical engineering, building and administration. This would enable the university to dispose of the Chambers Street building after phase 3. The first three phases of the development plan were activated accordingly (Table 8.1).

In June 1971, as a result of prompt action by the redoubtable Lord Balerno, the university purchased Hermiston House for £41,050 and the court sanctioned its use as a staff club, a decision that was never subsequently implemented because of the conversion costs. Hermiston House, now home of the principal of the university, had come into the Craig's family possession in 1686 and was for many years the dower house of the Riccarton estate. William Burn, the architect who designed the extension to Riccarton House, rented Hermiston House from the Gibson-Craigs from 1828 and made alterations to the property.[93]

The Secretary of State for Scotland, the Rt Hon. Gordon Campbell, laid the foundation stone of the university buildings at Riccarton on 25 June 1971. The Core I component of phase 1 (the Hugh Nisbet Building) included three central

Table 8.1 The first three phases of the development plan

Phase 1	Phase 2	Phase 3
Sports centre and playing fields	Mechanical engineering	Biological sciences
Actuarial mathematics and statistics	Civil engineering	Chemical engineering
Mathematics	Petroleum engineering	Building
Physics	Core II (balance of Hugh Nisbet Building and bridge link)	Library
Chemistry	Maintenance depot	Administration
Core I (part of Hugh Nisbet Building)	Spine for temporary library	
Residence blocks 1 to 3		

lecture theatres with a capacity of 200, 140 and 100, respectively, and a dining facility in which initially there was no separation of staff and students. Appropriately, the academic buildings for phase 1 were topped out by Lord Balerno, the first chairman of court, at a ceremony on the roof of the chemistry building in April 1972. There was clearly a mood of confidence in the institution and on 5 September 1973 the secretary wrote to Midlothian County Council inquiring if they would take the necessary steps to acquire the westerly fields excluded following the public inquiry in 1968, since the university was now planning for 5,000 students by 1981–82.[94] Midlothian confirmed in December 1973 that the four fields, totalling 52.2 acres, would be acquired and gifted to the

Lord Balerno, chairman of court, and construction workers celebrate the topping out of the chemistry department building, 1972. Photograph: John K. Wilkie

Table 8.2 New capital building programme, Riccarton, 1969–82

Project	Building start	Occupation date
Sports centre	April 1971	October 1973
Academics I	April 1971	December 1973
Core I	April 1971	October 1973
Mechanical engineering	April 1972	October 1975
Core II	October 1972	March 1976
Library I	May 1973	January 1976
Civil engineering	August 1973	July 1976
Residences I	April 1971	April 1974
Residences II	October 1972	March 1975
Petroleum engineering	October 1975	August 1976
Chaplaincy centre	March 1976	May 1978
Computer centre	May 1981	November 1982

university.[95] The departments of chemistry, mathematics, actuarial mathematics and statistics, and physics moved into the new phase 1 buildings, which had been built by John Laing Construction Ltd, in December 1973 (Table 8.2). A temporary Students' Union building, funded by the McRobert Trust, was opened in 1974.

Phase 2 of the development comprised academic buildings for the departments of mechanical engineering (occupied by October 1975) and civil engineering (July 1976); a further 197 residential places in the form of student flats occupied in March 1975; a major extension to the original core building to provide additional lecture theatres, offices, dining and bar facilities, and some shops (March 1976); the first section of the library (January 1976); and a building for petroleum engineering aided by a grant of £300,000 from the Department of Energy (August 1976).

In 1970 agreement was reached between the DES and UGC on a formula for regular supplementation of university costs against the ravages of inflation.[96] The value of the grants would be guaranteed, although the average grant per student had been drifting downwards since 1968, and the traditional system for funding universities sailed steadily on towards the next five-year period of 1972–77. The university system was in a fragile state and in the first 18 months of the new five-year period it received two crippling blows. During the winter of 1973–74 the UK was plunged into an economic crisis. In December 1973 Mr Barber, Conservative Chancellor of the Exchequer, announced large reductions in public expenditure, one of which was the cancellation of half the recently agreed compensation for increased university costs.[97] Worse was to follow only two weeks later. The rapid

The campus takes shape in this aerial view from the mid 1970s

rise in oil prices introduced by the Organisation of the Petroleum Exporting Countries (OPEC) led to the cancellation of the surviving 50 per cent of this compensation, and a reduction of one-half in equipment and furniture grants. After the election of a Labour government in 1974, the UGC managed to recover about £4 million a year for the universities, perhaps one-third of the amount that had been lopped off the compensation for inflation in university costs.[98] One of the first acts of the incoming Labour government in 1974 was to reduce university building starts of £30.6 million authorised for 1974–75 to £11.5 million, to be followed by only £6 million in 1977–78 and £10.5 million in 1978–79.[99] The building of subsidised residences for students virtually ceased from 1973 onwards. Against such a background, it was hardly surprising that the UGC imposed a moratorium on new building at Riccarton. The Heriot-Watt ship had sustained severe damage but it was able, with a somewhat demoralised crew and nervous passengers, to resume a limping and slower course towards a haven to the west of Edinburgh; but it was visibly lower in the water than when it set sail, and never again did the grant reach the level in real terms that had been proposed by the White Paper of 1972.

There had been a substantial overspend on phase 1 of the building programme at Riccarton. The UGC appointed a committee under the chairmanship of Professor David Flint of the University of Glasgow to investigate procedures and controls in relation to building projects at Heriot-Watt. The committee report in November 1976 considered that

there have been breakdowns of procedure, communications and control of the university's system for handling projects, accompanied by some lack of acceptance of the need to keep within UGC expenditure limits. ... In our opinion the Finance Committee, the Development Committee and the First Phase Building Sub-Committee have not been sufficiently rigorous and demanding in this monitoring of expenditure on the building projects we have considered.[100]

The report urged the court to impress in the clearest possible terms on all concerned the need to conform to both the university's and the UGC's procedures.[101] The largest project, with an estimated overexpenditure of £186,058 on an expenditure limit of £1.445 million, was phase 1 (mathematics, physics and chemistry). The excess for physics alone exceeded the authorised UGC limit by £179, 911.[102] Some two years later, on 22 June 1978, the chairman of the UGC, Sir Fred Dainton, wrote that the UGC 'have reason to believe that expenditure of the order of between a half and three-quarters of a million pounds has been incurred in excess of capital grants'.[103] The UGC was also concerned that additional expenditure on the phase 1 buildings 'may have been met at least in part from the university's recurrent grant'.[104] The First Phase Building Subcommittee was not made aware, however, of all the expenditure which had been incurred.[105] The UGC accepted that the major problem was that the quantity surveyors did not meet their responsibilities, but the university's development officer and the First Phase Building Subcommittee should have recognised that

Reverend Tom Scott, university chaplain, adopts a hands-on approach to the building of the new chaplaincy centre.
Photograph: John K. Wilkie

The end of an era: the Heriot-Watt University plaque is removed from the Chambers Street building, 1989

there were inadequacies requiring attention yet failed to do so.[106] The university had falsely assumed that the UGC would fund the overspend. This incident seriously undermined the university's reputation for financial rectitude; at a time when limited resources were available for new buildings, the UGC was not going to invest in a university that was improvident, so that twin-site working was prolonged. Even as late as 11 September 1980, the chairman of the UGC, Dr Edward Parkes, in response to representations about delays in the construction of the computer building, argued that what the UGC had to do

> in view of the unsatisfactory history of past projects, is to satisfy itself that the arrangements which you have for your computer building are best calculated to avoid the difficulties the University has incurred on the last two schemes.[107]

In a situation of national economic stringency, Treasury pressure on the UGC resulted in the committee withholding the expected repayment of much of the excess spending by the university. As a consequence, interest payments on the capital debt became a first charge on the university's income at a time when the costs of operating on two sites also escalated. It was not until 1982–83 that the capital debt and the accumulated revenue deficit were eliminated.[108] There had been a price to pay for R. A. Smith's entirely laudable desire to build a strong physics department.

Estimates of student numbers were revised downwards by the Department of Education in January 1974 to give credibility to government policy.[109] There was hope that the Labour government, elected in February 1974, might reverse the

Table 8.3 New capital building programme, Riccarton, 1983–2002

Project	Building start	Occupation date
Offshore engineering	October 1984	March 1985
Supplies office	December 1984	July 1985
Petroleum engineering II (Conoco Building)	November 1984	December 1985
Printing unit	May 1986	December 1986
Administration (Lord Balerno Building)	October 1985	June 1987
Petroleum engineering III	October 1986	July 1987
Building engineering	June 1985	October 1987
Residences III (Leonard Horner Hall)	December 1985	October 1987
Chemical engineering	July 1986	May 1988
Esmée Fairbairn Research Centre	January 1987	May 1988
Library, languages, TV centre	July 1986	August 1988
Economic and social studies	November 1987	July 1989
Biological sciences	December 1986	July 1989
Entrance complex	July 1988	August 1990
Extension to the Hugh Nisbet Building	January 1989	August 1990
Physics extension	April 1990	October 1990
Students' Union	November 1989	April 1991
Electrical engineering and computer science	June 1989	May 1992
Residences IV (Robert Bryson Hall)	September 1990	July 1992
Petroleum engineering IV (Enterprise Building)	July 1992	June 1993
Esmée Fairbairn Research Centre: Residences	November 1992	October 1993
Residences V (George Burnett Hall)	June 1994	September 1995
Residences V (Robin Smith Hall)	June 1994	September 1995
Sports centre extension	July 1994	March 1995
School of Languages	August 1996	August 1997
Scotch Whisky Research Institute	October 1996	August 1997
Extension to the Students' Union	August 1997	July 1998
Edinburgh Business School	January 1997	August 1998
Residences VI (Lord Home Hall)	June 1998	September 1999
Residences VI (Lord Thomson Hall)	June 1998	September 1999
Extension to the James Watt Centre	September 1998	September 1999
Medical centre	September 1998	September 1999
George Heriot Wing	September 1998	September 1999

policy of economies but this was soon dashed. The moratorium on new development was a severe blow to Heriot-Watt, greatly prolonging the acute practical problems of twin-site working and frustrating attempts to develop courses on the interfaces between disciplines. The petroleum engineering building, completed and occupied in August 1976, brought construction work to an end at Riccarton (Table 8.2). The computer centre, operational in November 1982, was the only building of significance funded by the UGC between 1976 and the mid 1980s.[110]

The financial drought ended when a letter from the UGC of 5 October 1983 confirmed its commitment to fund all the projects necessary to complete the move to Riccarton.[111] The UGC estimated that the transfer and outstanding building work would cost £11 million at 1983 prices. The 1980s were also a time of fresh approaches in the briefing and commissioning of the university's buildings. Rather than use the services of one or two practices repeatedly, a range of new architects was appointed. It was decided to vacate the Chambers Street building first, and also to locate the department of languages within an extension to the library building.[112] The building norms for departments in the Faculty of Economic and Social Studies were lower than those agreed with the UGC in 1975 and these tight physical constraints were to haunt the university when demand for management disciplines from home and abroad expanded rapidly in the 1990s. The sequence of building completions during the final phase of development (summarised in Table 8.3) included the administration block (Lord Balerno Building), opened by the Queen in 1987. With the completion of the building for electrical engineering and computer science in May 1992, all departments were finally located at Riccarton. The completion of the move after 20 years finally presented the long-sought opportunity for constructive

Principal A. MacFarlane, Donald MacDonald, Duncan Cameron and colleagues filling a 'time capsule' to be placed in plinth of statue of James Watt, 1990

Peter Kingston, managing director of Enterprise Oil, Principal MacFarlane, Professor Adrian Todd and Peter Wilson, secretary of the university, celebrate the award from the company to build a new petroleum engineering building, 1991

A rare view from the sunken garden towards Riccarton House in the early twentieth century

A similar view from the 1970s showing the university library on the site of Riccarton House

consolidation. The university's Chamber Street building was closed for the last time on 31 July 1989, ending over 116 years' ownership of the site.

Lord Mackay of Clashfern, destined to become chancellor of the university in 1991, opened the James Watt Centre and the new £3.8 million entrance complex and conference centre on 12 October 1990. The centre's multi-purpose hall with retractable seating for over 620 is nested within a range of associated smaller seminar rooms and meeting areas. The centre embodies the university's challenging philosophy of openness and flexibility to the world beyond its precincts. The statue of James Watt that had graced the university's building in Chambers Street since 1854 was also relocated to a plinth outside the new entrance complex in 1990. Inside the plinth, Principal MacFarlane placed a time capsule containing memorabilia, including the event which most stirred Scots in 1990, the video highlights of Scotland's grand slam rugby victory over England at Murrayfield.[113] Here, close by the magnificent Hungarian oak, it is hoped that James Watt will extend his fatherly gaze for further centuries over generations of students entering the university.

Demand for older residences with single and double bedrooms, communal sanitary facilities and students' eating in the university refectory had fallen. The university responded by providing accommodation to meet the changing lifestyles of its students. All the residences built in the 1990s had individual bedrooms with en suite shower rooms and self-catering facilities. Robert Bryson Hall became available in 1992 and Gavin Hastings opened two further halls in 1995. A further £7.8 million expansion of student residences, the Lord Thomson and Lord Home halls, was opened in 1999, bringing on-campus accommodation to over 1,927 places (including 165 rooms with 211 bed spaces for conference delegates in term time), thereby enabling the university to guarantee a room at Riccarton for every first-year student. The conference centre was also expanded at a cost of £2.5 million in order to capitalise on the popularity of Edinburgh as a venue; the sports centre and the Students' Union were extended; and Enterprise Oil donated £270,000 towards the cost of a new building for petroleum engineering, opened in 1993. Two new academic buildings arose on the southern edge of the campus: a languages building equipped with laboratories, and the imposing Edinburgh Business School, dominating the southern skyline and enjoying a vista over the playing fields (Table 8.3). A new £1.2 million health centre was also opened in 1998, and in keeping with the university's commitment to partnership, the new centre serves both the university and the local community.

The north academic blocks are a high-density development up to four storeys, all interlinked. This grid structure of the spur and spine system, resonant of the 1970s, was set to trample uncompromisingly all over the campus. The only benefit of the government's moratorium on new building in the mid 1970s was to rescue the campus from such a monotonous aesthetic fate. The academic buildings to the south were constructed at lower density with lawns and varied planting in between and with characteristic pitched aluminium roofs that, like the flat roofs in phase 1, leak frequently in wet weather. The university has been at the forefront of good landscape design practice (if not architecture) but it has also implemented measures to enhance environmental quality. Evidence of the university's successful management of the campus is available from a habitat survey of the ecology in 1998. Over a 25 year period, bird species recorded on campus have risen from 66 to 85, partly due to sensitive management of the woodlands.[114]

Europe's Pioneering Research Park

Since the nineteenth century, the institution has remained steadfast to two important principles: the delivery of industrially relevant applied courses to the most rigorous academic standards, and a research mission tailored primarily to the needs of industry and society. After the award of university status in 1966, the mission to transfer technology, techniques and ideas to industry has focused on three complementary strategies:

1 After a visit to the University of New South Wales in 1968, where he discussed how they organised university and industry links, Duncan Cameron prepared a paper for the Principal and Deans Committee which led in 1969 to the establishment of Unilink, one of the pioneering industrial liaison units in British academe.[115] How interesting that an Australian university should transfer a model of university–industry collaboration to Heriot-Watt some 150 years after former students of the Edinburgh School of Arts implanted the idea of mechanics' institutes in Australia. The first director of Unilink, Mr T. M. Chalmers, died after only a few months in post but his successor, Mr Arthur C. Gardiner, made a valuable contribution to the development of Unilink. It became a focus for fostering links between the expertise within departments and industry; through Unilink, industry was enabled to benefit from consultancy services of appropriate academics, use testing facilities for equipment or materials, or arrange for experimental work to be carried out.

2 Dedicated technology transfer units were developed in specific activities to provide an educational, research and development service to industry. Such

units, including the Institute of Offshore Engineering, Computer Applications Services, the Medical Laser Unit, and the Marine Science Unit, were an integral part of the university.

3 A research park was created on the Riccarton campus.

The concept of developing part of the campus as an area where companies could locate their research and development (R&D) activities in immediate proximity to the facilities and expertise of a university was first explored in the USA in the mid 1960s when there were only three such managed science parks in existence (Stanford, Research Triangle and Philadelphia Urban Park), although there was also an upsurge of knowledge-based enterprises along Route 128 near MIT in Boston. The original idea for a research park was articulated by Principal Nisbet in 1966 at a meeting with Duncan Cameron and Sandy Hodge of the Chamber of Commerce.[116] Professor Childs and Vice-Principal Smart then visited Stanford Research Institute and MIT in September 1966.[117] Principal Smith, who assumed office in June 1968 having worked at MIT, was convinced that the acquisition of the Riccarton site offered an ideal opportunity for Heriot-Watt to pioneer such a development not only in Britain but also in Europe. Research parks reflect an assumption that technological innovation stems from scientific research in a university and that parks can provide the catalytic incubator environment for the transformation of 'pure' research into production. Adherents of this 'linear model' assume a chain of successive interrelated activities. These begin with basic scientific research, pass through applied and more developmental research activities, the development of new product and process ideas, the evolution and testing of prototypes, to commercial production and finally to diffusion. As a result, the local technological environment can attract and encourage the formation and development of technology-based firms.

The activities of the companies on the research park (growth of which is shown in Figure 8.2) are focused on one or more of the following: research, development, design of new products or processes, prototype manufacture, and the provision of relevant training for both the final producers of the new product and their users. Given the university's location in the green belt, the research park precludes specifically 'manufacture on a scale intended for commercial distribution'. It is not, as is often the case in science parks, a manufacturing site for small science-based companies. The criteria for acceptance as a tenant on the park are stringent, confining development opportunities to projects having the following characteristics:

- only R&D activities of companies;
- of these, only companies that share some common scientific interest with the university;

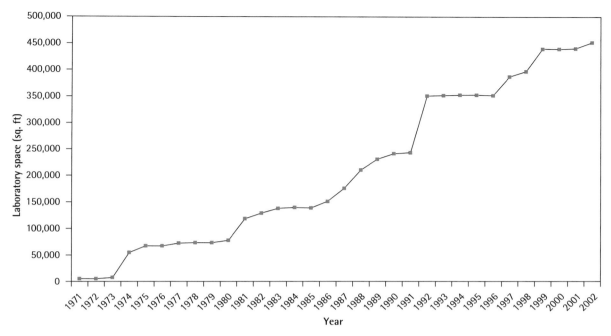

Figure 8.2 Growth of the research park, 1971–2002

• of these, only those willing to collaborate with the university;
• of these, only companies that are acknowledged to be acceptable as potential collaborators by the relevant academic departments;
• of these, only companies that undertake not to engage in competitive activities with the university.

Although these onerous criteria were not always implemented to the letter, they effectively constrained the pool of potential clients to a small subset of companies and placed the park at a competitive disadvantage relative to other later initiatives with much less restrictive covenants. Even the second UK university science park at Cambridge, which became operational two years after Heriot-Watt in 1973, adopted much looser criteria, permitting for example 'light industrial production'. The criterion concerning willingness to collaborate with university departments in research was only binding initially and, in practice, two-thirds of companies have no active research links with the university, partly because many industrial clients require academics to sign confidentiality agreements.[118]

The research park infrastructure in phase 1 was developed on a 12 hectare (30 acre) site north of the academic buildings. The park became operational when the first company, Inveresk International (conducting biological research), opened in April 1971. The second company, Edinburgh Instruments Ltd, was a spin-off formed to develop and assess the viability and application of instruments whose design derived from research work in space instrumentation, non-linear optics and spectroscopy by the department of physics under Professor S. D. Smith, who had been conducting major research programmes at Riccarton (in temporary accommodation) since 1970. Initial progress was modest for several reasons. First, when this pioneering initiative was launched in 1971 there was no public policy interest whatsoever in technology transfer between the groves of academe and the marketplace.[119] Second, although initially Riccarton lay within an intermediate area and qualified for 20 per cent building grants, Livingston then enjoyed the extra inducements of special development area status. Later, when Riccarton was excluded from the regional policy map, the university was to be solely responsible for its development. The infrastructure was largely financed through bank borrowings. The need to balance cash flows has governed the rate of growth of the park; the university has been reluctant to invest in advance laboratory buildings for lease to companies. Third, the birth of the park coincided with a major oil price recession during the early 1970s. Fourth, the university had little or no investment capital so was unable to provide speculative space for rent. Fifth, since the university restricted its own investment in the park to land and infrastructure (but excluding buildings except in highly favourable circumstances), potential tenants

The university research park, 1975. Photograph: John Dewar Studios

Aerial view of Edinburgh campus and research park, 1999. Photograph: Air Images

had to be willing to construct their own premises on a leased site or to be acceptable to a commercial property investor. The policy, therefore, was to provide serviced sites for lease by owner-occupiers or by the financing of a building for rent to approved tenants. As a consequence of those factors and the inevitable time lag before industry appreciated the potential of the concept, growth of the park did not accelerate until after 1980 (Figure 8.2).

Nevertheless, by the mid 1970s it was apparent that a further area would be needed, and the 9 hectares (22.5 acres) that now form the North Park were acquired.[120] This second phase of development was spearheaded by the attraction of Syntex Pharmaceuticals to the campus in 1976. By 2003 this company, now called Quintiles, was by far the largest employer on the park; 75 per cent of its 600 staff are graduates.[121] This initiative was complemented by the Scottish Development Agency, which constructed seven buildings on a 4 acre site in the 1980s; one of these buildings was for multi-occupancy. The third phase of expansion began in the late 1980s with the attraction of the Forth River Purification Board, later to become the Scottish Environmental Protection Agency, and the speculative construction of the Origo Centre incorporating sixteen 1,500 square foot units designed to encourage university spin-outs.[122] Only six of the spin-out units were taken up for their original purpose and the centre is now occupied totally by Inveresk International.

The fourth phase of expansion was ushered in with the purchase of the whole area of 44.5 hectares (110 acres) to the north of the academic buildings. The acquisition was made at agricultural value, the land to be taken up as required on payment of an agreed development uplift, and the residue leased for farming purposes to the former owner on an annual basis. The university decided to develop this area in stages, and planning permission for the first of these phases of 17 hectares was obtained in April 1992.[123] Development of the infrastructure, financed by the university on a loan, was completed in November 1992. Several major organisations have blossomed on this northerly site, including the Scotch Whisky Research Institute, Scottish Water and Renishaw Metrology.

Three types of organisation have populated the research park: technology transfer agencies, such as the Institute of Offshore Engineering, owned by the university; spin-off companies from the university, such as Edinburgh Instruments; and external companies. The nature of companies locating on the park has altered somewhat over its 30 year life. Prior to 1990, offshore engineering, petroleum engineering, pharmaceuticals, optoelectronics and computing were predominant; recently there has been increasing demand for sites from the biotechnology sector.

In the past, the research park as a straight financial investment did not secure and was never intended to secure a commercial rate of return for the university, but as the first such venture in Europe, it has brought substantial non-financial benefits of prestige and attention to the institution.[124] However, in 2002–03 it generated a net income of £300,000. Building on the park is now dependent on commercial development. The range of research capability offered by the university as an attraction to outside companies is limited and does not compare with larger institutions, especially those with bioscience and medical schools. Furthermore, the research programmes of the university's departments are not dependent strategically on links with research park companies; knowledge transfer from the university to firms is patchy. Physical proximity is a necessary but not sufficient condition for close collaboration. Nevertheless, the Heriot-Watt research park was seen as 'the most successful one in Scotland because it was led by "can do" people who had vigorously managed it'.[125] Given that the criteria for acceptance as a park tenant are stringent and that no manufacturing is allowed, the scale of development to 2,000 employees is impressive, especially as Lothian & Edinburgh Enterprise Limited (LEEL) decided in the 1990s to support the development of a science park for Edinburgh University in direct opposition to Heriot-Watt, a decision that did not appear to be based entirely on rational argument.

The university has always encouraged staff to translate their ideas and new innovations into marketable products. How successful has the university been in generating spin-off firms, defined as limited companies using intellectual property developed within the university or by university employees? To what extent have they located on the research park as originally envisaged? Edinburgh Instruments Ltd was the first campus company to spin out in 1971, initially locating on the research park but subsequently moving to Livingston, where it now employs 47 people. During the three decades since 1971 some 18 companies have spun off from the university's departments, of which four subsequently closed and two were acquired by other firms.[126] Fifteen of these 18 ventures were established between 1998 and 2002 (inclusive). This upsurge in spin-off activity coincided with the establishment of Technology and Research Services (TRS) by the amalgamation of the Institute of Technology Management (ITM) and Unilink, with the availability of resources from Scottish Enterprise to fund three staff to liaise with academics in order to facilitate the spin-off process, and with dynamic leadership of TRS by Gillian McFadzean. Of the 18 spin-offs, only three located on the university's research park. Most of them, unlikely to be able to provide the guarantees required by commercial investors, have been attracted to other locations serviced by economic development agencies and new towns where short-term leases and development grants were available. The companies successfully formed included technology development covering acoustic monitoring of rotating components within high-value capital equipment, optical device design and manufacture for the telecom markets, sophisticated machine language translation, textile design software, biotechnology conversion of albumen, underwater camera technology, unique animation technology, and drug discovery development. The 14 surviving spin-off companies employ a total of only 140 people,[127] half of which are in Edinburgh Instruments and Edinburgh Petroleum Services Limited (a spin-off from the department of petroleum engineering). The level of spin-off activity has now fallen as most commercially viable projects have been identified. The limited success of the policy has led to a reappraisal and to development and implementation of a new strategy – the licensing of new product innovations arising from university departments to outside firms.

The sunken garden at Riccarton, 1937. Photograph: The Scotsman Publications Ltd

The sunken garden, Riccarton, 1998. Photograph: Ken Paterson

Conclusion

Riccarton is much changed from the days before the Second World War when it was a quiet family residence. Some 1,800 people work on the campus and in term time around 7,000 people are present each day. Yet the atmosphere of tranquillity and the stately beauty of the setting remains. With the vista towards the Pentland Hills to the south, place names in the immediate vicinity such as Weaver's Knowe and Hermiston House, residence of the university's principal, recall the spirit of somewhere so famously evoked by R. L. Stevenson. The concern for knowledge and for truth has always led universities to seek a certain isolation. At Riccarton, research and education can be pursued for their own sake. They need no justification – they are an end in themselves.

Alumni will recall the campus in early summer: sunlight cascading through the glorious avenue of lime trees; the sturdy statue of James Watt, whose name is inscribed in abbreviated form on every light bulb; the sylvan setting of graduation garden parties in the sunken garden, a haven of tranquillity brightened by specimen trees and birdsong, the rhododendrons, a frothy billow of blossom. The outline of the modern buildings blend in harmoniously with the nineteenth-century gardens, symbolising the way in which Heriot-Watt continuously modernises itself, carrying forward the best of the old in distinguished synthesis with the new. And there is continuity with the past. In a shady secluded corner of the parklands, unseen by the passer-by, there still remains the wooded glade that Leonard Horner visited in June 1841 where the Gibson-Craigs of Riccarton lie at rest. Around them, their estate is again a centre of learning. There could be no more appropriate future, for in this inheritance of the Craigs and their descendants, academic excellence has found a home. The completion of the campus was the final vindication of Leonard Horner's vision of 180 years ago, founded as it was on Enlightenment principles and philosophy and on the practical demands of the Industrial Revolution.

Notes

[1] HWUA, HWC 1/2/79A, *Minutes of the Meetings of the Governors of the Heriot-Watt College*, 5 November 1965, p. 135.

[2] HWUA, *Academic Advisory Committee, Minutes of the Tenth Meeting*, 16 December 1965.

[3] *Ibid.*

[4] HWUA, Box 64, *Site Development.*

[5] HWUA, *Academic Advisory Committee, Minutes of the Tenth Meeting*, 16 December 1965, *op. cit.*

[6] HWUA, *Academic Advisory Committee, Minutes of the Seventh Meeting*, 18 March 1965.

[7] *The Scotsman*, 25 July 1964.

[8] HWUA 25/1, Box 64, *University Developments* (Sites/Brown Square House Correspondence) 1965–71, Letter from Mr D. Cameron, Secretary, to Mr A. R. McLeod, 27 November 1965.

[9] *Ibid.*

[10] *Public Record Office*, UGC 7/535.

[11] *The Glasgow Herald*, 24 February 1966.

[12] *Public Record Office*, UGC 7/535.

[13] HWUA, Box 64, *Site Development.*

[14] *Ibid.*

[15] *Public Record Office*, UGC 7/535.

[16] HWUA, Box 54, *Riccarton Site (1)*, June 1966 to December 1967.

[17] *Public Record Office*, UGC 7/535.

[18] *Ibid.* Letter from Principal Nisbet to E. R. Copleston, 18 July 1966.

[19] *Public Record Office*, UGC Paper 225/66.

[20] *Public Record Office*, UGC 7/535.

[21] I am most grateful to Ann Jones, university archivist, for much of the material in this section.

[22] HWUA, Reid, N. H. (1985) *Riccarton: An Illustrated History*, p. 1.

[23] Reid, *op. cit.*, p. 1.

[24] HWUA, Tweedie, J. J. (1979) *Riccarton: The Story of the Midlothian Estate on Which Heriot-Watt University Now Stands*, with additional notes by Alex Anderson, p. 4.

[25] Reid, *op. cit.*, p. 2.

[26] HWUA, GC1/9; Reid, *op. cit.*, p. 3.

[27] Tweedie, *op. cit.*, p. 4, note A; Donaldson, G. and Morpeth, R. S. (1977) *A Dictionary of Scottish History*, Edinburgh, p. 191.

[28] Tweedie, *op. cit.*, p. 5, note B; Reid, *op. cit.*, p. 4; Langwill, R. B., Currie Parish Supplement, *Parish Annals*, No. XVII, May 1895.

[29] Reid, *op. cit.*, p. 6; Tweedie, *op. cit.*, p. 6.

[30] Boyle, J. S. (1973) *Heriot-Watt University: From Mechanics Institute to Technological University*, Edinburgh, p. 67.

[31] Reid, *op. cit.*, p. 7; Lynch, M. (1992) *Scotland: A New History*, p. 264.

[32] Langwill, R. B., Currie Parish Supplement, *Parish Annals*, Nos XXIV, XXX, XXXI (May 1896, March 1897, April 1897); Tweedie, *op. cit.*, p. 7.

[33] Tweedie, *op. cit.*, p. 8.

[34] Reid, *op. cit.*, p. 10.

[35] *Ibid.*, p. 10.

[36] Third, B. (1957) The significance of Scottish estate plans and associated documents. *Scottish Studies*, Vol. 1, pp. 39–64.

[37] Reid, *op. cit.*, p. 10.

[38] *Ibid.*, p. 12.

[39] *Ibid.*, pp. 8, 12.

[40] HWUA, *GC Estate Papers*, 3/2, Contents and Estimated Yearly Value of the Farm of West Hermiston, 1825.

[41] Letter from Dr Norman Reid to Prof. P. N. O'Farrell, 13 August 2003.

[42] Boyle, *op. cit.*, p. 67.

[43] Reid, *op. cit.*, p. 12.

[44] HWUA, R. B. Langwill, Riccarton, n.d., p. 41.

[45] *Dictionary of National Biography*, Vol. XII (1887) London, p. 442.

[46] *Ibid.*, p. 442.

[47] Crombie, B. W. (1882) *Modern Athenians*, Edinburgh, p. 57.

[48] Lyell, K. M. (1880) *Memoirs of Leonard Horner*, London, Vol. 2, p. 27. Letter from Leonard Horner to his daughter Susan, 11 June 1841.

[49] The paintings were purchased with the aid of a grant from the Heritage Lottery Fund.

[50] Reid, *op. cit.*, p. 13.

[51] Jones, A. (2003) *From Robert The Bruce to Research Park: a brief history of Riccarton*, p. 2; Coats, A. M. (1963) *Garden Shrubs and Their Histories*, p. 144.

[52] HWUA, transcript of 1891 census returns for Riccarton; Jones, A. E. and Edgar, A. M. (2003) *Riccarton's Other Residents: Below Stairs*.

[53] Tweedie, J. and Jones, C. (1975) *Our District: The Historical Background of Currie and Ratho Parishes*, p. 61.

[54] HWUA, Edgar Jones, *op. cit.*

[55] Reid, *op. cit.*, p. 13.

[55] *Ibid.*, *op. cit.*, p. 14.

[56] Jones, *op. cit.*, p. 2.

[57] Salmon, P. (ed.) (1995) *Britain and Norway in the Second World War*, London, p. 199.

[58] Personal communication from Mr Donald MacDonald, former university press officer.

[59] HWUA, D. C. MacDonald, The King and Queen of Norway's Visit to Heriot-Watt University 6 July 1994. Heriot-Watt University press release.

[60] *Ibid.*, p. 2.

[61] HWUA, Kelvin, B. D. A and Jones, A. E. (1997) Account of interview with ex-servicemen Corporal John Watson and Private David Parsall of the Royal Artillery Third Anti-Aircraft Group, 7 June 1997.

[62] HWUA, Box 54, *Riccarton Site (1), op. cit.*

[63] *Public Record Office*, UGC Paper 225/66.

[64] *Ibid.*

[65] *Ibid.*

[66] *Ibid.*, 19 January 1967.

[67] *Public Record Office*, UGC 7/535, Memo to Miss Graham, 15 February 1967.

[68] *Public Record Office*, UGC 7/535.

[69] *Public Record Office*, UGC 7/535.

[70] *Public Record Office*, UGC /7/192.

[71] HWUA, Box 54, *Riccarton Site (1)*, Letter from Dundas & Wilson to the Secretary, Scottish Development Department, 16 February 1968, and Letter from Mr R. E. Smith, Secretary, Scottish Development Department, to Midlothian County Council, 17 December 1968.

[72] *Ibid.*

[73] HWUA, Box 54, *Riccarton Site (1)*.

[74] HWUA, Box 54, *Riccarton Site (1)*, Letter from Sir John Wolfenden to Principal R. A. Smith, 11 June 1968.

[75] HWUA, Box 64 (Sites/Brown Square House Correspondence) 1965–71, Letter from Principal R. A. Smith to Sir John Wolfenden, 21 June 1968.

[76] HWUA, Box 54, *op. cit.*, Letter from E. R. Copleston to Principal Smith, 31 January 1969.

[77] HWUA, *Development Report No. 2*, December 1968, p. 5.

[78] Light, liberty and learning, *The Architects' Journal*, 18 February 1970, p. 395.

[79] HWUA, Ms A. E. Jones, Interview with Mr Peter Smith, former development officer, 17 August 2001.

[80] *Ibid.* The idea to link the buildings was sparked by Peter Smith's October 1967 visit to MIT, Boston, where buildings are linked underground.

[81] McWilliam, Colin (1978) *The Buildings of Scotland: Lothian (except Edinburgh)*, Harmondsworth, p. 406.

[82] Letter from Prof. B. G. Gowenlock to Prof. P. N. O'Farrell, 15 May 2003.

[83] *Ibid.*

[84] McWilliam, *op. cit.*, p. 406.

[85] *Ibid.*, p. 406.

[86] HWUA, *Court Minutes*, 4 February 1969, p. 38.

[87] HWUA, Ms A. E. Jones, Interview with Mr Peter Smith, former development officer, 17 August 2001.

[88] HWUA, *Court Minutes*, 21 October 1969, p. 6. The sports centre was ultimately to cost over £200,000.

[89] HWUA, *Court Minutes*, 12 May 1970.

[90] Boyle *op. cit.*, p. 73.

[91] HWUA, *Senate Minutes*, 20 January 1970.

[92] HWUA, Box 54, *Riccarton Site (3)*, Correspondence, March 1969 to December 1972, Letter from UGC to Principal Smith, 30 October 1970.

[93] HWUA, Tweedie, J. (1979) *Riccarton: The Story of the Midlothian Estate on Which Heriot-Watt University Now Stands*, Edinburgh.

[94] HWUA, *Riccarton Site (4)*, Correspondence, January 1973 to December 1978.

[95] *Ibid.*

[96] Carswell, J. (1985) *Government & Universities in Britain*, Cambridge, pp. 145, 139.

[97] *Ibid.*, p. 145.

[98] *Ibid.*, p. 147.

[99] *Ibid.*, p. 152.

[100] HWUA, *Report to the University Court on Procedures and Controls in Relation to Building Projects*, November 1976.

[101] *Ibid.*

[102] *Ibid.*

[103] HWUA, Letter from Sir Fred Dainton to Principal Burnett, 22 June 1978.

[104] *Ibid.*

[105] HWUA, *Court Papers*, 1 November 1977, Building Projects: Procedures and Controls.

[106] HWUA, Letter from Mr M. V. Pettett of the UGC to Mr Duncan Cameron, 4 August 1978.

[107] HWUA, Letter from Dr Edward Parkes, UGC Chairman, to Sir Douglas Haddow, 11 September 1980.

[108] HWUA, Box 72, Alex Anderson's Papers.

[109] HWUA, Letter from Prof. F. S. Dainton, UGC Chairman, to all universities, 18 January 1974.

[110] The university purchased a further 26 acre plot for £56,000 lying north of the research park and south of the Calder road and west of Riccarton Mains Road.

[111] HWUA, *Senate Minutes*, 25 October 1983.

[112] *Ibid.*

[113] HWUA, *Press Information*, 18 April 1990.

[114] HWUA, *Master Plan 2000*.

[115] HWUA, Prof. P. N. O'Farrell, Interview with Mr Duncan Cameron, 26 June 2001.

[116] *Ibid.*

[117] HWUA, *Court Minutes*, 12 July 1966.

[118] HWUA, Prof. P. N. O'Farrell and Ms A. E. Jones, Interview with Mr J. Coyle, 8 October 2002.

[119] Johnston, T. L. (1986) The exploitation of academic research on science parks. Paper presented to the UK Science Parks Association Annual Conference, London, p. 1.

[120] HWUA, Ct. 1-01 1193 Paper N, Research Park, Annual Report 1992–93.

[121] HWUA, Prof. P. N. O'Farrell and Ms A. E. Jones, Interview with Mr J. Coyle, 8 October 2002.

[122] *Ibid.*

[123] HWUA, Ct. 1-01 1193 Paper N, Research Park Annual Report, 1992–93.

[124] HWUA, Scott, J. (1995) Future of the Research Park (minuted).

[125] Clark, B. R. (1998) *Creating Entrepreneurial Universities: Organizational Patterns of Transformation*, October, p. 72.

[126] I am grateful to Mrs G. McFadzean, director of TRS, for supplying this information.

[127] Employment data kindly provided by Mr Derek Brown, TRS.

Chapter Nine

The Flexible University

I don't know Ma'am, why they make
all this fuss about education if none
of the Pagets can read or write, and
they get on well enough.
Lord Melbourne to Queen Victoria

MBA graduates, July 1995. Photograph: Ken Paterson

Bye Bye Blackboard

Heriot-Watt University has developed a reputation as the pre-eminent institution in Scotland and a leader in the UK in the development of distance learning courses. Before the concept of distance learning became a fundamental component of the university's strategy in the 1990s, there had been one or two local departmental initiatives by dedicated enthusiasts. The earliest of these was the Computer Assisted Learning in Maths (CALM) programme pioneered by Professor Cliff Beevers in the early 1980s with a £125,000 grant from the Computer Board for the UK.[1] CALM took three years to develop and the computerised tutorial system was introduced into first-year service classes (not honours) in mathematics in 1986. CALM was especially helpful to middle-range students, and the software, which won the first Bank of Scotland Award to Higher Education in 1985, was sold to several other universities.

Another novel initiative, with the aim of widening access in the Highlands and Islands, which was implemented in collaboration with the University of Aberdeen, was an undergraduate Pathways to Higher Education in Science project. This programme, for which SHEFC provided £60,000 for course development, was introduced in 1995 and offered a flexible approach with teaching in the evenings at the two main university campuses and at study centres throughout the Highlands and Islands of Scotland. Students studied part-time in order to accumulate 24 credits which enabled them to enter the second year of a full-time degree programme at one of the two universities, or elsewhere. Heriot-Watt provides courses in mathematics, biology, computer science, and physics, while Aberdeen supplies geology, chemistry, land management and contributions to biology and computer science. The courses use a range of specially developed learning materials but the core of the programme is the interactive workshop. Students come together with a tutor and other students for simultaneous workshop sessions at 11 study centres on the mainland and 13 on the outer islands which are connected to each other by a variety of systems, initially whiteboard technology and later videoconferencing. The mathematics course has been taught since its inception by Professor Jack Carr, a dedicated scholar, who paradoxically has more interaction with his students in the virtual workshops than with his undergraduates in the lecture theatre even though, when using whiteboard technology, he could not see them.[2] The students attend local libraries, village halls, community centres and schoolrooms scattered across the far reaches of the Highlands and Islands. Among Professor Carr's early students was Martin, an oyster and scallop fisherman on the island of Stronsay in Orkney, who wished to understand the population dynamics of his fish farm, but being two hours by ferry from the nearest college, he had abandoned the idea of further study.[3] Professor Carr's coursework is also used in the university's first-year mathematics programmes and has enabled the lecture load for students to be reduced from four lectures per week to one lecture per week.[4]

MacFarlane's Vision

When Alistair MacFarlane become principal of Heriot-Watt University, he articulated a vision of a major shift away from the lecture and inflexible timetabling towards self-learning, with interactive computer-assisted learning revolutionising university teaching. To this end, Principal MacFarlane, with the support of the Scottish Development Agency, established an Institute of Computer-Based Learning (ICBL) in 1990 with the following aims, among others: to pursue research in computer-based learning with respect to its impact on teaching and training processes; to develop a range of highly supportive and flexible self-learning environments; and to utilise advanced software techniques within the learning and training environments being developed.[5]

The aims of this initiative to facilitate lifelong learning and access were consistent with the philosophy championed by Leonard Horner in 1821. Principal MacFarlane, who expended considerable time and energy on this project, intended that ICBL would stimulate the development of computer-based learning throughout the university, and conduct research and teaching. ICBL ran the Impact Programme in the early 1990s, funded by all the UK funding councils, in which Heriot-Watt staff were seconded to the training programme for a term after which they returned to their departments with an understanding of the potential for applying CBL to their subject area.

Professor Roy Leitch became director of information services in 1996 with responsibility for ICBL; he subsequently became assistant principal for teaching and learning in 1998. Much of the inspiration for Professor Leitch's thinking and motivation came from Principal MacFarlane, who 'altered the culture of Heriot-Watt and placed it ahead of other Scottish universities in computer-based learning'.[6] Professor Leitch adopted Alistair MacFarlane's basic approach and implemented it, with the 'strong support' of Principal Archer since 1997.[7] The

Professor Roy Leitch and Principal John Archer watch a student demonstrate the Scholar programme to Education Minister, Dr Sam Galbraith, 2000. Photograph: Douglas McBride

learning technology strategy articulated by Principal MacFarlane adopted a holistic approach with student learning at its core. The policy was not technology-driven but was inspired by educational objectives to enable on-campus students to study flexibly at their own pace, and to initiate a shift from an intensive lecture mode to student-centred learning. To implement this strategy, the university established the Learning Technology Centre (LTC), an umbrella organisation under the direction of Dr Roger Rist, to integrate the activities of ICBL, the Television Centre and Media Services Units, and a new Teaching and Learning Technology Service (TLTS). While the role of ICBL was redefined to develop a portfolio of research on pedagogical approaches using mainly external funds, TLTS was created to train staff and to help departments within the university to produce computer-based educational software for undergraduate and postgraduate courses. The university strategy was to adopt an integrated approach to flexible learning by establishing a central service to facilitate the adaptation and diffusion of best practice across the institution.[8]

The establishment of the LTC was a recognition that profound cultural and organisational change was needed to increase the use of CBL in a systematic way throughout all departments. This approach differentiated Heriot-Watt from most other universities where the adoption of new technology in teaching tended to be a craft-based activity confined to enthusiastic individuals. Here the process was more holistic and industrialised; the TLTS operated in partnership with academic departments in developing course materials and assessment methods in an organised and professional way. The TLTS introduced its Innovation in Teaching and Learning Programme in 1994, in which departments submitted proposals and a committee funded those where new methods and tools were being developed. This was superseded in 1996 by the Strategic Open Learning Development Programme (SOLD) with funding from the university of £2 million over six years. The departments supplied the authors who worked with the technologists of the LTC to develop the materials. The outputs from this programme included five undergraduate degree courses in management education, a paper-based programme supported on the web and delivered through support centres, with 1,200 students in two Malaysian universities; an MSc in IT; an MSc course in Arabic interpreting and translating, an MSc in construction management; and the Scholar programme. Notwithstanding, other important distance learning initiatives were developed outwith the SOLD programme, most notably the Next programme in petroleum engineering and an MSc in brewing and distilling.

The Scholar Programme

The concept of the Scholar programme, although clearly informed by earlier developments, such as the CALM project in mathematics, was formulated by Professor Roy Leitch in 1998.[9] This was a period of change in Scottish education with the introduction of Advanced Highers and a new Higher curriculum. Professor Leitch's notion was to develop courseware that would be compatible with Advanced Highers, HNC and the first year of Scottish university honours courses. Scholar, an academic collaboration designed to increase access and social inclusion in further and higher education while offering support to pupils and teachers, was launched in June 2000. It provides pupils and staff with flexibly delivered interactive materials over the internet and was piloted from August 2000 in four education authorities – City of Edinburgh, Midlothian, East Lothian and Scottish Borders – and five further education colleges – Stevenson, Telford, Jewel and Esk, Lauder, and Fife.

The majority of the authors were schoolteachers who were seconded to the programme. Each subject team was headed by a subject leader and they met fortnightly under the convenership of Professor Philip John with representatives from the LTC (Nils Tomes) and Gerry Toner.[10] This group managed the authoring process to meet the tight deadlines and was responsible for developing the e-learning pedagogy, quality assurance and assessment policy. The quality of the materials, the associated staff development programme – which first introduced the concept to somewhat sceptical teachers – and the missionary work of Gerry Toner, a former teacher and advisor to schools on education and industry, played an important role in convincing schools to participate. Through a major feat of organisation, the Advanced Higher materials were launched in August 2001 and the Higher materials one year later. By autumn 2002, all 32 local education authorities in Scotland were subscribing to the Scholar programme, making it one of the largest online interactive learning programmes in the world,[11] with 9,600 Advanced Higher students, 36,000 at Higher level in over 400 schools, 120 Higher National students, and 700 teachers and lecturers. The university is also delivering the Scholar programme to the Open University of Malaysia, where 1,000 science teachers have been upgraded, and to Agder University College in Norway. Finally, in 2004, a contract was signed with the Department of Education and Science to introduce the Scholar programme into all state schools in England. The Learning and Skills Council has funded a pilot project in three areas – Cumbria, Kent and the West Midlands. It is intended that Scholar will be implemented countrywide following an evaluation of the pilot programme.

The Scholar interactive courseware is designed to enrich the curriculum and to reduce the barriers faced by some students in the transition from school to further or higher education. Students can choose to study at their own pace in the classroom, online through networked computers, or from the associated printed study guides at a time and place that suits them. The online complementary text materials were developed by teams of subject specialists from schools, colleges and the university. Scholar has also fostered a virtual learning community with e-discussion groups where pupils and staff can communicate with others around the country. The Scholar virtual network encourages students to take responsibility for their own learning, thereby easing the transition from school to university. The Scholar programme offers five core subject that provide a route into science and engineering courses: biological science, chemistry, computer science, mathematics and physics.

The Scholar Forum, a not-for-profit organisation composed of representatives from schools, colleges and the university, was established in May 2000 to deliver the Scholar materials within the partner institutions. It is essentially a 'virtual college' giving access to the online facilities complemented by local tutorial support provided by the teachers and lecturers within the participating institutions. The online facilities include online texts with embedded activities and examples, automatically marked formative assessments, simulations to promote understanding of more challenging areas, animations and visualisation to bring diagrams and equations to life, interactive tutorial exercises, online discussion groups that link together learners and teachers, and an online professional development forum where teachers can share their expertise and discuss issues.

The Scholar materials are under continuous development; the study guides and the web materials are revised every year informed by teacher feedback at the annual training programmes. The university has also integrated Scholar material into its on-campus courses. LTC technologies and production techniques therefore underpin the Scholar programme and make it feasible to undertake a project on the scale envisaged.[12] LTC provides support in the form of staff training materials, access to laboratories and equipment, and assessments.

The Interactive University

To support the e-business sector in Scotland and to assist the globalisation of Scottish education, Scottish Enterprise invested £2.3 million to establish the Interactive University in 2002. The objective of this initiative is to stimulate the development, marketing and delivery of Scottish educational programmes, especially abroad. Professor Roy Leitch has been appointed chief executive and, since Heriot-Watt was the original subscriber, the Interactive University promoted its products exclusively during the first year. The LTC has been seconded to the Interactive University for three years and Heriot-Watt's computer-based technology and part of its intellectual property rights have been licensed to it. The Interactive University is the mechanism through which Heriot-Watt and other Scottish universities aim to globalise their courses using the distributed learning model. Much depends on this initiative if Heriot-Watt is to achieve a return on its investment of over £2 million – of which £700,000 was provided by the Scottish Executive – to support the development of the Scholar Forum.

One Man Changes the MBA Landscape: the Genesis of an Academic Entrepreneur

The Heriot-Watt distance learning MBA (DLMBA), the only MBA programme that penetrates all continents and cultures, is one of the most innovative and successful learning initiatives in the UK. It has effectively doubled the size of the university. Such a radical change in a university, for the most part, is not accidental or incidental. Transformation normally occurs when a number of senior individuals come together across a university over several years to change, by means of organised initiative, how the institution is oriented.[13] Acting from below, individual faculty members and administrators are limited in what they can achieve. Because universities are so resistant to innovation, it is rare that a solitary entrepreneur can sustain the energy and ethusiasm needed to effect a radical transformation in both the pedagogy and scale of a university's provision. Yet such a phenomenon has occurred at Heriot-Watt University.

Keith Lumsden was born in 1935 in Bathgate, an unpretentious town some 18 miles west of Edinburgh. His father, Robert, sometime actor and policeman, eventually opened a florist's shop in the town. By the time Keith was 12, it was apparent that there was 'something quite special about him – a degree of self-confidence that set him apart from his peers'.[14] Lumsden went up to Edinburgh University in 1954 to read engineering, a subject that he did not find congenial. A car crash and severe concussion caused him to miss a year of university, and during this time he decided to switch to economics. While he was a student, Lumsden would rise twice weekly at 5.00 A.M. and drive from Bathgate to the flower market in Glasgow. Here he faced the problem of deciding what quantities of various flowers to purchase, given that most varieties have a shelf life of only a week. Although the dates of weddings are known in advance, deaths are totally unpredictable; yet the florist business lives by people dying as unsold flowers can be used in a wreath. Hence the young student learned one of the fundamental characteristics of entrepreneurship – first observed by the Irish financier Richard Cantillon in 1755 – that the key role of the entrepreneur is to bear uncertainty and to take the action required to make a profit (or loss).[15] After graduating from Edinburgh University, he moved to Stanford University in 1960 to become an instructor in economics and to embark on a PhD.

In 1962 George Stigler, a future Nobel laureate, visited Stanford and suggested that the methods of teaching economics were both inefficient and ineffective.[16] This raised serious questions (and doubts) about the traditional approach to teaching the subject – three lectures and one tutorial per week.[17] Serendipity, not for the only time in Keith Lumsden's career, intervened in the form of an approach from a psychologist, Allen Calvin, who introduced Lumsden to the programming technique, a methodology developed to disaggregate complex ideas into small, carefully constructed steps, each one requiring written responses, thereby ensuring continuous participation by the student. McGraw-Hill published Lumsden's book *The Free Enterprise System* (with accompanying test booklet and teacher's manual) in 1963, the first ever programmed text in economics. He subsequently wrote other programmed texts for the school and university markets. Although chance encounters can lead to fruitful cooperation, it was also highly beneficial that Lumsden was embedded in the rich scholastic networks centred on Stanford University, interacting with scholars of the calibre of Stigler, Calvin and Kenneth Arrow.

Lumsden conducted a controlled experiment on programmed learning and showed that it was at least as effective as conventional lectures and textbooks, as measured by performance in a common examination.[18] This study served as a benchmark for the application of scientific method in economics education and helped to establish the legitimacy of research into a hitherto neglected field. Meanwhile in 1968 Lumsden completed his PhD on 'The Effects of Excess Demand and Excess Supply in the Tramp Shipping Industry' while simultaneously publishing programmed learning texts, conducting research on the factors influencing student learning in economics, and also research at the Stanford Research Institute on the economic potential of countries deemed to be a nuclear threat.

In 1967–68 Keith Lumsden spent nine months at Stanford's Italian campus in Florence. While in Italy he received a letter written in a spidery hand and archaic English from a Mr Paul Stobart, eldest son of Esmée Fairbairn and a trustee of the Esmée Fairbairn Trust, a man who was always proud to say that he had a grey pinstripe suit made in Savile Row in 1931 which still fitted him.[19] Esmée Fairbairn had been born a Bethel, from a landowning family of some antiquity in Yorkshire. She married Hugh Stobart, a director of the North Eastern Railway, and their son Paul, the first of four, was born in 1911. In the early 1920s, Hugh sent Esmée (properly chaperoned) to Kenya to inspect a property he had purchased there.[20] En route to Nairobi, in the best traditions of a romantic novel, Esmée fell in love with a dashing young Australian called Ian Fairbairn. He joined the unit trust company M&G as a director in 1934. In 1941, once her sons had grown up, Esmée left Hugh and married Ian Fairbairn. During the war, they lived in a small flat in Kensington; Ian doubled up his City work with an administrative post in uniform and Esmée pioneered the development of the Citizens' Advice Bureau service. One night in August 1944, a V1 'buzz bomb' cut out over the Thames and glided down towards the Kensington flat.[21] Esmée was killed and Ian, alone with her in the sitting room, was left unhurt but disconsolate for the rest of his life. A trust in Esmée's memory was established in 1961. Ian made over to it the bulk of his own holding in M&G. Paul Stobart purchased enough of the outstanding shares to give the trust 50.1% of the total capital, and ultimate control of the M&G Group came to rest in non-commercial hands. The primary objective of the trust has always been to enhance an understanding of the issues of finance and economics at all levels of the population.

Paul Stobart's letter to Keith Lumsden referred to articles by Professor Alan Thompson in the *Times* and Harold Wincott in the *Financial Times* which described the research into methods of teaching economics that Lumsden had been doing in Stanford. Stobart invited Lumsden to a lunch at the City Club in London, hosted by G. P. S. MacPherson (an honorary graduate of Heriot-Watt and a former Scottish rugby international); Harold Wincott, John and Ian Fairbairn were also in attendance. Lumsden was invited to prepare a paper on the current state of economics education. With characteristic candour, he argued that economists were 'quite unscientific about teaching economics; there should be more specification of objectives, more controlled experiments and some evaluation of how efficiently resources are being used in teaching economics'.[22] Keith Lumsden, even as a 32-year-old, was articulating an ambitious research agenda, envisaging a national study at secondary level to answer these six questions:

- What economics is being taught and by whom?
- How well is it being taught?
- How much economics do secondary school pupils and their teachers know?
- What economics should be taught?
- Can multiple-choice tests be developed to discriminate between students and help schools evaluate their performance against national norms?
- How can the efficiency of different methods of teaching including conventional teaching, programmed instruction, television and computers be evaluated?

The Esmée Fairbairn Trust responded by offering a grant of £50,000 for the Economics Education Project (EEP). While visiting friends in Edinburgh, Keith met Professor Tom Johnston (who had taught him at Edinburgh University) and he offered to host the research at Heriot-Watt. Together with Dick Attiyeh, Lumsden returned to Britain for the academic year 1969–70. The sheer scale of this research was a reflection of Lumsden's organisational ability and effectiveness. The sample included 4,000 students in 40 universities and 6,000 students in

Charles Ritchie, Principal Tom
Johnston, Professor Keith
Lumsden and Professor Richard
Attiyeh contemplate the future
of economics education, 1969.
Photograph: John Dewar
Studios

colleges and schools across the UK. Each student completed an intelligence test
and sat special exams at the beginning and end of their first-year economics course.
The study concluded that the factor which determines how far a student progresses
in economics was primarily individual aptitude, not type of school, course
organisation or teacher qualifications.[23] The Esmée Fairbairn Trust awarded a
further grant of £87,000 to extend the research by conducting a longitudinal
study. Since Keith Lumsden was returning to Stanford, Alex Scott, a classical
music loving economist, was recruited as a research assistant to work on the project
and so began a fruitful working relationship that has lasted for over three decades.

The Esmée Fairbairn Research Centre (TEFRC) was established in the
economics department in 1970. Keith Lumsden returned full-time as director in
October 1975. The key project in progress was that funded by the DES to test the
impact of various innovative teaching techniques on different types of students in
various educational settings. The techniques included TIPS (a teaching
information processing system that provided feedback to staff and students), case
studies, programmed learning, and computer simulations. Nine universities, five
polytechnics and one business school cooperated in designing and implementing
innovative courses and three institutions acted as controls; over 2,500 students
were involved in 19 innovative courses. Participating institutions adopted one of
four teaching strategies: a conventional course (three lectures and one tutorial per
week) was taught by the control group; the conventional course was scrapped and

innovative techniques were substituted for tutorials and essays; conventional inputs were reduced and innovative techniques were partially substituted; and innovative techniques were added on to existing conventional inputs. Each of the 15 institutions set a common examination comprising multiple-choice questions, a case and essays.[24]

The most radical finding was the lack of any relationship between the mix of teaching techniques used and performance outcomes in the examinations. Students on courses with high resource inputs, such as tutorials and lectures, did not perform better than those where innovative techniques were deployed.[25] A significant proportion of the first-year students in the samples were effectively distance learners as they seldom attended lectures or tutorials, confirming that there are people who are capable of learning at a distance. This provided an important research underpinning for the pedagogy that Professor Lumsden was developing for a distance learning MBA programme, as did another important finding that the correlations between scores on various *types* of assessment (cases, essays and multiple choice tests) were low, suggesting that different types of questions measure distinct aspects of economics comprehension.[26] The optimal exam should therefore incorporate all three modes of assessment: multiple choice, testing knowledge and simple applications; case studies examining complex applications and synthesis; and essays exploring synthesis and evaluation. These research findings were subsequently embedded in the design of the distance learning materials.

TEFRC Diversifies

In the mid 1970s, Professor Lumsden diversified the portfolio of services offered to the business community by TEFRC by introducing business executive courses. One methodology in which TEFRC specialised and used as the core of its executive courses was simulation. The first of these, *Running the British Economy*, was published by Longman and became the most widely used economics software package in the UK. It was originally disseminated through an annual competition for school economics students which started in 1976; sponsored by BP and Hewlett-Packard, some 407 schools were participating by 1988 sending over 1,000 teams and around 5,000 students to 31 regional centres. The software package had sold over 3,000 copies worldwide by 1988. Another simulation, *Stratship*, a strategic planning simulation of a shipping company, was developed in 1980 and was soon afloat providing a programme of management training for Scandinavian shipping companies. These and other simulations brought TEFRC to national and international prominence. Two of them, *Running the British Economy* and *Stratship*, are still in use to this day.

In order to continue developing its standing as an international centre for intensive executive programmes, the university needed suitable accommodation: a restaurant, quality bedrooms and specialised teaching facilities. The university provided the restaurant and bedrooms and Professor Lumsden raised the money for the teaching facility. The cost of the Business Executive Centre (BEC) was £764,000, of which the Esmée Fairbairn Trust granted £100,000. A further £200,000 was raised from companies, and several corporations, including Volvo Transport, Hewlett-Packard, Atlantic Container Line, Pieda, and Transtema, donated £25,000 each for seminar rooms. The building was opened by Paul Stobart, following an eloquent speech, on 13 June 1988. However, by 1992 it was apparent that the campus had a shortage of bedrooms suitable for executives. Keith Lumsden again made a case to the Esmée Fairbairn Trust and received a £500,000 grant and an interest-free loan of £500,000 repayable in five annual instalments from 1998. The Paul Stobart building was opened in December 1993. This was the final grant from the trust; its support between 1968 and 1993, both for research and infrastructure, totalled £3.7 million at 2002 prices, and was the essential foundation on which a global MBA was built.

The World's First Global MBA

The concept of distance learning is far from new. The English phonographer Isaac Pitman started teaching by correspondence in the UK in 1837, and in 1850 the University of London began to offer distance courses to the inhabitants of British colonies such as India and Australia.[27] Keith Lumsden was convinced that there was a large latent demand for education from individuals and organisations for whom the opportunity costs of attendance at an on-campus programme were prohibitive – a niche of mature, ambitious and motivated people, usually married and in their thirties. He drew on his wealth of research findings to design a distance learning MBA that would enable anyone to undertake the programme using self-contained course texts and without attendance.

The award of a grant of £186,000 from the Esmée Fairbairn Trust in 1978 to develop distance learning materials heralded a change in the governance of TEFRC: it ceased to be part of the Department of Economics and was reconstituted in 1979 as an independent research centre managed by a board. Keith Lumsden specified that the course texts be written to conform to a basic pattern which would embed the radical innovations derived from his research. First, a concept was introduced, expanded and applied to real business situations; it was then rounded off with a variety of examples. Theoretical exposition, therefore, was always accompanied by example. Second, all the texts were divided into modules, each of which was accompanied by a set of multiple-choice questions to test basic understanding and application of the concepts, and short essays and case studies with worked solutions to test higher levels of comprehension and synthesis. Model answers were provided for all types of question. Third, all courses included final practice exams with solutions so that students could assess their preparedness for sitting the university's exams. Fourth, all compulsory courses had accompanying comprehensive software packages: interactive programmes designed to provide the kind of feedback normally supplied by a tutor together with simulations and real-world databases.

MBA programmes tend to be very homogeneous across institutions, but while there is general agreement on content, there are substantial differences of emphasis and pedagogy. Keith Lumsden realised that conventional routes to higher education – on-campus programmes using traditional textbooks – did not meet the diversity of educational needs of the 1990s and beyond. The originality of his contribution was to invent, test and develop a pedagogy that was highly differentiated from the competition: dedicated, self-contained materials with accompanying software, designed specifically for distance learners. Most competitors were using conventional textbooks with additional readings, assignments and some live tuition; but Lumsden realised that it was very difficult for distance learners to study on their own using conventional textbooks. True distance learning – no provision for live teaching on campus and no assignments to be returned – was desirable to allow participants optimum flexibility to pursue their careers without interruption while putting new knowledge to work immediately. Students may study at their own pace; they may sample one course to judge if it is suitable for them, with or without examination; or they may accumulate examination passes towards the MBA. It enables students to cope with situations such as changing jobs, travelling constantly, relocating to another country, or taking on more responsibilities at home or work.

Open access is permitted to any individual part of the programme, but it requires evidence of academic ability before the prospective student is permitted to matriculate, i.e. to become part of the institution's academic community. Students have matriculated by four routes: 45 per cent have an undergraduate degree with first- or second-class honours; 9 per cent have a higher degree; 15 per cent have a professional qualification of at least degree standard; and 31 per cent have obtained passes in two compulsory courses, or one pass and one exemption. Up to December 1994 the pass rate in the examinations of those with no prior qualifications who matriculated via the two-course route was 84 per cent. This was the same as for those students who matriculated with undergraduate degrees and for those with higher degrees. The filter of the two-course route is therefore efficient in two ways. First, it maintains the academic standards of the degree by eliminating those individuals who, judged by their own performances in the MBA courses studied and examined, are unlikely to obtain the degree. Second, it prevents such individuals from engaging in further expenditure which, in the view of the university, will not yield them the expected return.

Keith Lumsden outlined his strategy for the DLMBA to the Faculty of Economic and Social Studies in 1979. Many staff of the university were sceptical, if not hostile, to the concept of awarding an MBA to students who would never appear on campus to attend a class. The issue, however, was not distance learning versus on-campus programmes but, more fundamentally, how different groups of students learn. Professor John Small, chairman of the Esmée Fairbairn Research Centre, 'had faith in this wild idea'.[28] Moreover, since Keith Lumsden had raised the money to conduct the research and develop the materials, the university was not at financial risk. It is highly unlikely that an 'old established university would have taken this on ... because of vested interests and the innovativeness of the ideas'.[29] The support of Principal Alistair MacFarlane, an expert on computer-based learning, was 'really consistent' and he was prepared to give Professor Lumsden the 'autonomy he wanted because he believed Keith could deliver'.[30] Principal MacFarlane regarded it as 'a genuinely innovative and imaginative development' and that 'it would never have succeeded had it been embedded in a conventional department'.[31]

A contract was signed with Pitman Publishing in 1989. Each course was offered initially at £250, to give a total cost of £2,250 for nine course texts; the accompanying software packages were sold separately. After 12 years of research and development, recruitment of authors from leading business schools throughout the world, and persuasion of a sometimes reluctant Heriot-Watt administration and faculty, the distance learning master of business administration (DLMBA) programme was launched in November 1990. The Open University, Manchester University, Henley Management College and Strathclyde University all had small programmes for distance learners at the time, but each required live tuition. Yet the uniqueness of the Heriot-Watt product, with its highly differentiated pedagogy, conferred a first-mover advantage in the marketplace. Other institutions did not try to replicate it precisely, in part because of high development costs and in part because of the difficulty of persuading academics to set aside a year to write true distance learning materials, so radically different from conventional textbooks. Pitman, in contrast to competing universities, was prepared to invest expertise and finance into marketing the programme.

A key element of continuity has been provided by Alick Kitchin, who has been in charge of marketing the MBA from its inception and who managed the totality of the relationship between Edinburgh Business School (EBS) and Pitman from 1993 to 1999, and subsequently with publishers Financial Times Knowledge until August 2001, and Pearson since August 2001. Kitchin, in consultation with Keith Lumsden, made a bold decision not to sell the course texts as books but to distribute them through a network of educationalists, private sector colleges, and training institutions.[32] They took it to the market niche themselves with rapid early take-up, especially in Hong Kong, Singapore and Australia. The second phase of marketing started in 1991 and involved mailing individual people such as doctors, dentists, lawyers, engineers, accountants and so on. Sales grew rapidly, with 3,459 texts sold in 1991 (Figure 9.1). Within three and a half years of its launch in November 1990, there were more than 8,000 students in over 100 countries worldwide. This performance earned TEFRC the Queen's Award for Export Achievement in 1994.[33] Growth of the DLMBA continued unabated, with course text sales peaking at 18,692 in 1997, until a decline caused by the currency collapse in South-east Asia (Figure 9.1). Sales started to recover in 2001, further

Principal Alistair MacFarlane, Professor Keith Lumsden and Rt Hon. Lord Provost Norman Irons with the Queen's Award for Export Achievement, 1994. Photograph: Ian Southern

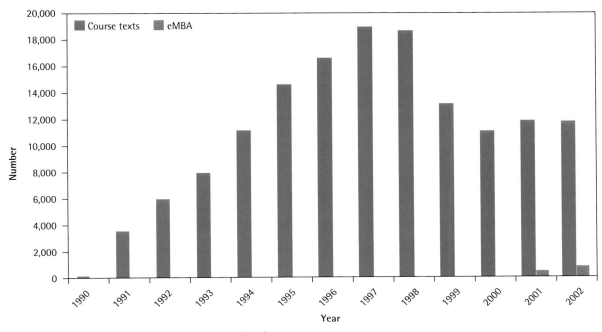

Figure 9.1 Total course text and eMBA sales by year

boosted by the launch of the internet-based MBA. Since the launch in November 1990, a total of 145,725 course texts had been sold worldwide by 2003. A second Queen's Award for Export Achievement followed in 1999, making EBS the only UK university department to win two of these prestigious awards.

By 2003 some 50 per cent of sales were via third parties and 50 per cent to individuals.[34] Some students received live tuition from the start, and the proportion of students studying for the MBA via the distributed learning model, whereby they attend an institution for classes, has now risen to around one-third of the total. Under a new UK quality regime from the mid 1990s, Heriot-Watt is responsible for the learning experience in the support centres, all of which must be approved. This prompted a third phase of the marketing in which the university rationalised provision by closing down poor performers and expanding better quality providers so that there are now 20 approved support centres globally. The 10 largest accounts now generate 80 per cent of the turnover of £2 million annually through third parties; sales to individuals total around £4 million each year.[35] By April 2003 some 6,671 people had been awarded an MBA by distance learning from Heriot-Watt University, averaging around 1,000 per annum in 1999–2002 (Figure 9.2). Students are 82 per cent male, 18 per cent female and have an average age of 34, ranging from an 84-year-old man in Illinois to a 15-year-old in Ontario.

The University of Phoenix, with 10,984 students in 2003, and Heriot-Watt,

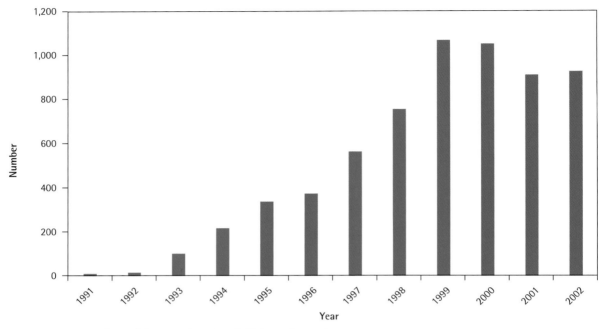

Figure 9.2 Number of distance learning MBA graduates by year

with 10,376, are the two largest distance learning MBA programmes in the world.[36] The Heriot-Watt programme is unique, however, in its degree of global penetration, transcending boundaries of language and culture to a greater extent than any competitor in the world. It is the only MBA that is successful in Europe, Asia, the Middle East, Africa and North America, with students currently registered from 150 countries worldwide (Figure 9.3). In terms of active students, defined as those who have taken an exam in the past year, there are 1,200 in Singapore and Malaysia, 1,000 in Israel, over 1,000 in the UK, 1,100 in Canada, 900 in the USA, and 650 in the West Indies (Figure 9.3). There are also a few students whose immediate whereabouts are unknown because they are on the high seas, and several more whose whereabouts are known with certainty because they are guests of their respective governments. Indeed some of the 300 examination centres worldwide are located inside the walls of penitentiaries. Payment of fees can sometimes be difficult for students from countries with exchange rate problems. One student offered to pay in carved African hippos, an offer rejected on the grounds that the relationship between carved hippos and pounds sterling had not yet been established.[37]

Markets such as Hong Kong, Malaysia and Singapore, where the university was originally successful, are now mature, with at least 50 competitors. In Asia the competition is primarily from Australian universities offering a low-price distance

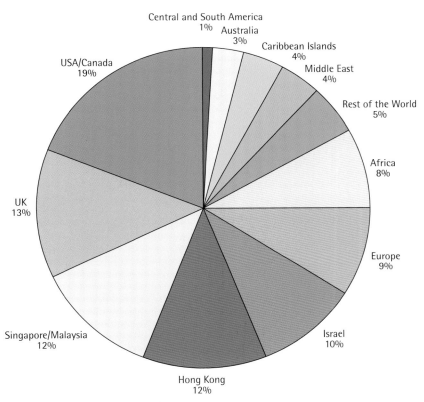

Figure 9.3 Distribution of MBA students by area

learning product for £3,000–£4,000 (compared with £5,400 for the current Heriot-Watt programme, rising to £7,200 in 2004) with faculty flying in to provide parts of the programme.[38] The school competes successfully against the cheaper Australian MBA because the brand reputation permits the university to charge a price premium. The fastest-growing markets in 2002 were Trinidad and Tobago, Zambia and India. The thrust of the marketing strategy is to open up new markets, especially in China, where a strategic alliance has been forged with Shanghai Jiao Tong University. The course texts have been translated into Chinese, Hebrew and Spanish (to develop the South American market) and will soon be available in Arabic.

One key element in the success of the distance learning MBA programme is the administrative support infrastructure. This coordinates three sets of examinations each year in 300 centres worldwide, manages the grading of 20,000 exam scripts, and efficiently processes all appeals. No batch of exam scripts has ever been lost. Another important factor behind the reputation of this course has been the maintenance of standards. As grade inflation has swept through British higher education like a bush fire, the failure rate on the Edinburgh Business School MBA exams has remained remarkably constant at approximately 25 per cent.

By the mid 1990s, senior staff were aware that the internet would transform dramatically the distance learning landscape and that TEFRC needed to be in the forefront of competitive changes. Professor Lumsden made a decision regarded as very risky by Pitman; he invested £300,000 per annum over three years to develop an e-based MBA. Some providers assumed that an exclusively e-based product was the solution, forgetting that people learn in different ways. Students opting for the e-based MBA also receive the course texts, since the combination of e-learning and distance learning is a powerful and complementary learning tool. Furthermore, the Heriot-Watt version harnesses the new technology's intrinsic capabilities rather than merely apes bankrupt classroom teaching forms. The Heriot-Watt e-based MBA supplies enhanced content, more examples and past papers and is an interactive product that provides targeted feedback as the student works through it. The MBA became a single product in January 2004 by integrating the web-based materials with the complementary course texts; the price per course rose from £600 to £800, or £7,200 for the complete programme. The MBA was therefore repositioned in a higher market segment to capture the joint benefits of the computer and the course textbooks. Also in 2004, EBS introduced specialist MBAs, more electives, masters courses and a doctorate in business administration, available by a variety of modes, including distance learning.

The Esmée Fairbairn Research Centre evolved into the Edinburgh Business School in 1995 and two years later it became a charitable company limited by guarantee as a wholly-owned subsidiary of Heriot-Watt University. It had become a 'university within a university'. This new organisational structure was necessary to manage rapid growth, while the academic branding of the courses remained under the auspices of the university. At the request of Principal MacFarlane, EBS agreed in 1996 to assume responsibility for the taught on campus MBA programmes, previously located in the School of Management. This enabled EBS to integrate the full-time, part-time and consortium MBAs with the distance learning version to produce one flexible MBA programme with a common syllabus, course texts, examinations and external examiners. This permits all MBA students to study for the same degree under a variety of modes, with the additional opportunity to transfer between modes of study during the time of enrolment. Since distance learning and on-campus MBA students sit common examinations, those who pass demonstrate that there is equality of learning in its cognitive aspects. To integrate the MBA courses and provide adequate teaching space, the university granted EBS consent to construct a prestigious 4,400 square metre building to its own specification using accumulated reserves of £6 million. This was opened in 1998.

The Edinburgh Business School.
Photograph: Tarquil Cramer

The public persona that Professor Lumsden projects is that of the brash, domineering chief executive who tends to ride roughshod over people, who pays scant attention to what they think, and is very effective at getting his own way. In reality he is more complex. Professor Alex Scott, a deep-thinking stalwart of EBS who has made a profound contribution to the development of the MBA programme and has worked with Professor Lumsden on many research projects, reports that Lumsden has a unique insight into the human condition and 'an amazing touch with people'.[39] His management style is, unsurprisingly, an

Opposite: The atrium at Edinburgh Business School

extension of his personality, so he is not an instinctive delegator; he tends to interact regularly with a large number of staff and to work closely with them. Many of his appointments were made largely on the basis of personal qualities rather than qualifications. Professor Gavin Kennedy, for example, an expert on Adam Smith and an authority on negotiation, who came to Heriot-Watt in 1982 to a chair in defence economics research, moved to TEFRC in 1988 largely because Keith Lumsden realised, among other things, that he had a unique expertise in negotiating and writing contracts.

Professor Lumsden articulated a global vision to create the largest distance learning MBA in the world. He had the organisational flair and determination to mobilise the resources necessary to create a world-class global business, and the qualities of leadership necessary to persuade able people to work with him to deliver the vision. He has done more than anyone at Heriot-Watt to shift the emphasis from teaching to learning, from set ways of doing things to flexibility. A rebel in a university setting, he exhibits the restlessness of the entrepreneur, and a latent desire for independence that makes him fundamentally antipathetic to the rules, procedures and committee decision-making processes of universities. The university, after much soul searching, ultimately had the foresight to tolerate an

MBA graduates, July 1995.
Photograph: Ken Paterson

iconoclastic entrepreneur and to give him just sufficient autonomy to create an MBA programme that has generated more than £100 million in income between 1991 and 2003 and boasts thousands of satisfied alumni in more countries across the world than any other.

The MBA and Other Distance Learning Initiatives

The DLMBA has influenced the whole direction of the university's strategy on distance learning, both directly and indirectly. The success of the MBA and the two Queen's Awards for Export Achievement have influenced distance learning initiatives across the university by showing that a professional operation of large scale could be launched and efficiently delivered worldwide from Edinburgh. This helped to create a climate of confidence and to build a momentum within the institution that enabled other distance learning programmes to be introduced, programmes which might not have happened otherwise. The undergraduate distance learning course in management – like the MBA a paper-based product with internet support – was modelled on the MBA, although being undergraduate all students must also enrol for tuition at approved support centres. The methodology of the distance learning MSc in brewing and distilling, originally developed by Professor Graham Stewart at the behest of South African Breweries and introduced in 1997, was initially paper-based following the example of the DLMBA. Subsequently, an e-based version has been introduced. Similarly, following discussions with the staff of EBS, the distance learning MSc in petroleum engineering, launched in 1999, also adopted a paper-based product and uses the MBA learning centres abroad. The DLMBA also influenced the development of the Scholar programme in two respects: it demonstrated the value of using high-quality content and it emphasised the importance of closely controlling the exam process.[40] Conversely, the department of building engineering, which launched its first distance learning MSc programme in acoustics in the early 1980s using videos supplemented by a summer school, introduced an MSc in construction management in 1992, based initially on course notes and later developed into textbooks. Building engineering, in terms of the evolution of distance learning, has been the Gondwanaland of Heriot-Watt (although on the north side of the campus) in that it developed its programmes completely independently of the DLMBA. All the distance learning programmes outwith EBS generate approximately £3 million per annum, of which the BA in management contributes £1 million.

Notes

1 HWUA, Prof. P. N. O'Farrell, Interview with Prof. Cliff Beevers, 27 January 2003.

2 HWUA, Prof. P. N. O'Farrell, Interview with Prof. Jack Carr, 24 January 2003.

3 *New Scientist*, 25 May 1996, p. 14.

4 HWUA, Prof. P. N. O'Farrell, Interview with Prof. Jack Carr, 24 January 2003.

5 HWUA, *Senate Minutes*, 24 October 1989, Appendix B.

6 HWUA, Prof. P. N. O'Farrell, Interview with Prof. R. Leitch, 17 January 2003.

7 *Ibid.*

8 HWUA, Prof. P. N. O'Farrell, Interview with Dr N. Tomes, 7 January 2003.

9 I am grateful to Prof. Philip John for detailed comments on the Scholar programme.

10 The subject leaders were biology (Dr Roger Stark, later superseded by Dr Phil Meaden), chemistry (Prof. Philip John), computing (Dr Peter King), mathematics (Prof. Cliff Beevers) and physics (Dr Mike Steel).

11 HWUA, Prof. P. N. O'Farrell, Interview with Prof. R. Leitch, 17 January 2003.

12 HWUA, Prof. P. N. O'Farrell, Interview with Dr N. Tomes, 7 January 2003.

13 Clark, B. R. (1998) *Creating Entrepreneurial Universities: Organizational Pathways of Transformation*, Oxford, p. 4.

14 HWUA, Prof. P. N. O'Farrell, Interview with Mr Charles Ritchie, 12 March 2003.

15 O'Farrell, P. N. (1986) *Entrepreneurs & Industrial Change*, Dublin, p. 144.

16 HWUA, Prof. P. N. O'Farrell and Ms A. E. Jones, Interview with Prof. K. G. Lumsden, 17 September 2002.

17 *Ibid.*

18 Lumsden, K. G. (1967) The effectiveness of programmed learning in elementary economics, *American Economic Review Press and Proceedings*, Vol. 57, pp. 652–59.

19 HWUA, Prof. P. N. O'Farrell, Interview with Mr Charles Ritchie, 12 March 2003.

20 HWUA, *Heriot-Watt Now*, June 1979.

21 *Ibid.*

22 HWUA, Prof. P. N. O'Farrell and Ms A. E. Jones, Interview with Prof. K. G. Lumsden, 17 September 2002.

[23] Lumsden K., Attiyeh, R. and Scott, A. (1980) *Economics Education in the United Kingdom*, London, pp. 204–28.

[24] Lumsden, K. G. and Scott, A. (1983) The efficacy of innovative teaching techniques in economics: the UK experience, *American Economic Review*, Vol. 73, pp. 13–17.

[25] *Ibid*, p. 14.

[26] *Ibid*, p. 17.

[27] *Financial Times*, 24 March 2003.

[28] HWUA, Prof. P. N. O'Farrell and Ms A. E. Jones, Interview with Prof. K. G. Lumsden, 17 September 2002.

[29] *Ibid.*

[30] HWUA, Prof. P. N. O'Farrell and Mrs P. McIntyre, Interview with Prof. C. M. Brown, 24 June 2002.

[31] HWUA, Prof. P. N. O'Farrell, Interview with Prof. Sir Alistair MacFarlane, 11 September 2001.

[32] HWUA, Prof. P. N. O'Farrell, Interview with Mr Alick Kitchin, 14 March 2003.

[33] Prof. Lumsden was awarded the Henry H. Villaud Research Award of Economics America in 1994 in recognition of outstanding contributions to economics education through research. It was the first time that the Villaud Research Award had been made to a person from outside the USA.

[34] *Ibid.*

[35] *Ibid.*

[36] *Financial Times*, 24 March 2003.

[37] HWUA, Edinburgh Business School Files.

[38] HWUA, Prof. P. N. O'Farrell, Interview with Mr Alick Kitchin, 14 March 2003.

[39] HWUA, Prof. P. N. O'Farrell, Interview with Prof. Alex Scott, 25 February 2003.

[40] HWUA, Prof. P. N. O'Farrell, Interview with Prof. Roy Leitch, 11 September 2003.

Chapter Ten

Into the New Millennium: 1988 to the Present

It is part of the function of education to help us to escape, not from our own time – for we are bound by that – but from the intellectual and emotional limitations of our time.
T. S. Eliot

Entrance to the James Watt Centre, Edinburgh campus. Photograph: Laurence Winram

A Caring Visionary

Alistair MacFarlane, who became principal in January 1989, was born in Edinburgh in 1931, the son of an accountant who spent his working life with the Co-operative Movement, and educated at Hamilton Academy in the suburbs of Glasgow. He was advised to undertake an engineering apprenticeship in Motherwell before proceeding to the University of Glasgow, where he graduated with first-class honours in electrical engineering in 1953. He worked as a radar engineer with Metropolitan Vickers in Manchester and was then appointed a lecturer in electrical engineering at Queen Mary College, London, in 1959. From 1966 he was reader in control engineering at UMIST and from 1969 he was professor. He was elected to a chair of engineering at the University of Cambridge in 1974 and he became head of the information engineering division and vice-master of Selwyn College. Professor MacFarlane's international reputation in the fields of interactive computing, multivariable feedback control, and dynamic systems led to numerous distinctions, including election to Fellowship of the Royal Society in 1984 and the award of the prestigious Faraday Medal in 1993. His appointment as principal of Heriot-Watt University enabled him to return after 30 years to his native Scotland and brought him closer to his main recreational activity, long-distance walking in the Scottish Highlands with his wife Nora. Nora was also to make an important contribution to the university as hostess, ambassador and fundraiser, adding style and colour to official functions with her infectious sense of humour.

Alistair MacFarlane is arguably the most outstanding intellectual to have been principal of Heriot-Watt since its foundation as the original mechanics' institute in 1821. A person with great clarity of thought and breadth of education who was able to discuss research issues with academics across the spectrum of subjects from mathematics to civil engineering, he had a rare ability to synthesise concepts and ideas from many disciplines and to articulate a strategic vision, usually years ahead of his peers. When he assumed office in 1989, he enunciated a vision of the structure and funding of education and the role of educational technology in the future of tertiary education that was not widely appreciated in this or any other university at the time. His views were encapsulated in what has come to be known as the MacFarlane Report, *Teaching and Learning in an Expanding Higher Education System,* commissioned by the Committee of Scottish University Principals and published in 1992. The report made a major impact across the world, except in Scotland, underlining the dictum that a prophet is not without honour, save in his own country. Principal MacFarlane established several objectives to be achieved during his tenure of office: to complete the move to Riccarton; to expand and diversify the university by negotiating associations or mergers with other institutions; and to take a major initiative focused on the role of educational technology in the future of learning.[1]

Points Mean Prizes: An Assessment Culture

The Conservative government resented the role of the UGC acting as a buffer between government and universities, while the civil servants of the DES disliked its independent attitude.[2] It increasingly looked like an anachronism in the machinery of government of the 1980s as it was liberal and respectful of university autonomy, and included in its terms of reference a requirement to advise government, something that the Thatcher administration did not need. The government abolished the UGC in 1989 and replaced it with the Universities Funding Council (UFC), which was tasked to achieve economy in the use of public money and effectiveness in university management. The UFC would be more managerial, more subordinate to government and less responsive to the universities; it would have more muscle to implement policy and much less to make it.[3] The 1987 White Paper *Higher Education: Meeting the Challenge* made it clear that the UFC's 'essential responsibilities should relate to the allocation of funding between universities rather than its overall amount, which is a matter for the Government to decide after considering all the evidence'. Despite the government's free-market rhetoric, intervention in the internal affairs of universities by public agencies was widespread by the early 1990s. Concern that society received value for money was one alleged motive; another was the belief that universities did not respond adequately to the needs of their client groups, students and employers.[4] The balance between dirigisme from government and the autonomy of universities to make decisions about the best use of resources had swung heavily towards interventionism. The freedom to pursue truth, to undertake research and to nourish thousands of students without the continual harassment of bureaucratic reporting requirements was now seriously at risk. The DES was now firmly in control and the buffer principle yielded to the requirements of Thatcherism.

The Research Assessment Exercise (RAE) caused the greatest anguish as the contractual obligation to do research became quantified in terms of number and type of publications required. The RAE has unquestionably been the single largest influence on academic life in Britain since the mid 1980s. Soon after it began in 1986, research ratings became an obsession in common rooms across the country. Heriot-Watt University was no exception. It was not simply that higher ratings meant more money in increasingly frugal times. RAE grades represent a commodity for which some academics yearn: a craving for reputation and the respect, if not adulation, of their peers. For academic staff with hopes of building a research career, the RAE has been a key measure of success. The formulaic basis of the exercise, where quality ratings and other measures are combined to calculate RAE income, only adds to its academic irresistibility, with staff devising ever more sophisticated tactics to maximise their chances of higher grades. The RAE has a symbolic power to influence income from other sources, it carries authority outside academe, and it acts as a signal to other funding bodies and to a range of markets across the globe as to the location of the leading research departments. It was largely the creation of a co-opted academic elite responding to new requirements from the state for public accountability and recognising the need to protect the competitiveness of British research in the context of growing demands on scarce resources.

The RAE in 1989 was more sophisticated than the first one in 1986, with panels appointed to conduct a peer review of each subject area and award a score from 1 (bottom) to 5 (top), which would then be used as a multiplier in the formula to calculate the research element in the recurrent grant. Each academic member of staff was invited to return two publications and two other forms of

Colin Moynihan, Energy Minister, visits the Conoco Centre, 1991. Photograph: Ian Southern

public output produced between 1 January 1984 and 31 December 1988. All staff were returned, including those who were not active in research, and total departmental output was also recorded. The results for Heriot-Watt were mediocre, as they were for the majority of Scottish universities. Heriot-Watt scored only one 5, in petroleum engineering. It was rated 4 in applied mathematics, offshore engineering and IOE. There were four 3 ratings: physics, mathematics, computer science and electrical engineering. There was real disappointment in parts of engineering and economic and social studies. Chemical engineering, civil engineering, mechanical engineering, chemistry and languages all scored 2s; and there were 1s in economics, business organisation, accountancy and biological sciences. Heriot-Watt's average rating across all cost centres placed it 48th in the UK, with only six universities lower, including Stirling. The Research Advisory Committee asserted that there had been a bias against technological universities and that greater weight had been given to research council income than to industrial contracts.[5] Principal Alistair MacFarlane, with typical candour, concluded:

> I see no grounds for believing that we have been treated other than in broadly the same way as everyone else in terms of fairness and consistency. . . . I now accept . . . that in very broad terms, the assessment gives a fair picture of our research standing.[6]

The university reacted by creating a number of initiatives to improve research in selected departments. Firstly, biological research was grouped into four areas: yeast physiology, cereal utilisation, aquaculture and bacterial physiology. The transfer of Professor Ian Cowie's group to chemistry as part of the Stirling University rationalisation in 1988 strengthened its ability in polymer and solid-state chemistry. The prospects for physics were boosted in 1990 by the establishment of the Scottish Collaborative Initiative in Optoelectronics, based on five universities. Led by Professor Andy Walker of the physics department and with rolling grants totalling £2.6 million, it conducted research into semiconductor optoelectronic devices and diffractive optics. The International Centre for Mathematical Sciences, a joint initiative of Heriot-Watt and Edinburgh Universities, was inaugurated in March 1991.

An era came to an end with the retirement of Duncan Cameron as secretary in 1990 after 25 years in post. His successor, Peter Wilson, a Lanarkshire man who was a colonel in the Royal Army Educational Corps, assumed responsibility on 1 October 1990. This was a time of change as power was moving away from university secretaries to senior academics with the changes in governance that swept through British academe following the Jarratt Report. Peter Wilson, a man of great energy, loyalty and dedication, has made a very significant contribution to the university, although his willingness to tackle a vast number of problems, with limited scope for delegation, has burdened him with a prodigious workload. The following year, 1991, Lord Thomson completed his term of office as chancellor to be replaced by Lord Mackay of Clashfern, a charming former Lord Chancellor of agile intellect, who has brought a calm and witty presence to the university's public occasions.

Mrs Thatcher was ousted as leader of the Conservative Party in October 1990 and succeeded as prime minister by John Major. In spring 1991 yet another White Paper was published. *Higher Education: A New Framework* projected a rise in student numbers in higher education of 16 per cent over the next five years.[7] It proposed the abolition of the binary divide between universities and polytechnics and the creation of separate funding councils in the four regions of the UK. The system of dual support for research was preserved, although greatly weakened by cuts in the block grant, and there was also a proposal to establish a UK teaching quality audit unit. The new Scottish Higher Education Funding Council (SHEFC), a non-departmental public body responsible to the Scottish Executive through the Scottish Executive Enterprise and Lifelong Learning Department, took over the functions of the UFC in Scotland in October 1992 and became

David Sturgeon, Academic Registrar, Eric Milligan, Convener, Lothian Regional Council, Lord Thomson of Monifeith, outgoing chancellor, and his successor, Lord Mackay of Clashfern, Eleanor McLaughlin, Lord Provost of the City of Edinburgh, Principal Alistair MacFarlane and James Miller, Chairman of Court at the opening of the James Watt Centre, 12 October 1990

responsible for the allocation of public funds to Scottish universities. Higher education in the UK became a highly managed system. Like the other funding councils, but independent of them, SHEFC exercises a degree of control and surveillance over the system that would have been unimaginable in the 1960s. The increasing dirigisme took four main forms: (i) funding formulae became detailed, explicit and transparent; (ii) funding councils developed initiatives in areas such as additional student numbers, widening participation and research for which institutions must bid, thereby breaching the principle of the block grant; (iii) funding councils conducted a range of assessments, either directly by means of the RAE, or through the Quality Assurance Agency, as with reviews of teaching quality; and (iv) strict financial regulations were imposed on universities.[8]

The results of the third RAE in 1992 revealed some improvement over the university's 1989 performance. Two subjects achieved a 5: physics, and civil and offshore engineering. Three scored 4: petroleum engineering, building engineering and mathematics. And eight recorded a 3: actuarial mathematics and statistics, computer science, electrical engineering, mechanical engineering, chemical engineering, business organisation, economics and languages. There was concern, however, that chemistry and biological sciences were both rated 2, and accountancy only 1. Although this was a better performance, especially in the Faculty of Economic and Social Studies, the problem was that other universities had also improved, thereby reducing the amount of resources to be distributed.

When Alistair MacFarlane assumed office as principal in 1989, the university still had a small deficit of £207,000. He invited Professor John Small, a shrewd and clear-thinking accountant with good judgement and an idiosyncratic managerial style, to become deputy principal in February 1990 with the responsibility of ensuring that the university returned to surplus. John Small did not court personal popularity. If staff came to his office demanding an immediate response, he always replied, 'If you want a quick decision, the answer is no.'[9] Maintaining the university's finances in equilibrium became even more difficult since the Conservative government abandoned further growth in 1994 and cut the per capita allocations for courses in humanities, law and social sciences by 30 per cent on the dubious assumption that this would somehow encourage universities to persuade students to study science and technology. Cuts continued apace and in November 1995 the government announced that, in addition to the 3 per cent efficiency gains required, a further 2 per cent cut was likely.[10] SHEFC then followed this by imposing real reductions in funding for teaching and research of 3 per cent and 2.75 per cent, respectively, for 1996–97.[11] Despite these difficult circumstances, essentially produced by real reductions in the resources made available by government, the university finances were effectively managed. The accounts returned to surplus in 1991–92 and remained in substantial surplus

Professor John Small, president
of the Watt Club, with his
predecessor, David Purves, 1985

during the rest of Principal MacFarlane's tenure (Figure 10.1). Alistair MacFarlane typically acknowledged that the financial success was entirely due to John Small, 'an extremely loyal, effective and congenial person to work with;[12] while Professor Small recalls how Professor MacFarlane never made a major decision about resources without consulting him.[13]

Over a period of many years the academic income of Heriot-Watt has not been sufficient to cover academic expenditure, although the three social science departments – accountancy and finance, business organisation and economics – together with computer science, were net contributors. Professor John Small conceded:

> We did not look as rigorously as we might at departments that were in deficit
> ... there were sacred cows in Science and Engineering and no one was prepared
> to face up to them.[14]

Some recognition of this disparity was acknowledged in the creation of four strategic new chair appointments in 1994 in molecular biology, mechanical and chemical engineering, languages, and in the Centre for Economic Reform and Transformation within Economics. This was the first occasion on which the university management had made an attempt to address years of underfunding of the Faculty of Economic and Social Studies. This confidence was not misplaced as both Professor Ian Mason (languages) and Professor Mark Schaffer (economics) have made important contributions to the university's mission. The chair in molecular biology was never filled and the person appointed in chemical engineering moved elsewhere after a brief period.

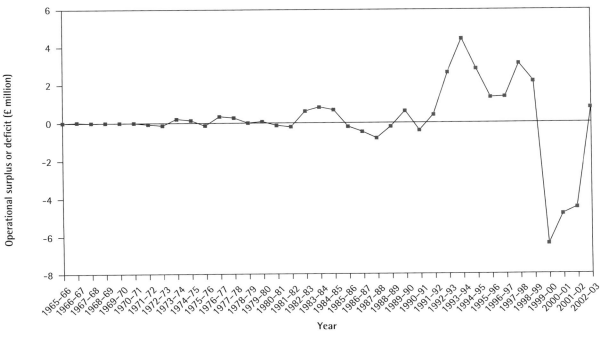

Figure 10.1 Operational surpluses and deficits for 1965–66 to 2002–03

The university created a Centre for Combined Studies in 1991 – headed initially by Professor Gareth Owen, a gregarious Welshman with degrees in engineering and theology and for many years a stalwart of the university choir, and later by Sarah Charlesworth, the first woman to graduate from Cambridge University with a first-class degree in engineering – as an initiative to introduce a degree, based on credit accumulation to cater for students who, for whatever reasons, could not progress on a specialised honours programme.[15] This development was complemented by modularisation. A modular system, in which the academic year for all courses consists of 12 modules, was devised by a committee under the chairmanship of the indefatigable Vice-Principal Robin Knops in 1992 and grafted on to the pre-existing three-term structure in 1994. Each module was conceived as 100 hours of student effort made up of eight weeks of teaching (not in the original regulations), self-study, one week of reading and revision, and a week of assessment, including a written exam. Advocates of the system pointed to its advantages of offering students flexibility and maximum choice; that more students would use the portability of their credits and transfer between universities (a prediction that has not been borne out); and that it would encourage breadth of study and the division of subjects into manageable units, making it less daunting than the traditional degree structure, especially for weaker students. The major benefits were parity of student effort across subjects and

Professor Robin Knops and family at his honorary graduation, 1999

constraining the length of engineering courses. Although the Heriot-Watt scheme was cleverly constructed and functioned efficiently, the university's staff, not renowned for their advocacy of radical ideas, were clearly influenced by their peer institutions and tacit pressure from SHEFC to implement a Scotland-wide credit transfer system and to adopt a politically correct and ill-conceived American innovation.

Although the Heriot-Watt system was popular with students, there are some major disadvantages, in common with other modularised courses. The teaching year is restricted to 24 weeks, although not by original regulation; knowledge is not compartmentalised but has a gestation period. However, term-length modules leave no time for unstructured intellectual discovery and constrain students from reading widely to acquire a deeper understanding of their subject. There is insufficient time for formative assessment, subjects lack coherence, and examination and assessment take priority over learning. A combination of modularisation and teaching quality audits has created a rigid system in the UK that threatens to undermine creativity; the syllabus has become a fixed menu, presented as a form of contract between professor and student, which has led to the 'McDonaldisation' of British higher education.

Any lingering hopes that the establishment of a separate funding council for Scotland would end a period of frequent intervention by the UFC shifts in policy and performance measurement were soon dashed. SHEFC, from the outset, developed its own separate formula for funding. It also initiated a methodology to evaluate teaching. Universities had entered the era of dubious league tables where unless judgements could be quantified, they were not regarded as meaningful. The university agreed in 1991–92 to allow SHEFC to pilot studies in electronic and electrical engineering and economics so that the proposed methodology for Teaching Quality Assessment (TQA) could be tested and refined. Following this exercise, the university adopted an arm's-length relationship with the TQA process, as no staff wished to be seconded as assessors. Although the methodology of teaching assessment was flawed and raised many questions about quality and how to measure it, SHEFC compounded this problem by devising a ranking system different from that in the rest of the UK. The RAE and the TQA bred a league table culture. The English press then published league tables for all UK universities to the great disadvantage of the Scottish institutions as they did not make allowances for the different methodology used in Scotland.

An autumnal view of the Edinburgh campus featuring the Cippico fountain, sculpted by James Butler in 1990. Photograph: Ken Paterson

SHEFC initiated a rota of visits to departments to assess teaching quality. The first 'excellent' came in electronic and electrical engineering in August 1993, with eight departments graded as 'highly satisfactory'. The grading taxonomy was subsequently changed twice. Under the current system – failing, approved or commendable – the subjects of chemical engineering, civil engineering, computer science, electronic and electrical engineering, mechanical engineering, offshore engineering, and petroleum engineering were collectively rated commendable (equivalent to excellent) in 2002.

Audit of all kinds (internal, external, institutional), assessment (of research and teaching), evaluation (of strategies that universities were now required to have), accountability (for special initiatives of all kinds) had become the inescapable condition of higher education, a culture inconsistent with creative and intellectual freedom. Is this audit culture inimical to performance? It implies that targets can be defined in advance. They must be not only predictable but also largely uncontested. If research outcomes were predictable, there would be little point in doing research in the first place. Research is about taking risks, exercising creativity and challenging academic orthodoxies, all of which are stifled by the RAE. The performance culture imposed on universities tends to measure everything except the things that really matter.

To Merge or Not to Merge?

Two of Principal MacFarlane's main objectives on assuming office in January 1989 were to increase the size of the university and to diversify its portfolio of subjects.[16] The university had been approached by the Scottish College of Textiles in Galashiels and Moray House College in Edinburgh, prompted by the termination of Council for National Academic Awards (CNAA) and the need to seek university accreditation. Edinburgh College of Art, with which there was already an association agreement, was an obvious candidate for a potential merger. In 1906 the Scotch Education Department had approved a major reorganisation of art education in Edinburgh, which at that time was provided by the Trustees Academy School of Art, Heriot-Watt College and the Royal Scottish Academy. Under the scheme, art teaching was combined in one institution, Edinburgh College of Art, opened in 1908, which served as a central institution for the south-east of Scotland. Sixty years later, on 1 October 1968, the college forged a formal link with Heriot-Watt University, creating a new joint faculty, the Faculty of Environmental Studies, to teach degree courses in architecture and town planning. The Faculty of Environmental Studies expanded by the formation of a separate department of landscape architecture in 1985. The university and college further extended their relationship to include the validation of art and design courses, and in 1986 the Faculty of Art and Design was established. The subjects taught at Edinburgh College of Art then resided within two faculties of the university. The college boasts a roll-call of distinguished alumni, including Sir Basil Spence, Eduardo Paolozzi and John Bellany.

The Scottish College of Textiles traced its origins to classes in technical subjects first introduced to the Borders with limited success by the mechanics' institute in 1867.[17] Hence, like Heriot-Watt, the institution shared a mission to provide education for industrial workers. The Galashiels Manufacturers' Corporation started classes in weaving, dyeing and chemistry in 1883 and these evolved into the Galashiels Combined Technical School in 1889.[18] The range of classes available and the number of students grew steadily and were boosted in 1904 when the Scotch Education Department extended its sphere of influence to include technical classes and made grants available.[19] The school moved to a new building at Victoria Mill in 1909 and changed its name to the South of Scotland Central Technical College. The new college building was opened by Lord Rae at a splendid ceremony attended by 3,000 people on 4 May 1909.[20] The curriculum had now been extended to include pattern and fibre analysis, textile testing, dyeing, colour, mechanics, physics, machine drawing, art, chemistry, electricity and building. The college was redesignated as the Scottish Woollen Technical College in 1922, and a year later, under its first principal, Thomas Oliver, it was granted central institution status. By the 1960s students studied management and computing as well as the latest developments in textile design and technology. Under the leadership of Principal James Martindale, the college moved to a new campus at Netherdale in Galashiels, which opened in 1965. Three years later, it was renamed the Scottish College of Textiles (SCOT).

Dr Chris Maddox was appointed principal of SCOT in 1988 and rapidly concluded that it needed an external partner, experienced in legitimising degrees at other institutions, to validate its programmes. He made overtures to Heriot-Watt and held meetings in 1988 with Professor Brian Gowenlock, dean of science, and Duncan Cameron, secretary. Brian Gowenlock had taught Chris Maddox on a laboratory course in chemistry when he was a student at Birmingham University. Principal Maddox found Cameron and Gowenlock to be 'open and generous' and agreement was reached within six months,[21] aided by the realisation that SCOT fitted well into the Heriot-Watt structure with its combination of science, engineering and business subjects. The accreditation of the college's degree

Textile students, 1913

programmes was transferred from CNAA to Heriot-Watt University. The senate meeting of 24 October 1989 approved the creation of the Faculty of Textiles and the degree programmes were accepted as approved courses of study for Heriot-Watt degrees; Principal Maddox and the vice-principal were appointed to the senate; and an Academic Advisory Committee was established.[22] Mutual interests were fostered by the appointment of Duncan Cameron and Professor Robin Knops to SCOT's board of governors. This body always displayed a commitment to full merger with the university.

In 1988 the university was approached by the chairman of the council of Moray House, a respected college of education, to explore the possibility of collaboration. A joint working party presented a rosy picture of the future:

- The college would be established as an associated college of the university, located at Riccarton, retaining initially its own academic board, board of governors, and SED funding.
- Students embarking on approved programmes from October 1991 would qualify for awards of Heriot-Watt University.
- In the longer term, the college, while retaining its identity, would be incorporated within the university.[23]

A draft ordinance was agreed in June 1991 regulating the association with Moray House. From the academic year 1991–92, Moray House College was recognised as an associated college of the university, while retaining its own academic board, board of governors, and continuation of Scottish Office funding.

Prinicipal MacFarlane was convinced of the need to continue the process and ultimately to merge the four institutions.[24] Discussions proceeded until Principal MacFarlane, in tripartite negotiations with principals of the three associated colleges, produced a discussion paper in October 1992, 'Towards a More Fully Integrated University'. This paper envisaged that the associated colleges would be incorporated within the university under the authority of a single senate and court while seeking to preserve the identity of the colleges. When the colleges responded in February 1993, having consulted their staff and governing bodies, the Scottish College of Textiles was the only one that wished to pursue merger negotiations.[25] Principal Maddox observed:

> Principal Alistair MacFarlane was extremely supportive of the relationship . . . and the time he devoted was far beyond that which you could expect to be devoted towards a small College by the Principal of a major university. . . . He and his wife made a point of visiting and talking to the students.[26]

However, both Edinburgh College of Art and Moray House College were unwilling to move towards fuller integration but wished to build on the existing arrangements as associated colleges. Moray House also proposed the creation of an alternative form of institution based on a federal structure of four equal partners, with arrangements to preserve the identity and maximum autonomy of each.[27] This form of governance was unacceptable to the university.

The existing arrangements of associated college status for the three institutions as faculties of the university continued but were fraught with minor problems, most notably the reluctance of the colleges to acknowledge the university's responsibility to insist on quality in appointments and promotions, in selection of external examiners, and in following up reports and recommendations of external examiners. This position, clearly unsatisfactory to all parties, was regarded by the university as unstable and was likely to evolve along one or two lines: merger or a move towards a looser form of association, such as validation on an institutional basis.

Moray House signalled its intention to move to a two-semester system in 1996–97, a further harbinger of difficulties to come.[28] Then, on 30 October 1996, Principal MacFarlane informed the senate that discussion had been taking place between Moray House and Edinburgh University to explore the possibility of merger and that Heriot-Watt had not been informed.[29] This crisis was extremely annoying for Alistair MacFarlane as 'the first thing I knew about it was when I read it in an Edinburgh University press release'.[30] He believes that Heriot-Watt

Procession to Old Gala House to celebrate the merger of the university and the Scottish College of Textiles, 1 October 1998. Photograph: Ken Paterson

management 'were deliberately kept in the dark as to what was actually going on'[31] by the senior staff of Moray House. This lack of candour on the part of Edinburgh University and Moray House College towards Heriot-Watt was magnified when it subsequently emerged that Moray House accepted merger terms with Edinburgh University that varied significantly from the federal structure of equal partners that it had sought with Heriot-Watt.

The merger discussions with SCOT, which had been ongoing, were suspended in 1994 by mutual agreement for a period of three years. At the invitation of Principal Maddox, Principal Designate John Archer visited SCOT during the summer of 1996 when Chris Maddox reaffirmed his commitment to merger. The subsequent failure of the Moray House relationship in autumn 1996, the unpleasantness surrounding it, and the advent of John Archer as principal prompted the university to revive merger discussion with SCOT in 1997. The Heriot-Watt University Court and the governing body of SCOT agreed a joint declaration of intent to seek merger of the institutions by 1 August 1998. In constitutional terms, it was clear what was at stake: the college had to agree to give up its independence in exchange for appropriate representation of staff on the senate; the college's governors had to be willing to relinquish their powers; the senate had to approve the establishment of the Faculty of Textiles; the University Court had to accept responsibility for the Galashiels campus; SHEFC had to be satisfied that the merger met its criteria; and the Secretary of State for Scotland had to give his approval. The college had some 48 staff and 700 students, including 70 postgraduates and others following HNC/HND courses in business studies and computing.

A joint working party evaluated the feasibility of the merger in all its aspects. Inevitably there were problems to be resolved: staff were represented by different unions; conditions of service such as lecturing hours undertaken by staff; holiday entitlement; and expectations about research were examples where there were clear disparities. A degree of goodwill prevailed in the negotiations, in no small part due to the forbearance and negotiating skills of the two main actors, Professor Charlie Brown for the university and Professor Chris Maddox for the college, who coincidentally had been undergraduate contemporaries while reading biochemistry at the University of Birmingham. Eventually the Secretary of State, Donald Dewar, approved the merger in August 1998. The two institutions processed down the aisle after a joyous graduation ceremony on 1 October 1998 to mark the inauguration of the Scottish Borders Campus. The merger scheme incorporated the department of textiles within the Faculty of Engineering; provision of management studies and computing in the Borders was placed under the control of the relevant Riccarton departments; all administrative, student services and commercial undertakings at Galashiels were integrated with those at Riccarton; and Professor Chris Maddox became assistant principal for welfare within the merged institution.

Although there has been considerable cooperation between the staff of the Borders campus and the senior management of the university following the merger, the development of a more relevant portfolio of educational provisions and improvements in research performance have been slow to emerge. The research grading of the staff returned to the RAE in 2001 failed to improve on the 3b awarded in 1996. The difficulty of attracting high-quality staff (and students) to a small town location in the Borders, however charming the surrounding countryside, has hindered attempts to transform the former college. At the time of merger in 1998, the textile courses were heavily oriented towards manufacturing and technology despite the fact that textile manufacturing in Scotland (and the rest of the UK) had been in long-term decline for many years. Courses have been restructured towards a greater emphasis on fashion and design, in which the UK has a competitive advantage. The university is committed to the challenge of providing a higher education presence in the Borders, and to the creation of a research capability of international standing in textiles. To this end, with the help of a £2.5 million Strategic Change grant from SHEFC, a serious attempt was made to improve student facilities. A new Students' Union was built, welfare and other services were provided, and a free transport link to Riccarton was introduced.

Heriot-Watt's orientation to 'useful learning' helped to give a favourable cast to the work of blending the culture of a college of textiles with the research-centred culture of the university. A major breakthrough occurred in June 2000 when a four-way collaboration, backed by the Department of Trade and Industry and the Engineering and Physical Sciences Research Council (EPSRC), brought together the three leading British universities in textile technology – Leeds, UMIST and Heriot-Watt – to win a Faraday Partnership award for technical textiles. The partnership won funding of £2.2 million over four years as seedcorn for an intensive programme of research training and technology transfer.[32] One strand of the funding stream financed posts to interact directly with industry; the other strand was a £1.2 million grant from EPSRC to the three universities to research new technologies and applications in technical textiles and materials, with the aim of transferring these advances to industry. A programme of research has developed that will greatly enhance the profile of the School of Textiles and Design.

Meanwhile, Principal Archer pursued a vigorous campaign during 1999 to promote the advantages of full merger with Edinburgh College of Art. The college governors voted to enter merger negotiations in October 1999. Despite Principal Archer's enthusiastic championing of the perceived benefits of merger, there had always been a majority of the governors of the College of Art who resisted the notion of losing its independence. The board of governors of the college disengaged from merger talks on 9 October 2000 and successfully applied for small

*Modelling clothes from School
of Textiles and Design Fashion
Show, 2003. Photograph:
Douglas McBride*

specialist institution status from SHEFC, which was followed by a validation agreement with the university. The School of Planning and Housing in the College of Art merged with the university to form part of the new School of the Built Environment from August 2002. Subsequently, the College of Art opted to become an associated college of Edinburgh University. Consequently, the relationships with the three colleges resulted in two divorces and one merger. Merger with Heriot-Watt was clearly in the strategic interest of SCOT, whereas the strategic case was less convincing with respect to Moray House and the College of Art.

The Managed Institution

The 1985 Jarratt Report, *Report of the Steering Committee for Efficiency Studies in Universities* (produced by a committee including Principal Tom Johnston), was critical of the sluggish decision-making of British

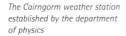

The Cairngorm weather station established by the department of physics

universities: they lacked a 'clear view of what they wanted to do' and they 'did not have the structure to effect adequate rates of change and the will to produce it'.[33] Jarratt recommended that universities and the system as a whole must work with clear objectives and achieve value for money. It advocated the introduction of performance indicators; made far-reaching recommendations about the governance of universities, primarily structures and processes of decision-making; and called on universities to adopt a more managerial style. It also emphasised that the vice-chancellor had to be recognised 'not only as an academic leader but also as chief executive' and that 'there ought to be a central planning and resources committee of strictly limited size . . . with the Vice-Chancellor as chairman'.[34]

Like most UK universities at the time, overall direction in Heriot-Watt was diffused in a labyrinth of committees that blossomed as offshoots of the senate, the court and the Principal and Deans Committee. Principal MacFarlane decided to create a proactive managerial group at the centre that could be likened to a cabinet. He established an executive board in 1989 consisting of Vice-Principals Small and Knops, the secretary and the academic registrar. Both Professors Small and Knops carried heavy artillery which they were not afraid to level even at the vice-chancellor, if necessary; but they would always loyally support the ultimate policy decision. This committee evolved in 1993 when the three elected deans were added, creating a more inclusive Executive and Deans Committee. Further changes occurred in 1995 with the appointment of two assistant principals, Professor Charlie Brown (who became vice-principal from August 1995) and Professor Patrick O'Farrell. Professor Brown was responsible for resources and Professor O'Farrell was responsible for research, quality and recruitment.[35] The executive was not an instrument of the court or the senate but became the centrepiece of a strengthened managerial core, thereby reducing rule by committees. Principal MacFarlane found the academics on the central management team to be 'a tower of strength'. He continued, 'I worked closely with this team and found them all immensely likeable, pleasant and utterly reliable people.'[36] Principal MacFarlane, in turn, provided 'quite outstanding leadership'.[37] In the Executive and Deans Committee meetings he had the temperament to function as *primus inter pares* among his colleagues; he was always interested in everyone's views; he fostered healthy and vigorous debate of issues in a friendly atmosphere; and he welcomed his own opinions being examined and challenged to arrive at a reasoned judgement. Alistair MacFarlane also delegated effectively, did not interfere, and trusted his team members to deliver.

Professor Charlie Brown brought a range of administrative qualities to his role as vice-principal: patent honesty and openness, a reputation for fairness in resource allocation, and an acute strategic vision combined with wise judgement. With the next RAE a year away, Principal MacFarlane sought to improve the university's

Professor Adrian Todd, department of petroleum engineering, receives OST award for collaboration with industry from Prime Minister John Major, 1996

processes for submitting returns. He appointed Professor O'Farrell as chair of the Research Advisory Committee primarily to manage the preparation of the 1996 RAE submission (with excellent assistance from Richard McGookin). The five-point scale in 1992 was expanded to a seven-point scale in 1996 and 2001. The 1996 RAE required a list of 'research active' staff, four selected publications from each of those staff, and information concerning the number of research students and studentships, amounts of external research income, and statements of the research environment and plans. This represented a shift towards a more qualitative rather than quantitative judgement.

A failure to improve was likely to have drastic consequences. When the results were published in December 1996, petroleum engineering was one of only nine departments in the whole of Scotland graded 5*. The department had won the prestigious Queen's Anniversary Prize for Higher Education (1994) for 'an education and research activity which is world class and exemplary collaboration and involvement in industry' and also a DTI/Office of Science and Technology award in 1996 for growth of industry–academe collaboration. Two subjects achieved 5: applied mathematics and built environment. Five scored 4: food science and technology, physics, civil engineering, electrical and electronic engineering, and computer science. Five recorded 3a: statistics and operational research, chemistry, economics, business management and education. Chemical engineering was the one unit to score 3b. Heriot-Watt achieved more subjects

*Opening of George Burnett Hall
with Vice-Principal Charlie
Brown, Nan Burnett and Gavin
Hastings,1995. Photograph:
Tony Gorzkowski, Whitehouse
Studios*

graded 4 or better in engineering and technology than any other Scottish
university.

The failure of chemistry to score a 4 and physics a 5, after years of generous
funding, were the only disappointments. In the *Times Higher Education
Supplement* league table of the 1996 RAE results, based on a weighted average of
the ratings, Heriot-Watt was ranked 33rd of the 99 universities listed. This was the
university's best ever performance relative to competitor institutions, third equal in
Scotland with Glasgow and better than competitors such as Liverpool, Newcastle-
upon-Tyne, Exeter, the Open University, Swansea, Leicester, City, Hull, Queen's
Belfast, Strathclyde, Stirling, Dundee and many others. The results of the
university, like those of some other institutions, were buttressed by accurately
targeted submissions, in particular by excluding research not deemed to be of an
appropriate quality.

The justifiable pride in the greatly improved ratings was tempered by the
announcement of the university's grant from SHEFC for 1997–98. Because
most universities had improved their ratings to some degree, the proportion of
grant allocated to higher grades was reduced. Since the multiplier for 5 and 5*
departments was reduced, those with 4s, one-third of Heriot-Watt
departments, were further disadvantaged. But Heriot-Watt returned only

69.5 per cent of its staff (Edinburgh submitted 94 per cent and Glasgow 76 per cent), and consequently the university, despite good grades, lost out on volume. The importance of raising the participation rate by 2001 was clear. There was also a need to increase the number of staff in each department capable of winning research grants. Research leadership in most departments was too dependent on a small number of people. The priorities for the next RAE were (i) to increase the participation rate to over 80 per cent, (ii) to maximise the number of departments rated 4 or better, (iii) to raise research income, and (iv) to encourage growth in research students graduating with a PhD. As subsequent events will show, the university succeeded in priorities (i) and (ii) but not in (iii) and (iv). To help achieve these priorities, the research outputs and grant winnings for all staff members were monitored, and the performance of departments reviewed annually from 1996 onward to prepare for future external evaluations of research. The level of intervention was at a micro scale: the assistant principal and the director of technological research services, Mrs Gillian McFadzean, were involved directly in decisions about which staff to enter in the 2001 submission.

The path of a principal is not always smooth and Alistair MacFarlane endured his share of frustrations. A man of vision, he did not always command the universal support of staff to enable him to realise it. There was scepticism among staff about the need to move from an 'administered' university to a 'managed' university, following the creation of the senior executive committee, as recommended by the Jarratt Report. Some staff perceived Principal MacFarlane, a shy person, as a rather distant figure. Coming from the leading engineering school in the UK at Cambridge, Alistair MacFarlane considered that the engineering departments at Heriot-Watt were too small to compete effectively and that they should diversify their research base. The engineers frustrated him in both of these aims – perhaps he underestimated the power of department heads at Heriot-Watt – and although mergers of civil and offshore engineering (1991), mechanical and chemical engineering (1994) and electrical engineering and computer science (1992) were implemented, only the amalgamation of mechanical and chemical, largely due to the leadership of Professor John Simmons, proved to be unambiguously successful. Meanwhile the departments of accountancy and finance, business organisation and economics were also merged within a new School of Management in 1997, and that has proved beneficial. The outcome of the negotiations with Moray House profoundly disappointed him. There was also difficulty with the physics department. The physics department had been operating a deficit for years and Principal MacFarlane sought to control its size.

Despite these challenges, when Alistair MacFarlane retired in December 1996 the university finances had a surplus of £1.35 million; a £5 million regeneration fund had been built up; the move to Riccarton was complete; the research park had expanded; Professor Keith Lumsden had been granted the autonomy to develop and launch the distance learning MBA;[38] the university had recorded its best ever RAE performance; a bold initiative on computer-based learning had been implemented (it did not bear fruit until after MacFarlane's departure, but the university is now acknowledged as a UK leader in applying this technology); Professor Des Smith, Professor John Ball, Professor Oliver Penrose and MacFarlane himself were Fellows of the Royal Society; and above all, he had raised the profile and the aspirations of the institution. After full consultation, especially among the senior management team, he was prepared to take difficult decisions and manage the consequences. He did not shrink from introducing stringent financial controls that caused some pain but which returned the university to surplus by 1991–92. He exhibited patience and a dry humour at senate, where he always ensured that opinions were freely expressed. Alistair MacFarlane was at his most impressive in small meetings with people he knew and trusted, where he would outline his ideas and strategic vision with persuasive rigour and clarity. He was witty and charming socially and he and his wife, Nora, were sparkling companions at the dinner table. Alistair MacFarlane was one of the most effective principals of Heriot-Watt, although like many visionaries, his achievements were not fully recognised at the time.

After many years of offering a very narrow range of subjects, as restricted as in any British institution, the university, in part responding (somewhat reluctantly) to market demands, established a department of psychology in the Faculty of Economic and Social Studies. The first entrants to the new degree in applied psychology were recruited in October 1997. The department's growth in funded numbers was dependent on the reasonable assumption that SHEFC would relax the consolidation policy on undergraduate numbers. This did not happen and the university suspended recruitment to the new degree after October 1998. Psychology continued to supply crucial modules to the new degree programme in sports science, and to the postgraduate diploma in occupational health and safety. The continuing crisis in recruitment to science and engineering, however, prompted a new psychology phoenix to rise from the ashes, having migrated to the science faculty, with recruitment to a degree programme initiated from October 2003.

The sports science programme will be considerably enhanced by the development of a football academy as a joint venture with Heart of Midlothian FC. Investment of £3.5 million from Hearts and £1.5 million from the university will provide Premier League quality pitches, a floodlit synthetic grass pitch, an indoor training hall, seminar rooms, a fully equipped sports medicine and sports science centre, and office accommodation.

Peter Wilson, secretary of the university, Chris Robinson, chief executive, and Craig Levein, head coach of Heart of Midlothian FC, with a young footballer at the turf cutting ceremony to mark the start of the sports academy construction, October 2002. Photograph: Douglas McBride

The Conservative government brought expansion to a halt in April 1996 and at the same time adopted a very tight fiscal stance. This resulted in severe cuts at English universities and slightly smaller reductions in Scotland. There was widespread concern over these cuts at a time when it was widely recognised that the sector was severely underfunded; the government responded by setting up an inquiry into the funding of higher education chaired by Sir Ron Dearing, with a parallel inquiry in Scotland chaired by Sir Ron Garrick.

An Evolving Student Profile

The university started on a very modest scale; there were only 1,031 full-time undergraduates in 1965–66 and a mere 22 postgraduates. In defiance of the UGC, the university expanded to over 2,500 students by 1972 (Figure 10.2). Growth was then steady, if unspectacular, until the imposition of the UGC cuts in 1981–82, when undergraduate numbers fell back over five years – compensated by growth in postgraduates – until the Faculty of Art and Design was incorporated in 1986–87 (Figure 10.2). Since then postgraduate numbers have increased by 131 per cent to 1,230 by 2000–2001, while total undergraduates rose 74 per cent to 5,759 (Figure 10.2).

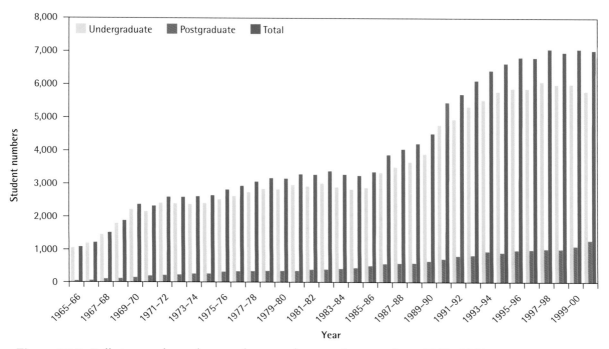

Figure 10.2 Full-time undergraduate and postgraduate student numbers, 1965–2001

In the late 1960s, only 10 per cent of the students were females, a proportion that rose to 21 per cent by 1979–80 as the Faculty of Economic and Social Studies expanded. Even by the mid 1980s, when women were entering the British university system in large numbers, only one-quarter of Heriot-Watt's students were female, the lowest proportion in Scotland (Figure 10.3). Women were even under-represented in science and engineering subjects relative to the national average for these disciplines. The inclusion of the Faculty of Art and Design from Edinburgh College of Art in 1986–87 and textiles in 1990–91 raised the female share to around 38 per cent, but despite many imaginative special initiatives to recruit women into science and technology, the Riccarton campus remains a predominantly male environment.

When Heriot-Watt emerged as a university, some 78 per cent of the full-time students were Scottish, 10 per cent were domiciled in the rest of the UK and 12 per cent were from outside the UK. The Scottish proportion fell steadily to 56 per cent in 1994–95 and then stabilised as grants were phased out (Figure 10.3). The university, however, has become more cosmopolitan; the share of overseas students (including the European Union) rose to one-quarter by 2001–02, while the proportion from the rest of the UK, having peaked at around 27 per cent in 1997–98, has declined to 20 per cent since these students must now pay tuition fees in Scotland.

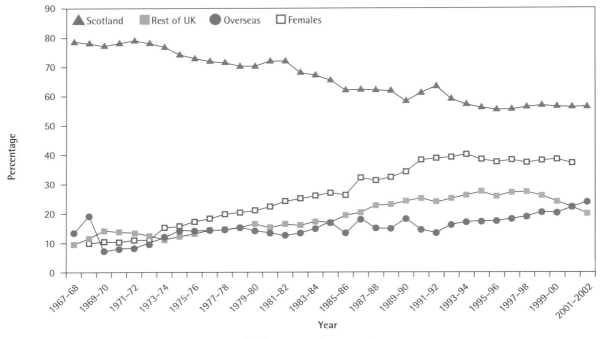

Figure 10.3 Home domicile and gender of full-time students, 1967–2002

The university established an international office in 1989 and appointed
Dr David Boak, a Heriot-Watt graduate who had worked for the British Council
for many years, to direct it. Initially this office was concerned with helping
academics to access European Union funds for research and with administering

*Alison Goligher, managing
director of Schlumberger UK
with Schlumberger engineering
scholarship students, 2003.
Photograph: Ken Paterson*

exchange programmes; it also became responsible for international student recruitment. Subsequently, the overseas recruitment function was integrated into the recruitment and admissions office in 1998. Overseas fee income has remained healthy, tending to increase marginally. This is partly explained by the perceived quality of Heriot-Watt degrees abroad, but in an extremely competitive marketplace, where not all universities have acted with integrity, the recruitment and admissions team have been very successful, initially under Charlie Woods and from 1994 under the dedicated leadership of Elizabeth Lister and the faculty schools liaison officers (posts created in 1978) plus academic colleagues in departments. As a consequence of the long-term fall in demand for science and engineering students, certain departments in the university have experienced problems in meeting the UK- and EU-funded numbers each year. Staff from the recruitment and admissions office, in cooperation with academics, make strenuous efforts to meet these targets by regularly visiting schools and colleges throughout the UK and attending fairs and conventions at home and abroad. They are also centrally concerned with implementing a range of access-widening initiatives – outreach to schools and communities that traditionally send few pupils to university – including the delivery of innovative programmes to recruit more female students to science and technology courses. There has been a healthy recovery in on-campus student numbers in the two years to October 2003, with growth of 5 per cent for undergraduates and 4.6 per cent for postgraduates.

Norway has traditionally supplied the largest number of overseas students. The association between Norway and the university started before the Second World War, when a small number of Norwegians came to study mechanical and electrical engineering at Heriot-Watt College. In fact, the very first Norwegian to enter the college was Alfred Bjorn-Hansen as early as 1908. During the Second World War, many Norwegians fled across the North Sea to Scotland, and Norwegian units were trained there and operated from Scottish bases; indeed Riccarton House was used to plan the liberation of Norway. After the war, when higher education in Norway was recovering from the effects of the Nazi occupation, the Norwegian government awarded a scholarship to its citizens to go abroad and study engineering. Numbers fluctuated but by 1968–69 there were 132 Norwegian students enrolled, some 7 per cent of the total student numbers. The peak year for recruitment was 1989–90, when there were 265 Norwegians on campus; since then numbers have declined somewhat as more courses are provided in Norway and Norwegians started to attend Australian universities in large numbers. Nevertheless, Heriot-Watt is now educating some third-generation Norwegian students. Many of those who have returned to Norway have made a major contribution to the life of the university and have taken back not only degrees but

Students celebrating Norwegian Constitution Day, 2003. Photograph: Robert Travers

sometimes Scottish partners. Norwegians have won laurels for the university on the sporting field, especially in skiing, athletics and orienteering, and have been conscientious and dedicated students whose ability in spoken and written English has often surpassed that of their British peers. Norwegian Constitution Day, 17 May, is firmly established in the university's calendar and Edinburgh continues to have the largest celebration outside Norway.

A New Style

Professor John Archer, former deputy rector of Imperial College, London, assumed office as principal in January 1997, the first English person to hold the post since the institution was founded in 1821. Born in London in 1943, the son of a teacher and the eldest of three children, John Archer spent his childhood in Hounslow and attended the County Grammar School, Chiswick. A swift sprinter, he played wing three-quarter on the rugby team and, on finishing school, was awarded sponsorship by ICI for a four-year honours degree sandwich course in industrial chemistry at City University. This programme involved six months of academic study until February each year, when the young Londoner moved to the ICI works at Widnes. After graduating, he became a doctoral student at Imperial College, where he explored how fluid drops would burn under high-intensity combustion, a thesis supervised by Paul Eistenklam, a major influence and 'academic anarchist'.[39] After obtaining his PhD from the department of chemical engineering in 1968 and completing one year of postdoctoral research, John Archer and his wife, Lesley, moved to Canada in 1969, where he worked for Imperial Oil (Esso) in Calgary. Returning to London in 1973, he worked for the Gas Council (British Gas) and then helped to establish the London office of a

Professor John S. Archer,
Principal and Vice-Chancellor.
Photograph: Ken Paterson

Canadian petroleum company, D&S Petroleum Consultants. He co-founded Energy Resource Consultants (ERC) in 1977, having spotted a gap in the UK for a consultancy operating on the interdisciplinary boundary between geosciences and engineering. This blossomed from 6 employees at the outset to 30 by the time he left to join Imperial College in 1980, where he was Mobil reader in petroleum engineering. He was appointed professor of petroleum engineering in 1986 and head of department of mineral resources engineering from 1987 to 1994. Professor Archer developed his research in reservoir characterisation, in particular the multiphase flow of fluids in porous media. More managerial responsibilities followed: he served as dean of the Royal School of Mines 1989–91, was appointed Imperial's pro-rector in 1991, with responsibility for resource allocation, and deputy rector in 1994.

An engaging, witty and convivial person, Principal Archer has made considerable efforts to further raise the profile of Heriot-Watt University in the wider Scottish community. He also moved decisively to make the university a more managed institution. Elected deans, as at Imperial College, were dropped from the senior management group, and assistant principals were changed from having an executive role to a strategic and monitoring role.[40] Principal Archer brought all the senior management team together in a new wing constructed above the medical centre. A man of considerable energy, he adopted a hands-on management style to the development of policy at a micro level, working with each academic member of the management team. The Principal's Advisory Group, in which deans and senior administrators participate, meets every fortnight to provide a wider forum for discussion. The role of the senate also changed to reflect the more managerialist culture by becoming less of a meeting for exchange of views and debate and more of a forum for the university management to inform staff of policy changes and initiatives. Together with the chairman of court, Ewan Brown, a highly effective person, John Archer rationalised the division of responsibilities between court and management, with the management more clearly responsible for running the university.

Principal Archer also sought to enhance the research strength of the university. In March 1997 he received the support of the court and the senate for a £3.5 million regeneration scheme to appoint new staff active in research and to encourage the non-active research staff to relocate or take early retirement.[41] By 31 December 2002, after five years of the regeneration programme, the university had invested £4.606 million, overwhelmingly on new academic appointments. The programme created some 20 full-time academic posts, 11 studentships, 7 research associates and 1 postdoctoral position. These new appointments were expected to be self-funding after three years in post through their research earnings from the SHEFC grant and from research overheads.[42] The regeneration scheme was also used to extend the university's PhD scholarship programme. The major beneficiaries of this munificence were the departments of chemistry (£1.033 million), physics (£636,000) and petroleum engineering (£583,000). Some £2.06 million (44.7 per cent) was invested in the engineering faculty, £2.48 million (53.9 per cent) in science and £62,000 (1.4 per cent) in the Faculty of Economic and Social Studies. The School of Management, which had 22 per cent of the university's undergraduates, received £18,800 from the regeneration scheme, 0.4 per cent of the total expenditure.[43] Hence the net result of the regeneration scheme was to allocate 98.6 per cent of the expenditure on new staff to science and engineering, parts of which have been unable to recruit sufficient students.[44]

After the Labour Party won a landslide victory in the general election of May 1997, there was an expectation that the new government would reverse the trend of cuts in university funding. There was great disappointment, therefore, when Gordon Brown, the new Chancellor of the Exchequer, committed the government to the Tory public expenditure targets for the following two years. Worse was to come. Dearing and Garrick reported in June 1997 and recommended the introduction of a flat-rate tuition fee of £1,000 a year, with an exemption for the poorest students. The government's response was a total surprise. Student fees were

Students using languages laboratory, 1999. Photograph: Ken Paterson

to be introduced, as Dearing proposed, but means-tested maintenance grants were to be abolished and replaced entirely by loans – confirmation, if such was needed, that universities were as low a priority for Labour as they were for the Conservatives. This new funding regime was allegedly intended to facilitate further expansion of higher education as part of the government's commitment to lifelong learning. This disappointment did not prevent the university from taking new initiatives, most notably the establishment of the Scottish Institute for Sustainable Technology in 1998, under the leadership of Professor Paul Jowitt and in partnership with Scottish Enterprise.

The people of Scotland voted overwhelmingly in favour of devolution in a referendum during autumn 1997. The first elections to the new parliament were held in May 1999, and since a system of proportional representation was used, Labour did not win an overall majority. The Liberal Democrats entered a coalition on condition that the whole question of student fees would be investigated. The subsequent committee of inquiry under Andrew Cubie recommended the abolition of upfront tuition fees, a concession also extended to European Union students, except those from the rest of the UK, from the academic year 2000–01.

The university returned 83.4 per cent of staff to the 2001 Research Assessment Exercise. The results demonstrated that some 90 per cent of the staff submitted

Table 10.1 Results of the 2001 Research Assessment Exercise

RAE grade in 2001	Subject	Ranking
5*	Petroleum engineering	Top in Scotland, equal top in UK
5	Actuarial mathematics and statistics	Equal top in Scotland
5	Applied mathematics	Equal top in Scotland
5	Built environment	Top in Scotland
4	Business and management	Equal top in Scotland
4	Chemical engineering	Equal top in Scotland
4	Chemistry	
4	Civil engineering	
4	Computer science	
4	Electrical and electronic engineering	
4	Food science and technology	Top in Scotland
4	Languages	
4	Mechanical engineering	
4	Physics	
4	Town and country planning	
3b	School of Textiles	

Table 10.2 Percentage of research-active staff at RAE grade 5 or 5*

	RAE 1992	RAE 1996	RAE 2001
UK (Scotland)	23	31	55 (50)
Heriot-Watt University	17	17	23

and all departments at the Edinburgh campus were assessed at grades 4, 5 or 5*, i.e. competitive by national and international standards (Table 10.1). The exception was the research in textiles at the Scottish Borders campus. The achievement resulted in a 28 per cent increase in recurrent revenue funding for the university from 2001–02 onwards, yet this consolidation of Heriot-Watt's research profile did not keep pace with increasing competitiveness at the highest level.

The proportion of research-active staff in the UK graded at 5 or 5* increased by over 30 percentage points between 1992 and 2001, whereas the percentage at Heriot-Watt rose by only 6 percentage points (Table 10.2). Consequently, the university fell from 33rd to 50th in the *Times Higher Education Supplement* league table, although 20 of the institutions ranked above Heriot-Watt returned lower proportions of their staff. Two factors contributed to this outcome. First, there were relatively low levels of research grants per capita in almost all departments. Figure 10.4 shows that research grant income at 2001 prices was approximately £800,000 per annum lower in the RAE period 1996–2001 than for the RAE period 1992–96. However, there has been some increase in research income since 2001 (Figure 10.4).

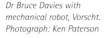

Dr Bruce Davies with mechanical robot, Vorscht. Photograph: Ken Paterson

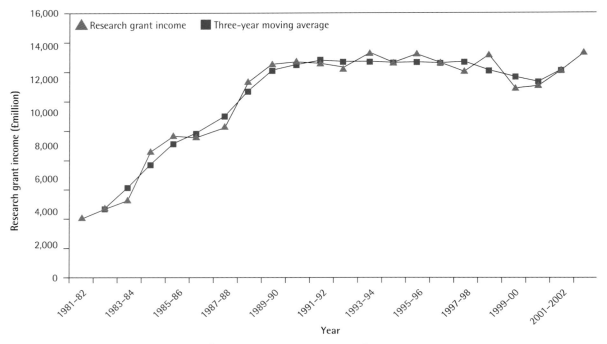

Figure 10.4 Research grant income for 1981 to 2002 at 2001 prices

Second, most Heriot-Watt departments recorded below-average numbers of PhD graduations per research-active member of staff between 1996 and 2001. Although the RAE has certainly increased the volume of research outputs and, arguably, has enhanced the quality of research (in a narrow technical sense), it has probably undermined the creativity and vitality of research across the UK by discouraging radical thinking and the development of new ideas, especially in interdisciplinary domains. This has been a disadvantage to Heriot-Watt.

Flowers of Scotland

During the past few decades Heriot-Watt has educated a number of students who have become eminent in their subsequent careers for highly contrasting reasons. The university has nurtured some of Scotland's foremost rugby internationals on its windswept pitches, including Jim Telfer, Jim

Calder, Craig Joiner and Duncan Hodge. It was, however, a sportsman who failed to break through at the highest level who has conquered the corporate world at a very young age. When the teenager Adam Crozier was on trial for Hibernian FC and playing for the Edinburgh team's reserves, he recalls racing into the penalty area, being fouled by a huge centre back and immediately getting up and going for goal.[45] His manager, Bertie Auld, the legendary hot-headed former Celtic midfielder, was angry and ordered the entire team to turn up the next day for training . . . in cheating. Crozier never made it on the football field; this slim, logical man was too small for the rough and tumble of the Scottish game.[46] Born on the island of Bute in 1964, Crozier graduated from Heriot-Watt with a degree in business organisation in 1984, after which he has followed a seemingly glittering career that saw him made chief executive of Saatchi and Saatchi at just 31 and chief executive of the Football Association (FA) at 36. He made a major reputation as a modernising chief executive of the FA who brought in a foreigner, Sven Goran Eriksson as England manager, and increased FA turnover by 250 per cent during his three-year tenure.[47] In 2003, and still under 40, Crozier became chief executive of the Royal Mail, charged with the enormous task of returning the organisation to profitability and restructuring it to compete effectively in the future. The Celtic supporter and fan of Van Morrison is facing a far greater challenge than he ever encountered as a footballer, in the exam halls at Heriot-Watt, or in his previous business career.

Following his first degree in physics at the University of St Andrews, David Miller, who had been brought up in Perth, made an enlightened decision to research for a doctorate at Heriot-Watt. Completing a doctoral study on the fundamental properties of semiconductor material under the influence of a laser flame in 1979, Miller demonstrated experimentally a phenomenon called optical bistability.[48] Optical bistability and the fabrication of optical transitions opened up the possibility of building optical computers. After lecturing at Heriot-Watt for a year, David Miller moved on to AT&T Bell Laboratories in New Jersey in 1981. Miller remained there for 15 years, becoming head of the advanced photonics research department, while simultaneously directing the Bell Labs jazz big band, playing clarinet and saxophone.[49] He migrated westwards to a chair in electrical engineering at Stanford University in 1996, where he continues to work on wave theory, while also pursuing engineering topics. A Fellow of the Royal Society and of the Institute of Electrical and Electronics Engineers, David Miller exemplifies the best multidisciplinary traditions of Heriot-Watt in being both a practising scientist and engineer.

Born in 1961 on a working-class housing estate in Muirhouse, Edinburgh, the young Irvine Welsh grew up among the harsh economic realities of a jobless, depressed area. He left school disillusioned at 16. These bleak beginnings had been

Irvine Welsh, acclaimed author and MBA graduate. Photograph: Gordon Wright

nurturing the most celebrated writer of his generation, leader of the 1990s group of Scottish realists. Leaving Edinburgh in 1977, Welsh gravitated to London to follow the burgeoning punk rock scene. In the late 1980s, Welsh moved back to Edinburgh, and while backpacking in American one summer seriously took to writing. After completing an MBA at Heriot-Watt in 1991, Welsh established himself as a British literary maverick with the publication of *Trainspotting*, to widespread critical acclaim, in 1993. One of the most influential books to come out of Britain in the past 30 years, it is a harrowing journey through the mental and physical tribulations of Scottish drug addicts. The book captured the helplessness of an unemployed and politically disenfranchised generation and their prodigious talent for drug-taking. When the film adaptation starring Ewan McGregor and Robert Carlyle opened in America, it was given subtitles.[50] *Trainspotting* turned Welsh into the king of British youth literature. His sophisticated messages of post-Thatcherite urban desolation, unemployment and political disillusionment were eagerly courted and simplified by the rising tide of British lad magazines. His latest novel, *Porno*, brought him back to the familiar Edinburgh territory of *Trainspotting*. No stranger to controversy, Welsh recently described Edinburgh as a 'shortbread Disneyland', a modern-day 'Brigadoon' and a 'cultural desert'.[51]

Renewal

In one year between 1998–99 (when there was a surplus of £2.2 million) and 1999–2000 the university plunged to its largest ever deficit of £6.4 million (Figure 10.1). This was a consequence of several factors, including investment in new staff under the regeneration scheme, writing off £0.7 million to develop distance learning materials, increased expenditure on scholarships, shortfall in the recruitment of science and engineering students, the lowest level of research income since 1988–89, and lower than expected growth in other income streams, notably the distance learning MBA programme, consultancy and conferences. Conference income increased after opening the new extension in September 1998 but it was insufficient to cover rising costs. Above all, for a highly labour-intensive organisation, the rise of 17.2 per cent in staff costs between 1998–99 and 2000 against an increase in total income of only 5.4 per cent was simply unsustainable. The attempt to recruit heavily to influence RAE results was commonplace throughout the university system. Consequently, further deficits occurred totalling £4.8 million in 2000–01 and £4.5 million in 2001–02.

This serious financial crisis prompted Principal Archer to implement a strategic restructuring of the university by reorganising the traditional structure of the faculties and 15 departments into six enlarged multidisciplinary schools:

- Built Environment;
- Management and Languages;
- Engineering and Physical Sciences;
- Mathematical and Computer Sciences;
- Life Sciences;
- Textiles and Design.

Additionally, two existing departments were designated as postgraduate institutes:

- Edinburgh Business School;
- Petroleum Engineering.

The restructuring involved a reduction of 120 in the staff complement. This was achieved by voluntary means so the cuts were not aimed selectively at activities which were unviable. This was the preferred solution from the perspective of staff morale, although the benefits from restructuring may take longer to be realised. Restructuring has helped to return the university to a surplus of £0.8 million in 2002 (Figure 10.1). The disappearance of traditional subject-based departments and the faculty structure created a different kind of university environment: a pan-institutional focus for undergraduate studies and postgraduate studies was established; and a new breed of head was appointed to run each school, with a clear job description and responsibilities. In conjunction with the consolidation of academic activities into larger units, the administrative support infrastructure was strengthened at school level, involving some devolution from centralised functions. Principal Archer introduced a more representative management structure in which the school heads and principal officers of the university together comprise the university's senior executive board, and this coordination of school, academic and management concerns was mirrored in similarly constituted new research, learning and teaching, and services boards. Although the department, with its sense of collegiality, had been the main loyalty base for staff, there was relatively little resistance to the restructuring into larger schools, perhaps as a consequence of the severity of the financial situation.

The large deficits that emerged in 1999–2000 may in the long run prove to have been the salvation of Heriot-Watt by prompting it to fundamentally appraise its performance and to finally confront narrow vested interests at departmental level that were obstructing change. The new School of Engineering and Physical Sciences, for example, comprises the former departments of physics, chemistry, electrical engineering, and mechanical and chemical engineering. It took a major financial crisis to sweep away lingering disciplinary protectionism and subject fragmentation. Hence, by merging five previous departments and eliminating course duplication, the School of Engineering and Physical Sciences has reduced the number of first-year modules by one-third. Each school and every other grouping throughout the university accepted a level of reduction calculated on the basis of the locally sustainable cost base, thereby reducing (but not eliminating) the cross-subsidy among schools and proportionate reductions across central and school costs. The success or failure of the new structure will depend on the extent to which the multidisciplinary schools reap the potential benefits from an integrated teaching and management structure that looks outwards and embraces the interdisciplinary opportunities in teaching and research between disciplines, and uses this broader funding base to exploit them. It will be at least five years before the relative success of the restructuring process can be fairly evaluated.

Social and Cultural Life

The students' association celebrated a landmark event on the symbolic date of May Day 1991, with the formal opening of its new Students' Union building at Riccarton. Funded largely from the sale of the former union premises at Grindlay Street, the £1.7 million new union became the hub of the campus student community.[52] Although students could now gather in Liberty's or the Freedom Bar to plan campaigns against student loans or fundraise for the Nicaraguan Solidarity Campaign, earnest political debate was seldom top of the agenda. The students' association continued to permit strip shows to be performed in the union up to the 1990s. The climate of opinion, however, was changing. Eventually, on 28 October 1993, a general meeting of the students' association, attended by over a hundred students, discussed the issue of pornography in the union. The motion before the meeting called for the association shop to stock pornographic magazines and for the union to stage male and female strip shows on a regular basis.[53] The meeting voted overwhelmingly against the motion. The

A cartoon from the Students'
Association handbook showing
the Students' Union under
construction

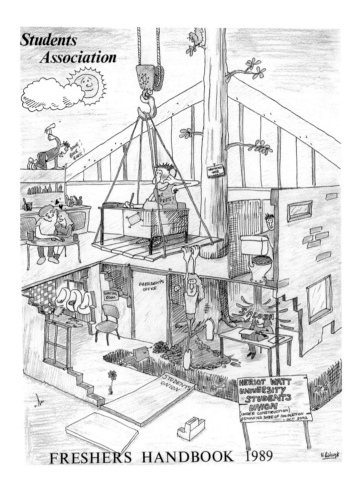

students' association established a Women's Committee in 1990 to provide advice
on such issues as contraception, self-defence and poor lighting on campus.

The programme of students' social events in the 1990s was dominated by
promotional evenings for various beer, cider and wine manufacturers.[54] The
attitude to this type of function was summarised succinctly by a report presented
to a meeting of the Services Core Committee on 7 March 1989 on a rugby club
function:

> Rugby club evening went excellently. . . . Vomit everywhere and girl locked in
> building until 4.00am (had passed out in toilet).[55]

Even the sectarian division characteristic of Scottish football had penetrated the
union, leading to fights in Grindlay Street and prompting the banning of football
colours on union premises from December 1988. A basic macho male culture
prevailed except when one or two more radical students came to prominence and

Students collecting for charity, 1990

issues other than whether to have Murphy's or Guinness emerged through the alcoholic haze. These generally focused on student concerns (grants, loans, the poll tax) but also national and international problems such as the Birmingham Six, Northern Ireland, Third World debt, and the plight of Nelson Mandela. The honorary president of the students' association, Robbie Coltrane, gave a show to raise money for a scholarship fund set up by the students to enable a South African student to study at the university.[56]

The students' association launched *Watt's On* in November 1986. Signalling a change in emphasis from *Omega*, it was more staid, more responsible, but less interesting. In 1988–89 Gary Younge, a languages student and now the prize-winning New York correspondent of the *Guardian*, was elected vice-president (welfare) and he became editor of *Watt's On* in October 1989. A thorn in the side of those who preferred apathy to action, he championed a range of student causes and did his best to challenge the campus conservatism of the Thatcher-dominated late 1980s. Younge raised the tone of the paper by writing serious pieces on issues such as racism and voting reform, but the burning question of the day was whether students should pay the poll tax (community charge). On 21 April 1988 *Watt's On* advised them to seriously consider not registering for the poll tax: 'This is illegal but if the Poll Tax is to be defeated now you should strongly consider this option.'[57] These sentiments were echoed by Robbie Coltrane's successor as honorary president, the august but no less radical Ian Hamilton QC, who had refused to pay the poll tax as he could not support 'this iniquitous exaction on the poor'.[58]

During the late 1990s, the serious cultural content of *Watt's On* was squeezed out by an increasing emphasis on reviewing pop music, articles on drinking games, crude sexist jokes, drink promotions and, a sign of the times, a column advertising

Left: Award winning Guardian journalist and Heriot-Watt alumnus Gary Younge. Photograph: The Guardian

Right: Steve King, musician in residence. Photograph: Ken Paterson

part-time casual jobs. *Watt's On* reached its nadir in 1999 when it introduced an item encouraging students to be photographed naked on campus for publication in the paper, and a new column where male students were interviewed on how they would 'pull a bird'. There was no longer an outlet for articles on issues such as racism, injustice and underdevelopment. Eventually, in May 2001, a new Watt Culture section was introduced into *Watt's On*, including theatre listings, reviews of plays, information on classical concerts, and Waterstone's list of top 10 best-selling books. A series called Watt Word was initiated, including articles on the arms trade and globalisation that signalled a more active engagement with political issues.

The Music Society had become moribund by the late 1980s. One of Principal Archer's major achievements has been to revive musical life on campus. He negotiated sponsorship of £25,000 per annum from Amerada Hess and the charismatic Steve King, viola player with the Scottish Chamber Orchestra, was appointed as musician in residence in October 1998. Steve King has transformed the cultural life of the university by running an orchestra and choir, an upper voices choir, chamber choir, a wind ensemble and string group, and organising a lunchtime concert series. He has raised the quality of performances, involved the local community and taken choirs and the orchestra to perform all over Scotland.

Dr Andy Hunter, a former lecturer in languages, was the university's piper since the early 1980s and wrote and performed special tunes for two kings of Norway and Lord Thomson of Monifieth. Dr Hunter advertised a class for pipers in February 1995 and ten students, including four experienced players, enrolled. A pipe band was formed and, in conjunction with Sandy Richardson, development

The university choir and orchestra perform in the James Watt Centre, November 1998. Photograph: Ken Paterson

and alumni officer, a university tartan was designed and produced by D. C. Dalgleish of Selkirk. The pipe band raises the profile of the university, performs for local events and charities, and has even attracted foreign students to its ranks, some of whom now play in pipe bands in Germany and Norway.

Principal MacFarlane, who steered the university through the final phase of relocation from central Edinburgh to Riccarton, initiated a policy of commissioning one sculpture every year from Edinburgh College of Art as a mark of the association.[59] He began in 1992, employing Stanley Wilson to create two sculptures from Kilkenny marble: A Stone for Ravenscraig and A Stone for the Whales. Later, two sculptures by William Edmonds, produced while he was a student, were acquired to diversify the collection.

Principal Archer has also been a champion of the arts at the university. First, the university agreed to accept seven paintings allocated under the Scottish Arts Council gifting scheme, a welcome windfall, including works by Eduardo Paolozzi, William Watson and David McClure. Second, Heriot-Watt was awarded a Heritage Lottery Fund grant of £50,400 in 2001 to purchase three portraits of the Gibson-Craig family, former owners of the Riccarton estate. Mrs Lesley Archer donated the partnership funding necessary to enable the university to take up the grant. The paintings, by Sir Henry Raeburn RA PRSA, depict Sir James, first Baronet Riccarton (1765–1850), his wife, Lady Anne Gibson-Craig (m. 1796, d. 1837), and their son, Sir William Gibson-Craig, second baronet (1797–1878).

Lord Thomson of Monifieth, chancellor of the university, and Dr Andrew Hunter, university piper, present to HM King Olav V of Norway the manuscript of the pipe march 'The King of Norway's Welcome to Riccarton' composed for his visit in November 1979

The university pipe band wearing the Heriot-Watt tartan. Photograph: Ken Paterson

All three are buried in the family graveyard at Riccarton. The paintings are from a once extensive collection of family portraits displayed at Riccarton House for many years prior to its demolition in 1956. The university's acquisition of the paintings has ensured that three of the most significant and closely related portraits will be

kept together as part of a permanent public museum collection. The parkland environment at the university's Edinburgh campus owes much to the foresight and dedication of Sir James, first Baronet Riccarton, who inherited the estate in 1823, and his son Sir William, second baronet, who landscaped the gardens around Riccarton House and introduced many fine and exotic tree species that survive today. The university's collection forms a part of Scotland's cultural and artistic heritage, and is useful not only for teaching and research purposes, but also in the way it gives the university a sense of patronage of the arts for the intellectual and aesthetic benefit of students and staff as well as the general public.

Conclusion

The university of the nineteenth century was the proclaimed defender of a set of civilised values; it was an autonomous institution – collegial in style and gentlemanly in tone – living by the ethic of academic responsibility. Translated to the twenty-first century it all becomes a lost set of expectations, conjuring a mental picture of an unworldly ivory tower. The intellectual sparkle and dialectic of the 1960s has fallen silent; the culture of external accountability has laid a thick blanket of dull conformity over UK universities. The British university system has had its autonomy sharply restricted and subjected to increasingly intrusive accountability regimes: an academic army in retreat, probably defeated. The alma mater has become a brand, students have become consumers, lecturers speak of products, the corporate presence is everywhere, together with the corporate mindset and the performance measurement culture. Meanwhile the fashionable trend in UK higher education is for collaboration or mergers between neighbouring institutions. Will higher education in Edinburgh and central Scotland turn towards new forms of association and governance through collaboration between institutions? Or will intense competition persist between institutions, between subjects and between individuals? Size remains a critical issue for the university. Small institutions – even with a record of excellence in niche subjects such as actuarial mathematics, petroleum engineering and languages emphasising interpreting and translating – will struggle to thrive in the twenty-first century unless, like the London School of Economics and Political Science, they are world leaders.

During the first phase of the university's development, pressures from the UGC

Entrance to the James Watt
Centre, Edinburgh campus.
Photograph: Laurence Winram

and a cold financial climate combined to make growth and diversification a highly
restrictive exercise. Yet some opportunities were seized: a new department of
accountancy and finance; the seeding of actuarial mathematics and statistics; the
creation of a department of languages emphasising interpreting and translating; the
establishment of petroleum engineering and the Institute of Offshore Engineering;
and the link with Edinburgh College of Art. Conversely, over the past two
decades, the university was only prepared to contemplate diversification into
applied psychology and sports science when science and engineering consistently
failed to recruit sufficient students. There is now a free market in subject provision
and the risks are higher. There is no longer a UGC making plans for controlled
expansion in strategically important areas, nor is there a UGC subcommittee to
rationalise the number of centres for important small subjects so as to ensure viable
centres of excellence. Will Heriot-Watt be sustainable without any further
diversification of its subject mix? Heriot-Watt as a university has reached early
middle age when a major issue facing institutions is renewal.[60] With an ageing staff,
where do new ideas and initiatives come from and who will have the willingness to
take risks and meet challenges? Michael Beloff warned that 'yesterday's experiment
will become tomorrow's tradition', with the 'new map of learning' beginning to
'curl and fray at the edges'.[61]

Having grown to an effective size, every institution develops its rigidities,
whether it has been in existence for thirty years or five hundred. It is a profound
truth that universities do not continue to be successful unless they change and
respond radically to new pressures. A major lesson to be taken from this book is
that the more ruthlessly a university pursues radical change, the more successful it

Jubilant graduates celebrate in
the sunken garden: Photograph:
Karen Larter

will become. Under Principals R. A. Smith and George Burnett, Heriot-Watt was
transformed from a central institution serving overwhelmingly a local Edinburgh
market into a recognisable university, with academic staff selected primarily on the
basis of their scholarly reputations and students chosen increasingly for their
intellectual achievement and potential. Then under Principals Johnston,
MacFarlane and Archer this meritocratic culture became overlaid by a global one.
This sought for Heriot-Watt an increasingly international presence: research
pursued all over the world, scientists ever more involved in commercial ventures, a
distance learning MBA with students in 150 countries, and a rising proportion of
overseas students on campus. Above all, a conscious recognition that for a
university to be attractive, it must be integral to contemporary economy and
society and engage vigorously with it, something which had been a fundamental
part of the thinking behind its foundation in 1821. Especially fertile periods of
vision and drive were the mid 1970s, when the IOE, the department of offshore
engineering and the department of petroleum engineering were created within 18
months, and the early 1990s, when Professor Keith Lumsden had the boldness and
commitment to launch the distance learning MBA worldwide. The recent radical
restructuring presents an opportunity for new creative initiatives to bubble up
from below. The future will call for bold, imaginative ideas and for the university

to be more ambitious than in the past. In fast-moving times, the prudent course of action for Heriot-Watt is to be steering instead of drifting, and shaping the impact of demands made on it rather than reacting to them. The greatest risk is to stand passively in place.

The affection for the institution which is felt by many who have shared even a small part of its history rests on more than nostalgic memories of Chambers Street, the Grindlay Street Union, the Grassmarket, Riccarton and the people who brought it all to life. Heriot-Watt has made a difference to those who studied, taught and worked there, and it has made a difference to the world at large. It has attracted thousands of students from every part of the world. The institution gave its members from the beginning a sense of belonging, of being more than passers-by who come and go. The unstinting work of the chaplaincy, Ann Trotman and successive welfare staff has been crucial in creating and maintaining a friendly and supportive community. One thinks of the friendships and marriages struck at Heriot-Watt. The janitors and receptionists have much to do with the community called Heriot-Watt, not only as the first port of call for those who return to the university as well as those who are there, but as a visible, tangible expression of the institution. The university has always been more than the sum of its parts.

No institution is without its warts, and I have not sought to hide them. But the reality at the start of the new millennium is that this complex palimpsest of a university – its original aim to offer educational opportunities that did not otherwise exist for the working classes of Edinburgh – successively overwritten by technical college utilitarianism, meritocratic striving and worldwide engagement, has survived for over 180 years. Heriot-Watt, despite its expansion, retains many of the admirable qualities of an elite system. There continues to be a close and creative relationship between teaching and research, a strong commitment to undergraduate education, and a tradition of academic concern reflected in teaching styles, patterns of pastoral care and relationships between staff and students. Heriot-Watt and its ancestors have provided routes of access and opportunity for generations of students from Scotland, the UK and across the world. An ethos of 'useful learning' still permeates the university. It is possible even now to sense that the first ever mechanics' institute is the spiritual ancestor of Heriot-Watt and that Horner's noble utilitarian aim to enable 'industrious tradesmen to become acquainted with such of the principles of Mechanics, Chemistry and other branches of Science as are of practical application in their several trades' still resonates through the lecture theatres and seminar rooms to this day.

Notes

[1] HWUA, Prof. P. N. O'Farrell, Interview with Prof. Sir A. G. J. MacFarlane, 11 September 2001.

[2] Letter from Prof. B. G. Gowenlock to Prof. P. N. O'Farrell, 15 September 2003.

[3] Shattock, M. (1984) *The UGC and the Management of British Universities*, Buckingham, p. 140.

[4] Butt, J. (1996) *John Anderson's Legacy: University of Strathclyde and Its Antecedents 1796–1996*, East Linton, p. 134.

[5] HWUA, *Executive Board Notes*, 22 March 1990.

[6] HWUA, *Executive Board*, 30 August 1989, Memorandum from the Principal.

[7] *Higher Education: A New Framework*, 1991.

[8] Scott, Peter (2001) 'Conclusion: Triumph and Retreat' in Warner, D. and Palfreyman, D. (eds) *The State of Higher Education: Managing Change and Diversity*, Buckingham, p. 188.

[9] HWUA, Prof. P. N. O'Farrell, Interview with Prof. John R. Small, 28 June 2001.

[10] HWUA, *Senate Minutes*, 28 November 1995.

[11] HWUA, *Court Minutes*, 18 March 1996.

[12] HWUA, Prof. P. N. O'Farrell, Interview with Prof. Sir Alistair MacFarlane, 11 September 2001.

[13] HWUA, Prof. P. N. O'Farrell, Interview with Prof. John R. Small, 28 June 2001.

[14] *Ibid.*

[15] A general degree had been introduced in 1970–71, an initiative of Prof. Brian Gowenlock, dean of science.

[16] HWUA, Prof. P. N. O'Farrell, Interview with Prof. Sir Alistair MacFarlane, 11 September 2001.

[17] HWUA, Records Management and Museum Service: Chapters in the history of textile education: The origins of the Scottish Borders Campus, December 2002.

[18] *Ibid.*

[19] Oliver, T. (1911) *A Phase in the Rise of Scotch Tweed Technique*, Galashiels, p. 11.

[20] *Ibid.*

[21] HWUA, Prof. P. N. O'Farrell and Mrs P. McIntyre, Interview with Prof. C. Maddox, 7 April 2001.

[22] HWUA, *Senate Minutes*, 24 October 1989.

[23] HWUA, *Minutes of Joint Meeting of Senate and Court*, 19 March 1990.

[24] HWUA, Prof. P. N. O'Farrell, Interview with Prof. Sir Alistair MacFarlane, 11 December 2001.

[25] HWUA, *Minutes of Court*, 15 February 1993.

[26] HWUA, Prof. P. N. O'Farrell, Mrs P. McIntyre and Ms A. E. Jones, Interview with Prof. C. Maddox, *op. cit.*

[27] HWUA, *Papers of Court*, 15 February 1993, Letter from Prof. Gordon Kirk, Principal Moray House College, to Mr P. L. Wilson, Secretary, Heriot-Watt University.

[28] HWUA, *Minutes of Senate*, 24 January 1995.

[29] HWUA, *Minutes of Senate*, 30 October 1996.

[30] HWUA, Prof. P. N. O'Farrell, Interview with Prof. Sir Alistair MacFarlane, 11 September 2001.

[31] *Ibid.*

[32] HWUA, *Press Information*, 28 June 2000.

[33] Committee of Vice-Chancellors and Principals (1985) *Report of the Steering Committee for Efficiency Studies in Universities* (Jarratt Report), London, p. 12.

[34] *Ibid.*, p. 36.

[35] The finance director also became a member of the management group.

[36] *Ibid.*

[37] Prof. P. N. O'Farrell, Interview with Prof. R. J. Knops, 5 July 2001.

[38] HWUA, Prof. P. N. O'Farrell and Mrs P. McIntyre, Interview with Prof. C. M. Brown, 24 June 2002.

[39] HWUA, Prof. P. N. O'Farrell, Interview with Principal J. S. Archer, 30 January 2003.

[40] HWUA, *Principal's Management Group Notes*, 20 August 1998.

[41] HWUA, *Court Papers*, 24 March 1997.

[42] *Ibid.*

[43] The highly regarded Logistics Research Centre, under the leadership of Prof. Alan McKinnon, made the first of four bids for support from the Regeneration Fund in August 1998, none of which were granted.

[44] The Finance Committee was satisfied on 21 October 1999 that the distribution of the investment was over a 'good spread of disciplines'.

[45] *The Guardian*, 9 August 2003.

[46] *Ibid.*

[47] *Ibid.*

[48] HWUA, Laureation for Prof. David Miller by Prof. B. Wherrett, 17 July 2003.

[49] *Ibid.*

[50] *The Observer*, 11 August 2002.

[51] *Ibid.*

[52] HWUA Press Information, 29 April, 1991.

[53] HWUA, *Watts On*, 5 November 1993.

[54] On 22 November 1991, 1,200 vodkas were sold at 50p each. Demand was such that the price was increased to 65p.

[55] *Watt's On*, 7 March 1989.

[56] HWUA, *Heriot-Watt University Students Association Handbook*, 1990–91.

[57] HWUA, *Watt's On*, 21 April 1988.

[58] HWUA, *Watt's On*, 2 May 1991. As a student at Glasgow University some 40 years previously, Ian Hamilton had taken part in a daring plot to remove the Stone of Destiny from Westminster Abbey and return it to Scotland. The stone, a powerful symbol of Scottish identity, is the seat on which Scottish kings had been inaugurated until 1296, when Edward I of England took it to London to serve the same function for kings of England. The British government returned the stone to Scotland as a devolutionary gesture on St Andrew's Day 1996. It is now displayed in Edinburgh Castle.

[59] I am grateful to Rachel Vincent, who provided me with invaluable information on the university's art collection.

[60] Rich, Tony (2001) The 1960s new universities. In Warner, D. and Palfreyman, D. (eds) *The State of Higher Education: Managing Change and Diversity*, Buckingham, p. 56.

[61] Beloff, M. (1963) *The Plateglass Universities*, London, p. 37.

Appendix: Recent Research at Heriot-Watt University

This appendix was edited from summaries of the research achievements of each subject written by leading academics from across the University.[1]

Mathematics

Professor R. J. Knops was largely responsible for transforming the Department of Mathematics from its predominantly teaching function in 1971 to one led by vigorously pursued high calibre mathematical research. The subject, which achieved grade 5s in both RAE 1996 and 2001, has an international reputation for innovative research in applied mathematics, especially nonlinear applied analysis and mechanics. Two explicit examples must suffice to illustrate the nature of the research undertaken. The first concerns the outstanding contributions of John Ball, appointed in 1972. Nonlinear elasticity is central to understanding the behaviour of all solid objects wherever they occur and irrespective of use. In his seminal paper published in 1977, Dr Ball developed a rich set of tools and concepts for studying these models. This research hugely influenced not only nonlinear elasticity but also nonlinear partial differential equations and multidimensional variational calculus. His theory and methods are now vital to worldwide interdisciplinary endeavours exploring matter at many different scales, and his impressive achievements earned him election to the Royal Society in 1988 and appointment to the Serleian Chair of Mathematics at Oxford University. The second development was focused and accelerated by the appointment in 1997 of Professor Jonathan Sherratt who has expertise in the mathematical modelling of wound healing, cell dynamics and tumour growth, informed by strong links with clinical medical research. The research has extended into brain tumours, using stochastic systems, and into the examination of the temporal and spatial evolution of disease as an aid to its management. Medical interests are complemented by studies into the effects of climate change on terrestrial ecosystems and the construction of models for the dynamics of global vegetation. The bias towards applications continues to be reflected in the evolution of present research into five main, but flexible, divisions: applied nonlinear analysis, computational applied mathematics, mathematical physics, mathematical medicine and biology, and algebraic topology.

Actuarial Mathematics and Statistics

Professor Jimmy Gray, as Head of the Department of Actuarial Mathematics and Statistics from 1972 until his retirement in 1989, laid the foundations for what is today recognised internationally as a centre of excellence for research which combines novel theoretical advances with practical applications in genetics, actuarial mathematics, financial mathematics, statistics and applied probability. This research was awarded a grade 5 in the 2001 RAE.

A major research theme has been work on mortality and morbidity. This was initiated by Professor John McCutcheon, who succeeded Jimmy Gray as Head of Department. For many years up to his retirement in 2001, John McCutcheon chaired the Mortality Sub-Committee of the Continuous Mortality Investigation Bureau (CMIB). The CMIB is a research committee set up by the UK actuarial profession. It is responsible for collecting and analysing mortality and morbidity data from insurance companies and then publishing the standard tables which are used by the companies to calculate life and health insurance premiums. John McCutcheon was succeeded as chair of the CMIB's Mortality Sub-Committee by Professor Angus Macdonald. In 1999, Angus Macdonald established the Genetics and Insurance Research Centre (GIRC) at Heriot-Watt. Funded by industry, but with all its work in the public domain, GIRC has established a unique position internationally for actuarial and financial research into the consequences of human genetics, and its work informs the policy-making debate going on in this area. Professor Howard Waters has made important research contributions to the stochastic modelling of life, health and non-life insurance. In particular, through his involvement with the CMIB's Income Protection Insurance Sub-Committee, he helped to bring modern stochastic process models into actuarial practice.

In the mid 1990s, the Department of Actuarial Mathematics and Statistics made the strategic decision to develop teaching and research in financial mathematics. Professor Andrew Cairns has published important research on the modelling of interest rates, which is particularly relevant to long-term financial planning and risk management.

The department has had a very long and fruitful association with Professor David Wilkie. In the late 1970s, David Wilkie was a part-time member of staff; currently he is a research consultant. David Wilkie was a member of the CMIB committee from 1964 to 1994. His work for the CMIB included producing several standard mortality tables and, together with Howard Waters (and Mr P. H. Bayliss), writing a seminal paper on the modelling of Income Protection Insurance, published in 1991. David Wilkie has made many major contributions to actuarial science and is best known for the 'Wilkie Investment Model', a stochastic investment model first detailed in a paper in 1986. Stochastic investment models are now being developed widely within the actuarial profession and the Wilkie model is the standard by which other models are judged.

In statistics and applied probability, there is an impressive track-record of achievement that combines theoretical developments with application and collaborative research with scientists from other disciplines. Professor Denis Mollison was an early pioneer in the modelling of biological populations in space and time. Following his retirement in 2000, Professor Gavin Gibson, formerly Deputy Director of Biomathematics and Statistics Scotland, was appointed to the Chair in Statistics. His research has focused on statistical inference for stochastic epidemic models, and has contributed to the understanding of host–pathogen interactions in populations of plants, animals and humans. A key feature of his work is the use of modern statistical computing techniques to enable complex models to be fitted to data within a statistically rigorous framework. The appointment of Professor Gibson has led to interdisciplinary collaborations with UK life scientists at Cambridge and Edinburgh, and internationally at Queensland University of Technology and the US Department of Agriculture.

Professor Serguei Foss is one of the world's leading applied probabilists. His vast array of achievements contains important contributions to many areas of probability including asymptotic analysis and perfect simulation, and his ideas have found application in the study of complex queuing and communication systems.

Computer Science

Following the appointment of Professor Howard Williams in 1980, the Department of Computer Science's active participation in the UK '5th Generation' Alvey programme led to substantial growth in research, building on established work in databases, graphics and software engineering. Intelligent knowledge based systems activity included the use of logic programming in databases and its support by hardware. This was complemented by Professor Fred Heath's development of hardware for free text retrieval. Innovative research in human–computer interaction (HCI) explored adaptive user interfaces. The department also co-hosted the Scottish HCI Centre with Strathclyde University, which sought to transfer HCI practice to industry.

In the 1980s, research growth was further consolidated by the appointment of new staff. Dr (now Professor) Andy Wallace established computer vision research, investigating low and high level machine vision and their relationships to human perception. HCI research was strengthened by the appointment of Professor Alistair Kilgour with expertise in interactive system design. Dr (now Professor) Alex Gammerman augmented machine learning and expert system activity through the application of advanced statistical techniques. In the late 1980s, SERC support provided a reconfigurable parallel system which was applied to vision and graphics research, bridging established activities with emerging interests in formally motivated software development.

The early 1990s also saw growing European funded activity, with major projects in tele-medicine, deductive databases, statistical expert systems and large image terminals. After the merger with Electrical Engineering to form the Department of Computing and Electrical Engineering, good synergy was exploited in the areas of intelligent systems, evolutionary techniques, and computer vision and image processing. Activity was also initiated in computer-based learning and in internet applications, especially information visualisation. There was also consistent funding in established areas, supporting novel research in active and multi-media databases, and 3D vision.

The late 1990s saw the appointment of staff with funded activity in automatic theorem proving, parallel and distributed functional programming, natural language generation, software engineering and information systems. Dependable systems research, which integrated much of the department's formally motivated software engineering activity, was strengthened with the 1998 appointment of Professor Rob Pooley, working on system modelling. Professor Fairouz Kamareddine's 1998 appointment initiated research activity into the Foundations of Computing, focusing on logics, term rewriting and type systems. This period also saw further collaboration on interactive media with the University's Learning Technology Centre, and new research in bioinformatics. In 2001, the Computer Science cognate area again recorded a grade 4 in the RAE.

Biological Sciences

In biological sciences, Professor Charlie Brown, supported by Principal Johnston, engaged in long and ultimately successful negotiations with the Brewers Society, the Scotch Whisky Association, the Maltsters Association of Great Britain and with a number of industrial companies, including the Suntory company of Japan, in order to fund the International Centre for Brewing and Distilling (ICBD). The Centre, established in 1988, is an industry–University collaboration that provides improved undergraduate and postgraduate courses in brewing and distilling, and research services for the brewing and distilling industries. The Scotch Whisky Association agreed to invest £500,000 over five years, which prompted the Brewers Society – anxious to support a University initiative after the closure of the unit at Birmingham University – to pledge £300,000. Suntory agreed initially to invest £500,000 over five years; their commitment has been renewed twice and they currently provide around £50,000 per annum as do the Brewers Society and the Scotch Whisky Association. United Distillers donated a distillery and a small-scale brewery was constructed. The provision of this infrastructure enabled the volume of research to be increased and stimulated the flow of Research Council Grants.

Professor Graham Stewart was appointed Director of ICBD in 1994 and supported an active yeast group working on the genetics and physiology of sugar uptake during brewery and distillery fermentations. This was extended by Dr Jamieson into the molecular biology of stress responses in yeast, in particular oxidative stress. Simultaneously, Professor Priest's research group has been studying the diversity of lactic acid bacteria in malt whisky fermentations and their contribution to whisky flavour. Research into brewing raw materials, especially barley, was pioneered by Professor Geoff Palmer with his studies of the physiology and technology of malting for which he received an OBE in 2003. Dr Peter Morris, in collaboration with the Scottish Crops Research Institute, has extended that work into the genetic basis of malting quality in barley as well as various projects involving genetic modification of barley to aid our understanding of germination and the malting process. The research of ICBD complemented that of the aquaculture group under Professor Brian Austin which conducts basic research on the ecology, taxonomy, identification and pathogenicity of fish diseases. This prompted a reorientation of the research focus towards food and technology, which was to yield a dividend of grade 4s in the RAEs of 1996 and 2001.

There is also an active research programme in the area of marine biodiversity and pollution. Dr Kingston is an international expert on the biological effects of marine oil spills and his expertise has been requested for most of the major international oil spills since the mid 1980s. Dr Moore is also involved in assessing the impact of pollution on marine copepods. This expertise in marine biodiversity was central to the award of £479,000 in 1999 by SHEFC for the establishment of the Centre for Marine Biodiversity and Biotechnology that has acted as a focus for research in marine ecology and biodiversity as well as the sensitive exploitation of marine organisms for biotechnological purposes led by Dr Burgess.

Chemistry

The materials chemistry group, under the direction of Professor Ian Cowie, has performed pioneering work in polymer blends and molecular composites. This led to the discovery of liquid crystalline polymer composite films that reflect ultraviolet light and can act as stable protective coatings. This was extended with the discovery of new polymer gel electrolytes that could be used on an industrial scale for 'smart windows' which undergo rapid reversible changes of colour for use in car sunroofs, mirrors and other display devices. Thermoplastic elastomers were also made from commercially available telechelic starting materials to produce plastics exhibiting a high elongation-to-break property. Elastic recovery of the materials was similar to commercially important fibres such as Lycra. Professor Viney's biomimetic materials group focused on the properties of silk fibres from silkworms and spiders. This group uncovered the limitations of silk as an engineering material, namely its poor creep properties and sensitivity to moisture, which hamper the long-term stability demanded by most engineering applications. Professor Phillip John, in collaboration with Professor John Wilson in Physics, gained international recognition for the low temperature growth of diamond. They were the first group in the UK to build a microwave plasma reactor in the late

1980s for diamond thin film growth, and the first academic group to demonstrate epitaxial growth of diamond on a silicon wafer.

After the retirement of Professor Grant Buchanan from the Chair of Organic Chemistry, Professor Pat Bailey brought a new impetus to a number of research areas. One of these was in molecular recognition, leading to the synthesis of molecular buckets derived by linking amino acids into cross-linked peptides to selectively bind other molecules. He also instigated a productive collaborative research programme with biologists in Oxford and York on investigations of proteins involved in the active transport of aminoacids and short peptides across the wall of the human gut. Another important programme in organic chemistry is to design a system to generate nitric oxide in a clean, highly regulated and localised manner within biological systems. The work, funded by a major pharmaceutical company, aimed at the synthesis of small molecules targeted at key biological receptors of significance in a number of diseases. An active research programme in nucleic acid chemistry, with the aim of developing DNA-binding agents, utilised the class of compounds know as peptide nucleic acids that can selectively modulate gene expression. The aim is to contribute to the treatment of human diseases, notably cancer.

Professor Welch's research in heteroborane chemistry has contributed to a greater understanding of the mechanisms of isomerisation of such species. Culminating in the synthesis of the first 13-vertex carborane, the 12-vertex to 13-vertex barrier has been overcome for the first time. The study of chiral and asymmetrically functionalised macrocyclic complexes led to the discovery of a novel isomer of the Jager 16 membered macrocyclic ring, and the first mesogenic dendrimer materials. In computational chemistry, low-valent transition metal amides and alkoxides have been modelled thereby allowing an understanding of the unusual properties of these mis-matched organometallic species, which are of key importance in catalysis.

In physical chemistry, Professor Josef Pfab applied laser induced fluorescence to study the detailed dynamics and spectroscopy of nitroso-compounds. In the era before 'technology transfer', he showed that the ultra-sensitive techniques developed to study molecular disassociation could be used to detect gases present at extremely low levels for uses in drug and explosive detection. The existing expertise on electron–molecule collisions and the applications in mass spectrometry was enhanced by the establishment, under the direction of Professor John, of a unique facility for post-ionisation laser mass spectrometry for both research and commercial activities.

Physics

Research in physics was developed by Professor Des Smith and his colleagues in the 1970s in nonlinear optics and infrared satellite meteorology. The latter experiment – based on the Nimbus series of satellites flown by NASA – successfully mapped the global temperature of the atmosphere in three dimensions by measuring the emission of atmospheric carbon dioxide from an altitude of 600 miles. It led to the discovery of temperature waves on a planetary scale, one of the most significant meteorological observations of the 1970s. Remote atmospheric sensing was continued using microwave satellite instrumentation, and yielded the first measurements of increases of chlorine monoxide concentrations which directly result in the destruction of the ozone layer over Antarctica. The major early activity was in the research and development of tuneable infrared lasers for ultra-high resolution spectroscopy. An allied development led directly to the subject of optical computing, and then optoelectronic computing; the world's first demonstrator of an 'all-optical' computer was constructed. In 1987, there was a further expansion in optoelectronics and in the related subjects of semiconductor growth and device physics, optical fibre physics and nonlinear dynamics. Professor Bob Harrison and collaborators have been leaders in the study of chaos in optical systems, particular optical cavities and lasers, and made the first observations of chaos in real lasers. Professor Brian Cavenett and Dr Kevin Prior were the first to develop blue diode lasers in Europe. Professor Denis Hall's group has developed new ultra-compact high power lasers that have transformed important sectors of laser surgery and industrial laser-based manufacturing. A fibre optics group, led by Professor Julian Jones, has carried out important research involving the development of innovative fibre optic sensors for turbo-machinery instrumentation, and miniature probes for measuring temperature pressure and flow in jet engine research. Industrial research collaborations include BT, Rolls-Royce and BMW. Since 1990, Professor Carl Pidgeon has led the UK condensed matter physics programme, utilising ultra-short high intensity light pulses at the Dutch free electron laser.

Built Environment

The Department of Building, formed in the 1930s, and renamed the Department of Building Engineering and Surveying in 1989, had developed an identifiable research ethos by the 1980s in the areas of acoustics, construction management and thermal environment assessment. This portfolio was extended in 1985 with the addition of work on building drainage systems and water conservation. Much of the work was directed towards applications and while this has to some extent continued up to the present time, more recently there has been an emphasis on mathematical modelling and simulation that has resulted in the recognition of the department's research as being of international standard.

Acoustics research, led by Professor Bob Craik and David Mackenzie, has concentrated on the development of the Statistical Energy Analysis simulation for sound and vibration transmission within building structures with applications to such diverse structures as aircraft and train compartments and ship hulls. The analysis provided the basis for an understanding of noise transmission within buildings that has informed codes and standards internationally. In parallel, work on audibility in open spaces, particularly open-plan classrooms, was fundamental to both the design process and specification of materials.

Research in construction economics and management has been strengthened by the arrival of Professor Kaka and Dr Fortune who have initiated work in the area of construction economics and sustainability. The mixed model of simulation development and applications-led research has continued with particular attention being paid to the effects of Public Private Partnerships and the Public Finance Initiative.

Climate change and the need to conserve water brought the work of the drainage research group to prominence. The group, led by Professor Swaffield, Dr Jack and Dr Campbell, has developed mathematical simulations based on the method of characteristics to describe the air and water unsteady flow conditions encountered within building drainage and vent systems and within roof drainage systems, including the siphonic systems found in such prestigious buildings as the Sydney Olympic Stadium. In parallel with these simulation developments, the group has contributed to water conservation and sustainability in the UK and overseas through ODA and World Bank contracts, by component and appliance design, and by Professor Swaffield's chairmanship from 1996 to 2003 of Defra's Water Regulations Advisory Committee that was responsible for the technical content of legislation for England and Wales that has introduced significant water conservation measures.

The Environmental Science Research Group led by Professor Aspinall has pioneered research across a wide range of user orientated design issues, ranging from early work by Roy Webb and Peter Aspinall on the effects of lighting on decision-making through to Professor Aspinall's work in conjunction with medical consultants at the Edinburgh Royal Infirmary on visual impairment. Parallel work on way finding, accessibility and audibility in public spaces has potential for future expansion. The group also has an active thermal modelling interest represented by Dr Harris and Dr Wang's research on below-ground buildings and airflow both within and around structures, the latter again featuring a synthesis of the analytical and experimental approaches through the use of the group's large low-speed wind tunnel.

Materials research has been led by Professor Banfill and has concentrated on the chemical and rheological properties of cement-based materials and has featured collaborative projects to produce a database of mix design guidance for high performance concrete optimised for workability, flow under vibration and hardened properties. The group's involvement with historic buildings led to the construction of the only fully instrumented lime kiln in the world for the production and characterisation of traditional lime binders.

International recognition for the work of the acoustics, drainage and environmental groups, together with the achievements of the construction economics and materials groups, secured the retention in 2001 of the RAE grade 5 awarded in 1996, confirming and strengthening the position of the university as the leading Scottish centre for research in the built environment.

Chemical Engineering

Chemical engineering, among other engineering disciplines, can be considered unique in its rooting to the micro cosmos of atoms, molecules and product formulation. Chemical engineering provides the link between design and manufacturing and it plays a fundamental role in industries such as petrochemicals, pharmaceuticals, food, and plastic. Research in chemical engineering at Heriot-Watt University reflects the paradigms of the discipline as well as their evolution. Indeed, while research at the industrial scale is carried out, the last decade has seen the flourishing of research areas which reflects the current status of a discipline which is redefining its boundaries.

The chemical engineering group at Heriot-Watt University has been recognised internationally for the activities on offshore processing and particle technology which was led by Professor Brian Waldie and is now headed by Dr Pekdemir and Dr White. Research on elimination/minimisation of detrimental effects of sea motion on oil and gas processing equipment and on floating mobile processing plants has an international reputation. The research group at Heriot-Watt University is the only one in the UK and among very few worldwide that is carrying out this type of work on large-scale experimental test rigs.

The shifting of the paradigms from the industrial level to the micro and macro scale has seen new development in experimental research in particle flocculation, crystallisation, bio-processing and bio-manufacturing carried out at the Centre for Oscillatory Baffled Reactors, led by Professor Ni.

At the nano-scale level, molecular simulation, spectroscopy and diffraction are being applied to a wide range of industrially significant engineering issues, which cover the full spectrum of modern chemical engineering research from oil and gas to pharmaceuticals. Molecular simulations aimed at understanding crystal growth and morphology are being applied to scale formation, polymorph prediction and control. This culminates in a major industry/academia project – 'Chemicals Behaving Badly' – aiming at the production of particles on a larger scale.

Another emerging area that is flourishing is at the interface with biology and life science under the direction of Dr Bustard. Research has been conducted in biomanufacturing, fermentation processes, biotechnological applications of microalgae, pollution abatement technologies, membrane bioreactors, electric field stimulation of biological systems, and bioprocess intensification strategies. Research has been carried out in dynamic modelling and simulation of fluidised bioreactors systems. Finally, modelling techniques for flow instabilities and particulate systems are being extended to biological systems by analysing the regulatory equations of the cell cycle.

Civil and Offshore Engineering

Research in civil and offshore engineering has been diverse both in terms of the range of topics and in coverage from the theoretical to highly practical. Civil engineering has received around £10m of research funding since 1980 from industry, the EU, EPSRC and other government agencies. On the experimental side, world class laboratory facilities have been developed for subsea pipeline engineering (with the capacity to simulate water depths of 2200 m and temperatures of 140 °C), the development of pavement (road surfaces), the testing of concrete slabs and reinforced concrete chemistry. A new multidirectional wave basin has been built that can produce larger waves than in any comparable European University facility. This has been complimented by research on the deterioration of concrete in coastal structures, remote monitoring of the behaviour of bridges and aquaculture cages. A wave and wind monitoring station was set up on a North Sea offshore platform in 1994 and the School now has the world's largest database of fast-sampled wave and wind data.

Pavement surfaces for many roads in Scotland have been developed in our labs and this research has led to a new spin-out company – Pavement Technology. Our concrete research has led to changes in European design codes for concrete structures and a novel method of quality control of fresh concrete. It is also leading to revision of practice in the way existing structures – including bridges – are assessed and maintained later in their lives. Similarly, research using the wave basin and the offshore wave database is leading to changes in the assessment of the risk of structural failure of offshore platforms in extreme storms.

In structural engineering, experimental work has been complimented by theoretical and numerical development of finite element methods. This has led to improvements in the modelling of cracking in concrete and its performance under impact and blast loading. Theoretical and numerical work on modelling the response of structures to earthquakes (undertaken in conjunction with Imperial College, London) is influencing the design codes for earthquake zone structures. In geotechnics, finite element modelling of soil behaviour under roads and rail tracks is leading, in conjunction with our development of new aggregate binders, to novel and cost-effective methods for the ground support of roads and railways. Other research in geotechnics has focused on modelling the movement of pollutants, both liquid and gaseous, through soil and this work has found practical application in the management of landfill sites and modelling the effects of land contamination.

In the area of sustainable water management, research has taken an holistic approach with theoretical, numerical, statistical and experimental modelling and management methodology development. Theoretical and numerical development has led to a model that can predict the three-dimensional dispersion of pollutants in rivers and waterways. Theoretical and statistical models have been developed that consider the impact of rainfall variations and climate change on reservoir planning and management.

Flood risk modelling and flood plain management has grown rapidly following the appointment of a new professor in environmental engineering in 2000. Models have been developed to support real-time flood forecasting and experimental facilities in this area and will soon be upgraded with SHRIF2 funding. The sustainable development of water resource systems has long been a research theme and a multi-objective approach to decision-making in the water industry has been developed and tested. Interest in safety and reliability has grown over the last decade with considerable work on the theoretical and numerical modelling of fires. A particular interest has been tunnel fires (such as that in the Channel Tunnel) and the university has representation on Home Office groups investigating fire modelling. Research has also been undertaken into the reliability of offshore safety systems in conjunction with the offshore oil and gas industry and there is ongoing research into the management of safety offshore and on the railways.

Electrical and Electronic Engineering

The discovery of North Sea oil stimulated research by electrical engineers on underwater vehicles under the Marine Technology Directorate of SERC. The manned underwater vehicles that perform tasks at ocean depths have an obvious application for oil exploration. The research addressed the generic theme of applying automation principles and technologies to improve the efficiency and safety of subsea tasks. Three interrelated research areas formed the basis of the programmes, namely, the intelligent control of autonomous underwater vehicles, through-water communications, and sonar data processing and interpretation. Later the emphasis moved to the investigation of systems required to provide an autonomous robotic vehicle capable of navigation and control using the interpretation of sonar sensors and able to communicate video image data through the sea. There are now four research groups in electrical and electronic engineering: microengineering, under the leadership of Professor Sangster, vision and image processing, led by Professor Andy Wallace, ocean systems, headed by Professor David Lane, with a major emphasis upon remotely operated underwater vehicles (this group has developed the world's first dexterous underwater robot hand); and the electrical power group, led by Professor Barry Williams, which is at the forefront of generic research in the development of faster and more efficient designs for motors, drives, switches and integrated circuits.

Mechanical Engineering

Research in mechanical engineering at Heriot-Watt University has evolved from being strongly discipline-based founded in the engineering science of thermodynamics, fluid mechanics, mechanics of materials and dynamics, towards the more applications based, especially in manufacturing. In the mid 1980s, the dynamics and mechanics effort was mostly in offshore engineering, CAD/CAM and thermodynamics, and heat transfer. Since about 1990, this has developed into a much wider portfolio including surface engineering, micro-mechanics (with applications in medical engineering), computational mechanics and machinery monitoring. Researchers in thermodynamics and heat transfer have made major contributions to the understanding of boiling and condensation; this developed through the 1990s to involve materials engineering. Manufacturing has also been an important area since the mid 1980s with the major developments in CAD/CAM. The Advanced Manufacturing Unit has been used for research in tool wear monitoring which is known internationally for its application-driven work in acoustic emission sensor development. This has led to collaboration with physicists in optical instrumentation, including those for shape and flow measurement. Work has also developed since 1990 in more generic manufacturing issues especially computer-aided design and manufacturing.

Institute of Petroleum Engineering

The Department (now Institute) of Petroleum Engineering was established in 1975 following a government working party study into the manpower needs of the quickly developing UK offshore oil and gas business. One of the recommendations was the establishment of a postgraduate centre in petroleum engineering based in Scotland to provide masters-level education in this sector and for such a group to be active in relevant research. Funding for research from the outset was not exclusively from conventional research council sources but from the oil operating companies involved with the considerable technical challenges associated with oil exploration and production in the North Sea. A government decision in the 1980s to the effect that in order to qualify for a licence to develop North Sea, oil companies –

including those from abroad – had to furnish evidence they were supporting UK research, provided an impetus for companies to sponsor research. Much of this funding involved collaboration between firms with common research problems.

The department pioneered the operation of joint venture research projects where industry, alongside the public sector research council and the DTI, formerly the Department of Energy, funded research focused on issues facing oil companies. The department was seen to be ahead of the game when, in the 1993 UK government white paper on 'Realising our Potential', universities were encouraged to partner in research. Awards by the Scottish Offshore Industry, the DTI and culminating in 1994, in its first year, the prestigious Queen's Anniversary Prize for Higher Education, gave recognition to this institute's outstanding partnership with industry in research.

The Institute's research in oilfield scale, started by Professor Adrian Todd in 1979, is world leading. The formation of deposits (like the furring of a kettle or in hard water conveying pipes) is a serious and expensive issue in oilfield production, where water injected into the reservoir to aid oil production mixes with water already in the reservoir resulting in deposits which can severely reduce the throughput of wells and the operation of equipment. The Institute's contribution, now supported by over 20 oil and service companies and led by Professor Ken Sorbie since 1988, towards understanding the mechanisms of behaviour and chemical treatment has led to software which is used across the industry in the design of treatments and laboratory practice to evaluate potential treatments.

Oil is contained within the microstructure of porous rocks, not unlike the rocks used in the construction of typical Edinburgh flats and houses. The understanding of the behaviour of oil, water and gas in such micropores to the extent that one can predict how fluids will flow and ultimately to how much might be recovered is no small challenge. In the mid 1980s, the Institute developed glass etched models of porous media and used them at the high pressures of reservoirs to examine how oil, gas and water were distributed. Some rich gas reservoirs, for example, when they produce, cause liquids to condense in the rock, like condensation forming on a window in a 'steamy' room. If this occurs, these valuable liquids might be left in a reservoir unrecovered. Under the leadership of Professor Ali Danesh, supported by Professor Dabir Tehrani and using micromodel technology, state of the art simulation experiments and computing resources developed inhouse, liquid condensation and flow understanding in complex reservoirs has been revolutionised. Commercial computer programs used by the industry in designing these very expensive developments have adopted equations developed by the Institute to ensure that the programs are consistent with the mechanisms established in its research.

The combination of oil, gas and water at the low temperature and high pressure conditions of, for example, a pipeline running along the seabed of the

North Sea can give rise to solid ice-like material called hydrates. Such formations can be costly to remove and dangerous if allowed to occur in vessels and flow control equipment. The Institute's research in this topic started in 1986. The Centre for Gas Hydrate Research, led by Bahman Tohidi, is internationally recognised. Two very significant outcomes have resulted from the research. Hydrates are formed by molecules small enough to fit within the hydrogen-oxygen structure of water. The research group proved experimentally that hydrates could form with larger molecules like a benzene, opening up such possibilities to other previously considered non-hydrate forming compounds. Hydrates were considered to be possible only when gas was present with water. The group has been the first to demonstrate that when the 'gas' is dissolved in the water, hydrates can still form.

Whereas in the 1970s the disciplines of engineering and geology were isolated in their contributions to oilfield exploration and development, over the last twelve years or so the industry has recognised the importance of an integrated approach in field design and management. Through the vision and enthusiasm of Professor Patrick Corbett, Professor Brian Smart and other colleagues, the institute has been at the forefront of this approach and geology, geophysics and rock mechanics are now significant disciplines contributing to its international research and teaching profile. This is evidenced by the biannual research forum hosted alternatively by Stanford University, USA and Heriot-Watt.

The broadening of the Institute's research profile is demonstrated by the inclusion now of a major research effort in geophysics under the leadership of Professor Colin McBeth. Characteristic of worldwide oil and gas field development is the quantification of uncertainty. Professor Mike Christie, with particular expertise in this area, and using high performance computing capability, is leading a team which is quickly establishing an international reputation in this important and developing area. The internationally outstanding quality of the Institute's research has been recognised in the 5* Research Assessment ranking over the last ten years.

School of Management and Languages

The Centre for Economic Reform and Transformation (CERT) was established in economics in 1990 by Professor Paul Hare in response to the radical economic and political changes taking place in Central and Eastern Europe. The aims of the Centre are not only to increase academic understanding of the economic transition to a market economy in Central and Eastern Europe but also to provide valuable expertise and economic advice to policy-makers in the United Kingdom, other countries and international organisations. Since 1997 CERT researchers have continued to expand and develop this knowledge under the directorship of Professor Mark Schaffer. The Centre's work has involved its researchers in studies of privatisation in Russia and other countries in Eastern Europe; labour market reform; competitiveness and industrial restructuring policy advice; enterprise reform; employment forecasting; food sector requirements and agriculture reform in Russia, and many other topics. CERT has become widely recognised as a leading international centre for the study of economic transition with a particular strength in applied microeconomic research.

A Logistics Research Centre was established within the School of Management in 1998 under the directorship of Professor Alan McKinnon. In addition to generating over £600,000 in funded research, an MSc in Logistics and Supply Chain Management was launched in 1997. The Centre has a strong reputation in the analysis of links between logistical restructuring and freight traffic growth. Professor McKinnon has tackled the problem of the growth of lorry traffic at different levels, from strategic management of logistical systems to the design of lorry trailers. His analysis of the benefits of increasing maximum lorry weight to 44 tonnes formed the basis for the Government's decision to increase the weight limit in 2001; and his seminal paper on the development of retail logistics resulted in the creation of the Government's Retail Logistics Task Force, to which he was subsequently appointed chairman. The research in logistics, together with that of CERT and other individuals, resulted in a grade 4 in RAE 2001.

In the 1970s and since, one strand of languages research has been involved with the theoretical underpinning of pedagogical materials such as *Le Français en Faculté*, *Lyon à la une*, *En fin de compte*, *Nuffield French for Scientists*, *Rus* and *French/German/Spanish through Interpreting*. A major shift in direction came in the 1980s with work in text linguistics and pragmatics (Professor Mason and Professor Hatim), leading to pioneering research in the applied linguistics of translating and interpreting and cementing Heriot-Watt University's reputation as an international player in research in this field. A PhD programme soon followed and in 1995, the Centre for Translating and Interpreting Studies in Scotland (CTISS) was created. Countless international invitations have resulted and a series of major publications are among the most cited research outputs in the field.

More recently, research has diversified. Semiotics, which was already central in translation research, provided a link to Dr Grant's work in interdisciplinary communication science. A number of international invitations, monographs, edited collections of essays and international conferences have already emerged from this new area.

In 1999 the research portfolio diversified into second language acquisition with the appointment of a Chair. Professor Sharwood Smith is recognised as a leading international player in this field, and the international journal, *Second Language Research*, is now based in the department.

In the field of European studies there has been significant recent output on aspects of political science, film theory and European cultural identities. A new research group in this area has been formed. Languages has gained the award of grade 4 in the last two Research Assessment Exercises.

Textiles and Design

The research base in the School of Textiles and Design, which evolved from the Scottish College of Textiles, has led to significant achievements in a diversity of areas. The school has emerged as an important international centre for research in textiles and allied topics ranging from the science and technology of textiles and colour, through clothing technology to the creative aspects of textile design and fashion.

An important trend which has emerged in the last decade within the UK textile industry has been the growth in technical textiles, a sector encompassing functional textiles for a wide range of applications including military, medical and agricultural applications. The school's research activity in this area, in particular the work of Dr Don Brydon and Dr Bert Mather, led, for example, to the development of significant improvements in the processing and technical properties of polypropylene, arguably the key growth fibre for technical textile applications. The EPSRC and the DTI recognised the importance of this industry sector by setting up the TechniTex Faraday Partnership in 1999, involving Heriot-Watt University as the lead partner, with Professor George Stylios as director, together with the University of Leeds, UMIST and British Textile Technology Group (BTTG) to work in partnership with industry.

The school has engaged in important research activity in the area of colour science. Dr Roger Wardman has contributed to the development of numerical methods for the specification of colour to replace the traditional methods of colour matching by eye. Dr Bob Christie, in collaboration with several industrial organisations, has made contributions in the chemistry of dyes and pigments, for example in the area of the development of computer-aided modelling methods for designing new colouring materials with improved performance.

There have also been significant achievements in the textile design area. In the early 1980s, the computer-aided design system known as ScotWeave emerged and has subsequently developed into a sophisticated commercial CAD system used worldwide. ScotWeave Limited is now a limited company based in Galashiels.

The school had had notable success in the development of systems for the 3D visualisation of humans, clothing and textiles, through the involvement of Professor George Stylios in the Research Institute for Flexible Materials, and a multidisciplinary programme between Mark Timmins and the School of Mathematics and Computer Sciences to explore 3D visualisation for fashion and furnishing applications. Sarah Taylor's work over many years in exploring sculptural weaving of optical fibres was recognised by her short-listing for the prestigious Jerwood Applied Arts Prize in 2002.

Note

[1] I am grateful to the following members of staff who wrote summaries of the research achievements within their respective disciplines: Prof. I. Cowie and Prof. P. John (Chemistry); Prof. C. Pidgeon (Physics); Prof. R. J. Knops (Mathematics); Prof. H. Waters and colleagues (Actuarial Mathematics and Statistics); Prof. C. Brown and Prof. F. Priest (Biological Sciences); Prof. J. Swaffield (Building Engineering); Prof. R. Reuben (Mechanical Engineering); Prof. B. Williams (Electrical Engineering); Dr G. Michaelson and colleagues (Computer Science); Prof. R. Ocone (Chemical Engineering); Prof. B. Smart and Prof. A. Todd (Petroleum Engineering); Prof. I. Mason (Languages); and Dr R. Christie and Ms S. Taylor (Textiles and Design).

Picture Credits

Scanning and image editing: Graphic Services, Heriot-Watt University.

All images are held by Heriot-Watt University Archive, Records Management and Museum Service except the following:

Pages 3, 14, 25, 36, 41, 75, 85, National Galleries of Scotland; p. 40, John R. Hume collection; pp. 68, 73, St Cecilia's Hall, Edinburgh; p. 65, photograph by David Octavius Hill, originally published in *Lilliput*, 1938; p. 80, Aberdeen University; pp. 106, 108, 109, originally published in Smiles (1885) *James Nasmyth*, John Murray; pp. 134, 143, Trustees of the National Library of Scotland; p. 138, originally published in Pryde, D. (1893) *Pleasant Memories of a Busy Life*, W. Blackwood & Sons; p. 160, originally published in Hole, W. (1884) *Quasi Cursores*, Edinburgh University Press, pp. 175, 204–5, Professor David Manners collection, photograph M. Wane and Co.; p.182, originally published in Maret, P. (1957) *Pioneer of Sociology; the life and letters of Patrick Geddes*, Percy Lund, Humphries & Co. Ltd, London; pp. 183, 462, Gordon Wright; p. 235, Curr (1946), *Modern Athenians*, McLagan and Cumming, Edinburgh; p. 247, The Scottish Brewing Archive; pp. 354, 356, Sudlow collection.

We gratefully acknowledge permission for the publication of the following images held by the university:

Pages 3, 5, 6, 63, 66, 99, 102, 149, 157, 236, 254, 259, 309, 318, 328, 402, 443, 450, photography by Douglas McBride; pp. 233, 256, 271, 305, 392 upper, © The Scotsman Publications Ltd; p. 244, McLagan and Cumming; pp. 299, 300, 301, 320, 371, 388, 409, John Dewar Studios; pp. 286, 289, 310, 312, 341, 372, *The Herald* (Glasgow); p. 362 upper and lower, John Tweedie collection; pp. 375, 378, John K. Wilkie; p. 389, Air Images; pp. 392 lower, 399, 420, 435, 440, 452, 455, 457, 459, 467 right, 468, 469 lower, Ken Paterson; pp. 414, 428, Ian Southern; p. 419, Tarquil Cramer; pp. 425, 471, Laurence Winram; p. 442, Derek Lunn www.dereklunn.com; p. 447, Tony Gorzkowski, Whitehouse Studios; p. 454, Robert Travers; p. 467 left, *The Guardian*; p. 472, Karen Larter.

The engraving shown in the background of the jacket is of the Watt Institution and School of Arts, Adam Square, Edinburgh, with the statue of James Watt in the foreground, circa 1854. Images featured in the strip at the head of the jacket are excerpts from: *rear*, left to right: *The Heriot-Watt College Magazine*, 1939; Women munitions workers in the Mechanical Engineering Department during the First World War; The University Choir and Orchestra (photograph: Ken Paterson); The room in which the first lectures of the Edinburgh School of Arts were delivered in the Freemasons' Hall, Niddry Street (image: St Cecilia's Hall); George Heriot, jeweller and moneylender to the Royal Family (portrait by George Scougall); *spine*: Heriot-Watt College in the early twentieth century (Professor David Manners collection, M. Wane and Co); *front*, left to right: Model from School of Textiles and Design Fashion Show, 2003 (photograph: Douglas McBride); students in Chemistry laboratory, 1900; Leonard Horner, founder of the Edinburgh School of Arts (print from a crayon drawing by Samuel Lawrence); jubilant graduates of 2003 (photograph: Karen Larter); James Watt (painting by Sir William Beechley). Author photograph by David Manton, Photodrome Ltd.

Whilst every effort has been made to trace the owners of copyright material, in a few cases this has proved impossible and we take this opportunity to offer our apologies to any copyright holders whose rights we may have unwittingly infringed. If any rights holders have been inadvertently overlooked, the publisher will be pleased to make the necessary arrangement at the first opportunity.

Index

Bold page numbers denote references to chapters. *Italic* page numbers denote references to illustrations. Sub-entries are in *chronological* order